SUMMERHAYS' ENCYCLOPAEDIA FOR HORSEMEN

Summerhays' ENCYCLOPAEDIA for HORSEMEN

COMPLETELY REVISED EDITION

Illustrated with specially commissioned line drawings

Compiled by R. S. Summerhays
Revised by Valerie Russell

, R.S

THRESHOLD BOOKS

Editions one to six published 1952 and 1975
by Frederick Warne & Co. Ltd
London and New York

This completely revised edition
published in Great Britain by
Threshold Books Ltd
661 Fulham Road
London SW6 5PZ
1988

First published in Australia by
Greenhouse Publications Pty Ltd
122-126 Ormond Road
Elwood, Vic 3184

Summerhays, R.S. (Reginald Sherriff), 1881-1976
   Summerhays' encyclopaedia for horsemen.

   Rev ed.
   ISBN 0 86436 191 2.

   1. Horses – Dictionaries. 2. Horsemanship –
Dictionaries. I. Russell, Valerie. II. Title.
III. Title: Encyclopaedia for horsemen.

636.1′003′21

CREDITS
Veterinary consultant: P. Ellis Jones, B VET MED, MRCVS
Illustrations: Dianne Breeze
Design: Alan Hamp
Editors: Barbara Cooper
Lesley Gowers

Typeset in Concorde by
Rapid Communications, London WC1
Printed in Great Britain by
Adlard & Son Ltd,
Letchworth, Hertfordshire

CONTENTS

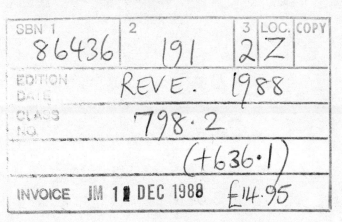

PREFACE

This wide-ranging revision of the 1975 edition of the *Encyclopaedia* reflects the considerable changes which have taken place in the horse world in the intervening years. The veterinary entries, in particular, have undergone extensive revision, and many new entries have been included. Because of the enormous increase in veterinary knowledge and the technical (and frequently changing) nature of modern procedures, the previous practice of including 'do-it-yourself' treatments has been abandoned for all but the most minor ailments. Also, because of the vast field of contemporary veterinary knowledge, only those topics most likely to be encountered by the average horse owner have been included. The veterinary consultant was Mr P. Ellis Jones (B VET MED, MRCVS), to whom sincere thanks are due.

The entries on breeds have been extensively revised and enlarged. Horse clothing and saddlery entries now include mention of the modern materials used.

The entries on feeding reflect the present-day scientific approach to the subject, while not eliminating the older (and still relevant) 'rule of thumb' methods.

In the years since 1975, dressage has become much more popular, and combined and scurry driving and endurance riding have developed enormously; entries take these into account.

Entries dealing with equestrian art, the historical aspects of horses and horsemanship, and some old-fashioned terms now out of general use have been retained, as they contribute much to an informed picture of the horse world.

The full-length articles, a feature of the earlier edition, have been deleted, as it was felt that they did not fit altogether happily into the format of an encyclopaedia. The information contained in them has, however, been included in the text under separate headings. Acknowledgement is therefore still due to the original contributors: Bill Curling, Jean Edmunds, Jean Froissard, Ecuyer-professeur, FFSE, Dorinda Fuller, E. Hartley Edwards, Cherrie Hatton-Hall, FBHS, Lady Anne Lytton, D. Machin-Goodall, Francis McIlhney Stifler, M. Popp, C. Richardson, FWCF, Mary Rose, FBHS, M.A.P. Simons, MRCVS, R.H. Smythe, MRCVS,

Glenda Spooner, Marylian Watney, Sheila Willcox, Dorian Williams, Henry Wynmalen and I.M. Yeomans. Special thanks are due to Mrs Stella Walker, who revised the previous edition and contributed much of the material on equestrian art and history.

The illustrations have been revised and redrawn to be more directly informative, with the inclusion of more labelling where appropriate.

The results section has been dropped as being too unwieldy. The section on foreign terms, however, has been extended to reflect the increasingly international nature of equestrianism.

When using the *Encyclopaedia*, it is important to remember that it is intended to give an *overall*, not a detailed, specialised picture. Readers requiring specialist knowledge are referred to the many books on most equestrian and equine topics.

Valerie Russell
May, 1988

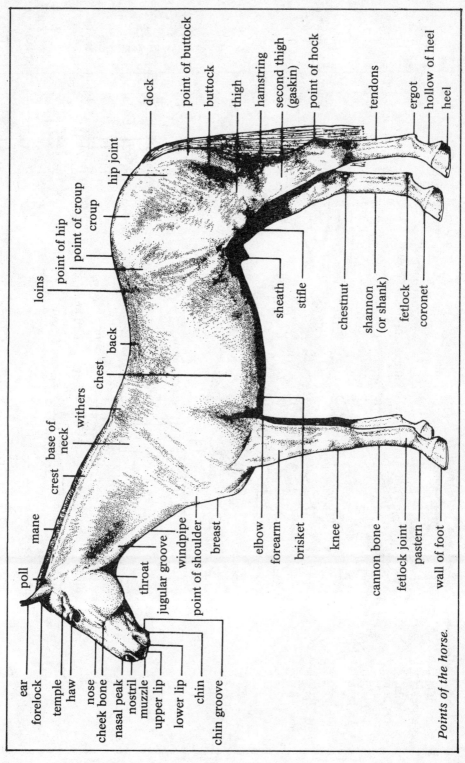

Points of the horse.

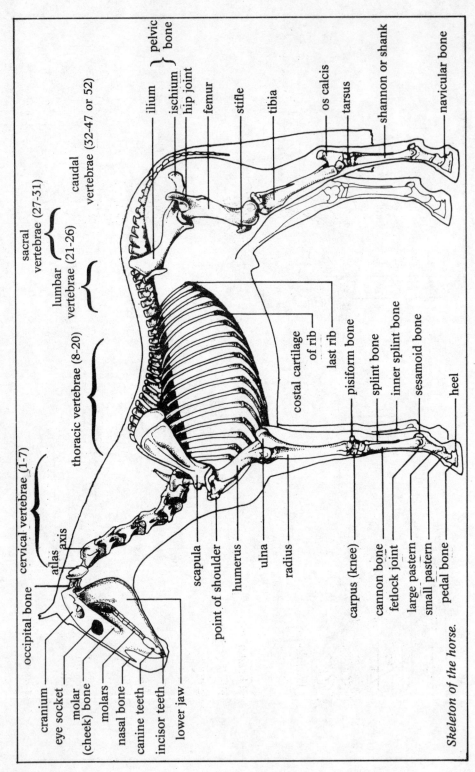

occipital bone
cranium
eye socket
molar (cheek) bone
molars
nasal bone
canine teeth
incisor teeth
lower jaw

cervical vertebrae (1-7)
atlas
axis

thoracic vertebrae (8-20)

lumbar vertebrae (21-26)

sacral vertebrae (27-31)

caudal vertebrae (32-47 or 52)

ilium
ischium } pelvic bone
hip joint
femur
stifle
tibia

os calcis
tarsus

shannon or shank

navicular bone

scapula
point of shoulder
humerus
ulna
radius

costal cartilage of rib
last rib
pisiform bone
splint bone
inner splint bone
sesamoid bone

heel

carpus (knee)
cannon bone
fetlock joint
large pastern
small pastern
pedal bone

Skeleton of the horse.

10

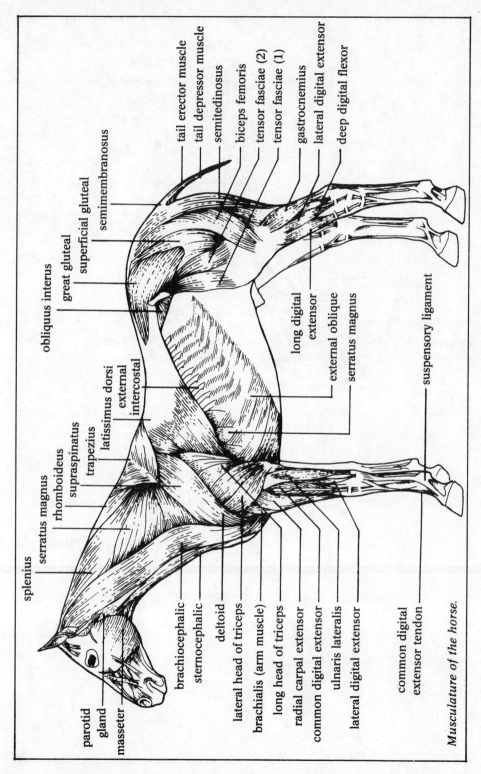

Musculature of the horse.

splenius
serratus magnus
rhomboideus
supraspinatus
trapezius
latissimus dorsi
external
intercostal

parotid
gland
masseter

brachiocephalic
sternocephalic
deltoid
lateral head of triceps
brachialis (arm muscle)
long head of triceps
radial carpal extensor
common digital extensor
ulnaris lateralis
lateral digital extensor

common digital
extensor tendon

obliquus interus
great gluteal
superficial gluteal
semimembranosus

tail erector muscle
tail depressor muscle
semitedinosus
biceps femoris
tensor fasciae (2)
tensor fasciae (1)
gastrocnemius
lateral digital extensor
deep digital flexor

long digital
extensor
external oblique
serratus magnus

suspensory ligament

11

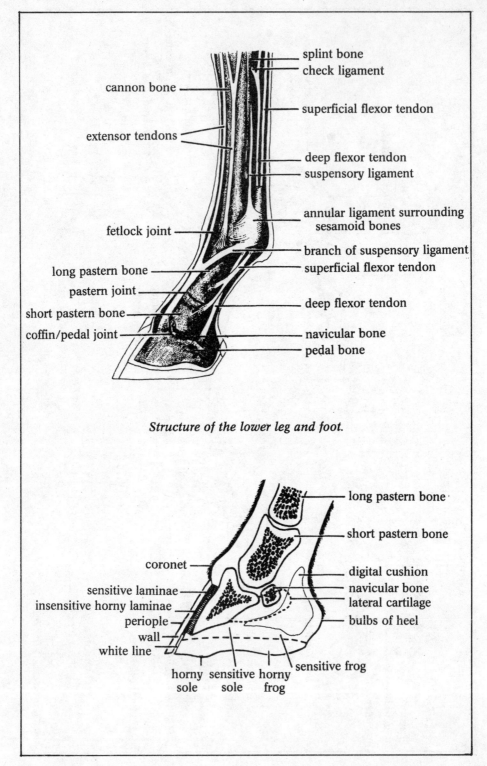

splint bone
check ligament
cannon bone
superficial flexor tendon
extensor tendons
deep flexor tendon
suspensory ligament
annular ligament surrounding
sesamoid bones
fetlock joint
branch of suspensory ligament
superficial flexor tendon
long pastern bone
pastern joint
short pastern bone
deep flexor tendon
coffin/pedal joint
navicular bone
pedal bone

Structure of the lower leg and foot.

long pastern bone
short pastern bone
coronet
digital cushion
sensitive laminae
navicular bone
insensitive horny laminae
lateral cartilage
periople
bulbs of heel
wall
white line
horny   sensitive horny   sensitive frog
sole   sole   frog

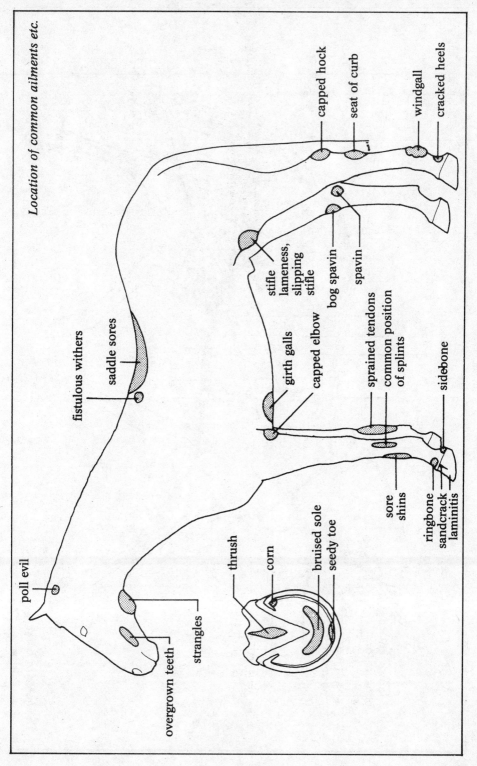

Location of common ailments etc.

poll evil

overgrown teeth

strangles

thrush

corn

bruised sole

seedy toe

fistulous withers

saddle sores

girth galls

capped elbow

stifle lameness, slipping stifle

bog spavin

spavin

sprained tendons

common position of splints

sore shins

sidebone

ringbone
sandcrack
laminitis

capped hock

seat of curb

windgall

cracked heels

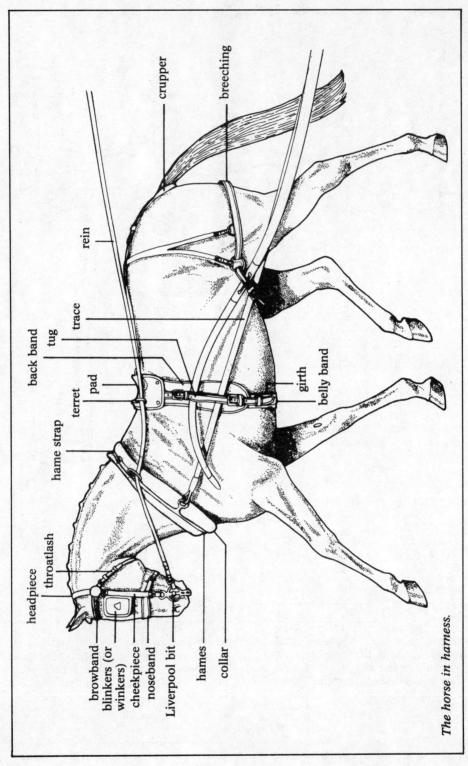

crupper

breeching

rein

trace

tug

back band

girth

belly band

terret

pad

hame strap

throatlash

headpiece

browband

blinkers (or winkers)

cheekpiece

noseband

Liverpool bit

hames

collar

The horse in harness.

A

AASB Anglo-Arab Stud Book.

ABRS Association of British Riding Schools (see under **British Riding Schools, Association of**)

AHS Arab Horse Society (q.v.).

AHSA American Horse Shows Association (q.v.).

AHSB Arab Horse Stud Book.

Abbot-Davies balancing rein A form of schooling tackle intended to develop the horse's muscles so as to obtain balance and good performance. It is claimed that the rein cuts the amount of time necessary for the basic schooling of the horse.

Abortion Loss of the foal before 300 days of gestation. It can be caused by bacterial, viral or fungal infections. Non-infectious causes include twinning, hormonal disturbance, inadequate feeding, and abnormalities of the foal.

Above the bit The horse is above the bit when his head is raised with the nose in front of the vertical, and thus with the mouth above the rider's hands. It is an evasion of the bit and a serious fault entailing lack of balance on the part of the horse and poor control on the part of the rider.

Abscess A cavity containing pus (bacteria, fluid, and cellular débris) which may occur anywhere in the body. It may be acute – i.e. forming and bursting rapidly – or chronic, forming slowly and not bursting unless near the surface. Treatment depends on the site of the abscess, and may involve poulticing (q.v.) treatment with antibiotics (q.v.), or draining.

Acceptance In horse racing, entries for all races are made some time before the race takes place. There may be one or more acceptance stages according to the conditions of the race. Five days before the race, horses have to be declared to run. Their names can be withdrawn or cancelled without additional cost up to 10 or 10.30 a.m. on the day before running. Acceptances and Declarations to Run have to be made at the Racing Calendar Office or the Overnight Declarations Office of the Jockey Club.

Account for The number of foxes killed during a season.

Accumulator In racing, a bet in which two or more horses are backed collectively, and all have to win.

Accumulator competition (show jumping) The course in this competition consists of six, eight or ten obstacles of progressive difficulty. Points scored increase accordingly.

'Acey deucey' American racing term for riding in flat races with one stirrup leather longer than the other.

Acland, Sir Thomas Founder of the famous Acland herd of Exmoor ponies (q.v.). In or about 1818 a Mr Knight purchased the Crown lands of Exmoor Forest. Outbid, Acland, retained the best twenty of the 400 ponies said to be then running on the Moor, to form the nucleus of a new herd. The official brand is an anchor on the near quarter.

Acne A skin eruption usually associated with bacterial infection. It causes small lumps under the skin, which often exude pus, and which are found underneath the saddle or where hair is rubbed; also on face and withers.

Action Good action when on a hard road at a walk produces a regular succession of 1-2-3-4 beats, and should appear as follows. Feet flat on the ground, toes reaching ground a fraction before heels; forefeet, toe and heel in line with body, turned neither in nor out, with straight and full extension of forelimbs, and free shoulder action; hindquarters free and loose, with feet carried under the body by perfect flexion of the hocks, which should have a slight inward tendency with toes turned slightly outwards; the distance between forelegs and hocks neither narrow nor wide. The whole should be free, easy, smooth and slightly languorous. At the trot, the legs of each diagonal must be raised and set down simultaneously, producing a regular succession of two-time. Daisy-cutters (q.v.) are prone to stumble, while exceedingly high action saps energy unnecessarily. The good horse trots from the shoulders, not the knee, legs moving on a straight line, toeing neither in nor out, hindlegs engaging themselves freely and with suppleness. At the canter the stride must be ample, smooth and regular, covering maximum ground with minimum effort, without becoming disunited (q.v.), and sounding three distinct beats: 1-2-3. See also **Action, free**; **Action, cramped**; **Action, extravagant**.

Action, cramped A term used when a horse fails to move freely.

Action, extravagant The very high knee and hock action of a Hackney, or the pronounced action – often verging on the excessive – of throwing the forelegs forward with toes pointed, as sometimes seen in show pony and hack classes.

Action, free Description of a horse's movement when there is plenty of propelling power behind and proper use of the shoulders. A free mover uses the shoulders, knees, pasterns, stifles and hocks to the best advantage and places the forefeet well out in front.

Action, round Showing little liberty or dash in movement. Many high-movers have this fault, and cover the ground very slowly in harness.

Added money In racing, money actually contributed towards the stakes by the racecourse or from other sources as distinct from money contributed by the owners of horses engaged.

Advance flag In racing, where starting stalls are not in use this flag is raised by an assistant stationed in advance of the starting line about 1 furlong's distance (220 yards; 201 m) down the course. In the event of a false start the horses are returned.

African horse sickness This disease, to which only the horse family is naturally susceptible among animals, is caused by a mosquito-transmitted virus. It is endemic in Africa, and has been present in the Middle East and Asia since the 1960s. Nine strains of virus cause four types of the disease, which may affect the heart and lungs. Each begins with a fever, and death from the acute form is common. Protection is offered by vaccination.

Against the clock A show-jumping term indicating that the result will be decided in favour of the competitor completing the course with the least number of faults in the fastest time.

Aga Khan Trophy Competed for by the international teams in the Prix des Nations Show Jumping event at the Dublin Horse Show (q.v.).

Age, a horse's The age of an ordinary horse or pony is reckoned from 1 May of the year in which it was foaled. The age of a Thoroughbred (i.e. one entered in the General Stud Book (q.v.)), dates from 1 January of the year in which it was foaled. South of the equator the age of a Thoroughbred dates from 1 August.

Age, to tell The horse has six incisor teeth above and six below. In the lower set, for example, the following applies (calling the middle pairs of teeth 'centrals', the next on either side 'laterals', and the two outer teeth 'corners'); centrals – cut at two and a half, fully up (level) at three years; laterals – cut at three and a half, fully up (level) at four years; corners – cut at four and a half, fully up (level) at five years. At two years, a horse has six incisors in each jaw – milk teeth with necks – and five cheek teeth on either side of each jaw. At five years it has six permanent incisors and six cheek teeth. A notch appears on the hinder edge of each corner tooth at seven years, wears down and reappears at eleven years (see also **Galvayne's groove**). At six years the

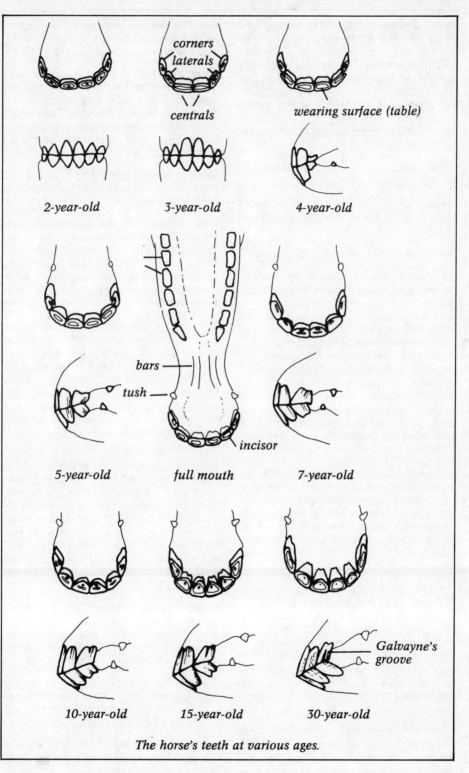

The horse's teeth at various ages.

upper and lower incisors meet at a right angle. As the years pass they become longer and are inclined in a forward direction until at twenty and over they are almost parallel. In the male, tushes appear at about four years. By eight years the grooves in the tables of the incisor teeth have worn away, and from then on the tables begin to become triangular rather than oval.

Aged Describes a horse when it reaches the age of seven years or over.

Ageing The process of telling the age of a horse by its teeth. See **Age, to tell** and diagrams on page 17.

Agist To take in horses or cattle to graze.

Agisters Persons employed by the Verderers (q.v.) of the New Forest in Britain to supervise the welfare of all commonable ponies and other animals turned out on the Forest, and to collect fees (called marking fees) paid by the Commoners in respect of each animal depastured. On payment of the fee, the agister cuts the tail of the pony (tail-marking) in a specific way. Each agister has his own pattern of cutting, which confirms that the fee has been paid, and also indicates in which district of the Forest the pony has been turned out.

Aids Signals by means of which the rider directs and conveys instructions to his horse. There are three principal aids: the legs, the reins or hands, and the seat. These are used in conjunction with the auxiliary aids – the spur, the whip, and the voice.

Aintree The historic racecourse on the outskirts of Liverpool, where the Grand National (q.v.) has been run since 1837. The present distance of the race is 4 miles 856 yards (7.219 km). Races on the flat and over hurdles are also run at Aintree. There are two steeplechase courses – that over which the Grand National is run, and the Mildmay course, which does not include the famous Grand National fences.

Aintree breast girth A simple web breast girth used to prevent the saddle slipping back. Also made of elastic.

Air The correct bearing of a horse in its different movements and paces, being also the correct rhythm in each of these.

Airer, saddle A wooden stand for holding a saddle so that the panel will dry more readily. A more sophisticated modern type is made of fibreglass, into which electrical heating elements are incorporated. This type can also be used to air and dry clothing.

'Airing' A term applied to horses which run in a race but are not intended to show their best form.

Airs, artificial These consist of paces other than the normal gaits of walk, trot and canter. They can only be obtained from the horse at the will of the rider, by careful schooling in the classical manner. Examples are passage and piaffe. (See **High School**)

Airs above the ground Airs above the ground are those movements sometimes called 'school jumps', which are performed with either the forelegs suspended off the ground or all four feet off the ground. They consist of the levade, the courbette, the capriole, the ballotade, and the croupade (qq.v.). (See also **Spanish Riding School** and **Cadre Noir**).

Akhal-Teké A breed of saddle horse found in Southern Turkmenia. One of the first Russian horses to have its own Stud Book. A beautiful horse, with good bone and carriage. Standing between 15-15.2 hh (152.4-157.5 cm), the breed has a sparse, short mane and forelock. Bay, chestnut, grey and black predominate, and the original strikingly attractive dun with a golden sheen is said now to be less common.

Albert headcollar A well-known English pattern of headcollar (q.v.). It is made with either brass or galvanised ('tin') mountings and the cheeks have either two or three rows of stitching.

Albino A congenital deficiency of colouring pigment in a horse's skin and hair which results in white hair, pink skin and blue eyes (sometimes brown).

Albino Horse Since 1937 the White or Albino Horse has been fostered and developed in the USA by the American Albino Horse Club. The foundation horse is said to be 'Old King' foaled in 1906. His breeding is unknown, but he is believed to have been from Arabian-Morgan stock. The Club has developed a riding horse of pure white. The Albino is not a breed but a colour type.

Al Borak The mythological winged horse of Mohammed. It was supposedly white in colour with a human head, and of dazzling splendour and incredible speed.

Alcock Arabian All grey Thoroughbreds are descended in direct (though not exclusively) male line from the grey Alcock Arabian.

Aldin, Cecil Charles Windsor (1870-1935) A prolific sporting artist, one-time Master of the South Berkshire Hunt. His pictures of hunting and famous English inns brought him great popularity. He illustrated his own books including *Ratcatcher to Scarlet* (1927) and *Scarlet to MFH* (1913).

Alfalfa (lucerne) A leguminous plant known and cultivated for more than two thousand years. It has a red and purple flower standing on a strong stalk and in Britain is more generally known as lucerne. Whether in a green state or as hay, it is a very valuable crop, and can be mown four times a season. It survives any drought, as its roots, many feet long, find water at a great depth. Nutritionally it is high in protein (q.v.). It contains naturally-occurring oestrogens (q.v.).

Alken, Henry Thomas, Snr (1785-1851) The most talented of the famous Alken family of sporting artists. He was born in Soho, London, was a pupil of John Thomas Barber, and first became a miniaturist to the Duke of Kent. He visited Leicestershire and hunted from Melton Mowbray, where he obtained first-hand experience of the sporting scene. He also wrote sporting articles under the pseudonym of 'Ben Tally-ho'. His pictures in both oils and watercolours are full of incident, specialising in hunting, racing, and some coaching scenes. He illustrated several books including *National Sports of Great Britain, Jorrocks' Jaunts and Jollities*, and *Memoirs of the Life of the late John Mytton*.

Alken, Samuel, Snr (1756-1815) Senior member of the Alken family of sporting artists, and uncle of Henry Alken, Snr. His pictures covered many sports, including hunting; he was an admirable horse artist, and also an engraver in aquatint.

Alken, Samuel Henry Miscalled Henry Alken Junior (1810-1894). Son of Henry Alken, Snr, born in Ipswich, he depicted similar sporting subjects to those of his father, but was of inferior talent. Confusion is caused by his deliberate use of the same signatures 'H. Alken' or 'H.A.'

'All on' Hunting term used by the whipper-in to indicate that every hound in the pack is present.

'All right, the' After a race, when the jockeys have weighed in to the satisfaction of the Clerk of the Scales, the Stewards authorise a signal (blue flag) to be hoisted over the number board. All bets can then be settled. The flag is not hoisted until the five minutes allowed for an objection has elapsed. Also known as 'Weighed In'.

'All-round my hat' cast See **Smith, Tom**.

All-weather rug See **New Zealand rug**.

Aloes By tradition the horse's purgative, but now superseded by safer and less drastic drugs.

Also ran Any horse which started in a race but finished unplaced.

Alter-Réal A Portuguese riding horse standing 15-15.2 hh (152.4-157.5 cm), known for its spirited temperament. Based on Andalusian (q.v.) mares brought in from Spain to the Villa de Portel Stud some 300 years ago, the breed flourished. It was used in classical haute école until invading Napoleonic troops stole the best horses. The Stud was abolished in 1834. Attempts to revive the breed using Hanoverian, Norman and Arabian blood were unsuccessful, but in 1932 the Ministry of Economy introduced further Andalusian blood, strict culling took place, and the breed improved considerably. It is once again being used in haute école.

Alter, to To castrate or geld a horse or colt.

Amateur According to FEI (q.v.) rules, any person aged 18 and over not attempting to make a profit through competition and not engaging in activities of the Professional, ranks as an Amateur. (For details, see **Professional**)

Amateur rider A person who holds a permit from the Jockey Club to ride as an amateur. This may be limited either to flat races or steeplechases and hurdle races. Any person who has ever held a professional jockey's licence or has been paid for riding in a race or has within the period of the preceding three years been paid as a stable employee in a licensed stable or as a groom or a Hunt servant, is considered to have 'ridden for hire' and is not eligible to ride as an amateur.

Amble An irregular trot produced by the alternate play of the right and left limbs. The limbs on the right are raised and lowered simultaneously, the left limbs alternating with them, the body thus always being out of equilibrium. Ambling is regarded as a serious fault in dressage. Great rapidity is gained by the amble, the smooth and gliding motion of which is very pleasant. Though it is tiring, over-worked and fatigued horses will sometimes amble. From ambling developed what in trotting circles is called 'pacing' (q.v.).

Amble, broken Essentially an American term applied to the gait of four beats as displayed by the five-gaited saddlehorse (q.v.). Each beat of the foot operates separately. It is also known as the single-foot.

American Horse Council A national trade organisation representing over a million American horsemen. It advises on government legislation regarding equestrian affairs.

American Horse Shows Association The controlling body in the USA of all recognised shows. It also evaluates and lists judges as Registered (Senior) and Recorded (Junior), publishes annually a rule book of correct conduct of all concerned with horse shows; and also records addresses of all breed organisations.

American Quarter Horse See **Quarter Horse**.

American runabout A strongly built, but light, four-wheeled, seated utility carriage which once enjoyed great popularity.

American Saddlebred A breed of American riding horse developed during the nineteenth century in the Southern states of the USA, particularly Kentucky, as a comfortable, well-mannered, durable horse on which estate owners could ride round their huge plantations. Originally known as the Kentucky Saddle Horse, the breed was produced by selective cross-breeding of Canadian and Narragansett Pacers, Morgans, Arabs, and Thoroughbreds. The Canadian Pacer, Tom Hall, was a famous sire, but the English Thoroughbred, Denmark, imported in 1839, was selected as the official foundation sire. Now bred almost exclusively for the show ring, the horse competes in either three or five-gaited classes. Three-gaited horses are shown hogged (roached), and five-gaited with full mane. The characteristic tail carriage is obtained by nicking the muscles of the dock and setting the tail in position with a crupper (a practice which is illegal in Great Britain). The horse exhibits great brilliance, and has a high, proud head carriage. The breed stands between 15.2 and 16 hh (157.5-162.6 cm); prevailing colours are bay, chestnut, black or grey, with occasional roans or palominos. Saddlebreds have been exported to Australia in recent years, the first ones being introduced by Mr and Mrs R. Besaw of Sutton Farm, New South Wales. The Australian Saddlebred Association was formed in 1977, and classes for the breed are now held at a number of major shows. Saddlebreds have been winning in both harness and ridden classes in Australia. See **Rack**; and **Gait, Slow**.

American Saddlehorse See **American Saddlebred**.

American Standardbred See **Standardbred**.

American Stud Book (Thoroughbred) This was founded by Colonel Sanders D. Bruce in 1868, and taken over by the New York Jockey Club in 1898.

American Trotting Championship See **Trotting Championship, the American**.

Americas, Pony of the See **Ponies of the Americas**.

Amnion The innermost membrane enclosing the foetus before birth.

Amulets See **Brasses**.

Anaemia/Anemia A condition arising from reduced circulating red blood cells resulting from (a) blood loss (b) haemolysis (destruction of blood cells in the circulation), or (c) bone marrow depression. Signs include paleness of mucous membranes, weakness, and increased heart rate. It may be caused by mineral deficiency, infection, external or internal haemorrhage, poisoning, or parasites such as red worms (q.v.). Treatment by a veterinary surgeon is necessary. See also **Haemolytic disease**.

Anaesthetic (a) General anaesthetic: a drug which renders the animal unconscious to painful stumuli, thus enabling surgery to be performed, (b) Local: a drug injected into the region of a nerve or nerve trunk, causing loss of sensation to the region served by the nerve.

Analgesic Drug which relieves or diminishes the feeling of pain.

Andadura See **Paso Fino**.

Andalusian/Andalucian The origin of this Spanish breed is uncertain. Spaniards assert that it is a purebred native horse with no outside blood in its ancestry. Others suggest that though it is certainly descended from the native horses of the Iberian peninsula it was considerably influenced by the introduction of Barb blood brought to Spain by the Moorish invaders. There is general agreement that the breed contains no Arab blood. The Andalusian, in addition to being an elegant riding horse with great presence and excellent paces, has exerted an influence on other breeds which in all probability is only exceeded by the Arab and the Thoroughbred. It has been used in the development of, among others, the Nonius, Alter-Réal, Lipizzaner, Hanoverian, Oldenburg, and Holstein. The breed's greatest influence was in the Americas, where it was introduced by the Conquistadors, and played a part in the development of such breeds as the Appaloosa, Paso Fino, Criollo and Paint Horse. In Spain, it is still used as a riding horse, and is associated with mounted bull-fighting. It is also used in the *ferias* or fairs, which are still so much a part of Spanish life. The Andalusian is usually grey or bay, with occasional blacks and roans. It stands 15-15.2 hh (152.4-157.5 cm), is a strong, deep-bodied horse, normally having a good front and high, strong quarters. Its temperament is excellent, it has great presence, and is a good and attractive ride.

Aneurysm Dilation of arterial wall as a result of mechanical damage.

Angleberry See **Warts**.

Angle pelham A pelham bit which has a straight bar mouth with right-angle bends at each end. The best-known is the Scamperdale (q.v.), perfected by Mr Sam Marsh.

Anglo-Arab The Arab Horse Society in Great Britain rules that an Anglo-Arab is the cross from a Thoroughbred stallion and an Arab mare, or vice versa, with their subsequent re-crossing; that is, they have no strains of blood other than Thoroughbred and Arabian in their pedigrees. Australia, Canada and Sweden follow this designation, but in other parts of the world a certain minimum percentage of Arabian blood is demanded: in the USA not less than 25% of Arabian nor more than 75% Thoroughbred; in France, South Africa, and the USSR a minimum of 25% Arabian; in Poland 12½% Arabian. The Anglo-Arab is a horse of outstanding quality, possessing all the best attributes of the Thoroughbred and with the more classic head, vivid tail carriage and intelligence of the Arab. It is successful as hunter, hack, in dressage, horse trials, and show jumping.

Anglo-Argentine Horse or polo pony; a cross between a Thoroughbred stallion and Criollo (q.v.) mare. Is an excellent stock horse and outstanding polo pony, and the bigger type make good jumpers.

Anglo-Donetz See **Don**.

Anglo-Kabardin Russian horse developed and bred in the Stavropol region and the Kabardin Republic (North Caucasus) by crossing Kabardin (q.v.) and Karachaev mares with Thoroughbred stallions. There is now between 25% and 75% Thoroughbred in the well-bred Anglo-Kabardin. The average height is 15.2-15.3 hh (157.5-160 cm).

Anglo-Kozakh A Russian agricultural horse developed by crossing Mongolian mares with English Thoroughbreds.

Anglo-Norman This breed was developed in Normandy during the early nineteenth century by crossing English Thoroughbred, half-bred, and Norfolk Roadsters stallions with native mares. (The native mares were descended from the ancient heavy Norman draught horse, which, during the seventeenth century, was itself crossed with Arabs and Barbs.) The light, active horse so produced was a fine trotter, and was used in the development of other breeds such as the Comtois (q.v.), the Freiberger (q.v.) and the Latvian Harness Horse (q.v.).

Animalintex Proprietary name of a type of veterinary poultice.

Ankle The fetlock joint.

Ankylosis Loss of joint movement caused by new bony deposits around the joints. Usually associated with arthritis, it is in reality a terminal healing process, and a horse may be almost free from pain after the affected bones have become fused together and ankylosis is complete, although there may be some loss of joint flexion.

Anne, Queen (1665-1714) Established the Royal Buckhounds Kennels at Ascot and hunted enthusiastically, driving herself in a chaise with a fast horse. At her command in 1711 the racecourse on Ascot Heath was laid out.

Anodynes Medicines which relieve and soothe pain. See **Anaesthetic** and **Analgesic**.

Anoestrus A state in a mare when no signs of season are exhibited. (See **Oestrous cycle**)

Ante-post betting The placing of bets at an agreed price before the day of a race.

Anthelmintics Drugs or substances which kill internal parasites.

Anthrax A notifiable disease (q.v.) rare in horses and humans. It is caused by the anthrax bacillus.

Antibiotics Drugs which kill or inhibit the multiplication of bacteria in the living animal.

Antibodies Proteins (q.v.) produced when a certain kind of substance – an antigen (q.v.), which is foreign to the animal's tissue – gains access. The antibody combines with the antigen, rendering it ineffective. Antibodies are usually specific, i.e. they will combine only with one particular antigen.

Anti-cast roller A stable roller in which the pads are connected by an iron hoop or arch. It is claimed that the hoop prevents a horse from becoming cast in the box. More importantly it ensures that the spine is not subjected to any pressure. The best type is where the plates on to which the pads are attached, are hinged on to the hoop, so making the roller adjustable to any shape of back. Also known as an 'arch roller'. See also **Rollers**.

Antigen A substance, usually a protein (q.v.), which stimulates the body to produce antibodies (q.v.).

Anti-histamine A drug which counteracts the effects of histamine (q.v.).

Anti-lug bit A jointed snaffle bit in which one side of the mouthpiece is shorter than the other, and in which the curve is greatly accentuated. It is used mainly on racehorses which hang to one side. The short side is fitted on the opposite side to that on which the horse hangs.

Antiphlogistine A proprietary name given to Denver clay, and similar to all kaolin poultices widely used for sprains.

Anti-rearing bit A circular bit which, if carefully adjusted, is said to correct rearing. It is known by racing men as a 'Chifney', and its use is confined to led animals who may be difficult to control.

Anti-sweat sheet A mesh cotton sheet which when used under an outer covering creates insulating air pockets next to the body and prevents 'breaking out' (q.v.).

Anvil A base or bed for shaping a horse shoe. Made of wrought iron, it has a face or working surface with a steel plate welded to it, and measures approximately 2 ft x 6 ft (60cm x 90cm). It has a rounded beak or bick used for shaping the shoes.

– but are not required for registration purposes.

Spotted horses have been known through the ages in many parts of the world and are shown in Chinese paintings of 3000 years ago. Other breeds in which spots are either characteristic, or are likely to occur include the Danish Knabstrup (q.v.) and the Austrian

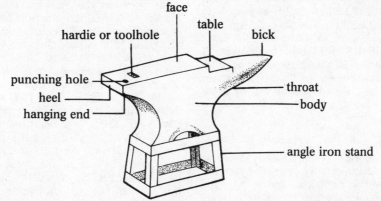

Anvil.

'Apocalypse, Four Horsemen of the' Described by St John in *Revelations*, Chapter 6, as riding a white, red, black, and a pale horse, symbolising conquest, war, famine, and death.

Appaloosa Horse The name derives from a breed of spotted horses developed by the Nez Perce Indians in the Palouse County of Idaho, USA. All spotted horses are not Appaloosas, and to be recognised for registration a horse must possess; (a) the mottled pink and black skin, most clearly seen around the nostrils, lips, and genitals; (b) the distinctive white sclera around the eyes; (c) one of the recognised coat patterns. The five principal patterns are: (1) blanket spotted – a white rump or back on which there are spots of any colour; (2) leopard-spotted – spots of any colour or mixture of colours, e.g. black and chestnut, on a light or white background; (3) snowflake – white on any coat colour except grey; (4) frost – white on a dark background; (5) marble – mottled all over the body. Appaloosa foals may be born with a solid colour coat and may develop one of the required patterns later in life. Other Appaloosa features may be present – e.g. vertically-striped hooves, a fine but sparse mane and tail

Pinzgauer (q.v.). Appaloosas, which are excellent riding horses, are best known in the United States, where they are much used in Western riding. There is now a very active Appaloosa Society in Great Britain, and after a slow start they are gaining popularity in Australia.

Apperley, Charles James (1778-1843) The most important sporting journalist of his day. He worked for *The Sporting Magazine* and *Sporting Review* under the *nom de plume* of Nimrod. Author of several sporting reminiscences including *Post and Paddock*, *Scott and Sebright*, and *Memoirs of the Life of John Mytton*.

Appointment card The hunting programme of forthcoming meets, showing dates and places.

Appointments A term generally referring to the harness and saddlery which a horse wears when at work. The award of a percentage of marks for the care of appointments in turn-out, harness and other classes is a recognition of this. In the USA the term applies to the garb of rider as well as of the horse. These may count for 15% of the marks in classes such as Corinthian (q.v.) Appointments.

'Apprentice, The' Colloquial name for a severe whip, formerly used by drivers of heavy coaches. (See **Short Tommy**)

Apprentices' allowances All lads who have signed an Apprentice Riding Agreement with a licensed flat-racing trainer and who are between 16 and 24 years of age may hold an Apprentice Jockey's Licence. Holders of such licences may claim the following allowances in flat races: 7lb (3.17 kg) until they have won 10 flat races; thereafter 5lb (2.26 kg) until they have won 50 flat races; thereafter 3lb (1.36 kg) until they have won 75 flat races. In all the above cases apprentice races are excepted. These allowances cannot be claimed in some of the more valuable races, as set out in the Rules of Racing.

Appuyer French word for half-pass (q.v.).

Apron, astride riding Usually made in double-texture mackintosh. The material is cut and shaped as an apron, intended to fall about 8 ins (20 cm) below the level of the knees. It is cut away between the legs to allow for the astride position. It is fastened by a belt at the waist on the right side. Leg straps are also fitted to keep the apron in a secure position while riding.

Apron, driving Made of lightweight material for summer driving, and of heavy boxcloth for winter use. It is worn over the knees by the coachman or coach passengers.

Apron, farrier's A divided apron reaching below the knees, usually fitted with a pouch and made from tough horse hide.

Arab/Arabian Arabian horses are those in whose pedigree there is no blood other than Arabian. They are the purest and most beautiful of the equine races, of great antiquity, and unrivalled in their influence on other breeds world-wide. The breed is known to the Arabs as 'Kehailan', the Arabic word for 'pure' or 'thoroughbred', and this purity of blood has been jealously guarded for centuries. Arabians are divided into a number of strains e.g. Saglawi, Ubayar, Hamdain, Managhi and Hadbar. They are possessed of great soundness of wind and limb, extreme powers of endurance, and the ability to thrive in frugal conditions. Because of these qualities, nearly every breed – ranging through types as diverse as the Welsh Mountain Pony and the Percheron – has had an infusion of Arab blood, and every Thoroughbred has Arab blood in its pedigree. Arabian prepotency (q.v.) is most vivid and persistent.

The Arabian is said to be one of the world's oldest established breeds, and it is believed to stem from the primitive wild horse of the Arabian peninsula. Horses with Arabian characteristics are featured on ancient Egyptian monuments of around 1300 BC, and there is an earlier statuette dating back to 2000 BC. The great Arab scholar and publicist Lady Wentworth claimed that the breed was established as far back as 5000 BC. The desert tribes of the Arabian peninsula developed the breed over many hundreds of years, but it was the prophet Mohammed (who died in AD 632) who was probably one of the most significant influences. He raised the status of the Arabian horse by decreeing that as an article of faith particular attention should be paid to the care of horses. After his death, the warlike followers of Islam left the Arabian peninsula and in conquering much of North Africa gained access to Spain and then France, taking their horses with them. Because of their superiority over the indigenous horses of the invaded lands, the Arabians were much used in improving native stock, and so began the influence of the breed – an influence which in time became world-wide.

It is well known that the 'founding fathers' of the English Thoroughbred are the three stallions – the Byerley Turk, the Godolphin Arabian, and the Darley Arabian (qq.v.) – imported into Britain in the last quarter of the seventeenth and the first quarter of the eighteenth centuries. They are almost invariably referred to as Arabs, but because of the former interchangeability of the terms 'Arabian', 'Turk' and 'Barb', some doubt has been expressed about the *true* breed of the illustrious trio. However, it seems certain that the Darley Arabian was a purebred Arab of the Menaghi strain, and that the Godolphin Arabian also was a purebred. What is not in dispute is that all Thoroughbreds can trace direct tail-male lines back to them. They are thus regarded as the foundation stallions of the Thoroughbred breed, although other stallions, such as Darcy's Arabian, the Unknown Arabian, the Leedes Arabian, and the Lister Turk all played significant roles.

The importation of the three foundation stallions was of major significance to the Thoroughbred breed, but it was not until 1878 that further imports occurred. These were made by Wilfred Scawen Blunt and his wife Lady Anne Blunt, the parents of the redoubtable Lady Wentworth. Realising that the quality of Arabian horses in the Middle East was beginning to decline, due chiefly to the owners selling off their best colts, the Blunts made a series of journeys into Arabia from 1878 until about 1896, buying up the finest mares and stallions that they could find, and bringing them back to Britain to found their famous Crabbet Park Stud in Sussex. By so doing they not only saved the purebred Arabian from almost certain extinction, but provided the foundation for subsequent breeding of Arabians in Britain, and also, in due course, in the USA, Australia, South Africa, the USSR and much of Europe. To underline the importance of Crabbet to the world of Arabian horse breeding, animals from the stud were exported to Egypt in 1920 and again in 1938 to improve the native stock. In 1920, another horse which was to exert considerable influence on Arab breeding in Britain was added to the Crabbet Stud by Lady Wentworth. This was the Polish stallion Skowronek, who had been imported by Mr Walter Winans and owned for some years by Mr H. V. Musgrave Clark who founded the famous Courthouse Stud. Showronek proved to be a highly prepotent and prolific stock-getter, and is regarded as the most influential sire of modern times, as he also had a great influence in America, largely through his inbred son, Raffles.

The next significant importations did not come until the 1950s, when another infusion of Polish Arabian blood was introduced by horses brought in by Miss Patricia Lindsay of Stockings Farm Stud, Northamptonshire. The influence of Stockings mares such as Karramba,

Czantoria and Celina, and stallions such as Grojec, Argos and Gerwazy has been considerable.

In more recent times, attempts have been made to enhance what is known as the 'dry desert look' by out-crossing to Spanish Arabs of Syrian and Polish lines.

The Arab horse stands, on average, about 14.3 hh, or 149.9 cm (although some of Lady Wentworth's (q.v.) stood up to 16 hh (162.6 cm), and is of distinctive appearance. The head is small, with a very broad forehead tapering to a fine muzzle, the skin of which is exceptionally soft. The profile is markedly concave (dished), a feature due largely to the 'jibbah'. This is a bulge between the eyes extending from a point between the ears down across the first third of the nasal bone – and is a formation of the frontal and parietal bones in the shape of a shield. It is most pronounced in young animals up to two years, becomes modified at maturity, and is rounder and more prominent in mares. The nostrils are very wide, thin-edged and mobile, allowing considerable flare on exertion or in excitement. The ears are small and finely modelled in a delicate curve. The jowl is deep, circular, and very clearly defined, with the throat set into it in a distinctly arched curve, particularly noticeable in the stallion. The angle at which the head meets the neck is distinctive, and is referred to as the 'mitbah'. The neck makes a slight angle at the top of the crest and from that point rises in a gentle curve to the head. The chest is broad and deep, the ribs well-rounded, and the body deep and roomy. The shoulders are long and sloping, with well-defined withers which are, however, generally less prominent than in Thoroughbreds. The back is short and level, and the tail set on level with the back and carried characteristically high, with a perfect arch when the animal is moving. Arab limbs are typically hard as iron, with steel-like well-defined tendons, and dense, fine bone. Poor hindlegs are not unknown in the breed, but the good ones are strong, with good hocks. The compactness of the Arabian is due to the fact that the breed has five lumbar vertebrae compared with the usual six in other breeds, and seventeen ribs instead of eighteen. There are also sixteen caudal (tail) vertebrae, instead of the usual eighteen.

The action of the Arabian is unmistakeable, particularly at the trot. It is exceedingly free at the shoulder, with the foot thrown well forward, the stifles swinging forward with hocks well lifted, the whole appearance giving a dancing, floating movement as if on springs.

Arab Horse Society Founded in England in 1918 to promote the breeding and importation of pure-bred Arabs and to encourage the re-introduction of Arab blood into English light-horse breeding. The Society holds an annual breed show and twice yearly publishes the *Arab Horse Society News*. It also publishes three stud books – for Arabs, Anglo-Arabs and part-bred Arabs.

Arab, Part-bred In the British Isles these are horses other than Anglo-Arab (q.v.), which have a minimum of 12½% Arabian blood in their pedigree, the remaining ingredient being from any breed other than Thoroughbred. From 1 January 1974 the Arab Horse Society (UK) ruled that requirements for registration of part-breds foaled after that date must be a minimum of 25% Arab blood. In Continental countries definitions vary widely. In the USA, and Canada the part-bred is known as the Half-bred Arabian, and the sire or dam must be pure Arabian, this giving a minimum of 50% Arabian blood. Australia also requires this percentage, with the sire or dam either pure Arabian, a registered Anglo-Arab with at least 50% Arab blood, or of registered part-bred Arabian parentage.

Arabs, in Australia The Arab is one of the oldest-established breeds in Australia, the first ones having been brought in from India around the beginning of the nineteenth century. It had considerable influence on working horses throughout the last century and for most of the period of Australia's development. Until 1960 anyone wishing to register a horse used the English Stud Book, but the breed now has its own Australian stud book. Most of the Arabians in Australia came – at least until comparatively recently –

from English stock (notably from Crabbet Park), but Polish, American and Egyptian blood lines are now playing a significant role. There are now Arab Horse Societies in most Australian states, and the breed is used in a wide variety of competitive events such as endurance rides, Arab racing, barrel-racing (q.v.), and camp-drafting (q.v.). Arabians have also been used as stock horses.

Arabs, in the USA Since World War II the numbers and popularity of the Arabian horse have increased enormously all over the USA. There has been an important introduction of Polish-bred horses and Egyptian blood lines, especially during the 1960s. With breeders living as far apart as Maine and California, there has been in some cases an unfortunate diversion from the classic Arabian conformation of the small fine head, deep chest, short back and high-set tail. Arabian classes at shows include various divisions with Park, English Pleasure, Western, costume, and driving events.

Arch-mouth pelham A bit with an arched mouth, giving maximum tongue room.

Arch roller See **Anti-cast roller**.

Archer, Frederick (1857-1886) Born in Cheltenham, Fred Archer became champion English jockey for thirteen seasons. From the age of 13 in 1870 until his death he rode 8084 races and won 2748. He was nicknamed 'The Tinman' because of his love of money. His will was proved at £66,662. He was a great believer in the persuasive powers of the whip.

Ardennes/Ardennais The Ardennes draught horse has developed in the mountainous region on the French/Belgian borders. It is a very ancient breed. Although at one time the French and Belgian Ardennes were considered a single breed, they have now gone their separate ways. In the French breed, three types have developed: the 'classic' and smallest Ardennes standing 15-15.2 hh (152.4-157.5 cm), found in the east of the country; the Auxois Ardennes, a larger and more powerful version of the 'classic'; and small numbers of the Northern Ardennes, formerly known as the 'Trait du Nord'. The Belgian Ardennes, regarded as a separate breed, is registered with the Royal Belgian Heavy Horse Society. It differs from the Belgian Heavy Draught (q.v.) particularly in outline, being more square, compared with the Belgian's more rectangular shape.

Ariégeois A small French bred, standing between 13.1-14.3 hh (134.6-149.9 cm), from the French Pyrenees, close to the Spanish border. Originally used as a pack animal, the Ariégeois is now used in agriculture and as a riding horse. The breed is sure-footed and exceptionally well adapted to the cold weather, but it cannot stand heat. The colour is solid black, with white flecks on the flanks.

Arkle A champion and very popular steeplechaser, by Archive out of Bright Cherry. Foaled in 1957, he stood 16.2½ hh (167 cm) and was bought by Anne, Duchess of Westminster, trained in Ireland by Tom Dreaper and ridden in his many triumphs by Pat Taafe. During his brilliant career he won 27 out of 35 races. He retired in 1966 after fracturing a bone in his foot when running (and still managing to finish second) in the King George VI chase at Kempton. At the age of 14, and suffering increasingly from rheumatism, he was put down. He is commemorated by a life-size statue at Cheltenham racecourse, and by the Arkle Trophy steeplechase at the same course.

Arkwright bit A curb bit with the curb rein hanging directly from the cheek, without a neck. Also known as the Lowther Bit.

Armlets/Arm-bands The programme number of each racehorse paraded in the paddock must be worn on the arm of the lad in charge.

Armour, George Denholm, OBE (1864-1949) A well-known sporting artist and author whose drawings, mostly in pen and ink, appeared in leading periodicals of the day.

Arterxerxes 'A stiff bay with white legs and a bang tail', the second horse of John Jorrocks, MFH. So called because he came 'arter Xerxes' when driven tandem. (See also **Jorrocks; Xerxes**)

Arthritis Inflammation of a joint, caused by stress, injury or infection.

Articulation Where two or more bones meet, forming a joint.

Artzel Obsolete term for a horse with a white mark on its forehead.

Arve A call to a horse to turn left; 'gee' is the call to turn right. Both are used mainly with agricultural horses. Different terms are used in other districts.

Ascarids See **Worms**.

Ascot/Ascot Heath Ascot Races were founded by Queen Anne (q.v.) in 1711, and have consistently been supported by the Royal Family ever since. The four-day Royal meeting in June is known as Royal Ascot, during which the Monarch drives in procession down the course before the racing begins. The other Ascot meetings are sometimes known as Ascot Heath races.

Ascot Gold Cup The principal long-distance race of the English flat-racing season. Founded in 1807, it is run over 2½ miles (4 km) at the Royal Ascot meeting in June. From 1845 to 1853 it was known as the Emperor's Plate.

'As hounds ran' The distance covered by hounds in a run, measuring each turn from field to field as opposed to 'as the crow flies', which is a straight line from start to finish.

'Asking the question' When a horse has been well tested in a gallop or in a race: i.e. when it has been pushed to its limits.

'Ask off' A term used, especially in show jumping, for the aids given by a rider to the horse at the point of take-off for a fence, i.e. asking the animal to jump.

Asl/Asil An Arabic word implying a horse of illustrious race – a horse of noble lineage.

Ass/Donkey There are more than half a dozen breeds of wild ass living in the world today, falling into two distinct groups, the African and the Asiatic. All breeds of domestic ass (*Equus asinus*) are believed to be descended from the wild ass of Nubia and other parts of North Africa between the Red Sea and the Nile. Though the Egyptians used them before horses, they were long in reaching Europe.

The most common colour is grey/brown, but broken-coloured donkeys are being bred, virtually all bearing a dorsal band/stripe and shoulder stripe. As distinct from the ergots (q.v.) on horses, which tend to be pointed, those on the ass resemble pads. The ass varies in height according to the strain. It is generally docile, intelligent, and very long lived. The male is commonly known as the jackass or 'jack' and the female as the she-ass.

The ass or donkey has become very popular in Britain in recent years, as a pet, for riding, and for driving. The Donkey Breed Society is very active, running a full programme of shows etc.

Assateague See **Chincoteague**.

Astley, Philip (1742-1814) Creator of the modern circus. An ex-Sergeant-Major turned trick rider. He left the Army at the age of 24 with the gift of a fine white horse, Gibraltar, which formed the nucleus of his first circus in a field near the present Waterloo Station. Astley's Amphitheatre eventually became the scene of one of London's most popular diversions where spectacular equestrian dramas and daring feats of horsemanship were staged. He appeared before the French Court and toured Europe as far east as Belgrade.

Atherstone girth A baghide girth shaped at the elbows to prevent galling. Similar to a 'Balding' girth (q.v.).

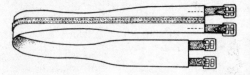

Atherstone girth.

Atlas The first (top) vertebra of the spine.

Australian cheeker See **Noseband, Australian**.

Australian Draught Horse From the days of the early settlers, draught horses played their part in the development of Australia. The breeds most common-ly used were Clydesdales, Shires, Percherons, and a few Suffolks. A Draught Horse Stud Book was started in 1912, but foundered through lack of support, and it was not until 1979 that the Australian Draught Horse Stud Book Society was founded. The Australian Draught Horse is not yet a breed in the generally accepted meaning of the word, being largely a mixture of part-breds, but if the present policy is continued, in which suitability for draught work is a prime requirement, a true breed will no doubt emerge.

Australian loose-ring snaffle A cheek snaffle fitted with a broad, jointed mouthpiece and loose, i.e. traversing, rings. This bit is now better known as the Fulmer snaffle due to the extensive use made of it by Robert Hall (founder of the Fulmer School of Equitation) who virtually reintroduced it to Britain.

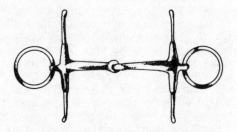

Australian loose-ring or Fulmer snaffle.

Australian Pony Now recognised as Australia's national pony, with its own Stud Book Society founded in 1931. The pony evolved from a variety of pony breeds imported over the last 190 years. Horses and ponies are known to have arrived with the early settlers, although the first *recorded* arrival of a pony was 1803. Early selective breeding, dating from the 1880s, was based on Timor ponies, Shetlands, and some East European breeds referred to as Hungarian. Subsequently, much more British native pony blood was infused, notably Welsh. Hackney stallions were also used. By about 1920 the Australian Pony had evolved as a definite type. The breed has a maximum height of 14 hh (142.2 cm), and is a quality pony of riding type, showing good, straight movement, without exaggerated knee or daisy-cutting action.

Australian Stock Horse The work-horse of the Australian outback, working sheep and cattle, this breed's ancestry includes Arab, Thoroughbred, Percheron and pony blood, with more recent additions of Quarter Horse. It is regarded as the modern descendant of the famous Waler (q.v.). The Australian Stock Horse also competes in many show classes, including the spectacular camp-drafting (q.v.), and is successful in endurance riding. The Australian Stock Horse Society was founded to promote and standardise the breed, and has well over 15,000 registrations in the main book and its appendices.

Australian Stud Book (Thoroughbred) In 1859 the Stud Book of New South Wales was published by Fowler Boyd Price, and the first all-Australian Stud Book was produced by William Yuille in 1878. Horses eligible for the General Stud Book (q.v.) were accepted, plus nineteen families which had produced notable performers but whose pedigrees had been lost in the early colonial days.

Austria, Elizabeth, Empress of (1837-1897) An accomplished horsewoman, who studied equitation seriously and took lessons at the Spanish Riding School in Vienna (q.v.). She hunted with great enthusiasm in England and Ireland between 1876 and 1882, when her skill, courage and elegance created a minor sensation. She is remembered for her remark to her pilot (guide), Captain 'Bay' Middleton, 'I don't mind the falls, but, remember, I will not scratch my face'.

Autorisation spéciale (show jumping) A pink card which riders must obtain from their national federation before competing at an international horse show.

Autumn double The coupling of the winners of the Cambridgeshire and the Cesarewitch. (See **Double**)

Avelignese A stocky, heavily-built pony bred in the mountains of Italy, and not unlike the Austrian Haflinger (q.v.) in appearance. The two breeds have a common ancestor in the Arabian stallion, El Bedavi. Standing 13.3-14.3 hh (139.7-149.9 cm), with great bone and substance, the Avelignese is chestnut, usually with flaxen mane and tail.

'Away from you' A ditch on the far side of a fence is 'away from you'; on the near side is 'to you'.

Azoturia Also known as 'setfast', or 'tying up'. A degenerative condition of the muscles, especially of the back and hindquarters, believed to be caused by excessively rapid conversion of muscle glycogen to lactic acid. It occurs in animals on a high protein diet, and develops during exercise after a day or two of rest. Some horses appear pre-disposed to the condition. The horse is reluctant to move forward, sweats profusely, and is stiff. The muscles of the back and hindquarters are hard and painful. There may be paralysis. The pulse and respiration rates are increased, and the temperature rises. The animal may with difficulty pass dark red, strong-smelling urine. Veterinary treatment is essential.

—B—

b. Bay. (See **Bay (colour)**)

BDS British Driving Society (q.v.).

BEF British Equestrian Federation (q.v.).

BEVA British Equine Veterinary Association (q.v.).

BFSS British Field Sports Society (q.v.).

BHS British Horse Society (q.v.).

BHSAI British Horse Society Assistant Instructor.

BHSI British Horse Society Instructor.

BHSII British Horse Society Intermediate Instructor.

Bl Black. (See **Black (colour)**)

BMPS Brood Mare Premium Scheme (q.v.).

BPS British Palomino Society (q.v.).

Br. Brown. (See **Brown (colour)**).

BSHCA British Show Hack and Cob Association (q.v.).

BSJA British Show Jumping Association (q.v.).

BSPS British Show Pony Society (q.v.).

BVA British Veterinary Association.

Babbler A hound which throws its tongue too much, either when it is not sure of the scent or when it is very far behind the leading hound.

Babieca The white horse of the legendary Spanish warrior Diaz de Bivar (d.1099) known as El Cid.

Back, hollow When the natural concave line of the back is exaggerated and unnatural.

Back, sore Caused by bad stable-management and poor horsemanship, e.g. the use of ill-fitting saddles, creating pressure or friction on particular parts of the back; slack girths; working unfit horses, etc. Prevented by ensuring the back is hard, that the saddle fits, and that the rider is sufficiently competent to sit squarely without rolling in the saddle.

Back, to (racing) To make a bet on a horse.

Back, to A term commonly used when an unbroken horse is first mounted.

Back, to To make a horse move backwards.

Back at the knee See **Calf-knee**.

Backband A strap going over or through the pad and carrying the weight of shafts or traces.

Back blood/Back-breeding A term applied to a hereditary trait in any particular family of horses which is liable to influence constitution and conformation of succeeding generations.

Back, cold Said of a horse when he dislikes the pressure of a cold saddle and 'plays up'. Warming the saddle first will often prevent bucking. Saddling up and girthing loosely some time before mounting helps.

Back, dipped This occurs in a horse when the dip between the withers and the croup is abnormally pronounced. It is often noticeable in old age.

Backgammon board Seat on the roof at the rear of a coach.

Backing Stage in breaking and training when the trainer ultimately succeeds in sitting on a horse's back.

Back strap See **Tugs**. The term is sometimes used outside the saddlery trade to denote the backband (q.v.).

Back straps Strips of leather which run from the top of the counter and up the back seams of riding boots to cover and protect them.

'Back up' See **Back, cold**.

Badger-pied A lightly marked cream or lemon hound with back and ears shading into fawn and black.

Badikins An arrangement for harnessing a horse to the plough, a crossbar to which the traces are fixed, also known as suppletrees, swiveltrees and whippletrees.

Badminton (Badminton House, Gloucestershire, ancestral home of the Dukes of Beaufort) The name is synonymous with the very soul of fox-hunting. In 1949 it was here that the first three-day event in Great Britain took place (other than the Olympic competition at Aldershot the previous year). It is now held annually in spring and attracts numerous competitors and many thousands of spectators.

Bag-fox (colloquially known as a Bagman). A fox kept temporarily in captivity and turned out for the purpose of being hunted on a given day in a given locality. Generally deemed a disreputable practice. In the nineteenth century there was a considerable demand for bag-foxes by poachers who sold them again to the hunts. A recognised source was Leadenhall Market in the City of London, hence another name for a bag-fox – a 'Leadenhaller'.

Baghide Name given to the cowhide which has an imprint or pattern on it and which covers any imperfections of the hide. Used for well-known three-folded (baghide) girth.

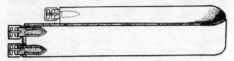

Baghide or three-fold girth.

Bahram Unbeaten winner of ten races, who won £43,000 in stakes for the Aga Khan. Won the 2000 Guineas, Derby and St Leger in 1935, and thus became the fourteenth winner of the Triple Crown (q.v.) in English racing history.

Baigi See **Buzkashi**.

Baily's Hunting Directory The annual directory of the hunts of the British Isles, Commonwealth, Europe and the USA.

Bait When a horse is stood in a stable for any brief period, and provided with food, it is said to be 'at bait'. Primarily a draught-horse term.

Balance This is achieved when a horse carries its own weight and the weight of its rider in such a way that it can use and control itself to best advantage at all paces and in all circumstances. To achieve this, the horse must maintain the distribution of its weight almost equally over the forehand and the hindquarters.

Bald face A horse with an entirely white face.

'Bald-headed' On 31 July 1760, Lieutenant-General the Marquis of Granby when leading the 6th Inniskilling Dragoons in a cavalry charge at the Battle of Warburg, lost his wig and so originated 'Going at it bald-headed'.

Balding gag bridle A large-ring gag snaffle. The size and weight of the rings prevent the gag effect coming into play until

Balding girth.

considerable pressure is used. Perfected by the late William Balding of Rugby (a well-known polo player).

Balding girth A cleverly constituted non-gall girth. The girth is split into three and plaited, thus giving maximum freedom for the horse's arms. Perfected by the late William Balding of Rugby.

Balearic An ancient and very distinctive type of horse found on the island of Majorca in the Balearic group, and most abundant in the Palma district. Differs from all other breeds in its slender limbs, free graceful carriage, short, thick, arched neck, delicate head, Roman nose, ears directed backwards, and thick, upright mane. Believed to be a descendant of the horses depicted on ancient vases and Greek coins.

Bales Very stout, oblong lengths of timber hanging from stable roof to convert any space (possibly a loose box) into stalls.

Balios See **Xanthus**.

Balking (or Baulking) When a horse refuses to jump or refuses to move at all. (See also **Jibbing**)

Balling A method of administering medicine in the form of a ball by means of a balling gun. Nowadays administration is with liquids through a stomach-tube.

Balling A hard 'caking' of an ice-like lump of snow found within the confines of the shoe, when a horse is ridden in snow. May be alleviated by greasing the soles of the feet thoroughly before the horse leaves the stable.

Balloon bit A hack bit with fancy cheek, in shape of balloon; similar to well-known Globe cheek pelham (q.v.).

Ballotade High School air above the ground when the horse is almost parallel to the ground at the summit of its leap. The forelegs are bent at the knees, hindlegs showing their shoes, as happens in a kick, except that the legs are not stretched as they would be in kicking. (See **Airs above the ground**)

Ball's Bridge (Dublin, Eire) Headquarters of the Royal Dublin Agricultural

Society and showground of the Dublin Horse Show.

Balmerino Top-class New Zealand racing Thoroughbred by the French-bred Trictrac. An unimpressive yearling, kept by his owner/breeder, Mr Ralph Stuart, partly because he was thought unsuitable to sell, and partly because of a lump in his leg which needed removal. As a two-year-old in the 1974-75 season he won only one of four races, but as a three-year-old he was the first horse to be placed top of the Free Handicaps in both Australia and New Zealand. He won fourteen times in eighteen races, including the New Zealand 2000 Guineas, the New Zealand Derby, and the Wellington Derby. Brought to Britain as a four-year-old, he won at Goodwood, and then came second in the French Prix de l'Arc de Triomphe. He retired to stud in New Zealand.

Bampton Fair (Devon) One-day annual fair held in October and dating from 1258.

Banbury bit Revolving and sliding mouthpiece found in both curb and pelham bits. Encourages the horse to 'mouth' the bit and prevents his 'catching hold' of it.

Bandages Bandages are used for a variety of purposes: on the tail for protection and to keep the hairs in place; on the legs of sick or lame horses for warmth, to help reduce heat and inflammation, and for support; on the legs during exercise and work for support and protection.

EQUIHOSE BANDAGES: Tubular, elasticated socks and stockings, similar to human surgical stockings, used for exercise, and in the stable for support. Made specifically for hocks, tendons, and fetlocks.

EXERCISE/WORKING BANDAGES: Similar to tail bandages (i.e. elasticated) and applied, over gamgee, from the knee to just above the fetlock joint.

STABLE/TRAVELLING BANDAGES: Woollen (occasionally stockinette) bandages, approximately 5 ins (12.5 cm) wide and 8 ft (240 cm) long, with tape or Velcro fastenings. Applied to the leg from knee to coronet.

STARCH BANDAGES: Ordinary linen bandages dipped into liquid starch and applied to an injured limb whilst still wet. When dry, they become hard, and hold the limb as if in a splint.

TAIL BANDAGE: A long elasticated bandage with either tape or Velcro fastening at one end. It is applied to keep the tail slim and neat. Tail bandages should not be damped or put on too tightly or they will damage the hair and cause discomfort. In polo, bandages are worn on tails to prevent the hair being caught by the stick in course of play.

Bang-tail A tail with hair squared-off close to dock or solid part of tail. Those connected with heavy horses refer to banging up the tail in the sense of tying it up.

Barb A horse originating in Morocco and Algeria. A large number of Barbs were taken to Spain by the Moslem invaders in the eighth century. From there, in due course, they spread to many other European countries, and finally, with the Conquistadors, to South America. Many were imported into Britain, including, for example, Richard II's Roan Barbary, and there is little doubt that Barbs were influential in the development of the Thoroughbred – although less so than the Arab. Other breeds which were almost certainly influenced by Barb blood include the Andalusian, the Criollo, and the Mustang. Barbs are still found in North Africa, but the purity of their breeding is open to question. They stand between 14-15 hh (142.2-152.4 cm) with flat shoulders, a rounded chest, relatively long head, and tail set lower than an Arab, with the hair of the tail and mane very profuse. The breed is of hardy constitution, and docile in temperament, less spirited than the Arab and of far less refinement and quality.

Bard/Bardel Covering of armour for the breast and flanks of a warhorse. Also a term occasionally used for an ornamental covering for a horse, and for a stuffed pack saddle for an ass or mule.

Bardot French term denoting offspring of pony or horse sire and female ass. (See **Hinny; Genet**).

Bare-back riding Riding without use of saddle or blanket.

Barême French term for the two tables of show-jumping faults set by the FEI (q.v.). Table A is judged on the normal system of 4 faults for each fence knocked down, etc., while Table C is for speed classes in which penalties are scored in seconds added to each competitor's time over the course.

Barley A very fattening high-energy food, containing sugar, more starch than oats, protein, and cellulose. It is one of the chief constituents of most horse nuts. It *must* be boiled if used whole, but if crushed or rolled it may be fed uncooked. To prepare whole barley, it should be soaked overnight and boiled until it forms a jelly. Too much barley can cause colic and kidney damage. Useful in tempting a shy feeder.

Barlow, Francis (c.1626-1702) Considered to be the earliest artist of the British Sporting School. He worked in London as an etcher as well as a painter of English country sports. Some of his finest pictures can be seen at Clandon Park, near Guildford, Surrey.

Bar mouth Name describing any straight mouthpiece. It can be found in either the snaffle, pelham or curb bit, but the name usually refers to a stallion bit.

Bar muzzle Two bars laid over the open end of the muzzle. They allow the horse to drink, but make bed-eating, crib-biting, rug-tearing, etc., impossible.

Barnet Fair (Hertfordshire) Annual fair for horses, ponies and cattle held by Charter granted in 1199 by King John to the Abbot of St Albans. Well-known market for small tradesmen's and costermongers' horses and ponies.

Barnum A schooling device named after the American circus owner, it is similar to a bridle used by the horse trainer, Jesse Beary. It consists of a leather head strap sewn to the offside rings of a rubber snaffle and a cord arranged so that it pulls the bit upwards and tightens on the head should the horse resist or attempt to break away from the trainer. It can also be used as a form of twitch.

'Bar one' (or any number) A racing expression indicating a wager offered or accepted on any runner except the selected one or more.

Barouche Large open carriage of family capacity with a high box-seat. Used from Regency to early Victorian times with four horses or a pair.

Barouche-sociable See **Vis-à-vis**.

Barra Pony A breed of Highland pony once indigenous in the Outer Hebrides but no longer recognised as a separate breed.

Barrage See **Jump-off**.

Barraud, Henry (1811-1874) and William (1810-1850) Two brothers who painted individually and also collaborated in sporting pictures. A well-known work is their splendid portrait 'Charles Davis, Huntsman to Queen Victoria's Buckhounds on his Grey Hunter, Hermit'.

Barrel Body of the horse, extending from behind forearms to loins.

Barrel-racing A form of horseracing which is practised in Australia and North America, where competitors race between and around barrels laid out in a standard pattern. The countries concerned have their own associations which issue governing rules and conditions of entry.

Barren Incapable of conceiving and producing a foal. See **Fertility**.

Bars Wooden poles to which leaders' (lead horses') traces are attached when pulling a carriage. The main bar is hung on the pole hook, and two swing bars hang between the main one. The pole hook is called the 'swan-neck' and is also known as stradstick, swingletree, singletree, whippletree and badikin.

Bars (of bits) The cheekpieces or arms of all forms of curb bits.

Bars (of foot) Partial outer surround to frog. Inflection or turning in of wall at heels.

Bars (of mouth) Space between tushes and molar teeth on which the bit lies in the mouth. The portion of the lower jaw where the gums are devoid of teeth.

Bars (of a saddle) Metal strips under the skirts of a saddle to which stirrup leathers are attached.

Bar shoe See **Shoes**.

Bascule The action of a horse when clearing the summit of an obstacle. He drops his head and neck, which acts as a balance, and folds up his front legs. Derived from the French *basculer*, to see-saw.

Bashkir/Bashkirsky A Russian pony/ horse of the southern foothills of the Urals used for pack and agricultural work. They are extremely hardy and tough, living out in temperatures more than 30° below freezing, and are capable of long journeys without sustenance. The mares' milk is used in making a fermented liqueur. The ponies are strong and solid, with massive heads and short, thick necks. Average height 13.3-14 hh (139.7-142.2 cm).

Bass brooms Stable brooms; made of South African bahia.

Basse École The phase preparatory to haute école (q.v.) during which the horse is exercised on one and two tracks in order to develop its natural paces which must attain perfect regularity. See also **Lower School**; **Campagne School**.

Bastard strangles This may follow Bacteraemia (bacteria in the bloodstream). It is associated with strangles (q.v.). Abscesses may develop in any of the internal organs.

Basterna A Roman horse litter with poles attached to a horse in front and behind, as in a form of sedan chair.

Basuto A hardy breed of South African pony. It is not indigenous to the country but is descended from four Arab and Barb horses imported from Java to the Cape by the Dutch East India Company in 1653. They in turn became founders of the Cape horse, the direct ancestor of the Basuto pony. Importation of Arabs, Barbs and Persians continued until 1811, when English Thoroughbreds of the very best lines were introduced. The pony was much bred and respected up to the time of the Boer War, since when it has declined in numbers and has deteriorated, through lack of interest. It has great powers of endurance and can carry 13-14 stone (883-889 kg) for 60-80 miles (95-130 km) a day.

Batak (or Deli) Pony bred in Batak Hills of Sumatra and exported from Singapore in large numbers. It has a handsome, high-bred looking head and a high-crested neck. Bataks differ considerably from Mongolian and Yarkandi ponies which are ewe-necked, the difference being due to a heavy infusion of Arab blood. Average height is about 11.3 hh (119.4 cm) or slightly larger. Brown is the predominating colour. A stouter built pony (Gayoe) with shorter, thicker legs and heavier hindquarters is found in the Gayoe Hills at the northern end of Sumatra.

Bath and West and Southern Counties Society (founded 1777) Holds an annual four-day show, with many classes for horses, on a permanent showground at Shepton Mallet, Somerset.

Batys A word used by Irish tinkers (gipsies) when referring to piebalds or skewbalds.

Baucher, Francois (1796-1873) Famous French horseman and instructor. Author of *Principes d'équitation*. Has had great influence on modern riding.

Baucher's snaffle See **Fillis bridoon**.

Baulking See **Balking**.

Bausonned (Archaic Northern and Scottish term of French derivation) Having any large white marking not amounting to piebald or skewbald. Stockings (q.v.) but not socks (q.v.), a white face, or a big blaze (q.v.) and snip (q.v.). Not just a star (q.v.).

Bay Essentially angry, baffled cry of hounds.

Bay See **Brow, Bez and Trez**.

Bay (colour) Bay varies considerably in shade from dull red approaching brown, to a yellowish colour approaching chestnut, but can be distinguished from the chestnut by the fact that the bay has a black mane and tail and almost invariably has black on the limbs.

Bay (to be or stand at) Where a hunted stag or boar turns to face and challenge hounds.

Bayard The battle charger of Renaud, eldest of the four famous sons of Aymon, Duke of Dordon, who lived in France in the time of the Emperor Charlemagne (AD 742-814). The horse was of phenomenal strength and extraordinary intelligence and figured in many mediaeval songs and stories. Another Bayard belonged to Fitzjames in Sir Walter Scott's *The Lady of the Lake*.

Bay-brown (colour) Where predominating colour is brown, with bay muzzle, black limbs, mane and tail.

Bayo Criollo (q.v.) term to describe cream colour in horses.

Beagles Small hounds used for hunting hares on foot.

Beam Dimension of main antler of stag, i.e. heavy beam or light beam.

Beaning Coper's trick. When an animal was lame on one front foot, a small piece of metal or sharp stone was placed in between sole and wall of the sound hoof in order to cause temporary pain so that, being tender in both front feet, the horse appeared to go sound.

Beans (and peas) These are highly nutritious, as they are rich in protein, and therefore should be fed only in small quantities of 1lb (0.45 kg) or so at a time. They should be at least a year old, hard, dry, sweet to the taste, and free from weevil or split. They are not much used these days.

Beans The black centres of incisor teeth.

Bearing The surface of the shoe in contact with the foot. Also the surface of the foot in contact with the ground.

Bearing rein Rein from pad to bridle, used when necessary to stop the horse lowering the head beyond a certain point. Much used at one time to induce and retain high head carriage in harness horses.

Bearing rein (full) Gag-like rein for supporting the head of a harness horse. Unlike bearing rein (simple), it runs from a billet stitched to a 'head' and is then passed through the swivel on the bridoon bit, from which it is taken through another swivel to the terret (q.v.).

Bearskin cape A cape worn by coachmen of the best class private 'town' vehicles in cold weather.

Beast Name applied to a horse by some people, but not by horsemen, except to an animal justifying the opprobrious term.

Beaufort, Henry Arthur Fitzroy Somerset, 10th Duke of (1900-1984) Master of the Horse to Edward VIII, King George VI, and Queen Elizabeth II, for a record forty-one years. The office was also held by two of his ancestors: the 4th Earl of Worcester, who was Master of the Horse to Queen Elizabeth I, and the 8th Duke of Beaufort, Master to Queen Victoria.

Educated at Wixenford, Eton, and Sandhurst, 'Master' (as he was universally and affectionately known) served in the Blues. He succeeded to the Dukedom on the death of his father in 1924.

Master of the Beaufort Hunt for sixty years until his death, he was a brilliant huntsman and a great breeder of foxhounds, winning some thirty-seven championships at Peterborough Royal Hound show. He was President of the British Field Sports Society for fifty-five years from its formation, Chairman of the Master of Foxhounds Association from 1940-50, President of the British Horse Society in 1958, of the Royal International Horse Show for thirty years, and of the Royal Windsor Horse Show for forty years.

Having watched with interest the 1948 Olympic three-day event at Aldershot he offered Badminton Park as a venue for an annual event from 1949 – and, in effect, laid the foundation for subsequent British successes in international horse trials.

Away from the horse world the Duke held many important offices, including Lord Lieutenant of Gloucestershire, President of the MCC, and Chancellor of Bristol University. He was created a GCVO in 1930, a Privy Councillor in

1936, and a Knight of the Garter in 1937.

Beaulieu Road Sales Near Lyndhurst in the New Forest, where periodical sales of New Forest Ponies take place under the auspices of the New Forest Pony Breeding and Cattle Society.

Beberbeck Stud Originated from the region of the same name in North West Germany, and famed for the excellent natural conditions for breeding horses. The stud of that name existed for 100 years before the First World War, but was subsequently bought by the Polish Government. Local mares were crossed with Arabs, and later Thoroughbred horses were used. Somewhat like a heavier type of Thoroughbred, they proved very useful cavalry horses. Of good conformation, deep girth, and with much bone, they stand over 16 hh (162.6 cm), and make good cart horses.

Becher, Captain Martin William (1797-1864) Served abroad for three years with the British army of occupation after the Napoleonic wars. He made his first appearance in cap and jacket in 1823, and was one of the greatest steeplechase riders of his day. In the third Grand National at Aintree, in 1839, he rode Conrad. At the fence with double rails and a large ditch dammed on the far side, the horse hit the rails, and the Captain went over its head. The brook has been called 'Becher's' ever since.

Beckford, Peter (1740-1811) Eminent sportsman and Master of Foxhounds. He described the whole system of the sport of hunting minutely, accurately, and in scholarly style in *Thoughts on Hunting*, published in 1781. 'Never', wrote Sir Egerton Brydges, 'had fox, nor hare the honour of being chased to death by so accomplished a hunter, nor a huntsmen's dinner graced by such urbanity and wit. He would bag a fox in Greek, find a hare in Latin, inspect his kennels in Italian and direct the economy of his stables in exquisite French'. His writings on hunting are recognised today as classics for all time.

Bedded down Implies that the horse's bed is 'set' and comfortable for the night.

Bedding Used in loose boxes to prevent draughts, to provide warmth, to prevent injury when the horse lies down, and to assist drainage. Good bedding should have the following qualities: soft, dry, warm, non-toxic to skin or if eaten, absorbent, drains well, clean and relatively dust free, easily disposable. The principal materials used are:

WHEAT STRAW: Traditionally considered the best, as it is light, drains well, is durable, and is not usually eaten. Good quality straw is clean and relatively dust-free.

OAT STRAW: Less good than wheat straw, and is often eaten. It is inclined to be dusty, less durable, and less well draining than wheat straw.

BARLEY STRAW: Similar to oat straw, but can cause skin irritation, and also colic if eaten.

SAWDUST: Economical and easy to work, but it must be dry. Care must be taken that it does not contain any impurities from the sawmill, such as wood treatment material or pieces of metal. It tends to clog drains; it becomes hot and wet. Easily disposable by burning.

WOOD SHAVINGS: Less dusty than sawdust; is not eaten, but frequent removal of droppings is essential. Easy to handle and is now available in bales. Easily disposable.

PEAT: Expensive, but now dry peat is used it is less heavy to handle, warm, and a comfortable bed.

SHREDDED PAPER: Dust free and often used for horses with allergies and wind problems. Not very easy to manage. Easily disposable.

DEEP LITTER SYSTEM: A bed made with a deep foundation of e.g. peat or moss, with a good layer of straw on top. Droppings are removed, but little or no mucking out is done. The bed is 'topped up' from time to time with straw.

Bed-eating A pernicious and to some extent harmful habit acquired by some horses. The use of a muzzle (q.v.) at non-feeding times is suggested.

Bedford cord Very hard-wearing material used for breeches, originally manufactured in the town of Bedford. The rounded cord effect is produced in the weave with sunken lines which run lengthwise. For exceptionally hard wear, cotton thread is introduced into the warp. Bedford cords, however, can be made of all wool, all worsted or all cotton, or a combination of any of them. Nowadays it is being superseded by man-made fibres.

Behind the bit The horse is behind the bit when, refusing to keep the contact with it, he draws his head behind the vertical towards his chest, and thus evades its action. (See **Overbent**) It is the consequence of a lack of impulsion and a bad hand.

Belgian Heavy Draught A horse of great weight and traction power, standing 16-17 hh (163-173 cm), originating in low-lying country in Belgium where there is fertile soil and succulent herbage. This heavy horse has a good temperament, a strong constitution, and is a willing worker. It was formerly exported to England, where it is claimed to have had a certain influence on the Shire. In recent years, the breed has been exported to the USA, where breeders have produced them selectively to achieve a lighter, more 'refined' animal, considerably removed from those still bred in Europe. Belgians were used in America in the famous Forty Horse Hitch, driven by Dick Sparrow in 1972.

Belgian Warmblood A breed developed in Belgium after World War II based on Dutch Gelderlanders, Hanoverians, and French warmblood breeds, and bred primarily as a performance horse. Registration is subject to inspection and performance testing, and in 1987 a total of 140 stallions and 8000 mares had been included in the Stud Book. The success of the breed may be judged by the performance of such horses as Cyrano, ridden by top show jumper Edgar Cüpper, and Jet Lag, by Nick Skelton. In the 1976 Olympics there were two warmbloods, Gai Luron and Porsche, in the Belgian team which won the show-jumping bronze medal.

Bell boots Another name for over-reach boots (q.v.).

'Belling' Weird and somewhat terrifying

note uttered by stags in the mating season.

Bell-mare Usually a steady and reliable old mare, around whose neck is a hung a bell which acts as a signal and guide to other horses in a herd, so that they will follow her.

Bellyband (harness) In single harness, usually one long piece of double-sewn leather forming bellyband and backband, sliding through pad or saddle. In double harness it is attached to the pad.

Belmont Stakes This is the senior of the three American Classic Races (q.v.), having been launched in 1867 at Jerome Park, which is no longer in operation. It was run at Morris Park from 1890 until Belmont Park opened in 1905. It has been run at various distances, starting at 1⅝ miles (2.6 km) from 1867-1873, but since 1926 it has been over 1½ miles (2.4 km). The race was not renewed in 1911 and 1912, when New York racing was closed by anti-gambling legislation. The Belmont Stakes conditioned for three-year-olds – geldings were excluded until 1957 – and is held in early June.

Belvoir tan Foxhound of dark rich mahogany and black with no white unless in the form of a collar. Derived from Senator, a hound whose mounted head adorns a wall in Belvoir Castle.

Benches Kennel term for broad wooden shelves or platforms on which hounds sleep.

Bending tackle Form of breaking tackle specifically used for altering 'carriage' of horse. The best known is called the Gooch Set, perfected by the late J. E. Walker MRCVS. Tension is from the horse's hindquarters, and a device incorporating the use of a Jodhpur curb (q.v.) is used to raise the horse's head to prevent over-bridling. A Wilson bit (See **Wilson snaffle**) in a special bridle is always used with this tackle so that tension is brought on to the nose and not the mouth.

Benjamin A coat consisting of as many as six capes, often with big pearl buttons, worn by coachmen. It had a double layer of cloth extending the full length of the outside of the sleeves for extra warmth.

Bennett, Godfrey D. S. (1884-1953) known authority on hackney horses and ponies of his time, having been a lifetime student of the breed. He had an expert knowledge of pedigrees, and wrote *Famous Harness Horses* which is regarded as the most important contribution to the subject.

Bentinck Benevolent Fund Lord George Bentinck was largely instrumental in an objection to Running Rein in the Derby of 1844. It was proved that the horse was a four-year-old, entered in a race restricted to three-year-olds. As a result of this, and several other contemporary scandals, the Jockey Club tightened up its rules regarding fraudulent practices. In appreciation of his services a public subscription was started and £2100 was collected, but he refused to accept anything. So in 1847 it was decided that the amount subscribed should be applied to form the nucleus of a charitable fund. Beneficiaries are licensed flat-race trainers and jockeys in needy circumstances, and their dependants. It is administered by Weatherbys (q.v.).

Bentinck bit A ported curb mouth with additional gated port attached.

Berenger, Richard (d. 1782) Author of *The History and Art of Horsemanship*, London, 1771.

Beresford Trust Founded in 1902 by Mr William Whitney of New York in memory of Lord William Beresford. To create the fund, Mr Whitney gave investments and securities equivalent to the Derby Stakes won by his horse Volodyovski, in 1901. Beneficiaries are unlicensed stable and stud employees, or their dependants, who are no longer able to work because of old age or ill-health. Administered by Weatherbys (q.v.).

Berkley bit A pelham with rings attached to existing top ring, similar to a Rugby pelham bit (q.v.), usually with a mullen mouth (q.v.).

Betting In horse-racing, betting is of two kinds: 'post', when wagering does not begin until the numbers of the runners are hoisted on the board; and 'antepost', when wagering opens in advance of the race day.

Betting shop Prior to the Betting, Gaming and Lotteries Act of 1963 all off-course betting in Britain was illegal. This Act legalised betting in shops licensed for the purpose.

Bhutan A pony bred in parts of Nepal and other Himalayan regions from Punjab to Darjeeling. It has much the same characteristics as the Spiti (q.v.) though is slightly bigger, averaging 13.3 hh (135 cm). Predominant colours are grey and iron-grey.

Bianconi car A public passenger vehicle of large capacity, used in place of stage coaches in Ireland before the advent of railways. Sideways seating is provided as in a jaunting car (q.v.), but the vehicle has four wheels and is drawn by a team or unicorn (q.v.). It was introduced and popularised by an Italian who gave it his name.

Bib A stout leather or plastic protection strapped beneath the stable headcollar to prevent a horse from biting its clothing.

Bib martingale See **Martingale, bib**.

Bicorne Two-cornered hat of Napoleonic origin worn by the riders of the Imperial Spanish Riding School of Vienna (q.v.).

Bidet A term used during the eighteenth century for a small saddle horse hired out for riding.

Big head Also known as osteodystrophia, osteoporosis, or miller's disease. Found in horses on unbalanced diets of cereals, hay, or bran, high in phosphorus and low in calcium. Untreated cases show enlargement of the face and swelling of the lower jaw. The symptoms are lameness, creaking joints, and arching of the back, with fractures and sprains in severe cases. It is treated by correcting calcium and phosphorus ration, feeding lucerne, or clover and limestone.

Big leg See **Lymphangitis**.

Bigourdan See **Tarbenian**.

'Bike' Hunting pronunciation of 'back'. 'Tally-ho bike' means 'back'.

Bike (USA) The two-wheeled, pneumatic-tyred, steel-spoked sulky (q.v.) used for trotting and pacing races for Standardbreds or racing ponies, or Roadster classes at shows.

Bilgoraj See **Konik**.

Billesdon Coplow Run A famous hunting episode dating back to 1800, when Hugo Meynell hunted the Quorn. After finding in the Billesdon Coplow covert the run lasted 2 hours 15 minutes over a distance of 28 miles (45 km).

Billet A term for buckle and strap attachment on a bridle.

Billet The excreta of a fox.

Binder A hunting term given to the top horizontal branch of a cut-and-laid fence (q.v.).

Biped The combination of two limbs. There are six bipeds: fore biped – the two forelegs; hind biped – the two hindlegs; near lateral bipeds – near fore and hind; off lateral biped – off fore and hind; near diagonal biped – near fore and off hind; off diagonal biped – off fore and near hind.

'Bird-eyed' An expression, now little used, denoting a horse whose manners may in other respects be impeccable, but which shies, usually violently, at imaginary objects in hedges.

Birth (or Parturition) Is the normal process of foaling. The signs of approaching birth include the filling of the udder, formation of wax on the teats, relaxation of the vulva, and softening of the muscles around the tail (slackening). The birth itself is divided into three stages. In the first stage the wall of the uterus goes into rhythmic contractions. During this, the mare may be restless – sweating, pawing the ground, looking at her flanks, etc. – but may feed in between bouts of discomfort. When birth is imminent, the vulva becomes relaxed and long, the mare sweats profusely, and milk drips from the udder. Finally the placenta ruptures and the placental fluid escapes – the process of 'breaking the waters'.

Stage two is the actual birth, normally lasting from 30 to 60 minutes. The foal is expelled by uterine contractions, with the forelegs and head presented first. The foal is surrounded by the shiny, membranous amnion – the membrane normally being broken after birth by the foal's front feet.

The third stage is the expulsion of the after-birth (placental membrane), and it is essential that this 'cleansing' should be complete.

Bishoping Filing or otherwise altering the exterior or cups of a horse's teeth to give a false indication of age. Where black marks have disappeared with age they can be reproduced artificially by burning with a hot iron.

Bit, action of See **Rein aids**.

Bit burr See **Brush pricker**.

Bit connectors See **Bit-straps**.

Bit covers Tubular rubber which covers and enlarges the mouth of any bit.

'Bite' Coaching term for a wet whipthong when it is caught up.

Biting A horse given to biting humans, clothing, and other horses can be effectively deterred if fitted with a muzzle.

Bitless bridle See **Bridles**.

Bits The word covers all the varieties used in riding and driving. The snaffle, pelham and Weymouth (qq.v.) are used on the riding horse. Driving bits are usually of the curb type, such as the Liverpool (q.v.), the cheek of which permits the placing of the rein in one of three levels. Buxton bits (q.v.) are still used in dress vehicles and sometimes in coaching. Snaffles are rarely used in driving except in cases of very light-mouthed horses, when a Wilson ring is the most common.

The basic definition of the bit, or hand aids, is that 'in conjunction with the other aids, i.e. the influences of the legs, back, seat and body weight, it controls the speed and direction and assists in the positioning of the head and neck.' These objects are achieved by the bit exerting pressure upon one or more of seven parts of the horse's head. The seven parts are: (1) the lips or corners of the mouth; (2) the bars of the mouth; (3) the tongue; (4) the nose; (5) the curb groove; (6) the poll; (7) the roof of the mouth. This latter, most properly, is rarely used, and would, in any case, require the use of a curb bit having a very high central port.

For a full list of 'bit' entries, refer to cross-references on page 317.

Bit shields/guards Originally these were oval leather 'safes', fitted around the mouthpiece of the bit and lying against the face, to prevent chafing of the corners of the lips. They are now made as circles of latex rubber which can be stretched over the bit ring, and being of rubber are softer and more satisfactory.

Bit-straps Small straps used to connect a bit to the squares of a headcollar. Oval spring hooks are also used for this purpose and are known as bit connectors.

Bitted See **Ears, identification marks**.

Black (colour) This occurs when black pigment is general throughout the body, coat, limbs, mane and tail, with no pattern factor present other than white markings.

'Black and Tan' Colloquial name for the well-known Irish Scarteen foxhounds; also known locally as 'Kerry Beagles'.

Black Beauty This children's classic, published in 1877, was written by Anna Sewell (1820-1875), the daughter of a Quaker grocer in Yarmouth. It is perhaps the best-known and best-loved work of fiction on the life of a horse.

Black Bess The high-quality mare of Dick Turpin the highwayman (q.v.). Their famous ride from London to York is fictional, owing its origins to Harrison Ainsworth's vivid account in his novel *Rookwood*, published 1834.

Black-brown (colour) This occurs when the predominating colour is black, with muzzle, and sometimes flanks, brown or tan.

Blacking, liquid and paste Only used on leather finished on flesh side. Surface grease must be 'killed' with an acid such as vinegar and a black 'filler' containing ingredients such as carbon and dextrose. Application of bone anneals fibres of leather, removes scratches and gives a surface finish similar to patent leather. (See **Boning**)

Black marks The term used to describe small areas of black hairs among white or any other colour.

Black masters Horse funeral furnishers, who used black sterilised stallions for drawing funeral carriages.

Black saddlers See **Saddlers, black**.

Blacksmith See **Farrier**.

Blacque-Belair (Lt. Col. Henri Louis – 1862-c.1920) Chief instructor at the Cavalry School, Saumur, France. Author of a number of books on equitation, such as *Cavalry Horsemanship and Horse Training*, which was translated from the French by J. Swire in 1920.

Blanket See **Rugs**.

Blanket clip See **Clips, types of**.

Blanket-marking See under **Appaloosa**.

Blanket riding The horse is ridden with a bridle and a blanket held in position by a surcingle. It is safer, more comfortable than, and preferable to, bareback riding.

Blaze A white marking covering almost the whole of the forehead between the eyes and extending down the front of the face over the whole of the nasal bones, usually down to the muzzle.

'Blazers, the' Famous foxhound pack in County Galway, Eire, founded early in the nineteenth century.

Bleeder A horse which has a tendency to break blood vessels or suffer from nosebleeds (see **Epistaxis**). Also, a horse used to provide blood serum for laboratory work.

Blemish A permanent mark left by an old injury, or possibly by a disease. In the show ring it is probably of little detriment in a hunter class, but is important in hack, all riding and show pony classes; of no importance in breed classes.

Blind A hunting term indicating that the fences (hedges) are still in leaf and the ditches ill-defined – a condition existing in autumn.

Blindness Many blind horses are excellent workers provided they are carefully driven. They usually pick up their feet well.

'Blind of an eye' See **Sight**.

Blinkers A head covering with leather eye-shields which allow the horse to see only to his front. Blinkers are made with either full or half cups or occasionally with very large ones known as 'wide-eyes'. Used in racing on 'doggy' horses. Sometimes, probably unfairly, referred to as the 'rogue's badge' (q.v.).

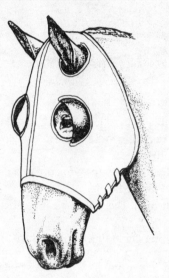

Blinkers.

Blinkers or Winkers (harness) A blocked-leather covering for eyes to confine the vision of a harness horse.

Blister A counter-irritant producing a severe form of inflammation. These products were once used to treat tendon injuries. It has no place in modern veterinary medicine, and its use is to be strongly condemned, as it serves no useful purpose in the repair process. The theory propounded was that blistering produced a counter-irritant, the effect, it was said, being to draw blood to the affected surface, thus expediting the process of repair. The 'blister' consisted of red mercuric chloride or an ammonia compound.

Blood The amount of blood that a horse's body contains is about one-eighteenth of its total weight. It is carried by arteries from the heart to all parts of the body, returns through veins to the lungs and – after oxygenation – to the heart, to be pumped round the body again. The blood transports oxygen and nourishment to the body tissues, and carries carbon dioxide and other waste materials to the kidneys and lungs for excretion. It consists of the fluid plasma (about 60%), in which is suspended red cells (erythrocytes) and white cells (leucocytes), and the smaller platelets, which are concerned with clotting. See also **Anaemia**.

Blood, to A term applied when young hounds are given their first taste of blood of their hunted fox.

Blooded A hunt ceremony when young people on the first occasion of following hounds mounted are blooded by the huntsman, who touches each cheek with blood of the hunted fox. The origin of the custom is uncertain; it has now almost died out.

Blood-horse Name universally used to indicate the English Thoroughbred.

Bloodstock Horses bred for racing. See **Thoroughbred** and **Thoroughbred Racing**.

Bloodstock Breeders' Review An annual illustrated world-wide survey of the British Thoroughbred founded by Ernest Coussell and Edward Moorhouse of the British Bloodstock Agency.

Blood weed Thoroughbred of low standard – often the gassy, shallow, and light-of-bone type, known to old-time dealers as 'blood tit'.

Blower See **High blowing**.

Blower, the Telephone service between a Bookmakers' office off course, and Tattersalls' enclosure on course.

Blowing away The huntsman blows hounds away on to the line of a fox which has left the covert.

Blowing out The huntsman blows hounds out of a covert in which they have drawn blank or in which they have lost their fox.

Blue Cap A black-pied Cheshire foxhound who, aged four, won the challenge match against Hugo Meynell's Richmond and another over the Beacon Course at

Newmarket in 1763, for a stake of 500 guineas a side. The partner of Blue Cap was his daughter Wanton, but the partner of Richmond was unnamed. Hounds ran a drag.

Blue eye See **Wall-eye**.

Blue feet A dense blue-black colouring exemplified by the feet of the Percheron, Fell and Dales.

Blue grass country An area in the State of Kentucky, USA, centred roughly on Lexington. The grass there, rich in lime and phosphates, is ideal for breeding horses; its 'blue' sheen is most noticeable in spring.

Blue riband of the turf The Derby Stakes (q.v.).

Bluff A bandage with leather eye sockets, put over heads of bad-tempered or excitable horses to keep them quiet.

Blunt, Wilfred Scawen (1840-1922) Traveller and man of letters. With his wife, Lady Anne Blunt, he made several visits to the Arabian desert in the late 1870s and 1880s. They brought back to England the finest selected Arabian horses to found the Crabbet Park Arabian Stud, which passed on to their daughter, the Rt. Hon. the Lady Wentworth, and which became a vital influence in the improved breeding of the Arabian horse (q.v.) all over the world.

Boadicea (d. AD 62) Said to have been the first British Queen to maintain a racing stud. She also bred horses for export to Rome.

Boards (polo) Used in England, the USA and Argentina to define the side lines. In India and the East they are not generally used.

Bobbery pack An expression, believed to have originated in India, used to describe a mixed pack of hounds or dogs for the purpose of hunting any available quarry. (Bobbery – a noisy row.)

Bobby-backed See **Sway-backed**.

Bob-tailed Used to describe a fox with no brush or only a very short one.

Bocado (South American) A leather bit made of rawhide, usually passed through the mouth and tied under the chin.

Bodenricks See **Cavalletti**.

Body brush An oval brush made of short, closely set bristles, used for removing dust, dirt and sweat from a horse's body, neck and quarters.

Body brush.

'Boiler, the' The kennelman who makes the puddings and skins and boils the flesh for hounds.

Bolt a fox To force a fox out of a drain or an earth.

Bolt-hole The hole in which the perch bolt on a coach is secured.

Bolting Galloping out of control. A horse that has once bolted is for the remainder of its life a source of danger, as it is likely to repeat the offence.

Bolting food May be a result of decayed teeth, and is a source of indigestion which leads to other troubles. The cause requires investigation.

Bona-fide Term used in point-to-point races signifying that a particular horse holds a certificate from the appropriate Master of Fox Hounds confirming that it is a genuine hunter.

Bone A measurement of bone immediately beneath the knee or hock (i.e. 'Good bone', 'plenty of bone'.) The term is applicable also to a hound.

Bone, flat A term of commendation indicating legs or knees of clean, hard and chiselled appearance – the reverse of round bone.

Bone, light Insufficient circumference of bone immediately below the knee, suggesting weakness; described as 'short of bone'.

Bone in the ground A hunting term,

describing the state of the ground during or following immediately after frosty weather – still hard even under a soft surface.

Bonheur, Marie Rosalie (Rosa) (1822-1899) French artist, born in Bordeaux. Her masterpiece *The Horse Fair*, shown at the Paris Exhibition in 1855, was many times reproduced. She is also celebrated for *The Duel*, illustrating the fight between two stallions Hobgoblin and The Godolphin Arabian for possession of the mare Roxana.

Boning After cleaning and polishing Bordeaux calf-leather boots or shoes with liquid or paste blacking (q.v.), a bone (preferably the shank bone of a deer) is rubbed over the leather. Finally the surface is brush-polished, and a silk or chamois leather is applied, resulting in a patent leather sheen. The process is used only on leather which is finished on the flesh side.

Bonnet A term applied to one who expatiates on the merits of a horse with a view to assisting owners to sell it. Most copers employed a bonnet, who was sometimes known as a 'Chaunter'.

'Book, in the' Expression indicating that the horse or mare has been entered or accepted for entry in the General Stud Book (q.v.).

'Book, the' A colloquialism for the General Stud Book (q.v.).

Bookmaker One who, on or off the racecourse, will accept bets either in cash or on credit, and will lay agreed odds against a horse or a greyhound winning a race. In Britain there is betting through bookmakers or the Totalisator (Pari-Mutuel), but in the USA, France, and many other racing countries, legalised betting is through the totalisator only.

Boot (of a vehicle) A built-in receptacle for luggage etc. A coach has a hind boot beneath the rear seats and a fore boot below the box. In Royal Mail coaches the hind boot was designed for mail bags.

Boot hooks Bone-, wood- or ivory-handled metal hook for pulling on top boots.

Boot jack A wooden or metal device used in removing riding boots.

Boot lift A metal device made to facilitate the top of a high boot passing over the legs of the breeches.

Boots, horse These exist in great variety and are designed either to give protection to a particular part of the leg, and/or support. For full list of individual types, refer to the cross-references at the back of the book.

Boot-tops See **Hunting boots**.

Boot trees See **Trees, boot**.

Bordeaux (waxed calf) Vegetable-tanned leather used for all first-grade black riding boots. It is the only leather on which a bone should be used. (See **Boning**)

Boring When a horse in action appears to carry the full weight of the forehand on the bit. Leaning heavily on the bit.

Boring (racing) This occurs when a horse, to improve its position, pushes another to such an extent that it interferes with its chances. It can be the subject of an objection.

Bosal A bitless bridle or hackamore which acts on the nerves of the nose and under the jaw.

Bosnian Native mountain pony bred in the Balkans, resembling the Hucul (q.v.); some Arab blood has recently been introduced.

Bots The larval stage of the bot which lays its eggs on the horse's forelegs in summer. The eggs are taken in when the horse licks its legs. They find their way into the stomach, where they develop into the bot larvae and attach themselves to the stomach wall. In spring they are passed out with the droppings, mature to adult form, and the cycle re-starts. Bots cause general unthriftiness and restlessness. When seen, the eggs should be removed with a paraffin-soaked cloth or a knife. Anti-fly preparations may be beneficial. Products are available which are very effective against bots.

Bottom A hunting term. In the Midlands it generally denotes a fence with a big and deep, though jumpable, ditch under it. In other parts of Britain and Ireland it may mean a quite unjumpable ditch or brook running at the bottom of a deep gulley or ravine.

Bottom A term denoting staying power and endurance in a horse.

Boulnois cab A London hackney cab which was in use before the introduction of the hansom. It was two-wheeled, with a door at the rear, as on an omnibus. The driver's seat was on the roof in front.

Boulonnais One of the more elegant of French draught horses, found chiefly in the region between Dunkirk and Le Havre. The breed, which still shows traces of early Arab influence, is divided into two types – the Large Boulonnais (Gros Boulonnais) and the Small Boulonnais (Petit Boulonnais), with a height range between 15.2 hh (157.5 cm) and 16.3 hh (170.2 cm). Some of the small Boulonnais became famous for express deliveries of fresh fish from Boulogne to Paris. The Boulonnais faced virtual extinction following the two World Wars, but, thanks to the enthusiasm of a small band of breeders, is now increasing in numbers. It is used in agriculture, particularly on small holdings, but is bred primarily for meat. A sturdy, thick-set animal, the Boulonnais is now predominantly grey, due possibly to the selective breeding of the colour from the days when they were used as coach horses, and greys were more easily seen at night.

Box See **Loose box**.

Box Coachman's seat. Alongside this, to the left, is the box seat, a privileged seat for an honoured passenger.

Boxcloth A material similar to Melton (q.v.) produced in the West Country. Boxcloth has a smoother face and is suitable for liveries. It was once used extensively for gaiters, leggings and horse boots. In earlier days the material was considered ideal for outdoor wear in the worst of weathers, especially for coach driving.

Boxing The transporting of a horse from one place to another, in a horsebox or in a trailer drawn by a car or four-wheel drive vehicle.

Box-seat See **Box**.

Box spur A type of spur which fits into regimental, dress and other boots used for riding. The heel has a small 'box' into which the spur is fitted.

Boxy foot (Also known as club, donkey or mule foot) A foot that is markedly upright, with the angle of the toe exceeding 60° in the front foot and 65° in the hind foot; it also has a small frog.

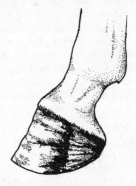

Boxy foot.

Brace (of foxes) The fox-hunting term for two foxes. One fox equals half a brace – e.g. two and a half brace equals five foxes.

Brace, the A term used in polo to denote the stance from which a stroke is played.

Bradoon See **Bridoon**.

Braids Term used in the USA for plaits (q.v.).

Brake A large vehicle for team or pair driving. There are several types, the Waggonette Brake being the most frequent in use; behind a high box it seats a number of people facing each other.

Brake, to To retard the progress of a vehicle. A hand lever or a foot pedal activates a block which presses on the surface of the tyres of the rear wheels.

Bran A by-product of the milling of wheat. It is used to encourage mastication of the food, to add bulk, and to assist digestion. The nutritive value of bran depends on the amount of flour that it contains; with efficient milling this is low, but it may contain up to 9.5% protein. If fed dry it is somewhat constipating but when fed damp it acts as a mild laxative. (See **Bran mash**) The best bran (broad bran) has large, flat flakes. Very fine bran (known as wheatings or millers' chaff) should not be fed to horses. Good bran is dry, sweet, flakey, free from lumps, and 'floury'. A bad sample is sour, lumpy, and dangerous to feed. Excessive quantities of bran can cause bone abnormalities.

Branch The surface of the shoe from toe to heel on each side of the foot.

Branding Hot-iron branding is the traditional means of distinguishing horses belonging to different owners who turn out stock to graze on common land. Brand marks are often made on the saddle patch, hindquarters, neck, or hoof. Gum tattooing is another method. A more modern process is freeze-branding (q.v.).

Bran mash Bran mash is ideal for a tired horse, and has slightly laxative properties. It is made by placing 2-3 lb (1-1.3 kg) of bran in a bucket, adding boiling water, and stirring well with a stick. The bucket is then covered with a sack until the mash is cool enough to feed. Correctly made, the mash should be 'wringing wet', but not sloppy. It is made more palatable by the addition of e.g. salt, black treacle or coarsely grated carrots.

Brasses, horse See **Horse brasses**.

Break A horse's action is said to break when it changes from one gait to another.

Breaking The education of a horse to the various purposes for which it is required, e.g. breaking to saddle or to harness. The term more popularly used nowadays is 'schooling'.

Breaking cart See **Skeleton break**.

Breaking out Profuse and unnatural sweating which occurs in spite of previous drying. The usual causes are strenuous exercise or unusual and excessive excitement.

Breaking tackle The complete set consists usually of a cavesson breaking head-collar with metal nose part and ring and padded noseband; a bridle for later use; a roller, adjustable each side; side reins, crupper and driving reins; and lungeing rein.

Break-up When hounds are eating the carcase of their hunted fox they are said to 'break-up' their fox.

Breastbone The sternum. A keel-shaped bone consisting of seven fused segments, each giving attachment to the lower ends of the corresponding rib. It lies between the forelimbs, and forms the lower boundary of the thorax.

Breast collar In some harness, but not coaching, this broad band of leather across the breast takes the place of collar and hames (q.v.).

Breast girth See **Aintree breast girth**.

Breastplate or Breast piece A leather neckstrap attached to the Ds of the saddle by short straps and to the girth, which passes through a loop. It is worn a few inches below the withers to prevent the saddle from slipping back. Inexperienced riders find it useful for holding on to when riding uphill. Lightweight breastplates for racing are made from either very thin leather or webbing.

Breathing bridoon See **Wind-sucker's bit; Flute bit**.

Breeches The accepted form of covering for the rider's legs when riding. Breeches are worn with hunting or riding boots, or (more rarely these days) with leggings and high-lows (q.v.). Jodhpur breeches are worn with jodhpur boots.

Breeches ball A cloth ball (colour according to choice) used in the cleaning of strappings on breeches, which are first scrubbed in warm, slightly soapy water, and allowed to dry partially before the ball is applied. Drying is then completed and surplus ball brushed off.

Breeching A broad leather band behind a horse's quarters which takes the weight of a vehicle when pulling up, backing, or descending a hill.

Breeching harness (long) More suitable for a four-wheeled vehicle and adjusted by a 'square' of metal through which the breeching strap passes. It is very neat, and acts as a kicking strap if correctly fitted.

Breeching harness (short) The best-known type is attached to the shaft through the shaft staples.

Breeching proper This consists of crupper, crupper dock, hip straps, breeching body, and breeching straps.

Breed classes These are always shown in-hand at shows, and are open to stallions, mares, colts and fillies. The entry of geldings occurs more often nowadays, more as a guide to their forebears, and an indication of the breed's suitability for riding, driving, etc.

Breeding (See also **Oestrous cycle**; **Birth**) Breeding horses can be a very interesting and rewarding aspect of ownership for those with the necessary knowledge. Successful breeders pay great attention to the selection of both mare and stallion, to the care of the mare during pregnancy, and, if stallion owners, to the correct management of the animal throughout the year, and more particularly to its preparation for stud duties.

SELECTION OF A MARE: Ideally, sentiment should not enter into the choice of a mare for breeding purposes. A potential brood mare is one that not only has good all-round conformation, and is robust and healthy, with good action, but has good *breeding* conformation, with enough depth and width to allow proper development of her foal. The latter automatically excludes a flat-ribbed, herring-gutted, narrow-hipped animal.

A veterinary examination of the mare's genitalia, to establish normal development of the genital tract and ovaries, is often recommended. More easily observed features should also be checked: e.g. the conformation of the vulva and anus, which, if they do not lie in the same vertical line, may allow excreta to pass into the vulva, with the accompanying risk of infection. The udder should also be checked for normality.

Temperament is important, particularly in a pleasure horse, for not only can a foal *inherit* its outlook on life, it can be influenced adversely by its dam's behaviour.

If possible, the mare's pedigree and her relatives should be investigated.

Exceptions to almost all the above are made, especially in the case of racing Thoroughbreds, where a mare is retired to stud almost entirely on the basis of her performance on the track. Where exceptions are made, even more care needs to be taken in the selection of the stallion to which the mare is sent.

SELECTION OF A STALLION: The majority of stallions in Britain are now approved by their respective breed societies, or have been passed as fit, and free from hereditary disease, by a veterinary examination. Attention must be paid to their conformation, action and type, as well as to their freedom from vice. The mare owner has to make further assessments, based on the qualities and faults of the potential brood mare, and on the background and record of the stallion. The wise owner will look not just at the stallion but, if possible, at some of his near relatives, to gain a more complete picture of the characteristics of his line. Where it is not possible to see, for example, the stallion's sire or dam, it is in most instances at least possible to study his pedigree, and to enquire from various sources concerning the general suitability of his line. Where the stallion has progeny, viewing some of these can, of course, be very revealing, and will show if he stamps his own type and quality. If it is found that the progeny consistently show a particular fault or faults, it must be assumed that it comes from the stallion or his forebears. As no animal is perfect, a stallion should be chosen that is strong on points in which the mare is weak. This presupposes that the owner not only has a good eye for a horse, but also is able to acknowledge defects in the mare. Other very important points to consider before selecting a stallion include his temperament, action, and fertility.

USE OF A STALLION: In general, a three-year-old colt may be allowed to cover a few experienced mares; a four-year-old might be expected to cover up to twenty; a five-year-old up to forty; while an older stallion may take more. The young stallion is expected to cover just one mare a day; an older horse may cover one in the morning and one in the afternoon.

STALLION MANAGEMENT: Stallions are divided into two basic groups: (1) those who are segregated, stabled, and cover mares in-hand – the most common practice in Thoroughbred and most large studs; (2) those who run out with the mares. A stallion in the first group should be stabled in a good, roomy box, ideally where he can see other horses, to prevent him becoming bored. A stallion requires daily exercise throughout the year. During the non-breeding season this may consist of being turned out (alone, or with barren mares) for long periods every day. If this is not possible, he will need to be lunged, ridden, or walked to prevent him becoming fat and flabby.

For the covering season, the stallion must be really fit. In Thoroughbred studs (and some others) the traditional way of getting him fit is to walk him. This starts about 8-10 weeks before the season, with ½ hour a day, gradually increasing to 1½ hours of good, energetic walking. Ideally, this should be preceded by his being turned out for a while, so that he is settled before being led. Alternatively, stallions may be lunged or ridden to get them hard and fit. Obviously, increased feeding accompanies increased exercise, with the emphasis on protein immediately before and during the season. Stabled stallions must always be thoroughly groomed after exercise. Those running out should not be groomed.

STUD FEES (these normally include the covering fee, plus a small amount for the groom): The most common arrangements are: (1) no foal, no fee – the covering fee is returned if, on an agreed date, the mare is tested and found not to be in foal; (2) No foal, free return – the covering fee is payable, but the mare may be returned to the stallion the following year without further payment; (3) No live foal, no fee – no fee is payable if the foal does not survive beyond 48 hours.

Breeze along, to A term used in the USA for galloping.

Breeze fly See **Horsefly**.

Breton The most numerous of present-day French draught horses. Native to Brittany, the breed has a long history of drawing carts laden with seaweed for use as a fertiliser on coastal farms. Bretons are very heavily built and short-legged,

yet with a hint of pony about them. They have developed three types – the Trait Breton, or Breton Draught Horse, standing 15.3-16.3 hh (160-170.2 cm); the Petit Trait Breton or Small Breton Draught Horse, standing 14.3-15.2 hh (149.9-160 cm), and the Postier Breton or Coach-horse Breton, which is about the same height as the Trait Breton but of lighter build. All three types are renowned for their willing temperament and their active, vigorous action, particularly at the trot. The principal colour is chestnut, with an occasional roan or bay. The breed is still used on smallholdings and vineyards, and is also highly regarded as a meat-producing animal.

Brick paving The hardest and non-absorbent Stafford Blue makes the best flooring for the stable.

Bridle A complete snaffle bridle consists of bit, one pair of reins, a pair of cheekpieces, a headpiece, in which is incorporated the throatlatch, a browband and a noseband. A pelham bridle has an additional pair of reins, the curb rein

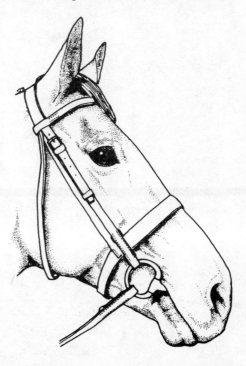

Snaffle bridle with cavesson noseband.

always being ⅛th in. (3 mm) narrower than the bridoon. A Weymouth or double bridle has, in addition to a second pair of reins, an extra head strap and cheekpiece known as a 'slip head', to which is fastened the bridoon. Bits are attached to the bridle by sewing, studs, buckles, occasionally snap billet hooks, and sometimes by a loop arrangement.

Bridle, bitless As the name implies, any bridle which is used without a bit. There are a number of varieties, including the American Bosal (q.v.). See **Hackamore**.

Bridle, double A common term for the Weymouth bridle (consisting of curb and bridoon).

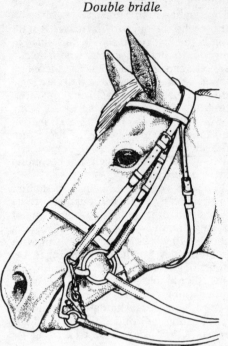

Double bridle.

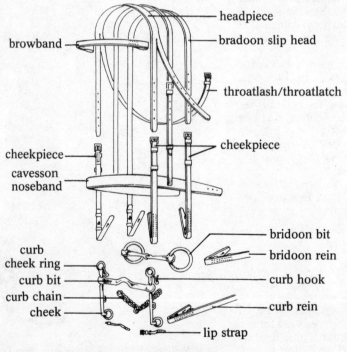

Parts of a double bridle.

Bridle, inventor of See **Pelethronius**.

Bridle back A full length of cowhide taken from the top of the back from tail to head. The extra length so obtained is useful for full-length reins. Backs of heavier substance are used for body rollers etc.

Bridle bracket A japanned or plastic-covered stable fitting which carries the bridle and the ends of the reins.

Bridle butt The best bridle leather is sold in pairs of butts. A butt is cut on either side of the spine from the tail to the beginning of the shoulders. The finest leather is that nearest to the spine; the lower part of the flank where the hide is coarser is not part of a butt.

Bridle hand The hand in which the reins are carried, generally the left hand.

Bridle trail See **Trail ride**.

Bridleway or Bridlepath A path over which the public have a right of way on horseback or leading a horse.

Bridoon The name given to the small snaffle bit used in double or bridoon bridles. Varieties include plain, twisted, ring in centre, egg-butt and turn-cheek. Known also as bradoon.

Brisket The lowest portion of the chest.

British Driving Society (BDS) Founded in 1957 and affiliated to the British Horse Society to encourage and assist those interested in the driving of horses, ponies and donkeys.

British Equestrian Federation (BEF) Founded in 1973 to bring together the major policy interests of common concern and benefit to the British Horse Society (q.v.) and the British Show Jumping Association (q.v.). The Federation's headquarters are at the British Equestrian Centre, Stoneleigh, Warwickshire.

British Equine Veterinary Association (BEVA) A society of veterinary surgeons formed in 1961 to promote veterinary and allied sciences for the welfare of the horse, to provide a forum for discussion and the exchange of ideas on the management, health and diseases of the horse, to encourage research into equine problems; and to co-operate with other bodies interested in these objectives.

British Field Sports Society (BFSS) Founded in 1930 to further the interests of all field sports.

British Horse Society (BHS) Founded in 1947 through the amalgamation of the National Horse Association of Great Britain, the Institute of the Horse, and the Pony Club (qq.v.). It is the authority and parent body of almost all horse and pony interests in Great Britain.

The Society's activities are directed by an elected council from the headquarters at the British Equestrian Centre, Stoneleigh, where a permanent executive staff is maintained. The Society has established a network of Regional Committees, each of which deals with a variety of horse activities within its own area, including bridleways and land access, riding and road safety, welfare, and development. There are also a number of national executive committees directing the activities of the various BHS groups – dressage, driving trials, horse trials, long-distance riding, and the horse and pony breeds committee. Similarly, the Pony Club and the Riding Clubs have national committees with executive officers and staff based at the British Equestrian Centre.

The Society has a system of approval for riding establishments throughout the country.

The training and examinations committee is responsible for the system of examinations run by the Society. Some are recognised as full professional qualifications: ranging from the British Horse Society's Assistant Instructor's (BHSAI) certificate, which is regarded as the first step on the professional ladder, through to the Fellowship of the British Horse Society (FBHS) – the highest qualification available. Other examinations and/or tests are organised for the non-professional, through the Riding Clubs and the Pony Club.

British Jumping Derby An annual competition which was first held at Hickstead (q.v.) in 1961 and is open to international riders. The course includes the famous 10 ft 6 in. (319 cm) high Derby Bank, and the Devil's Dyke, generally acknowledged as the most difficult obstacle on the sixteen-fence course.

British Palomino Society (BPS) See **Palomino**

British Riding Schools, Association of An organisation founded in 1954 by professional riding school proprietors *for* professional riding school proprietors. It is the only such organisation in Britain, and membership is open only to those whose establishments have been approved by the Society as meeting the required standard, and who are licensed by the relevant local authority. The principal aims of the Society are to look after its members, and to maintain standards for both horses and clients. The Society conducts a series of career-orientated examinations for those already employed in riding schools. These are: Horse Care and Riding Certificates I and II; Assistant Groom's Certificate; Groom's Diploma; Riding School Principal's Diploma; Riding Master's Diploma. The Society's address is: 44 Market Jew Street, Penzance, Cornwall, TR18 2HY.

British Show Hack and Cob Association (BSHCA) Founded in 1938 to further the interests of owners and breeders of hacks and cobs.

British Show Jumping Association (BSJA) Officially founded in 1925 to improve the standard of show jumping. It is the controlling body of show jumping in Great Britain, with headquarters at the British Equestrian Centre, Stoneleigh, Warwickshire.

British Show Pony Society (BSPS) Founded in 1949, this is the controlling body for improving and regulating the showing of children's riding ponies.

British Spotted Horse Society Founded in 1947 to promote the interests of the British Spotted Horse of riding type. Superseded by the British Appaloosa Society. Spotted ponies may now be registered with the British Spotted Pony Society.

Britzchska A type of travelling carriage similar to the Dormeuse (q.v.) in which passengers could lie flat for sleeping. It was postillion driven, with a rumble (q.v.). The vehicle was introduced from Germany *c.* 1820.

Brocket A male deer at two years. (Also known as a knobber or knobbler: terms which are now almost obsolete.)

Broken-coloured A colloquial term applied generally to donkeys who are piebald (q.v.) or skewbald (q.v.).

Broken-kneed Description of any horse having knees scarred by some type of injury.

Broken wind Also known as 'heaves', or chronic obstructive pulmonary disease (COPD). A condition of the lungs characterised by difficult breathing. It is thought to be an allergic reaction to fungi – especially those found in mouldy hay or in straw. The fungal spores induce muscular spasms in the walls of the air ducts and sacs of the lungs, which may eventually rupture. The symptoms are frequent, often spasmodic, long, deep, and hollow coughing. Breathing is wheezy and laboured. On expiration the flanks appear to heave twice. Management includes use of dust-free bedding and food. This is always a serious problem and veterinary advice should be sought without delay. See also **Coughs**.

Bronco (Mustang, q.v.**)** Western American cow pony. The name, derived from the Spanish (rough and rude), was originally applied to the wildest, untamable mustangs, but is now a generic term. It is sometimes shortened to 'Bronc'.

Bronco-busting Breaking-in a mustang for riding.

Brood mare The name given to a mare used for breeding. She should have a sound constitution, a good roomy middle, a set of good, short legs, and should be entirely free from hereditary disease.

Brood mare premium schemes First initiated by the Arab Horse Society in 1948. Premiums at various centres are given annually to suitable mares in foal to registered Arabian or Anglo-Arabian stallions and likely to produce a good foal from the mating. Adopted by other breed societies.

Broomtail A Western American term for a small horse not worth breaking. Sometimes applied to all mustangs.

Brothers and Sisters Full brothers and sisters, or own brothers and sisters, are those having the same sire and dam. Half brothers and sisters are animals out of the same dam by a different sire. Threequarters brothers and sisters or three-part brothers and sisters are animals out of the same dam and having as their sires animals who were half-brothers or were by the same sire out of a different dam.

Brougham The most popular of closed carriages, for pair or single. The first was built by Lord Brougham *c.*1839.

Brougham.

Brough Hill Fair A famous old fair held annually in Westmorland (now Cumbria). Particularly associated with Fell ponies, who were often known as Brough Hill ponies.

Brow, Bez (bay) and Trez The side branches or tines on the antlers of a stag. They are known as 'rights', and differentiated from points 'on top'. There are generally three points 'atop'.

Browband (also known as 'Front') A leather strap attached to the bridle through loop-ends forming a semi-circular fitting immediately under the horse's ears. It is used to prevent the bridle from slipping back on the neck. In harness it is usually ornamented with brass, and in road coaching with coloured leather to match the coach. For hunting the browband should be of plain leather. For racing and hack classes it is permissible to have the front covered in silk or plastic in the stable colours. (See **Fly front**)

Brown (colour) This occurs where there is a mixture of black and brown pigment in the coat, with black limbs, mane and tail.

Browne, Hablot Knight ('Phiz') (1815-1882) Illustrator of many Victorian novels, including most of Dickens, Ainsworth and Lever, and some of Surtees. He showed a talent for drawing horses in some of his book illustrations and in many independent drawings of the hunting field. Most, but not all of his sketches were in a humorous vein, and were usually signed 'Phiz'.

Brown Jack Winner of the Queen Alexandra Stakes at Ascot in six successive years: i.e. 1929-1934. (See **Donoghue, Steve**)

Brown saddlers See **Saddlers, brown**.

Brucella abortus A bacterium that causes abortion in cattle, and which has been the subject of a rigorous eradication campaign. The bacterium has been implicated in poll evil (q.v.) and fistulous withers (q.v.), and may cause abortion in mares. It also causes infection in joints, leading to stiffness. Diagnosis is by blood tests.

Bruce Lowe Figure System This system was originated at the beginning of the twentieth century by an Australian of this name. It is the medium for tracing descent through the mares in the General Stud Book, from which some thirty families have been enumerated. These tap-root mares were allotted numbers according to the amount of times their descendants had won classic races. All the families trace their origin to one of the three Arab sires: the Byerley Turk (1689), the Darley Arabian (1704), and the Godolphin Arabian (1730) (qq.v.).

Brumby A term originating in Australia. In the days of the first settlers a certain number of horses wandered off into the bush and they and their offspring became entirely wild and were known as Brumbies. Though some have proved to be excellent, most are considered to be of very little use – even if broken-in – because of their wild nature. On Australian racecourses a wild and uncontrollable horse is referred to sometimes as a Brumby.

Brush The tail of a fox.

Brush fence An obstacle, either natural or artificial, composed of brushwood or some other suitable hedging plant.

Brushing This occurs when a horse in motion strikes the fore or hind leg with the opposite one inside the fetlock joints. It is usually the result of faulty conformation or action. Turning the toes out can be responsible for it in front, going too close, behind. Other causes are lack of condition, fatigue, bad riding or driving, youth, old age, rough ground or faulty shoeing.

Brushing boots Boots of leather, felt or PVC which protect the inside of the lower leg, particularly the fetlock, when a horse brushes, i.e. it knocks one foreleg against the other. The boots are made in several different lengths and styles. See also **Fetlock ring**.

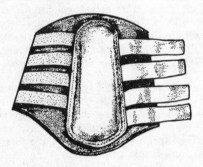

Brushing boot.

Brushing ring See **Fetlock ring**.

Brush pricker/ Bit burr A circular piece of leather studded with bristles which is fitted round the mouthpiece of the bit, bristles inwards, to discourage a horse from hanging to one side.

Brute Term applied to a horse, but not by horsemen, except in the case of an animal justifying such an opprobrious reference.

Bucephalus The horse of Alexander the Great. He was bought for 13 talents by Alexander's father, Philip of Macedon, but no-one was able to ride or break him in except the young Alexander. He carried his master through his Asian cam-

paigns, died in India in 326 BC, and was buried on the banks of the Jhelum River.

Buckboard General utility vehicle in country districts in the USA.

Bucked shins (USA) See **Shins, sore**.

Buckeroo (USA) One who is engaged in the breaking of broncos. The term is applied also to rodeo riders.

Buckets, stable These were often made of teak or oak, varnished or painted, and with a metal rim fixed around the inside to prevent the horse chewing the wood. Modern stable buckets are of rubber or plastic, which are lighter, less likely to cause damage, and more hygienic. They must be kept clean.

Buck eye A term applied to a prominent eye. At one time the phrase referred to a small-eyed animal.

Buckhounds Hounds used for the pursuit of deer.

Buckhounds, Royal Originally established about 1154 in the reign of Henry II, and reached a peak of popularity under George III when, soon after his accession, Parliament granted £5000 a year towards their upkeep. They were finally disbanded by Queen Victoria.

Buckjumping (Bucking, USA) The action of a horse in trying to unseat his rider by arching his back like a spring and jumping into the air with all four legs at once, the whole achieved in one violent movement and repeated with rapidity. Not to be confused with pig-jumping (leaping and kicking). The term is of American origin but the word used in the USA is bucking. True buckjumpers are generally only found among ranch horses in America and among station horses in Australia, but many fresh horses on a cold morning or when over-excited or under-worked will occasionally buck.

Buck knee Also known as 'calf-knee' (q.v.) or 'back at the knee'.

Buckskin A term used by farmers in the American West for the colour a shade darker than cream (q.v.). The accepted term in showing is dun.

Budyonovsky/Budenny Russian horses

from the Rostov region, bred in the 1920s by crossing Don and Chernomor mares with Thoroughbreds. Originally used in the army, they now compete in various sports. The average height is 16-16.1 hh (162.6-165 cm). They are riding horses of some quality. Mostly chestnut.

Buffalo Bill See **Cody, William**.

Buggy In England, a two-wheeled gig-like vehicle. Overseas, various four-wheeled traps are called buggies.

Bull A horse which grunts when tested for wind by feinting a blow across the ribs. (See **Grunting**)

Bulldogging A competition in rodeos in which a cowboy, after chasing a steer, jumps from his horse and throws the steer to the ground by grasping the horns and twisting the head.

Bullfinch A thick, high hedge fence which cannot be jumped over but must be scrambled or pushed through.

Bullfinch.

Bumper race A race for amateurs.

Bumping A jockey is guilty of bumping in a race when he collides, deliberately or otherwise, with another competitor in such a way as to interfere adversely with the latter's chances in the race.

Bunbury, Sir Charles (1740-1821) Noted racing character of his day and a close friend of the Duke of York. With his horse Diomed he won the first Derby in 1780. He also owned Smolensko, the first colt to win the Derby and the 2000 Guineas, and Eleanor, the first filly to win the Derby and the Oaks. He was a leading member of the Jockey Club and exercised great influence on racing.

Bunbury Mile The straight mile on the Newmarket (July) course, which is used during the summer months. The Newmarket Rowley Mile course is used in the spring and autumn. The courses are separated by The Ditch. The Bunbury Mile is named after Sir Charles Bunbury (see above).

Bung tail A docked tail. (See **Docking**)

Burford saddle See **Saddle, Morocco**.

Burghley Horse Trials Annual autumn three-day event held at Burghley House in Lincolnshire, home of the Marquesses of Exeter. Considered second only to Badminton in prestige, the Burghley event was first held in 1961.

Burmese (or Shan) Ponies bred by the hill-tribes of the Shan States and believed to be closely related to the Mongolian ponies, though modified by foreign blood. They are strong, but somewhat slow. A still smaller pony, closely allied to the Manipur, is much faster and used for polo, of which game Manipur is one of the original homes. (See **Manipur**)

Burnisher A device for cleaning and polishing steel bits, stirrup irons, and other articles of steel. It consists of a small square of close, interlinked steel chains with a backing or base of leather. It is seldom used nowadays, as the items mentioned are made of stainless steel or other non-rust metals.

Burro (Spanish) A donkey.

Bursae Blind sacs containing synovial fluid (q.v.) at places where tendons run over joints and bony prominences, to minimise friction. Through irritation, strain, overwork, etc., they are liable to become distended, giving rise, for example, to windgalls, capped elbows, capped hocks (qq.v.).

Bursitis Inflamed bursa (q.v.).

Burst In hunting, the first part of a run when hounds get away close to their fox, hence: to burst him, i.e. to kill a fox in the burst.

'Butcher' A rider with excessively heavy

and rough hands, also termed 'mutton-fisted'.

Butcher boots Plain black, high riding boots without tops.

Bute Colloquial name for Phenylbuta-zone (q.v.), a drug used as an anti-inflammatory and analgesic agent.

Butterflies Short-distance public coaches.

Butterfly snaffle See **Spring mouth**.

Buttock The part of the horse which lies at the back of the thighs. The point of the buttock projects a few inches below the root of the tail.

Buttress The angle formed by the inflexion of the wall to form the bar of a horse's foot. What is known as 'buttress foot' is caused by the fracture of the pyramidal process of the pedal bone, which sometimes occurs in low ring-bone.

Buxton bit This bit is characterised by a long, bent cheek. It is principally used for driving, and there are many variations. A few were used for riding.

Buzkashi (From *buz* – a goat, *kashi-dant* – to pull). A rudimentary form of rugby football on horseback. Its origin appears to be unknown, but it survives today in Central Asia where it may well have originated. It is to be seen from time to time in the neighbourhood of Kabul, the capital of Afghanistan. It is played by teams, each of which may exceed twenty-five in number, and several teams may play at the same time. The riders carry a whip with a short wooden handle which they may use to hit an opponent but not his pony. The ground is unlimited in size, and rocks and precipitous hills are looked upon with favour. Two single goal-posts lie about ½ mile (0.8 km) apart. Around each is drawn a circle of about 50 yd (46 m) in diameter. The 'ball' is a stuffed goatskin, and the object of the game is to pick it off the ground without dismounting, tuck it under the knee, then gallop round the far goal-post and back to the circle. The game starts with the 'ball' thrown into the 'scrum' as in rugby. Umpires decide which is the winning side. In Turkestan the game is known as *Baiga*, and is played regularly in Samarkand and generally in High Asia. It is sometimes called 'Dragging the Goat'.

Bye-day An extra hunting day which has not been advertised on the appointment card.

Byelorussian Harness Horse A strong, heavy, working harness horse produced by using Ardennes, Belgian Heavy Draught and Gudbrandsdal stallions on local breeds. They are exceptional workers, noted for their longevity and high fertility.

Byerley Turk The first of the three stallions considered as the founders of the Thoroughbred. It was imported into England by Captain Robert Byerley in 1689, having been captured from the Turks at the Siege of Buda and ridden by him at the Battle of the Boyne. This stallion established the Herod line, one of the most important in the breeding of the Thoroughbred racehorse.

C

C Colt (q.v.)

CA Concours d'Attelage (q.v.).

CCI Concours Complet Internationale.

CCIO Concours Complet Internationale Officiel.

CDI Concours de Dressage Internationale.

CDIO Concours de Dressage Internationale Officiel.

CEM Contagious equine metritus (q.v.).

Ch. Chestnut (q.v.).

CH Concours Hippique (q.v.).

CHI Concours Hippique Internationale.

CHIO Concours Hippique Internationale Officiel.

COPD Chronic obstructive pulmonary disease. (See **Broken wind**)

CS Concours de Saut (q.v.).

CSI Concours de Sauts d'Obstacles Internationale. Officially replaces CHI (q.v.).

CSIO Concours de Sauts d'Obstacles Internationale Officiel. Officially replaces CHIO (q.v.).

Cab Originally an abbreviation of Cabriolet (q.v.). (See **Hackney carriage**)

Caballo (Spanish) A horse.

Cabriolet High, single-horse, two-wheeled, hooded vehicle for two, with rear platform on which the 'tiger' (midget groom) could stand. Fashionable in the early Victorian era. In 1823 David Davies, Coachbuilder of Albany, put the first licensed cabriolets on the streets.

Cacolets Iron-framed, adjustable chairs used by the army for transporting the sick and wounded. They are carried on either side of the horse.

'Cad' A slang term for conductors of London's early horse buses. They were not noted for good manners. Also the name given in posting days to men working in stable yards which supplied the post-horses. Their work was to look after the horses, wash the post-chaises, call the post-boys at night, light the lamps and, when short of a rider, to ride a stage. This name was also given to the footmen of a stage coach whose main job was to apply the brake.

Caddis A worsted ribbon used by carters for binding horses' manes.

Cade A foal brought up by hand.

Cadence Dressage term referring to the rhythm and tempo of a horse's paces: the horse covering an equal space of ground in equal amount of time.

Cadre Noir Group name of the riding instructors of Saumur in France, who wear a black uniform. The group was an integral part of the cavalry school of Saumur until 1968. Since then it has been attached to the Institut Nationale d'Equitation (a part-civilian, part-military organisation), which in 1972 changed its name to École Nationale d'Equitation. Its purpose is the training of civilian instructors and the advanced training of riders for competition. The school is now situated at Terrefort, outside Saumur.

Cajol Norwegian dog cart.

Calashe/Caleche A light, low-wheeled carriage with a folding top and cee-springs (q.v.).

Calcutta Cup Light Horse Challenge Trophy Awarded to the owner of the horse gaining the highest number of points during one season at any officially recognised three-day event or horse trial.

Calf Name for red deer stag and hind in their first year. The young of fallow deer are called fawns.

Calf, brown-stained Vegetable tanned leather similar to polo brown calf but with slightly more dressing in it, therefore more hardwearing and waterproof.

Calf-knee Forelegs which, viewed from the side and having an imaginary line drawn through them, tend to concavity below the knees. (Also known as 'back at the knee' and 'buck knee').

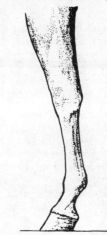

Calf-knee.

Calgary Stampede Held each July and considered to be Canada's top rodeo. Attractions include the drums and dancing of the Indians, the Thoroughbred racing and the stage show. Of great interest are the chuck wagon races which have their origin in groups of resting cowboys under sudden attack by Indians, when they threw all equipment including the cooking stove into the back of the wagon and, with four horses pulling the wagon, raced for safety. But the highlight is the rodeo, which includes bronco (q.v.) riding, bare-back bronc riding, steer wrestling, calf-roping, wild horse racing, wild cow milking, Brahma bull riding, and even wild buffalo riding.

Another feature of the Calgary Stampede and an integral part of the Canadian scene is the musical ride of the Royal Canadian Mounted Police.

Calkins/Caulkins/Caulks Projections from the heel of the shoe (usually the hind shoe only, except in draught horses), formed by drawing down the extremity of the shoe, or welding on a piece of steel. They are used to provide a good foothold on soft ground.

Calling In polo, calls come from the captain or member of the team in the best position to see, and must be instantly obeyed. Examples: 'Take him out', 'turn back', 'leave it', 'get on', 'back-hander', (or 'back it'), 'mine'. The expression 'all right' is never used. Good calling wins matches.

Call over A practice in which bookmakers determine ante-post prices for betting on a number of the chief races throughout the year. The odds against the horses engaged are 'called-over', and altered from time to time according to the amount of money bet on them.

Camargue Horse (Camarguais) Officially recognised as a breed in 1968, the 'wild white horses of the sea' used by the *gardiens* (French herdsmen) working the black fighting bulls of the Camargue, the desolate marsh region lying at the mouth of the Rhône in southern France. As they are very sure-footed they are also used as mounts for tourists viewing the rich wildlife of the area. This breed, of very ancient origin, may be descended from the Solutrean 'ram-headed horse', the prototype of the modern Barb (q.v.). They are nearly all grey, are exceptionally hardy, and seldom exceed 15 hh (152.4 cm).

Camarillo Type of albino horse with pink skin and black eyes, found in California.

Cambridge mouth Trade name for a ported mouthpiece as used in a curb bit.

Camera patrol A movie camera is used to film the running of races both from head on and from the side to enable the stewards to pinpoint incidents in a race. The introduction of this system has put jockeys on their mettle and has led to less interference in racing.

Camp, to To stand a horse with fore and hind feet spread as far apart as possible which made them immobile when passengers entered or left a carriage. Also known as to 'spread' and to 'stretch'.

Campagne (*Equitation de Campagne*) Riding out of doors.

Campagne School A standard of dressage below haute école (q.v.). See **Lower School, Basse École**.

Camp-drafting A sport of the Australian outback in which a rider on a highly manoeuvrable horse selects a beast from a mob of cattle and drives it to a spot known as the 'yards'. In competitive camp-drafting, the contest takes place around a course marked by oil-drums, and the rider completing the course in the fastest time with the fewest false moves wins.

Canadian International Championship An open race for three-year-olds and upwards. In 1938 it was run as the Long Branch Championship for three-year-olds. From 1938 to 1952 the distance was 1 1/16 miles (1.71 km). In 1953 and 1954 it was 1 1/8 miles (1.81 km) and in 1955 1 3/16 (1.91 km). Now it is run over 1 5/8 miles (2.61 km) (turf). It is Canada's richest race, and is run at Woodbine in October.

Canadian Mounted Police, The Royal (The 'Mounties') The famous police force of Canada, founded in 1873 to 'Maintain the Right'. Their proud claim was, and is, that they 'always get their man'.

Canas An equestrian sport introduced into Spain by the Arabs. Riders threw spears at one another simultaneously, warding off their opponents' spears with leather shields.

Canes, riding These are made of Malacca, Whangee (knobbed), Nilgeri, black thorn, etc. They are sometimes leather covered. Not to be confused with whips (q.v.).

Canker See **Thrush**.

Cannon bone (shin bone) Bone of the foreleg below the knee ending at the fetlock. The corresponding bone in the hind leg below the hock is termed the shannon or shank. It should be short for strength, broad and flat when looked at from the side. If there is insufficient measurement immediately below the knee, the horse is said to be 'short of bone' or 'tied in at the knee'. Owing to the unobservable but exceptional density of texture, lightness of bone (within reason) is no great defect in the Arab.

Canteen A case used in hunting to carry a sandwich box and flask. It is attached to the saddle by Ds (q.v.).

Canter A contraction of 'cantering gallop', which was an easy gallop used by the pilgrims on their way along stretches of the South Downs to the shrine at Canterbury. It is a three-time pace, in which the hoof beats are heard in the following sequence: near hind, near fore and off hind together, off fore (leading leg), followed by a moment of suspension in which all four feet are off the ground; or, off hind, off fore and near hind together, near fore (leading leg), followed by the moment of suspension. The canter is incorrect if four beats are heard, which is caused by lack of impulsion through faulty collection. In dressage, four canters are recognised: working, medium, extended, and collected (qq.v.).

Canter, aids for Depending on the degree of the horse's training and the rider's skill, different aids may be used. The most elementary are the lateral aids (q.v.), but the classical diagonal aids, resulting in a strike off from a state of balance are preferred. For the left canter, for example, which is initiated by the off hind leg, the horse's head should be turned very slightly to the left, the rider's legs closed onto the horse's sides, with the outside (right) leg further back than the inside, the seat is well down in the saddle, and the weight of the rider's seat is transferred slightly over the off hind leg, to urge that limb forward.

Canter, change of leg at the See **Flying change (of leg)**.

Canter, collected Cantering slowly with much impulsion, head carried high and flexed, quarters low, the horse moving in a true pace of three-time.

Canter, disunited The sequence of hoof beats when a horse is cantering disunited – i.e: off hind, near fore and near hind together, off fore (leading leg); or near hind, off fore and off hind together, near fore (leading leg). In other words, the horse performs a left canter in front and a right canter behind, or vice versa.

Canter, extended The stride is noticeably lengthened, without the cadence becoming precipitous. The entire topline lengthens somewhat, without the head changing to a great extent from its vertical position.

Canter, false The horse is following a curve at the canter on the outside lead: e.g. the near lead turning right. This, when performed purposely is called counter canter.

Canter, medium A pace of moderate extension between the collected (q.v.) and extended (q.v.) canter, with longer strides than the former, but shorter and more rounded than the latter.

Canter, true The horse is following a curve at the canter on the inside lead: e.g. near lead turning left.

Canter, working The pace between medium (q.v.) and collected (q.v.). Used in relatively untrained horses not ready for collected paces, and from it the other canters are developed.

Cantle Back of saddle.

Canvas rug See **New Zealand rug**.

Cap A hunting term indicating the collection of money from persons who follow hounds but who are not subscribers to the hunt. Subscribers can be capped for special funds: e.g. 'Poultry', 'Wire' etc. The amount varies with the hunt. In the USA it is often referred to as the 'Capping Fee'.

Cap Rider's peaked headwear with the owner's distinctive colours covering the skull cap (q.v.), or a hard, peaked velvet-covered cap.

Cap curb See **Jodhpur curb**.

Cape-cart Similar in type to the curricle, being the only recognised two-wheeled cart drawn by two horses to a single pole and yoke. Much used at one time in South Africa.

Cape Horse Found in the Cape Colony when Great Britain took possession in 1806. The original stock consisted of Barbs, Persians, or Arabs imported by the East India Company who first colonised the country. At a later date English roadsters and Thoroughbreds, and American-bred stallions, were imported. In 1807 Spanish horses were captured from a ship en route for Buenos Aires, and are said to have been the progenitors of the red roans and odd colours, later renowned for their hardiness and endurance.

Capel Thick-set farm horse used in mediaeval times.

Capel Wen-like swelling on the heel of the hock or point of the elbow. Also known as a 'capulet'.

Capping fee See **Cap**.

Caprilli, Federico (1868-1907) Italian cavalry officer, instructor at the Cavalry School of Pinerolo (1904) Caprilli is the undoubted inventor of the modern forward style of riding, which he introduced in 1890, and which has been known since 1907 as the 'Italian' or 'forward' seat. His *Principi di Equitazione di Campaghna* was published in 1901.

Capriole High School air above the ground in which the horse makes a half-rear with the hocks drawn under and very flexed, jumps forward and up in the air to a considerable height, then kicks his hindlegs with great energy and lands collectedly on four legs. A difficult exercise

to perform, making great demands upon the firmness and balance of the rider and the strength of the horse. Performed by riders of the Spanish Riding School in Vienna and of the Cadre Noir in France. (See **Airs above the ground**)

Capulet See **Capel**.

Carbohydrate An energy-producing constituent of certain foodstuffs. Carbohydrates include sugars and starches, which are found in oats, barley, hay etc. See **Feeding**.

Carholme, the Former racecourse at Lincoln, but now only used for point-to-points.

Carlburg tackle A simple form of breaking/mouthing tackle, which operates from the rump and incorporates side reins, but, as it has no means of elevating the head, it may lead to overbending.

Carousel/Carrousel A musical ride performed in unison by a group of riders. The series of movements are designed to resemble old-fashioned dances such as the quadrille (q.v.) and the Lancers, and the riders often wear period costume.

Carriage museums A number of carriage museums now exist in the British Isles. Among the most notable ones are The Tyrwhitt-Drake Museum, Maidstone, Kent; the Shuttleworth Museum, Biggleswade, Bedfordshire; Dodington Park, Chipping Sodbury, Glos; Breamore House, Fordingbridge, Hants; Arlington Court, Barnstaple, Devon; Aysgarth Museum, Richmond, Yorks; Shibden Hall, Halifax, Yorks; Transport Museum, Hull, Yorks; Transport Museum, Glasgow, Scotland; Transport Museum, Belfast, Northern Ireland; Carriage Museum, Luggala, Roundwood, Co. Wicklow, Ireland. There is also a fine collection at the Royal Mews in London.

Carries the scent Said of a hound which actually smells the fox's line when the pack is running.

Carrots A root vegetable much enjoyed by horses, rich in vitamin A (carotene) (q.v.), and also contains some protein. Carrots must be fed sliced lengthwise to avoid choking on a piece too large to be swallowed.

Carry Ploughland is said to 'carry' when it is sticky and is picked up on the feet of hounds or foxes.

Carry both ends See **Wear**.

'Carrying a scent' Said of good scenting country or of a hound which works with its nose when the pack is running.

'Carrying the bar' An old coaching term for a horse whose bar is an inch or two in front of his partner's.

Cart The general term for any two-wheeled vehicle. See **Waggon**.

'Carted' A familiar term describing a rider whose horse has run away.

Cartilage (gristle) Skeletal tissue consisting of cells and fibres scattered in a firm but flexible matrix. It is one of the components in the structure of the joints, and is present as a rubbery cap to the end of the bones to provide a smooth surface for movement. Most joints are bathed in lubricating synovial fluid (q.v.). Cartilage is also present in young animals at the 'growth plate'. It is in these areas near the ends of the bones that growth takes place, the cartilage gradually being replaced by bone as the bone grows.

Cartilage, articular The cartilage which forms a cap around the ends of the bones of joints to provide a smooth surface for movement. Most joints are bathed in lubricating synovial fluid (q.v.). The spinal vertebrae have pads of cartilage (intervertebral discs) between them, but without synovial fluid.

Cartilage, lateral Two plates of cartilage, concave on their inner surfaces, one on each side of the foot, holding between them the plantar cushion. The lateral cartilages spread outwards each time the horse's weight lands on the horny frog. Inflammation of the pedal bone or coronet bone may extend to the lateral cartilage, causing calcification. This hardening of the cartilage is termed 'side bone' (q.v.). A certain amount of calcification occurs quite normally in many horses after the twelfth to fourteenth year of life without giving rise to lameness.

'Carty' A cold-blood and any heavy draught horse. A 'carty sort' means common-bred.

Caspian Horse In 1965 a small number (fewer than forty) of miniature horses were re-discovered in a remote and mountainous area of Iran near the Caspian Sea. It is said that this breed dates from about 3000 BC, but they have been 'lost' for the past 2000 years. Careful scientific examination suggests that technically they are miniature *horses*, not ponies, and it is further suggested that they may have been the forerunners of the hot-blood horses (Arabians etc.) of today. Careful breeding on studs to re-establish the numbers in Britain has been undertaken, and it is a condition of the British Caspian Society that pure mares are bred *only* to purebred stallions. The horses stand 10-12 hh (100-121.9 cm) and may be bay, grey, or chestnut, with occasional white markings on head and legs. The head is short and fine, with a vaulted forehead, a fine, tapering muzzle, and large, low-set nostrils. The ears are short. The body is slim, and the limbs are fine, with dense, strong bone and little feathering. The feet are exceptionally strong and never need shoeing on any surface. There are Caspian studs in the USA and Australia.

Cast Said of a horse when it is lying in the stall or box and is unable to rise without assistance, either through lack of space or because it is lying too close to an adjacent wall or division.

Cast An effort made by hounds, either on their own initiative or at their huntsman's direction, to recover the scent at a check.

Cast A horse considered to be inferior or unsuitable.

Casting (coat) A horse casts its coat twice a year, in autumn and spring. The actual time is governed by the arrival of cold weather, the thickness of the horse's coat, whether it is stabled or at grass, and whether it is an early or late foal.

Casting (horse) Throwing a horse to the ground. This is generally resorted to for the purpose of a veterinary operation. An unbroken colt is best cast (for castration usually) by the use of rope sidelines.

Cast metal Bits, stirrup irons, etc., cast in a mould as opposed to being hand-forged. The latter is now almost a dead art.

Castors See **Chestnut**.

Castration The operation of emasculation of the male horse: i.e. gelding. It is best carried out in the spring or autumn, to avoid infection of the wound by flies.

Catch To find a mare 'in season' when running out at grass.

Catch The bringing in of horses off grass.

Catch hold A horse is said to 'catch hold' when he pulls.

Catch hold A huntsman is said to 'catch hold of hounds' when he lifts the pack. (See **Lift**)

Catching (or folding) a whip The act of lapping the thong of a team or tandem whip round the crop by a skilful turn of the coachman's whip. (See **Double thong**)

Catch pigeons Racing term for sprinters.

Catch weights Racing term usually applied in a race where two owners have challenged each other to a match where no weights are specified. It follows that the Clerk of the Scales (q.v.) is not concerned.

Cat-hairs The long, untidy hairs which grow in a horse's coat after the second clipping and which show early in the new year. They can be removed by singeing (q.v.).

Cat-hammed Descriptive of a horse with weak hocks that stand back and away from the natural stance.

'Cattle' Slang term for horses.

Cattlemen's carnivals Australian rodeos.

Caulkins/Caulks See **Calkins**.

Cavalcade A procession of people on horseback.

Cavalier A horseman, especially a horse soldier. A name (originally reproachful) for the supporters of King Charles I in the Civil War.

Cavalletti Low, movable wooden jump or series of jumps, similar in appearance to a knife rest. They are invaluable for

Cavalletti.

schooling young horses. Nine-foot (2.7 m) poles or logs are rested at each end on stout Xs. The 'arms' are crossed not quite at right angles, and by changing from close to open stance the height is lowered. In Germany they are known as 'bodenricks'.

Cavalry Horse soldiers. A troop of horses or horsemen.

Cavalry twill Cavalry twill is a development from the double twill used before 1914 for blue uniform breeches. It was first made of khaki material in the West of England during the early part of the First World War to be worn by cavalry regiments.

Cavendish, William See **Newcastle, William Cavendish, Duke of**

Cavesson (from French *caveçon***)** The word can either refer to a cavesson noseband or a breaking cavesson, and should be so qualified. A breaking or lungeing cavesson is a superior form of headcollar

Lungeing cavesson.

used in the training of a young horse. It has a padded nosepiece on to which is set a metal plate fitted with three swivelling rings. The lunge rein is fastened to any one of these rings. A cavesson noseband is the simplest form of leather noseband on a bridle.

Cavings See **Chaff**.

Cavvy Bunch of horses on a cattle ranch in North America.

Cayuse A strong, hardy Indian pony descended from a Spanish horse.

Cee-spring A C-shaped spring to which is attached a leather strap, situated at the back of early horse-drawn vehicles. Used before the invention of the elliptic spring.

Celle Stud Near Hanover, in West Germany. More than two centuries' old, it is now the state-run stud for the Hanoverian breed.

Centaur According to Greek legend, the centaurs were an ancient race of savage men living in the hills of Thessaly who were the offspring of Ixion and a cloud. In ancient works of art the centaur was represented as a man from head to loins, with the remaining part of the body that of a horse. Jason, hero of the Argonauts, was educated by Chiron the Centaur.

Chaff Chaff is chopped hay prepared by passing good-quality seed hay or hard meadow hay through a machine called a chaff-cutter or a 'choppy'. It is used to add bulk to food and to encourage the horse to chew. Chaff can also made from the residue of corn after thrashing (also known as 'cavings') but it has little value as a food.

Chaff cutters Machines which cut hay or straw into short lengths, for mixing with oats etc.

Chafing See **Gall**.

Chain, rack See **Rack chain**.

Chain, stallion A brass or steel chain about 18ins (45.7 cm) long, with a swivel-fitting on one end to which is fastened the lead rein, and a spring hook on the other. Its use gives more control, and prevents the stallion biting through the lead rein.

Chain-mouth snaffle A bit of which the mouthpiece is a chain rather than a solid metal bar.

Chair, The An open ditch of 6ft (1.8 m) followed by a fence of 5ft 2ins (1.6 m) on the steeplechase course at Aintree. The biggest fence on the Grand National, (q.v.), it is situated in front of the stands and is only jumped once, on the first circuit of the race. It derives its name from the iron chair which used to be placed by the jump for the use of the distance judge.

Chaise A pleasure or travelling carriage, especially a light open carriage with a top, for one or two persons, originally drawn by one horse.

'Chalk-jockey' One who has not ridden sufficient races to warrant his name being painted on a board for insertion in the frame of the course's number-board (q.v.). His name is lettered in chalk on a black-board.

Challenge A hound which 'opens' (q.v.) is said to 'challenge'.

Chalon, Henry Bernard (1770-1849) Born in London of Dutch parentage, a talented animal painter also noted for his sporting pictures. He painted racehorses and hunting scenes in a style much influenced by Stubbs.

Chamber horse An exercise chair used in the bedroom in Georgian times. It simulated the up and down motion of horse riding.

Chambon A schooling device of French origin. A strap from the girth passes between the forelegs and divides at the breast into two cord attachments which pass through rings on a poll pad and are then connected to the bit. The object is to induce a gradual lowering of the head, a rounding of the back, and engagement of the quarters.

Chamfrain Protective armour for a horse's head in mediaeval times.

Chamois leather Name sometimes given to natural wash leather produced from sheepskin. Leather from a Chamois goat would be a rarity.

Champ, to To chew and mouth the bit.

Change in the air See **Flying change (of leg)**.

Change of leg See **Flying change (of leg)**.

Chaparajos (Spanish) See **Chaps**.

Chapman Horses A name (no longer in use) for Cleveland Bays. They were very popular with itinerant 'chapmen' (travelling salesmen) a century ago.

Chaps (Spanish *Chaparajos*) A garment worn by South American cowboys. Made of calf-skin, and covering the trouser legs but not the seat, they were designed primarily for protection against thorns, heat and cold. They are now universally popular for wear when schooling.

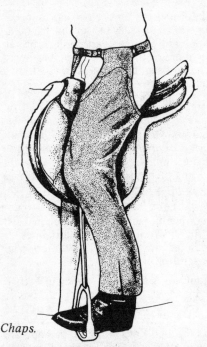

Chaps.

Check apparatus Ligaments forming part of the stay apparatus (q.v.), which help support the lower part of the leg.

Check rein A rein used for harness horses, to correct the carriage of their heads. It runs from the bit to the harness pad, or through Ds attached to the crownpiece, and so to the pad. It also acts as a valuable means of control.

Cheek (of bit) Shank, or leg, of bit, of varying length. Also refers to the cheek

of a snaffle bit: i.e. Dee cheek, eggbutt cheek.

Cheek guards For snaffles these consist of circular leather or rubber pads. For pelhams they are pear-shaped. They prevent chafing.

Cheekpiece Part of bridle to which the snaffle and bridoon bits are attached (sewn, billeted or hook-studded), and which in turn is buckled to the slip-head or headpiece.

Chef d'équipe Captain, or manager, of a competing team of horsemen.

Cheltenham gag A gag snaffle with eggbutt rings or cheeks rather than loose, traversing rings.

Cherries See **Roller mouth**.

Cheshire martingale See **Martingale, Cheshire**.

Chesnut Variant spelling of chestnut (colour) (q.v.), traditionally used when referring to the Suffolk breed (q.v.).

Chest Situated behind the forearms. It must be deep for the heart and lungs to function properly.

Chester (city) One of the earliest homes of horseracing in England, the first races dating back to about 1540. The same course, known as the Roodeye, is still used today.

Chestnut (or castor) Small, horny prominence found on the inside of all four legs, some 3 ins (7.5 cm) above the knees on the inside of the forelegs, and on hindlegs on the inner and lower part of the hock joint. It does not appear on the hocks of a hybrid.

Chestnut (colour) This colour consists of yellow hair in different degrees of intensity (golden and liver). A 'true' chestnut has a chestnut mane and tail, which may be lighter or darker than the body colour. Other chestnuts may have flaxen manes and tails.

Cheval de Selle Français See **Selle Français**.

Chevasse, Pierre French loriner, an associate of Benjamin Latchford (q.v.), who settled in Walsall in the latter part of the last century. His work gave impetus to the local craft.

Chifney, Samuel (1753-1807) Born in Norfolk, and entered Foxe's Stables at Newmarket. Won the Derby on Skyscraper. Wrote of himself in 1773: 'I can ride horses in a better manner in a race to beat others than any person ever known in my time', and in 1775: 'I can train horses for running better than any person I know in my time'. His theory was to ride with a slack rein. He was the first jockey to adopt the method of riding a waiting race, coming to the finish with a tremendous rush. He also invented the bit which bears his name (see **Anti-rearing bit**). Later he became involved in scandals, and died in poverty. His two sons, William and Samuel, were both successful jockeys.

China-eye See **Wall-eye**.

Chincoteague These and similar Assateague ponies are named after the islands which they inhabit off the coast of Virginia and Maryland, USA. The islands are owned by the Chincoteague Volunteer Fire Department. In July the ponies are rounded up for an annual auction sale. Many are pinto colours (piebald and skewbald), and they have degenerated through in-breeding to a small, narrow pony lacking in bone and quality, and rather stubborn in character. Average height: about 12 hh (121.9 cm).

Choke or Oesophageal impaction Usually caused by a lump of dry food: e.g. insufficiently soaked sugar-beet pulp, or a large piece of carrot or apple. It may occur if the horse is fed when still breathing very deeply after hard exercise. Choking is indicated by convulsive swallowing movements accompanied by much arching of the neck and the muzzle turning in towards the sternum. Because saliva cannot be swallowed it usually dribbles from the mouth and sometimes from the nostrils. One of the dangers is pneumonia from inhalation. Veterinary assistance is required at the earliest opportunity.

Christian, Dick A celebrated Leicestershire horsebreaker and steeplechase rider in the first half of the nineteenth century. He rode Clinker (q.v.), in the famous match against Squire Osbaldeston (q.v.) on Clasher (q.v.). Christian maintained, 'The gentlemen get the worst falls as they ride on horses which fall like a clod and don't try to get out of a difficulty. I am safer riding twenty young horses than one old one'. See **Dick Christian bridoon**.

Chronic Obstructive Pulmonary Disease (COPD) See **Broken wind**.

Chuck wagon Western term for wagon which houses cooking and camping equipment.

Chukka or Chukker Polo term for periods into which the game is divided. In Argentina, USA and Great Britain, chukkas are now seven minutes. In Argentina a full game is eight chukkas, in Great Britain and the USA it is only six.

Chukker (USA) See **Chukka**.

Churn barrel Roomy; well-ribbed up.

Chute A stall in which rodeo horses are saddled, bridled, and mounted.

Cimarron (South America) A wild horse.

Cinch American term for the girth on a Western saddle. The cinch does not buckle on to straps as does an English girth, but is adjusted with a 'tie' knot on a ring.

Circle cheek snaffle A riding bit with cheeks similar to a Liverpool bit, but with a central rein loop. It is used for keeping a horse running straight.

Circus horses There are three categories of circus horse: Liberty horses (q.v.) appear unridden in groups of six to sixteen or more. Haute école horses are ridden solo or sometimes in twos or threes, performing complicated movements based on classical High School (q.v.) traditions. Costumes and saddlery are specially decorative. Rosinbacks (q.v.) take their name from the rosin (resin) rubbed on the horse's back to prevent the performer from slipping.

Citation bridle Bridle specially designed to prevent a horse putting his tongue over the bit. Also known as a 'Citation' after the horse who first wore it.

Claiming race A race in which every horse may be claimed for a certain price as laid down in the conditions of the race.

Clarence A carriage first produced in 1842. It was described as 'midway between a Brougham (q.v.) and a coach' (q.v.). Shortly after the introduction of the Brougham a more formalised vehicle was produced, known as a Surrey Clarence, with a hammercloth box and rear platform for footmen, and with the appearance of a hybrid chariot-Brougham.

Clasher A good-looking 15.3 hh (160 cm) brown hunter gelding owned by 'Squire' George Osbaldeston and ridden by him in the famous match in the Quorn Country against Captain Ross's Clinker (q.v.) in 1829. The stake was 1500 guineas a side and the riders carried 12 stone (76 kg).

Classics A term denoting the five classic races for three-year-olds: the 2000 Guineas and the 1000 Guineas (fillies only), run at Newmarket over 1 mile (1.6 km); the Derby and the Oaks (fillies only), run at Epsom over 1½ miles (2.4 km); and the St Leger run at Doncaster over about 1¾ miles (2.8 km). Races equivalent to some or all of these are run in many other countries, including France, New Zealand, Japan, Italy, Ireland, Germany, Argentina, and South Africa.

Classics (racing, Australia) Most states have their own classics. The best known include the AJC Derby and St Leger in New South Wales, and the Derby in Victoria. Unlike the system in most other countries, geldings are eligible for Australian classic races.

Classics (racing, France) These are all run at Chantilly: Prix du Jockey Club (Derby), Poule d'Essai (2000 Guineas), Poule d'Essai des Pouliches (1000 Guineas), Prix de Diane (Oaks) and Prix Royal Oak (St Leger).

Classics (racing, USA) The Kentucky Derby, run at Churchill Downs, Kentucky (geldings eligible), 1¼ miles (2.01 km); the Preakness Stakes, run at Pimlico, Maryland, 1³⁄₁₆ miles (1.91 km); the Belmont Stakes, run at Belmont, New York, 1½ miles (2.41 km); and the Coaching Club American Oaks, also run at Belmont, New York, 1½ miles (2.41 km) for fillies only.

Clean bred An animal of any breed whose pedigree is of pure blood.

Clean ground Hunting term indicating that land is neither foiled (q.v.) nor stained.

Clean leg Breed without hair in any abundance: e.g. Suffolk, Cleveland Bay, as distinct from Shire and Clydesdale.

Clean leg Free from blemishes.

Cleft An interruption of continuity of the wall of the foot, at right angles to the direction of the horn-tubes. Can be caused by injury to the coronet.

Cleft in the horse's foot, the space lying between the branches of the frog (q.v.).

Clench/Clinch Term applied to the points of nails when holding the shoe on the hoof. Clenches are formed by the blacksmith hammering sufficient protruding nail shank over and downwards.

Clench, risen When a clench (q.v.) rises and protrudes from a shoe through wear; it is vital that this is attended to immediately to prevent injury to a horse, and it is advisable to obtain a new set of shoes.

Clenching In shoeing, nipping off protruding nail points, leaving enough nail to make a clench (q.v.), and smoothing off with a rasp.

Clerk of the course (racing) Person solely responsible for the general arrangements of a race meeting. He requires an annual licence from the Jockey Club and is paid by the racecourse executive.

Clerk of the scales (racing) Official responsible for weighing out and weighing in the jockeys. He must provide the starter with the list of runners. He is responsible for all signals on the number-board, including variations in the weights, apprentice allowances, objections, enquiries, etc. He requires an annual licence from the Jockey Club and is paid by them. He was originally responsible for the draw designating places for flat racing, but this is now carried out on the previous day at the Racing Calendar Office.

Clerk of the scales (show jumping) The official responsible to the judge for seeing that each competitor scales the specified weight in relevant classes.

Cleveland Bay Ancient breed of uncertain origin but almost totally indigenous to the county of Yorkshire. A century ago it was probably the nearest to a fixed type as any breed in England; even then two types existed, for agriculture and coaching. In common with other harness and agricultural horses, the breed declined in numbers alarmingly after World War II, until in 1962 only four mature stallions remained in Britain. Due largely to Her Majesty Queen Elizabeth II, interest in the breed revived: the Queen bought the stallion Mulgrave Supreme, which was subsequently made available to breeders. The breed has made a good recovery, and some horses have been exported to the USA, Canada, Pakistan, South Africa and Australia.

A clean-legged active horse much used for breeding hunters. Average height 16-17 hh (162.6-170 cm) with short legs and always of a whole bay colour. The action should be straight and true and of the kind for getting over the ground; high action is not desirable, but knees must flex. Very hard, 'blue' (dense blue-black) feet are essential.

Cleveland Bay Horse Society of Great Britain Founded in 1884 to promote the interests of the breed, and of horse breeding generally.

Click A sound often made by a rider or driver to start or accelerate his horse.

Clicket Mating call of vixen.

Clicking See **Forging**.

Clinch See **Clench**.

Clinker A Thoroughbred 16.1 hh (165 cm) bay hunter gelding, up to 14 stone (89 kg), owned by Captain Ross and ridden by Dick Christian (q.v.) in the famous match against 'Squire' Osbaldeston's horse, Clasher, (q.v.) in 1829.

Clipping The removal, by hand or machine, of the coat or the mane. The object is to avoid excessive sweating, to facilitate drying after hard work, and to save labour. Clipping is carried out after the winter coat has grown, with subsequent clips before the summer coat begins to set.

Clipping machines These are nearly all electrically operated, having superseded the old hand clippers which required two men to operate them. Blades are either fine, for close clipping, or coarse, for use on legs. There are two types of machine: the hand variety and the larger and more powerful one suspended from the roof.

Clips, types of
FULL CLIP: the whole coat is removed.
HUNTER: the legs, to the elbows and thighs, and a saddle patch are left unclipped.
BLANKET: the underside of the neck, and belly only are clipped.
TRACE: the hair is removed from the belly as far as the traces, and from the legs to half-way down the forearm and thigh.

Clog A form of restraint once used in East Anglia to subdue kickers in a yard. It was made of wood and cord, and was looped round the horse's back legs. When the horse kicked, the clog came down and gave him a sharp rap across the hocks.

Close-coupled Indicating a short, deep, compact body with well-sprung ribs, showing no slackness or weakness in the loins.

Closing The conditions of every race under Jockey Club rules have to be published in the Racing Calendar (q.v.) before it closes for entries. The advertisement in the Racing Calendar before closing must state the dates on which a meeting is to be held, the dates for closing the races to further entries, and other particulars as laid down by rules.

Clothing (horse) Rugs, blankets, hoods, tail-guards, summer sheets, coolers, etc. worn by the horse. See under individual items.

Clothing-tearing See **Rug tearing**.

Cloud Dark mark on the face of a horse.

Club feet See **Boxy foot**.

Clucking Encouraging sound made by rider or driver. (See **Click**)

Clydesdale Scottish draught horse developed in the district of Lanark around the River Clyde. It dates from the middle of the eighteenth century, when the hardy native breed – through use of Flemish stallions – was graded up to meet the trade demand for more weight and substance. Clydesdales combine quality and size without grossness and bulk, possess exceptionally sound feet and limbs, and are active walkers. They stand about 16.2 hh (165 cm). Colours are bay, brown, and roan, with some greys and blacks. Large white patches often occur on the face and legs and the underpart of the body.

Clydesdale Horse Society of Great Britain and Ireland Founded in 1877 to maintain the purity of the Clydesdale breed, and to collect and preserve their pedigrees. The Society holds an annual stallion show and various horse sales.

Coach The coach is believed to have been introduced into England in the sixteenth century and named after Kotje, a small town in Hungary where it was first made.

Coach dog The spotted Dalmatian was trained to run between the wheels of a vehicle, immediately behind the horse's heels. It was originally a gun-dog in the Balkans and Italy. Around the middle of the seventeenth century it was used in France to guard against highwaymen, which probably led to its being kept under travelling carriages in England, where it was introduced in the eighteenth century.

Coach horse Except for the Yorkshire coach horse, now extinct, there is no one particular type: Hackneys, Cleveland Bays, and other harness horses being in many respects suitable for driving as a team. Since the rise in popularity of competitive carriage driving, a number of breeds and cross-breds have been used. These include Oldenburg and their crosses, Welsh Cobs and Welsh/Thoroughbred crosses, Lipizzaners, Cleveland Bay crosses, etc.

Coach house This should be airy, well-ventilated, but not cold, and should be heated when it is frosty. The sun should not shine directly on the vehicles. The floor should be level, made of cement or any smooth surface; the doors should extend the whole width of the house and should be provided with stops to keep them open when vehicles are being run in and out.

Coaching Until the mid-sixteenth century, travel in England was both slow and uncomfortable. The first vehicles were huge, cumbersome stage wagons drawn by teams of six to eight heavy horses urged on by a mounted drover. They ran only in summer, for the roads were no more than rough tracks.

The first coach, thought to have been introduced into England from the town of Kotje in Hungary during the reign of Queen Elizabeth I, was a large square vehicle, open at the sides. From then on more and more coaches were brought into service and road surfaces gradually improved. In 1784 the first mail coach service was established by John Palmer of Bath – the mail having previously been carried by post-boys on horseback, who were frequently attacked and robbed. Apart from the security that they offered, the mail coaches also became popular as a means of conveyance: not only were they speedy, but they also could carry up to nine passengers at a charge of five pence a mile for those on top – thus giving rise to the term 'an outsider'.

In 1815, the engineers Telford and Macadam perfected a new type of road surface, so that greater numbers of coaches, both stage and mail, were able to operate. Stage coaches, though similar to the mails in construction, could carry up to twelve passengers on top. For security purposes the space at the back of a mail coach was occupied solely by the mail-bag guard, whereas on a stage this area provided accommodation for eight or more passengers. Mail coaches were always painted in Royal colours – black, with maroon panels on which the monarch's cypher was inscribed, and scarlet wheels and undercarriage. Stage coaches, which plied solely for trade, were painted in brilliant colours with the names of their stopping places in gold letters; they were also given sporting names such as 'Tally Ho', 'Red Rover', 'Magnet', etc., and it became the fashion for young men-about-town to drive them. Like the mails, they carried a red-coated guard, whose job was to sound the horn, watch over the luggage, and keep the coachman up to time.

With the arrival of the railways in the 1830s, mail and stage coaches were gradually phased out, but the fashion for four-in-hand driving remained, and gentlemen's coaches, or 'private drags' (q.v.), were developed. These were lighter in construction than stage coaches, and painted in more sombre colours, with the owner's crest or monogram on the boots and door panels, while two grooms in livery sat on the back seat. Several driving clubs were formed, and wagers, concerning both skill and speed with a four-in-hand, were made. There was also a revival of stage-coaching as a sport, which reached its zenith during the reign of King Edward VII, and lasted until the outbreak of World War I.

The attraction of coaching and its immense history of early communications, or else the urge to drive a four-in-hand, has led subsequent generations of sportsmen to resuscitate the art. Apart from taking part in horse shows, where as many as sixteen coaches have been seen in the ring, long distance runs have also been planned, and journeys from London to both Brighton and Southampton Portsmouth to Scarborough, and even Edinburgh to London, have been achieved since the end of World War II.

Coaching Club Formed in 1871 under the Presidency of the 8th Duke of Beaufort, and the only remaining club of its kind. Members must be able to drive a four-in-hand, and drive *private* (as opposed to road or stage) coaches, which are known as 'drags' (q.v.). Meets are held at various shows, including the Royal Windsor in May.

Coaching crop Correct name for coaching whip.

Coaching marathon Marathon for four-horse coaches, first introduced at the Royal International Horse Show in 1909. Since then it has been a popular feature of this and other shows. Brief intervals separate the departures of the coaches from a given point, the drive usually ending in the show ring. Marks are given for horses, turn-out and condition of horses on arrival, not for speed, though the journey must be completed within a set time and without a change of coachman.

Coachman One who drives one or more horses.

Coachman's elbow In giving or returning a salute, a driver does not raise his hat. The hand holding the whip is raised to face-level, with the whip diagonal to the body, thus raising the elbow.

Coat In the Northern Hemisphere a horse's coat grows towards the end of September in preparation for the winter. There is new growth again in the spring. Underbreds and horses at grass grow the heaviest coats. A dull, staring coat is often an indication of ill-health.

Cob Not a breed, but a well-established type. A big-bodied, short-legged horse or pony. Under British Show Hack and Cob Association rules, cobs may be shown in two size classes – lightweights capable of carrying up to 14 stone (88.7 kg), and heavyweights, capable of carrying over 14 stone (88.7 kg), both with a height limit of 15.1 hh (154.9 cm). See also **Welsh Cobs**.

Cockade Ornamental rosette fastened to the side of top hats worn as a badge of office by liveried servants employed by members of the nobility and the armed forces (i.e. those entitled to bear arms). Introduced into England during the reign of King George III.

Cock-eyed stirrup irons Type with 'eye' 1¼ ins (31 mm) out of the perpendicular and 'tread' sloped outward towards the heel, thus encouraging the inward slope of the foot and the lowered heel. Often known as 'Kournakof' irons after the riding instructor who popularised them.

Cock fences (hunting) Thorn fences cut very low.

Cockhorse Extra horse used on very steep hills to assist a stage coach in ascent. It was attached ahead of the leaders and was ridden by a 'cockhorse-boy'. The origin of the name is obscure.

Cocking cart Extremely high-hung two-wheeled cart, designed to take fighting game cocks. Popular for tandem driving in the early nineteenth century, it usually seated two, with an additional seat for the groom at the rear.

Cocks eyes/Cockeyes Metal eyes at the end of the leaders' traces to hook on to the bars.

Cocktail A horse of racing qualities but not a Thoroughbred.

Cock-tailed Having the tail docked (see **Docking**). A term used in the eighteenth century.

Cock-throttled A term applied when the head is set at the wrong angle and the gullet stands out in convex shape as in the throat of a cock.

Cody, William Frederick (1846-1917) American showman, known as 'Buffalo Bill'. A rider in the Pony Express (q.v.), he became an army scout and guide, and served in the US cavalry. He killed the Cheyenne chief Yellow Hand in single combat. In 1883 he organised the Wild West Show, which first toured Europe in 1887.

Coffee-housing Hunting expression for the objectionable habit of chatting at the covert side.

Coffin A cross-country fence used in horse trials (q.v.), comprising a post and rails on the take-off side, a ditch, and another set of post and rails.

Coffin.

Coffin cab A London hackney cab in use before the hansom. It was two-wheeled, with a coffin-like body for two passengers. The driver's seat was between the body and the off wheel.

Coffin head Coarse, ugly face in which the jowl lacks prominence.

Coggin's test Official diagnostic test for equine infectious anaemia adopted by the US Department of Agriculture.

Coital exanthema Infectious disease of vulva or penis caused by equine herpes virus 3, which is transmitted during coitus, or by insects or handlers. The incubation period is three to six days. It takes the form of blisters on the penis or vulva. Sometimes the horse has a temperature and is depressed. The condition usually clears by itself after two to four weeks.

Coldblood A term referring to the ancient (immediately post-Ice Age) group of horses of Northern Europe from which the modern heavy or draught breeds are believed to have descended. (See also **Warmblood**)

Cold-scenting Term applied to hunting country which, irrespective of day-to-day conditions, is liable to carry little scent.

Cold-shoeing The shoe is nailed to the foot without having been heated and shaped immediately beforehand. Generally less effective than hot-shoeing. (See also **Shoeing**)

Colds (in horses) See **Influenza, equine**.

Colic Pain in the abdominal cavity. It usually stems from the gut, but may arise from a variety of conditions. The majority of cases respond to treatment very well. All cases require veterinary attention.

There are several types of alimentary tract colic:
(1) IMPACTED – stoppage due to dry gut content in the large colon and/or caecum. The symptoms include a gradual onset of mild to moderate pain, which may persist for days. A few hard droppings may be passed, unless the blockage is complete. Treatment usually consists of lubricating the bowel content with liquid paraffin. The condition normally subsides in up to two to three days, and the horse will start to pass droppings again.
(2) SPASMODIC – muscular spasms of the gut wall, which may cause an increase in bowel sounds. There is a sudden onset of mild to moderate or severe pain, accompanied by periods of near normality.

Treatment consists of bowel-relaxing drugs. The symptoms usually subside after four to ten hours.

(3) FLATULENT – the bowel becomes distended with gas produced by fermentation of the gut content. Pain is moderate to severe. The distension of the bowel may be so severe as to cause rupture of the nerves and blood vessels in the bowel wall, possibly leading to death of a portion of the bowel, which may be fatal.

(4) THROMBO-EMBOLIC – caused by blockage of the blood vessels supplying the bowel. The blockage is due to damage of the blood vessels by migrating worm larvae of the *strongyle* family. The part of the bowel supplied by the blood vessel dies and in the process of dying causes the horse severe pain. If the part of the bowel affected is small then the horse usually recovers. If the area affected is large then it may lead to bowel rupture and death.

(5) OBSTRUCTIVE – a variety of causes include twisted gut, leading to complete destruction of the bowel. There is severe unremitting pain which will not respond to treatment. Early surgical intervention is required to save the horse.

General signs of abdominal pain include loss of appetite, restlessness, sweating, looking at flanks, kicking at the abdomen, sudden rolling and groaning. These may be seen in any of the above types of colic.

Collar An item of harness made of heavily padded leather. It carries the hames, and correct fitting is most important.

Collar of a whip The metal band at the top of the leather hand piece. It should mark the place where the hand grasps the whip.

Collar work Driving term for any work uphill or calling for strain through the traces to the collar.

Collected A term applied to a horse when ridden well up to the bit, with its neck raised and arched, so that the head is slightly in front of the vertical. The jaws are relaxed, and the hocks are well under the animal, which has full control of its limbs at all paces, and is ready and able to respond to the aids of the rider.

Collecting ring A ring immediately adjoining the showing or jumping ring where competitors assemble with their horses. Usually there is a steward in charge.

Collection See **Collected**.

Collection classes Unknown at shows in Great Britain but popular in the USA. Open to three or more exhibits from one stable, each stable being judged as one entry.

Collier Type of west Wales pack- or draught horse once used in coal mines. Short-legged with feather, and with strong quarters. Also known as a 'pitter'.

Collier's horse A knocker (q.v.).

Collinge's axles Type of axle now seen on most carriages except coaches. The removable cap facilitates greasing.

Colostrum The first milk of the mare after the birth of a foal. It is highly nutritious and contains protein anti-bodies, especially globulin, which confer immunity on the foal for the first weeks of its life. The colostrum must be available to and taken in by the foal in the first twelve hours or so of life, otherwise the antibodies will not be absorbed into the bloodstream.

Colours, body The principal colours are black, brown, bay, chestnut and grey, although the latter is not a colour but a failure of pigment to produce colour. Where there is any doubt as to the colour, the muzzle and eyelids may be examined for guidance.

Colours, registration of Every owner, or part-owner, in whose name a racehorse runs, is required to register his racing colours annually on payment of a fee. Colours so registered cannot be taken by another person.

Colours, Royal The following are the racing colours used by the Royal Family: HM Queen Elizabeth II: purple, gold braid, scarlet sleeves, black velvet cap, with a gold fringe; HM Queen Elizabeth the Queen Mother: blue, buff stripes, blue sleeves, black cap with a gold tassel.

Colt Male, ungelded horse up to four

years old. It is usual to denote the male sex of a foal as a 'colt foal'.

Comanche twitch A variant of the gag twitch in which the cord is attached to the near-side D of the headcollar.

Combined training This used to consist of a dressage test and a show-jumping round. In 1974 the title was changed to Dressage with Jumping.

Combined martingale See **Martingale, combined**.

Combs Nowadays these are generally made of metal; they were once made of bone. A large comb is used for the mane and tail, a small one for trimming.

'Comes again' Said of a horse (whether hunting or racing) which, though apparently flagging, will suddenly 'take hold' of the bit and gallop on with renewed zest. In hunting it is also often referred to as 'second wind'.

Comfrey A type of herb specially cultivated for horse feed. It is high in calcium and phosphates and is sometimes used as a substitute for hay in summer. It is also valued by many for its medicinal properties.

Common riding See **Hawick Common**.

Commons, Open Spaces, and Footpaths Preservation Society (founded 1865). Objects: to protect commons; to ensure public enjoyment of them for recreation; to promote the extension of open spaces; and to provide for the preservation and proper maintainance of public footpaths, bridleways and other highways.

Comtois An active, small but chunky draught horse originating in the Comté mountain region of eastern France. During the eighteenth century the Comtois was used to upgrade other breeds, and also as a cavalry and artillery horse. It is now confined to light draught work, particularly in forestry and in the vineyards, as well as being bred for meat. It stands between 14.3-15 hh (149.9-152.4 cm), is bay or chestnut, and has a square, rather heavy head. It is renowned for its toughness and excellent temperament.

Concentrates Foods, such as oats, barley, and maize, which provide large quantities of energy when fed in comparatively small quantities. Cf. bulk food such as hay.

Concours d'Attelage (CA) Equestrian events in which the competitions are confined exclusively to driving.

Concours Complet d'Equitation See **Horse trials**.

Concours de Saut (CS) Equestrian events in which the competitions are confined exclusively to jumping.

Concours Hippique (CH) Equestrian events which include competitions of more than one discipline.

Concussion Injury of (a) the head, in which there is loss or reduction of consciousness due to a severe blow, or (b) the legs (usually the forelegs) due to fast work on a hard surface. The symptoms of (a), in addition to impaired consciousness, may be dilated pupils, and laboured and irregular breathing. Veterinary attention is necessary. Symptoms of (b) include heat, soreness and lameness.

Condition A horse 'in condition' is at its very best in both looks and health, showing plenty of muscle, which should feel hard to the touch when the hand is run along the crest and neck. The skin on the horse's sides should feel freely movable over the ribs. Good condition is produced by correct attention to details of management, feeding, exercise, teeth, and grooming.

Condition race A race that is not a handicap and is governed by some conditions, such as 'for horses that have not won a race value £500'. Sometimes called a 'terms race'.

Confidential A term applied to a horse which is suitable for a novice or elderly rider.

Conformation A horse's make and shape.

Conjunctivitis Inflammation, giving a reddened appearance, of the conjunctiva of the eye, i.e. the membrane which lines the eyelids and covers the eyeballs.

Connemara A pony of great antiquity, evolved among the mountains, bogs, and stony outcrops of the western part of Ireland, from which it takes its name. The breed shows signs of Andalusian, Barb and Arab blood, probably introduced three or four hundred years ago by merchants travelling from the Iberian Peninsula to the ports of Galway. Towards the end of the nineteenth century, Welsh stallions were introduced, and one of them, Prince Llewellyn, sired Dynamite out of a native mare. Dynamite in turn sired Cannon Ball, who is Number 1 in the Connemara Stud Book. The breed is hardy, docile, sound, and intelligent. It makes an excellent all-round performance pony, doing equally well under saddle and in harness. Grey is the predominant colour, but there are also browns, duns, blacks, and occasional chestnuts and roans. The maximum height is 14.2 hh (147.3 cm). Connemaras have been very successful in Britain, and ponies from both Ireland and the mainland of Britain have been exported to the USA, Europe, and to Australia, where there is a flourishing Connemara Breeders Society.

Connemara Pony Breeders' Society, the Founded in Eire in 1923 to encourage the breeding of Connemara ponies, and their development and maintenance as a pure breed.

Connemara Pony Society, The English Founded in 1946 to encourage the breeding and utilisation of Connemara ponies in England.

Conestoga wagon Primitive covered wagon (canvas over wooden hoops) of the western American plains, used in the nineteenth century. Also known as a 'Prairie Schooner'.

Conquistadores The name given to the Spanish conquerors of Mexico in the sixteenth century. This small cavalry troop brought the first horses to be introduced into the Western hemisphere since their disappearance thousands of years before. The indigenious people believed that horse and rider were one being and panic and terror spread in their ranks. Bernal del Castillo Diaz, contemporary historian of the invaders wrote: 'After God we owed the victory to the horses.'

Constipation Recognisable by small, hard droppings, or no droppings, and excessive abdominal straining in an attempt to pass the hard droppings.

Contact The link through the reins between the mouth of the horse and the hands of the rider. It should be positive yet light, and on a well-schooled horse may be maintained by the weight of the reins alone.

Contagious equine metritus (CEM) A highly contagious bacterial venereal disease affecting the inner lining of the uterus. The bacterium may also survive for some time in the clitoral sinuses of the vulva. The incubation period is from three to ten days. It is characterised by copious, purulent vaginal discharge. Mares who have apparently recovered may remain infective carriers. The disease was apparently unknown in Western Europe until the late 1970s.

Continental martingale See **Martingale, Continental**.

Continental panel A term used to describe a forward-cut saddle with knee and thigh rolls.

Cooling off A horse that arrives home hot and sweating following work should have the girths loosened, be covered with a sweat rug (or a heavier rug inside out) and be walked around quietly until he has dried off appreciably before returning to the stable. (Away from home, a hot, sweating horse should not be loaded into a horse box, as he will easily catch a chill.) A short drink of *chilled* water (water with the chill off) may be given on return to the stable, followed, approximately an hour later by a longer drink. The saddle should not be removed until the horse is dry.

Cooper, Abraham, R.A. (1787-1868) Son of a tobacconist. He was a self-taught artist, apart from some instruction from Benjamin Marshall (q.v.). He exhibited 352 pictures over 58 years at the Royal Academy, and is known for a variety of animal and sporting subjects, especially racehorses.

'Cope' A hunting cry – 'cope forrard', a cheer of the whipper-in.

71

Copenhagen The charger of phenomenal stamina whom the Duke of Wellington rode at the Battle of Waterloo. Copenhagen was by Meteor by the illustrious Eclipse (q.v.), and raced in the colours of General Grosvenor as a three-year-old, but his turf career was not very successful and he passed into the possession of the Iron Duke. The name 'Copenhagen' was expunged from the General Stud Book because of a fault in his pedigree. His dam, Lady Catherine, carried General Grosvenor at the Siege of Copenhagen (hence the name), and embarked for England in foal.

Coper A horse dealer. The modern use of the word is usually opprobrious, implying one who practises sharp or underhand methods to influence the sale of a horse. Also known as 'horse coper'.

Cording The cruel practice of fixing a hard piece of cord round a horse's tongue and attaching the ends to the bit in such a manner that a slight jerk caused the tongue to be cut. The idea was that the sudden pain would make the horse step higher. The practice is now prohibited.

Cordwainers' Company (after the Spanish name for 'cordovan' or 'cordwain' leather used in bootmaking) The first reference to this guild was recorded in 1272 and a Charter was granted by Henry VI in 1439. Originally the guild was composed almost entirely of shoemakers, and there are still today some practical bootmakers among its liverymen. The Company grants numerous pensions and takes an active interest in the training of saddlers at the Cordwainers' College in London.

Corinthian (USA) In American shows, a class for hunters, both show and working, 'to be ridden in full hunting attire by amateurs who are members of (or in cases of a subscription pack, fully accredited subscribers to) a recognised or registered Hunt'. The hunters are judged on performance and soundness, with emphasis on brilliance (85 per cent), and appointments (15 per cent) of both horse and rider. The horses are shown over 'natural' hunting field jumps in an arena.

Corinthians A name applied generally to the 'bloods' of Regency days, who delighted in driving well-horsed coaches, curricles and highflyer phaetons (q.v.).

Corium Membranous vascular tissue inside the horn of the hoof. It supplies nourishment to the coronary band, the surface of the pedal bone, and the frog.

Corn A bruise on the sole of the foot involving the laminae (q.v.), and most commonly found in the terminal portion of the wings of the sole between the bars and the wall at the heel. The front feet are more prone to the condition. Common causes are stones, structural faults of the foot – e.g. weak heels – or bad farriery, including excessive lowering of the heels, too much paring, or badly fitting shoes. The symptoms are lameness (increasing with work), heat, and pain on pressure.

Corn, seat of The terminal portion of the 'wings' of a horse's sole, between the bars and the wall at the heel.

Corn bin Receptacle for holding corn, usually made of metal.

Cornish snaffle See **Scorrier snaffle**.

Cornucrescine Proprietary name for an ointment used to promote hoof growth.

Coronary band/Corium Located at the top of the foot between the perioplic band and the sensitive laminae or fleshy leaves of the hoof. The band, or 'cushion', as it is also known, consists of fibro-fatty tissue covered by a vascular fleshy covering, which nourishes and from which grows the hoof wall. This lies in the coronary groove around the upper border of the wall.

Coronation Coach (correctly referred to as the Gold State Coach). It was commissioned in 1758 but took four years to build and was just too late for the coronation of King George III. The cost complete was £7562, of which £1673 went to the coachmaker, Butler, £2500 to the carver, Wilton, and £933 to the gilder, Pajolas. Cipriani, the painter of its lovely panels, received £315, and the balance was paid to harnessmakers, saddlers, drapers, cover-makers, etc. The back wheels of the coach are nearly 6 ft (1.8 m) in diameter and are modelled on those of an ancient triumphal car.

The original damask upholstery covering is still retained, but new sponge-rubber cushioning, modern lighting and special rubber tyres were fitted for the coronation of Queen Elizabeth II.

Coronet The coronary band surrounding the top of the foot at the lower extremity of the growth of hair.

Coronet bone See **Pastern, short**.

Coronet boot Boots of leather lined with felt, worn just above the coronary band to prevent treading or over-reach (q.v.) injuries.

Coronet boot.

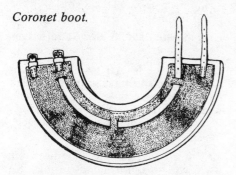

Corporal of Horse A rank in either of the two regiments of the Household Cavalry, equivalent in rank to a sergeant in other regiments.

Corral A high, stout, timber-built fenced-in enclosure for horses, cattle, etc. See **Pound**.

Cosh Familiar name for a stick carried for riding. Also known as a 'bat'.

Cottage windows The windows of a stage coach when they are divided into four small panes.

Cottonseed cake A valuable source of protein, common in the USA, less so in Britain.

Coughs These are caused by inflammation of the back of the throat and the windpipe or trachea. The various causative agents are nuisance dusts irritating the back of the throat, infectious diseases, and fungal spores. Several virus diseases cause coughing – equine influenza virus (EHVI) being one. The bacterium that causes strangles may produce a cough, along with one or two other bacteria.

The inhalation of fungal spores may lead to severe inflammation of the lung tissue, causing a deep chesty cough and a 'heaving' character to the breathing. Pneumonia can result from any of the previously mentioned conditions, of which one of the symptoms is a cough. Coughing may also be caused by the internal parasite lung worm (*Dictyocaulus arnfieldi*); this can be associated with donkeys, as they carry the lung worm without showing any marked symptoms themselves.

Coughing in the form of an epidemic is usually caused by the equine influenza virus. See **Influenza, equine**.

Counter canter See **Canter, false**.

Counter changes of hand on two tracks The half-pass (q.v.) executed in a series, alternately from left to right and right to left, with a predetermined number of steps.

Counter lead Cantering on the right rein with the near foreleg leading, or on the left rein with the off-foreleg leading. (See **Canter, false**)

Counters The heel portion of the leg of a boot. Stiffeners are used between these and the leg.

Country A hunting term indicating the area of a particular country over which any pack may hunt.

Coupé A short four-wheeled, closed carriage with an inside seat for two and an outside seat for the driver. Also the front or after compartment of a Continental diligence (q.v.).

Couple A term denoting two foxhounds. The number in a pack is reckoned in couples and couples-and-a-half: e.g. twelve-and-a-half couple. One hound is not described as 'half a couple', but as 'one hound'.

Couples Hound collars, joined by a metal distance link, carried on the 'D' of a whipper-in's saddle. The term can also refer to the two-buckle or snap-hook ends of a lead rein.

Couples, lead Leading couples, of either leather or chain, connecting the bit rings. They have a central ring to which the lead rein is attached.

Coupling-rein In pair and team they buckle to the insides of the bits at one end and join the draught reins (q.v.) at the other. The correct adjustment of their length to suit the horses is very important and not easy to achieve.

Coupling up Fastening the coupling reins in pair and team driving.

Courbette High School air above the ground in which the horse assumes the position of almost a full rear, jumps forward off his hocks, and lands again with hocks bent, maintaining the position of the rear, and so proceeds in short bounds. (See **Airs above the ground**)

Courier Seventeenth-century military term for a light horseman acting as a scout or skirmisher.

Course To course a fox is to run it in view: the opposite to hunting it by scent.

Cover A stud term. (See **Service**)

Cover A term referring to the web (i.e. the thickness and breadth of the metal) of a horseshoe. A shoe with a wide web is said to have plenty of 'cover'.

Covered school A building used for riding, with a suitable floor of tan, sand, sawdust and/or some proprietary mixture. A full-size school measures about 65 yds by 22 yds (60 m by 20 m).

Covering boots For use on hind feet of mares during service, to prevent injury to the stallion. They are made of thick felt, heavily reinforced with leather, and are strapped on.

Covert Pronounced 'cover'. A hunting term indicating any wood other than a very large one. (See **Woodland**)

Covert coat In earlier days hunting men hacked to covert side in a light top coat made of fine Venetian twill – hence the name. Later the cloth became known as 'covert cloth', and is now mainly used for lightweight coats for riders, usually thigh length. Covert is made with whipcord weave, the best quality containing warp threads of worsted twist which impart a flecked appearance. Formerly a product of the West of England.

Covert hack A horse formerly used to convey a rider to a meet of hounds. A good riding type, it had well-placed shoulders; short, sound legs, and a good back and quarters. It was up to weight, a nice easy mover at the trot and canter, and also was able to jump.

Cowboy/Cow-puncher A man employed on the big cattle ranches of North America to watch, guard and round up cattle which roam almost wild on the ranges.

Cow-collar A leather strap which circles the neck, with a ring attachment for lead. Though useful on horses which habitually slip their headcollars at grass, it wears down the mane.

Cow-gulleted saddle See **Saddle, Lane Fox**.

Cowhide The leather from which most saddlery is made. Its substance (i.e. thickness) varies according to the purpose for which it is used. Colours are: London – light, Havana – medium, and Warwick – dark.

Cow horn American hunting horn, still used with some foxhounds in the USA, mostly south of Philadelphia.

Cow-kick Forward kick which some horses give with the hindlegs. It can be a serious danger to a rider who is mounting or standing by the horse.

Cow-mouthed saddle See **Saddle, Lane Fox**.

Cow pony Mount of cowboy or cow-puncher, usually of great stamina and hardiness, though sometimes lacking in beauty. (See **Argentine Pony** and **Criollo**)

Cowt North-country term for a young male horse, derived from local pronunciation of colt (q.v.).

Crab Unfavourable criticism of a horse, likely to depreciate its value or prevent its sale.

'Cracking the nostrils' See **High blowing**.

Cracks A horse's foot is subject to various cracks which are distinguished (according to the location) as toe-cracks, side-cracks, quarter-cracks, bar-cracks, etc. See also **Sandcrack**.

Cradle A device consisting of several lengths of rounded wood fastened at intervals by straps to form a necklet around a horse's neck, from throat to shoulder. It is designed to prevent a horse which is suffering from irritation or under treatment from biting the afflicted area.

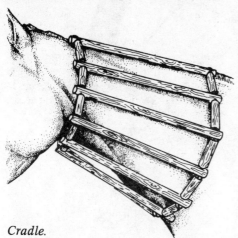

Cradle.

An improved version is known as the 'Cheshire cradle'. It consists of a padded, curved metal bar encasing the chest and fastened to the roller, with a further bar projecting from the centre fastening to the headcollar. It is more comfortable, and does not chafe.

Cradle stirrup irons Irons on which the tread is rounded, giving a circular appearance. Used for racing under both Rules. The shape allows for a lighter iron, which is more comfortable to a foot encased in a thin boot. Made from steel and, sometimes, aluminium.

Crash helmet See **Skull cap**.

Cream (colour) The body coat of a cream colour, with unpigmented skin. The iris is deficient in pigment and is often devoid of it, giving the eye a pinkish or bluish appearance. Also known as Cremello.

Cremello See **Cream colour**.

Crib A rack or manger in a stable.

Crib-biting A disagreable and harmful vice, which may be caused by boredom or copying another horse. The horse takes hold of the manger, door ledge, or any other projection, with its teeth, and sucks in air. It causes indigestion and general unthriftiness. A crib-biter develops worn front edges to the teeth. The habit can be discouraged by preventing boredom (e.g. by having hens in the stable), and by painting any protruding edges in the stable with anti-chewing substances. The animal should be isolated, if possible, to prevent other horses copying the vice. (See also **Wind-sucking**)

Crib-biting device This may be one of many patterns, all of which in some way or another bring pressure upon the horse's gullet in an attempt to prevent both crib-biting and wind-sucking.

Crinet Horse armour for the neck and throat.

Criollo A descendant of horses (mainly Barbs and Andalusians) brought over by the Spaniards in the conquest of South America. It is now regarded as the native horse of Argentina, although it is also found in other South American countries. It stands up to 15 hh (152.4 cm), and is usually dun with eel-stripe and zebra markings, but may also be roan, brown, or black. It is an extremely hardy, tough breed.

Crocker's bit See **Rockwell bridle**.

Cronet The hair growing over the top of a horse's hoof. Also part of the armour of a horse.

Crookedness See **Straightness**.

Crop See **Whip, hunting**.

Cross-breeding The mating of purebred individuals of different breeds.

Crossing feet A horse whose forelegs are faulty, and whose freedom of action is thereby impaired, is liable to cross its feet. Commonly called 'plaiting' or 'lacing'.

Crossing traces In driving, the inside trace of one leader fastening to the inside hook of its partner's bar. This levels up two leaders who are working unevenly.

Cross-saddle See **Saddle, astride or across**.

Croup The upper line from the loins to the root of the tail. It should be convex, even when a fairly heavy weight is carried.

Croupade High School air above the ground, almost identical to the ballotade (q.v.) except that the horse does not show its shoes. (See **Airs above the ground**)

Croupade.

Crowned Old term for a horse with 'broken' knees which exhibited an area of skin devoid of hair growth, usually following injury caused by 'coming down'.

Crudwell Flat racer and steeplechaser who won 50 out of 108 races from 1949-1960: more than any other racehorse in the twentieth century in Britain. Named after the Wiltshire village where he was born.

Crupper, breaking Made in the same way as those for riding, etc., but should have fastened buckles on either side of the dock piece so that it can be fitted and adjusted without upsetting the pupil.

Crupper, harness A leather loop which is passed under the tail and is attached to the 'D' on the pad of a harness horse to keep it in position. To prevent friction it is best to fill it with linseed, which exudes a certain amount of grease, or to keep it well oiled.

Crupper, riding A strap-shaped padded piece of leather which passes under the tail and is attached to the saddle to steady it. A riding crupper is frequently used on ponies when deficient withers make it difficult to keep the saddle in place. As with the harness crupper (above) it should be kept well oiled to prevent chafing.

Crust (of hoof or wall) The hard outside covering of the wall of the foot. The term refers to the *whole* of the crust, not just the outside portion.

Cry A hunting term indicating the sound made by the pack when actually hunting its quarry.

Csikos Hungarian cowboys who tend herds of horses during their long summer sojourn on the *puszta* or Hungarian grazing plains.

C-spring See **Cee-spring**.

Cub When applied to foxes the term indicates any young fox up to 1 November. Cubs are usually born in March, though they may arrive any time between Christmas and May. The average number in a litter is five, though as many as thirteen have been known.

Cubes, horse A manufactured compound of food substances made up into cubes, pellets or nuts of varying sizes and composition. The foodstuffs include oats, barley, bran, maize, linseed cake, molasses, beans, grass meal, etc., supplying all the necessary proteins, oil, fibre, carbohydrates, minerals and vitamins of the concentrate (q.v.) portion of the horse's diet. The cubes are manufactured in a number of grades to suit different animals performing differing amounts of work. The label on the bag generally shows the percentage of protein, oil, and fibre. The following table gives some indication of the percentage constituents in a range of nuts available in Britain.

	Protein %	Oil %	Fibre %
Horse and pony nuts	10	2.5	15
Racehorse	14	3.5	9
Complete	10	2.5	20
Stud	15	3.5	6
Concentrate	26	3.0	8.5
Horse and pony 'mix'	14	2.0	7

Horse and pony nuts are suitable for children's ponies and horses in light work. Racehorse nuts are suitable also for horses in heavy work, e.g. hunting, eventing, etc. A horse fed principally on nuts, which are very dry, will require more water to drink than an animal on a diet containing more moisture. Care must be taken, however, that the horse does not have a long drink after eating nuts, as they will swell in the stomach, causing colic.

Cub-hunting This may begin any time between the end of July and the end of September, depending on the harvest. The objects are to teach young, unentered hounds to hunt, and fox cubs to leave their coverts, as well as to reduce the fox population. There is no question of the huntsman showing sport, nor, strictly, should followers be there, except on invitation of the Master. It follows that no cap (q.v.) should be taken.

Cumeling A nineteenth-century name for a horse which, of its own accord, attached itself to, and became the property of, the lord of the manor.

Cup (show jumping) Shaped metal holder for fence pole.

Curb Abbreviation for curb bit.

Curb A soft, sometimes painful, thickening of the tendon or ligament on the back of the hock about a hand's breadth below the point. It is caused by strain – sometimes due to faulty conformation – or by injury. Heat may be present. If lame, the horse will go on his toes. When standing, he will raise the heel of the affected foot off the ground.

Curb chain A chain fitted to the eye of the curb or Pelham bit. It rests in the groove of the jaw just above the lower lip. Added pressure on the lower rein increases the leverage and tightens the curb chain. The chain itself consists of approximately seventeen flat or semi-flat links, with a ring in the centre through which the leather lip-strap passes. A less severe curb can be constructed from soft leather or doubled elastic. A jodhpur polo curb is a stronger chain with an oval-shaped device in the centre; it fits between the jaw bones and exerts pressure.

Curb hooks Hooks on the side of the curb bit, by means of which the curb chain is attached to the bit. Made in pairs, they vary from 1¼-2½ ins (32-64 mm).

Curb hook, circle A round flat disc, with the centre part taken away to enable the hook to fit snugly inside. Reputed to be gall-proof.

Curb hook, Liverpool Single hook, which can be used on either side.

Curb reins These are the reins attached to the lower rings of the curb bit. The curb rein is narrower in width by ⅛ in. (3 mm) than the snaffle rein.

Cur-dog Name applied in hunting to a dog of any breed other than a hound. It originated with 'care' dog: a dog which took care of sheep and which was usually responsible for coursing a hunted fox.

Curragh, The Site of the well-known racecourse in County Kildare, Eire, where the Irish Derby is run annually.

Curre-type Pronounced 'cur'. A type of foxhound predominantly English-bred with one or more strains of Welsh foxhound blood. The breed was originated by the late Sir Edward Curre.

Curricle The only English two-wheeled carriage designed for a pair of horses driven abreast. Applied to harnessing, the term denotes the putting of a pair to a two-wheeled vehicle by means of a curricle bar (q.v.).

Curricle bar A transverse bar over the horses' backs used to put to a pair-driven curricle.

Currier See **Curry, to**.

Curry, to To rub down or dress a horse with a comb – hence 'currier', an obsolete term for a groom.

Curry comb A flat piece of metal which has on one side either a handle ('jockey' pattern) or a webbing loop through which the hand is passed, and on the other side strips of metal into which blunt teeth are set at right angles. The

Metal curry comb.

comb is used for scraping the dust from a body brush, etc. Combs are now made of plastic and rubber and can be used on the body to remove a shedding coat or mud.

Curtal or Curtall In the sixteenth and seventeenth centuries a horse with its tail cut short (and sometimes its ears cropped) of a small size or breed. (See also **Ears, identification marks**)

Curvet A light leap in which the horse

raises its forelegs together, followed by a spring with the hindlegs. A leap: a frolic.

Cut Gelded. (See **Castration**)

Cut and laid A fairly low fence made by cutting thorn branches half way through and binding them in and out among stakes set into the middle of the fence.

'Cut a voluntary' Hunting slang meaning to fall off a horse as opposed to 'take a fall', which implies that the rider *and* horse fell.

Cutaway (coat) See **Shadbelly**.

Cut-back head Denotes a saddle, the tree of which is cut away at the head to provide clearance for the withers. Trees are made from quarter cut-back to full cut-back. The latter is known as a 'cowmouth' (See **Saddle, Lane Fox**)

'Cut 'em down' Nineteenth-century colloquial hunting term meaning reckless and ruthless riders.

Cutting horse Cow pony schooled in 'cutting out' (separating) selected beasts from a herd of cattle.

Cuttop In driving, the protections covering the tops of wheels, which shelter the axle-tree arms from dirt.

D

D (racing) Abbreviation for distance.

DBHS Diploma of the British Horse Society.

DBS Donkey Breed Society (q.v.).

D (or Dee) Metal fitting on the saddle, shaped like the letter D and to which can be attached the breastplate, hound couples, and sundry other items such as raincoats, flasks, etc.

'D'-shaped bit See **Snaffle bit**.

Daily double See **Tote double**.

Daisy-cutting Descriptive of a horse's action which at the walk or trot is close

to the ground and shows little elevation, e.g. typical of the Arab.

Dalby, David (1790-1840) A Yorkshire sporting artist popular with northern squires. His subjects included hunter and racehorse portraits, hunting, and, occasionally, driving scenes.

Dales British native ponies originally bred on the east side of the Pennine Hills in northern England. At one time they and the Fells (q.v.) who are bred on the west side of the Pennines, were considered a single breed, but the Dales have since developed into slightly larger and heavier animals with a maximum height of 14.2 hh (147.3 cm) compared with the Fells 14 hh (142.2 cm). Official recognition of the distinction came in 1916 with the formation of the Dales Pony Improvement Society. The Dales may be black, brown, or, more rarely, grey, and are exceptionally strong, sure-footed and particularly active at the trot. They have very good feet. They are excellent all-purpose family ponies, going well under saddle and in harness. A single pony is always referred to as a Dales, contrasting with their western neighbours, in which a single animal is a Fell.

Dales Pony Society Formed in 1963 by the reorganisation of the Dales Pony Improvement Society.

Dally An American expression used to denote the rapid passing of a lariat (q.v.) around the saddle horn.

Dam Female parent of a horse or foal.

Damage fund A small cap made by some hunts, usually at each meet, on all present, including foot followers, to compensate landowners and others for damage. It is often combined with a 'poultry fund'.

Dandy A horse-drawn railway-carriage used in Cumberland from 1861 to 1914.

Dandy brush A wooden-backed brush with strong bristles or plastic or nylon tufts, used for removing dried mud. It should not be used on manes or tails, for which a body-brush is more suitable.

Dandy brush.

Dandy cart Spring cart once used by tradesmen, especially milkmen.

Danebury mark An old racing expression applied to very light racehorses who often have to wear a breast-girth to keep the saddle from slipping forward and who show a deep mark or groove run-ning down the quarters on either side of the tail.

Dark horse (racing) A horse whose form is unknown outside his stable.

Darley Arabian, the Stallion imported into England in 1704 by Richard Darley, a Yorkshire squire. He was of the Managhi strain, one of the best breeds of the Anazeh Arabs, and became one of the most famous progenitors of the Thoroughbred (q.v.). He sired Flying Childers, and was the great-great grandsire of Eclipse (q.v.). See also **Arab; Thoroughbred racing**.

Dartmoor Pony A small native pony originating on the Moor whose name it bears, although very few purebreds remain in their native habitat. A pony of great charm and elegance, the Dartmoor makes an ideal children's mount and goes very well in harness. The breed has been exported to many European countries and to the United States. Dartmoors have a maximum height of 12.2 hh (127.0 cm). The most common colours are black, brown and bay, with a few greys. Excessive white markings are not encouraged.

Dartmoor Pony Society, The Founded in 1920 to promote and encourage the breeding of pure Dartmoor ponies.

Dartnall rein A specially soft plaited rein shaped to the rider's hands and used for show jumping. Handmade by the Dartnall family of Richmond, Surrey.

Dash board The upright protection in front of the coachman's feet in some vehicles. Made of stiff leather or wood.

Davis, Richard Barrett (1782-1854) A sporting artist born to a sporting atmosphere – being a son of Richard Davis, huntsman to the Royal Harriers, and brother of Charles Davis, huntsman to the Royal Buckhounds. Living most of the time at Windsor, he painted many spirited hunting scenes and numerous mounted portraits of Masters and huntsmen (often engraved), including the well-known portraits of his brother Charles on his horse, Hermit. Another brother, W. H. Davis, also painted sporting scenes, and horse and cattle portraits.

Day rug (blanket, USA) A rug worn in the stable or (sometimes) for travelling. Traditionally made of pure wool, and bound with braid or cloth in a contrasting colour. It is fastened across the chest with a leather strap and buckle, and has a fillet string under the tail. It requires a roller (q.v.) to keep it in place. Many modern materials are now being used for rugs, such as quilted nylon and various types of polyester-based fabrics.

Dead heat This occurs when two or more horses pass the winning post in a dead line. The dead heat is not run off. When two horses run a dead heat for first place, the prizes to which the first and second horses would have been entitled are divided equally between them. Each horse that divides a prize for first place is deemed a winner for penalties. Stallions siring the dead-heat winners are each credited with a winner.

Dead meat (racing) A term used when a stable decides that a horse shall not win.

Deafness Often associated with great docility, deaf horses being very easily controlled by the rein.

Deal A common term in the horse trade when a sale is completed.

Dealer's rug A jute rug, usually half-lined, rectangular in shape and fastening by means of a surcingle.

Dealer's whip A steel-lined drop-thong whip used by horse dealers, principally at fairs.

Decarpentry, General Albert Edouard Eugene (1878-1956) Instructor at Saumur; President of the FEI Panel of Dressage Judges; author of works on dressage and equestrian history and biography. *Piaffe and Passage*, and the famous *Academic Equitation* are available in English. During his lifetime Decarpentry was generally looked upon as the ultimate international authority. Today he is regarded as the greatest equitation master of the twentieth century.

Declaration (of forfeit) All entries of horses in races must be made to the Racing Calendar Office at Weatherbys by the owner of the horse or his authorised agent, who is usually his trainer. The terms of the races vary. Most big races have one or more forfeit stages, when it must be decided whether to pay more to keep the horse in the race or 'declare forfeit': i.e. forfeit the entry fee, etc., and take the horse out of the race.

Declaration (of runners) A horse entered in a particular race must be declared a runner in that race to the Overnight Declaration Office of the Jockey Club (Weatherbys), generally five days before the race is to be run: Sunday being a *non dies*. Declarations to run can be cancelled usually up to 10 or 10.30 a.m. on the day before the running of the race.

Dee See **D**.

Deep (hunting) A term indicating that the 'going' (q.v.) is soft or heavy. (See **Holding**)

Deep through the girth Descriptive of a horse who is well ribbed up with generous depth of girth behind the elbows. (See **Heart room**)

Dehydration Condition in which more water is lost from the body than is absorbed. It can be caused by excessive scouring, sweating, or fever.
SIGNS: A fold of skin when pinched returns to normal only slowly, the horse's pulse and respiration rates return to normal slowly after exercise. Severe dehydration can induce shock and collapse of the circulatory system. This is an extremely serious condition, requiring urgent veterinary attention.

Dejuger, Se French term implying that the hind feet touch down behind the imprint left by the forefeet.

Deli See **Batak**.

Demi-mail phaeton (or Semi-mail) A lighter and more elegant form of mail phaeton (q.v.), which had a wheel arch in the body and was without a perch. It was used in town as well as in the country.

Demi-pique Abbreviated term for the demi-piqued saddle which was used by heavy cavalry and ordinary travellers in the eighteenth century. It was a saddle with a half horn or low peak half as high as that on the original heavy cavalry saddle of the mid-seventeenth century, and correctly termed the 'Great Saddle'.

Demi-sang A term used in many countries to describe a first Thoroughbred cross.

De-nerve(d) See **Neurectomy**.

Dennett An early form of gig; an improved version of the Whiskey (q.v.).

Derby, Edward George Villiers, 17th Earl of (1865-1948) One of the greatest patrons of the turf and a most successful owner and breeder. He won twenty classics (1000 Guineas seven times, the Derby six, the Oaks and 2000 Guineas each twice) and gained £800,000 in stake money. He was the owner of Hyperion (q.v.), Fairway, Swynford and Phalaris, among others.

Derby Dinner (at Tattersall's) Richard Tattersall, head of the famous firm, gave an annual 'Derby Dinner' at which each guest was required to drink the toast 'John Warde and the Noble Science' in a silver fox's head which held almost a pint of port. No heel-taps were admitted. None stood the ordeal better than Richard himself.

Derby Stakes, the The Blue Riband of the Turf, run annually over a distance of 1½ miles (12 furlongs; 2.4 km), on Epsom Downs, traditionally on the first Wednesday in June. The race is for three-year-old colts, who carry 9 stone (57.15 kg). The race was first run in 1780 under the auspices of the 12th Earl of Derby, who won the privilege of using his name by tossing a coin with Sir Charles Bunbury (q.v.), winner of the first Derby with Diomed.

Dermatitis Inflamed skin caused by allergy, bacteria, fungus or virus. Eczema, ringworm, mud fever (qq.v.) and nettle rash (urticaria, q.v.) are all examples of the condition.

Dermatophilus infection Infection by the bacterium *Dermatophilus congolensis*, giving rise to (a) rain scald (q.v.) and (b) mud fever (q.v.). It may be prevented by good horse and stable management, and/or by stabling the horse.

Description of colour and markings In 1954 the Royal College of Veterinary Surgeons recommended the following sequence for certification of horses: colour; breed; sex; age; height; marks on head (including eyes); marks on limbs, fore first, then hind, commencing from below; marks on body, including mane and tail; acquired marks, congenital abnormalities, whorls or any other notable features.

Destrier A Norman warhorse which became extinct many centuries ago. The name derives from the Latin *dextrarius* (the right side), on which the squire led his master's horse. The destrier was primarily a trotting horse.

Destruction, humane This is usually carried out by intravenous injection or by humane killer. With the latter, the instrument is placed against the forehead at the intersection of an imaginary line from the base of the right ear to the top of the left eye, and similarly from the left ear to the right eye.

Devon Horse Show and County Fair (USA) An eight-day show held in Devon, Pennsylvania, run for the benefit of the Bryn Mawr Hospital. One of the premier horse shows in the USA.

Devonshire slipper stirrup This type accommodates the entire foot as in a leather slipper, and revolves on a bar. Benjamin Latchford (q.v.) in his treatise of 1883 illustrates a number of similar type. A modern version is used in riding for the disabled.

Diagonal aids Riding aids given when the rider uses the right rein with the left leg or, alternatively, the left rein with the right leg.

Diana A Roman divinity who was, amongst other things, the goddess of hunting.

Diarrhoea Loose, semi-liquid faeces. The condition indicates intestinal or stomach disorder due to a variety of causes such as incorrect diet; bacterial, fungal or viral infection; poisons; worms; chill; excitement. It may occur in foals when the dam is in season, due to the composition of the milk. *Salmonella* and *E. coli* infection lead to severe blood-stained, watery diarrhoea, resulting in dehydration and possible death. (See also **Purgatives; Scouring**)

Dick Christian bridoon or snaffle A bit with a ring in the centre which eliminates tongue pressure. See **Christian, Dick**.

Dickey The servant's seat at the rear of a vehicle.

'Dictator of the Turf' See **Rous, Admiral**.

Diligence A carriage used in pre-railway times in parts of Europe which served the same purpose as the stage coach in England: i.e. carrying passengers travelling long distances by stages. Diligences had various 'classes' at differing rates of fare for inside and outside passengers, and were cumbersome vehicles usually drawn by five horses.

Dioestrus The quiescent period between one oestrus and the next in the oestrous cycle (q.v.) of the mare.

Directory of the Turf Reference book, first published by Stud and Stable in 1961, which provides up-to-date biographical details of almost all of those professionally engaged in racing in Britain, with separate sections for owners, trainers, jockeys, studs, racecourses and the racing press.

Direct rein A leading or opening rein, the action of which turns the horse's head towards the direction in which it is required to move. A natural rein action.

Dirt tracks Unknown in Britain for either flat or steeplechasing, but in general use in many other countries. In the USA most 'big tracks' are dirt, a mile (1.6 km) in circumference (or longer) often with a turf course just inside the dirt track.

Dish-face See **Jibbah**.

Dishing A faulty action. The foot of one or both of the forelegs is thrown outwards and forwards when moving forwards.

Distance Applied when there are more than twenty lengths between horses at the finish of a race. (See next entry)

Distance, the 240 yards (219 m) from the winning post.

Disunited See **Canter, disunited** and **Galloping, disunited**.

Dixon, Henry Hall (1822-1870) English author who, under the pen-name of 'The Druid', wrote *Post and Paddock* (1856); *Silk and Scarlet* (1858); *Scott and Sebright* (1862); *Field and Fern* (1865); *Saddle and Sirloin* (1870).

Dock The flesh and bone part of the horse's tail.

'Docker, the' A slang term for the short whip used by poor-class drivers.

Docking The amputation of a portion of the tail. Although the after-effects were considered cruel by very many people and the practice was forbidden by law in most countries, it was permitted in England under the Anaesthetics Act and was practised on certain classes of horses. A portion of the tail, varying in length according to the owner's fancy, was clipped of hair and the end was removed by a docking knife or scissors, the bleeding being stopped by the application of a hot docking-iron. Great care was required, as tetanus or blood-poisoning might follow. The practice is now illegal in Britain under the Docking and Nicking Act, 1948. In ancient times this mutilation probably served some ritual purpose, and still does in West Africa. Docking was sometimes used in England as early as the mediaeval and Tudor periods, and became widespread for harness horses at the beginning of the eighteenth century.

Dr Bristol bit Originally 'trotting man's bit'. Its action is non-nutcracker, as it has an oval plate in the centre of the snaffle mouth. It is bent to ensure the maximum comfort for the tongue.

'Dr Green' A term used to suggest the benefits of new spring grass.

Dodman East Anglian name for a snail. The slowest working horse on the farm was often named 'Dodman'.

Doeskin Used for covering a saddle where the rider requires assistance in gripping or extra comfort. Foam knee-pads covered in doeskin are often inlaid into the flaps of modern saddles.

Doer A 'good doer' is a horse which

thrives and keeps its flesh and condition. A 'bad doer' is one which lacks these attributes in spite of every care.

'Dog' A sluggish horse which constantly has to be forced into his work. It is also applied to racehorses who have failed in public to reproduce home form.

Dog-cart A two- or four-wheeled trap for one horse. At full capacity it seats four people, the two at the rear sitting with their backs to the horse.

Dog-cart.

Dog fox Male fox.

'Doggy' horses See **Blinkers**.

Dole/Dole Gudbrandsdal This breed originated in the Gudbrandsdal valley of northern Norway. The two types have since been inter-bred to form one popular breed. Some authorities suggest that in Britain the Dales and Fells may have developed from ancestors of the breed. In Norway after World War II the Dole was in decline, but following the establishment of state studs in 1962 interest has been revived. The horse stands about 15 hh (152.4 cm), has a pony-type head, and is an all-purpose animal.

Dolls Portable, lightweight barricades of wood or plastic used on racecourses to keep horses to the desired course.

Domadir (South American) A horse-breaker or trainer.

Don/Donsky A Russian horse bred in the Don Valley during the eighteenth and nineteenth centuries. It is descended from local steppe horses crossed with Karabakh, Turkmen, Persian-Arab, and, later, Orlov-Rastopchin breeds, with some infusions of Thoroughbred blood. The breed is particularly associated with the Cossacks in the Napoleonic campaigns of the early nineteenth century.

In modern times the Don has been successful in long distance and endurance events. The breed stands about 16.2 hh (165 cm), is quite massively built, with a tendency to straight shoulders, upright pasterns, and poor hind limbs.

'Done' Said of a horse who is exhausted. Also refers to a horse whose grooming is completed.

Donkey Term for the ass (q.v.), first used colloquially in 1785.

Donkey Breed Society (DBS) Founded in 1967 to promote the breeding and showing of donkeys and to assist all those who breed, own, or are interested in them. (Formerly the Donkey Show Society.)

Donkey foot See **Boxy foot**.

Donoghue, Steve (Stephen) (1884-1945) Born in Warrington, Lancashire. He was champion jockey in England from 1914 to 1923. He won the Derby six times from 1915 to 1925, and had six successive wins in the Queen Alexandra Stakes at Ascot on Sir Harold Wernher's Brown Jack.

Donsky See **Don**.

Doorman An almost obsolete term for a farrier who prepares the feet, nails on the shoes, finishes off (clenches up) and helps to make new shoes. (See **Fireman**)

Doped fox (or 'touched up fox') A fox which, to ensure a hunt, is caused to tread in some strong-smelling liquid put at the exit of the place where he is known to lie.

Doping The practice of administering or causing to be administered, for the purpose of affecting the performance of the horse, drugs or stimulants, internally, by injection, or other methods. The administration of certain medicines properly prescribed by a veterinary surgeon may be regarded as doping if the horse is raced or competes while such drugs remain in the system and can be detected by analysis. The various ruling bodies, e.g. the Jockey Club, the British Show Jumping Association, the FEI (q.v.), etc. issue lists of forbidden substances. Random dope tests are now performed by a number of governing bodies.

Dormeuse A heavy four-wheeled vehicle, invariably drawn by four horses, used on the Continent in the nineteenth century by those who could afford to travel in their own carriages. A description given by a contemporary Duke of Beaufort was 'a travelling chariot with a long boot in front into which one could, by letting down the front of it, put one's legs, the front fixing under the seat – make a good bed, a rolled up mattress was kept in the boot, and this formed the cushions the travellers sat on. Imperials, bonnet-boxes, cap-boxes and wells under seats held the luggage. On the dickey behind was a cabriolet head to keep the servants dry.' The hooded-dickey gave almost the appearance of a separate carriage joined to the larger one.

d'Orsay A light carriage of the Brougham type, named after Count d'Orsay.

Dos-à-dos A two- or four-wheeled dog-cart with seats placed back to back.

Double (hunting) A fence or bank with a ditch on both sides.

Double (racing) The backer couples two horses to win in separate races. If the first horse wins, the amount won plus the original stake are placed on the second horse. Both horses must win or the bet is lost.

Double (show jumping) Two obstacles so spaced that they are judged as one obstacle.

Double bank Bank with a ditch on both the take-off and the landing sides.

Double bridle See **Bridles**.

Double harness Pair harness.

Double oxer (hunting) Any fence (hedge) having a protective rail just below the top on either side.

Double oxer (show jumping) A brush fence with poles on both sides, forming a spread fence.

Double the horn, to The notes made by the huntsman – short, sharp, and pulsating – which indicate that a fox has been roused, has crossed a ride, or has been holloaed away.

Double thong When a four-horse whip is 'caught on the crop' (as it is carried in normal use when not wanted for touching up the leaders), enough 'double thong' is left loose to reach the wheelers.

Draft Hounds selected for the day's hunting, or those which for some reason have been weeded out from the kennels.

Drag An artificial scent made by trailing an article which has been soaked in a strong-smelling liquid. For foxhounds the best drag is made from soiled litter from a tame fox's kennel, or a sack so impregnated. Aniseed is frequently used.

Drag A slang name for a private or park coach kept for one's own driving, as distinct from a stage or road coach (q.v.). They were painted in their owner's colours and with a monogram or crest

Park drag.

emblazoned on both doors and on the boot in the rear. Accommodation was provided on the back seat for two grooms dressed in livery to match the paintwork of the coach.

'Dragging the goat' See **Buzkashi**.

Drag-hunt To hunt with a pack of hounds on an artificial scent or drag laid by trailing material suitably impregnated. (See **Drag**)

Dragman A coachman.

Drag-shoe See **Skid-pan**.

Drag stick/Drag prop A round pole of wooden construction about 3 ins (7.5 cm) thick and headed with a sharp iron spike some 4 ins (10 cm) long. The stick is fitted to the back axle of a cart about half-way between the centre of the axle and the rear offside wheel. An eye in the axle joins an eye fitted on the end of the drag stick, which is some 3 ft 6 ins (1.06 m) in length. The purpose of the stick is to take the weight off the horse when the van is stationary on an incline, and to prevent the cart 'running back'. When not in use it can be hung up on the rear axle.

Draught horse A horse used for drawing any vehicle. The term is now more usually associated with the heavy breeds.

Draught reins The main reins in pair and team driving, running from the outside of the bits to the coachman's hand. To them are buckled the coupling reins (q.v.) that connect to the inside of the bit of the partner horse.

Dravelling bit A breaking bit with three movable ports (q.v.) of different sizes. Any one can be chosen to act as the 'port', while the remaining two act as 'keys' (q.v.).

Draw A term used when hounds seek their fox in a covert or in another place where it is accustomed to lie.

Draw The area selected for a day's hunting.

Draw The huntsman or whipper-in removes or 'draws' a hound from the pack.

Draw (racing) A draw for flat racing only is made by the Overnight Declarations Office (q.v.), to determine the stall or place which each jockey shall take at the start. Number 1 is always on the extreme left as the horses face the start.

Drawing knife A farrier's knife with a narrow blade and a point bent over for safety. The handle is made of horn or wood, with a V-shaped notch which is used to manipulate a hot shoe. The blade is used for lowering the wall and trimming ragged pieces of the frog and flakes of sole.

Draw-rein A rein attached to the girth which comes to the hand through the bit rings. It is an extremely severe means of control.

Draw yard The yard or other place in kennels where the hounds are collected before being drawn off by the huntsman to their respective lodging rooms.

Dray A low wagon without sides, used for carrying a heavy load.

Drench Liquid medicine administered by means of a bottle – preferably plastic, but if glass is used, the neck of the bottle must be bandaged to protect it from the horse's teeth. Drenching is a highly skilled procedure and should only be undertaken by a competent person.

Dress, hunting – general Hunts customarily have special designs for collars and buttons. The privilege of being invited to wear these rests with the MFH. For their own or other hunt balls, male subscribers may wear the livery of their hunt, whether scarlet or another colour, with collar and lapel facings and hunt buttons as decreed.

Given below are the traditional correct modes of dress, but in modern times they are rarely enforced. Hunt subscribers tend to follow tradition to a considerable degree. Members of the public (i.e. non-subscribers) may wear whatever they please, but it is regarded as a courtesy to the hunt to dress neatly.

Dress, hunting – ladies
SIDE-SADDLE: the habit may be black or navy with silk hat or bowler and veil; pale, primrose-coloured waistcoat; hunting tie (stock) with plain bar, gold tie-pin; black boots; crop with thong and lash; gloves; and a spur. When cub-hunting side-saddle: a tweed habit

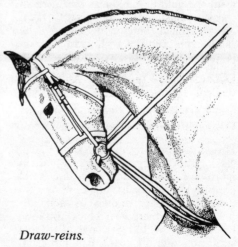

Draw-reins.

and bowler, discreetly coloured shirt and tie.

ASTRIDE: black or navy hunting coat; fawn breeches; collarless shirt; black bowler or velvet hunting cap; hunting tie (stock) with plain bar, gold tie-pin, waistcoat or dark V-necked sweater; black boots with black leather garters; spurs; hunting whip; and gloves.

Dress, for hunting – men's For hunting in Great Britain and Ireland the following dress is correct:

(1) Red or black swallowtail coat; collarless shirt; beige or Tattersall check waistcoat; white breeches; black hunting boots with mahogany tops; white leather garters; silk top hat; hunting whip with thong and lash attached; spurs; white hunting tie (stock) with plain bar, gold tie-pin; and gloves.

(2) Red or black hunting coat; collarless shirt; beige or Tattersall check waistcoat (optional); white breeches, black boots with mahogany tops and white garter straps; silk top hat, spurs; white hunting tie (stock) with plain bar, gold tie-pin; hunting whip; and gloves. The wearing of silk top hats has over recent years been the subject of discussion on the grounds of safety, as it gives little protection in a fall. In general, most hunts now accept some form of hard head-gear (bowler, velvet cap with harness, or crash-skull with dark cover).

(3) Hunting cap; black hunting coat; collarless shirt; white hunting tie with plain bar, gold tie-pin; beige or Tattersall check waistcoat (optional); fawn breeches; black 'butcher' boots and black garter straps; hunting whip; and gloves.

(4) Rat-catcher (only worn during cub-hunting); tweed coat; hunting tie or shirt with collar and plain tie; bowler hat or hunting cap; fawn breeches; black or brown boots, with garter straps; hunting whip; spurs; and gloves.

Dress, for showing In hunter and hack classes, rat-catcher is customarily worn in morning classes, but at formal shows and evening performances, full hunting costume is customary for men. In hack classes, however, men wear black swallow-tailed coats with black overalls (q.v.) strapped under the instep, 6 in. (15.2 cm)

black boots, white collar and grey tie, silk hat and showing stick.

In show pony classes, children generally wear a black or blue hunting cap, dark blue or black hunting coat, light-coloured jodhpurs, black or brown jodhpur boots, a collar and tie with plain tie-pin; dark leather gloves and a show cane. For both children and adults in Mountain and Moorland pony classes and in working hunter classes, tweed jackets with a collar and tie are considered correct, with light-coloured jodhpurs or breeches. Spurs are not worn in children's showing classes.

Dressage The word is derived from the French verb *dresser* – to train, to adjust, or to straighten out. Although it was not applied to horses until the eighteenth century, systematic training dates back at least to the fifth century BC, when the Greek philosopher, Xenophon, wrote two books on the subject: *On the Art of Horsemanship* and *On the Cavalry Commander*. These have become classics, and much of Xenophon's theory and practice – notably the philosophy of obtaining the best from horses by quietness and understanding – is still relevant in modern times.

Most training in ancient times was directed towards the manoeuvrability of cavalry horses, although the aesthetic side of horsemanship was not wholly neglected, and Xenophon described more advanced movements such as the piaffe.

With the decline of Greek influence and the rise of the Roman Empire, much of Xenophon's teaching and methods were lost, and it was not until the beginning of the Renaissance in early sixteenth-century Italy that an interest in equestrian skills, other than for the purposes of war or for jousting, was revived. As a result, Frederico Grisone, who was familiar with the works of Xenophon, established the first of the 'modern style' riding academies. This was attended by children of the aristocracy, so that they could acquire the elegant skills of horsemanship which were becoming an essential element of life for European courtiers.

From Italy the emphasis on classical riding moved to France. In the early seventeenth century Antoine Pluvinel de la Baume (q.v.), a student of Giovanni Pignatelli (Grisone's successor in Naples), founded a riding school in Paris which was attended by, among others, the future Louis XIII.

At approximately the same time, the first of the few Englishmen who have made any impact on classical riding opened a school in Antwerp. He was William Cavendish (later to become Duke of Newcastle), a friend of King Charles II. Cavendish is best remembered for his book *A General System of Horsemanship in All its Branches*. A brilliant horseman, he was the first person to make use of the shoulder-in (q.v.), although the introduction of this movement is more usually attributed to one of the most influential horsemen and teachers of all time, the Frenchman François de le Guerinière. A firm believer in the Xenophon philosophy of achieving results by kindness, de la Guerinière's principal claim to fame is his book *Ecole de Cavalerie*, published in 1729. It was a masterpiece – a treatise setting out clearly and concisely the classical method of riding and training, and embodying principles of horsemanship which have lasted to this day.

De la Guerinière's principles were adopted in the famous Spanish Riding School (q.v.) in Vienna – an institution dating from about 1572, when the Emperor Maximilian II imported Andalusian horses for use in his riding school. This magnificent building still accommodates the Spanish Riding School – the only establishment left in the world whose sole function is to preserve the classical form of riding.

In France the demise of the Napoleonic Empire in the early nineteenth century threatened the survival of classical equitation. To resuscitate the art, a new school was established at Saumur in 1814 – initially to train the cavalry, but later to undertake the advance training of civilian horsemen. At Saumur the famous corps of instructors, the Cadre Noir, taught all the classical skills, which they still demonstrate today all over the world, and which they teach to students from many countries.

The twentieth century has seen a definite change of emphasis in the aims of dressage riding. From being practised chiefly as a means of improving the agility and responsiveness of cavalry horses, and then as an important adjunct to the aesthetic quality of court life in Europe, it has, with increasing rapidity, come to be regarded as a competitive sport or art at both national and international levels. Its popularity, at first confined almost entirely to Continental Europe, has spread to Britain, the USA, Australia, New Zealand – and indeed, anywhere where equestrian sports are practised.

It was introduced as an Olympic competition, for both teams and individuals, in 1912, when Sweden took all three individual medals as well as the team gold. Analysis of subsequent Olympic successes underline the dominance of the Continental Europeans, with Sweden, France, Switzerland and Germany monopolising the top awards, and Denmark, Austria, Holland, Portugal and the USSR achieving some success. The only non-European country to win Olympic honours has been the USA, with a bronze individual and team award at the Los Angeles Games in 1932.

The outstanding feature of the last twenty-five years has been the success of the Germans, who have won the team gold in all but one of the seven Olympics during that period.

Britain has never won an Olympic dressage medal – a true reflection of the general lack of enthusiasm for this discipline until very recently. Since the early to mid-seventies, however, interest has gradually increased, until it has become the fastest-growing section of equestrian sport in Britain, participation at the lower levels of national competition being the largest growth area.

The discipline is also increasing in popularity in Australia, though – as with the British until very recently – Australians have tended to take less readily to dressage than to other equestrian sports.

Dressage, competitive In Britain, dressage takes place at two levels – national and international – the latter being governed by the FEI (q.v.) Dressage Bureau, and the former by the British Horse Society. Tests in both categories are divided into two types: (1) prescribed tests

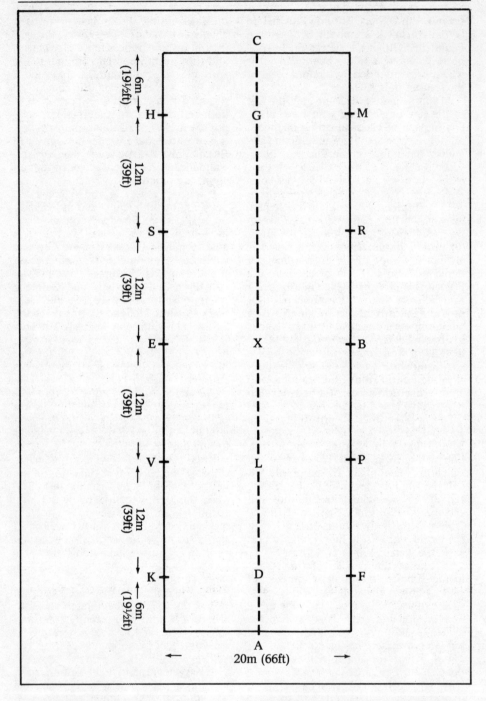

Plan of dressage arena, 60 × 20m (198 × 66ft). This is used in international competitions for tests from medium standard upwards, and including Grand Prix. NB: When a smaller arena (40 × 20m/132 × 66ft) is used, the markers R, S, V, P, L and I are not required.

in which the movements are dictated precisely by the relevant authority; and (2) freestyle or Kür, in which the rider devises the programme, which must occupy a specified time and contain certain designated movements.

In Britain, the national tests are graded as follows (in ascending order of difficulty): Preliminary, Novice, Elementary, Medium, Advanced (the latter including the official international tests).

The international tests are (also in ascending order of difficulty): Prix St George, Intermédiaire I, Intermédiaire II, Grand Prix, and Grand Prix Special. The Grand Prix is the Olympic Test, and the Grand Prix Special, a shorter even more difficult test, usually ridden only by the top ten to twelve competitors in the Individual Grand Prix. Marks are allotted for every movement or small section of movements, on the following scale: 0 – Not Performed; 1 – Very Bad; 2 – Bad; 3 – Fairly Bad; 4 – Insufficient; 5 – Sufficient; 6 – Satisfactory; 7 – Fairly Good; 8 – Good; 9 – Very Good; 10 – Excellent. Account is taken of accuracy, freedom and fluency of paces, suppleness, lightness, straightness, impulsion, the submission of the horse, the harmony between horse and rider, the rider's position, seat and application of the aids.

In Britain, national tests below Advanced level are performed in a rectangular arena measuring 20 m x 44 m, while Advanced tests and all international tests take place in a full size arena measuring 20 m x 60 m. The arena is marked around the perimeter by a standard, traditional pattern of twelve letters, while an additional five letters (three in the smaller arena) denote points on the centre line. At national level, one to three judges assess the tests, while at international level, five are usually required stationed at various points around the arena.

Dressage (driving) See **Driving trials**.

Dressage to music A comparatively new discipline in which riders devise their own dressage test (which must incorporate certain specified movements) and perform it to music of their choice. The test is marked in two sections – one for artistic impression; the other for techni-

cal merit. This type of dressage is gaining in popularity both nationally and internationally.

Dressage with jumping See **Combined training**.

Dress chariot Nobleman's carriage used for civic and state occasions (*c.* 1837).

Drift, the A term applied in the New Forest, Hampshire, and on the Moors of the West of England to the annual rounding-up of moorland ponies for branding, etc.

Drivers Those who drive. In an uncomplimentary sense, the term implies those with less art than 'coachmen'.

Driving Driving for sport, as distinct from driving as a means of transport, is enjoying great popularity in Britain, Europe, and the USA. In Britain, driving is divided into two principal sections for competitive purposes. The British Driving Society deals primarily with: (1) private driving, i.e. driving in which the horses and vehicles are judged in the show ring before setting out for a marathon, and assessed again on their return; and (2) concours d'elegance, in which the turn-outs are judged, as the name suggests, on their overall appearance, cleanliness, and manner of going. The Horse Driving Trials Group of the British Horse Society administers the official three-phase events for horses and ponies, which are based on ridden three-day events. (See **Driving trials**, **Driving, scurry**.)

Driving reins Reins (about 21-25 ft; 6.2-7.6 m) of web or leather for long-rein driving, buckled to the bit and passing through rings in a breaking roller. Plough lines are also used; these taper at the bit-end and put less weight on the mouth.

Driving trials The driving equivalent of ridden horse trials, which test the all-round ability of driver and horses. At present, international competitions are for teams of four and for pairs, but national federations cater for singles, with sub-sections for ponies. In driving trials there are three separate competitions:

COMPETITION A is divided into two sections: (1) Presentation, which is an assessment of the overall appearance of the turn-out of horses, driver, and grooms, with marks awarded in five categories – (a) driver and grooms; (b) horses; (c) harness; (d) vehicle and spare equipment; (e) general impression. (2) Dressage: judged by three or five judges in arenas measuring 110 yds x 44 yds (100 m x 40 m) for teams, or sometimes 65 yds x 44 yds (60 x 40 m) for singles and pairs. There are different standards of tests, lasting ten minutes in the larger arena, and eight minutes in the smaller arena at international level; and a five-minute novice test, and a British Driving Society test, both at national level. The tests are performed at ordinary walk; working, collected and extended trot, all with changes of direction; and a rein-back is included. Competitors are judged on accuracy, precision, and correctness of paces, and, in the case of pairs and teams, manner of working together.

SECTION B is the marathon, the driving equivalent of the ridden speed and endurance phase. Experienced competitors have specially designed vehicles which stand up to the rigours of the cross-country drive. In an international event the marathon covers distances of 14.3-16.8 miles (23-27 km), and is divided into three trot and two walk sections. The last section, at the trot, includes five to eight obstacles or hazards, each of which must be negotiated within a set time. A strict time limit is set for each section, with penalty points for finishing late, or for finishing earlier than a set time. All competitors are refereed, either from the vehicle or from the ground, with penalties for errors of course, breaking of pace, etc.

COMPETITION C: The equivalent of show jumping. Competitors drive through a course of pairs of plastic cones, spaced between 1-2 ft (30-60 cm) wider than the track width of the vehicle, and with balls on top which fall if a cone is touched. Tight turns and many changes of direction are included. The speed required is 220 / 275 yards (200-250 m) per minute, and penalties are incurred for dislodging balls, and for exceeding the time limit. The overall winner is the competitor with the lowest score over the three competitions. In many events prizes are also awarded for placings in each of the three constituent competitions.

Although *competition driving* (simi-lar to the above) has existed for many decades, it was not until 1969 that the FEI (q.v.) published the first set of international rules, at the instigation of HRH the Duke of Edinburgh (who was about to become President of the FEI), assisted by Colonel Sir Michael Ansell. The first international competition under the new rules took place in Lucerne in 1970, and in 1977 the Hungarians staged the first European championships. Since then the sport has expanded considerably at both national and international levels. European countries have competed from the early days of the sport, but the United States have only recently entered the field, and are now competing with success at the highest international level. The sport has not yet received Olympic recognition, but world championships are held every year of even date, with world pairs championships every year of odd date.

Driving, scurry Similar to the obstacle driving phase of a driving trials (q.v.), but staged against the clock, with penalties for knocking the balls off the tops of the cones. It is a very fast, exciting sport, at which ponies excel. One of the best known scurry driving competitions in Great Britain is held during the Horse of the Year Show at Wembley each October.

Driving with a full hand Having the reins passing through the fingers singly. This method is occasionally used in tandem, but incorrectly, since the same procedure should be used in tandem driving as with four-in-hand: the first finger should divide the leaders' reins and the second finger the wheelers'.

Drop (fence) A fence with the landing side lower than the take-off.

Droppings (dung, faeces) The solid waste eliminated by a horse. The droppings should be green/brown or golden brown according to diet, and should be formed into balls which just break on reaching the ground. Any change from the normal – such as a strong smell, sliminess, excessive softness or hardness – requires investigation. Heavy red-worm infestation may be seen as tiny red lines in the droppings.

Dropping the shoulder The action, usually at the canter, of suddenly dropping either shoulder, causing the rider to be unseated. It seems more or less impossible to anticipate this and to remain in the saddle.

Droshky A low, four-wheeled carriage much used in Russia.

Druid, The See **Dixon, Henry Hall**.

Dry single A hunting term indicating a bank without a ditch.

Dual paternity A term applied to the pedigree of an animal whose dam has been covered by two different stallions during the covering season in which it was conceived.

Dublin Horse Show (Royal Dublin Society, Ball's Bridge, Dublin) The show was founded in 1731 for a variety of agricultural purposes, but no horse-show classes were held for agricultural horses until 1861. The horse show proper was first held in 1868 on the site of the present Parliament of Eire, and moved to Ball's Bridge and opened there in 1881. It is held during the first week in August.

Dude An inexperienced horseman who takes up ranch life in the western states of America. The term originally meant a 'stranger'.

Dude ranch A cattle ranch in the western states of America which offers accommodation and riding facilities to guests. Many such ranches have become largely artificial.

Dülmen The only extant German native pony breed, which has lived in the Meerfelder Bruch in Westphalia since the fourteenth century. The herd is privately owned by the Duke of Cröy, who holds an annual sale following a round-up. The Dülmen stands up to 12.3 hh (129.5 cm), and is usually black, brown or dun.

Dumb jockey A wooden contrivance fastened on a young horse's back in the position of a saddle, from which reins are passed to the mouth in such a way that the head is placed in any desired position. This form of training used to be advocated by many horsemen, but has been violently opposed by others as being cruel and restricting, since it lacks the give and take on the mouth that the experienced rider can offer. It is now virtually obsolete.

Dumping Shortening of the toe by excessive rasping of the front of the wall of the hoof to make the foot fit the shoe. A bad practice, as the shoe should be made to fit the foot.

Dumpling An unusually large and comfortable box cushion fitted to some coaches.

Dun (blue) A horse whose black colouring, evenly distributed over the body, gives the appearance of blue. It can be with or without a dorsal band (list) or wither-stripes, but always has a black skin, mane and tail.

Dun (yellow) A horse with diffuse yellow pigment in the hair. The skin is black, as are the mane and tail, and there may or may not be a dorsal band (list), wither-stripes and bars on the legs.

Duncan gag (sometimes called the Duncombe) A plain or twisted mouth gag with a small upwards cheek with two round holes for a rounded gag rein. Designed for use in conjunction with a curb bit.

Duncombe gag See **Duncan gag** above.

Dung See **Droppings**.

Dung-eating (coprophagia) The unnatural habit acquired by some horses of eating their droppings. It may be due to lack of a particular substance in the diet; the most likely being phosphorus. A mineral and vitamin supplement may be tried. The use of a muzzle (q.v.) at non-feeding times is desirable.

Durban July Handicap The major flat race of South Africa which was first run in 1897 over 1 mile (1.6 km), by 1916 was gradually extended to 1¼ miles (2 km), and in 1970 became 1⅓ miles (2.2 km).

Dutch Draught Horse One of the most massively built and most heavily muscled of all European draught horses. A heavy horse existed in the Low Countries in the Middle Ages, but with the coming of gunpowder, their principal task – that of carrying noblemen in armour – declined, and so did the breed. Towards the end of the nineteenth century the need for heavy horses for agriculture and transport increased, and careful breeding of native mares with Belgian Heavy Draught stallions produced what is now called the Dutch Draught. In 1914 Stud Book Societies from the provinces combined to produce a national Stud Book Society, known as the Royal Association of the Netherlands Draught Horse. Standing up to 17 hh (170 cm) the horses have a small, compact head, a massive deep body, and short 'tree-trunk' legs, with feathering. Today the breed is much used in a number of European countries for pulling brewers' drays.

Dutch slip A simple form of headcollar, made of leather or tubular web, suitable for foals.

Dutch Warmblood An all-round riding horse, standing approximately 16-16.2 hh (162.6-165 cm) and produced by crossing Groningen and Gelderlanders, firstly with Thoroughbreds and later with French and German warmbloods. The result is a rather lighter animal than most of the German warmbloods.

Dwelling This occurs when hounds linger too long on the line of scent.

Dziggetai A species of wild ass, mule-like in appearance, inhabiting the elevated steppes of Tartary.

E

ECG Electro-cardiograph. Obtained by attaching an apparatus to the horse which measures the electrical impulses of the heart and records them on paper, so that abnormalities of heart function may be detected. It can also be achieved remotely by telemetry: the horse is exercised and the data transmitted from him to the recording apparatus by a radio transmitter.

EHPS Endurance Horse and Pony Society (q.v.).

Each way (racing) Abbreviation: ew. To back a horse 'each way' is to back it to win, or to be placed first, second or third.

Ears, identification marks From early times ears of animals were cut in various ways as a means of identification. For horses this practice continued until the sixteenth century (until much later in the northern counties and the south-west of England).

BITTED: A piece 'bitten' from the inner edge of the ear.

CROPPED: Cut straight across half-way down the ear, originally used purely for identification but continued in the eighteenth century as a mode of fashion to achieve a 'smart' effect.

FOLD-BITTED: Ear folded over and a piece removed from the folded edge.

FORK-STOWED: Nicked at the top in a fish-tail shape.

RITT: The top slit lengthwise.

STOWED: The tip cut straight across.

UNDER-BITTED: A piece 'bitten' from the outer edge.

Ears, lop Ears which tend to flop forwards and downwards, or downwards on each side, giving a dejected appearance. Horses having such are often quiet and generous, and it is often said that a lop-eared horse is never a bad horse. Many good racehorses are blemished in this way. It is a rare occurrence in Arabs.

Ears, prick Short, pointed ears normally directed to the front, and giving an alert and expectant appearance.

Ear-stripping Process of stroking or pulling hands over ears from base to tip to induce circulation and bring comfort to a cold or tired horse.

Earth The underground home of a fox.

Earth stopper A man employed by a hunt

to block the entrance to an earth when the fox is out during the night before a day's hunt. (See **Stopping earth**)

East Dean Run, the At Goodwood there is a quaintly worded manuscript telling of a run on 26 January 1739, beginning at 7.45 a.m. and ending at 5.50 p.m. near the wall of Arundel river with only three followers up.

East Friesian Produced during the eighteenth century and closely related to the Oldenburg (q.v.). A great mixture of breeds were used in its production – Spanish, Irish, Polish, Hungarian, Thoroughbred and, later, Cleveland Bay and Norman. Since World War II, Arab blood has been used to produce a more quality riding horse, and recently Hanoverian blood has also influenced the breed. It is a general purpose, riding/driving horse, standing 15.2-16 hh (157.5-162.6 cm), with strong limbs, and very powerful quarters.

Eastern horses The group which is roughly covered by the Arabian, Barb, Turkish and Syrian breeds.

East Prussian Horse See **Trakehner**.

Ecart An expression used in the Vuillier Dosage System (q.v.), meaning the degree of deviation from the standard number of dosage strains.

Eclipse A stallion bred by HRH the Duke of Cumberland in 1764, by Markse out of Spiletta, and a great-great-grandson of the Darley Arabian (q.v.). The horse was originally owned jointly by Mr William Wildman and Colonel Dennis O'Kelley. His first race was in May 1769 and his last in the autumn of 1771. He was never beaten, and the only horse said to have extended him in a race was Bucephalus, who never recovered from the effort. In racing and as a sire the phrase applied to him was 'Eclipse first, the rest nowhere', for he was immeasurably the greatest racehorse of his century and, if his predominating influence on the breed be taken into consideration, of all time; well over a hundred of his descendants have won the Derby.

Eclipse gag A veterinary gag used to keep the mouth open.

Eclipse Stakes First run at Sandown Park near London in 1886, when the winner was Bendigo. It is a race for three-year-olds and upwards over 1¼ miles (2 km) in July.

Ecuyer A riding master or instructor, particularly associated with the Cadre Noir in France (q.v.).

Eczema Any non-specific inflammatory condition of the skin, characterised by itching and scabbiness, and exudation of serum. See also **Dermatitis**.

Edward VII, King (1841-1910) Keen patron of the Turf, both as Prince of Wales and King. He won the Derby three times, with Persimmon (1896), Diamond Jubilee (1900), and Minoru (1909), and the Grand National with Ambush II (1900).

Edwards, Lionel Dalhousie Robertson (1878-1966) A talented sporting artist and painter of equestrian portraits, and also an author and press illustrator. He was a keen naturalist and foxhunting man, and his pictures exhibit unique perception of the English sporting scene. He was equally at home in watercolours and in oils. Many prints were published after his originals. He wrote several books, including *Reminiscences of a Sporting Artist*, and *Thy Servant a Horse*.

Eel stripe See **Stripe, dorsal**.

Eggbutt Term used for a hinge in the mouth of a bit, which obviates pinching of the lips. One version has slots in the

Straight bar eggbutt snaffle.

ring for a cheek attachment so that the bit keeps in the correct position. The simplest eggbutt snaffle is one with a jointed bit and fixed rings.

Egg link pelham A jointed pelham with an egg-shaped link in the centre.

Eglantine Trade name of a nickel-mixture metal used in the manufacture of bits and stirrup irons. It is rustless, does not turn yellow (in contrast with pure nickel), and is much less inclined to break than pure nickel.

Eight Horses, Legend of the (Chinese) An Emperor of the Chou Dynasty (ninth century, BC) was overcome with wanderlust. He wanted to travel all over the world. He chose eight horses, called Wah Lau, Luk Yee, Chik Kee, Pak O, Kue Wong, Yu Lung, Du Lee and Sam Chee (for each of these names there is a slightly different version). The horses were able to travel 30,000 li (Chinese miles) in one day, and the Emperor had a successful tour. At last he went to the West, and climbed the Kun Lun Mountains. There he met the goddess Si Wong Mu, with whom he stayed for rather a long time. The Lord of Chu, profiting by the absence of the Emperor, attempted to seize the throne. The Emperor heard of this treachery, and thanks to the eight horses was able to rush home in time to suppress the rebellion. After that he made no more expeditions, but from time to time the Goddess used to send him messages by a blue bird.

Eild Scottish term for barren mares or ewes. (See **Yeld**)

Ekka A one-horse cart used in India which is drawn without traces, the pad being prevented from slipping back by a broad strap which passes across the horse's breast.

Elastic curb See **Humane curb**.

Elberfeld Horses In 1900 William von Osten of Berlin, to prove his theories on equine intelligence, presented in public a Russian stallion, Kluge Hans, whom he had ostensibly trained to calculate by pawing the ground with his hoof. They proceeded to reading, colour differentiation, etc., up to the general standard of knowledge of a fourteen-year-old child. Enormous publicity resulted, and exhaustive tests by learned committees and societies for evidence of collusion proved negative. In 1904, however, Oskar Pfungst, the German psychologist, demonstrated that the horse answered to unconscious and almost imperceptible signs from his owner. At von Osten's death, a wealthy Elberfeld manufacturer inherited Kluge Hans, and with two Arab stallions and other horses he worked to prove von Osten's ideas, with apparent success; but most experts, though not all of them, remained unconvinced of the animals' mental capabilities. At the outbreak of World War I, the group of horses was dispersed.

Elbow The upper joint of the foreleg.

Elbow, capped A swelling (soft in the early stages, harder later) at the point of the elbow, due to inflammation of the bursae (q.v.). It is usually caused by the inner heel of the shoe bruising the elbow when the horse is lying on insufficient bedding or on a rough, uneven floor. It can be prevented by ensuring plenty of bedding, use of a 'sausage boot' (q.v.), or by shoeing with a threequarter shoe. It may require veterinary treatment.

Eldonian Trade name used by makers of cast stainless-steel bits, stirrups, spurs, etc.

Elecampane A herb used in mediaeval times to revive horses suffering from exhaustion, and to renew their appetite.

Electrolytes (blood salts) Essential chemicals such as potassium, sodium, etc., present in solution in the blood. Excessive loss of these salts by sweating may occur, for example, in long-distance riding or eventing in very hot weather. They must be replaced by adding them to the diet or water offered.

Electrotherapy Treatment of e.g. injuries by means of an electric current. (See **Faradism**)

Electuary The name given to a medicinal agent in which the drugs are made into a paste with a base of treacle or honey. It is excellent for sore throats. Dosage is by smearing paste on to the tongue, roof of mouth or back teeth with a smooth flat piece of wood.

Elephant ear sponge The popular name for a flat stable sponge.

Elijahs Straps worn by horsemen below the knees instead of leggings. An East Anglian term.

Elizabeth I, Queen (1533-1603) Was

known to be an excellent horsewoman, and encouraged the breeding of riding hacks and racehorses. The heavy armour of horse and man of the late Plantagenet and early Tudor times had become obsolete, and Queen Elizabeth, also, had not inherited the physical amplitude of her father, Henry VIII, so the massive 'great horse' of his reign was replaced by a lighter type of hack. Queen Elizabeth loved riding as a form of relaxation, and hunted with enthusiasm all her life until her seventieth year. On her many journeys across England, often as far afield as Warwickshire, Suffolk and Devon, she rarely used a litter, but rode on horseback, with her court. On some occasions, however, she rode pillion behind her Master of the Horse, and there are records of her travelling from Exeter to London, and also attending St Paul's in state in this manner. She maintained a racing establishment called the Barbary House Stables at Greenwich, where she kept forty Arabs, Barbs and Turks.

Elk lip A wide and somewhat loose and overhanging upper lip.

Elk lip.

Elliptic spring This ingenious device, made of laminated steel plates in an elliptical form, was invented by a coachbuilder named Elliot in 1804. It revolutionised carriage building.

El Morzillo The black horse belonging to Hernando Cortés, conqueror of Mexico in the sixteenth century. (See **Conquistadores**) The horse died during the expedition to Guatemala in 1524, and was deified by the natives in the form of a huge stone statue which was discovered and destroyed by Spanish Franciscan missionaries in 1697.

Embrocation A fluid preparation, often with an oily base, applied externally by rubbing.

Embolism The sudden blocking of a blood vessel by a blood clot that has been circulating within the blood system. See also **Thrombosis**.

Empty mare A mare who is not in foal.

Emston New Zealand rug The original type of New Zealand rug used in Britain. It is secured without a surcingle, which might cause chafing. (See **New Zealand rug**)

Endocarditis Inflammation of the lining of the heart valves and/or chambers, caused by redworm or streptococcal bacteria.

Endoscope An instrument which enables a veterinary surgeon to examine the upper part of the respiratory or digestive tract and associated structures.

Endosteum A very fine vascular membrane which lines the internal medullary cavities of the long bones, wherein lies the marrow, or medulla.

Endurance Horse and Pony Society The Society was founded in 1973 to hold endurance and long-distance rides and to encourage research into all aspects of the sport. The research was particularly notable in the veterinary field, where the Society's Veterinary Panel made significant contributions to the knowledge of horses' reactions to the various stresses of this type of sport. The EHPS introduced a variety of rides, run under several different sets of rules, which have expanded the horizons of distance riders in Great Britain, and which have contributed significantly to the greater understanding of the sport. In the New Forest in 1975 the Society staged the first 100-mile (160 km) endurance ride to be held in Britain.

Endurance riding See **Long-distance riding**.

Endurance tests Few have been held in Britain, but in 1920, 1921 and 1922 tests were held by the Arab Horse Society, open to Arab, Anglo-Arab, and part-bred Arab stallions, mares and geldings, to carry 13 stone (182 lb; 82.5 kg), over a course of 300 miles (480 km), with consecutive daily runs of 60 miles (96 km). (See **Long-distance riding, Tevis Cup, Quilty Cup**, and **Golden Horseshoe Ride**)

Enema Lubrication or flushing of the bowel by means of (usually) a special tube. It is carried out quite often in new-born foals to remove a sticky meconium which the foal is unable to pass.

Engaged (1) Of a horse, when entered for a race; (2) of a jockey – when he/she is retained by an owner or stable to ride in a race or races.

Engagement The hindlegs are advanced further under the body because the haunches have been lowered by the flexion of the principal joints (coxo-femoral, stifle and hock) of the quarters.

'Enlarged' The act of releasing the carted deer at a stag hunt.

Enlargements, bone These are chiefly found amongst horses raised on marshy ground.

Enter (hunting) A young hound is 'entered' from the time he is taught to hunt a fox.

Enteritis Inflammation of the small intestine caused, for example by bacteria, fungi, or other agents. It can be fatal, especially in foals, and veterinary attention is essential. Symptoms include loss of appetite; rigors (q.v.); frequent passing of liquid faeces; rapid, hard pulse; raised temperature; tense abdominal wall; and a tucked-up appearance associated with any abdominal pain. (See **Diarrhoea**)

Entire Term referring to a stallion (q.v.).

Entry (hunting) Young, unentered hounds.

Entry (racing) A horse has to be entered for racing in Britain through the Racing Calendar Office (q.v.) at Weatherbys. All entries close at noon on Wednesdays. Later, horses have to be 'declared to run' before they can take part in a race.

Eohippus The generic name given in the theory of evolution of the horse (q.v.) to the first equine ancestor.

Eohippus.

Epistaxis Bleeding from the nose due to haemorrhage in the nasal passages after fast work (more frequently seen in racehorses), the top of the throat, the guttural pouch. (See also **Bleeder**.)

Epona A Celtic goddess, patroness of horse breeders, whose cult was widely diffused in north-west Europe in Iron Age times and was spread still wider during the Roman era.

Equerry Originally the stable (écurie) of a royal establishment, but now refers to an officer of the Royal Household in occasional attendance on the Sovereign. The Crown Equerry is in charge of the horses and carriages in the Royal Mews and is responsible for their preparation for State and other Royal occasions.

Equestrian Pertaining to horses or horsemanship. One who rides on horseback.

Equiboots/Easy boots A type of protective boot with a hinged front fastened with a metal clip arrangement. Used when the hoof is damaged, or on rough or slippery going.

Equihose A proprietary name for elasticated socks used to give support to a horse's legs either in the stable or at work. See **Bandages**.

Equine Pertaining to a horse.

Equine Research Station Part of the Animal Health Trust at Balaton Lodge,

Newmarket, Suffolk. It was established in 1947 through the generosity of Lady Yule and Miss Gladys Yule.

Equine viral arteritis A viral disease of the respiratory tract, characterised by conjunctivitis (hence the common name 'pink eye'), fever, serous, watery nasal discharge, oedema (q.v.) of the eyelids and legs, and of the scrotum in stallions. Can cause abortion. Usually affects very young or very old horses. Modified live vaccines are available in endemic areas, but mortality is low.

Equipage A carriage and attendant retinue.

Equirotal phaeton Consists of two vehicles – a gig (q.v.) in front, and a curricle (q.v.) behind, which, by adding two couplings between the bodies, turned it into a phaeton (q.v.). Invented by W. Bridges Adams in 1838, it was given the name 'Equirotal' because the four wheels are of equal size.

Equus Caballus The forebear of the domesticated horse. See **Equus Przewalskii Przewalskii Poliakov** (Asiatic Wild Horse), **Equus Przewalskii Gmelini Antonius** (Plateau horse or Tarpan), and **Equus Przewalskii Silvaticus** (Forest or Diluvial Horse), **Equus Caballus Celticus**. See also **Evolution of the Horse**.

Equus Caballus Celticus Name given by Dr J. C. Ewart of Edinburgh University, to the type of Plateau horse he considered was the forebear of the Shetland,

Equiboot.

Connemara, Norwegian and Icelandic ponies.

Equus Przewalskii Gmelini Antonius (The Tarpan) Thought to be one of the ancestors of the modern horse. The Tarpan of today (different in some respects from the earlier horse) is limited to a single herd in Poland. It is relatively lightly built, standing about 13 hh (132.1 cm), with a blue-dun coat showing the primitive black dorsal stripe and zebra markings on the legs. The modern breed has a normal mane, but the original Tarpan almost certainly had the primitive upright mane as seen in the Norwegian Fjord pony. The dun coat turns white in winter.

Equus Przewalskii Przewalskii Poliakov (The Asiatic Wild Horse) Believed to be one of the ancestors of the modern horse. It can be seen in many zoos. It has the typical upright mane of the primitive horse, is light yellow dun shading to a cream belly, with black legs, mane and tail. The head is long, with high-set eyes. The wild horse is interesting genetically in that it has 66 chromosomes instead of the 64 of the domestic horse. It stands about 13 hh (132.1 cm).

Equus Przewalskii Silvaticus Also known as the Forest or Diluvial horse of Europe, now extinct, but generally regarded as the ancestor of the European heavy draught breeds. It lived in the wet, marshy lands of northern Europe.

Ergot A horny growth at the back of the fetlock joint. It is the remnant of a pad found behind the toe of Eohippus (q.v.), the earliest known ancestor of the horse.

Ermine marks Small black or brown marks on white, closely resembling ermine fur, which surround the coronet of one or more feet.

Escutcheon The division of hair which begins below the point of the hips and extends downwards on the flanks.

European Championships Championships in all the equestrian disciplines – i.e. horse trials, dressage, show jumping and driving – are held biennially, with different countries hosting the events each year. Equivalent junior champion-ships are held in all disciplines except driving.

Even money (racing) Where the odds are one unit for one unit.

Event horse Descriptive of a horse which is likely to prove suitable for the exacting tests required in one-, two-, or three-day events. (See **Horse trials**)

Evolution of the horse Up to a certain stage, the evolution of the horse is better known than that of most mammals. This is due to the remarkable completeness of the fossil record revealed in North America. It began with an exceptionally well-preserved example of Hyracotherium (more commonly known as Eohippus or the Dawn Horse), found in rocks of the Eocene period (dating from some 60 million years ago) in the southern USA in 1867. A further excellent fossil was discovered in 1931 in Wyoming. These almost complete skeletons showed an animal about the size of a fox, lightly framed, with a somewhat upwardly-curved spinal column, a comparatively short tail, and a long, low skull, contain-ing teeth adapted for browsing, not graz-ing. Hyracotherium had nineteen ribs, the limbs were slender, and adapted for running, with elongated feet in which the 'wrist' and 'ankle' joints were raised so that the animal's weight was on its toes – four toes in the front limb and three in the hind – each toe terminating in a small hoof-like structure. Behind each toe a pad-like structure aided the creature's movement through the soft wet ground of its habitat. (The ergots of the modern horse are the vestiges of these ancient pads.)

The fossil records show that Hyra-cotherium was found throughout North America, Europe, and Asia. However, it became extinct in the early (Lower) Eocene period, except in North America, and those horses which subsequently appeared in the other continents mi-grated from North America by means of land-bridges.

Throughout the following fifty or so million years, the evolution of the horse, *put in its simplest form*, followed a rela-tively straight line. This was characterised by an increase in size; a straightening and stiffening of the back; development and enlargement of the brain; complicated changes in dentition; a deepening of the front of the skull, including the lower jaw; a lengthening of the face in front of the eyes to accommodate the increasing-ly highly-crowned cheek teeth; a gradual reduction of the lateral toes, and develop-ment of the middle one.

The next stage of development from Hyracotherium was Mesohippus, a slightly larger creature, with three toes, followed by Meryhippus, which was markedly larger, standing about 3 ft 3ins (99 cm). The feet retained their three toes, but the two lateral ones were, to all intents, useless, and the animal walked on the single central toe with its terminal hoof. Meryhippus had also developed a post-orbital bar (i.e. a bony structure separating the orbit from the tempo-ral region of the skull), typical of later horses.

Following Meryhippus, the main line of evolution diverged. One branch, at the end of the Miocene and the begin-ning of the Pliocene periods, consisted of lightly built animals which retained the three-toed foot and spread to all conti-nents other than South America, becom-

Evolution of the horse.

Eohippus   Mesohippus   Meryhippus   Pliohippus   Equus

ing extinct in the Pleistocene period. The other, Pliohippus, developed in North America about six million years ago. It stood about 4ft high (122 cm), and was recognisably horse-like, with a single toe, the other two being vestigial splints similar to the modern horse; the teeth, too, were very similar to the Equus of modern times.

From Pliohippus developed, in one direction, the now extinct Hippidium of South America; from the other, in North America, developed Equus. It became extinct in America a few thousand years ago, but at the beginning of the Pleistocene period it had migrated to other continents, including Europe, and its descendants are the horses that we know today.

Tracing development from Pliohippus to our present-day breeds is not so simple and gives rise to theory rather than fact. There is, however, reasonable agreement that modern domestic stock is descended from three, possibly four, different forms of Equus Caballus. They are: EQUUS PRZEWALSKII GMELINI ANTONIUS, the Plateau horse, commonly known as the Tarpan, which evolved in Eastern Europe, and still exists as a herd in Poland; EQUUS PRZEWALSKII PRZEWALSKII POLIAKOV, the wild horse of the Asian Steppes, which can still be seen in a few zoos but is almost certainly extinct in the wild; EQUUS PRZEWALSKII SILVATICUS, the Forest or Diluvial horse from which the heavy horse of northern Europe is derived; and the TUNDRA HORSE, which does not feature prominently in modern theories, but remains are reported to have been found in Siberia. Soviet scientists (and no-one else, at present) believe that these horses may be the ancestors of the modern Yakut ponies of the region.

According to some theories, the light horses of today are descended from the Tarpan and Asiatic wild horses, while the heavy horses derive from the Forest or Diluvial horses.

By examination of skeletal structures and dentition Professor Speed (who carried out much research on the Exmoor pony) and others have enlarged on these theories. They suggest that modern domestic horses descend from four subspecies: PONY TYPE 1, found in north-west Europe, and very similar in many ways to the modern Exmoor pony; PONY TYPE 2, a much heavier, larger, animal standing up to 14.2 hh (147.3 cm), found in northern Eurasia, with some similarities to the modern Highland; HORSE TYPE 3, originating in Central Asia and akin to the Akhal-Teké in some respects – although considerably less elegant, being very narrow and goose-rumped; HORSE TYPE 4, an animal of refinement, coming from Western Asia, and considered by some to be the distant ancestor of the Arab, possibly by way of the Caspian horse.

Ewe neck This occurs when the crest of the neck (between the poll and the withers) is concave rather than convex. An 'upside-down neck'.

Ewe neck.

Exmoor Pony One of the most distinctive of the nine Mountain and Moorland breeds of Britain. Its two most easily recognisable features are a mealy coloured muzzle and 'toad' eyes – the latter being very large, with heavy top lids and brows surrounded by light, buff-coloured hair. The Exmoors are a breed of great antiquity and, because of the remoteness of their native habitat on the high moors in Devon and Somerset, they are almost certainly the purest of the Mountain and Moorland breeds. They have suffered very little 'improvement' by infusion of outside blood, and are generally regarded as having undergone little change from their historic ancestors.

The Breed Society has strenuously defended the type and the purity of the breed, with rigorous inspections which ensure that no animal with white hairs, or with white streaks in the hoof, or lacking in type, is registered as purebred. The breed therefore remains the most uniform of all the native ponies. All ponies, when passed for registration, have the Breed Society's star brand imprinted on their shoulder, and below this, their own herd number. Each individual's number in the herd is branded on the near flank.

There are just three herds of purebred ponies still running out on the native habitat, although efforts are being made to introduce further stock. Exmoor stallions and geldings stand up to 12.3 hh (129.5 cm) and mares to 12.2 hh (127.0 cm). The breed makes good children's riding ponies, and as they are well up to weight they are also ridden by small adults. They are being used increasingly in harness.

Exmoor Pony Society Founded in 1921 to improve and encourage the breeding of Exmoor Ponies of the Moorland type, to institute shows of breeding stock, and to examine and approve all potential stallions.

Exotosis A bony growth on the surface of a bone. (See **Ringbone**; **Splint**)

Export of horses and ponies The regulations are complicated. The Ministry of Agriculture, Fisheries and Food provides *Notes for the Guidance of Persons Intending to Export Horses and Ponies*. In the case of permanent export (i.e.

other than a temporary exit, such as for competition purposes) a certificate of minimum value from a recognised valuer or breed society inspector is required; also reservation at approved lairage (q.v.) for a specified period of time, and examination there by a veterinary surgeon.

Extension A lengthening of a horse's stride while maintaining balance and rhythm and without the pace becoming hurried. (See under **Walk**; **Trot** and **Canter, extended**)

Extension stirrup leathers Leathers in which the mounting-side leather is fitted with a metal hook and an extra web length, to enable the rider to mount with a longer leather. It is hooked up to a normal position when the rider is in the saddle. Also known as 'hook-up' stirrup leathers.

Eye The eyes of the horse, situated as they are, one on each side of the head, give the animal a very wide field of view. The vision is, however, principally monocular (*cf.* human binocular vision), except when looking at very close objects. The horse finds lateral vision easier than direct forward sight which requires the head to be slightly raised in a straight line with the body for both eyes to focus on an object ahead. When both eyes simultaneously look ahead the horse's ears prick forward; when lateral vision is being used they tend to lop a little or point backwards. When grazing, a horse can see between its legs in every direction. The horse is believed to have a relatively poor appreciation of distance and of colour.

F

f. filly

F (racing) Fell.

FBHS Fellow of the British Horse Society. (See **British Horse Society**)

FEI Fédération Equestre Internationale (q.v.).

FFSE Fédération Française des Sports Equestres.

FRCVS Fellow of the Royal College of Veterinary Surgeons.

FS Foundation stock.

Face-piece Harness decoration consisting of a metal crest or other device set in a pear-shaped leather foundation which falls from the bridle headpiece.

Fadge Pace which is neither walk nor trot. Sometimes called 'hound jog' or 'hound pace' (q.v.).

Fairly hunted See **Point-to-points**.

Faking Improper tampering in order to conceal some fault, or fraudulently altering the appearance of a horse.

Falabella A miniature horse developed by the Falabella family on Recrio de Roca Ranch near Buenos Aires in Argentina by crossing small Thoroughbred stallions with Shetland mares. The breed does not exceed 30 ins (76.2 cm) in height, but has horse characteristics in spite of its size. Any colour is permitted. They are popular in America and there is now a Falabella Society in Britain.

Fall, a (in competition) A horse is officially judged to have fallen when the shoulders and quarters on the same side touch the ground or (in show jumping) touch the obstacle and the ground. A rider technically falls when he is separated from the horse and has to remount. In ordinary parlance a rider does not fall but comes down with his horse.

Falling horses A term used in the film world to describe horses which are specially trained to make spectacular falls. They are first taught to lie down on a sand or sawdust bed; they then do so at a walk, and finally at a gallop, without hurting themselves. Few horses have the nerve to accomplish this successfully, and those with the necessary ability command high fees.

False nostril A blind sac at the entrance of the nostril on the upper surface, which one can feel by inserting a finger gently into the sac. (See **High blowing**).

False quarter A term used of the hoof when an injury has occurred to the coronary band, affecting the horn's oil secretion, and thus leaving a permanent weakness in the hoof wall. There must be no pressure from the shoe on the affected part; the gap in a bar shoe prevents this.

False ribs Ribs to the rear of the eighth rib. (See **Ribs**)

Fan Extension at the rear of military saddles for the attachment of equipment.

Fancy curb Name for all single-rein curb bits with fancifully designed cheeks: e.g. globe, heart, acorn.

Fanning A term used when a cowboy rides a buckjumper, waving his hat (Stetson) in the air and slapping his horse with it. This encourages the horse to buck harder, and also helps the rider to retain his balance.

Fanning Old coaching term for the light use of the whip.

Fan tail The tail of a docked horse which is not squared but is cut shorter at the sides near the root, presenting the appearance of a fan. (Docking (q.v.) is illegal in Great Britain.)

Far North-country term for the offside (q.v.) of an animal.

Faradism Electrical therapy, named after Michael Faraday, which produces rhythmical contractions of the muscles. It is used therapeutically to induce circulation in injury sites, to reduce adhesions, and to assist in correcting muscle imbalance. It is also used diagnostically, as when it is applied to the site of painful muscles, the horse reacts.

Farcy An old term for glanders (q.v.).

Faroe Islands Pony Somewhat similar in type to the Icelandic Pony (q.v.).

Farrier From 1356 this name was applied by the Worshipful Company of Farriers to the man who attended a sick horse, and today in the army it is the farrier who, under the supervision of the veterinary surgeon, attends to sick horses and mules. Used today for a shoeing smith. The symbol of the farrier is the axe, as carried in ceremonial processions, e.g. the Trooping the Colour.

Farriers' Registration Act, 1975 Introduced to ensure proper standards of farriery. It prohibits shoeing of any equines by unqualified persons.

Farriers, The Worshipful Company of

One of the ancient livery companies of London, dating back to the fourteenth century. It received its Charter from King Charles II in 1674. The Guild is now closely involved with the education of potential farriers, and before any farrier may practise he must serve an apprenticeship and pass the examinations necessary to be awarded the Diploma of the Worshipful Company (Dip.WCF).

Fast cheek See **Fixed cheek**.

Fat See **Condition**; also **Feeding, general principles of**.

Fault, at When hounds lose or run out of scent.

Favouring a leg When a horse in movement avoids placing its full weight on one of his limbs. This varies according to the extent of pain or injury in the favoured limb, and is a clear indication of lameness.

Feather All fetlocks are covered with hair, but when this is found abundantly long – as in Shires and Clydesdales – it is termed 'feather'. (See **Hair**)

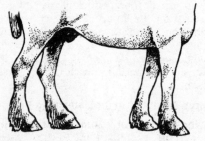

Feather.

Feather (hunting) When a hound believes it owns the scent, but is uncertain, he will not speak to it, but will 'feather', indicated by waving his stern and by driving along the presumed line with his nose to the ground.

'Feather edging' Driving near to anything.

Fédération Equestre Internationale (FEI) International equestrian federation which governs equestrian sports worldwide. It is composed of representatives of the affiliated national bodies of all the leading equestrian countries.

Feeding, general principles of The purposes of feeding are (1) to provide material for the formation and replacement of body tissues, such as muscle, bone, skin, etc., and to put flesh on the horse; (2) to provide energy for movement, work, and the body processes; (3) for development.

The basic rules of feeding are: (1) Water before feeding, never after. (2) Do not feed a hot or tired horse. Allow it to cool off. (3) Feed little and often, to suit the horse's small stomach. (4) Feed at regular times. (5) Feed plenty of bulk, such as hay or grass, to aid digestion. The capacity of the gut of the average horse may approach 50 gallons, and digestion depends upon the greater part of this being occupied. (6) Do not work the horse for at least one hour after feeding. (7) Feed according to the work being done, and the size and weight of the horse. (8) Weigh the food. Do not guess. (9) Feed only the best quality food available, and ensure that it is fresh, wholesome, and fed in clean containers. (10) Treat each animal as an individual.

The horse requires three principal groups of nutrients – proteins, carbohydrates and fats, plus a variety of minerals, and vitamins. Water is essential to health and to efficient digestion. (See **Water**)

The principal sources of protein include oats, beans, barley, flaked maize, sugar-beet pulp, hay, grass, horse nuts, and protein supplements such as soyabean meal, dried skim-milk powder, fish meal, and linseed. Carbohydrates are found in oats, barley, maize, sugar-beet pulp, hay, horse nuts, molasses, and mollassine meal. Linseed is one of the best sources of fat (oil), together with soyabean meal, milk pellets, horse nuts, grass meal, barley and maize.

Essential minerals such as calcium, potassium, etc., are found in grass and grains, but the addition of common salt (sodium chloride) to the food is usual. Some parts of the country are deficient in natural minerals in the soil (and hence in the grass or hay), which may be remedied by a salt lick containing the missing minerals.

Vitamins normally occur naturally in the various foodstuffs, including carrots.

As a *very* general guide, a horse or pony

in work may be fed 2½ lb (1.1 kg) of food per day for every 100 lb (45 kg) the animal weighs. This is divided between hay and concentrates (q.v.), *depending on the work being done*. Animals in light work require approximately 70% hay, in medium work 50-60%, and in hard work 20-30%.

Feet The feet of a horse need the utmost care. They are recognised as being the most important part of the anatomy, as witness the well-known saying 'No feet, no horse'.

Feet, odd Many otherwise good horses have odd feet, due to malformation or to varying causes. Although they are unlikely to cause unsoundness, they count as blemishes and faults in the show ring. They may indicate that a horse has previously suffered severe lameness, with consequent resting and lack of growth.

Feet, rings on Ridges running round the outside walls of the hoof. They should be regarded with suspicion as they may be the result of laminitis. They are sometimes caused by the horse having been turned out on damp land. If the coronet has been blistered (q.v.), rings may appear on the hoof, but will grow out.

Feet, shelly Brittle and thin-soled feet, which are liable to lameness. Such feet are difficult to shoe.

Fellow/felloe (pronounced 'felly') On a carriage or cart, the section of the wheel rim which holds the spokes and carries the tyre.

Fell Pony A pony which was once identical with the original Dales pony (q.v.), but was bred on the western side of the Pennines in northern England. It is now slightly smaller and less heavy than the Dales, standing a maximum of 14 hh (142.2 cm). During the eighteenth century the breed was used extensively as a pack pony, carrying lead, iron ore and coal – a load of 16 stone (101 kg) per pony being transported in panniers to the coast. Some carried wool and butter as far as London. The ponies are good, fast walkers, and exceptional trotters, the latter probably attributable to early Friesian blood. The Fell is an excellent ride-and-drive pony, and ideal for a family, as it is well up to weight, yet easily managed and sensible. It is a strong, powerfully built pony with profuse mane, tail and forelock, and with hard, 'blue' feet. Most Fells are black or dark brown, but there is a strain of grey Fells dating back, it is said, to ponies bred by Cistercian monks in Tudor times.

Fell Pony Society Founded about 1916 to promote the breeding and registration of pure-bred Fell ponies. The animals are entered in the Fell Pony Stud Book, the first volume of which was published in 1981; before that the ponies were registered in the National Pony Society Stud Book. The Society holds an annual stallion show, breed show and performance trials.

Femur The thigh bone which extends from the hip joint to the stifle.

Fence The general term applicable to all obstacles met in racing (except hurdles), hunting, horse trials, and show jumping. There are many types of fence, e.g. open ditch and water in racing, bullfinch and oxer in hunting, coffin in horse trials, and triple bar in show jumping.

Fence, to The act of leaping over an obstacle.

Fen Trotter See **Lincolnshire Trotter**, the definition of which is probably applicable in this case.

Ferneley, John, Snr (1782-1860) A very gifted painter of horses, hunting scenes and portraits, particularly associated with Melton Mowbray. A wheelwright's son, he became a pupil of Ben Marshall and gained great popularity with the hunting aristocracy of the Shires. His horses have great natural dignity, and he evokes the atmosphere of the golden age of foxhunting in the Shires probably more successfully than any other artist. He painted a few racehorses and several driving subjects. Three of his children inherited some of his talent: two sons, John Ferneley, Junior (1815-1862) and Claude Lorraine Ferneley (1822-1891), both painted horse portraits and hunting subjects of merit. A daughter, Sarah Ferneley, produced paintings and lithographs.

Ferrule The 'shaft' of a hunting horn.

Fertility The ability to conceive. The average fertility rate of stud stallions is between 60% to 80%, while the average percentage of mares foaling is given as between 65% to 70%. Fertility is affected by age, condition, time of year, physical abnormality, disease, and quality of management.

Fetlock Tuft of hair behind the fetlock joint (q.v.).

Fetlock joint This lies at the lower extremity of the cannon bone, joining it to the pastern (q.v.).

Fetlock ring A rubber anti-brushing ring fitting just above the fetlock joint. Also known as 'brushing ring'.

Fever See **Temperature**.

Fever in the feet See **Laminitis**.

Fiadore (western) Equivalent of a throatlatch (q.v.).

Fibula The smaller of the two bones (the other is the tibia) which extend between the stifle joint and the hock. The tibia goes the whole length, to articulate with the astragalus of the hock joint, but the fibula terminates two-thirds of the way down the tibia.

Fidding/figging A discreditable method of making a mare carry her tail higher by applying ginger or cayenne pepper to her sex organ. It constitutes an act of cruelty. (See **Gingering**)

Fiddle-headed A large, plain, coarse, ugly-shaped head.

Field A hunting term indicating all the mounted followers of both sexes assembled to hunt on any particular day.

Field (racing) 'The field' in betting implies all the competitors in a race. If a bookmaker offers '2-1 the field' it implies the shortest price offered, that is, on the favourite.

Field boots Item of Army uniform, made of brown and sometimes black leather, generally of a tougher tannage than polo boots, to withstand campaigning.

Field Master Master of the Pack, or, if he is hunting his hounds, someone appointed to control the field when hounds are drawing or hunting.

Field money Tip given to hunt servant, also a cap (q.v.) or capping fee.

Field shelter During the winter months horses at grass will rarely use a shed, no matter how bad the weather, but a shelter of some kind should be provided for the summer as a refuge from fly torment.

Fiennes, Celia (1662-1737) She made extensive tours on horseback throughout England, visiting every county and recording her impressions in a diary. In the summer of 1698 she covered 1551 miles 'many of them long miles' from Salisbury to Newcastle and Cornwall.

Fifth leg A horse which is clever in recovering from a mistake at a fence is said to have a fifth leg.

Filing teeth See **Rasping**.

Fillet strap An ornamental piece of leather harness which hangs from the back strap in pair-horse harness.

Fillet string The cord attached to the corners of some rugs. It passes under the tail to help keep the rug in place and to prevent it blowing in the wind. It is also known as a 'tail string'.

Fillis, James (*c.* 1850-1900) A well-known equestrian authority, who wrote *Breaking and Riding* and other instructional works. An Englishman who lived most of his life in France, he was at one time instructor at the Imperial School of Russia. Though he was undoubtedly a great horseman, much of his work belonged more to the circus than to classical riding.

Fillis bridoon A bit, named after James Fillis (above), with a low, wide port, hinged on both sides and having a separate eye for the cheekpieces. It is suspended in the mouth rather than resting on it. Baucher's snaffle is similar.

Filly A female horse under the age of four.

Find (or unkennel) To dislodge a fox, to get him moving.

'Fine' (harness class, USA) Harness classes in the USA in which saddlebreds are shown with wagons or traps.

Finnish Horse This breed has two varieties: (a) draught, and (b) universal. Both have been developed by crossing native ponies with various other breeds to produce tough, strong horses.

Fino-Fino See **Paso Fino**.

Fireman A nearly obsolete term for a farrier whose work is to make and fit shoes. (See **Doorman**)

Firing A treatment once used for certain types of leg conditions and injuries, e.g. splints, curbs, tendon injuries. It consisted of burning the overlying skin with a red-hot iron or an acid, to induce the formation of scar tissue. Firing should not be undertaken as it causes needless suffering and has no benefit in the treatment of lameness.

Firing irons See **Firing**.

Firr, Tom Famous huntsman of the Quorn from 1872 to 1898. He said it was a piece of gross impertinence to interfere with hounds until they had made their own cast.

First-cross The progeny of any two animals of separate breeds registered in the stud books of such breeds.

Fistula A type of ulcer which typically occurs over bursae or fluid-filled pockets: i.e. the poll or over the withers – fistulous withers. An operation is necessary, and a cure can only be affected by draining the ulcer and removing the diseased tissue. *Brucella* bacteria have sometimes been implicated in this condition. It carries a poor prognosis. See **Withers, fistulous**.

Five-barred gate Any gate in the hunting field.

Five-gaited Saddlehorse See **American Saddlebred**.

Fixed cheek/Fast cheek A curb bit where the mouth bit is immovable, i.e. does not slide.

Fjord Pony See **Norwegian Fjord Pony**.

Flagging Another term for docking (q.v.).

Flags The floor of hounds' kennel courts.

Flanchard Primitive armour covering the flanks of a mediaeval warhorse.

Flank That part of the horse's body behind the ribs and below the loins, extending down to the belly.

Flapping meeting Any race meeting which is held without the sanction of a recognised turf authority.

Flask (hunting) This can be one of several shapes and is carried during hunting in a leather holster or in a sandwich case, either being attached by short leather straps to the Ds on the saddle.

Flat, on the Applied to a race without obstacles.

Flat-catcher A horse having outwardly good looks and virtues but whose hidden defects appear on closer acquaintance.

Flat-footed A horse is said to be flat-footed when, owing to the lowness of the wall of the hoof, he goes on the heels more than on the toes, instead of putting the feet squarely and evenly on the ground. The fault is usually associated with a large, soft frog and brittle horn, and horses reared on soft ground are most subject to it.

Flat race See **Flat, on the**.

Flat ring A flattened bit ring as opposed to a round or wire ring. Both are loose rings. The disadvantage of the former is that it requires a larger hole in the mouthpiece, through which it passes, and this factor can cause pinching of the lips.

Flat-sided A horse is said to be flat-sided when the ribs are not rounded or 'well-sprung'. Also known as 'slat-' or 'slab-sided'.

Flatulence/'Wind' Distension of the alimentary tract with gas. See also **Colic**.

Flea-bitten Description of a horse with a grey coat flecked with hairs of darker tones.

Fleam A mid-sixteenth century lancet used for bleeding horses.

Flèche, à la A circus act in which a rider drives a horse in the lead on long reins.

Flecked Where small collections of white hairs occur, distributed irregularly on any part of the body, it is described as 'flecked'.

Flehmen position Extended neck and head and curled upper lip, seen typically in sexually aroused stallions or colts; in mares in early stages of labour; and sometimes when a horse is suffering from colic.

Flemish/Flanders Horse The descendant of the bulky Forest or Diluvial horse found in the Low Countries. It is generally accepted as the ancestor of many European breeds of heavy horses, including the Belgian, the Shire, and the Clydesdale.

Flesh A kennel term indicating the meat on which hounds are fed.

Flesh cart Vehicle for conveying to kennels the carcases of animals on which hounds feed.

Flesh hovel A kennel term indicating the room where carcases are skinned and jointed and where the meat is hung.

Flesh marks Patches where the pigment of the skin is absent.

Flesh side The inside of a piece of leather. Nourishment in the form of oil, etc., should be applied to the flesh side where the pores are unsealed. The grain side (outside) of the leather is waterproofed and does not absorb oil so readily.

Flexalan A brand of oil dressing for leather containing lanolin.

Flexing hocks Often applied to Hackney action, as this horse, more than other breeds, bends the hocks and gets the legs further under its belly.

Flexion A horse flexes when it yields its jaw to the pressure of the bit, with its neck held high and bent at the poll.

Flies Fences which, when hunting, are not jumped on and off, i.e. they are jumped in one single action.

Flight (of hurdles) A row of hurdles. (See **Hurdle race**)

Float A country vehicle, low to the ground like a governess cart (q.v.). It has a forward-facing driving seat. The term is also used in the USA and Australia for a motorised horsebox.

Floating An American term for tooth rasping. See **Rasping (teeth)**.

Floorman A racecourse bookmaker's runner.

Flute bit A perforated hollow mouthpiece bit used to prevent wind-sucking.

Fly A one-horse four-wheeled, covered carriage plying for hire.

Fly, to See **Fly fence**.

Fly-cap A net worn over the ears as a protection against flies.

Fly fence A hunting term indicating any fence which can be cleared (jumped).

Fly front/Fly fringe A browband laced with hanging lengths of cord or strips of leather to keep flies away from a horse's eyes.

Flying change (of leg) A change of leading leg at the canter, during the fourth or 'silent' time of the movement when the horse has all four legs in the air. For the movement to be correct, forelegs and hindlegs must change together during the fourth time, though the hindlegs should slightly precede the forelegs. Flying changes may be performed singly or in quite close succession, and spaced regularly by a given number of strides; at every fourth, third or second stride, or at every stride.

Fly-link The link on a curb chain through which the lip-strap passes.

Fly sheet A sheet or net worn over the back and quarters as a protection against flies.

Fly-terrets (harness) A terret made of matching brass or other metal with a 'swing' fitting in a circular ring. It was primarily ornamental, but was sometimes fixed to the slip-head in the hope of deterring flies which would otherwise cause discomfort to the horse.

Fly whisk A horse-hair switch carried by a rider for removing flies from the horse. It is often dyed in bright colours.

Foal A colt, gelding, or filly up to the age

of twelve months, described accordingly as a colt-foal or filly-foal.

Foal bit See **Tattersall bit**.

Foal headcollar Made of light leather or tubular web, adjustable at the head, throat and nose, and fitted with a hand tag at the rear. Also known as a 'foal slip' or Dutch slip (q.v.).

Foal headcollar.

Foal-heat Period from approximately the seventh to the fourteenth day after foaling when a mare's first heat may be expected.

Foaling time This old horseman's saying may be used as a guide:
She bags up her udder a few days before
She waxes and slackens some hours before
She sweats and she fidgets some minutes before
She foals.

Foal-lap See **Hippomanes**.

Foal slip See **Foal headcollar** and **Dutch slip**.

Fodder Any feeding stuffs normally fed to horses.

Foil (hunting) When sheep or other animals cross the line of a hunted fox,

obliterating the scent, they are said to 'foil' the ground.

Foix, Gaston de Author of *Le Livre de la Chasse* (1387), which became the textbook of hunting in France, and was circulated throughout Europe. The English translation, *The Master of Game* is the oldest book on hunting in England, and was made by Edward, Duke of York (1373-1415).

Fold-bitted See **Ears, identification marks**.

Fold the whip With one flick of the whip-hand the thong and lash of any driving whip can be twisted and wrapped lightly around the shaft, thus keeping it in control.

Fomentation Application of heat by means of cloths, etc., soaked in hot water.

Foot board On a coach, a board on which the coachman's feet rest.

Foot-stool See **Shoeing block**.

Forage Foodstuffs or, more specifically, bulk food such as hay or grass.

Fordham, George (1837-1887) Champion jockey nine times. He won the Derby in 1879 on Baron Lionel de Rothschild's Sir Bevys. His first big success was in 1852 when, aged fifteen, he won the Cambridgeshire, riding at only 3 stone 12 lb (24.48 kg). A brilliant jockey, he often contrived to deceive opponents out of a race. He rode fifteen Classic winners, and was the only serious rival of Fred Archer in his heyday. An owner presented Fordham with a bible and a gold-mounted whip inscribed 'Honesty is the best policy', which advice he always followed. See **Archer, Frederick**.

Forearm That part of the front leg which extends from the elbow to the knee. It contains two bones, the radius and the ulna.

Fore carriage The front part of the undercarriage of any four-wheeled vehicle which turns to the left or right with the front wheels.

Forecast (racing) A betting term denoting the prophecy of the experts on the prices which will be offered against each horse's chance of winning the race. The forecast, which appears in daily papers under the list of probable runners for each race, is based on past form and information, and is therefore apt to be incorrect. Bets may be placed by punters forecasting the winners in one, two or three races (i.e. singles, doubles, trebles, or accumulators), and on the first, second and third horses in a race. A straight forecast is the correct selection of the first two horses in a race in the finishing order.

Forensic laboratory (Newmarket) The laboratory where dope testing is carried out.

Forfeit (racing) See **Declaration of forfeit**.

Forfeit list (racing) A list of people owing money in entry fees etc., and the horses on which the arrears are due. The Unpaid Forfeit List is published regularly in the Racing Calendar. A winning horse whose owner is in the forfeit list can have an objection laid against him.

Forfeit stakes See **Declaration**.

Forefooted An American term used when a horse is roped by the front feet.

Forehand The head, neck, shoulders, withers and forelegs of a horse.

Forehand, turn on the The simplest of all turns on two tracks, in which the hindquarters move around the forelegs, which move in a very small circle.

Forehead drop/Forehead piece An ornament which hangs down the horse's forehead on some harness.

Foreign terms See **Glossary**.

Forelock A continuation of the mane which extends between the ears and hangs over the forehead.

Forging The collision of the hind shoe with the fore shoe when the horse is trotting. It can be recognised by the clicking noise as one shoe strikes against the other, and occurs when the horse is young and green, when it is uncollected, unbalanced, or fatigued, or when it is being ridden or driven in a slovenly manner. When a horse is liable to forge,

the inner borders of the fore shoes may be bevelled off and concaved, and the hind shoes made with a bevelled square toe and two clips, and be let back at the toe wherever possible. A flat hind shoe, thinnest at the heel, is best.

Fork Stable forks are usually 4 ft (121 cm) in length with blunted prongs; they are sometimes made of split wood.

Fork-stowed See **Ears, identification marks**.

Form A hollow or indentation in the ground in which a hare will lie.

Form (racing) Record of a horse's achievements by which its chances in a race are assessed.

'Forrard' A huntsman's cheer to hounds: 'Forrard'; 'Forrard on'; 'Hark forrard to. . .' (a reliable hound).

'Forty Thieves' An old term for the gipsy and hawker fraternity to be found at horse fairs.

Forward seat A term applied to the seat of a rider. It is the reverse of one who sits on the back of the saddle and whose feet and legs from the knees downwards are in front of the girth. The forward seat is the *balanced seat*. In jumping the term refers specifically to the modern practice of sitting forward, with the seat bones clear of the saddle and closing the angle between the upper part of the rider's body and that part of the horse's back which is in front of him. This relieves the weakest part of the horse's back – the loins – of the rider's weight. It contrasts with the old-fashioned 'sitting back' jumping seat, in which the rider's weight, especially on the descent, was on the back of the saddle, with the rider leaning back. This is sometimes still used, in a modified form, in steeplechase riding. See **Seat, balanced**.

Fothering-time A corruption of foddering-time, i.e. feeding time in hunting and farm stables. It is rarely used in racing establishments, where the equivalent is 'morning' and 'evening' stables. The passage in front of cattle stalls is called the 'fother-gang'.

Foundation mares (racing) See **Bruce Lowe Figure System**.

Founder Another name for laminitis (q.v.).

Four-in-hand A team of four horses: two wheelers and two leaders. The term is sometimes used to describe a coach-and-four as a complete turn-out. A four-in-hand coach can be either a mail, park, road, or stage coach. See **Coaching**; **Mail coach**; **Park drag**; **Road coach**; **Stage coach**.

Four-time Applied to the definition of a pace. A pace of four-time is so called because it is marked by four hoof-beats.

Four-wheeled dog-cart A popular trap with body and seating as in a dog-cart but on four wheels, for a single horse or a pair.

Four-wheeler See **'Growler'**.

Fox A wild animal of the genus *Vulpes*. Its body is red-brown to reddish-grey.

Foxhound A hound bred and kept for hunting the fox. Measuring from 22-25 ins (55.8-63.5 cm) at the shoulder, it is usually white with black, tan and light markings on the head and body.

Foxhound Kennel Stud Book This was first compiled in 1841 by Mr Vyner, and a subsequent volume in 1866 by Mr Cornelius Tongue. By a resolution passed at the Annual General Meeting of members of the Masters of Foxhounds' Association held at Tattersall's on 28 May 1906, these two volumes were republished. Subsequently, and at frequent intervals, other volumes have been added. The first volume contained a list of His Majesty's Buckhounds and of forty-six packs of foxhounds.

Foxhunter Outstanding international show jumper of great personality. He was owned by Lt. Col. H. M. (now Sir Harry) Llewellyn. Foaled in 1940, Foxhunter, a bay gelding, 16.3 hh (167.5 cm), was by the Thoroughbred sire, Erehwemos, out of Catcall, who went back to a pure Clydesdale mare. He represented Great Britain 35 times and had 78 international wins to his credit. He won the King George V Cup (q.v.) three times and a team gold medal in the Helsinki Olympics. Semi-retired in 1953 he made his final appearance in 1956, when he won the final Committee Trophy at the Dublin Show. He died in 1959.

Foxhunter competition (show jumping) An adult event for registered horses in Grade C who are owned by and ridden by members of the BSJA (q.v.). The highest-placed horses (the number according to the number of entries) are eligible to compete in one of the regional finals. The highest-placed horses (also according to the numbers competing) in each regional final qualify to compete in the Foxhunter Championship at the Horse of the Year Show in October. There is also a Junior Foxhunter competition, for registered JC ponies. See also **Grading, of horses**.

Foxhunting See **Hunting**.

'Foxhunting, the Father of' See **Warde, John**.

Fox trot A four-beat gait, but not evenly spaced as in the walk; the stride is not as long as in the running walk, nor as speedy; it is between a square two beat and a square four beat. The left hind foot strikes the ground followed quickly by the diagonal or right foot, then a slight pause, after which comes the right hind, quickly followed by the left fore. In the United States the fox trot was accepted in early Plantation Horse Classes as a substitute for the running walk.

Frampton, Tregonwell (1641-1727) He supervised the racing stud of William III, managed that of Queen Anne, and enjoyed similar patronage in the reigns of Kings George I and George II. Known as the 'Father of Racing', he was an acknowledged authority on the sport.

Fredericksborg One of the oldest and best known breeds from Denmark, where it was used as a cavalry charger, in haute école, in harness, and on the land. The Fredericksborg Stallion Pluto (foaled 1765) founded the famous line of Lipizzaner horses which still bear his name. In recent times Thoroughbred blood has been introduced into Fredericksborgs to produce horses more suitable for modern equestrian sports. They stand 15.3-16 hh (160.0-162.6 cm), and are riding horses of good conformation. The colour is predominantly chestnut.

Free handicap Three Free Handicaps are published at the end of the flat-racing season by the handicapper to the Jockey Club: one for two-year-olds, one for three-year-olds and one for four-year-olds and upwards. Those for three-year-olds, and four-year-olds and upwards, are published for information only. The one for two-year-olds is run the following spring at the Newmarket Craven meeting over 7 furlongs (1.4 km). There is no initial entry fee, hence the name.

Freeman, Frank For twenty-five years huntsman to the Pytchley, Freeman was acclaimed by many to be the greatest huntsman of all time; some disputed this in favour of Tom Firr of the Quorn (q.v.). He died in 1947.

Free return A term meaning the right of an owner of a mare which has failed to conceive to send the mare next season to the same stallion for service without further payment.

Freestyle dressage (Kür) See **Dressage, competitive**.

Freeze branding/marking A system of permanent identification introduced in Britain in 1978. It is the application of a super-chilled marker to a clipped area on the left side of the saddle area. The intense cold kills the pigment cells of the hairs, which re-grow white within a few weeks. Light-coloured horses are marked in a similar fashion, but the *hair* is killed, leaving a bare area.

Freiberger This light farm horse originated in the Jura region of Switzerland, where before World War II it was worked as a pack and saddle animal. It is still used on small farms in the mountains. Threequarters of all Freibergers trace their descent from the stallion Vaillant, foaled in 1891, whose great grandsire was an English half-bred, and whose granddam was of French Thoroughbred and Anglo-Norman breeding. Further Anglo-Norman blood was used around 1889. Later some heavy horse blood was introduced, and since World War II further Anglo-Norman and some Arab have also been used. The Freiberger stands between 15-15.3 hh (152.4-160.0 cm), is strong, short-coupled, and with good feet and limbs. It moves well and is very sure-footed.

French bridoon or French link A term used for a simple mouth bit with a connecting link in the centre to prevent nutcracker action.

French chasing boots A form of speedy cut boot, usually made of leather and lined with rubber or sheepskin.

French clip See **Stud fastening**.

French panel Another name for a Saumur panel. (See **Saddle panel**)

French Saddle Pony The result of crossing French native pony mares with Arab, Connemara, and Welsh stallions, and mating the progeny back to Arabs. They stand 12.2-14.2 hh (127.0-147.3 cm), and are quality, hardy ponies.

French Stud Book (Thoroughbred) Founded in 1833 by royal decree, and administered by the Ministry of Agriculture.

French Trotter Developed in the early nineteenth century by crossing imported English Thoroughbreds, half-breds and Norfolk Roadsters with native mares, to produce, initially, an Anglo-Norman trotting horse; later, American Standardbreds were used. The breed was recognised in 1922, and produces some of the world's most successful trotting racers. Those who are unsuccessful as racers make excellent riding horses. The Trotter has also been used for breeding the Selle Français (q.v.). The breed is very similar to a Thoroughbred in appearance, and the most usual colours are bay, brown and chestnut.

Fresh A term descriptive of a horse which is bright and alert, somewhat excitable, and probably short of exercise.

Fresh fox A term applied when hounds of their own accord change from the fox they are hunting to another.

'Fresh-legged' A term, used chiefly by dealers, indicating an unworn – and usually a young – horse.

Frideriksborg See **Fredericksborg**.

Friesian A small (15 hh/152.4 cm), very strong and thick-set horse bred in the Friesland district of the Netherlands, where 3000-year-old remains of what are believed to be its cold-blood ancestors have been found. The breed was used in mediaeval warfare to carry soldiers in heavy armour, and it was also much in demand as an agricultural animal. As well as showing docility and strength it had (and has) the advantage of being a very economic feeder. Friesians came to Britain with the Romans, and were of great importance in the development of what are now the Fells and Dales breeds. Infusions of, firstly, Eastern blood at the time of the Crusades and, later, Andalusian blood were made. Later still, a lighter type was produced for trotting races, a sport at which the breed excels. The Friesian Stud Book was founded in 1879, but the breed suffered a serious decline between World Wars I and II, until farm horses were once again in demand. A few Friesians have been imported into Britain in recent years, and the breed is well-established in the USA. Friesians are always black, and are noted for their profuse manes, which may reach the ground. The legs are quite heavily feathered.

Frog See **Hoof, frog of**.

Frog-cleft A natural depression in the centre of the widest part of the frog.

Front A term indicative of that portion of the horse which lies in front of the rider.

Frost nails Nails with large, pointed or wedge-shaped heads which are fixed in a horse's shoes to prevent him from slipping. There are two basic types: (a) nails with flat surfaces under the head and (b) nails with a conical neck. The former are for use in an emergency to replace the normal heel nails; the latter require specially prepared holes which enable the nails to be inserted into the shoe without penetrating the hoof.

Full brother (or sister) Progeny having the same dam (q.v.) and the same sire (q.v.).

Full cry Indicating that the whole or main body of any pack of hounds is in strong and relentless pursuit of its quarry in the open and is giving tongue.

Full mouth A horse at six years old.

Full panel One which follows the shape of the saddle flap to within 2 ins (5 cm) of the bottom edge. The part under the flap of the saddle is usually quilted.

Full pass A movement on two tracks (q.v.) in which the horse moves sideways without going forward. (See also **Travers**; **Renvers**)

Fulmer saddle See **Saddle, Fulmer**.

Fulmer snaffle See **Australian loose-ring snaffle**.

Funk A temperamental horse which gets on its toes, breaks out in sweat, or shows other signs of nervousness on a hunting morning or when saddled for a race.

Furioso A good type of general-purpose riding, and also carriage, horse developed in the part of the old Austrian Empire which is now Hungary. The breed was founded by the mating of Hungarian mares with two English Thoroughbred stallions in the mid-eighteenth century. Furioso, from whom the breed takes its name, was the first and North Star, a descendant of Waxy, the Derby winner of 1793, was the other. The two bloodlines were kept separate until about 1885, since when they have intermingled, the Furioso line being dominant. The breed is now produced at the Apajuszter Stud in Hungary, and in other Central European countries. Average height is about 16 hh (162.6 cm).

Furlong A unit of distance used in racing, equivalent to 220 yds or ⅛ mile (200 m).

Furniture The metal mountings on harness and saddlery. It may be galvanised, brass, or plated.

Furze A poor food for horses. The green tips are sometimes collected, chopped, and mixed with chaff, and are considered by some to be both fattening and appetising. Gorse is a natural food of Mountain and Moorland ponies, especially in the winter.

Futchells The fastenings which secure the splinter bar to the axle-tree bed of a coach, where the pole is inserted.

G

G Gelding.

g Grey.

GD (USA) Good track.

GSB General Stud Book (q.v.).

Gadfly See **Horsefly**.

Gag The term 'gag' denotes any bit used with a rounded leather cheekpiece which passes through holes in the bit ring or through rollers, pulleys, etc., its primary purpose being to raise the head. There are numerous designs. Those used in place of a bridoon on a double bridle are the Duncan and Shrewsbury patterns.

Gag-twitch See **Twitch**.

Gait Horse gait, at-gait, gaited-out – all refer to animals pastured out for payment.

Gait Term for 'pace'. A horse normally has three gaits: walk, trot, and canter. The

American five-gaited horse (American Saddlebred, q.v.) also has rack (q.v.) and slow gait (q.v.).

Gait, slow A high-stepping, four-beat gait executed in a slow, restrained manner.

Gaited horse (USA) A horse which is schooled to artificial as well as natural gaits.

Gaiting strap (USA) Strap running inside the shafts of a trotting sulky from rear to front to prevent a horse moving sideways in its gait. Also known as 'side-strap'.

Galiceno It is claimed that this breed, which is now established in both North and South America, originated in Galicia in north-west Spain and was among those brought by Cortez when he landed in Mexico. Referred to as a horse, although standing only 12-13.2 hh

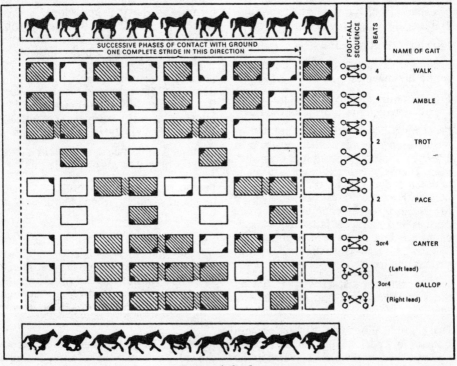

Gaits of the horse.

(121.9-137.2 cm), the Galiceno is a tough, hardy and courageous type, yet docile and easy to handle. Used for ranch work and in harness, it is found in all solid colours.

Gall A sore place caused by harsh or ill-fitting tack or harness; usually found under the girth or saddle. See also **Girth galls**; **Saddle sores**.

Gallop A faster canter. The fastest is the racing gallop in which the diagonal sequence is broken and the pace becomes four-time, followed by a moment of suspension. The sequence (when leading with the off-foreleg) is: near hind, off hind, near fore, off fore, followed by the moment of suspension.

Gallop, false See **Canter, false**.

Galloped for wind To ascertain whether a horse's respiratory system is functioning normally it is galloped in circles, during which time, and immediately following, clinical signs in the respiratory system can be heard by an experienced person.

Galloping disunited See **Canter, disunited**.

Galloping sheet See **Quarter sheet**.

Gallops, training Stretches of grass, heath or downland of varying lengths where trainers gallop their horses in preparation for racing. There are public and private gallops. The former are maintained through trainers paying fees per horse per season.

Galloway A riding pony, well-known for many years in Galloway, S.W. Scotland, standing about 14 hh (147.3 cm). Daniel Defoe, in his *Tour Through Scotland* (1706; Letter XII) wrote: 'Here [in Galloway] they have the best breed of strong low horse in Britain, if not in Europe, which we call pads (pacing as distinct from trotting saddle horses) and from whence we call *all* truss, strong, small, riding horses Galloways; these horses are remarkable for being good pacers, strong, easy-goers, hardy, gentle, well-broke, and above all, that they never tire; and are very much bought up in England on that account.' (The word truss probably meant compact.) The breed became extinct by the end of the nineteenth century, but until quite recently it was remembered in parts of the Lake District, where Fell ponies are still sometimes called 'Fell-Galloways'. The term is used in pony or Galloway racing to denote the height limit, and it was formerly used to describe undersised Thoroughbreds in racing outside Jockey Club or National Hunt Rules.

Galloway (show classes) In Australia, pony classes are limited in height to 14 hh (142 cm). Those exceeding 14 hh (142 cm) and not exceeding 14.2 hh (144 cm) are termed Galloways.

Galton's law Sir Francis Galton (1822-1911) expounded a theory of ancestral contribution in breeding: the premise being that on an average both parents contribute one half to the issue's make-up, the four grand-parents a quarter each, the great-grand-parents, one-eighth, etc. Galton's Law is often used as a stamina index amongst bloodstock breeders.

Galvayne, Sydney A renowned student of the horse, horse breaker, and trainer, who came to England from Australia in 1884 and introduced a humane system for the training of unbroken and vicious horses. He utilised scientifically the horse's superior strength against itself, and stated that he had never had a failure. He held over three hundred classes in Great Britain, and in 1887 he appeared before Queen Victoria.

Galvayne's groove/mark A brownish-coloured groove which runs down the length of the corner incisor teeth. It

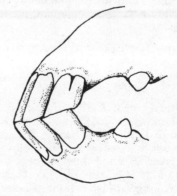

Galvayne's groove.

appears when the horse is nine to ten years old; at fifteen years it is halfway down; at twenty it has reached the bottom; at twenty-five it has disappeared from the upper half of the tooth; and by thirty-two it has gone completely.

Galvayne strap A device (often a piece of rope) used for connecting a headcollar (q.v.) to a horse's tail. When a horse is tied in this manner he can only move in a circle and soon tires, which makes subjugation simple.

'Galway Blazers' See **'Blazers, The'**.

Gambler's choice See **'Take your own line'**.

Gambo A two-wheeled farm cart used in Wales for carrying hay.

Gamgee Cotton wool covered with gauze. Used under bandages, and also for veterinary purposes.

Gammon board See **Backgammon board**.

Garden-seat bus The last type of passenger horse-bus used on London streets. The outside passengers were accommodated on double seats facing the front of the bus, with a central gangway.

Garranos (or Minho) A breed of pony bred in the Portuguese provinces of Garrano do Minho and Traz dos Montes, and in western Spain. They are used in light agriculture, also in the army as pack ponies, and are very strong. Arabian blood was introduced some years ago. They stand between 10 and 12 hh (100-121.9 cm), are predominantly chestnut, and have good bone and plenty of substance.

Garron (Gaelic, *gearran*) A general name for the native ponies of Scotland and Ireland: or, more accurately, for a gelding.

Garter A narrow leather strap and buckle on hunting or riding boots. It passes through a loop at the back and, in front, between the second and third button of the breeches, and is buckled on the outside of the leg. Made of white buckskin for wearing with white hunting breeches; of patent or black leather for patent 'tops' (q.v.); and of black leather for black butcher boots (q.v.).

Gascoigne, Chien de A blue-mottled hound, said to be the oldest strain in France. Origin of the Holcombe (Lancashire) Harriers.

Gaskin The portion of the hind limb above the hock and extending upwards to the stifle. Often called the 'second thigh'.

Gate stop Sharp brass or nickel stud fixed on the crook point of hunting whips.

Gato A Criollo pony who with Mancha took part in Tschiffely's historic ride. (See also **Criollo** and **Tschiffely**)

Gaucho South American cowboy or mounted horseman of mixed European and South American Indian blood. He is considered by many to be the world's finest rough-rider.

Gay Said of a horse when the head and tail are carried gaily and the animal moves with an airy walk.

Gee See **Arve**.

Gelderland This horse originates from a very old native breed of the Dutch province of Gelderland, and was crossed, many years ago with Thoroughbreds, Holsteins, and Anglo-Normans. The modern breed, used in the production of the Dutch Warmblood (q.v.), is wide and deep, yet of beautiful build, with a very stylish action. Height ranges from 15.2-16hh (157.5-162.6 cm), although larger animals are also seen. An excellent saddle horse, but particularly admired as a carriage horse, and used in competitive carriage driving.

Gelding An emasculated male horse. (See **Castration**)

General Stud Book (GSB) Founded in 1791 by James Weatherby and published ever since by the same family firm. The GSB includes all Thoroughbred mares and their progeny foaled in the British Isles. A new volume of the book is produced every four years, and there is an annual supplement listing the year's foalings. Since 1970, blood typing has been mandatory for all entries.

Generous Descriptive of a horse who gives of his best in any equestrian sport, or when used commercially.

Genet/Jennet A small Spanish horse, or the offspring of a horse-sire and female ass, sometimes called a 'hinny' or bardot (qq.v.). Also a type of horse known in the twelfth century – an ambling hack.

Gentle, to To handle a horse – particularly a young one – quietly and with understanding.

George III, King (1738-1820) See **Buckhounds, Royal**.

George IV phaeton See **Park phaeton**.

George V, King (1865-1936) He took a keen interest in racing, as did his father, King Edward VII, but he did not have the same good fortune. In 1928 he won the 1000 Guineas, with Scuttle.

George VI, King (1895-1952) He was not so keen on racing as his father, King George V, but he had more luck. In 1942 with the colt Big Game and the filly Sun Chariot, both leased to him from the National Stud, he won four of the five Classic races – all run at Newmarket in wartime. The filly won the 1000 Guineas, the Oaks and the St Leger; the colt won the 2000 Guineas and started favourite for the Derby, but failed to stay. Four years later, the King's homebred filly Hypericum, trained for him by Sir Cecil Boyd-Rochfort, won the 1000 Guineas.

German mouthpiece A broad, comfortable mouthpiece covering a large area of sensory nerves and so distributing the pressure rather than confining it to one area, as may be the case with a thinner mouthpiece. The mouthpiece is often hollow.

German panel See **Melbourne facings**.

German rein Similar to the Market Harborough martingale (q.v.). In Germany it is known as the 'English rein'.

German snaffle A popular snaffle bit using a German mouthpiece as described above. It is made with eggbutt cheeks or ordinary wire rings; in the latter case the holes in the mouthpiece through which the rings pass are specially small in diameter to prevent pinching the lips.

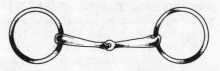

German or loose-ring snaffle.

Gestation, of donkey mare (jenny) Approximately twelve and a half months.

Gestation, of mare The period between conception and foaling is about eleven months.

Get The progeny of a stallion.

Get under, to A term used in jumping, meaning to take off too near the obstacle.

'Getting hanged' A coaching term for catching the thong of the whip in the bar or harness.

Gidran A Hungarian breed tracing back to Gidran Senior, an Arab stallion imported in 1816 and mated with the Spanish-bred Arrogante, to produce Gidran II – regarded as the breed's foundation stallion. Later, Thoroughbred and more Arab blood was infused, together with other blood, to produce an excellent riding horse of some 16 hh (162.6 cm), with an Arab-type head showing the dished profile. Gidrans are also bred in Rumania and Bulgaria.

Gig A two-wheeled carriage seating two people only. There are many variations. (See **Lawton**, **Liverpool**, **Murrieta**, **Stanhope** and **Tilbury gigs**).

Gilbey, Tresham (1862-1947) A noted polo player, polo pony breeder, and past-President of the National Pony Society (q.v.).

Gilbey, Sir Walter, Bart (1831-1914) A well-known horseman who wrote many books, including *Thoroughbred and Other Ponies*; *Horse Breeding to Colour*; *The Harness Horse*; *Horse Breeding in England and India*; *George Stubbs*; *The Old English War Horse or Shire Horse*; and *Animal Painters*. He devoted much of his life to fostering interest in all breeds of horses, and was one of the founders of the Hunters' Improvement and National Light Horse Breeders' Society in 1885.

Giles, Godfrey Douglas (1857-1941) Painter of military and sporting scenes. Retired from the Indian Army as Major in 1884. Studied painting under Carolus Duran in Paris and exhibited in London. Accredited with being the originator of the hunting countries series, expanded later by Cecil Aldin (q.v.) and Lionel Edwards (q.v.).

Gilpin, Sawrey, RA, FSA (1733-1807) Born in Carlisle, an important painter of animal and sporting pictures, and of some historical subjects. He worked in London and studied under William Scott. Most of his paintings were commissioned by three important patrons: HRH The Duke of Cumberland; the renowned English eccentric, Colonel Thornton; and Samuel Whitbread, the brewer.

Gimcrack A famous and very small Yorkshire horse, 'The Hero of the North', whose name is perpetuated in the Gimcrack Stakes for two-year-olds, run at the York summer meeting. The winning owner of this race is guest of honour at the annual Gimcrack Dinner and traditionally makes a speech giving his ideas for the improvement of racing.

Gingering The practice of forcing an irritant, such as ginger or pepper, into the horse's rectum to impel a high tail carriage. Rated as cruelty.

Gin horse A mill-horse. (The gin is the machine which separates the cotton from the seeds.)

Girth The circumference of a horse measured from behind the withers and around the lowest line of the body: e.g. 'a good girth', 'lacking girth'.

Girth, fitting of The placing of the girth is largely decided by the conformation of the back and withers. The girth should be as far back from the elbows as possible.

Girth extension A strap about 14 ins (35.6 cm) long with holes punched in the two buckles and the bifurcations. It is used to extend a tight girth when a horse has become fat after summer grazing.

Girth galls A sore on the soft skin behind the elbow in the girth area. The causes of it include badly fitting girths, dirt or dried sweat in the girth areas, working an unfit or fat horse, or sensitive skin. They can be prevented by careful girthing (q.v.), by covering the girth with rubber tubing, sheepskin or cotton wool (see **Girth sleeves**), using nylon or Balding girths (q.v.) on an unfit horse, and applying surgical spirit to the healed area, to harden the skin.

Girthing Care should be taken to girth up gradually. There should be at least two stages before mounting, and one when in the saddle. Most horses are ridden with the girth too tight. If a horse has to be girthed tight, as before a race, stand in front of him and pull his forelegs forward as high as they can be raised, to make sure that there are no puckers of skin.

Girths Girths are used to secure the saddle, and pass under the horse's belly, buckling on to the girth straps on each side of the saddle. The main varieties are nylon or cotton, webbing (always used in pairs), lampwick, tubular web (i.e. two of 1¼ ins (31 mm) web joined in the centre and the join overlaid with pimple rubber, giving a good grip), elastic (used in pairs), and, best of all, leather. For racing, web or elastic girths, between 2-3½ ins (50-89 mm) wide are used. Most patterns can be inset with elastic to allow a little 'give'. Principal leather varieties are the Atherstone, Balding, and three-fold (qq.v.).

Girth safes Safes which prevent the girth buckles from penetrating the saddle flaps. (See **Safes**)

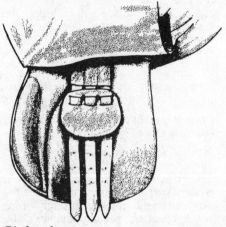

Girth safe.

Girth sleeve A sleeve of rubber or sheepskin passed over the girth to prevent galling. (See **Girth galls**)

Girth straps The straps to which the girth is attached on any saddle. There are usually three on a full-sized saddle. Show saddles have an extra one upon the point of the tree. Lightweight saddles have only one. (See **Lonsdale girth straps**)

'Give a lead', to To ride ahead in order to encourage a reluctant horse.

Give with the hand, to To open the fingers so that the tension of the rein is relaxed, thus reducing the pressure of the bit on the bars of the horses mouth.

Giving the office See **Office**.

Glanders (also known as 'farcy'). A very serious (and notifiable) contagious disease of horse and man caused by the *Loefflerella mallei* bacterium. It has been unknown in Britain since 1925, but is found in Asia, North Africa, and Eastern Europe. In its acute form, death occurs within a few days. Symptoms include a purulent discharge from the nostrils, ulcers on the mucous membranes, and abscesses in the angles of the lower jaw. There is no specific treatment.

Gleet, nasal Chronic catarrhal discharge from the nose.

Glass-eye (USA) See **Wall-eye**.

Glitters, Lucy A character in *Mr Sponge's Sporting Tour* by R. S. Surtees (q.v.). A great horsewoman, she married Mr Sponge.

Globe-cheek pelham This is usually a fixed-mouth cob or pony riding-curb, with a large eye and an even larger globe-like bottom ring (presumably to balance the bit). It is frequently seen in a good show-pony bridle.

Gloster bars An arrangement fitted to the saddle comprising two shaped, padded and sprung bars which fit over the top of the rider's thighs. Intended to teach beginners jumping, and for the incapacitated. Virtually obsolete.

Goal posts (polo) These are generally made of basket work and should be at least 10 ft (3 m) high, erected so that they collapse easily in a collision. They are usually painted a light colour at the base and dark at the top. There is no cross-piece as in football or hockey. A goal is held to be scored if a high ball passes between what would constitute the upward prolongation of the goal posts.

Goat-snatching See **Karabair**.

Godolphin Arabian Imported into England in 1730 from Paris by Mr Edwin Coke and now generally accepted as a pure-bred Jilfan Arabian standing just under 15 hh (152 cm). He was later acquired by the second Earl of Godolphin to become one of the three famous progenitors of the Thoroughbred (q.v.), and established the Matchem line. (See **Bruce Lowe Figure System**, **Arab**; **Thoroughbred**; and **Thoroughbred racing**)

'Goes well into the bridle' Said of a horse who is not afraid of going up to its bit and who does not avoid its pressure by throwing up his head, carrying it too high or too low, or going behind its bridle.

Go-go race Gymkhana event in the USA involving riding between poles placed 6 ft (1.8 m) and 12 ft (3.6 m) apart down the length of the arena.

Gogue, de An extension of the principle employed by the Chambon (q.v.) schooling device. It differs from the latter in that the horse can be ridden and jumped while wearing the martingale.

Going A term indicating the nature of the ground over which a horse travels, whether hunting, racing or otherwise: e.g. 'going heavy', 'going good'.

Going amiss A racing term applied when a mare in training comes in season at the time of her race.

Going gauge See **Pilling going gauge**.

'Going short' This results from pain anywhere in the leg or associated muscles, tendons or joints, or from bony thickenings around the joints. The gait is shortened so that the affected leg or legs do not strike the ground as far forward as they should and are picked up more quickly when extending backwards.

Golden Horseshoe Ride First organised

117

in 1965 by the *Daily Telegraph*, later under the jurisdiction of the British Horse Society and the Arab Horse Society, and in the early years held at a different venue each year (usually a racecourse). It is now under the jurisdiction of the British Horse Society Long Distance Riding Group. The Golden Horseshoe Ride takes place annually over two days on Exmoor on the Devon/Somerset borders. Until 1985 the total distance was 75 miles (120 km), with 50 miles (80 km) being ridden on the first day, and 25 miles (40 km) on the second. In 1986 the distance was increased to 100 miles (160 km) – 50 miles (80 km) each day. See **Long-distance riding**.

Golden Horse Society Founded in 1947 to create an interest in the breeding and showing of Golden Horses, and to register suitable animals. The British Palomino Society now fulfils these functions.

Golden Miller Famous steeplechaser owned by the late Hon. Dorothy Paget. Foaled in 1927 by Goldcourt out of Miller's Pride. Winner of twenty-nine races, including the 1934 Grand National and the Cheltenham Gold Cup, which he won five years in succession from 1932 to 1936.

'Gone away' When a hunted fox has broken covert and is running.

'Gone in the wind' An indefinite term, loosely applied to any affliction of wind, more particularly whistling, roaring, and broken wind. It indicates that a horse is 'unsound in its wind'. See **Roarer**.

'Gone to ground' Said of a fox which has gone into a drain or earth.

Gooch wagon A very light and elegant four-wheeled, single-horse vehicle of the spider phaeton type, designed and made by Mills and Sons. Their 'Viceroy' was a pneumatic-tyred adaptation of this.

Goodall, Stephen (1757-1823) A renowned huntsman with the Pytchley and the Quorn. He weighed over 20 stone (280 lb; 127 kg). His career, with that of his grandson, William, is described in *Huntsman of a Golden Age*, by Daphne Machin Goodall.

Goodall, William (1817-1859) Grandson of huntsman Stephen Goodall (q.v.). At the age of twenty-four he became huntsman to the Belvoir Hunt, where he won great admiration and respect.

Good front See **Good rein**.

Good head Hounds are said to 'carry a good head' when they hunt fast on a wide front.

Good horse A 'good horse' is one with many good, few indifferent, and no bad points.

Good nick A term for good condition in a horse.

'Good night' (after hunting) Traditionally said on parting at the end of a hunting day, even in the early afternoon. After cub-hunting: 'Good day' or 'Good morning'.

Good outlook See **Good rein**, below.

Good rein A term applied to a horse which because of the excellent position in which he carries his saddle, and his good sloping shoulders and generous length of neck, gives his rider all that can be required of a well-fronted horse. Also referred to as a 'good front' or a 'good outlook'.

Good roof A term denoting a good line of back and general excellence of body. Also called 'good top'.

Goose-rumped Said of a horse when the slope from the highest point of the quarters runs acutely to the root of the tail. (See also **Quarters, drooping**)

Goose-rumped.

Gordon, Adam Lindsay (1833-1870)
Born in the Azores and educated at
Cheltenham College, Gloucestershire.
After a career as a gentleman rider in
steeplechases, in 1853 he emigrated to
Australia. He achieved little success in
various jobs, but became well known for
his bush ballads, galloping rhymes, and
songs of the open air, of steeplechasing,
racing and hunting. His best-known and
most evocative poem was 'How We Beat
the Favourite'. After a series of bad falls
and financial troubles he committed sui-
cide.

Gorse Can be fed to horses when
chopped. (See **Furze**)

'Go spare', to When a horse goes off
alone without its rider.

Gotland/Gothland or Skogsruss Pony
The oldest breed of pony in Scandinavia,
originating on the island of Gotland.
They still run wild in the forests of Lojsta,
but for the last few hundred years many
have been bred selectively with the introduction of Oriental blood. Utility ponies
with quality heads, but lacking in depth
of body and in bone, they are also used
for light farm work. They stand 12-13.2
hh (121.9-137.2 cm), and may be black,
brown, chestnut, grey dun or palomino.
Their most natural gait is the trot, and
annual trotting meetings are still held in
Gotland.

Governess cart A light, low-hung, two-
wheeled trap for a single horse or pony.
It seats four passengers facing each other.
Access is by a rear door, only one step
from the ground. It is also known as a
'tub-cart' or 'car'.

Grade horse Indicating one which is not
purebred (USA).

Grade Thoroughbred An American expression indicating that a horse has half
or more Thoroughbred blood in his
breeding.

Grade-up, to To breed a stallion of
superior blood to an inferior type of mare.

Grading, of horses In Great Britain,
horses in different disciplines are graded
according to the points or the money
they have won. In show jumping they are
graded on the basis of prize money won,
from Grade C (the lowest), through
Grades B and A. Ponies 14.2 hh (147.3
cm) and under are graded from Grade JD
through JC to Grade JA. Dressage horses
are graded according to points won,
starting at Novice and progressing up
through Elementary, Medium, Advanced
Medium, and Advanced. Horse trials
horses are also graded according to
points won, starting as Novices, and
progressing through Intermediate to
Advanced.

Grain (in leather) The outside surface is
known as the 'grain side'. In the currying
process the finish is put on this side,
sealing the pores and waterproofing the
leather.

Granddam The mother of a horse's sire
or dam (qq.v.).

Grand National, the The most famous
steeplechase in the world, run at Aintree
(q.v.) on the outskirts of Liverpool over
a course of just over 4 miles (6 km), with
thirty fences, including the water jump in
front of the stands. Founded in 1837 by
a Liverpool innkeeper with the backing
of the 2nd Earl of Sefton, who was then
the owner of the course. It was not until
1847 that it acquired its present name:
the Grand National Handicap Steeplechase. It is popularly referred to as 'The
National'.

Grand Pardubice A steeplechase in
Czechoslovakia founded in 1874 by
Count Kinksky, run over 4½ miles (6.9
km) with thirty-one fences over much
newly ploughed terrain.

Grand Prix The most demanding class
in both show jumping and dressage. In
the former it usually takes place over the
biggest course of the show. In dressage it
is a set test of a standard only exceeded by
the Grand Prix Special. (See **Dressage,
competitive**)

Grandsire The father of a horse's sire or
dam (qq.v.).

Grant, Sir Francis, PRA (1810-1878)
His portraits won him the distinction of
becoming President of the Royal Academy. Early in his career he studied with
John Ferneley Snr (q.v.) and painted
sporting scenes. *The Melton Hunt*

Breakfast (1834) was one of his first Academy exhibits.

Grass The natural diet of the horse (together with other herbage), which it needs, either fresh or as hay (q.v.) to supply bulk and roughage and to ensure digestion. The best grasses in Britain are considered to be perennial rye, Timothy, cocksfoot (American Orchard), meadow fescue, sweet vernal, and common foxtail. Grass is fed by grazing or as green feed; the latter *must* be freshly cut and fed immediately, before fermentation begins. Grass provides an adequate complete diet during the summer months when it is at its best, but some concentrates (q.v.) are necessary if the horse is doing anything other than the lightest work. Grass on which horses are grazing should be kept free from droppings.

Grass, dried Grass that is cut and immediately dried by artificial means. Also available as meal or nuts.

Grass, hydroponic Grass grown in specially designed machines under rigidly controlled conditions of moisture, temperature, etc., with only water as the growing medium.

Grass crack A split from the wearing surface of the hoofs upwards. Also known as 'split hoof'.

Grass rings Circular ridges on the hoof allegedly caused by sudden changes in a horse's diet (i.e. being brought in from grass), or moving from wet to dry standing conditions. Laminitis also causes rings.

Grass sickness A sudden and almost invariably fatal illness which, in spite of its name, is not confined to horses at grass. The general symptoms include depression, lethargy, difficulty in swallowing, inflamed membranes, evil smelling green mucous discharge from nostrils owing to regurgitation of the stomach contents, dribbling, muscular tremors, distended stomach, little or no bowel activity, with impaction of the colon. The cause is unknown, but is thought to be an as yet unidentified nerve toxin. There is no effective treatment, and death is usually inevitable.

Grass yard A paddock enclosed by wire netting, and perhaps an acre in extent, where in warm weather hounds and puppies can be left to bask in the sun and to air themselves.

Graze To feed on grass.

Grazing Pasture.

Grease An excessive discharge of grease from the sebaceous glands of the heel, which can lead to infection. It is usually caused by dirty, wet bedding and is historically associated with heavy horses such as Shires, who carry profuse feathering (q.v.). It is closely allied to mud fever (q.v.).

Great Horse, the See **Shire**.

'Green' Applied to a horse whose education is incomplete.

Green meat A general term referring to grass, lucerne, clover, green wheat or green barley.

Green ribbon Sometimes worn on the tail of a horse out hunting, to indicate that it is young and unschooled, and therefore unpredictable.

Grey (colour) This occurs when the body colour of a horse is a varying mosaic of black and white hairs with a black skin. With increasing age the coat grows lighter in colour. Grey is not strictly a colour, but a failure of pigment to produce colour. Every grey Thoroughbred is descended from the Alcock Arabian (q.v.).

Grey-ticked Where white hairs are sparsely distributed through the coat in any part of the body.

Grid See **Tongue grid**.

Grief Term indicating a fall or falls.

Griffen Term applied in India to a newcomer or novice pony.

Gripes An old term for colic (q.v.).

Grisone, Frederico Italian nobleman who established a riding school in Naples in the mid-sixteenth century. He was one of the first exponents of the use of combined aids and of the use of the leg as opposed to the spur.

Grissel A colour also known as 'rount' (q.v.).

Grogginess See **Knuckling-over**.

Groningen A Dutch farm horse which can be used successfully as a heavyweight saddle horse and as a first-rate carriage horse. It has good conformation, a strong back, and a deep body, with legs and feet of excellent substance, and a very refined head and neck. Height ranges from 15.2 hh to over 16 hh (157.5 cm to over 162.6 cm). In spite of its comparatively heavy weight, the horse was once primarily a light draught horse of pure breed and elegance, but it is now used in the production of the Dutch Warmblood (q.v.), and in competitive carriage driving.

Groom One who is engaged in the general care of the horse.

Grooming Grooming is the daily attention needed for the coat and feet of the stabled horse, and is of vital importance to the animal's health. It is necessary to maintain condition, prevent disease, ensure cleanliness and the absence of external parasites, and to improve the appearance of the horse. It removes waste products from the skin, stimulates circulation of blood and lymph and improves muscle tone. The necessary tools are: *hoof pick*, for cleaning out the feet; *dandy brush*, for removing heavy dirt and caked mud; *body brush* for removing dust, scurf and grease from the coat, mane and tail; *curry comb*, either metal or rubber, to clean the body brush – the rubber variety may also be used on horses with heavy coats, and helps to remove caked mud and dirt; the *water brush*, to lay the mane and tail – also used in washing the feet; two *sponges*, one for cleaning eyes and nose, the other for cleaning the dock and sheath; a *wisp*, woven out of hay, used to promote circulation and for massage; a *mane and tail comb*, generally metal, used in pulling manes and tails; a *stable rubber*, for final polishing; and a *sweat scraper*, used to remove excess water from the coat after washing the horse.

The stabled horse should be brushed off, his feet should be picked out, and his eyes, nose and dock sponged each morning before exercise. This is called 'quartering'. He should receive a thorough grooming (approximately threequarters of an hour), including extensive use of the body brush and the wisp, after work. This is sometimes known as 'strapping'. He should be lightly brushed off each evening and day rugs should be changed for night rugs before evening feed.

Horses or ponies kept at grass should have their feet picked out daily and be brushed lightly with a dandy brush only. The body brush removes the natural oils from the coat, and should not be used on horses living out. Horses at grass also appreciate the spongeing of eyes, nose and dock regularly. Nowadays in some countries grooming machines are used on horses every second or third day; on other days they are hand groomed and wisped.

In hot climates, and before shows etc. horses may be bathed. (This is an increasing practice in Britain, though it was once frowned upon.) Bathing is not a short cut to good grooming. A horse should never be bathed unless he can be thoroughly dried. If the horse is sweaty after work he will enjoy a bath, but he must not be washed until he has been walked cool, if not dry. After bathing, which should be in warm water, and a shampoo or mild soap, he should be given a thorough brushing with a body brush.

Grooming pad A circular leather pad filled with hay. It has an elastic hand-loop. Also known as a 'massage' or 'strapping' pad.

Ground line The line of the base of an obstacle from which a horse assesses its take-off.

'Growler' A slang name for the four-wheeled, one-horse London cab. Also known as a 'four-wheeler'.

Grow out, to At maturity young stock may exceed the height limit of his type and/or breed.

Groy/Groi A gipsy term for a horse.

Grullo An American colour description for a slate- or mouse-coloured horse, the most characteristic running into a blue. Nearly all grullos have barred legs and a dorsal stripe.

Grunting ('grunt to the stick') This occurs when, because of his breed (such as heavy draught), or lack of opportunity, a horse cannot be galloped for wind (q.v.). He is held by the head and a pretence is made to deal him a violent blow in the stomach with a stick. If of faulty wind, in its fright the horse will 'grunt to the stick'. If he makes no noise, soundness can be assumed. A hunter which grunts on landing over a fence may arouse suspicion. 'Grunting to the stick' is not universally accepted by the veterinary profession as evidence of respiratory unsoundness. (See **Bull**)

Guarantee See **Warranty**.

Guard Armed attendant on a mail coach (q.v.). On a road (stage) coach (q.v.), this term also applies to the footman or 'cad' (q.v.), whose main job was to apply the brake.

Guard rail A stout pole placed before an open ditch in racing jumps, to make the horse 'stand back' and spread himself.

Gudbrandsdal See **Dole Gudbrandsdal**.

Guideless pacing On 29 June 1903, at Whitegate Park, Blackpool, in a match against time, a mare called Lady R, with a flying start, guideless, paced, a mile (1.6 km) in 2 minutes and 14⅖ seconds.

Guide terrets Upright metal rings fastened into the top of the pad encircling the body of the wheelers in a team. Through them run the reins from the leading horse.

Guinea hunter Dealer's 'tout'. Intermediary between buyer and seller. Found in large numbers at Irish horse fairs, and mostly of the gipsy or tinker fraternities.

Guineas Money unit still used in racing and in the sale of horses. Equivalent to £1.10p in decimal coinage.

Guineas, the Colloquial name for the Two Thousand Guineas (q.v.) race.

Gulf Arab See **Shirazi**.

Gullet Lower end of a horse-collar.

Gullet plate Strengthening plate in the head of a saddle.

Gullet plate A device used in conjunction with a strap to prevent crib-biting.

Gut, twisted See **Colic**.

Gymkhana, mounted A contest consisting of one or more mounted events, the winning of which depends largely upon the skill of the rider and the agility and obedience of the horse or pony. Such events include musical chairs, bending, ball and bucket, potato race, etc.

Gypo horse A term used in some part of the country to describe a horse of whom one parent belongs to a heavy and the other to a light breed.

—H—

HB Half-bred Stud Book (q.v.).

Hd (racing) Head.

HH Popular abbreviation for the Hampshire Hunt.

hh Hands high. (See **Hand**; and **Height**)

HIS Hunters' Improvement Society (q.v.).

HOYS Horse of the Year Show (q.v.).

hp Horse power (q.v.).

Habit Side-saddle costume for a lady or girl.

Hack This is not an established breed but a recognised type – with the refinement of the riding horse – and not to be confused with the Hackney (q.v.) which is a harness horse. The name 'Hack' is essentially English, and of ancient origin. Show Hack winners are mostly Thoroughbreds or nearly so, and are required to be as perfect in conformation as possible, and to have impeccable manners. The ideal hack should have a small, very refined head, an elegant neck, a good, sloping shoulder, and should present an overall picture of the ultimate in elegance and grace. The action must be straight and smooth, and at the trot a floating, almost extravagant action is demanded. Under the rules of the British Show Hack and Cob Association, hacks are judged according to a scheme of marking which allocates 40% of the marks for conformation, presence, type, and action in-hand, and 60% for ride, training test, and manners.

Hack, ladies' A horse exceeding 14.2 hh (147.3 cm) but not exceeding 15.3 hh (160 cm), suitable for carrying a lady side-saddle.

Hack, large Exceeding 15 hh (152.4 cm) but not exceeding 15.3 hh (160 cm). To be ridden astride.

Hack, small Exceeding 14.2 hh (147.3 cm) but not exceeding 15 hh (152.4 cm). To be ridden astride.

Hack, to General term implying to go for a ride.

Hackamore (Western) (From the Spanish *jaquima*.) Generally a 'mechanical' bitless bridle. Cheekpieces of varying length with curb straps (not chains) are used to control the horse by exerting pressure on the nose, the poll and the chin groove. There are at least four types of hackamore in Western riding. The bosal hackamore derives its name from the bosal – a heavy braided rawhide noseband with a large adjustable knot known as the 'heel knot', which fits under the chin. It is a 'non-mechanical' hackamore and has a lightweight headpiece which may go over both ears or which may have a slit allowing it to fit over one ear only.

Hack bit A fancy cheek-curb bit.

Hack classes Competitions for the best Hack, held at all important horse shows (q.v.).

'Hackles up' A hound is said to have its 'hackles up' when it is angry. The hair along its back and the back of its neck stands on end, and its stern curves stiffly over its back. Hounds have their hackles up when they are close to their fox and running for blood.

'Hack on', to To ride one's own horse to a meet of hounds.

Hackney carriage A licenced carriage which plied for hire.

Hackney Horse The immediate ancestors of the Hackney horse were two famous trotting breeds of the eighteenth and nineteenth centuries – the Yorkshire Hackney and the Norfolk Roadster. Both breeds trace back through a horse known as The Original Shales, to the Darley Arabian (q.v.). The Original Shales was out of a mare described as a Hackney – the name possibly deriving from the French *haquenée*. The Yorkshire and the Norfolk breeds developed independently, the latter being a powerful, heavily-built cobby animal, and the former showing more quality. In time the two types merged to produce the spectacular showy trotting horse, the Hackney.

The spectacular trot shows free shoulder movement with high, ground-covering knee action, the foreleg being thrown well forward, not just up and down, with that slight pause which gives a peculiar grace of movement, the horse appearing to float over the ground. Action must be straight and true, with no dishing (q.v.), or throwing of hooves from side to side. Hackneys must possess a small convex head, a small muzzle, large eyes and small ears, a long, thick-set neck, powerful shoulders, low withers, a compact body, short legs, and compact, well-shaped feet. The most usual colours are dark brown, black, bay, and chestnut. The height varies between about 14.3-15.3 hh (149.9-160 cm).

Hackney Horse Society Established in 1883 to promote and improve the breeding of Hackney horses, Hackney ponies, harness and driving horses; to hold shows offering prizes in competition; and also to compile and publish Stud Books.

Hackney Pony Of more recent origin than the Hackney horse. It was developed during the second half of the nineteenth century by crossing Hackney stallions with carefully selected native pony mares. It stands up to 14 hh (142.2 cm) and shows the unique pony quality, together with the brilliant action of the Hackney horse.

Haemoglobin The red pigment in the

oxygen-carrying red blood cells (erythrocytes).

Haemoglobinuria See **Azoturia**.

Haemolytic disease/Jaundice A comparatively rare disease of the newborn (usually approximately 24-hours-old) foal. It is caused by destruction of the foal's red blood cells by antibodies in the mare's colostrum (q.v.). Symptoms include jaundice (yellowing) of the whites of the eyes and visible membranes, rapid pulse and respiration – especially on exertion – sleepiness, signs of severe anaemia (q.v.), and red urine. *Immediate* blood transfusion is required if the foal is to survive.

Haflinger A Tyrolean breed of mountain pony originating in the village of Haflinger in Southern Austria and produced by the crossing of Alpine heavy horse mares with Arab stallions. The principal modern stud is in Jenesien, where the ponies are turned out on Alpine pastures, thus enabling their native sure-footedness to develop to the full. The ponies stand up to 13.3 hh (139.7 cm), and are always palomino or chestnut with flaxen mane and tail. They are very thick-set, with plenty of bone and with a neat head showing a slightly dished profile. The head is carried close to the ground when climbing. The breed is still used on farms and as a pack pony, but its newest role is taking tourists on treks through the Tyrolean countryside. A number have been exported to Switzerland and Germany, and the Indian Army is about to replace its mules with Haflingers. There are a small number in Britain, and the Haflinger Society of Great Britain was founded in 1971. All Haflingers passed for registration are branded with the breed's emblem – the Edelweiss, Austria's native flower, with the letter 'H' in the centre.

Haggin Cup (USA) See **Tevis Cup**.

Hair/Feather The hair which all horses carry to a greater or lesser extent on their legs and heels. Shires and Clydesdales and some other heavy breeds have a profuse growth. The hair should be fine in texture, free from curl, and extending from the pastern almost to the back of the knee and hock. Light breeds have on the fetlocks a shorter growth of hair, which may be removed by pulling. Hair on the heel, which is a sign of cold blood, should never be cut.

'Hairies' A friendly name for the heavier breeds of horse and pony which show some hair around the fetlocks. A term of affection used by troops in World War I for Shire and similar horses.

'Hairy' A straggly high fence of the 'bullfinch' (q.v.) variety.

Half-bred A term loosely applied to a horse which is an admixture of breeds. It is also applied to a Thoroughbred horse not eligible for entry in the General Stud Book.

Half-Bred Stud Book (H-B Stud-Book) Compiled by Miss F. M. Prior, this illustrated book is a register of the produce of mares of winning blood in the female line who are not eligible for the General Stud Book. It contains the histories, pedigrees and racing performance of all the best-known half-bred families of racehorses. Published from 1914 until 1972, it has been superseded by the Non-Thoroughbred register compiled by Weatherbys.

Half-brothers and sisters See **Brothers and sisters**.

Half halt This has been described as 'the momentary collection of the horse in motion' (von Blixen-Finecke), and is used to increase the attention and balance of the riding horse. It is achieved by a scarcely visible, virtually simultaneous action of the rider's seat, legs and hands: the horse is driven forward with the seat, loins and legs but momentarily restrained by the hands; this is followed by a momentary release of rein pressure before restoring the original contact. The result is an increase in collection. See **Collected**.

Half-pass A movement on two tracks performed at the walk, trot or canter. The horse travels sideways and forwards, its head turned slightly towards the direction of movement, legs crossing, shoulders preceding haunches, in the oblique direction.

Half pirouette See **Pirouette**.

Half pirouette renversée See **Pirouette renversée**.

Half speed The usual pace of a horse doing fast work in training. It is rather more than half a horse's full speed, but the horse is not fully extended.

Half volte A figure consisting of a half circle of given radius and an oblique following it, entailing a change of hand. It may be performed on either one or two tracks (q.v.).

Hall, Harry (app. 1838-1886) Sporting artist well known for his faithful portraits of hunters and racehorses. He also painted shooting and coaching scenes, etc. In style he owed much to the influence of J. F. Herring, Snr. (q.v.).

Halt, the This is brought about by the rider maintaining impulsion through seat and leg pressure and eventually stopping the forward movement by the tactful restraining use of the hands on the reins.

Halter A hemp or cotton head (q.v.) for leading an unbitted horse or for tying a horse up in a stall. The best type is a Yorkshire halter which, unlike the normal adjustable pattern, does not tighten

Half-pass.

up on the head and is fitted with a cord throatlatch to prevent its being pulled across an eye. In the USA halters are usually of heavy leather with brass fittings.

Halter classes A term used in the USA and elsewhere (but not in Great Britain) for in-hand classes (q.v.).

Hame Detachable, plated, metal arm in cart-horse harness. The hames link the traces and the collar. (See **Neck collar**)

Hame-rein In cart-horse harness a short rein to which hames are attached. It covers the points of the hames, and is released when a horse is pulling a load up an incline, thereby giving him full freedom to stretch his neck.

Hame-strap A strap used for fastening the hames at the top, to keep them in position on the collar.

Ham-fisted See **Mutton-fisted**.

Hammer-cloth A cloth covering the driver's seat or box in a state or family coach.

Hamshackle, to To shackle a horse or cow with a rope or strap which connects the head with one of the forelegs.

Hamstring The tendon of the gastrocnemius muscle, which runs down the back of the second thigh to the point of the hock. Often referred to as the Achilles' tendon, it is the most hardworked in the horse's body.

Hand The measurement by which the height of a horse is reckoned. It equals 4 inches (10.16 cm). (See **Height**)

Hand gallop A fast, smooth canter in which a horse settles down at a pace which does not quite approach his fastest speed.

Hand horse Offside (q.v.) horse, or horse who is led in a postillion (q.v.) ridden pair.

Handicap (polo) Players are handicapped according to individual ability, the best players being accorded the highest handicap. The maximum is 10, the minimum is –2. In handicap games, the individual handicaps of the team members are added together and the lower total is subtracted from the higher to establish the number of goals 'start' conceded to the team with the lower handicap.

Handicap (racing) A race in which the weights to be carried by the horses are adjusted by the Handicapper for the purpose of equalising their chances of winning.

Handicapper A Jockey Club official who equates the weights to be carried by horses in races for the purpose of equalising their chances of winning. He must attend the meeting to which he is appointed.

Handiness The ability of a horse to turn quickly and willingly.

Handled Said of a young horse which has been haltered and led before breaking.

Handley Cross The immortal story by R. S. Surtees, published in 1843, relating the adventures and misadventures of John Jorrocks, a grocer, as Master of the Handley Cross Hunt in the 1830s. (See **Surtees, Robert Smith**)

Handling (foals) All foals should be handled from their earliest days, when they will grow up less shy and timid. They should be led from both sides, and should be accustomed to having their feet picked up.

Handling from the near-side Custom or habit causes practically every horseman to perform ninety per cent of his tasks from the near-side, thus giving the horse a left-handed complex. The wise horseman will do everything possible from both sides, including mounting and dismounting. When leading a horse through traffic, the safest way is to keep to the left side of the road, therefore the horse must be taught to lead comfortably from the offside.

Hand-rubbing Most useful for reducing fullness of the legs, as well as for warming when cold, or to alleviate pain. When rubbing, follow the direction of the hair of the coat.

Hands, good Hands which rely on no greater strength than that of the fingers, which are light and which know how to give and take the pull of the horse on the bit. It is essential for the true horseman to possess good hands and a strong seat.

Hand sale Where the outstretched hand of the person making the offer is struck by the hand of the one accepting it on the sale of the horse.

Handy hunter class Often included, though not officially recognised, in many smaller shows. Horses prove their obedience and handiness with obstacles that include hunting-type jumps, gates to be opened and shut, slip rails removed, etc. Judging is on performance and time, not conformation.

Hanging off An old coaching term used when a horse hangs away from his pair.

'Hang up your bars' An old road term applied to someone who gives up coaching.

Hanoverian/Hannoverian The first records of this German warmblood breed date back to 1714, King George I, who was also Elector of Hanover, sent Thoroughbred horses from England to improve the mares in German studs which were said to be descended from the Great Horse of the Middle Ages. In 1735, King George II founded a stud at Celle with some Holstein stallions of mixed Neapolitan and Andalusian blood. During the next thirty years these stallions produced an all-purpose animal to work on the land, under saddle, and in harness, until further Thoroughbred blood was introduced, resulting in a lighter breed. The stud suffered varying fortunes in the Napoleonic and two World Wars, but the breed still remains at Celle, where the principal aim is the production of top quality competition riding horses.

Hanoverians are renowned as show jumpers (e.g. the Olympic gold medallist Warwick Rex and the 1974 World Champion, Simona). They also excel in dressage, producing outstanding horses such as Slibowitz and Woyceck. The breed has also been used to produce Westphalian warmbloods which, in effect, are Hanoverians bred in Westphalia, particularly at Warendorf (q.v.).

Hanoverians stand up to 16.2 hh (165

cm), are of good riding horse conformation with powerful quarters, and an energetic ground-covering action.

Hanoverian bit Any bit of any design which has a double-jointed and ported mouth and which is not attached to cheeks.

Hanoverian mouth A bit, either curb, or more usually pelham, which has a fairly high port jointed to the mouthpiece on either side. The mouthpiece has metal rollers set round it.

Hansom A two-wheeled vehicle on which the driver is seated high up at the back. Originally a huge clumsy carriage it was designed in 1834 by J. A. Hansom, an architect. Its improved, more familiar shape is owed to a Mr J. Chapman. Used extensively as a public cab for hire, the Hansom was known as 'the gondola of London'.

Haras French word meaning a stud for breeding horses.

Harbourer (stag hunting) Through a great knowledge of venery and the habits of the stag, the Harbourer is appointed to advise the Master where a warrantable stag is likely to be found on the day of the hunt. By the size and shape of the slots (q.v.) of the stag, and by other signs, he is able to tell the probable age and weight of the quarry and where it may be found.

'Hard and fast' A term used by American cowboys to denote the double half-hitching of the rope round the saddle-horn.

Hardel, to To couple hounds. An old term no longer in use.

'Hark-to' Huntsman's cry calling a hound's attention to that of another hound who is speaking (acknowledging the scent). Also 'hark-back' and 'hark-forward'.

Harness A comprehensive term given to the bridle, collar, pad, etc., for a driven horse. There are different types for use with various vehicles. It is not applicable to riding horses.

Harness, black A trade term applied only to harness used on horses other than for riding.

Harness, brown A trade term for harness used on the ridden horse.

Harness classes Show classes generally embracing open driving, Hackney, Utility, Trade (Light and Heavy), and Concours d'Elégance.

Harras An Old English collective term for horses (French = stud).

Harriers A pack of hounds which hunts hares, followed by a mounted field.

Harry Highover's pelham An early and once popular bit in which bridoon mouths were individually attached to the 2-inch (5 cm) port of a curb bit.

Hart, stag A male deer at five years.

Hartwell pelham Now refers to a ported mouthpiece instead of the more usual mullen mouth. Older patterns had a bent mouthpiece.

Hat guard String of braid attached to the ring at the back of the brim of a riding hat and also to the loop inside the coat collar band. Rarely used nowadays.

Hausman gag A metal gag used for veterinary purposes.

Haute École See **High School**; and **Circus horses**.

Havana colour See **Tanning**.

Haw The third eyelid or nictitating membrane.

Hawick Common Riding A picturesque ceremony held in Scotland during the first full week in June, lasting several days. The date of origin is unknown, but the principal event, 'Cornet's Chase', re-enacts the capture of a standard from the English by the men of Hawick in 1514. The Cornet, a bachelor, is the standard-bearer; the chase a gallop by townsmen up the steep slope of Vertish Hill. Afterwards they ride the marches of the common to mark the bounds.

Hawkins, Jeremiah (1763-1835) An eccentric sportsman, born in Gloucestershire, and known as the 'Gloucestershire Mytton'. He was immortalised a century or so ago by his portrait on half the ale jugs in the country. Passionately devoted to hunting, Jerry Hawkins possessed amazing powers of endurance and was in the habit of swimming the river Severn on his horse when returning from a hunt. 'Nimrod' records that there was a ludicrous naïvety about him and that he was possessed of much goodness of heart.

Hay Young grass that has been cut before it has come into full flower, and dried in the field. (See also **Grass, dried**). It forms the staple bulk food of stabled horses, and a supplementary food for others. It contains between 4 to 7% protein in Britain, and 8 to 16% in the USA – depending on the quality – but more if it contains lucerne (alfalfa, q.v.). In poor hay, where the protein content is low, digestibility is also low, resulting in even less protein for the animal. The qualities of good hay are: (1) a sweet, not musty, smell. (2) A greenish to brownish colour, not colourless or yellow. (3) A sweet, not bitter, taste. (4) It should be crisp to the touch. (5) It should be clean, and without dust or mould. (6) It should contain good grasses such as cocksfoot, meadow fescue, rye grass, rough and smooth stalked meadow grass, timothy, etc. (7) There should be an absence of poor grasses, such as couch, bents, false oat and quaking grasses. (8) Weeds, particularly poisonous ones such as ragwort, should not be present.

MEADOW HAY is cut from permanent pasture which is never ploughed. It varies in quality and composition.

SEED OR MIXTURE HAY is cut from specially sown fields containing a variety of selected grasses or a single grass. It is usually free from weeds, of high quality, and clean.

Hay may also contain plants such as lucerne which are sometimes erroneously included under the general heading of 'grasses' used in hay-making, but do not belong to the grass family. Hay less than six months old (minimum) should not be fed as it is indigestible.

Hay, dust-free An alternative to hay, made from grass which is cut when at its nutritional optimum and baled in air-tight bags when half-dry – usually about 36 hours after cutting. This treatment dramatically reduces the amount of dust and mould found in ordinary hay, which can produce allergic reactions in some horses. It also ensures that approximately 95% of the feeding value of the grass is retained.

Hay, mowburnt Hay of a dark brown or yellow colour which has deteriorated due to over-heating – caused by baling before the hay is fully dry.

Hayes, Captain Matthew Horace (1842-1904) Qualified as a veterinary surgeon at New Edinburgh Veterinary College in 1883 and took his Fellowship in 1891. He wrote extensively on horse subjects, and his *The Points of the Horse* and *Veterinary Notes for Horse Owners* achieved great popularity.

Hay-net A thick, corded net made of jute or polypropylene; if of jute, it is often tarred. A hay-net is an economical

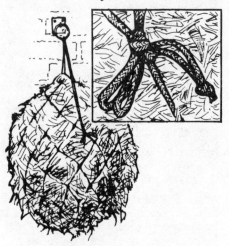

Hay-net and quick-release knot.

method of feeding hay, as it cannot be thrown about or soiled. The net must be tied high enough to prevent the horse's legs becoming entangled in it.

Hay rack See under **Rack, hay**.

Hay tea A very useful drink for a sick horse. A stable bucket is three-parts filled with the best hay available, topped up with boiling water, covered, and left to soak. When cold, the water is drained off and given as a drink.

Hazing-horse A cowboy term for a horse that is engaged in bulldogging (q.v.). The assisting rider uses it to keep the steer in a line so that the competing rider can jump on to the back of the steer.

Head A trade term for a leather or hemp headcollar or head stall. (See **Halter**)

Head The technical name for the hood of a carriage.

Head (distance) When a horse wins a race by a head it means that the length of its head was in front of the second horse. (See **Length**)

Head, bridle See **Headpiece (of bridle)**.

Head-cap See **Hood**.

Head carriage The natural position of the head and neck expected of a horse of true conformation.

Headcollar/Head stall A leather head (q.v.) used for leading an unbitted horse or for tying up a horse in a stable or stall.

Leather headcollar.

It consists of a noseband, cheekpieces, headpiece, and back strap, joined by metal rings or squares, and fastened by buckles attached to the headpiece. It is made of leather or nylon.

Headcollar rope A rope attached to the headcollar and running through a ring

in the manger. The other end is fixed, preferably, to a log of lignum vitae wood so that the rope may not become slack or get under the horse's legs. Rope or leather lines are superior to chains, as the noise of the latter running through rings disturbs other horses. Covering the rope generously with soap when first used will treble its life. The term is also applied to a rope shank with a tarred 'eye' which is used as a lead from a headcollar or for tying up.

Headed Said of a fox (or other quarry) which has seen or heard someone or something causing it to deviate from its original line.

Head halter (USA) See **Halter**.

Head lad In a racing stable the head lad is responsible for stable management, morning work, feeding, minor ailments, etc. The word 'lad' is no indication of age, as the nature and importance of the work involved necessitates the appointment of men of considerable and long experience.

Headland The uncultivated edge of a ploughed field, or the drier rim (close to the hedge) of a wet grass field.

Head lap See **Hood**.

Head of the saddle, the The front arch.

Headpiece (of bridle) That part of the bridle to which are attached the cheekpieces and the throatlatch (and the browband, if worn). When the bridle is on the horse, the headpiece fits over the top of the head behind the ears.

Head shy A term for a horse who will not allow his head to be handled or his bridle put on. This is usually when a horse has been subjected to rough treatment.

Head stall See **Headcollar**.

'Heads up' Said of hounds which are not feeling for the scent.

Head terrets On carriage horses, these originally were fixed upright metal rings between the wheelers' ears through which the leaders' reins ran. Now the rings more generally are on the outside of the wheelers' bridles. The objection to head terrets is that too much pressure is put on the poll (head) of the wheeler, and when the horse throws his head up, he interferes with the leader.

Head to the wall See **Travers**.

Health, indications of Signs of good health are head erect and alert, eyes bright, ears pricked, good appetite, well-furnished body with the skin supple and not tightly stretched, droppings fairly firm and not slimy.

Heart room A term of commendation indicating depth through a horse's girth, combined with a broad and open chest ('deep through the girth' is also used).

Heart sounds There are two normal sounds – the first when the heart muscle is contracting (*systole*), and the second when it is starting to relax and go into *diastole*. The former (termed 'lubb'), is low-pitched; the latter ('dupp') is higher pitched. These sounds may be heard by applying a stethoscope against the chest wall at the point of the elbow. They are made as a result of the closure of the heart valves. 'Lubb' is related to the closing of the main ventricular valves to prevent blood flowing back into the two atria. 'Dupp' is associated with the closing of the aortic and pulmonary artery valves at the end of systole. Any abnormality in heart-sound may indicate a problem in the heart, or reflect such things as anaemia and dehydration.

Heat (on or in) Said of a mare or filly when in condition to breed.

Heat treatment Application of heat in one of three ways – conductive, radiant, or conversive:
CONDUCTIVE is by direct application; e.g. hot poultices, hot-water bottle, etc.
RADIANT is by means of infra-red lamp.
CONVERSIVE is by high frequency electrical energy which generates heat in the tissues.

Heaves A term describing respiratory difficulty, when a horse appears to heave twice on exhalation; or, more severely, the chest appears to heave in order to force air in and out of congested airways. (See **Broken wind**)

Heavy horse Any one of the big draught horse varieties.

Heavy top Coarse neck, shoulders and light-boned limbs out of proportion to the size of the horse.

Heel (hunting) When hounds run the line of a fox in the reverse direction to which it was going. 'Running heel' or 'heel way'.

Heel boot A leather boot cupped over a horse's heel to protect it against a blow from a hind toe.

Heel-bug A skin condition affecting the heel and pastern, and sometimes the face and muzzle. The cause is infection in autumn by the harvest mite, *Trombicula autumnalis*. It appears in certain locations which may carry the infection, or possibly set up an allergy. In some instances the cases are complicated by secondary infection. The fact that a number of horses who are crowded together in a muddy lane or gateway will sometimes contract the disease suggests the possibility of contagion. White heels and white horses appear more susceptible, but it is uncertain whether this is due to photo-sensitisation or because white heels are more often washed with soap and water.

Heels The lower back parts of the wall of the hoof, together with the two soft bulb-like areas either side of the mid-line at the back of the foot.

Heels, contracted Heels which are too narrow. A condition usually caused by excessive paring of the frog – which becomes dry and not in contact with the ground – or of the bars and heels, leaving the toe too long. Reduction of the frog by thrush (q.v.) is another cause. It can be alleviated by increasing pressure on the frog by use of T or bar shoes, or by keeping the toe short.

Heels, cracked An inflamed area of the heel, with raw cracks often extending from one side of the heel to the other. The heel area may become scaly, and small blisters/vesicles may form, then rupture, causing the cracks. The horse is lame, tending to go on its toes. The condition is caused by bad stable management – allowing the horse to stand on wet bedding, or failing to dry the legs properly after washing or exercise. It can be prevented by better management, and application of Vaseline to heels before going out in wet conditions. (See also **Mud fever**)

Heels, opening up of Faulty farriery, in which the bars of the foot are cut out to a greater or lesser degree, to make the foot appear wider. This removes an important part of the anti-concussion mechanism of the foot and causes contraction.

Height The height of a horse in Britain is measured in hands and inches – one hand equals 4 ins (10.16 cm). See **Joint measurement scheme**.

'Hell-for-leather' To ride a horse 'all-out', pressed to extremes. The expression may derive from a state of 'all of a lather'.

Hemp The best halters are made of hemp, a natural plant fibre. Hemp is also used for good quality self-coloured night rollers, and by saddlers for sewing.

Henderson, Charles Cooper (1803-1877) Born in Chertsey, Surrey. A painter of coaching and harness pictures in oils and watercolours. Particularly successful with mail coach scenes at night, which combined animation and accuracy.

Hengest A mediaeval term for a horse, usually a gelding.

Henry VIII, King (1491-1547) A good horseman, keenly interested in hunting and an indefatigable and adept performer at the joust. He introduced legislation to improve the size and stamina of the native horses. He also imported Italian and Spanish breeding stock and established successful studs in different parts of the country (e.g. Malmesbury).

Hereditary diseases Serious conditions or ailments which a veterinary surgeon is normally asked to certify that a prospective purchase is free from, namely: under- and over-shot mouth, cryptorchidism, stringhalt, shivering, cataracts, upward fixation of the patella, and ring-bone.

Herring, John Frederick, Snr (1795-1865) Probably the most prolific of all painters of racehorses and famous for portraits of thirty-three consecutive winners of the St Leger and eighteen of the Derby. In his youth he was a stage-coachman on the Doncaster-Halifax route and was self-taught as an artist before studying with Abraham Cooper (q.v.). Though his pictures of Thoroughbreds tended to be static and lifeless, he attained great popularity and success. He lived in Doncaster, Newmarket, and London before retiring to Tonbridge, where he painted attractive farmyard scenes notable for their precise detail. His sons, John Frederick, Jnr, Charles, and Ben, also painted horses and sporting scenes; their work, though less able, is sometimes confused with that of their father.

Herring-gutted Said of a horse which has a mean, weedy body, flat-sided and running upwards sharply from the girth to the quarters (q.v.).

Hickstead Site of the All-England Jumping Course, established by Douglas Bunn in West Sussex in 1960. Venue of the British Jumping Derby, staged over a long sixteen-fence course, including some permanent obstacles and the imposing 10ft (3m) Derby Bank down the near-vertical face of which competitors must ride.

Hidebound The result of indigestion, worms, or some other cause through which horses become out of condition. The coat 'stares', the skin becomes tight over the ribs, and there are general signs of malnutrition.

High blowing A very distinctive sound heard sometimes at the gallop. It is often incorrectly suspected as a defect in wind, but actually due to fast movement causing excessive flapping of the false nostril (q.v.). Unlike 'roaring' (see under **Roarer**), it disappears as speed is increased. Sometimes referred to as 'cracking the nostrils' it is considered an asset by South American gauchos as denoting a horse of endurance.

Highflyer phaeton An exaggeratedly high-hung phaeton, popular in Regency days.

High jump record Set in 1949 by Captain Alberto Larraguibel of Chile, on Huaso, who jumped 8 ft 1½ ins (2.47 m) at Vina dé Mar (Chile). The British record is held by Nick Skelton and Lastic, who jumped 7 ft 7⁵⁄₁₆ ins (2.32 m) at Olympia, London, in 1978.

Highland Pony One of the strongest and heaviest of the British Mountain and Moorland breeds. It has been bred in the Highlands and Islands of Scotland for centuries, and in the course of its history has been infused with Arabian, American Trotting Horse, Clydesdale, and Norwegian blood. Until comparatively recently, the breed was divided into two types – the Western Isles pony, of lighter build and standing up to about 14 hh (142.2 cm), and the heavier mainland type, standing up to 14.2 hh (147.3 cm). Although the two types still exist to a certain extent, they are no longer recognised by the Highland Pony Society.

The breed is noted for its unusual colours, particularly the various shades of dun – yellow, golden, mouse, cream, and fox – in addition to the usual greys, browns and blacks. The original shade is believed to be yellow dun. Most ponies carry one or more of the so-called 'primitive features', which include the distinctive dorsal eel stripe and zebra markings on the inside of the legs – an indication of great antiquity.

Highland ponies have been used as pack animals, in harness, and under saddle. Their best-known use is perhaps in deer-stalking, where they carry sportsmen up into the hills, and then the shot stag (weighing up to 16 stone/101 kg) down. They are also used for pony trekking. Highland ponies are extremely sturdily built, with good bone, and are noted for the length and profusion of their manes, tails, and forelocks.

Highland Pony Society Founded in 1923 to promote the general interests of the breeders and owners of Highland Ponies, which are registered in their own Stud Book. The Society runs a performance competition annually.

High School (Haute École) The classical art of riding, in accordance with traditions transmitted by the great equestrian masters of the past, which today are still preserved and practised to the highest perfection by the Spanish Riding School, Vienna, and the Cadre Noir, Saumur, France (qq.v.). Specifically, the term High School refers to the more advanced movements of classical riding. See **Airs, artificial**; and **High School horse** (below).

High School horse One trained in accordance with the principles of the classical art of riding, and therefore able to perform the High School 'airs', such as piaffe, levade, courbette, capriole, etc. (qq.v.).

High-tailing Term for horses who gallop away with tails held high.

Highways and Locomotives (Amendment) Act 1878, Sec.26 This Act called for the use of a skidpan, slipper or shoe to be placed under the wheel of a wagon, wain, cart, or carriage when descending a hill.

Hind Female red deer.

Hind hunting See **Hunting seasons**.

Hindquarters See **Quarters**.

Hinny The progeny of a horse and a she-ass. Also called a 'genet', 'jennet' or bardot (qq.v.).

Hip, point of The bony prominence which lies a hand's breadth behind the last rib of a horse. In reality it is the external tuberosity of the pelvis and has no connection with the true hips or hip joint. (See **Hips, ragged**)

Hip down A term applied to the permanent result of fracture of the angle of the haunch, the most prominent projection of the pelvis, which can occur if the bone comes in contact with a protrusion such as a gate or doorpost.

Hipparchikos (Greek for 'The Cavalry Commander'). The title of a work produced about 365 BC by Xenophon (q.v.) explaining his duties and training. It is the earliest known book dealing solely with cavalry training.

Hipparion An early Pliocene mammal. In the theory of evolution is placed as one of the early ancestors of the horse. (**See Evolution**)

Hippike The *Treatise on Horsemanship* written by Xenophon (q.v.) in 365 BC 'to explain, for the benefit of our younger friends, what we conceive to be the most correct method of dealing with horses.' This work remains a classic in basic principles.

Hippocampus The sea horse.

Hippodame Obsolete term for a horse-tamer.

Hippodrome The Greek name for a race-course for horses and chariots.

Hippogriff A fabulous creature like the griffin, with the hindquarters of a horse.

Hippoid An animal resembling, or allied to, the horse.

Hippolith A concretion found in the intestines of a horse.

Hippological Hethica Earliest-known book on the horse (*c.* fourteenth century BC), written on clay tablets by Kikkuli of Mitanni, an expert trainer of chariot horses.

Hippology The study of horses.

Hippomanes Rubber-like oval or rectangular structure, approximately 1½ ins (38 mm) thick, found in placental fluid. It may be grey, brown or yellow/white, and consists of cells and salts. Its true function is unknown, but it is alleged to be an aphrodisiac. It is also known as 'foal-lap', and is sometimes found on the floor after a mare has foaled.

Hippopathology The science of veterinary surgery.

Hippophagy The act of feeding on horse flesh.

Hippophile A lover of horses.

Hippophobia A fear of horses.

Hippotherapy The use of riding as a therapy for the mentally or physically handicapped.

Hippotomy The anatomy or dissection of a horse.

Hips, ragged A term given to the points of the horse's hips when they are very prominent.

Hip straps Straps which pass over the rump of a cart horse to carry the breeching (q.v.).

Hireling A horse let out on hire.

Histamine A chemical substance released into the bloodstream in allergic reactions: e.g. in broken wind, where it causes small air tubules to constrict.

'Hit and hurry' competition (show jumping) Each competitor jumps the course in correct order for one minute. Three points are scored for each obstacle cleared and one point for every obstacle knocked down.

Hitchcock gag A neat head raiser consisting of a slip head with pulleys below the ears to which is attached a rounded leather rein controlled by the rider, to put pressure on the corners of the mouth. As with any form of gag and bit it has a strong controlling influence.

Hitch up, to To harness a horse or horses for driving (colloquial).

'Hit the line' When a hound strikes the line of the hunted fox, it is said to hit the line.

Hobbles These are made of rope, leather bound where they come into contact with the horse. The type used when covering mares consist of a loop around the neck, the ends passing between the forelegs to the hind pasterns, to which they are secured. There is also a pattern of service hobbles made from cotton rope or buffalo hide where a strap, passing through the forelegs and encircling the mare's neck, is fastened to the hind hobbles. This pattern can be fitted with a quick-release device. Hobbles to prevent horses from straying resemble hound couples, fastening the forelegs together. For surgical operations, etc. there are patterns for securing all four legs.

Hobby A description, originally given to a strong, active, rather small type of horse in the twelfth century, later applied to riding horses and hacks. It is still in use in some parts of Ireland.

Hobby-horse A stick adorned with the head of a horse, on which children used to 'ride'. (One of the chief parts played in the ancient Morris-dance.)

Hobday, Sir Frederick, FRCVS (1870-1939) A distinguished veterinary surgeon. Educated at Burton Grammar School and the Royal Veterinary College,

London. He served with the Royal Army Veterinary Corps in Italy and France from 1915 to 1918, was twice mentioned in despatches, and was awarded the CMG. He was principal and Dean of the Royal Veterinary College from 1927 to 1937, during the period of rebuilding, for which he was largely instrumental in raising funds. He was also the Royal Veterinary Surgeon to King George V and was knighted in 1933. He carried out pioneer work in veterinary anaesthetics, canine surgery, and the operation for the relief of roaring in horses, with which his name is associated. He was also the author of several surgical books.

Hobdayed An operation (named after its inventor, Sir Frederick Hobday) to relieve roaring/whistling when this is caused by the paralysis of muscles controlling the larynx. The operation is intended to allow a free passage of air into the lungs by attempting, through surgery, to get the vocal folds to adhere to the side of the larynx, thus preventing the paralysed chord from being sucked into the airway on inspiration. See also **Tracheotomy**.

Hobson's choice Tobias Hobson was an innkeeper, horse-dealer, and carrier in Cambridge at the turn of the sixteenth century. Whichever horse a customer tried to choose he invariably ended up with the next one in line, as fixed by Hobson. The phrase 'Hobson's choice' thus became a by-word for no choice at all.

Hock The joint lying between the second thigh and hind cannon, corresponding with the human ankle. It is the hardest-worked joint in the horse's body, and the most ingeniously constructed. It has two principal levers, the first being formed by the prolongation of the os calcis, equivalent to the human heel, which enables the gastrocnemius muscles to flex the hocks so violently that over half a ton of equine body can be propelled over a fence and for some distance through the air. The second lever works on the pulley principle; the doubly grooved astragalus (the uppermost of the two rows of bones) revolving around the matching grooves and ridges on the lower end of the tibia. It

is the extreme flexibility of the hock joints which enables the horse to change the position of the centre of gravity within the body and to maintain balance at all gaits.

Hock boots Boots which fit over the hock to protect against knocking in the box or when travelling.

Hock boot.

Hock, capped A similar swelling to capped elbow, but on the point of the hock, caused by bruising. It can be prevented

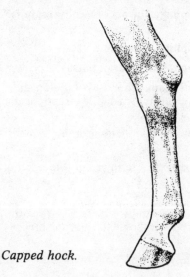

Capped hock.

by wearing a hock boot (q.v.), or by bedding on thick sawdust or peat. See also **Elbow, capped**; **Hock boots**.

Hock, sprung A swelling at the back of the hock caused by stress and concussion and resulting in lameness.

Hocks, cow Hocks which turn inwards at the points, as in a cow.

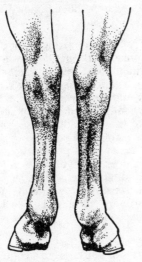

Cow hocks.

Hocks, curby An expression indicating hocks affected by curb trouble, or ones shaped so that they are liable to be sprained and thus spring a curb. False curbs are present when the head of the inner splint bone (small metatarsal) is larger than normal, causing the appearance of a curb.

Hocks, sickle Bent and weak-looking hocks which somewhat resemble a drawn-out sickle in shape.

'Hocks, well-let-down' A greatly prized item of conformation. The closer to the ground that the hocks are (if unblemished), the better, as it implies short cannon bones. The cannon bones of the hindlegs are termed 'hind shanks', or 'shannon' bones.

Hog-back See **Roach-back**.

Hogged mane A term used where the mane has been wholly removed.

Hog's back A timber jump with the cen-

tre pole higher than those on the take-off and landing sides.

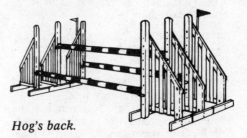

Hog's back.

Hog-tied An American term for a horse which has all four feet tied to prevent it from rising.

'Hoick'/'Huick' A hunting cheer, pronounced 'hike', meaning 'hark'.

'Hoick holloa' A cheer, pronounced 'hike holler', drawing hounds, or the huntsman's attention, to a holloa.

Hold, a Said of a covert in which a fox lies.

Hold, to When a huntsman makes a cast, he is said to 'hold hounds round'.

Holding A term which indicates that the 'going' (q.v.) is soft or heavy. In hunting it is usually described as 'deep'.

Hold-up, to To prevent foxes leaving a covert.

Holiday, Gilbert Joseph (1879-1937) Studied at the Royal Academy schools and became a talented sporting artist.

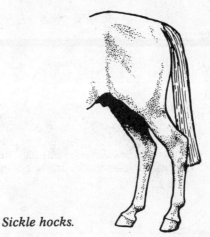

Sickle hocks.

His subjects included hunting, polo and military scenes. After a fall with the Woolwich Drag he was forced to work from a wheelchair.

'Holloa' A high, rousing, hunting cry given by someone who has viewed a fox. Pronounced 'holler'.

Holstein One of the oldest-established breeds of German warmbloods, bred in the Schleswig-Holstein region at least as early as the seventeenth century, by putting local native mares, descended from the Great Horses, to Andalusian and Oriental stallions. With the decline in the need for extreme weight-carrying war-horses and the increased need for harness animals, infusions of Yorkshire Coach Horse and Cleveland Bay blood were made in the nineteenth century, producing a handsome, high-stepping carriage horse. Following the more recent demand for riding horses, Thoroughbred blood was introduced to produce a handsome, very scopey and lighter horse, particularly suitable for competitive equestrian sports. In the 1976 Olympics, Holstein horses won individual gold and bronze medals and team silver medals in show jumping, horse trials, and dressage. Famous examples of the breed include the great show jumper Meteor, and the dressage horse Granat. Holsteins average between 16 hh (162.6 cm) and 17hh (170 cm), and resemble a quality hunter, with plenty of bone and substance. The most usual colour is bay with black points.

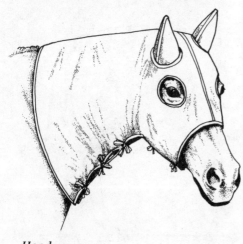

Hood.

Home-straight The run-in to the finishing post on a racecourse.

Hood A cloth covering for the head, ears and neck, used in cold weather. For wet weather a waterproof material is used. Known also as head-cap and head lap. Since the introduction of starting stalls on racecourses, hoods have been used on horses which are reluctant to enter the stalls. They are removed immediately the horse is in the stall.

Hoof The horny covering of the sensitive foot, from the coronet downwards. It is a continuation of the skin and contains within it a variety of structures. These are divided into two headings: *the external foot or hoof*, derived from the superficial layers of the skin and consisting of the wall, frog, sole and periople (qq.v.), and *the inner or sensitive layers*, derived from the deep layers of the skin (corium) and including the sensitive sole, sensitive laminae, sensitive frog, and the perioplic and coronary coria (qq.v.). The hoof, although continually growing, is dead matter.

Hoof, bars of The bars are a continuation of the wall of the hoof at the heels, where the wall turns inwards on each side of the frog, forming the bars. They continue towards the point of the frog, until about half-way, where they become lost in the sole. Their function is to strengthen the heels and to prevent contraction.

Hoof, bearing surface of The surface of the hoof which is in contact with the ground. When shoeing, the farrier prepares a level bearing surface for the shoe by rasping away excess horn. See **Shoeing**.

Hoof, coria of The sensitive and modified part of the deeper layers of the skin, containing blood vessels and nerves, and providing nutrition to the wall. There are both perioplic and coronary coria, the latter situated in the coronary groove.

Hoof, coronary groove/cavity of This runs around the top of the inner side of the wall to a depth of about ½ in. (12.7 mm) or a little more. The coronary band or cushion fits into it. Examination with a magnifying glass will reveal in this cavity a very large number of tiny holes – where the horn tubes of the wall begin.

Hoof, frog of The frog is the wedge-shaped mass of rubber-like horn situated between the heels, and normally it should contain about 42% moisture. Its softness is due to this high percentage of moisture, while its tough, rubber-like qualities are derived from the fatty frog or plantar cushion situated above and forming the bulbs of the heels. The functions of the frog, when allowed to come into play, are: (a) to grip the ground and prevent slipping; (b) to minimise concussion; (c) to assist expansion and prevent contraction of the hoof; (d) to help to carry the weight of the horse; (e) to promote (in conjunction with the lateral cartilages) a healthy and natural supply of blood to the foot.

Hoof, horny laminae of These are thin, flat plates of horn standing out at right angles from the anterior or inside surface of the wall of the hoof. They inter-lock with the sensitive laminae (thin fleshy vascular leaves) which cover the pedal bone and the lateral cartilages, forming a secure union of the hoof to the sensitive laminae.

Hoof, periople of The periople is a thin, varnish-like horn secreted by the perioplic ring, which is situated around the extreme upper border of the coronary cushion. The periople can be seen very plainly when distended with moisture. Its function is to protect the young horn of the wall, and to prevent undue evaporation of moisture from the wall. It also joins the skin with the horn of the wall.

Hoof, sole of The sole is composed of horn, but the horn tubes assume a more irregular wavy line than they do in the wall. The sole is about ⅜ in. (9.5 mm) thick, and contains about 36% of moisture. It acts as the floor of the foot and exists chiefly for protective purposes. It should be arched in shape, or when the foot is picked up should be seen to be somewhat hollow or concave; this gives greater strength and better clearance from the ground.

Hoof, wall of Generally speaking the wall grows from the coronary band or cushion; strictly speaking it does, excepting the laminal sheath, or innermost section, of the wall, which is secreted by the sensitive laminae. This is not quite the hard, solid substance it appears to be, but is really composed of three kinds of horn: (a) A mass of hair-like tubes called 'tubular horn' – all of these very fine tubes are attached to and grow from the papillae (cone-like points) of the coronary band or cushion. (b) An inter-tubular horn, also secreted by the coronary cushion, which is a glutinous horn substance cementing the horn tubes into the solid-looking mass we usually see. (c) The intra-tubular or cellular horn whose chief function appears to be as a conveyor of moisture.

The average thickness of the wall is about ½ in. (12.7 mm), thickest at the toe, thinner towards the heel. It should contain about 16-24% moisture; part of this natural moisture is derived from the blood and part by absorption from the soil, and therefore much depends upon the conditions under which the horse is kept. Conditions also affect the rate of growth, but roughly it may be said to take about 9 to 12 months for a new wall to grow from coronet to toe (ground surface).

Hoof, white line of This is a soft horn containing about 50% moisture and forms the connection of the sole with the wall. It denotes the exact thickness of the wall, and can be regarded as a guide for the farrier: nails can enter the white line, but on *no account* must they penetrate beyond it. In removing overgrowth, or in preparing the foot for the new shoe, the white line should not be seen too clearly, if at all. If it does show too much, the foot can be regarded as over-dressed, or over-lowered, and in that state grave risk is being run of tenderness, or even actual lameness.

Hoof oil A ready-mixed preparation of oil to enhance the appearance of the hoof and/or to prevent brittleness. Neatsfoot oil is used to prevent brittleness in white or light-coloured hooves.

Hoof-pick An implement for removing dirt, stones, nails, etc., from the hoof.

Metal hoof-pick (above) and plastic handled hoof-pick cum brush.

Hook fastening See **Stud-fastening**.

Hook-up stirrup leathers See **Extension stirrup leathers**.

Hooves, brittle The causes are neglect of the feet, mutilation in shoeing, or an hereditary disposition to grow poor horn. The use of biotin as a feed additive helps to cure this problem.

Hopples 'Straps' of leather in the racing harness of a pacer. They consist of loops on each leg, joined so as to allow adjustments to the correct length from front to hindleg, and buckled by further straps on to the strap from the crupper to the saddle pad. In addition, a very thin breastcollar is worn, the straps of which buckle on to the loops encircling each front leg. The four loops compel the horse to move at a lateral gait only. They should hang from 3-4 ins (7.5-10 cm) above the hocks and the knees.

Horn The outer surface of the hoof. It is also known as the 'wall'. See **Hoof, wall of**.

Horn, coaching The original horn used on mail coaches was issued by the Post Office. It was made of tin and was 3 ft (91.4 cm) long (hence the expression 'yard of tin'). As mail guards took great pride in their horn-blowing, they usually provided their own horns which were made of either copper or brass to produce a softer tone. Apart from playing tunes, there were special calls warning of the coach's approach, and signals such as 'Clear the road', 'Coming by', etc. Guards on road coaches, as well as the grooms on private drags, used these signals and tunes. See **Three feet of tin; Yard of tin**.

Horn, hunting Usually made of copper, with a nickel or silver mouthpiece, although some are made entirely of silver. The hunting horn is 9-10 ins (20-25.5 cm) long, according to the maker. The huntsman indicates many of his directions to the hounds through his horn, using a combination of different notes or blasts.

Horn, saddle See **Saddle horn**.

Horn basket A basket or leather case on a coach for the guard's horn, umbrellas, etc.

Horn case An open-end leather case fastened to the front of the saddle, to carry a hunting horn.

Horn tumour (keratoma) A lump which appears on the inner side of the hoof wall, most frequently in the toe region, and which presses upon the sensitive laminae covering the coffin bone. Usually it is cone-shaped, and consists of hard, dense horn. The afflicted animal tends to go on its heels. Veterinary attention is necessary.

Horse, biggest Believed to be a Belgian Draught horse bred in America, standing 19.2 hh (195 cm) and weighing 3,200 lb (1450 kg). It died in 1948.

Horse, to To provide with a horse or horses. To set out on horseback.

Horse and Pony Breeding and Benefit Fund Founded in 1945 by R. S. Summerhays. Objects: to solicit from horse shows, etc., a share of their profits or donations, to make collections, and to obtain donations, to make collections, and to obtain donations from individuals. To distribute such moneys to those causes which have for their purpose, and which achieve by their efforts, the breeding and benefit of horses and ponies.

Horse-bier A wheel-less bier drawn by two horses, which was used at burials in hilly areas, one horse being harnessed in front, the shafts extending to the rear into which the following horse was harnessed.

The coffin was placed between them on a platform over the shafts.

Horse-block See **Mounting block**.

Horse-boat A ferry boat for conveying horses or carriages. In the USA it applies to a boat drawn by horses.

Horsebox The original horsebox was for transporting horses by rail – a practice which in Britain has ceased. The modern motorised horsebox can provide accommodation for up to eight or more horses, as well as, in some cases, comfortable accommodation for riders and grooms. In Australia and parts of the USA it is known as a horse float or van.

Horse-boy Obsolete term (often contemptuous) for a stable-boy.

Horse brasses Brass ornaments said to have been used originally on camels in the desert, and now used on cart-horse harness. They were at one time believed to ward off 'the evil eye'. Although harness decoration has prehistoric origins, true horse brasses were first used in Britain (as far as can be established) at the end of the eighteenth century and reached the height of their popularity in the mid-nineteenth century. A great number of different designs existed; some depicted animals, some were in the form of heraldic devices, others represented the trade of the horse owner, etc. A number of 'award' brasses were made: e.g. those produced for the Royal Society for the Prevention of Cruelty to Animals. They are still used on heavy-horse harness, but are also popular among collectors, and as household decorations.

Horse bread A mixture of beans, wheat, yeast and water kneaded together and baked, which was formerly used as a feed for horses.

Horse-breaker (tamer) One who breaks or trains horses by teaching them to carry a pack or a rider, or to draw a vehicle.

Horse-coper See **Coper**.

Horse-corser A jobbing dealer in horses.

Horse dealer One who is engaged in the buying and selling of horses for profit or on commission.

Horseflesh This is widely eaten in certain European and various other countries, and is given as food to dogs and cats. A number of European heavy horses are bred with the horseflesh market very much in mind.

Horsefly Member of the Tabanidae family of Diptera (flies with two wings), erroneously called gadflies. The female sucks blood. (See **Warbles**)

Horse-gentler East Anglian term for one who breaks-in colts.

Horse Guards See **Household Cavalry**.

Horse latitudes This term originated in the sixteenth century at the time of the Spanish Conquest of South America, when on the voyages from Spain to Morocco and Brazil a prolonged calm caused shortage of water, necessitating throwing the horses overboard.

Horseman/Horsewoman One who rides on horseback. One skilled in the riding and management of horses. Also, formerly, a farm hand who worked with horses.

Horsemanship See **Riding, art of**.

Horseman's Sunday A religious service originated by R. S. Summerhays in 1949, held annually at Tattenham Corner, Epsom Downs (usually on the Sunday following the St Leger) during which horses, ponies and donkeys, ridden or driven, are blessed. Similar services are held at other places throughout the country and in many parts of the world.

Horse Marines An old phrase of derision – 'Tell that to the Horse Marines' – directed at someone guilty of gross exaggeration. Horse Marines are known to have long existed in the capacity of Honorary Horse Militia attached to the Cinque Ports Defence Units. The official journal of the Royal Marines recorded that the 17th Lancers were known as the 'Horse Marines' on account of service aboard HMS *Hermione*, and there were many instances of marines serving in a mounted capacity (e.g. Java, 1811; Crimean War, 1854; Egyptian War, 1882; British Honduras, 1913).

Horsemastership A comprehensive term

covering the care of the horse; in sickness, in health, and in all its activities, whether for pleasure or competitive and working uses.

Horse of the Year Show Founded in 1949 and organised by the British Show Jumping Association (q.v.). As the name implies, the Show seeks to find and proclaim the leading horse and pony of the year in all the usual show classes, as well as the Leading Jumper of the Year. It is held annually in October at the Empire Pool, Wembley. Its original venue was Harringay.

Horseplay Rude, boisterous behaviour.

Horse-posts (riding posts) Term applied to the horse and rider carrying mails, especially those from main road coach stopping-places in outlying country districts.

Horse-power The power which a horse can exert, or its equivalent. It equals that required to raise 33,000 lb avoirdupois one foot per minute, and is used as a standard for estimating the power of engines. The calculation is said to be based on the performance of a Clydesdale horse. In the USA a Tractor Denominator is used to test the power of draught horses in competitions. It records the total power exerted by a team of horses and also that of each member of the team.

Horserace Betting Levy Board Set up by the British Government in 1961, under the Betting, Gaming and Lotteries Act, to administer a levy from bookmakers and the Totalisator for the benefit of horseracing, the improvement of breeds of horses, and the encouragement of veterinary science and education. In consultation with the Jockey Club, the Board decides how the money should be spent, and contributions have been made towards photo-finish equipment, camera patrols, commentary systems, security, the Forensic Laboratory at Newmarket for dope testing and research, racecourses, and assistance for the transporting of horses to meetings, etc. The Board is responsible to the Home Secretary. It has a Chairman and two members appointed by the Home Secretary, three by the Jockey Club, and two *ex officio* members – the Chairmen of the Totalisator Board and the Bookmakers' Committee.

Horserace Totalisator Board Appointed under the Betting, Gaming and Lotteries Act of 1961 to administer the Tote. Under the Horserace Betting Levy Board it has a Chairman, appointed by the Home Secretary, three other members, and a Director General. It is successor in title to the Racecourse Betting Control Board established by the Racecourse Betting Act of 1928.

Horses and Ponies Protection Association Founded in 1937 to protect horses, ponies and donkeys from neglect and ill-treatment. It disseminates information promoting the stricter supervision of slaughter-houses and markets and better transport conditions by road, sea and air.

Horse-sense Sound common sense.

Horseshoe cheek A fancy cheek in the shape of a horseshoe used on straight-bar stallion show bits.

Horse show It is not known how horse shows originated, but they probably developed from fairs and other places where horses were assembled for sale. Except in the case of shows held by breed societies, the usual schedule includes such classes as Hunters, Hacks, Cobs, Mountain and Moorland Ponies, Children's Riding Ponies, and Show Jumping.

Horseshoes The origins of metal horseshoes are uncertain, but remains of iron shoes and nails have been found in Celtic barrows and Gallic graves, both in Northern Europe and in Britain. As Iron Age Man arrived in Britain about 400 BC it may be assumed that he brought the skills of shoeing horses with him. The typical Celtic shoe was the somewhat crude precursor (in structure) of modern shoes. Wherever remains of Roman settlements have been found, both in Britain and in Europe, protective devices for hooves (hipposandals) have been found. These consisted of flat iron plates with a grooved under-surface, two upright side plates, and hooks in front and behind, apparently for the attachment of cords which kept them in place. These were less than satisfactory, and were discarded, whereas the older metal rims, nailed to the feet have been refined, and over the centuries have developed into the modern style of horseshoes. (See **Shoeing**; and various entries under **Shoe**)

Horse-sick A term applied to pastures which have become infected with worm eggs by horses grazing on them for too long, and which usually gives rise to severe worm infestation. See **Worms**.

Horse sickness See **African horse sickness**.

Horse-standard Correct name for a measuring-stick (q.v.).

Horse trials Horse trials, sometimes known as events, provide an all-round test for horse and rider, incorporating the disciplines of dressage, show jumping and cross-country riding. Originally the competition was a test for military chargers, and on the Continent it is still known as the 'militaire'. A three-day event was first included in the Olympic Games in 1912. The British did not enter a team until the 1936 Berlin Olympics, and there were no *national* competitions in the United Kingdom until after the 1948 Olympics (when the equestrian events were held at Aldershot). The 10th Duke of Beaufort (q.v.) realised the immense possibilities of the development of this sport in Britain, and placed his estate at Badminton in Gloucestershire at the disposal of a committee to organise Britain's first national three-day event. It was run on lines exactly similar to the Continental 'militaire', the first day being devoted to dressage, the second to speed and endurance, and the third to show jumping.

Three-day event dressage is of medium standard, requiring the competitor to produce good collected and extended paces, work on two tracks, counter canter, and transitions from canter to halt.

The speed and endurance test on the second day is divided into four phases, covering a distance of about 17 miles (27 km) in national events and about 22 miles (35 km) in the Olympics.

PHASE A is roads and tracks, which must be completed at a specified speed requiring alternating steady trot and canter paces, with penalties for finishing outside the optimum time.

PHASE B is the steeplechase, with ten or twelve obstacles over a course of about 2½ miles (4 km) again with an optimum time.

PHASE C is a further section of roads and tracks, followed by a compulsory ten-minute halt during which the horse is examined for fitness to continue by a veterinary surgeon.

PHASE D, the cross country, is the final phase of the speed and endurance, and consists of thirty or more fixed obstacles, sited and constructed so that the courage, skill and judgement of both horse and rider are thoroughly tested. It is over 4 miles (6 km) long, and, again, must be completed in an optimum time, with penalties for exceeding this. There are a set of standards for the height and spread of the fences, and some will present competitors with alternative ways of jumping, with time being saved by boldness.

The final day is a show jumping test, and is included to demonstrate that after a day of tremendous effort the horse is still fit enough to continue. The course is made deliberately twisty, and although the size of the obstacles is relatively small, it is of sufficient difficulty to test both horse and rider. At the conclusion, the horse and rider with the least penalties over the three tests is the winner.

The British Horse Society is the governing body for horse trials in Britain, and since the first Badminton in 1948 there have been an increasing number of trials organised all over the country, and vastly increased numbers of riders wishing to compete. Most trials are one-day events, in which dressage, show jumping and cross-country are undertaken on the same day (though sometimes the entries are so great that two dressage days are required). The dressage test is ridden first, and then either the cross-country or the show jumping, at the discretion of the organisers. There are also a number of two-day events, which enable competitors to make the transition between the more novice standard one-day and the very demanding three-day event. The two-day event generally includes a steeplechase course and some roads and tracks.

In Britain, event horses are graded as Novice, Intermediate, and Advanced, depending on the points they have won in competition. The events, too, are graded to suit the varying standards of horses.

For a number of years when they first began to compete regularly in international horses trials, British riders, with their hunting background, performed extremely well across country, but were at a great disadvantage because of their lack of experience *and* interest in dressage. However, with instruction and advice from overseas, they began to improve, and from 1953 to 1957 Britain won the European Team Championship (1953, 1954, 1955 and 1957; there was no competition in 1956) and the individual gold medals in the same years with Major Lawrence Rook, Mr Bertie Hill, Major Frank Weldon and Miss Sheila Willcox respectively. Since then, the British team has won the team and/or individual titles on numerous occasions. Britain won the Olympic title for the first time in 1956, and again in 1968 and 1972. Mary Gordon Watson holds the distinction of winning Olympic, World and European gold medals all on the same horse (Cornishman V). Richard Meade has won both individual and team Olympic gold medals. Lucinda Green (née Prior-Palmer) as well as being World Champion in 1984 has the unique record of six Badminton wins on six different horses. Virginia Leng (née Holgate) has achieved a matchless run of international successes.

Horse trials are also popular in the USA, the team winning an Olympic gold medal for the first time in 1932, and again in 1948, 1976 and 1984. Outstanding American riders include Bruce Davidson, Michael Plumb and Tad Coffin.

Australian eventing hit the world stage in 1960, when Laurie Morgan, Bill Roycroft, Brian Crago and Neale Lavis won the Olympic team title, and Laurie Morgan took the individual gold.

New Zealand has entered the world eventing scene only very recently, with Mark Todd winning the 1984 Olympic individual gold medal. Since then the sport has increased greatly in popularity, and a number of excellent riders are now appearing.

Horse walker A mechanical device for exercising horses. It consists, in effect, of a giant wheel which rotates at walking pace and to the outside of which horses are attached. After suitable introduction, the animals walk quietly round with the wheel, and so are exercised.

'Horsing' A mare 'in use' or 'in season'. The period at which she is likely to breed.

Horsing stone See **Mounting block**.

Hostler (ostler) One who worked with horses stabled or baited at an inn.

Hot blood The Thoroughbred and Eastern breeds: i.e. Arabian, Barb, Turk, Syrian, etc., or an admixture of these breeds. (See also **Warmblood; Coldblood**)

Hot shot, to (Western USA) To use a battery-powered electric prod for training and moving horses. It is illegal and is forbidden by racing authorities for 'big tracks' or recognised shows.

Hound couples A contrivance for attaching two hounds, consisting of two hound collars and a distance chain and swivel. There is a lighter type which can be rolled up and carried on the saddle.

Hound hunt A hunt in which, with but little scent, hounds doggedly hunt their fox by skill and perseverance.

Hound jog See **Hound pace**.

Hound pace The pace at which hounds normally travel on the road: about 6 miles (9.7 km) an hour. Also known as 'hound jog' or 'fadge' (q.v.).

Hound show, first Held by the Cleveland Agricultural Society at Redcar in 1859.

'Hounds please!' A warning to the field to beware of hounds and to move horses, etc., out of the way.

Household Cavalry The Household Cavalry Regiment is one of the very few mounted regiments remaining in the British Army. The Regiment, based at Hyde Park Barracks in London, provides the Sovereign's escort and escorts for other members of the Royal Family on State Occasions, such as the Opening of Parliament; mounts the Queen's Life Guard every day at Whitehall; and appears (dismounted) at the Garter Ceremony at Windsor Castle. The Regiment consists of squadrons of the Life Guards (with full dress uniform consisting of scarlet tunics, cuirasses, helmets with white plumes, white breeches, and black jackboots) and the Blues and Royals (blue tunics, cuirasses, helmets with red plumes, white breeches, and black jackboots).

Housing An ornamental covering for a horse. A saddlecloth and the trappings of a horse (see **Shabrack**). Also the large pad of leather which is fastened on to the hames (q.v.) or collar of a heavy harness horse. In dry weather this leather apron stands up stiffly, but in wet it lies back on the horse's withers to keep him dry.

Hovels See **Field shelters**.

Howitt, Samuel (1765-1822) An Essex man by birth and a prolific painter and etcher of animals and sporting scenes. He engraved forty plates of *Field Sports of the East* and a set of twenty for Orme's *British Field Sports*.

Hucul/Huzul A primitive type of pony bred in the mountainous Carpathian area of Poland, where it was originally used as a pack animal. It is said to be a descendant of the ancient Tarpan (q.v.). The Hucul is now bred selectively, principally as a harness pony and for farm work, at the Siary Stud near Gorlice. The pony stands between 12.1-13.1 hh (124.5-134.6 cm) and is noted for its strength and docility. The most usual colours are dun and bay.

'Huick!' See **'Hoick'**.

Humane curb A curb made of leather or elastic instead of the usual chain.

Humane Disposal of Surplus Ponies, Society for the Founded in 1971 to protect unwanted ponies, especially youngstock and foals, from exploitation at public sales and elsewhere.

Humane slaughter See **Destruction, humane**.

Hummel A Nott Stag (q.v.).

Hungarian Shagya (or Shagya Arabian) The best Hungarian breed, the Shagya is, in fact, of Arab origin, the name being derived from a particular desertbred Arabian stallion which founded the strain. The main stud in Hungary is at Babolna. It is an extremely hardy horse, mostly grey in colour, standing 14-15 hh (142.2-152.4 cm). It is an excellent mover, thriving on little food, and with most of the qualities of the Arab. The foundation stock consisted of purebred Arabians and stock of undoubted Oriental blood and type, though not of authentic pedigree.

Hunloke bit Incorrect name given to a globe-cheek curb bit.

Hunt The territory hunted by a pack: i.e. the country.

Hunt, A The act of pursuing a fox is called a hunt or 'run'.

Hunt, The A collective term for Master, hounds, servants and field.

Hunt button A button with a design, monogram or lettering distinctive to a particular hunt, the right of a subscriber to wear it being vested in the Master. With scarlet, a brass button is worn. With a black coat, a black bone button (the design in white) is worn.

Hunt cap, velvet A peaked cap with a fibre-glass shell covered in velvet. Nowadays caps fitted with a chin-harness for safety are increasingly being worn.

Hunt Cup Short title for the Royal Hunt Cup, the chief betting race of the Royal Ascot meeting in June. It is run over 1 mile (1.6 km).

Hunter Not a breed but a type, which is largely influenced by the nature of the country over which it is used. However, the show hunter, which is the ideal, is Thoroughbred, or nearly so; he has power and scope, giving a good length of rein, and a strong back and loins, hocks of great propelling power, with the best galloping action. He must ride with balance and courage, carry his head in the correct position, and be responsive to his rider. In hunter classes, horses should be plaited and wear double bridles.

Hunter, good See **Warranty**.

Hunter (show, heavyweight) A mare or

gelding, four years or over, capable of carrying more than 14 stone (196 lb; 89 kg). To be ridden astride.

Hunter (show, ladies) A mare or gelding, four years or over, suitable for carrying a lady side-saddle. To be ridden by a lady, side-saddle.

Hunter (show, lightweight) A mare or gelding, four years old or over, capable of carrying not more than 12½ stone (175 lb; 79.37 kg). To be ridden astride.

Hunter (show, middleweight) A mare or gelding, four years old or over, capable of carrying from 12½-14 stone (175-196 lb; 79-89 kg). To be ridden astride.

Hunter (show, small) A mare or gelding, four years old or over, exceeding 14.2 hh (147.3 cm), but not exceeding 15.2 hh (157.5 cm). To be ridden astride or side-saddle, and to be judged as a hunter.

Hunter, working See **Working hunter**.

Hunter clip See **Clips, types of**.

Hunters' Improvement and National Light Horse Breeding Society (Founded 1885) Objects: to improve the 'breed' and promote the breeding of hunters and other horses used for riding and driving purposes. In recent years, because of an increased emphasis on *all* light horses, the Society is now known by the latter half of its original title i.e. The National Light Horse Breeding Society.

Hunter steeplechase A race confined to hunters and amateur riders, run only in the second half of the steeplechasing season. It is confined to horses certified by an MFH (q.v.) to have been fairly hunted during the season.

Hunter trials Competitive event held for horses and ponies across (as far as possible) a natural hunting country. Generally judged on performance within a specified time limit.

Hunt heels Heels for hunting boots are generally not more than ¾ in. (19 mm) high. They are built square and longer in the waist of the boots than walking heels, and are cut at an angle more to the inside. This ensures that the stirrup irons are in the correct position when ridden right 'home'.

Hunt hounds, to To direct, control and assist hounds in pursuit of their quarry.

Hunting Hunting of various quarries – hare, deer, and fox – has taken place in Britain for centuries. It was not, however, until the late seventeenth or early eighteenth centuries that packs of hounds began to be used exclusively for hunting the fox. By the middle of the eighteenth century, due in particular to enthusiastic landowners such as the Duke of Buckingham and members of the Royal Family, foxhunting was the most flourishing sport in the country. The areas hunted over were huge. The Earls of Berkeley hunted from Bristol to London, and the Dukes of Beaufort from Bath to Oxford – but even such wealthy landlords eventually found the expense too great, particularly as theirs were 'private packs' and they themselves bore the total cost. As a result of the Industrial Revolution during the nineteenth century, many of the 'new gentry' could afford to hunt, and subscription packs were started, hunting smaller areas. Although the nineteenth century was, in many ways, the heyday of hunting, it was also the most discreditable in its history. The fields were huge, and paid little attention to the farmers. Foxes, being in short supply because of poaching, were invariably bagged. With no traffic-ridden roads, no barbed wire, no artificial fertilisers to steady the chase, hounds were forced on at a tremendous pace, the field riding as if in a race, on unclipped horses many of which, their owners proudly boasted, died of exhaustion every season. The march of progress and World War I brought foxhunters to their senses, and when hunting was resumed after the war it was much more what those who – two hundred years earlier – first discovered the joys of the chase, had intended it to be. Between the wars there were still plenty of people who maintained large establishments, and foxhunting in those two decades was of a very high order, well-organised, producing excellent sport, the country still ridable. As a result of a few dedicated enthusiasts, hunting survived World War II, and is now a much more broadly based sport, with followers from a much wider social spectrum, including the farmers, without whom it could not survive. A new feature has been the introduction of Supporters' Clubs, who help with finances and act as ambassadors for the sport. There are now just under two hundred packs of foxhounds, and six packs of Fellhounds recognised by the Masters of Foxhounds Association. Other forms of hunting still exist in Britain, with twenty-three packs of harriers, eleven drag-hunts, and four packs of stag/buck hounds.

Hunting is also popular in the United States and Canada. Over one hundred packs of foxhounds are recognised by the American MFH Association. The sport began in the states of Virginia, Pennsylvania, and Maryland, hunting the indigenous grey fox, and later the red fox (imported, it is said, from Britain). In the Western states, fox and coyote are both hunted. George Washington owned his own pack, including some French hounds. The first Hunt Club, formed in 1766, was the Gloucester Fox Hunting Club in Delaware. Famous packs include the Middleburg, Essex, Elkridge/ Harford, Cheshire, Arapahoe (the latter two both with purebred English hounds), London, Old Dominion, Radnor, Blue Ridge, and Meadow Brook.

In Canada, since the British garrison days when Toronto was called 'Muddy York', the Toronto North York Hunt, formed in 1850, and then the Eglinton Hunt, have provided sport. The Montreal Hunt, established in 1826, had a French counterpart about 1890 in La Club de Chasses's Courre Canadien, and today has an excellent second hunt called Lac de Deux Monts, where English and French share their sport with great enthusiasm. Other hunts are the Ottawa Valley, the London, the Frontenac at Kingston, and Fraser River Valley, British Columbia. Canadian hunting has a short season with August cubbing, then only September-November, and with luck, part of December, before the weather drives all but the hardiest indoors.

Hunting in Australia takes place principally in the eastern and southern states of Victoria, New South Wales, South Australia, Tasmania and the Australian Capital Territory, although there is a Hunt Club in Western Australia. Drag hunting is popular in the country surrounding Sydney. Foxes were introduced from Britain. The oldest Australian hunt is the Melbourne Hunt Club, but South Australia has the largest number of hunts – eleven. There are also a number of hunts in New Zealand, but as there are no foxes, these are harriers. Jumping formidable wire fences (avoided wherever possible in Britain) is a feature of New Zealand hunting.

Hunting boots See **Dress, for hunting**.

Hunting-box, lodge, or seat A residence for hunting.

Hunting gate A narrow wicket erected for the use of riders.

'Hunting Jupiter' The name given to Hugo Meynell (q.v.) by members of the Quorn Hunt of which he was Master from 1753 to 1800.

Hunting monarch, first In England this was King Penda of Mercia; his huntsman lived near Pytchley Village.

Hunting seasons
CUB HUNTING: 4 August to 1 November (approx.).
FOXHUNTING: November-April.
FALLOW BUCK: 1 August to 30 April.
RED HIND: 1 November to 28 February.
HARRIERS AND BEAGLES: October-March (approx.)
COURSING: 15 September to 10 March.

Hunting spurs See **Spurs**.

Hunting tie A specially shaped cravat of white linen or piqué worn round the neck, the ends being passed through a loop at the back of the neck, then brought round and knotted in front, where they are crossed and held together with a plain, solid tie pin. Also called a 'stock'. (See illustration overleaf.)

Hunting whip See **Whip, hunting**.

Hunting year This runs from 1 May, when hunt subscriptions fall due.

Hunt livery The distinctive coat (usually scarlet), collar and buttons worn by the hunt staff.

Hunt secretary He fulfils (usually in an honorary capacity) the normal duties of

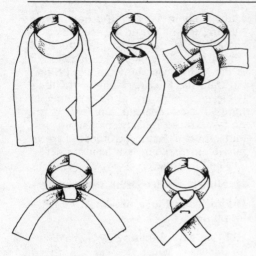

How to tie a hunting tie

a secretary but he also acts – according to the time he can spare and the inclination of the Master – as liaison between the Hunt and farmers, landowners and subscribers.

Hunt servants Huntsman (if professional), kennel huntsman (if any) and whippers-in.

Huntsman The Master, should he hunt his own hounds, may be the Huntsman, or a professional or any other person may be employed.

Hunt subscriptions These are payable in advance annually on 1 May. The amount varies according to the Hunt and the number of days normally hunted each week.

Hunt supporters' clubs Formed in support of local hunts by those who are keenly interested in the sport but who are unable to ride to hounds. Valuable work in marshalling cars, shutting gates and raising funds is performed by the members.

Hunt terrier A small short-legged and very courageous terrier attached to most

hunts and used to eject the hunted fox from any earth or drain which it may enter (See **Russell, Rev. Jack**; and **Terrier man**).

Hurdle race A race during the course of which a number of hurdles must be jumped. There must be no fewer than eight flights in a 2-mile (3.2 km) hurdle (the minimum distance for a hurdle race), and an additional flight for every extra ¼ mile (0.40 km) beyond 2 miles (3.2 km).

Hurlingham Polo Committee/Association Since polo is no longer played at the Hurlingham Club, London, the control of the game is now vested in the Hurlingham Polo Association which has jurisdiction over the game in England.

Huzul See **Hucul**.

Hybrids Crosses between a horse on the one side and an ass, zebra, etc., on the other. Such offspring are, with few exceptions, sterile.

Hydrotherapy Treatment by water, as in equine swimming pools, which allows exercise while keeping the weight off the horse's legs.

Hyperion Owned and bred by the 17th Earl of Derby (q.v.) this chestnut by Gainsborough out of Selene was only 15.1 hh (153 cm). He won the Derby and St Leger in 1933. The outstanding stallion of his generation, he was six times leading sire of the year. His sons included Aureole, Abernant, Sun Chariot, Hypericum, and Gulf Stream. He died in 1960 at the age of thirty.

Hyracotherium (Eohippus) A lower Eocene mammal, the size of a fox, with four toes on the front foot and three on the hind, but functionally, it may be said to have had three toes on all feet. It is recognised as one of the very early ancestors of the horse. (See **Evolution of the horse**)

Iberian Horse Ancestor of the Tarbenian horse (q.v.), which at the beginning of the nineteenth century was improved through the importation of Arabian stallions by Napoleon Bonaparte.

Icelandic Pony The breed is not indigenous, but is composed of immigrants, like the human inhabitants who in the ninth century migrated from Scandinavia to Iceland, taking their ponies with them. These immigrants were later joined by settlers from the Western Isles of Scotland, who brought with them ponies of Celtic stock. No outside blood has been introduced for at least eight hundred years, so the ponies are of exceptional purity. Until the beginning of the twentieth century they were the sole means of transport. They are very strong, agile and tough, and about half the total population live out in a semi-wild state. Selective breeding is based on improving their five gaits – the walk, trot and gallop, plus the pace, which is a lateral gait, and the 'Tolt', a running walk of four equal beats, used when covering rough ground. The Icelandic pony stands between 12.3-13.2 hh (129.5-137.2 cm). It is found in a remarkable variety of colours: officially there are fifteen basic colour types and combinations, including chestnut with flaxen mane and tail, a few skewbalds, and several varieties of piebald. Icelandic ponies are now used extensively as riding ponies, competing in all equestrian disciplines and in special show classes for four- and five-gaited animals.

Imperial crowner A bad fall.

Importation of horses Particulars are available from the Ministry of Agriculture, Fisheries and Food in England, and the Department of Agriculture and Fisheries for Scotland in Edinburgh.

Impulsion Forward propulsion created by the energetic use of the hindquarters, resulting in the hindlegs coming well under the horse's body. Impulsion passes through the horse's back, neck, and poll, and ends in the mouth, where it is contained and directed by the rider's hands through the reins. It should not be confused with speed.

In blood Hounds which have killed recently are said to be 'in blood'.

Inbreeding The mating of brother and sister, sire and daughter, son and dam.

Incisors The front or biting teeth. The age of a horse is determined from them. (See **Age, to tell**)

Incitatus The racing stallion beloved by the Roman Emperor, Gaius Caesar (AD 12-41), who was usually known as Caligula. The horse was first called Porcellus – 'little pig' – but when it began to win races, Caligula changed the name to Incitatus – 'swift-speeding' – and his admiration for its qualities became an obsession. The horse was given a marble stable with a manger of ivory and bucket of gold, trappings of purple cloth, and a collar of jewels. He was appointed a citizen of Rome, then a senator; and the final honour of a consulship was only prevented by the assassination of Caligula himself.

Independent seat A rider is said to have an independent seat when he has reached such a degree of balance that he is independent of the reins and stirrups as aids to the correctness of the seat.

Indigestion See **Colic**.

Indirect rein An opposite or bearing rein. The action of this is to press against the horse's neck on the side opposite to the direction in which the horse is required to move. Also known as 'neck-reining'.

Indoor polo This is popular in the USA, where international players and ponies participate in the winter. The game is played on tan (q.v.), on an area approximately 300 ft by 150 ft (91.44 x 45.72 m), with the goal posts 10 ft (3 m) apart. A leather-covered sponge 'ball' is used, and there are three players a side. It is a good schooling medium. The game has been played in Britain, but has never been widely accepted.

Influenza, equine An epidemic cold or cough due to a virus of which two main strains have been identified. It is highly infectious, and the spread among horses in a yard is extremely rapid. The first symptom is often a fever of about 104°F (40°C), which may go unnoticed. This is followed by a watery nasal discharge which becomes thicker, the mucous membranes of the eye becomes pink in the severe forms; there is shivering, loss of appetite, and a persistent hacking cough. Immediate veterinary attention is essential. Vaccination is available, and is compulsory for many competition horses. (See also **Cough**).

'In front of the bit' Said of a horse who hangs on the hands and pulls. Also known as 'heavy on the bit'.

Inhaling See **Steaming (the head)**.

In hand A horse is said to be in hand when it flexes its jaw to the pressure of the rein. Some instructors recommend obtaining this flexion in the earliest stages of training by gently 'feeling' the bit reins while standing or walking with the horse. Others prefer to educate the horse from the saddle.

In-hand Indicating a led horse.

In-hand Classes led into the show ring by rein and bridle or halter, unsaddled and without harness. They include stallions, mares and foals; also youngstock and geldings. The term is used to distinguish the class from a ridden class or harness class.

Injured Jockeys' Fund The original fund was set up in 1964 following the grave injuries to the National Hunt jockeys Paddy Farrell and Tim Brookshaw. Public response was so generous that with the consent of the two injured jockeys the fund was closed and the Injured National Hunt Jockeys' Fund took its place, its purpose being to help any injured steeplechase jockey or their families. The fund has again been broadened in scope and is now able to help all jockeys, both flat as well as jumping. In its first twelve years, £226,000 was distributed to help jockeys and their families.

Insemination, artificial The process of impregnating a mare by artificial means, as opposed to the natural act. Though becoming more widely accepted, it is not yet sanctioned in Great Britain, except for experimental purposes. The Jockey Club is opposed to the procedure.

Inside (racing) Nearest the rails marking the inside perimeter.

Inspector of Courses (racing) An official appointed by the Jockey Club to see that racecourses are kept up to the required standards.

Insurance Generally advisable for all horses and ponies and always for stables and contents. Under the Animals Act owners are liable for damage caused by their horses. Personal and third party insurance is advisable. Advice can be sought from the British Horse Society (q.v.).

Instinct See **Intelligence**; and **Memory**.

Institute of the Horse and Pony Club Ltd Founded in 1925 to be an authoritative centre of information on all matters relating to the horse, its training and management. Now absorbed by the British Horse Society.

Intelligence Experts differ entirely as to the intelligence possessed by a horse. Some claim that he has a very poor intelligence, and does everything from habit acquired by training, or in association with the comfort of the stable or the instinct for safety and protection. Others maintain that the horse is capable of applying his brain in a way that can only be attributed to great intelligence.

Interference In racing, dangerous, reckless, careless, or improper riding which impedes the progress of another horse or other horses. It may lead to disqualification of the horse and disciplinary action against the rider.

Interfering A general term used for the various ways in which a horse can injure itself by striking one foot or leg with another. (See **Brushing**, **Forging**, **Overreaching**, **Speedy cutting**).

International horse show (CSI) Any horse show which includes one or more competitions open to foreign riders who come as individual competitors authorised by their national federation, at the invitation of the host national federation, or by personal invitation. No team or individual competitor is sent officially to a CSI.

International horse show (CSIO) Any international horse show which, being authorised by its national federation, and having obtained consent of the FEI (q.v.), is entered in the FEI calendar. Riders are sent to it officially by national federations and with the approval of any government departments which may be concerned.

'In the money' Said of a racehorse, show horse, show jumper, etc., who receives any prize money offered in a race or class.

'In the soup' In difficulties. It originally referred to a hunting mishap, when a rider fell into a ditch of dirty water.

In velvet Descriptive of a stag whose antlers are growing and are covered in a velvety skin. (See **Velvet**)

In whelp The state of a hound or other bitch when she is carrying her young.

Iodine, tincture of A first-aid treatment for cuts and scratches, now largely superseded by the use of antibiotics.

Irish Draught The Irish Draught was bred in Ireland as a dual-purpose animal, suitable for farm work and for riding, and it was a type that evolved rather than a breed; thus there are no early records or stud books. In 1917 the Department of Agriculture in Ireland instituted a *Book of Horses of the Irish Draught type* in an attempt to regulate the breed. After a period of decline in the mid-1930s the breed revived, helped in 1976 by the establishment of the Irish Draught Horse Society. This was followed by the founding in 1979 of the Irish Draught Society (Great Britain) to register pure and part-bred stock, to keep progeny records, to undertake inspections, and to encourage the breeding of Irish Draught horses in Britain. The British numbers are still small, with fewer than one hundred purebred mares on the register, but the breed's success in producing excellent hunters and

competition performance horses when crossed with Thoroughbreds is now being recognised. As a result, the National Light Horse Breeding Society (q.v.) has appointed Irish Draught stallions to their Hunter Approved Scheme.

The Irish Draught Horse stands between 15-16 hh (152.4-162.6 cm), and is an active, short-shinned, powerful horse, with substance and quality. The forehead is wide, the eyes bold, the ears long and well-set, the neck is also well-set, the shoulders clean-cut. The girth is deep, the back, loins and quarters are strong. The limbs are strong with plenty of high-quality, flat bone. The action is smooth, active and free, without exaggeration. Any strong whole colours are permitted. The Irish Draught is known for intelligence, a gentle nature, and common sense.

Irish National Hunt Steeplechase Committee The governing body and recognised 'turf authority' responsible for controlling steeplechasing and hurdle racing in Ireland.

Irish riff Term used for small lumps on horses' shoulders which sometimes occur a few months after a horse arrives from Ireland.

Irish Turf Club Responsible for the rules of racing and disciplinary matters in the Irish Republic.

Irish Racing Board Responsible for the conduct of racing in the Irish Republic.

Iron See **Stirrup iron**.

Isabella/Y'sabella Bred since the fifteenth century when Queen Isabella of Spain formed a stud of gold coloured riding horses for herself and her ladies. Some of these 'Golden Horses of the Queen' were given by Isabella to America, which was then being colonised by the Spaniards. Originally of Arab stock, they vary in colour from light to liver chestnuts with white mane and tail, and those of real golden colour are now generally referred to as 'palomino' (q.v.). In Spain, palominos are still referred to as 'Isabellas'.

Italian Heavy Draught A heavy breed

based on the French Breton (q.v.) and formerly quite widely used in agriculture. It is now in demand principally for the meat trade. Standing 15-16 hh (152.4-162.6 cm), the Italian Draught is predominantly chestnut, with flaxen mane and tail.

Itching, of mane and tail Irritation may be due to the presence of lice or an indication of psoroptic mange. It can also be brought about by the bites of midges, and in some animals by photo-sensitivity (sensitivity to light, especially ultra-violet rays). (See **Sweet itch; Mange**).

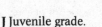

J Juvenile grade.

Jabbing See **Jobbing in the mouth**.

Jack See **Mule**.

Jack A term sometimes used to indicate a large bone spavin.

Jackass See **Ass**.

Jack-knifing A term used in buck-jumping when a horse clicks its front and hindlegs together whilst in the air, or when it crosses them so that their positions are reversed. (Also called 'straight bucking'.)

Jade/Jadey A sluggish or stale horse. A horse which lacks condition, courage and spirit.

Jagger A pedlar's or pack horse; a small horse-load in the north of England was known as 'a jaggin'. Many bridle paths once used by pack ponies carrying coal or lead are known as 'jagger' or 'jaggin' ways.

Jaggin See **Jagger**.

Jaivey See **Jarvey**.

Jaquama/Jaquima See **Hackamore**.

Jarde/Jardon A callous tumour found on the outside of a horse's hock.

Jarvey An Irish term for the driver of a Hackney carriage. Also Jaivey.

Jaundice A yellowing condition of the mucous membranes, visible in the eyes, mouth, and nostrils. The urine is brown and discoloured by bile pigments. The cause may be due to an obstruction of the flow of bile into the intestines. It may result from hepatitis (inflammation

of the liver), blocking of the bile duct, or thickening of the duodenum (the portion of the small intestine into which the bile duct opens). Veterinary advice is urgently needed in even the mildest case. See also **Haemolytic disease**.

Jaunting car A two-wheeled Irish vehicle in which the passengers sit facing the sides of the road with their feet on platforms which fold up.

'Jelly dogs' Colloquial term for beagles.

Jennet See **Genet; Bardot; Hinny**.

Jenny A female donkey.

Jerk-line string Jerk-line is a Western American term for any number from six to twenty horses strung out two abreast, and the jerk-line string is a single line run from the lead to the driver on the wagon who 'steers' the team by giving jerks on the line.

Jerky A small, low, American one-horse, four-wheeled vehicle of the buggy type which, when fitted with a top, is called a 'Surrey'. The Jerky is now almost extinct, having long been replaced by the first utility American motorcar. The name was probably acquired from folk-usage.

Jersey Act A resolution introduced by Lord Jersey to the Jockey Club in 1913, and passed by his fellow members, that Weatherbys, proprietors of the General Stud Book, should be advised to confine all future entries in the GSB to animals whose pedigrees could be traced at all points to strains already appearing in pedigrees in earlier volumes of the GSB. It was aimed at preventing certain strains from the USA gaining admission, and was acted on by Weatherbys. It caused much ill-feeling among breeders in America and France. In 1949, after World War II, when it was realised that some of the most successful racing families in France were not eligible, it was repealed. (See also **Thoroughbred racing**)

Jibbah See **Arab**.

Jibbing A most objectionable habit where the horse refuses to move forward and, in some cases, runs backwards. This may sometimes be checked by quickly circling two or three times and then pushing forward.

Jigging The action of a horse who refuses to walk and substitutes a short-paced, uneasy trot.

Jingle A cart with long shafts.

Jobbing in the mouth The act, deliberate or involuntary, of catching a horse with a sharp jerk in the mouth. In the USA it is known as 'jabbing'.

Jobey noseband See **Noseband, Brinekind**.

Job horses Horses (harness or otherwise) which are hired or 'jobbed' from a job master.

Job master One who offers horses for hire.

Jockette Colloquial term for lady jockey. (See **Ladies' races**)

Jockey Any rider, professional or amateur, who competes in a horse race. It is sometimes used colloquially for riders in other equestrian sports.

'Jockey' A thin sheet of metal curved to the shape of the front and rear tops of riding boots. Jockeys help ease the leg into the boot.

Jockey, dumb See **Dumb-jockey**.

Jockey, apprentice In Britain, boys and girls aged sixteen (sometimes a little older) train as flat race jockeys by becoming apprenticed to registered trainers. Suitable physique is vital, and at the age of sixteen the young boy or girl should, ideally, be under 5 ft (1.5 m) in height and weigh less than 6 stone (37.8 kg). Riding experience is essential, as few modern trainers will give elementary riding instruction. Usually, the potential jockey is given a three months' trial, and if considered suitable, signs apprenticeship papers, normally for a period of a year, renewable by mutual consent. The apprentice will learn stable routine and management, how to ride 'work' (i.e. how to ride racehorses at exercise and during training), and the theory of race-riding. Only the really able apprentice, however, will be allowed to ride in races, and a trainer is not obliged to give an apprentice rides in public. Some trainers send their apprentices to the British Racing School, Newmarket, financed by the Horserace Betting Levy Board. There is no formal apprenticeship scheme for National Hunt Racing, and many National Hunt jockeys start their careers as amateurs in point-to-point races.

Jockey Club The first recorded reference to the Jockey Club was in 1752. It is the governing body and recognised 'turf authority' responsible for controlling flat racing and steeplechasing in Great Britain. In 1968, it amalgamated with the National Hunt Committee, and in 1970 was granted a Royal Charter. The executive power of the Club is invested in nine stewards (q.v.).

Jockey Club (USA) An organisation similar to the Jockey Club of Great Britain. It is responsible for stud processing and produces the official Thoroughbred Stud Book.

Jockey Club Rules The rules issued by the Jockey Club refer to all meetings held under its sanction. They are procurable in book form from Weatherbys.

Jockey Club Stewards There are nine stewards of the Jockey Club, including a senior steward and two deputy senior stewards. The stewards have wide-ranging powers as laid down in Rules 1 to 4 of the *Rules of Racing*.

Jockey, first Principal jockey engaged to ride for an owner or stable.

Jockeys Hunting boots, usually of black, waxed calf, with fitted polished tops of various colours, black patent tops, or scouring tops. (The latter have a matt finish and are cleaned with a top powder.)

Jockeys Small black deposits of grease and dirt which accumulate on the flaps and sweat flaps of a saddle. They should be removed as soon as they become apparent. In stubborn cases a mild solution of washing soda crystals will help.

Jockeys' Association of Great Britain The body representing jockeys in British racing. Formed by the amalgamation of the National Hunt Jockeys' Association and the Flat Racing Jockeys' Association.

Jockey's valet See **Valet, Jockey's**.

Jodhpur boots A type of boot with elastic sides or a buckle-over front, designed to protect the instep from undue pressure by the stirrup iron.

Jodhpur breeches/Jodphurs A popular form of riding breeches, named after the Indian state of Jodhpur.
The leg is extended, unbuttoned and unlaced, down to the ankle, rendering unnecessary the wearing of high boots.

Jodhpur polo curb A curb chain with a large centre link which fits between the horse's jaw bones and exerts considerable pressure.

Jogger Training vehicle for Hackneys.

Jog-trot A gait somewhat short of a true trot. Similar to jigging (q.v.).

Joint evil/ill Also known as navel ill, infective arthritis, or pyaemia. An infection of the joints which may affect foals in the first three to six months of life. Caused by bacterial infection entering through the navel. More rarely seen in older horses as the result of a penetrating wound. The symptoms include swelling of the navel and failure to dry up, loss of appetite, fever, swelling of one or more joints – commonly the knee, fetlock, stifle or hock – with, in severe cases, the formation of abscesses, or even intractable hepatitis. Treatment by a veterinary surgeon is essential if lasting damage or death is to be avoided.

Joint-masters Two or more individuals sharing the Mastership of a pack of hounds.

Joint measurement scheme The scheme was set up in 1934 to provide measurements descriptions and classification of horses and ponies for competition purposes. Official measurers, all of whom have been members of the Royal College of Veterinary Surgeons for five years or more, and who are in equine practice, are appointed by the stewards of the Scheme. The stewards are appointed annually by the British Veterinary Association, the Royal College of Veterinary Surgeons, and the member societies (i.e. the British Horse Society, the British Show Jumping Association, the British Show Hack, Cob and Riding Horse Association, the British Show Pony Association, the National Light Horse Breeding Society, the National Pony Society, the Welsh Pony and Cob Society, and the Hackney Horse Society). The measurements are taken on an official measuring pad and under very strict rules of procedure. Measurement certificates are then issued and are accepted by practically every show in Great Britain. Annual certificates are issued for animals of four or five years of age, or those aged six or over which are presented for their first measurement. Life certificates are issued for animals six years and over, provided that they have held an annual certificate. The rules allow for objections to certificates under special circumstances and conditions.

Joint oil See **Synovial fluid**.

Joint Racing Board The most important policy-making body in British racing. It is under the co-chairmanship of the Senior Steward of the Jockey Club (q.v.), and the Chairman of the Horserace Betting Levy Board (q.v.). The Board also includes two Deputy Senior Stewards of the Jockey Club and two Government-appointed members of the Horserace Betting Levy Board.

Jointed pelham A pelham bit having a jointed mouthpiece.

Joints The meeting of two or more bones. These are classified as follows:
(1) FIBROUS: e.g. bones of the skull.
(2) CARTILAGINOUS: e.g. where the left lower jaw meets the right lower jaw.
(3) SYNOVIAL: e.g. all major articular joints of the body and legs. Synovial

joints move fairly freely in most cases.

The movements between two bones may be very complex. Where two bones slide over each other, a gliding movement is apparent. A hinge-type joint results in angular flexion or extension. Rotation may take place when a bone is able to rotate around a longitudinal axis. Most joints show combinations of some or all of these movements. See also **Cartilage**; **Synovial fluid**; and **Ligaments**.

Jones, Adrian (1845-1936) He occasionally drew or painted horse portraits, but is best known for his splendid sculptures of horses, with such impressive groups as the *Quadriga* at Hyde Park Corner and the *Cavalry Memorial* at Stanhope Gate; also for the beautiful statue of *Persimmon* at Sandringham.

Jorrocks, John An eccentric and extravagant sporting grocer – a citizen of St Botolph Lane and Great Coram Street in London. Created by R. S. Surtees in 1831, he appears in books such as *Jorrocks' Jaunts and Jollities, Handley Cross*, and *Hillingdon Hall*, and is one of the most quoted and best-loved characters in sporting fiction. See also **Surtees, Robert Smith**.

Jostling stone See **Mounting block**.

Joust A combat between two mounted knights with lances. Also a mock combat in a tournament (q.v.).

Jowl The part of the head contained within the branches of the jaw-bones.

Jowl sweater A form of cap with ear holes which overlaps under the throat. It is made from felt and lined with oilskin, plastic, or other waterproof material. Its purpose is to sweat off surplus fat which might make it difficult for a horse or pony to flex his head at the poll.

Juba port A rubber port (q.v.) which can be fastened on any mullen mouthpiece to prevent a horse getting his tongue over the bit.

Judge (racing) An official appointed by the Jockey Club to place the first four horses – or more if there are special prizes – in each race.

Judges, panel of Sometimes called a jury. Most societies and associations maintain a panel of judges, qualified to judge general and special breeds; the British Show Jumping Association has a panel for show-jumping classes under their rules. Lists are available to show executives.

Juger, se French term meaning that the hind feet touch down on the imprints left by the forefeet.

Jumart Erroneously believed to be the hybrid offspring of a bull and mare or she-ass, or of a horse or ass and a cow.

'Jumped' A term used by American cowboys. When a herd of wild horses are warned by a neigh from their leader (stallion) and gallop off, they are 'jumped'.

Jumper's bump A term applied to the protuberance at the top of the croup, a formation erroneously supposed to increase a horse's jumping power.

'Jumping' A coaching term for a wheeler which canters because it feels the pressure of the coach, which is 'overtaking' it.

Jumping blind A hunting term used to denote jumping through an untrimmed or overgrown (blind) ditch.

Jumping boots Boots of leather lined with rubber, with ridges inside to protect the tendons. The boots are fitted on the *backs* of the forelegs as support and protection.

Jumping-lane A long, narrow, fenced-in enclosure used in teaching a horse to jump. Different forms of jumps are placed at varying distances, and the horse can neither jump out of the lane nor run out at the jumps. The exit is at the end of the lane. (Also known as a 'Weedon lane'.)

'Jumping powder' See **Stirrup cup**.

Jump-off (barrage) When there is a tie for first place in a show-jumping competition a jump-off is held to decide the winner.

Jury See **Judges, panel of**.

Justin Morgan See **Morgan Horse**.

Jute rugs Night rugs are frequently made of jute, a natural fibre commonly used in the making of sacks. It is also used for rollers. (See **Rollers**).

Jutland The heavy draught horse of Denmark, bred chiefly in the peninsula from which its takes its name. The present breed is the result of a programme begun in 1850, when the English half-Shire, half-Suffolk stallion Oppenheim, was imported. He is regarded as one of the founders of the Jutland – his sixth generation descendant, Aldrupp-Munkedal, dominated the scene from 1890 to 1912 – and his chestnut colour is now typical of the breed.

The post-World War II years were disastrous, but a faithful few breeders retained their best horses, so that the Jutland has been re-established as a working agricultural horse, and is also used for pulling brewers' drays. It is a medium-sized active horse, solidly built, with very short legs showing moderate feathering and with good bone. The average height is between 15.3-16hh (160.0-162.6 cm). The common chestnut colour is accompanied by light-coloured mane and tail. There are also a few blacks and browns.

Juvenile show-jumping grades See **Grading, of horses**.

—K—

Kabardin These horses are found in the mountainous regions of the Northern Caucasus, where they have been bred from at least the sixteenth century through the crossing of native Mongolian stock with Eastern sires of Persian, Turkmen, and Karrabahk blood. The original small animal was used for riding in the mountains. Many Kabardins died during and after the Russian Revolution, but a re-established, stronger animal began to emerge in the 1920s at the Kabardin, Balkan, and Karachaev-Cherkass studs. Today the principal studs are at Malokarachaev and Malkinare. The breed stands between 15-15.2hh (152.4-157.5 cm), and is a strong, well-proportioned riding horse, often with a Roman nose. It is used for riding, particularly in the mountains, and in harness.

Kadir Cup The competition for the Kadir Cup for pig-sticking in India was instituted in 1873 and first competed for in 1874 when it was won by Mr White of the 15th Hussars on Hindoo. It was competed for annually at the Meerut Tent Club meeting. With the exception of breaks during the Afghan War in 1879 and 1880 and the First World War from 1915 to 1918 the competition was held continuously until 1939. On the outbreak of World War II the Cup was left in the Royal Artillery Mess in Meerut. It was subsequently taken to Kenya and was brought back to England on an aircraft of the Queen's Flight in which Princess Margaret was a passenger. It is now displayed in the Indian Army Memorial Room at the Royal Military Academy at Sandhurst. The competition took its name from the rough, uncultivated terrain of the Ganges-Kadir country, which provided an ideal habitat for wild boar.

Kaolin (China clay) A white, odourless powder used in poulticing. A ready-to-use preparation is available in a sealed foil envelope which can be easily heated. It is also available in tins. See also **Poulticing** and **Antiphlogistine**.

Kaolin poultice See **Antiphlogistine**.

Karabahk This beautiful breed is found in the Caucasus, and in the past it greatly contributed to the improvement of the Don horse (q.v.). In conformation, Karabahks are predominantly Arab, with the typical dished profile. The modern breed is crossed with Arab stallions at the Akdam Stud. The characteristic golden colour is found elsewhere only in the Akhal-Teké (q.v.).

Karabair A light, saddle and harness animal of mixed Mongolian and Arabian blood. Of good conformation, it is bred in the mountains of Uzbekistan and Tadzhikstan. The horses are kept in herds on mountain pastures and are particularly noted for their use in the traditional game of goat-catching (*kokpar*), in which teams compete at full gallop, the aim being to secure the carcass of a goat and carry it through the goal. Mares of the breed are crossed with Thoroughbred stallions to produce horses suitable for the more widely recognised equestrian sports and for flat racing. Karabairs stand between 14.2-15 hh (147.3-152.4 cm). The principal colours are chestnut and bay, with some dun, black, piebald and palomino.

Karacabecy The native horse of Turkey. It is bred at several state studs, and is a mixture of native Turkish and Arabian blood. It is a good all-purpose riding horse and is often crossed with Haflingers and Nonius horses to produce an animal suitable for agriculture, light draught, and pack work. The breed stands up to 16 hh (162.6 cm) and bears some resemblance to the Arab.

Kathiawari and Marwari These ponies are found in Rajputana, India. They have strong Arabian characteristics, including inward-pointing ears and, often, a long mane. All colours including piebald and skewbald are found. Height is about 14.2hh (147.6 cm).

Kave/Kaving See **Porting**.

Kay collar See **Rim collar**.

'Keep' Pasture for grazing.

Keeper(s) Stitched leather loops which retain the straps of the bridle. Also the leather loop on the top end of a hunting whip to which the thong is attached.

Kehailan (Kehilan, Kehaylan, Koheilan, Koheili) An Arabian generic term meaning purebred. Applied to the whole breed of pure Arabian horses.

Kelshie See **Klibber**.

Kennel A fox's bed above ground, or in a covert or hedgerow. To push the fox out is to 'unkennel' him.

Kennel huntsman He is responsible for the management and feeding of hounds in kennel, and is often the first whipper-in when the huntsman is an amateur.

Kennelman One who works in the ken-nels under the huntsman or kennel huntsman.

Kennels A collective term for the various buildings and yards in which a pack of hounds is kept.

Kentucky Derby One of the three Classic races (q.v.) in the USA. It has been run annually without interruption since its inauguration in 1875, and the only change was in 1896 when the distance was shortened from 1½ miles (2.41 km) to 1¼ miles (2.01 km). The race is for three-year-olds and is run at Churchill Downs, Kentucky, on the first Saturday in May.

Kentucky Futurity An important high-class trotting race for three-year-olds, run annually at Lexington, Kentucky.

Kentucky Saddle Horse See **American Saddlebred**.

'Kept-up' Said of a horse which is sta-bled during the summer. The converse is 'turned-out' or 'summered'.

Keratoma A horn tumour: i.e. a horny growth on the interior wall of the horn of the hoof. It is caused by excessive activity of the horn-producing laminae following an injury, or the pressure of irri-tating matter in the foot, usually near the toe. The symptoms are inflammation and lameness. A fistula may form which will exude pus. A veterinary surgeon should be consulted.

Kerry Pony A robust and extremely har-dy animal from Ireland, which up to the beginning of the century was in consider-able demand for riding and driving.

Kersey Coarse, narrow cloth used for leg bandages and Yorkshire boots (qq.v.).

Key bugle A copper wind instrument – in appearance like a large cornet but with keys instead of valves – much used by musically inclined guards on stage coaches. It is said that they were pro-hibited on mail coaches, but there are plenty of paintings by contemporary art-ists showing them in use.

Keys (players) Pieces of metal attached to mouthing bits to produce saliva and to soften mouths.

Kick over the traces, to To throw off control, such as when a horse gets a leg over a trace.

Kicking A vicious and dangerous habit. In the stable, the walls and door may be padded with rough leather packed with hay, straw, or some other padding. If kicking occurs when the horse is being ridden (when it is most dangerous), the head should be kept up, the corners of the mouth played on through the reins, and the whip applied to the shoulders. It is not possible to prevent a horse which is being led from kicking, whether he is moving or stationary.

Kicking strap (in harness) A strap which passes through the loop above the crupper and is buckled at both ends of the shaft. Its purpose is to inhibit kicking.

Kidney link The link at the bottom of the harness to which the pole chains are fastened.

Kimblewick/Kimblewicke (USA) A form of one-rein pelham. It has a straight mouthpiece with a small port, short cheekpiece and curb chain. Sometimes known as a 'Spanish jumping bit', from which it was adapted by Lt. Col. F. E. Gibson for Mr Phil Oliver of Kimblewick.

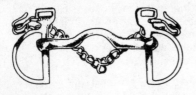

Kimblewick.

Kineton See **Noseband, Kineton**.

King George V Cup An individual show jumping award competed for annually under FEI rules at the Royal International Horse Show (q.v.) in London. It is the major competition for male riders.

King George VI and Queen Elizabeth Stakes First run at Ascot in 1951 in celebration of the Festival of Britain. It is a 1½-mile (2.41 km) race.

Kiplingcote's Race Founded and endowed by a body of foxhunters in 1619, this is the oldest endowed race in the world. It is run over some 4 miles

(6 km) of old tracks and roads on the Yorkshire Wolds. There is evidence that the race was held fifty years earlier, for a husbandman on oath stated 'that ninge at Kypplingcote Eshe [Ashes or Ash] about Shrovetide last (1555). . .'. Known as the 'Yorkshire Derby', the race was 'to be Ridd yearly in the third Thursday of March'. The winner takes the interest on the invested fund, the second, the entry fees, which may be greater in amount than that won by the winner. The race is open to any type of horse, each entry having to carry 10 stone (140 lb; 63.5 kg). A veteran in attendance in 1875 stated: 'We have sometimes to cut through snow seven or eight feet thick for a passage for horses to run through, but we have always had our race. . .'

Kirby Gate Traditional venue, 5 miles (8 km) from Melton Mowbray, of the opening meet of the Quorn Foxhounds.

Kirghiz See **Novokirghiz**.

Kladruber A breed which takes its name from the Imperial Stud of the Austro-Hungarian empire in Bohemia, where it was first bred in 1579. It is descended from Spanish horses (imported from both Spain and Italy), to which it owes its typical characteristics of conformation – high action, a Roman nose, and a powerful, heavy-crested neck. Selection was made for size (up to 17hh: 170 cm) and colour. The two permitted colours are grey and black, from the Italian stallion Peppoli, foaled in 1764, and the grey Imperatore. Used in their heyday primarily for ceremonial carriages, Kladrubers are now being bred as all-purpose horses for riding and driving.

Klebsiella An equine venereal disease.

Klibber A saddle for native ponies' in the Shetland Isles. It is made of wood and has panniers on either side called 'Kelshies', which are used for carrying peat.

Kluge Hans See **Elberfeld Horses**.

Knabstrup An old Danish breed of spotted horses which dates back to the Napoleonic wars. Around 1808, Spanish troops stationed in Denmark left behind a spotted mare, Flaebehoppen, of exceptional speed and endurance. She became the foundation mare of the breed, having been put to a Frederiksborg stallion. There are now only a few Knabstrup studs in Denmark. Some of the mares have been put back to Frederiksborgs, so the number of purebreds is small. Knabstrups stand 15.2-16 hh (157.5-

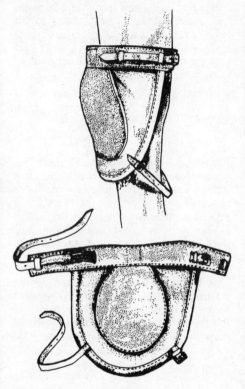

Knee-caps.

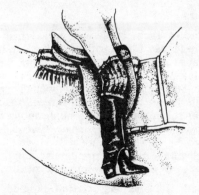

Polo knee-caps.

162.6 cm) and are a light- to medium-weight riding horse, of good conformation. They have always been popular with circuses.

Knacker A dealer who buys, sells, and slaughters old and worn-out horses. In East Anglia harness-makers were also known as knackers, as they used to slaughter horses and dress their own leather.

Knavesmire The racecourse at York.

Knee The joint between the forearm and the cannon bone.

Knee, true The stifle (q.v.), situated at the lower end of the thighs on the hindlegs, which corresponds to the human knee-cap (patella).

Knee-caps Felt protectors for the knees, reinforced with blocked leather and with two straps for fastening above and below the knee. They are used for walking exercise or for travelling, as protection against damage by slipping. The top straps should be fairly tight, the lower ones loose.

Knee-caps, jumping Stout leather protectors lined with ¾-in (19 mm) foam rubber. They have double, padded, elastic-set straps on the tops only, and are used when schooling young horses over fixed timber. Nowadays they are also available in neoprene rubber reinforced with PVC.

Knee-caps, polo Protectors designed to prevent injury to a rider who is being successfully 'ridden off' by an opponent. (See **Polo**)

Knee-caps, skeleton Lightweight, leather knee-caps, with no rugging surround to the blocked caps. They are used for jumping, exercise, etc.

Knee-halter, to To couple the head to one foreleg by attaching a rein or strap to the halter to prevent the horse from moving freely.

Knee-roll A pad or packing forming part of the front of the flap of a saddle. It can be of a thickness and length suitable to the rider's needs and is used for greater security in the saddle: e.g. for grip and steadiness when jumping.

'Knees and hocks to the ground' A term denoting good, short cannon bones and shanks. Also 'well to the ground', and 'near to the ground'.

Knife-board bus An early type of London horse-bus. The outside passengers (on the roof) sat back-to-back on long benches on either side. It was succeeded by the 'Garden-seat bus' (q.v.).

Knobber/Knobbler A male deer at two years old. (The term is now obsolete.)

'Knocker' A dealer's term of derision for a horse with cow-hocks, sickled, and standing far back. The latter defect causes them to become soiled and the cow-hocks, being so close together, 'knock' them clean. See **Hocks, cow**.

Knots Side-bones formed by the ossification of the lateral cartilages on the rear lateral aspect of the foot just above the coronet.

Knuckling over (Also known as 'grogginess' or 'overshot fetlock') 1. A condition found in foals or youngstock, caused by a contracted flexor tendon, in which the forelegs are straight and the fetlock joint permanently flexed. May be present at birth or develop in youngsters up to eighteen months. When present at birth it is usual for the condition to improve spontaneously. 2. Action when horse stumbles.

Kocholine A jelly-like grease for preserving leather.

Konik A native breed of Poland ('konik' means 'small horse'). It bears a strong resemblance to the Tarpan (q.v.) and retains several primitive features, including the dun colour. It is a very hardy animal, making the most of poor food, and has amazing endurance and strength for its size. Standing only about 13 hh (132.1 cm) it has a strong, very compact body, with a short neck, and short legs with good bone and a small amount of feather.

Kournakoff irons See **Cock-eyed**.

Kumel A fox bed above ground.

Kür See **Dressage, competitive**.

Kustinair A hardy Russian riding horse descended from the ancient Kazakh strain. Various programmes from 1898 onwards have improved the breed, with a gradual increase in size up to 15.2 hh (157.5 cm). Don and Strelet blood was used first, followed by Thoroughbred. Later, a reversion was made to using Don, Kazakh and Thoroughbred crosses. The breed is now noted as a strong endurance horse, and is used to improve other local stock. Bay and chestnut are the most usual colours, with occasional greys.

L

L (racing) Length.

Lace rein A rein in the hand-part of which a lace is passed over and through in 'V' shapes, giving a good grip.

Lacing See **Crossing feet**.

Lad A worker who looks after racehorses in stables, rides them out, and accompanies them to race meetings. The word 'lad' is not an indicator of age since stable lads will most certainly be adults. The job of 'lad' is now frequently undertaken by 'lasses'. (See **Head lad**)

Ladies' races These were sanctioned by the Jockey Club for the first time on the flat at a meeting at Kempton Park on 6 May 1972. The winner was Meriel Tufnell on Scorched Earth. In 1974 women were allowed to compete against men in amateur flat races. In 1975 applications for professional jockeys' licences were permitted. In 1976 National Hunt amateur permits were issued to women, and they may now hold professional licences.

Lady Jockeys' Association Formed in 1972.

Lady's phaeton See **Park phaeton**.

La Guerinière, François Robichon de (1688-1751) A leading master of equitation in the mid-eighteenth century who is considered to be the father of the modern classical school. Author of *École de Cavalerie*, published in Paris in 1733. (See also **Dressage**)

Laid-on (hunting) The place in a supposed line of scent at which a pack of hounds is urged to own the scent and to hunt on.

Lairage A horse transit camp. Also a place where horses and ponies are rested before being transported by sea or air.

'Lame hand' A bad coachman. Also known as a 'spoon'.

Lameness A disturbance of the natural gait of the horse in which the animal's weight is unevenly distributed. When the affected foreleg strikes the ground, the head and withers rise. As the affected hind limb strikes the ground, the head is lowered and the point of the hip rises.

Laminae These appear as fine, very sensitive leaves covering the external surface of the pedal bone, extending from the coronary cushion to the lower edge of the pedal bone. They interlock with similar horny laminae lining the interior surface of the wall of the foot, forming a secure union of the hoof with the sensitive foot.

Laminitis (Also known as 'founder' or 'fever of the feet') Inflammation of the sensitive laminae (q.v.) under the wall of the hoof. The principal causes of the condition are an excess of carbohydrate-containing food – i.e. grass, cereals or horse nuts – and lack of exercise. Other causes are exhaustion, reaction to drugs, or the aftermath of severe infection. Laminitis may become chronic, causing permanent changes in which the pedal bone rotates, leading to 'dropped sole'. The symptoms are lameness, heat in the feet, unwillingness to move, typical stance with forelegs extended and weight on heels, hindlegs forward. In extreme cases the animal sweats profusely, trembles, and shows increased pulse and respiration rates. A pulse may be felt in the digital artery at the back of the fetlock as the blood supply to the foot becomes restricted. Animals with a history of laminitis show the typical 'ringed' wall of the hoof, and the horn is usually poor and crumbling. Veterinary attention is essential. See also **Sole, dropped**.

Lampas Swollen condition of the roof of the mouth. It sometimes appears when the incisor teeth change in young horses. It is often mis-diagnosed by owners as an explanation of loss of appetite.

Lampwick girth A girth of strong but very soft tubular fabric, ideal for use in summer.

Lancer bit A plain cheek curb-bit with two rein slots. A military bit, sometimes used in polo. The '9th Lancer' is made with an elbow. It is also useful in driving, where the leaders catch hold and carry the cheek.

Landais A breed of pony which originated on the Barthes plains, and which may be descended from the Steppes pony (Asiatic Wild Horse). Before World War I Arab blood was introduced to upgrade the breed, but its numbers declined to around a hundred. At one stage it was threatened with extinction, but was saved by a few enthusiastic breeders, using Welsh Section B and more Arab blood to improve the stock. The Landais stands between 11.3-13.1 hh (119.4-134.6 cm), has a neat head with some Arab characteristics. Its fine silky coat may be black, brown, bay or chestnut.

Landau An open carriage fitted with adjustable leather hoods which can be raised when required. Invented at Landau, Germany, in 1757, it was very popu-

Landau.

lar in England from mid-Victorian times onwards, varying from the modest, single-horse type to the postillion-driven state vehicle.

Landing side The far side (from the rider) of any obstacle to be jumped.

Landseer, Sir Edwin Henry, RA (1802-1873) The most famous animal painter of his day, who received many commissions from Queen Victoria and other persons of note. His exceptional talents were often marred by sentimentality, but he painted a number of spectacular pictures, such as *The Hunting of Chevy Chase* and *The Stag at Bay*.

Lane creepers A term applied to New Forest ponies who, before the boundaries of the Forest were fenced and gridded in 1963-64, used to wander down the lanes and roads into nearby villages, grazing on roadside verges. They made nuisances of themselves by jumping into farmers' fields and private gardens in search of food, and were also a considerable hazard to traffic on the roads.

L'Année Hippique The French edition of this equestrian annual was first published in 1943 and included a unique collection of some 300 articles and 8000 original photographs. It ceased publication in 1972, restarted in 1978, was published in 1979, then ceased until 1984, since when it has been published annually.

Laporte, George Henry (1799-1873) A painter of animals, figures and hunting subjects. He was official animal artist to the Duke of Cumberland, the second son of George II. Forty-three engravings of his paintings were published in the *Sporting Magazine*.

Lapping traces The inside trace of one leader passes the inside of the other and returns to its own bar.

Lariat A lasso used by riders and others for securing a steer or any other animal.

'Lark' To 'lark' is to jump fences when hounds are not running, or on returning from hunting.

Lash A silk or whip-cord attachment at the end of the thong of a driving whip or hunting crop.

Latchford, Benjamin A well-known nineteenth-century maker of bits, stirrup-irons and spurs, whose place of business was in Upper St Martin's Lane, London. He wrote *The Loriner* (1871). In the nineties, spurs were known as 'Latchfords'.

Latchfords Spurs (see above). Jorrocks (q.v.) in one of the 'Sporting Lectures' talks of 'letting in the Latchfords'.

Lateral aids Combination of two aids on the same side: i.e. left hand and leg; right hand and leg. (See **Diagonal aids**)

Lateral movement Any sideways and forward movement in which the horse's hind feet follow a different track to those of the forefeet.

Latvian A breed which at present is produced at two studs, the Tervete and the Burtnieki, to meet a demand in the USSR for quality riding horses. Thoroughbred, Hanoverian and Arab stallions are being used on light harness-type mares.

Latvian Harness Horse A Russian breed produced in the 1920s and first registered in 1952. There are two types: the light harness horse, produced from the use of Hanoverian blood on native mares, and the heavier type, from Anglo-Norman, Norfolk Roadster and Oldenburg stallions.

Lawn clippings These should never be fed unless absolutely fresh and free from chemicals – and then very sparingly; to do otherwise invites an attack of colic.

Lawn meet (hunting) A meet held at a private house by invitation of the occupier.

Lawton gig A smart, well-sprung gig named after its maker. (See **Gig**)

Lay, to (racing) To wager; to bet.

Lay on, to To put the main body of staghounds on the line after the tufters (q.v.) have driven the stag from the covert. To set a pack of hounds on to the place where the scent of a fox may be expected or on to the line of any hunted quarry.

Lazyback The back-rest of the outside seat on a coach or similar vehicle. Generally it can be turned down when not in use, but on a road coach it is fixed.

'Leadenhaller, a' See **Bag-fox**.

Leader Either of the two leading horses of a team ('near leader', 'off leader') or a driven horse which leads one or more.

Lead harness Harness for leaders, as distinct from wheel harness.

Leading leg This always means the leading front leg: i.e. the leg which strikes forward during the 'second time' of the canter or gallop, while the three remaining legs are in support. In racing it is important for a horse to lead with his near-fore on a left-handed course, and with his off-fore on a right-handed course.

Leading on the road This should always be done from the leader's left-hand side, keeping the leader between the horse and the traffic. A bridle should always be used, not a headcollar.

Leading reins Paddock lead reins are made of webbing, with a buckle and billet fastening, a snap hook, or a Y-fastening which passes through the bit rings and a central 'D' before buckling. For stallions leather lead reins are used with a stallion chain. Paddock leads are 8 ft (2.43 m) long. Stallion leads are often considerably longer.

Lean head A head in which the muscles, blood vessels and bony protruberances show up distinctly. It is usually neatly formed and has a fine skin.

Leaping-head or leaping pommel See **Pommel**.

Lease a horse, to A recognised form of temporary ownership in breeding, racing, show jumping and showing. The fees and period of lease are subject to negotiation.

Leasing (racehorse) Horses may be leased from the owner for their racing career. The terms of the lease may be settled between the parties concerned, but the lease itself must be signed by the parties and lodged at the Racing Calendar Office.

Leasing (stallion) A practical means of introducing the blood of a certain horse in a district for a season or more, whether to be travelled or otherwise. Many are also leased without reference to introducing the blood to a district, but simply because of the lessee's particular fancy for the horse as a sire.

Leather COWHIDE is used in the manufacture of most saddles in Britain: sheephide, pigskin, and doe or buckskin are used in only small quantities. The upper or outside of leather is known as the 'grain' side. During the dressing process it becomes sealed and nearly waterproof, and at this stage the colour is also added. The inner side is known as the 'flesh' side.

A complete hide is divided into sections. The best part of a hide is found in the *butts* on either side of the backbone. The quality, texture, and substance (i.e. the thickness) of the hide deteriorates further down the flanks. Butt leather is used for bridles and for saddle flaps. For some long reins for driving, a full back from neck to tail is used.

The belly is thin, and is used for relatively unimportant straps. The shoulder, which is thicker and less pliable than the butt, is used principally for headcollars. In poorer quality saddles it may also be used for the flaps.

PIGSKIN, because of its elasticity and relative lack of substance, is used for saddle seats. DOE- or BUCKSKIN (both of which are extremely expensive) are sometimes used to cover the cowhide flaps and skirts. SHEEPHIDE is used for the linings, etc. of cheaper saddles.

RAWHIDE is cowhide which has undergone a special tanning, and is recognised by the lighter, untanned line running through the centre when viewed from the side. It is very strong, and is used for stirrup leathers and girths. HELVETIA LEATHER, which is greasy, tough, and yellow in colour, may be used in reinforcing martingales, nosebands, etc. REVERSED HIDE is cowhide mechanically roughened, and is sometimes used in saddles to give more grip.

Leather curb See **Humane curb**.

Leathers, stirrup Leather straps (of cowhide, rawhide, or buffalo hide) by means of which stirrup irons are attached to the saddle. Before mounting, the length of a leather can be gauged by placing the iron under the arm and extending the arm along the leather until the fingertips touch the side bar of the saddle. So that the stirrup irons will lie where the rider can readily 'pick them up', the leathers are twisted several times from right to left and then released.

Leech, John (1817-1864) Caricaturist and illustrator, who produced many coloured woodcuts of sporting subjects and illustrated *Mr Sponge's Sporting Tour, Handley Cross*, and other works of R. S. Surtees (q.v.). He was also a prolific contributor to *Punch*.

'Leery' Old-time horseman's expression for a horse who, – though not vicious or nappy – moves hesitatingly and seems not to have much heart in his work.

'Left at the post' Term describing a horse who is slow to take off at the start of a race and is left at the rear of other runners as they get away.

Left-hand course A course where the horses run in an anti-clockwise direction: e.g. Aintree, Cheltenham, Doncaster and Epsom.

Leggings These were made of various leathers – pigskin, polo calf, box calf, reversed calf (i.e. suede finish) – and also of such materials as box cloth and canvas. They were usually fastened with buttons or laces and hooks. A type fastened with metal thongs and slots were known as 'Richmonds'. Leggings were worn with breeches and 'high-lows' (ankle-length boots).

Legs The legs of riding boots, which may be lined or single.

Legs, filled Usually caused by over-feeding or lack of exercise. The limbs swell suddenly and become very tender and stiff. Young horses and those run down by over-work are the most prone to this ailment.

Legs, gammy/gummy The tendons below a horse's knees and hocks should stand out clearly under the skin like a taut cord. If the line of the tendons should be concealed because the legs are 'filled', or in a state of puffiness due to strain or hard work, the term 'gammy' or 'gummy' legs is used. See also **Legs, filled**.

'Legs out of one hole' Descriptive of

horses who are narrow-chested and go close in front.

Leg spray A circular piece of rubber hosing joined at the break by a T-connection to which a hosepipe can be fitted. The inside of the circle is perforated to allow water to be sprayed all round the leg. It is used to combat puffy legs.

Leg-up, to A method of assisted mounting. An assistant stands to the left of and somewhat behind the rider, and grasps the rider's left leg (which is sharply bent at the knee) above the ankle with the right hand. As the rider 'gives' or ducks to spring, the assistant lifts the leg firmly and somewhat sharply, enabling the rider to clear the saddle with his right leg. The rider's spring is essential to a neat and effective leg-up.

Leg yielding The yielding or obedience of the horse to the pressure of the rider's leg on or near the girth so that the animal's whole body moves away sideways from the pressure.

Lemon-pied A hound with a white body and lemon-coloured markings.

Length The measurement of a horse from end to end used as a unit of distance in racing. The distance separating the leading horses at the finish of a race is judged in lengths, half-lengths, neck, head, and short head.

Leopard marking Where darker spots are widely distributed on a lighter background in a horse's coat. See **Appaloosa**.

'Lepper' (Leaper) Colloquial Irish hunting term for a jumper – 'a good lepper'.

'Let down' A term used to imply a well-conditioned and normal body. It is the converse of 'tucked up' (q.v.). (See also **Hocks, well let down**)

Leucoderma A condition in which white patches appear on the hairless part of the horse (round the eye and under the tail) due to lack of pigment. They are unsightly, and permanent, but not harmful.

Leucocyte White blood cell.

'Leu-in', to (hunting) To put hounds into covert.

Levade High School movement in which the horse raises itself from the ground with the forefeet and then draws them in whilst the hindquarters, deeply bent in the haunches, bear the entire weight of the body.

Levade

Level mover A horse that is true and level at the walk, trot and canter. The toes of the forelegs point to the front, the distance between the pairs of fore and hindlegs is correct, and the hocks are firm and steady.

Liberty A horse shows liberty when it moves with freedom, using its shoulders and covering the ground freely.

Liberty horse A circus horse which performs a series of movements in the ring, unhandled and unridden, controlled only by the trainer or presenter. Because of their presence, beauty and honesty of work, and handy size, Arab stallions are often preferred.

Lice Parasites found commonly on horses, particularly in late winter and early spring. The horse rubs itself on any convenient object and the hair comes away, leaving bare patches, more particularly at the poll, throat, crest, shoulder and flanks. Two types are found – blood sucking lice, and biting lice which feed on skin and hair débris. Grooming a horse regularly reduces the chances of survival of the lice, as does good management and the judicious use of insecticidal louse powders.

Licence, racecourse This must be renewed annually, and all meetings must be sanctioned by the Stewards of the Jockey Club. Applications for fixtures must be made to the Jockey Club by 1 March and must be accompanied by an audited statement of accounts for the preceding year.

Licence, trainer's Every trainer of a horse running under the Rules of Racing must obtain an annual licence from the Stewards of the Jockey Club. Applications must be sent in for consideration before 1 March. Any trainer running a horse without a licence is liable to a fine or to be made a disqualified person at the discretion of the Stewards. Women were first granted licences to train under Jockey Club rules in 1966. (See also **Permit holders**)

Lifespan, horse's The length of life of a horse varies according to usage, care and attention, and, to some extent, breed. Light and regular work and good food have a large bearing on age. The greatest recorded age is that of Old Billy, who originally worked as a farm horse and was later purchased by the Manchester and Irwell Navigation Company, as a barge horse. He died aged sixty-two.

Lift A hunting term used when hounds are taken by a huntsman to a point where he thinks the fox has moved, or where the fox has been seen.

Ligament A band of fibrous tissue connecting two bones at a joint, or supporting internal organs. Many ligaments are found around the bones associated with a particular joint: e.g. collateral ligament of the knee joint. An example of an internal ligament in a mare is the ovarian ligament which supports the ovaries.

Ligamentum nuchae The long ligament, extending from poll to withers, which helps support the head. It is divided into two parts: a funicular (rope-like) portion, and a lamellar (fan-like) portion. It is the funicular portion which becomes necrotic and gives rise to poll evil (q.v.).

Light horse The name of a group comprising hunters, hacks and riding horses in general.

Lightness The horse's perfect obedience to the slightest indications of hand and leg.

Limekilns, the Situated at Newmarket, on the eastern side of the town, and well-known for its summer gallops. Usually open only in dry weather.

Limousin A half-bred horse of English blood, named after the region in France where it is bred.

Linch pin The pin passed through the end of a vehicle's axle-tree to keep the wheel in place. It is still used as the sole means of securing the wheels of some farm waggons and carts.

Lincolnshire Handicap The first big race of the flat-racing season, formerly run at Lincoln, now at Doncaster. It is the first leg of the Spring Double; The Grand National is the second.

Lincolnshire Trotter An extinct breed of trotting horse once well-known in the county. It was first bred after the Civil War and was much used as a coach and carriage horse in London. The breed probably became merged in the general light harness horse of the Eastern counties as typified by the Hackney of the period.

Line In hunting, the trail of scent on which a pack hunt their fox.

Line-breeding The mating of individuals who have a common ancestor some generations removed. It is used to intensify a desired hereditary trait.

Linen bearings A covering of linen sewn on to the serge panel of a saddle.

Linhay (cart-linhay) An open farm shed for housing farm-carts.

Linseed The seed of flax. It is rich in protein and oil, and is very useful for putting flesh on a poor horse as well as for putting gloss on the coat. It *must* be cooked before feeding, as in the uncooked state it may contain toxic substances. Generally it is used in the form of 'jelly', or 'tea', or with bran as a mash. Linseed oil may be fed as a supplement.

Linseed jelly is made by putting about a quarter pound of linseed in a large saucepan at least half filled with water, which is left to stand overnight. The next day it is boiled for several hours with regular stirring to prevent sticking. The jelly forms as the mixture cools. Linseed tea is made in a similar fashion, but with more water. NOTE: *Linseed jelly and tea do not keep for more than 24 hours.*

Linseed oil meal cake This has similar properties to cooked linseed, and may be fed with grain. (See above).

Lipizzaner The breed takes its name from the stud at Lipizza near Trieste founded by the Archduke Charles, son of the Emperor Ferdinand I of Austria. The origin of Lipizzaners is, however, much older. They came from the Iberian Peninsula and are believed to be the descendants of the Spanish (Andalusian) horses used for ceremonial duties by Roman emperors. At Lipizza, where nine stallions and twenty-four mares formed the foundation stock, outside blood (Italian and Arabian) was introduced in later years, resulting in the development of six lines, named after the six founding stallions: Conversano, Favory, Maestoso, Siglavy, Pluto, and Neopolitano – lines which exist to this day. They have achieved particular fame as the High School horses of the Spanish Riding School of Vienna (q.v.).

The Lipizzaner stands between 15.1-16.2 hh (154.9-165 cm), has a well-shaped head – often with a convex profile – a well-set-on neck, a markedly strong, compact and muscular deep body, with very powerful quarters, and a high-set tail. The limbs are short, with good, flat bone. Until the middle of the eighteenth century, Lipizzaners were bay, dun, cream, brown, spotted, or palomino, as well as grey, but now most are grey, and only grey stallions are used in the Spanish Riding School. Bays are still occasionally found. Foals are born black or very dark brown. The Spanish Riding School stallions are bred at Piber, in Yugoslavia, where the foals are branded: on the left croup with a P (for Piber) under the Austrian Imperial crown; on the left cheek with an L (for Lipizzaner); on the left side under the saddle with the initials of the sire's line and the dam's sire's line; on the right side with the registered number.

Lip markings See **Flesh marks**. In any written description of a horse it should be noted whether these markings embrace the whole or a portion of either lip.

Lip strap A thin leather strap fastened to one side of the ring of a curb bit. It is threaded through a special link provided in the curb chain, and buckled at the other end to the corresponding ring of the curb bit. The strap keeps the curb chain from overhanging the lower lip, and the cheeks of the bit from turning. It also stops the horse from catching hold of the cheek of the bit with its teeth.

Lip tattoo Identification marks tattooed on the lips of horses. Sometimes also used on the ear. In some cases animals have suffered permanent nerve damage from this tattooing.

Lips A horse's lips should be thin, and carried closed. A drooping under-lip is unsightly and is supposed to be a sign of lack of courage.

List A dark stripe along the back (see **Stripe dorsal**). Also the particular place on a horse's loins where the hair meets and runs in different directions.

Lithuanian Heavy Harness Horse This breed was developed for agricultural work in the first quarter of the twentieth century. The Swedish Ardennes with their size and strength, were crossed with Zhmud mares (q.v.), whose principal qualities are those of great hardiness and endurance. The third and fourth generations of the crosses were then interbred to produce the Lithuanian Heavy Harness Horse. It was registered as a breed in 1963. Standing between 15.1-15.2 hh (154.9-157.5 cm), it has a long head, a good, deep body, and strong, medium-length legs. It is very muscular. Chestnut is the predominant colour.

Litter A vehicle formerly used for the transport of invalids or the elderly. It contained a couch, and was enclosed by curtains. It was fitted with poles on either side and carried by men or horses.

Litter Straw bedding in stables.

Litter The puppies produced by a hound bitch at one whelping.

Liver fluke A flat-worm, parasitic in the liver which is usually found in cattle and sheep, but can affect horses. It occurs in wet conditions where the infected secondary host – a very small snail living in mud on the edges of wet places in pasture – is present. Horses may swallow the liver-fluke cysts which, in due course, will migrate to the liver, develop, and cause unthriftiness, anaemia, and diarrhoea.

Liverpool bit The most usual type of bit used for driving. It has two or three slots on the bar which provide an alternate amount of control on the horse's mouth.

Liverpool bit.

Liverpool gig Very similar to the Lawton gig (q.v.).

'Liverpool horse' A term implying that the horse referred to is capable of jumping the Grand National course (q.v.).

Livery, horse at A horse boarded out at a livery stable, to be fed, cared for, or turned out at the owner's request for an agreed sum.

Livery cloth A name given to the fine, faced wool cloth used in the manufacture of paddock clothing.

Livery stables/yard A term applied to an establishment which offers to take in horses at livery.

'Live with hounds', to A term meaning the ability of a horse to keep up with hounds when they are running very fast.

Loaded shoulder Excessive thickness of muscle lying over the region of the shoulder.

'Lobbing and sobbing' When a horse rolls about and is blown after an exhausting gallop.

Lobuno Criollo (q.v.) term for a dark blue colour with black points.

Lock The amount of turn possible in the forecarriage and front wheels of a vehicle. Coaches have a quarter-distance lock, but many other carriages have a full lock allowing it to turn in a small space.

Lockjaw See **Tetanus**.

Locote An outlaw horse of the American West. The name derives from locote, a poisonous prairie weed which, if eaten, is said to turn a horse mad.

Lodging rooms Hounds' sleeping quarters, containing benches about 1½ ft (45 cm) from the ground, running round three sides and almost completely occupying the floor space.

Log headcollar A solid block of wood with a hole bored down its centre through which a rope is passed and knotted. The other end is slipped through a ring in the manger, allowing limited scope for movement.

Loins The part of the back which extends down either side of the spinal vertebrae lying immediately behind the saddle.

Lokai A breed from the foothills and valleys of Southern Tadzhikstan which results from the crossing of Central Asian horses with those from the steppes. It is a dual-purpose pack and saddle animal: its sure-footedness, strength and endurance making it ideal for the mountainous terrain. Lighter, riding-type Lokais, using Arab, Thoroughbred and Akhal-Teké blood, have also been produced. The breed stands between 13.3-14.3 hh (139.7-149.9 cm).

London Cart Horse Parade Society See London Harness Horse Parade Society

London colour A trade term for the light colour usually used in new saddlery. See **Tanning**.

London Harness Horse Parade Society This was formed in 1966 by the amalgamation of two older societies, the London Cart Horse Parade Society (founded in 1890), and the London Van Horse Parade Society (1904). The Society holds an annual parade on Easter Monday in Regent's Park, London. The objects of the London Cart Horse Parade Society were: to improve the general condition and treatment of the London cart horses. Those of the London Van Horse Parade Society were: the improvement of the general condition and treatment of van and light draught horses employed for business purposes, and the encouragement of drivers to take a humane and individual interest in the horses under their care.

Lone Eagle See **Norton Perfection**.

Long-distance riding/Endurance riding A sport which has become very popular in Britain during the last twenty years. Rides of distances from 25 to 100 miles (40 to 160 km) are undertaken, and all horses competing must pass strict veterinary tests before, during and after the rides. Some rides are judged on a 'first past the post and fit to continue' basis; others on the basis of a minimum required speed, with penalties for failing to comply with certain veterinary requirements. The sport is now internationally recognised by the FEI (q.v.). In Britain, the British Horse Society Long Distance Riding Group and the Endurance Horse and Pony Society each organise rides. Principal rides run by the former include the GOLDEN HORSE-SHOE (q.v.), the NATIONAL CHAMPIONSHIP (held over 100 miles (160 km) to be completed within 24 hours), and the GOOD-WOOD INTERNATIONAL, recognised by the FEI (50 miles/80 km) on two successive days). The Endurance Horse and Pony Society's principal ride is the SUMMER SOLSTICE 100-miles-in-24-hours (160 km) ride. The sport was firmly established in Australia and the USA some time before it become popular in Britain and Europe. See also **Tevis Ride**; and **Quilty Ride**.

Longeing See **Lungeing**.

Longeing rein See **Lungeing rein**.

Longest race The longest race in Britain on the flat is the Queen Alexandra Stakes run over 2¾ miles (4.4 km) at Ascot in the summer.

'Long in the tooth' A term descriptive of an old horse.

Long jump record Held by Lt. Col. Lopez del Hierro of Spain on the Anglo-Arab Amado Mio, who jumped 27 ft 2¾ ins (8.30 m) at Barcelona in 1951 under FEI (q.v.) regulations.

Long-reining The driving of a young horse by a trainer on foot. Most movements can be taught without the horse suffering the weight of the rider's body. It is said to produce more finesse in training before backing than is obtainable by lungeing, though this is debated by some experts. The trainer has good control through the 'outer' rein and should be able to place the horse where he will, with complete control of pace.

Long reins These should consist of two separate webbing reins fitted with leather billets to prevent twisting. Each should be about 25 ft (7.6 m) long. They must not be fastened or buckled together.

Long Tom A racing term for a hunting whip. The trainer or his assistant carries one on the gallops to encourage horses to start.

Lonsdale, Hugh Cecil Lowther, 5th Earl of (1857-1944) MFH of the Woodland Pytchley, Cottesmore and Quorn. He may be said to have been associated with all activities in the horse world throughout his long life. He was for many years a predominant figure at the Royal International Horse Show (q.v.) at Olympia.

Lonsdale girth A very short girth, used with Lonsdale girth straps (q.v.).

Lonsdale girth straps Straps which extend well beneath the saddle flap. Used with a special short girth, they remove the bulk of girth buckles under the thigh, and are frequently employed on dressage and jumping saddles.

Lonsdale waggonette A luxurious form of waggonette (q.v.) with a low-hung rounded body and folding hoods. Introduced by the 5th Earl of Lonsdale (q.v.).

'Looker' One who for payment 'watches' horses or cattle on unfenced marsh land which is surrounded by dykes. The name has been used for centuries on the Romney Marshes, Sussex, but is now falling into disuse.

Loose box See **Stables**.

Loose-headed Said of a horse which runs out of control, e.g. while out at grass.

Loose rein A rein which hangs loosely without contact between the horse's mouth and the rider's or driver's hands.

Lope The characteristic gait of a cow pony; an easy, uncollected canter.

Lord Mayor's State Coach An elaborate processional carriage built in 1757 by Berry and Barker of Holborn. In the Lord Mayor's Procession it is drawn by six heavy horses wearing State harness made in 1833. It weighs 3 tons 16 cwt. The body of the coach is supported on four black leather braces fastened with gilt buckles bearing the Arms of the City of London. The paintings on the panels are attributed to Cipriani, but this is not an established fact. Brakes were first fitted to the coach in 1951.

Loriner A manufacturer of bits, spurs, stirrups and minor steel adjuncts of a horse's harness.

Loriners' Company, the The Masters, Wardens, Assistants and Commonalty of Loriners of the City of London, properly known as the Worshipful Company of Loriners. It ranks 53rd in order of precedence. The earliest known reference to the Loriners' Company dates back to 1245 and relates to the representation of those concerned in the manufacture of bits, spurs and stirrups.

'Lost shoes' A Leicestershire term implying 'dead beat'.

'Lot of horse in a little room, a' A reference to a horse that is close to the ground, compact, short-coupled, and with good bone.

Lower school Refers to the level of training immediately below High School attained by a dressage horse. Also known as Campagne School.

Lowther, Viscount In 1666 Lord Lowther took by road from Lowther Castle, Westmorland, the family pack of hounds to hunt what is now the Cottesmore country, with which the Lowther family have long been associated.

Lowther riding bit In curb bits this refers to the type of cheek where, instead of being of the usual pattern which has a neck, the curb rein ring drops from the hole in the cheek. (See **Arkwright bit**)

Lozenge A round piece of leather which may be fitted round a bit at the side of a horse's mouth. It is generally used to straighten a horse that hangs from its bit on one side, or to stop chafing at the angle of the lips.

Lucerne See **Alfalfa**.

Lugging bit See **Anti-lug**.

Lundy Ponies Selected New Forest mares and fillies and a Thoroughbred stallion were taken to Lundy Island in 1928 to establish a breed. Various other stallions were subsequently used, including Welsh and Connemara. The predominant colour was dun, and the ponies stood about 13.2 hh (137.2 cm) A few remain on the island.

Lungeing (previously known as 'longeing') With a single rein attached to a lungeing cavesson the horse can be circled to left and to right, made to walk, trot and canter, to halt, and to get used to and obey words of command. Especially useful in the early training of a young horse.

Lungeing rein This should be of tubular webbing, about 25 ft (76. m) in length, with a swivel billet at the bit end and a hand loop at the other. It is fastened to one of the rings on the noseplate of the lungeing cavesson. It is also available with a swivel snap-hook attachment.

Lungeing whip A long whip with a light thong. An essential part of lungeing equipment.

Lungworm A species of worm, *Dictyocaulus arnfieldi*, picked up by horses and donkeys from pasture in summer. Though a high proportion of donkeys may be infected, it rarely causes problems in them. In horses the lungs are affected by the adult worm, causing a dry cough and lung damage. Infection may be prevented by maintaining clean pasture, and particular care should be taken if horses and donkeys graze together. Veterinary advice should be sought. Treatment with modern worming compounds is effective.

Lurrie Lancashire name for a flat-bodied four-wheeler (dray).

Lusitano Originally the Portuguese Army horse, and probably based on Andalusian blood. It is used in light agriculture, but is best known as a mount for Portuguese bull-fighters. It stands between 15-16 hh (152.4-162.6 cm) and is a strong, compact riding horse, with a high action. Lusitanos are exceptionally agile; in Portuguese bull-fighting it is considered a disgrace for a horse to be injured by a charging bull.

Lymphangitis, epizootic Inflammation of the lymphatic vessels and nodes, most frequently in the hindlegs, but can occur elsewhere. Symptoms include hot, very painful swelling under the skin; the affected area sometimes extending from foot to stifle. The swelling may be marked, and there may be raised pulse and respiration rates, shivering, frequent movement of the legs, and extreme lameness. The most common cause is excess feeding with lack of sufficient exercise, but it may also be due to infection. Treatment with drugs may be necessary. The non-infective type may be prevented by cutting down food before a rest day.

M In racing, a mile.

M & M Mountain and Moorland. (See **Mountain and Moorland Ponies of the British Isles**)

MFH Master of Foxhounds.

MFHA Master of Foxhounds Association (q.v.).

MH Master of Harriers.

MRCVS Member of the Royal College of Veterinary Surgeons.

MSH Master of Staghounds.

Macs Mackintosh racing breeches sometimes worn by jockeys when racing in bad weather.

'Made' A horse is said to be 'made' when his education for riding and/or driving is complete.

'Made hunter' A hunter properly schooled to negotiate hunting country with comfort and safety. One definition is said to run thus: 'the outline and shape of a cob, the spirit and breeding of a racehorse, the size and scope of a carriage-horse, and the manners and action of a park hack'.

'Made the hit' Said of a hound when it has found the scent of the hunted fox. (See **'Own the line'**).

Madison Square Garden See **National Horse Show (USA)**.

Madrina See **Tropilla**.

Magenis snaffle (Often miscalled 'McGuinness'.) The mouth has slits into which are set revolving rollers which

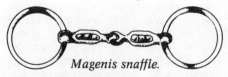
Magenis snaffle.

work loosely. It prevents a horse evading the bit by crossing its jaws. A popular bit for 'strong' horses.

Mahogany tops Brown leather tops on black hunting boots.

Maiden (racing) A maiden for flat racing is a horse of either sex which has never won a flat race, except for minor exceptions like matches. Similarly, a maiden for steeplechasing is a horse of either sex which has never won a steeplechase or hurdle race (point-to-points, matches, etc. excepted).

Maiden allowance A special allowance given in some races for a horse which has never won a race.

Maiden mare and Maiden Different definitions exist. The National Light Horse Breeding Society (HIS) gives 'a mare which has never been put to a stallion'; another: 'one carrying her first foal'.

Maiden race A race confined to maiden horses at the start of the race (See **Maiden (racing)**).

Mail axle The safest type of axle, as introduced on mail coaches, in which the wheel is secured by three nuts.

Mail coach Specially designed and painted as a Royal vehicle, i.e. black with maroon panels and scarlet undercarriage and wheels, and decorated with the Royal cypher. The mail coach was run under government contract before the invention of railways, and was introduced by John Palmer in 1784 to supersede the carrying of mail by men on horseback. The coach carried only nine passengers (four inside and five on top), as opposed to the sixteen on a road or stage coach (q.v.), no seats being available on the back since this area was occupied solely by the guard who had the mail under his care in the hind boot.

Mail phaeton The heaviest type of phaeton for a pair, this was built on a perch, with mail axles and coach springing as in a mail coach.

Main bar The largest of the three bars used in team driving. (See **Bars**)

Maize (corn in USA) A high-energy-producing grain, which in Britain is usually fed steam-flaked, but in the USA may be fed on the cob. It is very palatable, but because of its high starch content it can be over-heating, and should not be fed in large amounts.

'Make and break' A term sometimes used for breaking in a young horse.

'Makes a noise' Unsound in wind, i.e. whistling or roaring. See **'Roarer'**.

Malapolski A Polish riding and light draught horse developed from native Polish stock with infusions of Arab blood to produce a riding horse type. Furioso and Gidran blood was introduced to produce a heavier type.

Mallein test A test carried out to detect glanders in horses, mules or donkeys – usually suspects or contacts. It is applied by injecting mallein into or under the skin. Mallein is prepared from artificial cultures of *Pfeifferella mallei* – the causal organism of glanders – and its use is comparable to that of tuberculin for detecting tuberculosis in cattle.

Mallenders An old term for sub-acute or chronic inflammation of the skin at the back of the knee joint. A watery discharge causes the hair to stick out and eventually to fall off, leaving a scurfy thickening of the skin. It is a common complaint in cart-horses when out of condition and in those with thick, gammy legs. See **Sallenders**; **Legs, gammy**.

Mallet Polo stick (q.v.).

Mameluke bit A curb bit with a ported mouth, to the centre of which is attached a large ring. Sometimes confused with the Turkish curb, which is similar except for having loose eyes at the top of the cheek which reduces poll pressure.

Manada (South American) A group or herd of wild mares collected by a mustang stallion. Depending upon the virility, courage, and determination of the mustang concerned, this would vary from six or eight to fifty or more. Manadas of about 100 have been quoted.

Mancha A Criollo pony, joint hero with Gato of Tschiffely's Ride. (See also **Criollo**, and **Tschiffely, A. F.**)

Manchero A Spanish word denoting one who not only journeys on horseback, but also makes the schooling, care and comfort of his horse his first consideration.

Manchester team See **Trandem**.

Mane The long hair flowing from the top of the neck (crest).

Mane-drag A comb affixed to a handle, used primarily for trimming and dragging a rough mane.

Manège An enclosure for the teaching of equitation or the schooling of horses. In recent years this has come to mean an *outdoor* enclosure.

Manège figures See **School figures**.

Mane plaiting Manes may be plaited (a) to show the shape of the neck, or (b) to train a difficult mane to fall on the desired side of the neck. See **Plaits**.

Mane pulling Removal of hair from the mane to (a) shorten it; (b) thin it; (c) allow it to lie flat. It is done by winding a few long underneath hairs around a comb and pulling sharply. Hairs are never pulled from the upper layer, as a shortened fringe will form.

Mane thread Heavy linen thread used in plaiting manes.

Mange A highly infectious skin condition caused by mites of the order *Acarina*. There are four types – chorioptic, demodectic, psoroptic and sarcoptic. The disease is rare in Great Britain, but the veterinary surgeon *must* be informed if it is suspected, as sarcoptic mange is a notifiable disease (q.v.).
CHORIOPTIC MANGE occurs on the fetlock or pastern, particularly in animals with heavy feathering, and is characterised by scabs. The horse scratches or rubs the area, and stamps its feet.
DEMODACTIC MANGE is caused by *Demodex folliculorum*, and attacks the hair follicles and sebaceous glands of the skin, or the glands of the eye. The skin becomes scaly or covered with pustules. It is often found in parts of the mane or tail.
PSOROPTIC MANGE is caused by the mite *Psoroptes communis var. equi*, which burrows into the skin, causing very thick scabs.
SARCOPTIC MANGE is, as indicated, the

most serious, and is caused by the mite *Sarcoptes scabiei var. equi.* It burrows into the skin, eventually causing small red blisters. The hair falls out, leaving bald patches.

Manger For feeding horses, these may be of iron, hard wood, or plastic, wide enough to enable the horse to eat comfortably and deep enough to prevent the horse from wasting food by pushing it out with his nose. There are various designs, with or without a receptacle for water and a hay-rack attached; mangers are sometimes fitted into wall-angles (corners). Overhead hay-racks should be avoided, since falling dust and seed may affect the horse's eyes.

Manger log See **Log headcollar.**

Mangolds A root crop, which should not be fed during the year they are grown. Also known as mangel wurzels.

Manipur A pony bred for hundreds, possibly thousands, of years in Manipur State, E. India. Early manuscripts record that in the seventh century, the then reigning king of Manipur introduced polo played on ponies bred in that state. The pony is believed to be bred from Mongolian-Arab stock, and is small, 11-13 hh (111.8-132.1 cm), with a proportionate body, sturdy and sure-footed. The head is rather long, but of gentle appearance, and set on a clean, strong muscular neck; the legs are of good quality, with strong knees and hocks.

Manners A horse's obedience to the will of his rider, given in a generous, willing fashion.

Man O' War Arguably the greatest American racehorse. Bred in 1917 by August Belmont II, he was sold to Samuel D. Riddle as a yearling. Man O' War was by Mahubah, and was beaten in only one of his twenty-one races – and that defeat was blamed on the incompetence of his jockey. He won the Preakness and the Belmont Stakes, and broke seven records during his three-year-old season. His owner allowed him only twenty-five mares a season at stud, yet in spite of this restriction, he has had an enormous influence on racing, with horses such as Relko, Sir Ivor, and Never Say Die trac-

ing back to him. He was known as 'Big Red' because of his fiery chestnut colour and impressive build.

Manual of Horsemastership The well-known Army Manual of Horsemastership, Equitation and Animal Transport, on which, in pre-mechanised Army days, the whole British cavalry and artillery were trained.

Manure The accumulated excreta of the horse, and a most valuable fertiliser.

Marchador Gaucho (q.v.) term for a fast rolling gait between a trot and a canter.

Mare A female equine which has attained the age of four years.

Mare-colt The name more usually applied to fillies by the moormen of Exmoor and the Commoners of the New Forest.

Marengo The charger ridden by Napoleon throughout his Italian and Austrian campaigns, and at the battle of Waterloo. The horse's skeleton is now housed at the National Army Museum, Royal Military Academy, Sandhurst, Camberley, Surrey, England.

Mare's-nest A supposed discovery which proves to be false.

Mark The dark centre of the tooth of a young horse.

Market Harborough A type of martingale (q.v.) used to control headstrong horses. It has the normal neck strap

Market Harborough.

171

and girth fittings, but at the centre of the chest, where the two former straps meet, there is a ring. To this are attached, by means of a spring hook, two pieces of strong leather. These are led up through the bit rings, and fasten onto the reins by means of one of four metal Ds attached to them. Pressure is brought to bear on the bars of the mouth only when the head is thrown upwards; at all other times the appliance is inoperative.

Market Harborough In hunting circles, the centre for meets of the Fernie, Pytchley and Woodland Pytchley Hounds.

star

stripe

star and stripe

blaze

white muzzle

snip and lip marks

Face markings.

Markings, face Markings on the face and head include: face markings, covering the forehead and front of the face, extending laterally towards the mouth; muzzle markings, embracing both lips and extending to the region of the nostrils; and star markings, appearing on the forehead. The description should include reference to the shape, size, intensity and position. Stripe markings extend down the face, no wider than the flat anterior surface of the nasal bones. If the stripe is a continuation of a star, it must be described as a star and a stripe co-joined; if separate and distinct, as an interrupted stripe; it should be specified whether the stripe is narrow or broad.

Markings, limb Markings on the limbs include: coronet markings, where the hair immediately above the hoof is white; fetlock markings, comprising the region of the fetlock joint and downwards; heel markings, extending from the back of the pastern to the ergot; pastern mark-

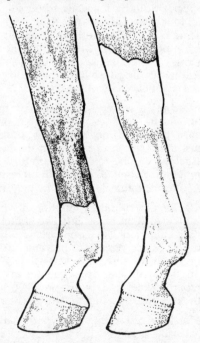

Sock (left) and stocking markings.

ings, comprising the area immediately below the fetlock joint and downwards, and which may be elaborated as 'half pastern', or 'threequarter pastern'; sock markings, extending to about half-way up the cannon bone; stocking markings, extending to the region of the knee or hock.

'Mark to ground' When hounds bay outside an earth or a drain inside which is a hunted fox, they are said to 'mark the fox to ground'.

Marocco Elizabethan performing horse exhibited in London. At a command it would dance, rear, lie down, and tap out with its foot numbers turned up on a dice. In 1600, ridden by its owner, Thomas Bankes, it climbed to the top of St Paul's. In Italy, Marocco's abilities were attributed to black magic and the horse and owner were ordered to be burnt to death. Bankes returned safely to England, but Marocco's fate is unknown.

Marshal (USA) Rider who leads a parade of entries in a race past the grandstand.

Marshall, Benjamin (1767-1835) Leicestershire-born sporting artist. First studied under L. F. Abbot, the portrait painter, and later painted with outstanding talent, hunters, racehorses, hacks, and sporting groups. His pictures possess a unique English quality and fetch very high prices. After a coaching accident, he wrote sporting articles under the pen-names of 'Observator', and 'Breeder-of-Cocktails'. His son, Lambert, also became a sporting artist.

Marshland Shales One of the most famous of the early nineteenth-century Norfolk and Suffolk trotters from which many of the modern Hackneys are descended. Marshland Shales was sired by Thistelton's Shales out of Jenkin's Mare, both of which went back to Original Shales, grandson of Flying Childers. Marshland Shales was a 15 hh (152.4 cm) bright chestnut of great stamina, a prolific sire, and capable of carrying 20 stone (127 kg). He had, reputedly, trotted 20 miles (32 km) within the hour. George Borrow in *Lavengro* has a moving description of Marshland Shales in his old age. (See **Original Shales**)

Martingale A device, in various arrangements, to regulate a horse's head carriage, claimed by Richard Berenger (d. 1782) to have been invented by an Italian riding master, Evangelista. A martingale usually consists of a strap or straps, attached to the girth at one end, and at the other to the reins or to the noseband.

Martingale, bib A running martingale having the split filled in with baghide to prevent young racehorses becoming

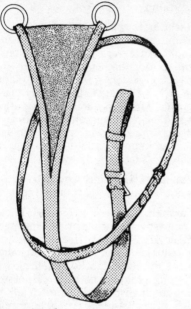

Bib martingale.

entangled in the martingale or catching it on their corner teeth. Also known as a web martingale.

Martingale, Cheshire A standing type (q.v.) which divides at the breast, the two extensions being connected directly to the bit rings, either by buckles or snap hooks.

Martingale, combined One in which both running and standing martingales are incorporated into one body and can be used together.

Martingale, Continental Of French origin, the body ends in a ring at the breast. A strap passes through the ring, fastening round the head behind the poll at one end, and attached to the noseband at the other. Used to assist in obtaining a lower head carriage and proper employment of the quarters.

Martingale, Grainger A martingale with

the branches directly and permanently attached to a nosepiece. The latter is fitted above the bit but lower than the normal cavesson noseband. There is a sliding fitment joining the branches which can be adjusted to give more or less freedom, as desired.

Martingale, Irish A loop of leather through which the reins pass, carried under the neck, thus preventing the reins being thrown over the horse's head in the event of a fall. There are usually two rings

Irish martingale.

attached by a piece of double-sewn leather 4½ ins (11.4 cm) long, but all-metal patterns are also made. Most racehorses run with Irish martingales, which are also called 'rings' or 'spectacles'.

Martingale, pugri A standing martingale, used only in polo, and made of turban (pugri) cloth. It is usually coloured, and all four ponies of the same team wear the same colour. The cloth prevents cutting or 'nipping' of the flesh, which, in the stress of the game, could happen with a leather martingale; a further advantage is the slight elasticity of the cloth.

Martingale, pulley A running martingale in which the rings are mounted on a cord passing through a pulley situated just above the breast level on the body. It allows a horse to make sharp turns, as in jumping competitions, without restriction to the opposite side of the mouth.

Martingale, running A martingale which is divided at the breast into two branches, each culminating in a ring through which the reins are passed. It prevents undue raising of the head by exerting pressure on the reins and consequently on the mouth. When used with a double bridle, the rings are attached to the curb rein.

Martingale, standing This type of martingale runs from the girth to the noseband. The best type is made with an additional adjustment just above the breast. The top strap, in this pattern, should be lined with rawhide.

Martingale, split The branches of a run-

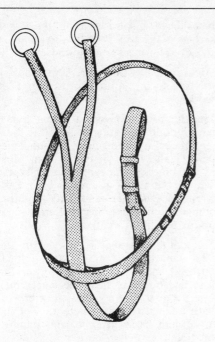

Running martingale.

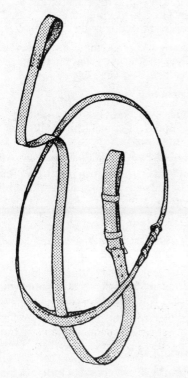

Standing martingale.

ning martingale fitted with a buckle and strap just beneath their point of junction. It is attached to the breastplate when it is desired to use a martingale as well as this latter. A similar standing attachment is also made.

Martingale ring A rubber ring fitted diagonally to encompass the point where the neckstrap and body of the martingale join. It keeps the neckstrap in place.

Martingale stop Leather or rubber stops fitted to the rein some 10-12 ins (25-30 cm) from the bit. They prevent the rings of running martingales sliding forward and becoming caught on either the rein fastening or a corner tooth.

Martingale triangles Metal, triangular-shaped fittings with a roller used in place of ordinary running martingale rings, usually when a martingale is to be used on the curb rein of a double bridle or pelham. The roller does not bend the leather as much as a ring.

Marwari See **Kathiawari**.

Maryland Hunt Cup (USA) Started in 1894 as a competition between members of the Elkridge Hunt and the Green Spring Valley Hunt, over farmland and natural fences. It was restricted to amateurs but now professionals are permitted to ride without payment. Often spoken of in the USA as the Grand National. The course is now flagged, covers 4 miles (6.4 km) over twenty-two 5 ft (1.5 m) post-and-rail fences. There has never been a grandstand, just natural hillside.

Mash See **Bran mash**.

Mask A fox's head.

Massage pad See **Grooming pad**.

Master See **MFH**.

Master of Foxhounds Association 'Headquarters' of the Masters of Foxhound packs, and publishers of the Foxhound Kennel Studbook. Founded in 1881 as the result of a dispute at Boodles Club in St James's, London, where affairs concerning hunting were previously discussed and decided.

Master of Hounds, first Sir Rustyn Villenove was appointed Master of

Hounds, Magister Canum Regis, to Henry IV at a salary of 12 pence per day.

'Master of the Game, the' See **de Foix, Gaston**.

Master of the Horse John Russell was the first to hold this office, in 1377, the reign of Richard II. A distinguished Master of the Horse was the 10th Duke of Beaufort (q.v.), who held the office for forty-one years. The duties of the Master of the Horse include attendance at all official occasions when the Sovereign is mounted or in a horse-drawn carriage, and responsibility for the overall turn-out of the men, carriages and horses on such occasions, as well as for the safety of the Sovereign. The Master of the Horse has the right to ride next to the Sovereign and is senior to all on parade on such occasions.

Mastitis Inflammation of the udder which usually occurs after foaling, at any time during which the foal is suckling, or immediately following weaning. During either of the first two the foal is much affected, and unless the owner has had practical experience of this trouble, veterinary advice should be sought.

Masuren horse An old type of Polish warmblood horse with much Trakehner blood, and used in the breeding of Wielkopolskis (q.v.).

Match A race between two horses, the property of two different owners, on terms agreed by them.

Match Book, the Keeper of the (racing) See **Weatherbys**.

McGuinness snaffle See **Magenis snaffle**.

Mealy nose Descriptive of a muzzle mainly oatmeal in colour. (See **Exmoor Pony**)

Measurement scheme See **Joint measurement scheme**.

Measuring stick or horse standard A straight shaft of wood, calibrated in inches and hands, having a sliding right-angle arm which is placed over the horse's withers. As the arm is raised or lowered on the upright, the exact height can be read. The best and most accurate types have a spirit-level on the upper surface of the arm. There is also a smaller size used for measuring hounds.

'Meat for work' An expression denoting the free keep of a horse in exchange for work.

Mecklenburg A German riding horse, with bloodlines dating back to the fourteenth century, and similar to, but somewhat smaller than, the Hanoverian. Most of the breed disappeared during World War II, but a stud was reformed in Schwerin in East Germany, and produces competition horses. Mecklenburgs stand up to 16.2 hh (165 cm).

Meconium The faecal material in the large colon of a foal *in utero* and at birth. It must be expelled within the first few hours of life. The faeces may be hard or soft, and yellowish or brown, with a slimy covering. Retention of the meconium leads to colic, and requires treatment.

Meet The appointed place for a pack to meet on a hunting day. Also used to describe a meeting of driving vehicles.

Meeting Any assembly of horses and jockeys at a given place for the purpose of racing.

Megrim See **Staggers**.

Méjuger, se French word meaning that the hind feet touch down in front of the imprints left by the forefeet. (See **Déjuger, se**, and **Juger, se**)

Melbourne Cup (racing) The most important race in Australia. A handicap run over 2 miles (3.2 km). Founded in 1861 and run annually at Flemington in Victoria, on the first Tuesday in November. The first winner was Archer, who also won the second running of the race.

Melbourne facings A saddle panel where a gusset is let into the rear to allow fuller stuffing of that part. Used in dressage saddles to ensure that the saddle remains level on the back. Sometimes called a German panel.

Melton A heavy coating cloth, originally a product of the west of England. It is extremely densely woven, thus ensuring both softness and shape. Often used for hunting coats, it was first made popular at Melton Mowbray (Belvoir, Quorn and Cottesmore Hunts) from which town it takes its name.

Melton Mowbray In Leicestershire, the centre for meets of the Belvoir, Cottesmore and Quorn Hunts.

Memory Horses are endowed with remarkable memories. In estimating this, regard must be paid to the possible influence of instinct, which in itself is most marked. (See **Intelligence**)

Metabolism The general chemical processes within the body by means of which energy is made available.

Metacarpal bone (large) The cannon bone, the main bone of the front leg from the knee to the fetlock joint.

Metacarpals, small (splint bones) Two in number, the small metacarpals are found at the posterior part of the large metacarpal bone, sometimes becoming attached to it by bony deposits.

Metatarsal bone The cannon or shank bone, the main bone of the hindleg, between the hock and the fetlock.

Metrication (racing) This has not afflicted British racing so far.

Metropolitan bit A term loosely describing a number of bits, e.g. Metropolitan Liverpool, Metropolitan Ashleigh, etc. It used to describe bits used by the Household Cavalry and inscribed *Honi soit qui mal y pense*.

Metropolitan Police, Mounted Branch It traces its origins to a small horse patrol, started in 1763 by Sir John Fielding, which was incorporated into the Metropolitan Police in 1836. The training headquarters at Imber Court in Surrey were opened in 1919. Here young horses are schooled for six months in an unhurried system based entirely on patience and reward, before taking up official patrol duties. The officers of the Mounted Branch (which now include women) are also trained at Imber Court.

Mettlesome Descriptive of a horse of spirit, courage and character – such an animal needs a skilled rider or driver.

Mewing A term used of a stag when shedding his antlers, usually at the end of April or the beginning of May.

Mews An area given over to stables. The word derives from the French *muer*, originally a place where moulting falcons were confined. In 1537 the royal stables at Charing Cross were called mews, having been built on a site where royal hawks were kept.

Meynell, Hugo (1735-1808) Became the second MFH of the Quorn Hunt (from 1753-1800). Among his own field he was known as the 'Hunting Jupiter'. He was one of the 'noble science' school, for he looked upon horses as machines which enabled him to keep company with his hounds.

Midden A dung-heap.

Middleton, Captain 'Bay' (12th Lancers) Piloted the Empress of Austria (q.v.) when she hunted with fashionable packs in the Midlands. He was killed when riding his horse Night Line in a House of Commons point-to-point race at Kineton.

'Midlands, the' Grass hunting countries, roughly in the Midlands, which include the following hunts: Bicester with Whaddon Chase, Grafton, Pytchley, Quorn, Fernie, Belvoir, Cottesmore, Meynell, North Staffordshire, Woodland Pytchley, Atherstone, Rufford, Albrighton, Croome, and South Nottinghamshire.

Midnight Steeplechase See **Moonlight Steeplechase**.

Mildew The most common fungus appearing on growing grain or plants, it manifests itself as dark spots which eat into the plant and turn it into black powder.

Mildmay, Anthony, of Flete (1909-1950) Lord Mildmay was the most popular amateur rider of his time, and was twice unlucky not to win the Grand National. In 1936 he was out clear on his own horse Davy Jones at the last but one fence when his reins parted at the buckle and his horse ran out at the final fence. In 1948 on his favourite horse, Cromwell, he finished third in spite of being attacked by cramp in the neck and riding almost

177

blind in the last mile. He was tragically drowned when swimming near his home in Devon.

Miler A horse deemed to be well fitted to stay the distance with credit in a mile race on the flat.

Militaire See **Horse trials**.

Milk The fluid secretion of the mare's mammary glands which provides food for the foal. Replacement milk is now available for foals. Otherwise, it is usual practice to find a lactating mare to act as foster mother to foals who have lost their mothers, as mares' milk is obviously the best food for the growing foal. See **Colostrum**.

Milk pellets Small white pellets which are much enjoyed by horses and particularly by foals. They are a good source of protein and oil (approximately 23% and 15% respectively). Up to 1 lb (0.45 kg) a day may be fed, according to the animal, and unlike many other protein products they do not 'hot up' the horse.

Milk teeth Two incisors with which a foal is born, together with those which appear within the first few weeks.

Miller Brothers, C.D., E.D. and G.A. These were great polo players and pig-stickers associated with the formation and subsequent history of the Roehampton Club, London.

Milling A coaching term for kicking.

Mill Reef American-bred racing Thoroughbred, who in 1971 won the English Derby, the French Prix de l'Arc de Triomphe, the Eclipse Stakes and the Queen Elizabeth Diamond Stakes. Owned and bred by Mr Paul Mellon, he was by Never Bend (by Nasrullah) out of Milan Mill; he was trained in England by Ian Balding. He also won the Coventry Stakes, the Imperial Stakes, the Coronation Cup and the French Prix Ganay. He was beaten only twice in fourteen outings, in the 2000 Guineas by Brigadier Gerard, and in France by My Swallow. He was joint holder (with San San) of the record for 1½ miles (2.4 km) at Longchamp. His racing career ended when he shattered his near foreleg at exercise; a remarkable operation allowed

him to walk again, and he retired to the National Stud. His progeny included the Derby winner Shirley Heights, Acamas, Glint of Gold, King of Clubs, and the 1987 Derby winner, Reference Point. At the time of his death in 1986 his progeny had won 400 races, worth about £4 million.

Milord A carriage, designed by David Davies of London, with a cab-shaped body hung on four elliptic springs with a low driving seat. It became very fashionable in England and on the Continent (*c.* 1835).

Ming horses Highly glazed models of horses, usually in fine white porcelain, produced in China during the Ming Dynasty, AD 1368-1644.

Minho See **Garranos**.

Mise en main Literally means 'bringing in hand', i.e. the relaxing of the jaw in the position of ramener (q.v.).

Misfetched Mistaught; descriptive of an animal which has been badly broken and possesses some vice.

Misfit A horse not representative of, nor suited to, the work required of its breed, e.g. one bred for racing, but sold as a riding-school horse.

Missouri Fox-trotting Horse A horse developed about 150 years ago in Missouri, USA, using Morgan, Thoroughbred and Arab blood, with later infusions of Tennessee Walking Horse and Saddlebred. It was bred specifically to cover long distances over rough ground, and the 'fox-trot' gait in which the horse walks in front and trots behind, was evolved. The hind feet, instead of moving in a normal trotting action, slide forward, and the result is a smooth, comfortable pace which can be maintained over long periods. A stud book was started in 1948.

Mitbah The term descriptive of the peculiar angle at which the neck enters the head of the Arabian horse. The neck makes a slight angle at the top of the crest, and from that point runs in a gentle curve to the head. The windpipe enters between the jaws in the same way. This gives the peculiar arched set of the neck, and allows free movements of the head in every direction.

Mixed pack A pack composed of dog hounds and bitches.

'Mob a fox' A term describing the hunting of a fox when it is given no chance of escape; to surround it or 'gallop it down'.

Mock feed A diet which includes no corn, for use when, for some reason, the horse cannot be exercised.

Model (USA) Term used for a show class judged on conformation.

Moff A waggon which can be converted into a cart by the addition of sideboards.

Mohawk attachment A straight bar covered with rubber ball washers, and two upturned hooks which catch upon the two eyes of pelham cheeks, increasing twofold the bearing surface upon the tongue and the bars of the mouth. A Mohawk hook is fastened in the middle of a pelham bar with an S-shaped rubber fitting allowing the horse to push it out of line with its tongue, a rubber spring returning it to its place. The chief object of the bit is to put pressure on the bars of the mouth.

Molars The large grinding teeth of the horse which lie beyond the bars of the mouth. The grinding surfaces slope outwards towards the cheeks, which are used to retain the food between the teeth. As a result the enamel of the teeth wears to sharp points on the outside of the upper row, and the inside of the lower row, rendering tongue and cheeks liable to laceration. This in turn inhibits efficient mastication. In such cases the services of a veterinary surgeon are required. (See **Rasping**)

Monday morning complaint, evil or leg See **Lymphangitis**.

Mongolian A pony, both domesticated and feral, found all over the vast desolate area of Mongolia, from Manchuria in the east to Turkistan in the west. The breed is extremely hardy, adapting well to the extremes of heat and cold found on the steppes and desert of its natural habitat. In winter, the herds are driven to pastures which offer shelter from the biting winds, but there is no water, so the ponies eat snow to quench their thirst. Because of the huge area in which they live, there are several different types of Mongolian pony. The smallest, standing up to 12.1 hh (124.4 cm), lives to the south of the Gobi Desert, and the largest, standing up to 13 hh (132.1 cm), is found in western Mongolia. In general, the breed has a large, often Roman-nosed head, with small eyes which reflect its rather uncertain temperament; the neck is thick, the chest deep, and the back and loins strong. The legs are short with good bone, with long feathers often starting at the knee. An unusual feature of the breed is side whiskers. The ponies are used as dual-purpose riding and pack animals.

'Monkey' A betting term implying a wager of £500.

Moon-blindness See **Ophthalmia**.

Moonlight Steeplechase This is said to have been run in 1803 from the Cavalry Barracks at Ipswich to Nacton Church, a distance of 4½ miles (7.2 km). There is, however, no real evidence that the event ever took place. Henry Alken (q.v.) painted a picture of the race, and the first prints, in which the riders are seen wearing starched nightshirts, appeared in 1839. (Known also as The First Steeplechase on Record or The Night Riders of Nacton).

Moray car A two-wheeled carriage hung especially low for easy access by ladies.

Morgan An American breed of light horse, unique in being descended from, and named after, a single stallion, Justin Morgan. He produced his own type, character and conformation with remarkable exactness. Justin Morgan was by True Briton, said to be a Thoroughbred, but it seems more probable that he was a Welsh Cob (True Briton being a common name in that breed). Morgan himself and his descendants have the typical cob high head carriage, known in Morgan circles as 'upheadedness'. Morgans have always been exceptionally versatile, and today are used as riding horses and in harness. Two types have developed – the Park Horse, and the Pleasure Horse. The former, so named because it was originally ridden in the parks of the southern American states, moves with a very animated high-stepping trot, which does not develop fully until the horse is about seven years old. The Pleasure Horse, although of the same conformation, does now show such spectacular movement. The Morgan stands 14.2-15.2 hh (147.3-157.5 cm) and is brown, bay, or black, with an occasional chestnut. The breed has recently become established in Britain in small numbers.

Morland, George (1763-1804) An artist of uneven talent. Horses figure frequently in the scenes of English rural life for which he is famed; hunting was an occasional subject. The countryman's horse 'in the rough' was Morland's choice; he had little use for a well-groomed Thoroughbred. His horses, like other animals, were painted as part of impoverished and unsophisticated country scenes.

Morning-glory (racing) A racehorse which goes well in its training gallops in the morning but performs badly on the racecourse.

Mountain and Moorland ponies of the British Isles The breeds of ponies native to the British Isles. Their ancestors are believed to have arrived while the land-bridge still existed between what is now Britain and Continental Europe. The breeds are: Welsh, Shetland, Dartmoor, New Forest, Highland, Exmoor, Fell, Dales, and Connemara (qq.v.). They are distinguished by hardiness, common sense and adaptability.

Mounties, the See **Canadian Mounted Police, The Royal**.

Mounting There are four normal methods of mounting: placing the foot in the stirrup iron; using a mounting block (q.v.); having a leg-up (q.v.); springing or vaulting from the ground over the horse's neck and withers. The latter is the common practice of racing lads and requires considerable agility. The spring must carry the body right on to the horse's back, and the right elbow must be well to the offside. It is useful on many occasions, especially when in a hurry, as it can be performed while the horse is

moving forward. The leg-up method is invariably used by jockeys in the paddock before a race.

Mounting block A small platform, some 2½ ft (76.2 cm) high, approached by two or three steps, on which a rider stands when mounting a horse. Its use makes mounting easier for the rider and more comfortable for the horse. It had a permanent place in every stableyard in Victorian times, and, of course, in pillion days. Sometimes known as a Horsing Stone, Jostling Stone, or Pillion Post.

Moustache A tuft of hair which appears on the upper lip of some heavy horses and of some Mountain and Moorland pony breeds.

Mouth In a horse this comprises the lips, tongue, teeth, hard palate or roof (which takes the form of ridges or bars running from side to side between the upper molar teeth), and the soft palate – a membranous muscle which separates the mouth from the pharynx when swallowing. The size and shape of the soft palate in association with the larynx probably explains why horses cannot breathe through their mouths.

Mouth/Mouthpiece That part of the bit which is in the mouth.

Mouth, full Term denoting that all the milk teeth have been finally replaced by permanent teeth. This state should be reached when the horse is five years old.

Mouth, good Said of a horse which is 'on the bit', yet can be ridden with a light, soft, but firm pressure.

Mouthing The process of introducing a young horse to the bit and encouraging it to mouth and champ to produce saliva. There are various forms and designs of mouthing bits (q.v.).

Mouthing bit A bit, made of metal, and of either the bar or the broken-mouth variety, with 'keys' or 'players' attached, which encourage a 'wet' mouth.

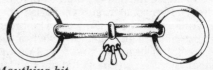
Mouthing bit.

Mucking out The process of removing droppings and soiled bedding from a box or stall and sweeping it out.

Muck sweat Describes a horse which has been ridden to such an extent that it is in a lather, and both dirt and sweat come out of its pores and impregnate its coat.

Mud fever Similar to and sometimes accompanying cracked heels (q.v.), but may extend to the inner sides of the forelegs and the front of the hindlegs, and also the belly and flanks. The cause is similar to cracked heels: i.e. wet legs leading to infection by *Dermatophilus congolensis*. It can be prevented by refraining from brushing the legs and belly of a wet, muddy horse; instead apply stable bandages and brush next day when dry, or wash with warm water and dry thoroughly. Established cases may require veterinary attention.

'Mug's horse' A horse which is easy to ride but which may look 'hot' and difficult.

Mulassier Horses used in France for breeding mules. Probably descended from Dutch stock. The stallions stand between 16.1-16.3 hh (165.1-170.1 cm), the mares rather less. A somewhat coarse-looking breed, characterised by thick, shaggy manes and tails, and sometimes with curly hair around the knees and hocks.

Mule The offspring of a male ass and a female horse; very rarely can a mule be bred from.

Mule feet Feet with small frogs and high heels. Known also as club or boxy feet.

Mullen mouth Half-moon shaped mouthpiece of a bit, otherwise known as a 'mulling mouth'. (See **Snaffle bit**)

Munnings, Sir Alfred James, KCVO, PRA (1878-1959) An artist of brilliant talent and great popularity, who painted in a vivid and fluent style all types of horses and sporting scenes, as well as landscapes. His pictures of the modern Thoroughbred, especially of racehorses, were unequalled in his day. He was President of the Royal Academy of Arts from 1944 to 1949, and was relentless and reckless in his denunciation of 'modern art'.

Murakosi Hungarian draught horse. In the eighteenth century, two types were developed by crossing German draught horses with Noriker-type animals. The smaller type stood 14-15 hh (142.2-152.4 cm), and the larger, slower type 15-16 hh (152.4-162.6 cm). They were unattractive animals, with piggy eyes, and poor feet and legs, so the authorities concentrated on producing the better quality Hungarian Heavy Draught until the 1960s. Then they turned their attention to improving the Murakosi breed, by introducing Fjord, Hucul and Haflinger blood. This was successful to some degree, but the breed is not expected to expand significantly.

Murgese An Italian horse, suitable for riding and light draught, and standing between 15-16 hh (152.4-162.6 cm), and predominantly chestnut. The original breed was used in the fifteenth and sixteenth centuries by the cavalry but disappeared some 200 years ago. The modern breed, produced in the 1920s, by use of imported Oriental blood on local stock, is found chiefly in southern Italy.

Murrieta gig Designed by C. J. de Murrieta, a member of the Coaching Club (q.v.). It had a more elegant but reduced form of the old curricle (q.v.) body, suspended on Stanhope gig (q.v.) undercarriage. It was fitted with a folding hood.

Muscles Connective tissues of the body consisting of collections of fibres arranged in bundles and surrounded by a strong fibrous sheath. They have the ability to contract and to exert a pulling force. There are three principal types in the horse:
1. CARDIAC MUSCLE – found in the heart, and having the characteristic rhythmic contraction.
2. SMOOTH or INVOLUNTARY MUSCLE – found in the walls of arteries, the alimentary tract, intestines, etc.
3. STRIPED or SKELETAL MUSCLE – a voluntary muscle under the control of the animal and found in the limbs etc.

Muscovy, anti-rearing bit This differs from the usual Chifney bit as its side rings are attached to knobs, which in turn are fitted loosely to a large bit ring. (See **Anti-rearing bit**)

'Music' The cry of hounds when hunting.

Mustangs The feral and semi-feral horses of the plains of western America and the pampas of South America. The name apparently derives from *mestengo*, i.e. 'stranger', which comes from the Spanish *mesta*, the name given to an association of graziers, one of whose functions was the appropriation of wild cattle which had attached themselves to the herd. Probably of Spanish origin, the horse, having been brought over by Cortès in 1519, was the first true specimen seen in the New World, and was of Spanish, Arabian and Barb blood. Seldom more than 14.2hh (147.3 cm), it was scraggy and tough, of no quality, and with an uncertain temperament, but it was hardy and courageous, and possessed a cast-iron constitution; it was represented by every known colour. Once domesticated, the Mustang made a useful light saddle horse, and was the original cow-pony. There are still some true wild Mustangs in western America, and some are also kept on ranches.

Mute A hound which does not throw its tongue when on the line of a fox is said to be mute.

Mutton-fisted Descriptive of a rider who is heavy-handed, but not necessarily rough.

Muzzle Protective covering for the nose, shaped like a bucket, made of netting, leather or plastic (the latter two with ventilation holes). It is attached and held in position by a slip-head. Net muzzles are used on harness horses which bite; leather or plastic muzzles are used on

Leather muzzle.

horses addicted to dung-eating, eating bedding or tearing clothing. Muzzles are also constructed from wire mesh and from fibreglass. (See **Bar muzzle**)

Muzzle That part of the head which includes the nostrils, lips, gums, and teeth.

Mytoon, John (Jack) (1796-1834) An eccentric, inveterate gambler and a remarkable sportsman, commemorated in *The Memoirs of the Life of the Late John Mytton, Esq.*, by Nimrod (Charles James Apperley, q.v.). At one time he kept twenty-eight hunters in his stable and hunted two countries. His feats of endurance were prodigious and his extraordinary exploits, many undertaken for bets, included driving his tandem across country at night, and putting his gig at a closed turnstile. He died in penury of chronic alcoholism at the age of thirty-eight.

N

NFFR No foal, free return. See **Breeding**.

NFNF No foal, no fee. An arrangement by which if no foal is produced from a mating, no stud fee is payable.

NH National Hunt.

Nk (racing) Neck.

NPS National Pony Society (q.v.).

NPSB National Pony Stud Book.

NSHA (USA) National Steeplechase and Hunt Association (q.v.).

Nag Derived from the word *negan*, Anglo-Saxon 'to neigh'; this is an old term for a saddle horse, but seldom used now.

Nagbut snaffle A jointed bit with a grid port in the centre to discourage tongue-over-the-bit evasion. Light enough for racing.

Nagging An old-fashioned term describing the process of training and schooling a horse for hunting or riding, and for good manners under all circumstances.

Nagsman A horseman who, by his skill, rides to improve a horse, whether as a ride, or on account of some vice or bad manners. He is usually a professional attached to a dealer's yard.

Nail-bind See **Shod too close**.

Nails (clenching) These are machine-made from the best mild steel. The principal parts of a horseshoe nail are (a) the head, which is wedge-shaped, with a flat upper surface and whose sides slope into (b) the neck, which is the junction between the head and the shank (c). The shank, which extends from the neck to the point, is slightly curved to ensure its correct passage through the hoof, and is twice as wide as it is thick. The point is bevelled on its inner surface, and the length of the bevelled surface determines where the nail emerges. The nail is always driven with the non-bevelled side (outer face) towards the outside of the shoe, so that the point emerges on the outside of the wall of the hoof.

'Nap' or nap selection Many racing correspondents in Britain normally give a nap selection each day, which they consider the best bet of the day at the probable odds.

'Nappy' A horse which, either from stubbornness or bad temper, refuses to carry out any of the aids properly given, e.g. refuses to leave its stable or the company of other horses, is inclined to turn for home, or refuses to pass certain points.

Narragansett Pacer From the founding of the American Colonies in the early seventeenth century until 1800, when roads were sufficiently improved to take wheeled traffic, the customary means of travel was by a pacing horse. The most popular strain was developed in the Narragansett Bay area of Rhode Island. These horses, noted for their speed and comfort, were also exported to the West Indies and the Southern colonies. George Washington rode one in his old age. They were used in the development of the American Saddlebred (q.v.) and the Tennessee Walking Horse (q.v.).

Narrow behind Where the croup and thighs are deficient in muscle, giving a narrow appearance when viewed from behind.

National Association of Farriers, Blacksmiths & Agricultural Engineers This was formed in 1905 by bringing together the several local associations then in existence. The founders regarded this as essential for the future of the trades, in order to ensure improved standards. Originally, the Association was for Blacksmiths and Farriers, but it was later found prudent to encompass firms who had turned to agricultural engineering. In 1945, in conjunction with other bodies such as the National Farmers Union, the Association formed a National Joint Apprenticeship Council for the relevant trades, laying down minimum standards of training and devising a syllabus. Further, with the help of the Worshipful Company of Farriers, the Association sought authority for the statutory Registration of Farriers; as a result, The Farriers Registration Act came into being in 1975, and the Association is represented on the Farriers Registration Council. The Association also promotes the study, practice and knowledge of the trades it represents, by arranging lectures and competitions throughout the country and giving prizes and medals for efficiency and expertise.

National Foaling Bank A service which introduces owners of mares suitable for use as foster mothers to owners of orphan foals, or vice versa. It is organised for all breeds of horses. Similar services are organised for their members by the Thoroughbred Breeders' Association and the National Light Horse Breeders' Society.

National Horse Show (USA) Founded in 1883 and held annually in November in Madison Square Garden, New York City, as the premier horse show of the USA. It features all classes including harness, equitation, international show jumping, and displays of various descriptions. It is referred to colloquially as 'The National' and 'The Garden'.

National Hunt Committee (racing) Formerly the governing body responsible for the conduct of steeplechasing and hurdle-racing in Britain, but now amalgamated with the Jockey Club (q.v.), which issues one rule book to cover both flat racing and steeplechasing.

National Light Horse Breeding Society See **Hunters' Improvement and National Light Horse Breeding Society**.

National Pony Society Originally known as the Polo and Riding Pony Society, founded in 1893, 'to encourage the breeding, registration and improvement of riding ponies and Mountain and Moorland ponies, and to foster the welfare of ponies in general'. In conjunction with the British Horse Society, it is the officially appointed liaison between the Government and all those concerned with ponies and is represented on all major horse and pony organisations. Through its council and numerous sub-committees, the Society organises the following: (1) The publication of a stud book and register of riding ponies. (2) An annual two-day show with classes for ridden and driven ponies as well as for those in-hand. (3) National Championships, with qualifiers throughout the country and finals held at important events towards the end of the season. (4) An affiliation scheme to encourage classes for registered riding and Mountain and Moorland ponies at shows all over England, Scotland and Wales. (5) An up-to-date list of qualified judges, reviewed annually in order to ensure that competence is maintained at a high level. (The Probationer Judges Scheme gives prospective judges an opportunity to gain knowledge and experience before being considered for inclusion on the panel proper.) (6) Sales for registered ponies which are held twice a year, in the spring and in the autumn. (7) The distribution of the Horserace Betting Levy Board Grant for the benefit of Mountain and Moorland ponies.

The National Pony Society Diploma Examination Scheme is designed to provide practical and technical training in all branches of pony management at inspected, approved establishments. The Stud Assistant's Certificate, which requires one year's training, and the full Diploma, which requires three, both demand a high standard of efficiency and knowledge, and provide the successful candidate with a qualification that is not only widely recognised but also highly regarded.

Study days are held at such venues as the British Equestrian Centre. A Junior Judging Competition is held annually and the Society takes part in parades and other similar activities.

All members receive a copy of the Annual Review, which includes reports from the breed societies, the sub-committees and the area chairmen. There is a register of breeders, a list of stallions at stud, and much useful and official information. A number of booklets, available from the office, cover various aspects of the work of the Society and the care of ponies.

The Society has its own welfare committee and is also represented on that of the British Horse Society.

All members are eligible to join in the activities of the twenty NPS areas covering Great Britain. These activities include shows, films, lectures and a variety of pony and social events.

The Scottish Committee organises an annual show, which attracts entries from south of the border as well as from all over Scotland. It also organises shows, open days, discussions, and many other local events. In all these ways, the National Pony Society's members throughout Great Britain, wherever they live, may participate in Society events, competitive, instructional and social.

National Steeplechase and Hunt Association Covers activities in the USA similar to those under the jurisdiction of the former National Hunt Committee (q.v.) in Britain.

National Stud Established in 1916 at Tully in Co. Kildare, Ireland, when Lord Wavertree presented his entire stud of bloodstock to the nation and it became Government sponsored. It was transferred from Ireland to Gillingham, Dorset, in 1943, and expanded in 1949 when the West Grinstead Stud in Sussex was bought. At that time the National Stud had both brood mares and stallions, and it was hoped that it would breed racehorses good enough to stand later at the stud as stallions. The best of the yearlings were, for many years, leased for their racing careers to the Monarch. The stud bred some very high-class horses, including Blandford, sire of four Derby winners, and the classic winners Big Game, Carrozza, Chamossaire, Royal Lancer, and Sun Chariot. There was regret among many when all the mares were sold in 1964, and the stud moved to Newmarket in 1966, where it became a stud for stallions only. Management was transferred from the Ministry of Agriculture to the Horserace Betting Levy Board.

National Trainers' Association A body formed to protect the interests of racehorse trainers in Great Britain.

National Trotting Association of Great Britain Founded in 1952 to promote the sport of horse-trotting races.

National Veterinary Medical Association of Great Britain and Ireland (Founded 1881) Founded to promote and advance the interests of veterinary and allied sciences.

Nations' Cup Prix des Nations (q.v.).

Native ponies Another name for Mountain and Moorland ponies (q.v.).

Nave The wooden centre of a wheel from which the spokes radiate to the fellow or felloe (q.v.).

Navel ill See **Joint evil/ill**.

Navicular bone A small bone in the foot situated transversely behind the pedal bone, and which articulates with the latter and with the pastern.

Navicular disease A disease of the foot in which the blood supply to the navicular bone is increasingly blocked by clots, leading to degeneration. The front feet are more prone to the condition than the hind. The causes are not fully understood, but concussion due to excessive work on hard surfaces, poor conformation (small feet with upright pasterns), or bad shoeing producing excessive pressure on the deep flexor tendon, have all been suggested. The condition is more common in animals over eight years of age. Symptoms include intermittent lameness, which in the early stages of the disease wears off with exercise; a shorter stride; stumbling; heat; and pain. Veterinary treatment is essential, and the most modern treatment is with Warfarin, an anti-coagulant, which prevents blood clotting in the vessels, thereby maintaining the blood supply to the navicular bone. In advanced cases, neurectomy (q.v.), may be necessary – making the horse legally unsound.

Near head See **Pommel**.

Near-side A committee appointed by the Royal College of Veterinary Surgeons strongly advised that the near- or left-hand side be described as the 'left-side' and the offside as the 'right-side'.

Neck (racing) A horse is said to have won by a neck when both its head and neck are in front of the following horse.

Neck collar (harness) This consists of an outer cover of patent or other leather, and an interior stuffed with selected straw to form a cushion to fit the shoulders. The stuffing is strengthened with a roll or 'whale' shaped to form a recess into which are placed the hames (q.v.).

Neck cradle See **Cradle**.

Neck reining See **Indirect rein**.

Neckstrap A circular leather strap worn at the base of the neck through which the martingale is passed and is held in position. Also a strap which novice riders may hold to prevent them 'jobbing' (q.v.) the horse's mouth.

Neck sweater A hood covering the neck and throat made of heavy felt lined with oilskin, plastic or waterproof material. Used to sweat off a thick neck. (See **Jowl sweater**).

Neigh A horse's call denoting surprise, pleasure or anxiety, though in a stallion more often indicating a mating call.

Nelson gag A gag snaffle with cheeks. The bridle cheeks are fastened to eyes on the top of the bit cheek, and not to the bit rings. As with most gags, two reins should be used.

Neopolitan See **Noseband, Neopolitan**.

Nerve Courage in the hunting-field; the reverse of 'nerves'.

Nerved (USA) See **Neurectomy**.

Nettle rash See **Urticaria**.

Neurectomy The nerve supply to the foot is sometimes severed surgically in the case of a horse suffering from chronic foot lameness. This method is sometimes resorted to as a relief from the pain of navicular disease (q.v.). The equivalent American term is 'nerved'. A horse so treated is legally unsound. The prognosis after neurectomy varies. It may make riding the horse dangerous, as he cannot readily feel the ground and may stumble. Complications from surgery arise in the form of a neuroma forming round the severed nerve ends. The neuroma may infiltrate blood vessels, blocking them, or it may itself cause pain.

Newcastle, William Cavendish, Duke of (1592-1676) An ardent Royalist who fled to the Continent when Oliver Cromwell came to power. When in exile he established a famous riding school at Antwerp and published there, in French, in 1658,

the first of many works on horsemanship: *La Methode et Invention Nouvelle de Dresser les Chevaux*. Translated into English in 1667, after the Restoration, this became, and still ranks as, a classic work on equitation.

New Forest Hunt Club Founded in 1789 for the purpose of hunting the New Forest country. In that year the Lord Warden of the New Forest (the then Duke of Gloucester) nominated Mr Gilbert's hounds the established pack of the country, in succession to his own, with prior rights to hunt the New Forest. Mr Gilbert's hounds had been granted permission to hunt the country since 1780, and in the season 1789-1790 they became a subscription pack under the New Forest Hunt Club.

New Forest Pony The New Forest is one of the nine breeds of ponies comprising the Mountain and Moorland group (q.v.) in Britain. Its origins are uncertain, but in the days of Canute (*c*.995-1035) mention was made of wild horses living in the Forest, which is in Hampshire in southern England. In contrast to nearly all the other native pony breeds (except the Exmoor and the Welsh Mountain pony), New Forest ponies are still bred in significant numbers in their native habitat. Some 2500 or so, belonging to the New Forest Commoners, roam the 145 square miles (375 sq. km) of the New Forest (excluded only from the fenced inclosures) and are, to all intents, wild ponies. They are, however, rounded up ('drifted' q.v.) annually, into 'pounds' (enclosed yards), so the owners may select those, mostly foals, for sale at the Beaulieu Road Sale Yards (q.v.). Other ponies are bred on private studs all over Britain. The New Forest are generally thought to be the least distinctive (and possibly the least uniform) of the native breeds, due largely to the introduction, as recently as the 1930s, but principally in the nineteenth century, of outside blood to 'improve' the stock. Other native breeds, a few Arabs and Thoroughbreds, and Hackneys were all used. Today, the New Forest is an excellent all-round family pony, at home under saddle and in harness. The sizes range from about 11.3 hh (119.4 cm) to a maximum of 14.2 hh (147.3 cm), and the ponies may be any colour except skewbald, piebald, or blue-eyed cream. The head tends to be large, on a short-ish neck, and the tail not particularly high-set. New Forest ponies have been exported to many countries in Europe, to the USA and Canada; and to Australia (where they are doing very well, and one has been entered in the Stock Horse Stud Book Appendix) and New Zealand.

New Forest Pony Breeding and Cattle Society Formed in 1938, amalgamating two older societies, The Association for the Improvement of the Breed of New Forest Ponies, and the Burley and District New Forest Pony and Cattle Society. The Society publishes a stud book, organises an annual stallion show and breed show, and runs an annual performance competition.

New Kirghiz See **Novokirghiz**.

Newmarket 'Discovered' by King James I in 1605 as a hunting, hawking and racing centre. Charles I continued the royal patronage of this sporting centre, as also did Charles II, whose first official visit after the Restoration took place in 1666, when he founded the Newmarket Town Plate (q.v.). Today, Newmarket is considered the headquarters of flat racing in England. It is the biggest centre for the training of racehorses and a large number of studs surround the town. There are two racecourses – The Rowley Mile course, which is used in spring and autumn, and the July course, which is used in summer. The chief races are the 2000 Guineas and the 1000 Guineas in the spring; and the Champion Stakes, the Cesarewitch and the Cambridgeshire in the autumn.

Newmarket bandages The name sometimes given to stockinette bandages which come in many colours. (See also **Bandages**)

Newmarket boots Of the regulation hunting-boot height, these have a waterproof canvas leg, and a strap attached to the heel which passes over the instep and buckles on the outside of the foot.

Newmarket bridle A schooling bridle using a mullen mouth Wilson ring (i.e. four rings) snaffle. The reins are attached to the outer ring and a noseband con-

nects the two inner rings. Pressure on the reins results in pressure on the nose which is consequently lowered.

Newmarket cloths Shaped pieces of box cloth which are sewn round a racehorse's legs to give support. They are usually placed round the forelegs between knee and fetlock.

Newmarket Sales The principal sales of Thoroughbreds in England now take place in Newmarket, conducted by Tattersall's, the most important being the Newmarket October Open Yearling Sales and the Premier Yearling Sales (formerly the Houghton Yearling Sales) in the autumn, and the Newmarket December Sales mostly for horses in and out of training.

Newmarket Town Plate This race was instituted in 1665 by King Charles II. No trainer, jockey, stable lad or groom can ride in it, but women are eligible; the weight carried by all horses is 12 stone (76 kg). It is run over 3 miles 6 furlongs (6 km) on the Round Course at Newmarket. The winner receives the Plate, and there is prize money for first, second and third places, a prize for the best turned out horse, and vouchers for other riders. The race is now sponsored.

New York Show See **National Horse Show**.

New Zealand rug The original New Zealand Rug introduced to Britain by the Emston Saddlery Company in 1928 was a weather-proofed, woollen-lined heavy canvas rug, to be worn by horses turned

New Zealand rug

187

out in the field. Similar rugs are available today. They are kept in place by a leather strap with a buckle fastening across the chest, adjustable leather straps with spring clips which link through the hind-legs and clip back onto metal rings on the rug, and some also have draw string round the croup to ensure a good fit. They are generously cut and carefully shaped so that, in the best quality rugs, no surcingle is needed. Cheaper versions are available, made from lighter canvas. See also **Emston New Zealand rug**.)

Nez Perce Indians See **Appaloosa**.

Nick Indicating a mating likely to produce the desired type – 'a good nick'.

Nicker A horse's call denoting pleasurable anticipation – to nicker or whicker.

Nicking The division and re-setting of certain muscles under the tail to produce a high tail carriage. Illegal in Britain, but many American gaited horses undergo this operation.

Nicking The practice whereby the blood of one family is combined with that of another to produce, certain desired results e.g. greater speed, better quality bone, greater or lesser height, etc.

Nidget A triangular horseshoe formerly used in Kent and Sussex.

Niggle A movement of the hands and reins to alter the horse's carriage or to induce a greater speed. The term is generally applied to jockeys when race riding. Also refers to 'playing' on a horse's mouth to prevent biting or to distract its attention.

Niggling A term used of a horse that persists in a very short, jerky trot.

Nigh A colloquial term meaning near or left side.

Night eyes Another, but little used, name for chestnuts (q.v.).

Night roller See **Roller**.

Night rug Usually made of jute or canvas, fully lined with a woollen-mixture cloth, although those of poorer quality may be of lightweight jute and only half-lined. They are kept in place with surcingle, and with a strap and buckle at the chest. In

very cold weather, a horse blanket may be worn under the night rug. This is usually of pure wool, weighing about 8 lb (33.6 kg), and traditionally is fawn-coloured, often with coloured stripes.

Nilgeri A knobbed riding cane frequently leather-covered.

Nimrod See **Apperley, Charles James**.

Nits See **Lice**.

Nobbling Interfering, by underhand methods, with a horse's chance in a race.

Non-hand-fed/Forest-fed classes Judging, during March and April, of New Forest ponies which have run out on the Forest, in the case of mares, all their lives, and in the case of stallions for the previous year and through the winter. The ponies are judged both on condition and conformation; the stallions are judged again in July on their progeny.

Nonius A Hungarian breed named after its founder, the Anglo-Norman stallion, Nonius Senior, foaled in 1810. There are two types: Large Nonius, a big-boned horse of 15.3-16.2 hh (160-168.4 cm), and Small Nonius, about 14.3-15.3 hh (149.9-160 cm); either type may come from one mare. Of a quiet disposition and an excellent action, they make good agricultural and riding horses, though they are not very hardy. Since the decline of their use in agriculture, the Large Nonius is now being used, very successfully, as a carriage driving horse. Usually bay in colour.

Non-Thoroughbred register Compiled by Weatherby and Sons in place of the Half-bred Stud Book (q.v.). Up to 1987 this was for the produce of Thoroughbred stallions out of mares who had been identified by Weatherbys. Entry has now been widened to include the produce of certain non-Thoroughbred stallions registered with Weatherbys.

Norfolk car A four-wheeled, one-horse vehicle with seats facing forward and back, being somewhat larger than the well-known dog-cart, but not measuring quite so high.

Norfolk Roadster See **Norfolk Trotter**.

Norfolk Trotter A strong, short-legged,

very fast-trotting and tireless horse of a breed that dates back to the fifteenth century. It had considerable influence on the Hackney (q.v.), especially through Marshland Shales and Phenomenon. Also known as 'Norfolk Roadster'. A few Norfolk Trotters remain today.

Noriker A medium-weight draught horse whose history began some 2000 years ago when the Romans, in their northward drive, occupied what is now Austria. They brought their heavy warhorses with them, and in time, inter-breeding with local stock occurred, to produce a hardy, sure-footed animal, well adapted to the rigours of their mountainous homeland. These animals became known as Norikers, from the ancient province of Noricum in which they developed. There are five main bloodlines of Norikers, including the Pinzgauer Noriker, now bred in Bavaria. The breed, which stands 15.3-17 hh (160-170 cm), is noted for its colour range, including dapple, brindle, and a few spotted, in addition to the more usual browns, chestnuts and blacks.

Norman Cob A type developed from half-bred horses, and considered suitable for light draught work. La Manche is the main breeding centre, and cobs are still used on local farms. They stand between 15.3-16.3 hh (160-167.5 cm), and are stockily built, active horses, but lighter than the true draught breeds.

North Swedish Horse A medium-sized, very compact draught horse which, although descended from the ancient Swedish work horse, has only been recognised as a separate breed since 1900. Early influences include the Norwegian Dole, and in the nineteenth century, Belgian and Clydesdale blood was used to impart more size and strength. The breed was, and is, used extensively in forestry work. The government-subsidised stallion-rearing institute at Wangen runs a programme by means of which top-quality stallions and mares which have passed rigorous selection tests for both conformation and qualities of endurance, are produced. The North Swedish horse stands up to about 15.3 hh (160 cm), and has a relatively large head, and very short, powerful legs. The predominant colour is bay.

Norton Perfection A racing bridle for a very hard pulling horse. The bit has four rings and two mouthpieces, one of which is very thin and sharp. To this latter is attached a low-fitting elastic noseband which is kept in place by thin straps fastening on the headpiece of the bridle. Sometimes called a 'Lone Eagle'.

Norwegian Fjord Pony A very attractive dun-coloured (occasionally bay or brown) pony which is believed to have inhabited Norway, and possibly other parts of Scandinavia since prehistoric times. It was used by the Vikings for the unpleasant sport of horse fighting. Its modern use is for light agricultural work, and its sure-footedness make it an ideal pack pony in mountainous areas. Fjord ponies are used in a number of other European countries, under saddle and in harness, and there is an enthusiastic breed society in Britain. They have a number of primitive features, including a black dorsal eel stripe, and, in some instances, zebra markings on the legs. One of the most interesting features is the mane and tail hair which consists of black hairs in the centre and silver hairs on the outside. The mane stands stiffly upright, and is often cut in a characteristic curve. The Fjord pony stands between 13-14 hh (132.1-142.2 cm), and is a short-coupled, compact pony, with good strong legs and plenty of bone.

'Nose' The ability of a hound to scent its hunted quarry – 'a good nose'.

Nose, Roman This gives a convex line to the face as in e.g. the Shire Horse.

Nosebag A portable manger which can be hung on the horse's head; useful for administering an inhalant.

Noseband A broad leather band worn under the cheeks and above the bit, and usually described as the cavesson. It should be adjusted to admit two fingers between the leather and the nose. Almost universally worn, it can be put on to provide an attachment for a standing martingale. To prevent a horse from opening its mouth too wide, it is better to have a drop noseband (q.v.) fitted below the bit to act on the cartilage of the nose.

Noseband, Australian A rubber device slipped over the bit rings on either side of the mouth, joining on the nose and running up the face to a fastening on the headpiece. It keeps the bit up in the mouth, preventing the horse getting his tongue over the bit, and exerts slight restraining pressure on the nose at the same time as pressure on the mouth. Also known as an Australian Cheeker.

Australian noseband.

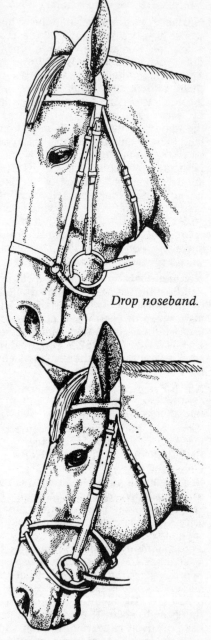

Drop noseband.

Flash noseband.

Grakle noseband.

Noseband, Brinekind By attaching each end to curb hooks this brings circular pressure around the nose: thus when the curb rein is pulled, pressure (which is sometimes highly desirable) is brought into play. The device was perfected by the late George Brine. It is also known as the 'Jobey' or 'Bucephalus' noseband.

Noseband, cavesson See **Cavesson**.

Noseband, cross A loose term covering Grakle or figure-of-eight nosebands (see below) which have intersecting straps.

Noseband, drop Attached round the muzzle below the bit, this is used to prevent a horse from opening its mouth or crossing its jaws, thus evading the action of the bit. Pressure placed on the bit through the reins results in pressure on the nose through the noseband, and the resultant correct positioning of the head gives the rider more control.

Noseband, figure-of-eight Similar to the Grakle noseband (see below), but of an improved pattern.

Noseband, flash An ordinary cavesson noseband in the centre of which are sewn two diagonally-crossing straps which fasten beneath the bit. Used when a standing martingale and drop noseband is required.

Noseband, fly A noseband laced in the same manner as a fly front (q.v.).

Noseband, Grakle A double noseband which prevents the horse from opening its mouth; it is designed for a horse which 'yaws', reaches for the bit with its mouth open, or swings its head. Named after the 1931 Grand National winner, who wore one.

Noseband, Kineton Sometimes called a 'Puckle' after its inventor, who lived at Kineton. A device attached to the bridle, which by means of two semi-circles of leather-covered metal brings pressure upon the nose before there is any bearing on the bars of the mouth. It is effective on a strong pulling horse.

Noseband, Neopolitan Similar to the Hackamore (Western) (q.v.). The loop encircling the nose is of metal with two metal shanks, allowing enormous lever-

age. A noseband of the same type but less severe is seen in Arabia.

Noseband, sheepskin (shadow roll) A noseband with a wide sheepskin covering on the front, and chiefly used for racing; it is believed to prevent the head from being thrown up, thus causing lack of balance. It also prevents the horse from noticing forward-cast shadows.

Nose-bleeding See **Epistaxis**.

Nose net A muzzle made of light cord attached to the bridle in such a manner that, when the reins are pulled, it will tighten over the nostrils. It is sometimes placed over the muzzle of a puller as a check – it stops the horse from opening his mouth, and acts as a restraining influence. (See **Muzzle**)

Notifiable diseases These are: anthrax, rabies, African horse sickness, contagious equine metritis, dourine, epizootic lymphangitis, equine viral encephalitis, glanders (including the form of glanders commonly known as farcy).

Nott stag A West Country term for a

Kineton noseband.

stag which never grows antlers; known in Scotland (and elsewhere) as a 'hummel'.

Novice A junior apprentice jockey, or a learner rider.

Novice (show classes) Breed societies and show organisers impose competition entry rules under which inexperienced horses and ponies are eligible for novice classes if their cash winnings or placings at previous shows or competitions up to a selected date do not exceed a specified limit. The rules vary according to the authority making them.

Novice (racing) For hurdle races it is a horse which has not won a hurdle race at the time of closing, and for steeplechases, a horse which has not won a steeplechase at closing. There are plenty of races confined to novice hurdlers and novice steeplechasers.

Novokirghiz The original Kirghiz horse, bred in the Tien Shan area of the USSR, was a small pony-type animal used in agriculture. In the 1930s unsuccessful attempts were made to improve the breed and increase its size. A new breed was, however, evolved in 1954, by crossing local mares with Don and TB stallions, and the best progeny were then re-crossed. Three types emerged: the basic, the heavy and the riding, standing up to 15.2 hh (157.5 cm). All are multi-purpose riding/harness/pack animals.

Number-boards These are on all racecourses and give, by means of numbers corresponding with the day's race card (q.v.), the names of the horses running in any particular race, as well as the name of the jockey for each. They give,

too, special information, e.g. that a certain horse will be wearing blinkers. (See **Chalk-jockey**)

Number cloth Every horse running in a race must carry a white linen saddle cloth bearing the number corresponding with its number on the race card. The cloth is supplied to the rider at the time of weighing out, and must be worn so that the number is clearly visible. The rider must put the cloth on the scale and include it with his weight.

Numbers (racing) See **Number-boards**.

Numnah A pad cut to the shape of, but rather larger than, the saddle, and worn underneath it, having leather, tape or nylon fastenings or loops which fasten it to the saddle. The traditional material is sheepskin, but modern numnahs may be of nylon simulated sheepskin, cotton-covered foam, acrylic fabric, or felt. The numnah prevents undue pressure from the saddle on a back which is sensitive, perhaps as the result of summering (q.v.), or other lack of condition. It is used for show jumping, eventing, etc., but continued use over a long period, as when hunting, can so overheat the back as to cause the very tenderness that its use seeks to avoid; rubber is particularly bad in this respect, although modern foam plastic does keep a back cool.

Nursery handicap A handicap race confined to two-year-old racehorses.

Nut-cracker A horse that has acquired the rare habit of grinding his teeth.

Nut-cracker action The squeezing action, across the lower jaw, of a jointed snaffle.

Oaks, the The Oaks is the chief race of the season for three-year-old fillies only. It is run over 1½ miles (2.4 km) at the Epsom Summer Meeting over the Derby course. Founded in 1779, it was named after the nearby residence of the 12th Earl

of Derby and was won by his filly Bridget. The race was founded one year before the Derby.

Oats A high energy food, containing approximately 8-9% protein, 4% oil, 9%

fibre, and 60% starch and sugars. Because of their high energy content, oats must be fed with caution to children's ponies and animals not in hard work. They are the most common cereal fed to horses in Britain and in many other parts of the world. Oats may be fed in one of four ways: (1) The most usual form is bruised or cracked, in which the hard kernel is cracked open, thus making it more readily digestible. (2) Whole. (3) Crushed – in which the oats are crushed heavily, and emerge looking like porridge oats. (4) Cooked, in which they are soaked overnight, then boiled. The whole forms a jelly, and is excellent for a sick horse or a shy feeder. In whatever form they come, oats should be clean and sweet-smelling. See **Feeding, general principles of**.

Obedience In a horse obedience is the one great essential for the safety and comfort of rider or driver.

Objection (racing) Various causes may justify an objection being lodged after a race, as laid down in the Rules of Racing. Normally an objection is made in writing by the owner, trainer or jockey within five minutes of the winner weighing in. The stewards of the meeting may at the same time order an enquiry into the running of the race. There can be other objections made later on grounds which have nothing to do with an incident in the race, such as a horse's ineligibility to run in a particular race. In America the term generally used is 'protest'.

Objection (show classes) Objections can be lodged for any alleged infringement of rules laid down by any society or show, which can require a specified sum of money to be lodged with each objection, and call for this to be made within a specified time.

Objection flags (racing) A red flag with a white 'E' hoisted on the number-board shows that an objection and/or enquiry has been lodged. A white flag in place of the red flag with white 'E' indicates that the objection has been over-ruled; a green flag denotes that the objection has been sustained.

Occipital crest The protuberance on the top of the head between the ears, i.e. the poll.

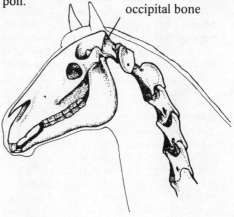

occipital bone

Occipital crest.

Odd-coloured Descriptive of a coat where there is an admixture of more than two colours tending to merge into each other at the edges of patches of colour, with irregular body markings. For two-colour coats, see **Piebald** and **Skewbald**.

Odds The proportion by which the bet staked by one party exceeds that of another. Prices are offered or 'laid' on or against the chance of a horse winning a race.

Odds, long Indication in betting that the chances of a horse winning or being placed are slender.

'Odds, over the' When a backer obtains a longer price than that which is offered at the start of the race.

Odds, short Indication in betting that the chances of a horse winning or being placed are good.

'Odds on' When the assumed chances of a horse winning are greater than even money.

Oedema Accumulation of fluid outside cells causing soft swellings which leave pits when the fingers are removed after applying pressure.

Oestrogen Female sex hormone which in mares is responsible for changes in the oestrous cycle (q.v.).

Oestrous cycle The sexual cycle of the

mare, in which periods of sexual activity (oestrus) alternate with those of inactivity (dioestrus). The cycle lasts about three weeks (five days of oestrus followed by approximately fifteen days of dioestrus) normally throughout spring and summer. It is controlled by the pituitary gland, which produces the follicle-stimulating hormone (FSH), and the lutenising hormone (LH). The former activates the ovaries to produce a follicle, which ruptures, releasing the egg into the fallopian tube (ovulation). At the same time as the follicle is developing, the ovaries produce the hormone oestrogen (q.v.), which produces oestrous behaviour: i.e. the mare comes into season. Ovulation occurs when the mare has been in season for approximately four days. Following ovulation, the site of the egg in the ovary forms a yellow body (corpus luteum) under the influence of the lutenising hormone. The corpus luteum secretes progesterone, a hormone which causes dioestrus. If fertilisation does not occur, the yellow body ceases to function after about the fifteenth day, more FSH is produced, and the cycle re-starts. Heat may be induced by the use of luteolytic hormones which cause the corpus luteum to regress and thus produce a heat in the mare. This technique may be employed in conjunction with inspection of the vagina and cervix using a special endoscope, to time a heat for optimal fertility.

Off When a horse has passed a certain year of its age, e.g. the fifth year, it is said to be 'five off'.

'Off, the' The actual start of a race. Formerly, the starter's assistant raised a white flag to show that the horses were under the starter's orders, and lowered it at the start of the race. Now, in most cases, the signal is given by radio, but the rules still provide for the white flag as an alternative.

'Office, the' The act of communicating to a horse the final indication for the 'take-off' in jumping.

Official, the See **OK**.

Offside The right-hand side of the horse. See **Near-side**.

Ogilvie, William Henry (1869-1963) A prolific writer of sporting verses. His best-known collections on horses and hunting are *Galloping Shoes*, *Scattered Scarlet*, *Over the Grass*, and *A Handful of Leather*.

'OK, the' The American colloquial equivalent of 'the all right' (q.v.). Also in the United States called the Official.

Oldenburg The heaviest of the German warmblood horses, sometimes standing over 17 hh (170 cm). Based on Friesian horses (q.v.), the breed was produced as a quality coach horse by the use of Spanish and Italian blood in the seventeenth century, and later by the introduction of Cleveland Bay, Thoroughbred, Hanoverian and Norman blood. With the decline in demand for coach horses in the early twentieth century, more Thoroughbred, Hanoverian and Trakehner blood was used to produce first an all-purpose farm horse, then a riding horse. More recently, the Oldenburg has once again been used as a harness horse in carriage driving events, notably by HRH the Prince Philip. There are a number of the breed in the Royal Mews at Buckingham Palace. Oldenburgs are brown, black and grey, and move with fairly high knee action.

'Old Rowley' A nickname given to King Charles II, owner of the stallion of that name which he often rode at Newmarket. (See **Rowley Mile**)

Olympic Games The equestrian section consists of: (1) The three-day event (formerly known as the Military), which has three phases, as in the British horse trials (q.v.) – (a) dressage; (b) cross-country; (c) show jumping. (2) Show jumping. (3) Dressage. Normally, each discipline has competitions for both team and individual awards, but in Rome in 1960 no team dressage was held. In 1956, lady riders took part in the equestrian section of the Games for the first time and are now eligible for all events.

Olympic Games and International Equestrian Fund Provides money for equestrian teams travelling abroad to compete in the Olympics and international competitions.

Omnibus See **Garden-seat bus**, **Knife-**

board bus, **Private omnibus**.

Omnibus, public See **Garden-seat bus**, **Knife-board bus**, **Shillibeer**.

One-day event See **Horse trials**.

One-sided mouth A mouth which is unresponsive on one side, and inclined to set with the bit on one side and pull. The cause usually arises from tenderness on the bars or lip corners, which causes the horse to take the bit and pull to one side. Unless care is taken, one side becomes calloused. The cause should be investigated and treated, resting the mouth, and bitting carefully.

One Thousand Guineas This Classic race is for three-year-old fillies only and is run over a straight mile (1.6 km) at the Newmarket Spring Meeting on the Rowley Mile course. The race was founded in 1814.

One-track A term indicating that the hindlegs are moving strictly in line with their respective forelegs, near hind following near foreleg, off hind with off foreleg. (See **Two tracks**).

'On its toes' A term describing a horse which is fidgety, excitable, keen, anxious and unwilling to keep to a walking pace.

'On the bit' A horse is on the bit when it takes a light and temperate but definite feel on the reins, without resistance, and with a relaxed jaw. The head must remain steady, slightly in front of the vertical,

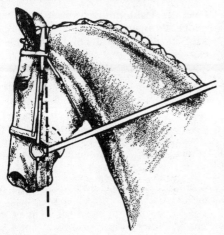

On the bit.

with the neck raised and arched according to the stage of training, with the poll being the highest part of the neck.

'On the leg' An expression to indicate that a horse is too long in the leg. This is generally associated with one which is shallow in the body. Implying the same defect is the expression 'showing too much daylight'.

'On the rails' (racing) Said of a jockey who is riding closest to the rails (q.v.).

Open A hunting term for a fox's earth which is not stopped.

Open The hound which first 'speaks' to a fox in covert is said to 'open' on it.

Open country Hunting term indicating that the country hunted is virtually free from woodland.

Open ditch (racing) All steeplechase courses have two or more open ditches, as opposed to plain fences which have no ditch on the take-off side. They have to be of dimensions approved by the Jockey Club.

Opening meet The first meet of the regular hunting season, generally held at the beginning of November. It is the first day on which the field wear scarlet coats and silk hats.

Open rein (or Opening rein) This refers to the use of one rein only for the purpose of guiding the horse, i.e. using the right rein to turn to the right, and the left rein to turn the left. Also known as the direct rein.

Ophthalmia Inflammation of the deeper structures of the eye, characterised by pain, closing of the eyelids, and a varying degree of discharge.

Opportunity race A race for young steeplechase jockeys over hurdles or fences, restricted to riders who have ridden only a certain number of winners.

Oriental horses A loose term, now rarely used, referring to the Arabs and Barbs imported from the Middle East to mate with home-bred horses in Stuart and Georgian times.

Original Shales Foaled in 1750 by Blaze out of a Hackney mare bred by Robert

Shales of Oxborough. Recognised as the progenitor of the modern Hackney (q.v.). (See **Marshland Shales**)

Orlov Trotter A famous breed of Russian Trotter, dating back to the 1870s, when Count Alexis Grigorievich Orlov crossed the white Arab stallion Smetanka with Dutch, Danish Mecklenburg and Thoroughbred mares at the Orlov Stud, near Moscow. Later, the stock was moved to the Khrenov Stud, where the breed became firmly established by crossing other Arab stallions with Danish and Dutch mares. The foundation stallion of the breed was Bars I, a grandson of Smetanka. There are now five distinct types within the breed, with the most typical being the medium-sized Khrenov. The breed stands between 15.3-16 hh (160-162.6 cm), is a large, well-proportioned animal, predominantly grey, with good limbs.

Ormonde The unbeaten horse belonging to the first Duke of Westminster. Ormonde won the Triple Crown (q.v.) in 1886. He competed in and won sixteen races, and won over £28,000 in stake money. Later he turned roarer (q.v.), but is only known to have sired one roarer, Gold Finch. He was sold to Argentina, then to the USA, where he was put down in 1904.

Osbaldeston, George (pronounced Osbal-*des*-ton) (1787-1866) Twice Master of the Quorn (1817-21 and 1823-27), Osbaldeston lived at Quorndon Hall. On a round course at Newmarket in 1831, for a bet of 1000 guineas, he rode 200 miles (321.8 km) on horseback in 8 hours 42 minutes. He rode in many matches across country; these included his ride on his own hunter, Clasher, against Dick Christian (q.v.) on Clinker (q.v.). Osbaldeston tried his hand at every sport, and was also famous at single wicket cricket.

Ostler See **Hostler**.

Ostrich bit A bit perfected in Walsall for the American market. It has a hollow tube mouthpiece in which rotates a longer mouthpiece to which the rings are attached. It is secured to the bridle by 'eyes' from the main mouthpiece. It is always used with a leather chin strap.

Mainly a racing snaffle and very useful on the sharp-cornered American tracks as it cannot slide through the mouth. A pelham (q.v.) bit with the same mouthpiece was also made.

'Out at elbow' A term describing a hound whose elbows project outwards; not a straight mover. This is a weakness.

Outcrossing The mating of less closely related or unrelated individuals.

Outlaw In Western America a term for an incorrigible horse; a rogue.

'Out of blood' Hounds which have not killed for some time are said to be 'out of blood', or 'short of blood'.

Outrider A mounted attendant who rides in advance of, or beside, a carriage. In America he is an official of the racetrack, usually in hunt livery, who leads a parade of racehorses past the stands before the start of a race.

Outside, the (racing) Furthest from the rails. A jockey is often said to make his challenge on the inside or nearest the rails, or on the outside or furthest away from the rails.

Outsider (racing) A term implying a horse with little chance of winning a race in which it is engaged. Also a term of opprobrium, believed to be derived from the unfortunate passenger who was compelled to ride on the top of a stage coach, exposed to all weathers.

Overalls Tight riding trousers strapped under the instep and worn as full dress with a silk hat and tail coat in hack classes.

'Over at the knee' A forward bend or curve of the knees which may be the result of excessive wear, but is often a matter of conformation. This was very marked in the case of the famous racehorse, St Simon, as well as in many others. It is a disfigurement which would count against a show horse.

Overbent Serious defective position of the head which approaches the chest to a point beyond the vertical. It may be caused either by the horse's attempt to evade the bit, or the awkwardness of the rider.

Over-carted A horse or pony drawing any vehicle which is too large (not necessarily too heavy), in regard to the animal's size.

Overcheck (driving) A thin leather or cord check from the bit through the rings to the pad; used by hackney horse and hackney pony drivers.

Overcheck (on Hackney buggy harness) Known among Hackney people as 'top-rein', familiar to show spectators as the rein which is released from the hook on the pad when the horse comes to a standstill in the line-up, and which is fastened again at the moment of moving off.

Overcheck (on racing harness) Used on pacers and trotters to keep the head up and the nose well forward, this position being an adjunct to speed.

Overcheck (riding) A thin leather or cord check, usually running from a small (broken or mullen) bridoon (q.v.) between the horse's ears to the saddle. This term is also used for a very thin (wire-mouth) gag snaffle, sometimes twisted, with cord cheeks, used by nagsmen, with a curb bit to raise the head.

Over-collected Showing too much collection, the horse's head position being behind the vertical.

Over at the knee.

Over-faced Descriptive of a horse who is asked to jump beyond its powers, either in height, width or number of jumps.

Over-horsed A term used to describe a rider whose horse is too large or too spirited for him.

Overnight Declarations Office This is the Jockey Club Office, now at Weatherbys, at which all horses have to be declared to run at the five-day stage before a race, and at which horses are withdrawn on the eve of a race.

Over-reach boot A circular rubber boot, sometimes laced, which prevents serious injury to the coronet when a horse over-reaches (see below).

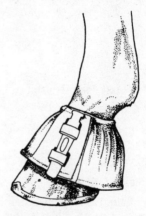

Over-reach boot.

Over-reaching This is caused by the rim of the toe of the hind shoe striking down against the heel of the forefoot. It may be prevented by a smooth concaved toe to the hind shoe, or, in exceptional cases, a specially made shoe. (See **Shoe, fullered**)

Over-ride Term used to describe hunt followers who ride too close to hounds when they are running.

Over-ride, to To ride a horse either at an excessive pace or for too long a period, having regard to its physical condition.

'Over-the-bridge' A dealer's term applied to steeplechasing.

'Over the sticks' A slang term applied to steeplechasing.

Overo (USA and South America) See **Pinto/Paint**.

Overshot fetlock See **Knuckling-over**.

Overshot mouth See **Parrot-mouth**.

Over-tracking In medium, extended and free walk, and medium and extended trot the imprint of the hind foot should be *beyond* the imprint of the fore foot on the same side.

Owner According to the Rules of Racing the owner of a racehorse, broadly speaking, may be a part-owner or a lessee but not a leasor.

Owner partnerships (racing) These are usually formed by two to four people to meet the costs of owning a racehorse. Details of all partnerships, the name and address of every person having any interest in a horse, and the relative proportions of such interest must be supplied, signed by all parties, and lodged at the Racing Calendar Office. All partners are jointly and severally liable for every stake or forfeit. See also **Syndicate (racing)**.

'Own the line' A hound which is on the fox's line is said to 'own the line'.

Ox fence/Oxer An ordinary hedge, with a guard rail set about a yard (1 m) from it on one side. (See also **Double oxer**)

—P—

PBAR Part-bred Arab Register.

PC Pony Club.

PDSA People's Dispensary for Sick Animals (q.v.).

POA (USA) Pony of the Americas.

POB Ponies of Britain.

PU (in racing) An abbreviation for 'pulled up'; a horse which for some reason or other is pulled up by its jockey and does not complete the course.

Pace Army requirements are: walk 4 mph (6.43 km/h); trot 8 mph (12.8 km/h); canter 9 mph (14.4 km/h); slow gallop 12 mph (19.3 km/h); gallop 15 mph (24.1 km/h). See also **Gait**.

Pace-maker A horse which leads and sets the pace in a race. In long-distance races other than handicaps, a trainer often puts in a pace-maker to ensure a true-run race.

Pacer A horse which, instead of trotting with a diagonal action, moves with near-fore and hind together, followed by off-fore and hind. A very comfortable gait for long-distance riding, and popular in American shows and trotting races. The old English name 'ambler' describes a horse with this action.

Pacing A term describing a form of racing in great vogue in the United States and to a lesser extent elsewhere (See **Amble, Pacer**).

Pack An undefined number of hounds kept for hunting.

Packhorse A horse used for carrying packs, either the kit of a horseman or merchandise. In ancient times, pack-horses were the chief, and often only, means of transportation for goods.

Pad The foot of a fox. To 'pad a fox' is to follow the pad marks, i.e. to track it.

Pad (harness) The saddle used in double harness; the centre-piece of a set of harness, bridging the horse's back. It should have a top of patent leather on an under-panel of oiled leather, and its pattern should match the blinkers and padcloths (q.v.).

Pad (roller) A rectangular piece of felt, 1 in. (2.5 cm) or so thick, which may be strapped under a roller, if the latter is not stuffed and maintained properly.

Pad (saddle) See **Numnah**.

Pad (wither) Also known as a Wither Pad. A temporary measure to prevent a saddle which is in need of re-stuffing from resting on the withers. Usually made of woven wool, but may be sheepskin.

Padcloth A cloth covering a horse's loins.

Padding Wool flock used as stuffing in saddles and rollers, now being replaced by plastic foam in many saddles.

Paddock An enclosed area of grassland used for rearing young horses, for turning out working animals when not required, and for restoring sick or lame horses to health or soundness. The term is synonymous with pasture, though the latter suggests something of a greater area. A paddock should afford a good growth of sweet and rich herbage and have a sound and safe surface and fence.

Paddock (racing) Every racecourse must have a railed-off paddock where the horses are paraded after they have been saddled, and where the jockeys assemble and mount.

Pad-groom The correct term for a hunt servant. Livery: white cord breeches; top boots with flesh-coloured tops.

Pad-horse An obsolete term for a horse used for riding on the road; an easy-paced horse.

Pad-tree The wooden or metal frame to which harness pads are attached.

Pair Two horses driven abreast.

Palate, soft Muscular membrane separating mouth from pharynx except during swallowing. The condition known as 'soft palate', when interference by the membrane in normal breathing occurs (see **Roarer**), may be alleviated to some extent by surgery, cautery (application of hot metal or electrical current), or injection of a sclerosing agent (which hardens the tissues).

Palfrey In mediaeval times a light horse, as distinct from a warhorse, especially a small saddle-horse which could amble (q.v.).

Palio of Siena See **Siena Races**.

Palmer, Lynwood (1868-1939) Educated for the diplomatic service, but went to Canada ranching and horse breeding. Artistic talent and a dedication to horses led to Canadian commissions for equestrian pictures. He went to New York and after a lapse of eleven years returned to England where he became established as a sporting artist, painting pictures for Edward VII and George V. He possessed a remarkable gift for capturing the individuality and character of Thoroughbred horses, and also included picturesque landscape effects in his backgrounds. Several of his pictures are owned by the Royal Jockey Club, Newmarket. In addition, Palmer was a leading authority on horsemastership, driving, shoeing and care of the horse's foot.

Palomino The 'Golden Horse of the West' is widely regarded as a colour type, not a breed, except in the United States. The colour, that of 'a newly minted gold coin', is found in many breeds, but animals of this colour do not 'breed true'. The mating of Palomino to Palomino produces one albino and one chestnut to two Palomino-coloured foals, and although the mating of *chestnut* to Palomino produces Palomino, the colour is often very poor, and not registrable by most Palomino societies. The colour, although never seen in modern Arabs, is thought to have originated in the ancient Arab breed, and may date back to the Homeric age. The first mention of it states that it was much favoured by the kings of Yemen, whilst Queen Isabella of Spain, the sponsor of Columbus, encouraged their breeding, and the horses were (and still are) known in Spain as 'Isabellas' (q.v.). The present name is believed to derive from Juan de Palomino, who received one of these horses from Cortés. They are now used extensively in America for saddle, parades, and spectacular purposes. In Britain, any suitably coloured horse or pony may be registered with the British Palomino Society. For registration with the Palomino Horse Association of America, the animal must be between 14.1-16 hh (144.8-162.6 cm).

Pan-American Games These events, based on the Olympic model, are limited to nations in North, South and Central America. They were first held in 1951, and take place every four years in the year preceding the Olympic Games.

Panel (saddle) See **Saddle panel**.

Pannade The curvet (q.v.) of a horse.

Papes pattern A method of securing any type of rug by means of straps from the rear flanks joined to a central belly ring, from which a further strap passes through the forelegs and is secured at the breast.

Parabola (show jumping) The arc through the air made by a horse on clearing any obstacle, from the point of leaving the ground to the point of contact on landing.

Parade-ring Area where horses are paraded before a race.

Parafilariasis A skin condition caused by a worm, *Parafilaria multipapillosa*, in the sub-cutaneous tissues, usually of the shoulders or quarters. Unknown in Britain, but found in the USSR.

Parallel bars A spread fence consisting of two lines of poles set parallel to each other.

Pariani Pariani was the name of Italy's foremost saddlemaker; he was the reputed originator of the spring-tree saddle. See **Saddle, Italian**.

Pari-mutuel A system of reciprocal betting similar to the totalisator; the only form of betting authorised in France since 1891. The odds returned are determined by dividing the total amount invested on a race by the number of winning units, less the percentage taken.

Park course A term to describe a racecourse which is entirely closed, like Kempton Park and Sandown Park in England, in contrast to Epsom which is partly open to the racing public without payment.

Park drag See **Drag**.

Park phaeton A low-hung phaeton for a

Park phaeton.

lady driver, otherwise known as a George IV's, Lady's, or Peter's phaeton.

Park railings (hunting) Any iron railing.

Parliamentary horse It was illegal for mail coaches (q.v.) to be driven at a gallop, but if one horse of the team was trotting the coach was within the law. Mail contractors therefore paid high prices for fast trotters, one of which they liked to include in each team. This trotter was known as the 'parliamentary' horse.

Parrot mouth A malformation of the upper jaw, where the front (incisor) teeth overhang the lower jaw, preventing proper mastication between the upper and lower incisor teeth and therefore indu-

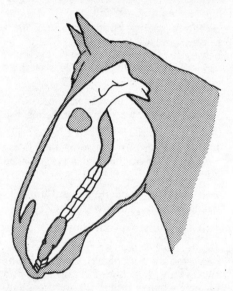

Parrot mouth.

cive to digestive trouble. The condition also prevents a horse from grazing. This congenital deformity is often known as 'overshot'.

Parthenon Frieze A masterpiece of Greek sculpture dating from the mid-fifth century BC. Carved on the top of the outer wall of the Cella of the Parthenon at Athens, it represents the ritual procession of the Pan-Athenaic festival, with many horses of different types. A part of the frieze can be seen in the British Museum, London.

Paso Corto See **Paso Fino**.

Paso Fino The Paso Fino originated or was developed in Puerto Rico, Columbia, Peru, and Florida, and is gaining ground in the USA; there are breed clubs in some parts of the country. The horses must *never* trot. They perform the *paso largo* and *paso corto*, and sometimes the *sobre paso* and *andadura*. The Paso Fino gait, sometimes called the *fino-fino*, is very slow, with extreme collection and a steady unbroken rhythm. The *paso corto* is a more relaxed gait, suitable for trail or pleasure riding with only mild collection – faster than the walk. The *paso largo* is the speed form of the gait, and adherents claim that the Paso Fino can pass cantering horses while maintaining the *paso largo*. The same 1-2-3-4 rhythm must be maintained, and the rider should appear motionless in the saddle as at all *paso* gaits. The *sobre paso* is the most relaxed form of the gait, with little or no style, but the horse must not hang his head. The rein is completely loose. This is not a show-ring gait. The *andadura* is executed when the horse is pushed for top speed, not into a gallop, but rather into a sort of pace. It is not a comfortable gait. The Paso Fino can walk in a free manner, and some have a delightful canter. Speed at a gallop is never part of showing. They are from 13-15.2 hh (132.1-157.5 cm) and weigh 700-1100 lb (312-454 kg).

Paso Largo See **Paso Fino**.

Pass See **Half-pass**.

Passada A wider, easier form of a half-pirouette or turn on the haunches used primarily as a training exercise.

Passage A High School air, consisting of a very cadenced, lofty trot, with a moment of suspension clearly marked.

Passmore and Cole bars A pattern of safety-stirrup bars designed to release the leather in the event of a fall.

Pastern That part of a horse's leg which lies between the fetlock joint and the coronet.

Pastern joint Formed by first and second phalangeal bones, i.e. the long pastern (os suffraginis) and the short pastern (os coronae).

Pastern bone, split Sudden and extreme lameness is caused by the fracture of the first phalanx. Other symptoms include sweating and great distress. Veterinary attention is required and may consist of applying a plaster support, followed by long rest. The prognosis for this sort of fracture is poor, but may be improved by screwing the bones together in an operation using modern internal fixation techniques.

Past mark of mouth A term meaning a horse is 'aged' (q.v.).

Patch A well-defined irregular area of hairs differing from the general body colour. The colour, shape, position and extent should be given on any written description.

Pate (Obsolete) The head of a fox.

Patent safety A description of a horse (often a hunter) that will carry its rider with maximum safety and comfort.

Pato A traditional mounted game played in South America.

Patten shoe A shoe with a wide raised bar across the heel, which may be used on a horse with sprained tendons, to raise the heel and reduce pain. Also known as platten shoe.

Pattern races (Also known as Graded Stake races in some countries.) An international method of grading leading non-handicap races according to their intrinsic importance. The idea is to provide races for the best horses of all ages, and, providing sufficient prize money is available, to encourage owners/trainers to keep them in training long enough to test properly the horses' constitution and soundness, and so raise the general standard. There are three groups of Pattern Races. Group 1 – championship races, including the Classic races, in which horses meet on weight for age terms with no penalties or allowances. Group II – races just below championship level in which there may be penalties and/or allowances. Group III – races of mainly domestic interest, including Classic trials, which are required to complete the series of tests for the best horses. The chosen races are published in Pattern

Race books, and the scheme operates in over twenty countries.

Peacock safety irons A type designed for children. The outside leg of the iron is removed and replaced with a stout rubber ring.

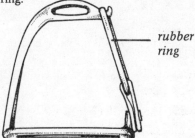

rubber ring

Peacock safety iron.

'Peacocky' Descriptive of a very high neck-carriage with the head bent strongly at the poll; a narrow and flash-looking appearance which attracts the unwary buyer.

Peas A nutritious horse feed which is rich in protein, but both heating and fattening. Peas are fed (in small quantities) split or crushed.

Peck A term denoting the act of stumbling. This can be at any gait and is the term commonly used when a horse stumbles on landing over a fence; hence the term 'pecked on landing'.

Pedal bone This is crescent-shaped and somewhat resembles the hoof. It lies within the hoof and with the navicular bone and lower portion of the coronet bone forms the pedal or foot joint.

Pedal ostitis Inflammation of the pedal bone, often causing pain and lameness. X-ray examination shows diminished density in areas of the pedal bone. Caused by – 1. concussion over a long period; 2. (sometimes) corns, laminitis or bruised/punctured sole. It is most common in one forefoot. The symptoms are similar to early navicular disease (q.v.).

Peel, John (1776-1854) A Cumberland yeoman farmer who hunted his own hounds in that country for forty-six years. He lived at Ruthwaite near Ireby and is buried in Caldbeck churchyard. He acquired fame through the popular song 'John Peel', written by Woodcock Graves in 1832.

Pegasus The winged horse of Greek mythology, offspring of Poseidon and Medusa, the Gorgon. He was caught by Bellerophon with a golden bridle, and ridden by him to kill the Chimera. From a mark where his hoof struck Mount Helicon sprang Hippocrene, the River of the Muses.

Pegasus Club Composed of members of the Bench and the Bar, this club holds a point-to-point annually on a different course.

Pegs See **Frost nails**.

Peg-sticking (USA) See **Tent pegging**.

Pelethronius King of the Lapithae, in Thessaly, said to have invented bridles.

Pelham Any bit designed to combine in one the action of a double bridle, i.e. curb and bridoon.

Jointed pelham bit.

Pelham roundings Curved leather couplings joining the bridoon and curb rings of a pelham bit so that one rein can be used instead of two.

Penalty (racing) In certain races, e.g. maidens (q.v.) at closing (q.v.), penalties can be incurred by horses winning between the closing of the entries and the running of the race concerned, in which they will have to carry more weight. Penalties vary considerably and conditions for these vary with different races. There are no penalties for the Classics (q.v.) and certain other races, nor can they be incurred by horses which have only been placed.

Penalty seconds (show jumping) Time added in some speed contests for faults incurred while jumping the course.

Pendulous lip Descriptive of the under-lip hanging low and lifeless.

People's Dispensary for Sick Animals Founded in 1917 by the late Mrs Maria Elizabeth Dickin, CBE, and incorporated in 1923, the PDSA claims to be the only society founded exclusively for the free treatment of sick and injured animals for owners unable to afford professional fees. Through its dispensaries, animal hospitals, mobile caravans and home treatment, it attends to a huge number of cases each year. It is supported entirely by voluntary contributions.

Perch The main timber in the under-carriage of coaches and some other old-time carriages, the perch runs from the front to the back of the vehicle, and usually curves downwards.

Perch-bolt This passes through the fore axle-tree bed and the fore transom holding the perch on a coach.

Percheron One of the most popular heavy draught horses. The Percheron originated in the La Perche district of France, and owes much of its undoubted quality to Oriental blood dating from the eighteenth century. Now bred in many countries outside France, e.g. USA, Canada, and Australia, it is one of the four main breeds of heavy horse in Britain. It is possessed of low draught, having a short, compact body of great depth, with short legs and good bone. It is a very active, elegant horse at its best. In France, there are two types – the Grand Taille and the Petit Taille (also known as the Gros Taille and the Postier). The Postier stands up to 16.1 hh (165 cm), and the Grand Taille up to 16.3 hh (170.18 cm). The colour is predominantly grey, with some black, and the occasional bay, chestnut or roan. In France, the Percheron, as in the case of so many Continental heavy breeds, is being bred largely for the production of meat.

Percheron Horse Society, the British Founded in 1919 to establish and maintain the purity of the Percheron breed in the United Kingdom.

Pericarditis Inflammation of the pericardium (the membrane surrounding the heart). It is caused by bacterial infection, or, in foals, by injury at birth. It is a very serious condition which may lead to accumulation of fluid in the pericardium – thus reducing the ability of the heart to work, leading in severe cases to death.

Perioplic ring See **Hoof, periople of**.

Permit holder Under Jockey Club Rules for steeplechasing and hurdle races, trainers who train solely for themselves and immediate members of their family can be granted a permit to train, as opposed to a full training licence. (See **Licence, trainer**)

Persian Arab See **Persian Horse**.

Persian Horse Known as a breed for many centuries BC, the Persian was claimed to be descended from the Tarpan (q.v.); it is also suggested that it was the ancestor of the Arab. It was a typical Oriental breed – beautiful, full of quality, high-spirited and speedy, and consequently much appreciated by Islamic warriors. Today there are several different breeds found in Persia (Iran), such as the Persian Arab, the Turkoman, the Shirazi, the Yamoote, the Bokhara Pony, and the Jaf.

Peruvian Ambler (Caballo de Paso Peruano) The horse claims descent from the horses brought over in the Spanish Conquest of Peru, which were mainly of Barb origin. In type the Caballo de Paso is similar to the Barb, but slightly bigger, with longer legs and a higher tail carriage, the legs being fine boned, strong and clean. These horses are extremely agile and sure-footed, a necessity for their rugged country. Their main pace, the amble (q.v.), is most comfortable and can be surprisingly fast. Each year there are competitions to find the best Caballo de Paso. These are enthusiastically supported.

Petechial fever Also known as *Purpura haemorrhagica* or putrid fever. An acute feverish condition accompanied by purple bleeding from the mucous membranes and swelling on the dependent parts of the body. It is generally the aftermath of diseases such as strangles – an acute infectious disease of the upper respiratory tract. The outlook is poor and veterinary attention is essential.

'Peterborough' To foxhunters, this means the Peterborough Royal Hound Show, which was founded in 1878. Held annually since then, the show has become established as the premier foxhound show of Great Britain, and is now incorporated in the East of England Show.

Peter's phaeton See **Park phaeton**.

Peytrel/Poitrel Breastplate armour for the horse.

Phaeton A four-wheeled carriage for personal driving, of which there are many varieties (See **Mail**, **Demi-mail**, **Park**, **Equirotal**, **Siamese** and **Spider phaetons**).

Phar Lap Great New Zealand-bred racehorse foaled in 1926 (by Night March). A big, backward, bright chestnut colt, he was gelded as a yearling, but matured as a three-year-old, and enjoyed a phenomenal racing career. In three years he won thirty-seven times in fifty-one starts. Known as the 'Red Terror' because of his colour, he won the Australian Jockey Club and Victorian Derbys and St Legers, and the Melbourne Cup. As a five-year-old he went to America, and won the 1¼ mile (2 km) Agua Cahenter Handicap in Mexico in a record time of 2 minutes 2.8 seconds. He died when turned out at grass in California, in circumstances that have been regarded as mysterious, but possibly as a result of eating sprayed grass. His skin is now in the Melbourne Museum, his heart in Canberra, and his skeleton in New Zealand.

Phenylbutazone An anti-inflammatory non-steroid drug, commonly known as 'Bute'. Since 1981 the drug has been the only one of its type permitted under FEI (q.v.) rules, but under current regulations it must not be present at levels in excess of 4 micrograms per ml of blood. 'Butazolodin' is a trade name for the drug.

'Phiz' See **Browne, Hablot Knight**.

Photo-finish A method of determining the order of placings at the end of a race. The finish photographed from both sides of the course to enable the judge to place with certainty the first four or more finishers.

Photo-sensitivity Caused by ingestion of photo-active substances and toxins: e.g. as found in St John's Wort. The characteristic signs are inflammation of the white or unpigmented areas of the skin, caused by the ultra-violet light in sunlight acting on these substances, which are converted into products causing the skin damage. The condition can be painful, and requires veterinary attention.

Piaffe A passage (q.v.) done virtually on the spot, with minimal forward movement. The action should be lofty, slow, and cadenced.

Pickaxe A slang term for a team of five horses with two wheelers and three leaders; also used for one wheel-horse and two leaders, as opposed to a unicorn, i.e. one leader and two wheelers.

'Picked-up' Racing term indicating a shortening of the reins by the jockey to balance and poise his mount for an increase in pace.

Pick up hounds To lift hounds.

Pie A foxhound colour, lighter than the rich Belvoir tan. There are three shades – lemon pie, hare pie and badger pie.

Piebald When the horse's body colour consists of large irregular patches of black and white. The line of demarcation between the two colours is generally well-defined. Piebalds and skewbalds are termed Pintos or Paints (qq.v.) in the USA and are separately named according to colour-grouping.

Pigeon toes Toes which turn inwards; horses having these never strike into themselves, but the condition results in excessive wear of the outside of the foot and shoe. A farrier may correct this by lowering the foot on the appropriate side.

Pig-eye A small eye, undistinguished in character and having a mean, uninterested and unintelligent outlook.

Pigskin The most desirable leather for the seat of a saddle, on account of its durability and elasticity.

Pig-sticking The sport of hunting wild boar on horseback with a spear, developed by British officers in India at the beginning of the nineteenth century, from the more ancient sport of spearing bear. The greatest centres were in the thick grass-grown old beds of the great rivers, i.e. the Jumna and the Ganges of the United Provinces, called the Kadir country, and in the Central Provinces, especially around Muttra. It was also practised in parts of the Punjab, of Bengal, and in North Africa. Doyen of clubs was the Meerut Tent Club, founded before the Mutiny. The premier competition was for the Kadir Cup (q.v.), an individual event instituted in 1873; the Muttra Cup was awarded for the best team results each season. A smallish animal of polo pony type was best for this sport, which required the highest degree of skill and courage in both horse and rider.

Pigtail In an American 'train' of mules, each animal is tied to a short rope with loops braided in each end, called a pigtail.

Pilentum Open carriage with the doorway very near the ground. Made in different sizes to carry four or six people, and drawn by one or two horses (*c.* 1834).

Pillar or Pillars Training of the horse by the aid of pillars may have originated in classical times. Eumenes (d. 316 BC), when besieged in his fort of Noras by Antigonus, feared his horses would suffer from lack of exercise. He therefore invented a method of working them in their stalls by placing a pulley in the stable beams and, with a running rein, pulling up their fore parts. Assistants at the rear urged the horses into motion on the one spot. Pignatelli, the famous Neopolitan master of equitation, to avoid the fatigue of holding the lunge rein, and having no manège (q.v.), used to tie his horses to a tree and work them round it. Antoine de Pluvinel de la Baume (1555-1620) copied this idea in France using a post or pillar, later adding a second one. Pillars are still used in training the horses of the Spanish Riding School (q.v.) in Vienna, and of the Cadre Noir (q.v.) in France.

Pillar reins A pair of brass-mounted reins, attached to stall-posts or pillars, to secure a horse when backed into its stall. When the horse is to be saddled, it should be turned round and placed with the reins attached to pillars (q.v.).

Pillars The supporting posts of the divisions between stalls to which pillar-reins are attached.

'Pillars of the Stud Book' The three Arabian sires, to one of which all entries in the General Stud Book trace their descent: the Byerley Turk (1689), the Darley Arabian (1704), and the Godolphin Arabian (1730) (qq.v.).

'Pill-box' A slang name popularly applied to a brougham of the smallest build, seating two persons within. It was particularly favoured by doctors of London's West End. (See **Brougham**)

Pilling going gauge An instrument designed to test the state of the 'going' (q.v.) on racecourses.

Pillion A type of saddle attached to the hinderpart of an ordinary saddle on which a second person (usually a woman) could ride. There are records of Queen Elizabeth I riding behind her Master of the Horse to St Paul's Cathedral. The pillion is stated to have been out of use in Britain since about 1830.

Pillion post See **Mounting block**.

Pindos Pony Bred in the Greek mountainous regions of Thessaly and Epirus for riding and light farm work. The mares are used for the breeding of mules. These ponies stand 12-13 hh (122-132 cm) and are predominantly grey.

Pinerolo Famous Italian Cavalry School near Turin, founded in 1823. It became the Royal Cavalry School. Federico Caprilli (q.v.) became its most renowned instructor.

Pin-firing/Point-firing See **Firing**.

Pink (hunting) Incorrect term for the colour of scarlet hunting coats. Origin of the term is uncertain, but possibly based on the fact that 'Mr Pink' was a fashionable nineteenth-century hunting tailor.

Pink eye See **Equine viral arteritis**.

Pinto/Paint The word 'Pinto' derives

from the Spanish word *pintado* (painted), and describes the characteristic irregular patches of solid colour and white which distinguish this type of horse. In America, they are regarded as a breed, but in many other countries they are a colour type. The American Paint Horse Association recognises two types of coat-colouring, depending principally on the location of the white markings. The white of the Overo type does not usually cross the back between the withers and the tail, at least one leg will be dark, the tail is usually one colour, and the white markings are irregular and rather scattered. The Tobiano type (which outnumbers the Overo by approximately 4:1) usually has all four legs white, at least below the knees and hocks, the head is marked like a solid-coloured horse, being either solid, or with a blaze or star, there will usually be dark colour on one or both flanks, and these dark spots are usually regular and distinct. Pintos were very popular with the North American Indians. The modern type traces its ancestry to the Quarter Horse, and there have also been infusions of Thoroughbred blood. Outside the USA, horses with predominantly black markings are called piebald, and those with brown and white markings, skewbald. They are usually half- or part-breds, but the Shetland Pony Stud Book is one of the few breed societies to accept 'broken-coloured' ponies for registration as purebreds. The Pinto Horse Association of America recognises four types according to use: (a) stock type; (b) hunter type; (c) pleasure type; (d) saddle type. Paint horses are also very popular in Australia, and a Paint Horse Society has recently been formed in Britain.

Pin toes See **Pigeon toes**.

Pinto Horse Society Formed in the United States of America by enthusiasts, to encourage the development of Pinto colouration into a breed of its own type by selection.

'Pint pot, muzzle in a' A popular phrase descriptive of a muzzle so small as to be capable of being 'put in a pint pot', e.g. the best type of Arabian horse has such a muzzle.

Pinzgauer See **Noriker**.

Pipe A branch or hole of a fox earth.

Pipe-opener A gallop to clear the horse's wind.

Pirouette A movement performed on two tracks, in which the forelegs describe a complete circle with a radius equal to the length of the horse. The forefeet and outside hind foot moves around the inside hind foot, with the latter being raised and put down on the spot or with a minimal forward movement. It may be performed at the walk, canter, or piaffe, with the rhythm, balance, and cadence of the pace being retained throughout. The movement is known as a half-pirouette when it is executed through 180 degrees instead of the full 360 degrees.

Pirouette renversée A movement where the hindlegs describe a complete circle, the centre of which is occupied by a foreleg serving as a pivot. It is performed only at the walk. It is called half pirouette renversée when the rotation of the quarters is through 180 degrees. Unlike the pirouette (q.v.), it does not figure in FEI dressage tests.

Pit ponies Not used before the nineteenth century, but when colliery 'lift' cages were installed these ponies worked underground in large numbers. Size was governed by the height of the pit workings; Shetlands, Welsh, Fells, Dartmoors, Exmoors, Norwegian and Icelandic ponies were used. Ponies have now been replaced by machines.

Pitter See **Collier**.

Pituitary gland A ductless gland situated at the base of the brain. It produces hormones which ultimately act on various organs of the body including the uterus, ovaries, testes, kidneys, mammary glands, and the adrenal and thyroid glands.

Place (racing) Any horse placed by the judge first, second or third in a race is a 'placed' horse. No horse passing the winning post after the judge has left his box can be 'placed'.

Place betting Backing a horse for a place – three places with eight or more runners, and two places with five to seven runners.

Bookmakers tabulate their own rules on place betting with various contingencies.

Plaited reins These reins usually have plaited handparts, as all-plaited reins cannot easily accommodate a running martingale. The handparts are normally plaited from five strands of leather.

Plaiting See **Crossing feet**.

Plaits Worn most generally in the show ring in the manes of hunters, hacks, show and working ponies and hackneys, to smarten the neck and general appearance, and to add refinement.

Plaits.

Plaits (hack) Similar to plaits for a hunter (q.v.) but the mane can be shorter and the plaits smaller and neater.

Plaits (Hackney) The mane is hogged on each side of the neck, leaving a very thin line of mane in the centre. This is plaited in a considerable number of small plaits with yellow, green or red wool.

Plaits (hunter) The mane must be a fair length and not pulled too short; the plaits, seven, or at the most nine, in number, should be turned back underneath and sewn with thread of the same colour as the mane.

Plaits (USA) Usually called braids. Great difference of opinion as to the correct number. It is likely to run from nine to thirteen on a gelding and from eight to twelve on a mare. Mares are supposed to have even numbers of braids, geldings odd.

Plantar cushion A mass of fibro-fatty tissue, filling up the space behind the pedal bone and forming the bulb of the heel; it acts as a shock absorber.

Plantation Walking Horse See **Tennessee Walking Horse**.

Plate (racing) A very light aluminium shoe used in racing. The most common form has a single groove; the 'double grip' has two grooves and is said to give a more secure footing.

Racing plate.

'Plate, in the' Descriptive of a rider when sitting in the saddle.

Plater A term for a horse which runs in a selling race (q.v.), so is normally of a low standard.

Platten shoe See **Patten shoe**.

Players See **Keys**.

Pleven A Hungarian horse of mixed ancestry but of considerable distinction. It exhibits Arab characteristics, having been based mainly on that breed. Average height about 15.2 hh (157.5 cm).

Plough A hunting term implying wheat fields, seed, stubble and fallow.

Ploughs The arable parts of East Anglia are known as 'the ploughs'; hence 'to hunt on the ploughs'.

Pluvinel, Antoine de (1555-1620) (Antoine de Pluvinel de la Baume) Riding instructor to the King of France, Louis XIII, and author of *The Instruction of the King in the Art of Riding*, printed in 1626, which is in the form of a dialogue between the King as his pupil and the author as riding instructor.

Pneumonia Inflammation of lung tissue, often following influenza or strangles. It is caused by organisms such as bacteria, fungi, viruses or migrating larvae. The symptoms are rapid respiration, loss of appetite, high fever, shivering, coughing, a rapid weak pulse, and nasal discharge. It is a very serious condition requiring veterinary attention.

Poached When the ground in front of a jump or in gateways is muddy and cut-up it is said to be poached.

Point In hunting the point of a run is the distance between any two points measured in a straight line. The *actual* distance, however, is termed 'as hounds ran' (q.v.).

Point-firing See **Firing**.

'Pointing' Standing with the toe of either foreleg pointing. A symptom of navicular disease (q.v.).

'Pointing your leaders' Giving the leaders in a coach team the hint that you intend to alter direction to right or left.

Point-to-points Steeplechase races confined to horses which have been regularly and fairly hunted with any recognised pack of hounds. For all races (except those confined to the hunt promoting the meeting, i.e. 'Members' Races'), the owners must obtain a Master of Hounds certificate stating that each horse has been hunted with his pack, and the owner must confirm that the animal has been 'regularly and fairly' hunted. The certificate must be registered at the Racing Calendar Office before the horse is eligible to be entered. Each hunt normally has its own point-to-point meeting on a course chosen by the Committee (courses are often shared with other local hunts). In addition to the Members', there are usually five races, including an Adjacent Hunts, probably two Open, and a Ladies'. Men and women now compete on equal terms in point-to-points, and carry the same weight (12 stone 8 lb; 80 kg) when they compete against each other; in Ladies' races, however, 11 stone (70 kg) is carried. The races are open to amateur riders only.

Originally all these races were run over natural country from one point to another, but now virtually all take place on a course over built-up fences. The minimum distance is 3 miles (4.8 km),

and the longest is the Ralph Grimthorpe Gold Cup of 4½ miles (7.2 km) at the Middleton meeting in Yorkshire. Almost 200 point-to-points are run in the United Kingdom during the season, which lasts from February to early June.

Points A term elaborating colour, e.g. 'bay with black points' indicates a bay with black mane, tail and lower portion of the legs.

Points Ready-knitted tips for whips.

Poisoning, acorn This happens after eating acorns, but the actual cause is uncertain: it is possibly due to an alkaloid. Symptoms include severe diarrhoea, often with haemorrhage, very high temperature (up to 106°F), pulse over 100, and rapid general collapse. Urgent veterinary treatment essential.

Poisoning, ragwort Occurs if horses eat dead ragwort plants: e.g. in hay. The symptoms include rapid pulse and respiration, constipation, jaundice, and dullness. It is usually fatal, as no treatment is available.

Poisoning, selenium (North America) Occurs after eating certain plants, such as some vetches, oonopsis (golden weed), and stanleya (prince's bloom). In the acute form death occurs in a few hours. Symptoms of the acute form are bloat, colic, and breathing difficulties. Symptoms of the sub-acute form include weight-loss, staggering, impaired vision, abdominal pain, and inability to swallow, followed by death. In the chronic form, there is loss of hair from the mane and tail, depraved appetite, rings on the hoof which in severe cases may lead to separation and shedding. There is no treatment.

Poisoning, sugar-beet Caused by eating fresh sugar-beet tops. Symptoms include restlessness, cold limbs, inability to swallow, and paralysis.

Poisoning, yew Yew contains an alkaloid which depresses the heart action, and horses which eat the foliage usually die almost immediately.

Poisonous plants The most dangerous poisonous plants are yew, laburnum, St John's Wort (responsible for photo-sensitivity, q.v.), hemlock, acorns, ragwort and deadly nightshade. If eaten in quantity, rhododendrons, damsons, meadow saffron, bluebell, horse-tails, green bracken, celandine, some buttercups, some vetches, ground ivy, water dropwort, foxglove, maple and coniferous trees are also dangerous. Weeds such as dog mercury, fat hen and water figwort, thorn apple, henbane and cowbane are also harmful but are usually absent from pasture. Fool's parsley (*Arethusa cynapium*) is poisonous, but although it is a common field weed, horses usually avoid it. See also various entries under **Poisoning**.

Poitevin A heavy horse bred in the Landes district of France, originally being brought from Norway, Denmark, and Holland. It is slow, quiet, and allegedly rather lazy. The mares are used to breed very large mules to the big Poitou ass.

Poitou ass An ass which sometimes attains 15 hh (152.4 cm) and may have 9 ins (228 mm) of bone below the knee. It has enormous ears which cannot be carried upright but poke outwards, and whose inner hair forms a series of curls called *'cadenettes'*, regarded as a sign of pure breeding. The usual colours are dark brown and black, but greys are seen. Bred to cart-mares, Poitou jacks throw very good heavy-type mules, some of which stand over 16 hh (162.6 cm).

Pole In driving, the timber between a pair of horses or the wheelers of a team.

Pole (aids for pacer and trotter) A pointed wooden pole placed on the side opposite to which the horse pulls. It is buckled to one of the rings on the saddle-pad and the pointed end is pushed through a ring on the headpiece, protruding a few inches beyond the nose of the horse.

Pole chains These are used in coaching and a few carriages to put-to wheelers. (See also **Pole pieces**)

Pole head A movable steel fitting on the pole of a coach (and some other vehicles) to which pole chains or pole pieces are attached.

Pole hook The hook on the end of a coach pole to carry the bars. In coaching parlance it is known as the 'swan-neck'.

Pole pieces Strong leather loops used in most private carriages for putting-to a pair, in place of chains. (See **Pole chains**).

Pole pin This secures the pole in place when fitted between the futchells (q.v.).

Poleys Pads on a Western (USA) saddle.

Poling Poling-up or pole-piecing: the act of attaching pole chains or pole pieces to the horses' hames.

Polish Arab The Poles have a great reputation as horse breeders and their horses have always been in demand in Europe, while their cavalry in the seventeenth century was invincible. The cavalry horses had Eastern blood in them – Arab, Barb, Turkish, Persian, etc., but the Arab has been held in the highest regard since the sixteenth century. Many great families of Poland founded studs of Arabian horses long ago, e.g. the Sangussgo Stud in 1506, while the name of Count Potocki and his stud is well known to Englishmen. A number of studs in America have been founded on Polish Arabs, while the famous and beautiful Arab Champion in England 'Skowronek', came from the Antoniny Stud in Poland. A characteristic feature of Polish Arab breeding was the constant introduction of fresh blood by importing the most valuable horses direct from the Arabian desert and by selection from racing at Levow. From the 1960s onwards, Polish Arabs have been increasingly purchased by breeders in many parts of the world, especially the United States and Germany, while in Britain, Miss Patricia Lindsay of the Stockings Stud first imported them in the 1950s.

Polish Half-bred The nature of the Polish country, wide agricultural lands, the type of soil, not always good roads, limited railway network, rendered heavy draught horses such as Percherons and Shires unsuitable. In consequence, Polish breeders, with care and system, developed a cross-breed to suit their requirements, using the English Thoroughbred, Arab, or Anglo-Arab to bring stamina and action. Before the 1939 war, this was done on a highly selective basis, and a very good type of half-bred was produced, and half-bred stud books or registers were kept. Types vary with provinces and general requirements. See also **Malapolski, Wielkopolski**.

Polish Thoroughbred The term indicates a horse of pure English Thoroughbred stock as bred and developed in Poland. The first English Thoroughbreds were introduced to Poland early in the nineteenth century and the Polish Horse Racing Association was formed in 1841. Breeding was at first confined to a few wealthy families, and many good brood mares were imported from England, France, Germany and Austria, and also the stallion Flying Fox from England at a cost of 37,000 guineas. Training stables on English lines became established. The two World Wars decimated the horse population of Poland, but today the Thoroughbred is being bred extensively in Government studs, and Poland is second only to the USSR in producing classic racehorses in Eastern Europe.

Poll The area of a horse's head between the ears; the seat of poll evil (q.v.).

Pollard, James (1792-1867) Son of Robert Pollard, an engraver and sporting artist. Painted angling and shooting scenes, but became particularly popular for his vast number of pictures of coaching and driving subjects, there being more coaching prints after Pollard than any other artist. His style was meticulous and seldom varied; often his human figures are curiously elongated and much of the charm of his pictures lies in the interesting London backgrounds and provincial inns.

Poll evil Swelling on one or both sides of neck below the poll. It is a serious condition usually caused by a blow, such as hitting the head on a low doorway, or excessive pressure of a heavy bridle. The area becomes infected with *Brucellus abortus*. Veterinary treatment is necessary, and usually consists of draining the abscess, followed by antibiotics.

Poll pad or guard A felt pad with leather or PVC backing which slides on to the headpiece of a headcollar or bridle to prevent injury should the horse throw up his head whilst travelling in a horsebox.

Poll pad or guard.

Polo A very ancient sport, with records of games played in 525 BC. It appears to have originated in Persia, and Manipur in E. India. It was introduced to England in 1869 by officers from the 9th Lancers, 19th Hussars, 1st Life Guards and Royal Horse Guards, and the first public game in this country was played at Hounslow in that year, although the game had already been adopted by Assam tea planters in India in 1850. Polo, was introduced to America in 1876 by James Gordon Bennet, and since the abolition of a height limit for polo ponies in 1919, Argentina has become the leading country, both in terms of the quality of its players and in breeding polo ponies, India was formerly the nursery of all British players, but the position altered between the wars, although first-class polo is still played in that country. After the war, the game in Britain declined sharply, but due largely to the efforts of Lord Cowdray, and the participation, first of Prince Philip, and later, the Prince of Wales, it revived, and is now in a very healthy state.

A polo ground measures a maximum of 300 yards (274 m) in length by 200 yards (180 m) wide, with goal posts at least 10 ft (3 m) high, set 24 ft (7.3 m) apart. The ball, which is just 3 ins (8 cm) in diameter, is made of willow or bamboo root and is hit with a stick (mallet in the USA) made of cane measuring 48-54 ins (120-137 cm) long, and with a cylindrical wooden head set at right angles to the shaft. The aim of the game is to hit the ball between the opponents' goalposts. The game is played by two teams of four players, each of whom has a handicap (q.v.). Each game is divided into a maximum of eight chukkas (q.v.) (although more usually between four and six) of seven and a half minutes in length, with three minutes between each chukka and a five-minute interval at half-time. Each time a goal is

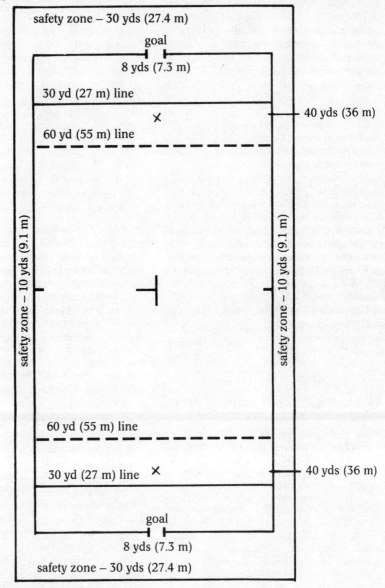

Layout of a boarded polo ground.

scored the teams change ends. Because of the pace of the game, each pony can only play two chukkas. The rules, laid down by the national boards such as the Hurlingham Polo Association in Britain, the US Polo Association in America and the Argentine Association in that country, are all essentially similar, and are designed to combat dangerous play in the game. Penalties (free goals and free hits) are awarded for such infringements as crossing the line of the ball in front of a player who has the right of way, dangerous riding, hooking of another player's stick unless he is on the same side of the opponent's pony as the ball. There is no 'off-side' rule in polo. The rules in a match are administered by two umpires, who are mounted to keep them close to the play, and by a referee who is off the field but in a central position. By mutual agreement, one umpire and the referee may be dispensed with.

The necessary equipment for the pony is as follows: boots or bandages on all four legs as protection, a pelham or double bridle, a standing martingale, and a saddle. For the rider, protective headgear in the form of a hard helmet is compulsory, and other necessities include a left-hand glove, a polo whip (about 42 ins (106 cm) in length), brown top boots, breeches, and, as further protection if required, padded leather knee-caps.

Polo breast girth Similar to an Aintree breast girth (q.v.) but made of leather, often padded with sheepskin, and having a slot at the centre of the breast, through which a martingale can be passed.

Polo brown calf High polishing leather, vegetable tanned, for polo boots.

Polo club (oldest) This is the Cachar Polo Club (India), founded in 1859 by British tea planters in Assam, who, since about 1850, had been taking part in local polo.

Polocrosse A mounted combination of polo and lacrosse which was played in Japan over 1000 years ago, and made a brief appearance as an indoor game in England in the 1930s. It is now very popular as an outdoor game in Australia. There are three players a side, using a soft ball and a polo-type stick with a net at the

end. Ponies are limited to 15 hh (152.4 cm), and the field is 160 yards (146 m) by 60 yards (54 m) with goal-posts 14 ft (4.27 m) high and 8 ft (2.43 m) apart.

Polo pit An enclosed 'cage' with a sloping floor, used for instructing beginners in the correct use of the stick for hitting purposes. The learner sits astride a saddled wooden horse in the centre of the pit, and the balls return to him after striking.

Polo pony A type rather than a breed. The height has varied from about 12-13 hh (121-132 cm) in the sixteenth century, up to 16 hh (163 cm) and over, the height limit having been removed. The average height for the modern game is 15-15.1 hh (152.4-155 cm). Over the years, variations in breeds have included Manipur ponies from E. India, mountain ponies from the Himalayas, Arabs, and English Thoroughbreds. At the end of the nineteenth century, a start was made to breed polo ponies by small Thoroughbred sires and good foundation mares selected for performance. For the modern British game, some owners still breed their own ponies, using small Thoroughbreds, but the majority come from Argentina, where Criollo/Thoroughbred crosses are bred in considerable numbers on the *estancias*. The requirements are: a long neck with good flexion at the junction of the head, good shoulders, a short, strong back with well-sprung ribs, elbows well away from the body, exceptionally powerful quarters, and hocks well-let-down. Ponies must have courage and playing temperament.

Polo pony boots Made of felt and leather (or PVC) with elastic or velcro fastenings. They envelop the legs from just below the knee and from 5 ins (12 cm) below the hock to the hoof, giving all-round protection against treading, blows from the stick, etc.

Pommel The raised, arched part of the front of an astride saddle. In a side-saddle, there are two pommels or projections, both on the near side. The right leg rests over the higher one (the top pommel or near head), which is fixed; the left leg rests under and against the lower one (known as the 'leaping head'), which is detachable.

Ponies Act, 1969 Presented by the late Lord Silkin in the House of Lords and ratified in 1970. Under the act it is unlawful to export any pony to any port outside the United Kingdom unless the Minister of Agriculture (or in Scotland, the Secretary of State) is satisfied that the pony is intended for breeding, riding or exhibition. Its aim is to eliminate the possibility of exportation for slaughter in Europe. Any pony to be exported must be of a certain specified value and must be rested immediately before being loaded on to the ship or aircraft.

Ponies of Britain (POB) Originally registered as a charity, the Ponies of Britain had, as its principal aims, the welfare of horses and ponies, and the revival of the British native pony breeds. It began, almost by chance, in the early 1950s, when the late Sir John Crocker Bulteel, then Clerk of Royal Ascot Racecourse, asked Mrs Glenda Spooner to stage a pony show in the paddock at Ascot. The first show was held in 1952. Thereafter, the late Miss Gladys Yule joined Mrs Spooner, and the Ponies of Britain quickly progressed from organising shows into an extremely active body that encompassed many facets of the native pony world, particularly welfare. Miss Yule was Chairman until her death in 1957. Mrs Spooner succeeded her and remained chairman until just before her death in 1981. Under the remarkable and energetic direction of Mrs Spooner, the Ponies of Britain ran three major shows a year (the Stallion, Scottish and Summer), together with cross-country events, instructional courses and lectures. The Ponies of Britain could be said to have played a major part in bringing to the attention of the horse world the serious plight of the Mountain and Moorland breeds immediately after World War II, and, by staging shows for them, in reviving their fortunes as excellent all-round performance animals. An Approved Trekking and Riding Holidays Scheme was also instituted. Glenda Spooner played a prominent role in getting the 'Ponies Act 1969' (q.v.) on to the statute book. In 1986, the Ponies of Britain, as founded by Glenda Spooner, ended. 'Ponies of Britain 1987' is now a show society, while the welfare side is a separate organisation known as The Glenda Spooner Equine Welfare Trust and is in no way connected with Ponies of Britain 1987.

Ponies of the Americas (POA) A new (1954) and very popular breed in the USA, which has spread from coast to coast. The first pony, Black Hand 1, was bred by crossing an Appaloosa mare with a Shetland stallion. There is now some Quarter Horse blood in the breed. The breed standard requires that the ponies should be between 11.2-13.2 hh (116.8-137.2 cm), with the conformation of a miniature Arabian/Quarter Horse, with Appaloosa colouring and characteristics. One parent must be a registered POA. The action at the trot requires extreme high hock movement reminiscent of the Hackney (q.v.) or American Saddlebred (q.v.). The Pony of the Americas is ridden primarily by the seventeen-and-under age group, and by members of the Pony of the Americas Club, but may be suitable for adults.

'Pony' A betting term implying a wager of £25.

Pony In the early part of the century the definition of a pony was 'a small horse less than 13 hh' (132.1 cm). The modern show pony is an animal not exceeding 14.2 hh (147.3 cm). It should be noted, however, that a polo pony, to which no height limit applies, is always a pony, yet an Arab horse, to which the same applies, is always a horse, however small it may be. The height designation of a show Hackney is that a pony must not exceed 14 hh (142.2 cm), and a Hackney horse must exceed that height.

Pony Club, the (PC) Founded in 1929 to encourage young people to ride and enjoy sport connected with horses and ponies and to receive skilled instruction. Membership is open to all under seventeen years and to Associate Members between seventeen and twenty-one years. Its success is phenomenal and branches are found in many English-speaking countries; it is the largest association of riders in the world. The Pony

Club in Britain holds annual championships in show jumping, horse trials, dressage, etc., as well as a tetrathlon championship, and the Prince Philip Cup Mounted Games; it also organises a series of tests and efficiency certificates to create enthusiasm, and ensure progress, ranging from the beginners' D Test to the advanced A Test for the highly competent.

Pony Express Established in 1860 by William H. Russell and Pike's Peak Express, as a fast mail service from St Joseph, Missouri, to San Francisco. Five hundred horses were in service, with 190 relay posts, each about 12 miles (19 km) apart. A rider rode three stages and was allowed only two minutes to change horses. The ponies travelled at the gallop and, in spite of snow, floods and marauding Indians, the mail had to get through. It is recorded that one Express rider covered 380 miles (610 km) and was in the saddle for thirty-six hours. The ponies used were mainly of native Western stock, and a distance of nearly 2000 miles (3210 km) was covered in ten days. The service, however, lasted only eighteen months, and it was never successful commercially.

Pony gout See **Laminitis**.

Pony racing No longer officially held; formerly run under the authority of the Pony Turf Club, which no longer exists. It was confined to Thoroughbred ponies not exceeding 15 hh (152.4 cm) and halfbreds which also ran under these rules.

Pony trekking A form of country riding holiday, started initially in Scotland, and which spread rapidly throughout Britain. It provides a fine opportunity for riding through beautiful countryside. Most trekking takes place from residential centres, with riders covering varying distances each day, according to ability, but mostly at paces no faster than a trot. Many centres use the native ponies of the areas in which they are sited.

Port An indentation of greater or lesser height in the centre of the mouthpiece of a bit, giving the horse sufficient room for its tongue.

Porting A term used by grooms for horses which paw their bedding to the rear of the stall and strike the floor with their forefeet. Also known as 'kaving'.

Post and rails Timber obstacle comprised of rails attached to posts fixed in the ground.

Post betting See **Betting**.

Postboy An attendant who, in posting days, rode one of a pair to a carriage, or, with another postboy, rode the leader or wheeler.

Postboy waistcoat A long, waisted garment usually cut high at the chest opening, and with 'flaps' on all four pockets.

Post-chaise A postboy-driven closed carriage of posting days.

Post entry No late entries are allowed under the Rules of Racing, entries for all races closing at a time laid down in the Racing Calendar (q.v.).

Post horse A horse which, in posting days, was let out for hire to the public for post vehicles.

Postillion A man who drives from the saddle, riding the near horse of a pair or team.

Posting A term, originating in America, indicating the rider rising from the saddle at the trot.

Posting In pre-railway days, posting was the method of travel used by the wealthy, who travelled in hired vehicles of various types, which gave them the privacy unobtainable in the stage coaches. Horses used for this purpose were travelled a certain distance or stage, usually about 10 miles (16 km), depending on the nature of the country, and either driven back with a vehicle travelling in the opposite direction, or were ridden back by a postboy.

Post master The owner, in posting days, of post horses (q.v.).

Post race A race for which a person, under one subscription, was able to enter two or more horses, and run any one or more of them, as the conditions prescribed. No longer in use.

Potatoes Potatoes provide both protein

and carbohydrate, and can be fed cooked (unpeeled but scrubbed), in relatively small quantities (up to 2 lb (1 kg) a day).

Pottock A French breed of pony formerly much used in smuggling, but now a popular children's pony and a good harness animal. Found chiefly in the mountains in the Basque region, to which it is well adapted. Three types are recognised – the Standard, the Piebald and the Double. The first two types are between 11.1-13 hh (114.3-132.1 cm), while the Double stands between 12.3-14.2 hh (129.5-147.3 cm). Principal colours are brown and white, chestnut and white, or black, chestnut and white.

Pouch In coaching the leather wallet slung over the shoulder of the guard. Among the small items carried was a small clock with a face exposed through a window cut in the leather surface.

Poultice boots Heavy rubber boots with a reinforced side for use when poulticing a foot.

Poultice boot.

Poulticing The application of a hot or cold substance to draw dirt, pus, or maggots from an affected area, or to alter the temperature of the site of an injury to assist in the healing process. Poultices may be made from linseed, kaolin, bran, etc., and proprietary poultices, e.g. Animalintex (q.v.) are also available. See **Poultice boots**.

Poultry fund A small cap made by most hunts, at meets, on all present, including foot followers, to compensate owners of poultry for damage done.

Pound A small, stout timber-built enclosure in which police or local authorities temporarily housed straying horses, ponies or other animals. Very little used in modern times, except under special circumstances, e.g. in the New Forest during the annual 'drifts' (q.v.) when the ponies are rounded up and driven into pounds to be branded, wormed and 'tail-marked' (q.v.).

Poznan horse An old-type Polish warmblood dual-purpose riding/agricultural horse, derived from Thoroughbred, Arab and Hanoverian blood. Best known as one of the two breeds from which the Wielkopolski (q.v.) has been developed.

Prad A Victorian term for a horse.

Prairie schooner See **Conestoga Wagon**.

Prance The action of a horse when bounding or springing gaily.

Preakness Stakes The Preakness, one of the three Classic Races (q.v.) in the USA, has had a most chequered career since its introduction as a 1½-mile (2.4 km) event at Pimlico, Maryland, in 1873. It was abandoned after the 1889 race at 1¼ miles (2.01 km), then revived as a 1 ¹⁄₁₆-mile (1.7 km) contest at Gravesend in New York in 1894. The race was run at a mile when it returned to Pimlico in 1909. The present 1³⁄₁₆-mile (9½ furlongs: 1.9 km) distance was not finally adopted until 1925. Two divisions of the Preakness were staged in 1918. The race is scheduled for the middle of May, and is conditioned for three-year-olds.

Prefix In many breed societies, prefixes and affixes are much used by breeders as a means of recognising by name all animals bred by them. Such prefixes and affixes are registered with the relevant breed society and, in recent years, with the central registry, and are transferrable on the sale of animals.

Pregnancy, diagnosis of The fact that a mare does not come into season or oestrus (q.v.) following mating is an indication that she may be in foal, but is not positive proof. A blood sample taken between 45 and 100 days, with a peak period of 60 to 70 days, reveals a high level of follicle stimulating hormone produced by the mare's uterus. The test is about 95% accurate. Physical examination of the uterus via the rectum by a veterinary surgeon after about 42 days will confirm pregnancy or otherwise, and is very accurate. The latest pregnancy detection device is an echograph by means of an ultra-sonic probe.

Preliminary canter All horses leaving the paddock before starting for a race, canter down to the start, except when there is a parade, as before the Derby, Grand National, Gold Cup, etc., when they canter to the start after the parade.

Premium stallion A stallion which has been awarded, through its breed society, an annual premium for merit. Originally, premium stallions travelled the district to which they were allotted, but this practice is now less common. See also **Brood mare premium schemes**.

Prepotency The strong power of transmitting hereditary features and qualities.

President's Cup An annual trophy, first given in 1965 by Prince Philip when he took office as President of the Fédération Equestre Internationale (q.v.), for the country gaining the most points in a year in Nations' Cup show-jumping competitions (q.v.).

Pretashka A galloping mate to a Russian trotter driven to a wagon or droshky (q.v.).

Price Odds quoted on a horse in a race.

Pricked Descriptive of a foot when a nail has been driven into the sensitive area, usually the sensitive laminae.

Pricker Obsolete term for one who follows hounds on horseback. Also a whipper-in (q.v.).

Pricker-pad or shield A cruel device to deal with a one-sided mouth. It consists of a washer, the inside of which is studded with sharp points and is attached to the side of the snaffle against which the horse leans. Now obsolete, and replaced by the 'brush pricker' (q.v.).

Pricket A male deer, at two years of age, with its first antlers.

Prime age A horse is said to be at its

prime age between the ages of six and ten years.

Prince of Wales Cup (show jumping) Up to 1914 known as the King Edward VII Cup. Competed for annually in Great Britain (initially at the Royal International Horse Show, now at the All-England Show Jumping Arena, Hickstead) under FEI rules, for teams of four riders of the same nationality. It is the British Nations' Cup trophy.

Prince of Wales spurs A modern spur with a drooping neck (with or without rowel, q.v.) with loop sides of uneven length, the longer one being worn on the outside of the foot.

Prince of Wales spur.

Prince Philip Mounted Games Inaugurated in 1957 at the suggestion of HRH the Duke of Edinburgh. The object is to provide members of the Pony Club with a competition for good and well-trained ponies that do not necessarily have to be of high quality or great value. The events are for Pony Club teams of five riders, and preliminary competitions are held during the summer. The finalists compete at the Horse of the Year Show in October for the Prince Philip Cup.

Prior's Half-Bred Stud Book See **Half-Bred Stud Book**.

Private omnibus A closed vehicle of varying size with seats arranged as in a wagonette (q.v.).

Private pack In hunting, where the Master, unsupported by subscription, bears the entire expenses of the pack.

Prix Caprilli A test, ridden in an arena of specified dimensions, judged on riding ability and not as a dressage test. Used in various forms in Riding Club competitions.

Prix des Nations (FEI) International team show-jumping competition; also called the Nations' Cup. The full team consists of four riders, men or women, from each country, the score of the best three competitors from each country in two rounds to count.

Prix St George See **Dressage**.

Professional (non-racing events under FEI rules) (1) A professional under the general regulations is any competitor after his eighteenth birthday who has been issued with a Professional licence by his national federation. (2) The following are also considered to be Professional competitors, and issued with Professional licences: (i) Competitors who train or instruct other competitors and/or horses for international competitions without the approval of their national federation. (ii) Competitors who are officially recognised by their national federation and issued with an appropriate certificate as a professional trainer or instructor of international competitors and/or horses. (iii) Competitors who enter any form of personal sponsorship agreement or advertising contract without the approval of their national federation.

Progesterone A female sex hormone produced by the ovaries, which prepares the uterus to receive the fertilised egg. It inhibits sexual activity, and is present during pregnancy, which it helps to maintain.

Prop, to Describes the slowing-up action of a horse reluctant to take off at a fence.

Prophet's thumb mark A pronounced dimple mark occasionally found in the neck of horses, especially Arabs. It is believed by some Eastern races to be a sign of great luck and a horse so marked is consequently greatly treasured.

Proppy A stilty mover not flexing at the knees or pastern joints, probably straight in the shoulders.

Proprietor One who owns a team, and drives his own coach.

Protein A complex organic compound containing nitrogen, and widely found in plants and animals tissue. Essential to all horses, as it is necessary for the building and repairing of tissues, and is a constituent of healthy skin, blood, bone, and hair. Proteins are present in oats, beans, barley, flaked maize, sugar-beet pulp, hay, grass, horse nuts and cubes, soya-bean meal, dried skimmed milk powder, fish meal, linseed, etc. Protein contains approximately 16% nitrogen, and the quantity of protein in a given food is estimated by measuring the amount of nitrogen present in it. This is expressed as the percentage of 'crude protein' present. Not *all* crude protein is digestible, and some food tables, etc. show the amount of digestible protein in a given food.

Protest (USA) See **Objection**.

Provinces The term applied to a hunting country anywhere in England, Scotland or Wales, except in the Midlands and the Shires (q.v.) in England.

Prussia-side stirrup iron A pattern of iron, unlike those commonly used in the United Kingdom (the sides of which do not vary in width). It narrows gradually on either side as far as the eye which receives the stirrup leather.

Przewalski/Przevalskii See **Wild Horse (Asiatic)**; **Tarpan**; **Equus Przewalskii**; and **Evolution of the Horse**.

Puckle noseband See **Noseband, Kineton**.

Pudding Oatmeal porridge, as boiled and fed to hounds.

'Puddle' A shuffling, 'footy' action seen in many underbred, common horses, and those with worn legs and unsound feet.

'Puffer' One who runs up the price of a horse at an auction on behalf of the seller, but who has no intention of buying (sometimes called a 'trotter').

'Puffing the glims' An expression used to

denote a method of making a horse look younger than its years by cutting a small hole through the skin of the hollow above the eye and blowing through a quill to fill the cavity.

Pugri See **Martingale, pugri**.

Puissance (show jumping) A competition to test horses' ability to jump large obstacles. The fences are fewer but much larger than other show-jumping courses.

Pulled tail See **Tail pulling**.

Puller A horse which pulls, usually through having had its mouth spoiled and therefore made insensitive, or from excitement (mostly in company with other horses). Methods to combat this are many and varied, but most of them are ineffective unless the rider is a good horseman. The elementary rule is 'give and take'.

Pulse The pulse of an adult horse at rest is normally 36-42 beats per minute, and 50-100 in a foal depending on age. It is taken either where the sub-maxillary artery passes under the jaw on either side, or at the radial artery inside the foreleg on a level with the elbow.

Pump handles Two curved iron handles at the rear of a coach to hold when jumping up on to the vehicle.

Punter One who backs or bets on a horse to win or gain a place in a race.

Puppy walker Someone who takes care of one or two hound puppies, from about ten weeks old until the following February or March, when they are returned to the kennels. Essentials for these puppies are absolute freedom, and good suitable food, thus giving them every chance to develop well. Lord Yarborough at Brocklesby (1746) was the first MFH to start the system of 'walking puppies' and of keeping hound pedigrees.

Purebred A breed or animal whose blood is unsoiled by that of other breeds, i.e. not of mixed race.

Purgatives Medicine (usually drugs) administered to stimulate evacuation of the intestinal tract. There are two principal types:
1. SALINE, which increases the bowel volume by forcing fluids into it from the bloodstream to dilute the salt solution. Together with the purgatives' softening effect, this enhances bowel movement.
2. OIL-BASED, which causes mild irritation of the bowel wall and thus encourages movement. Both should be administered by a veterinary surgeon.

Purging See **Diarrhoea**.

Pur sang Purebred, e.g. *le pur sang arabe* = purebred Arab; *le pur sang anglais* = the Thoroughbred.

'Puss' The name by which the hunted hare has been known to generations of those who hunt with harriers.

Puszta Hungarian plains, once great feeding grounds for herds of horses and cattle.

Put down, to A horse is put down when it is destroyed on account of old age, ill-health or injury. See **Destruction, humane**.

Putting-in Fox earths which are closed with the fox inside during the morning of a hunting day are said to be 'put to'. The process of closing the earth is 'putting-to'.

Putting-to The act of harnessing a horse to a vehicle.

Quad A slang term for a horse.

Quadrille The first 'horse-dances' recorded date back to 700-650 BC when quadrilles of two, four, or eight riders took part. For many centuries these were neglected, but in the early part of the sixteenth century a great revival took place which lasted until the latter part of the nineteenth century. The art was enjoyed by most of the nobles throughout Europe, and special music was composed to suit the superbly caparisoned horses and their riders, whose displays reached great heights of elegance and skill. Though far less practised in England, quadrilles were encouraged and performed in the reign of Elizabeth I. They have recently returned to the riding scene, and a quadrille competition for Riding Clubs now takes place at the Horse of the Year Show (q.v.).

Quarter Part of the hoof between the toe and the heel.

Quarter Horse, American A breed of horse developed in the USA and claimed to run the quarter mile faster than any other equine. The origin of the breed was in Virginia, where, in the early settlers' days, match racing was a popular sport. Race tracks, cut in virgin forest, were usually about a quarter of a mile in length, and the horses which raced over them were called 'Quarter Horses'. The name is now synonymous with a quick start and a fast sprint. They were bred originally from the horses brought to North America by the Spaniards, and from Thoroughbreds, Hobbies and Galloways brought by English settlers. The greatest and best known progenitor of the breed was Janus, a 14 hh (142.2 cm) English-bred horse by the Godolphin Arabian. The Quarter Horse's comparatively small size (in the early days) and remarkable manoeuvrability made him ideal for working cattle. The *modern* Quarter Horse, which may be up to 16 hh (162.6 cm), is still used for this purpose, but also for Western show riding, rodeo, trail riding, showing, jumping, and dressage. Quarter Horse racing, after a period in decline, is again keenly supported in America. The breed claims to be the most popular in the world, with a registry containing over 1½ million entries. Quarter Horses have been exported, notably to Australia, where the first ones arrived in 1954. There is now a number of large and successful studs. There is also a British Quarter Horse Association, and Quarter Horse racing has been introduced, but so far in a very small way.

Quartering An abbreviated form of grooming, in which the horse's roller is not removed. Eyes, nose and dock are sponged, and rugs turned back, so that the quarters and then the forehand can be groomed. The term also indicates the use of a water brush on soiled and ruffled hair on the lower part of the quarters, caused by the horse lying down during the night.

Quarter marks Fancy patterns, made solely for appearance, on the quarters of a horse, mostly seen on racehorses and show horses. Small areas of hair are brushed with a wet brush in the reverse direction of the hair growth, thus forming a design. A stencil plate may be used to achieve a specific pattern.

Quarter marks Marks placed along each side of a riding school denoting the quarter and threequarters distances. Useful when drilling a ride and schooling.

Quarters The area lying between the rear of the flank and the root of the tail, stretching downwards to the top of the gaskin.

Quarters, drooping A term applied to quarters which, instead of being level, fall away behind the croup, the result being a low set of the tail. (See **Goose-rumped**)

Quarters, false A longitudinal depression in the wall of the hoof, caused by the failure of the coronet to secrete the horny crust; this failure is the result of some injury such as a tread or quittor (q.v.).

Quarters (or haunches), turn on the An elementary form of pirouette at the walk, in which the forehand is rotated around the pivot of the hindlegs. The hindlegs should move up and down in the rhythm of the walk.

Quarter sheet.

'galloping sheet'. It can vary in weight according to the time of year and is also available in waterproof sheeting. A fillet string (q.v.) should be used to prevent the sheet being blown up.

Quarters out See **Renvers**.

Quarter strap Harness passing over a horse's quarters to meet the breeching.

Quarter straps An American term, the English equivalent being a loin strap or trace bearer (q.v.). In single harness, a loin strap buckles on to the shafts, whereas in pair harness it is across the loins and acts as a trace bearer. The State harness of the Lord Mayor of London's coach (q.v.) is fitted with loin straps. The loin strap is a form of kicking strap (q.v.).

Queen Alexandra Stakes The longest flat race in Britain. It is run over 2¾ miles (4.4 km) at Ascot in the summer.

Queen Elizabeth II Cup (show jumping) An individual award open to ladies only. Competed for annually under FEI rules at the Royal International Horse Show.

Queen's Birthday Parade, the See **Trooping the Colour**.

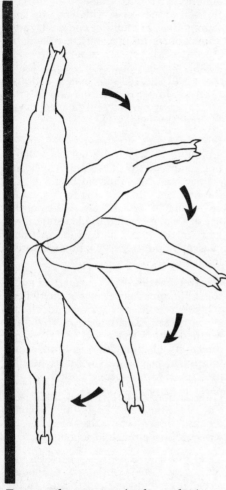

Turn on the quarters (or haunches) (right).

Quarters in See **Travers**.

Quarter sheet A rectangular sheet varying in length between 3 ft 6 ins (1.06 m) and 4 ft (1.21 m) for use in the paddock or when at exercise. In the paddock it is kept in place by a light 'race' roller and breast girth, at exercise the front corners are folded back under the girth straps. In the latter context it is also known as a

Queen's Plate, the Canada's oldest race, established in 1860, and considered the most fashionable event of the year. A large amount of prize money and 65% of all entry fees go to the winner, plus 50 guineas. The race was for three-year-olds and over up to 1938, when it was restricted to three- and four-year-olds. It is now open to Canadian-bred three-year-old colts, geldings or fillies, and run over 1¼ miles (2 km).

Quiddor A horse who drops food from

the mouth in the process of mastication. This is usually caused by some major abnormality of the teeth, and a veterinary surgeon should be consulted.

Quilty Cup The Tom Quilty Cup is an Australian 100-mile (160 km) endurance ride, first staged in 1966, and named after a famous horseman who sponsored it. It is a one-day ride, held over an exceedingly tough course in the Blue Mountains of New South Wales.

Quintain A mediaeval game in which riders on horses tilted at a bar swinging from a horizontal cross-piece erected on a pole.

Quirt (Spanish *cuarta***)** A blacksnake whip or bullwhip (American terms).

Quittor A chronic fistulous inflammation of the lateral cartilage of the pedal bone, caused by direct or indirect injury, in which the pus from a corn or prick travels upwards. The symptoms include lameness, tenderness of the coronet, and a pus-filled swelling. Treatment is by antibiotics or, in severe cases, by surgical removal of part of the lateral cartilage.

Quoiler A name for thill harness, the shaft horse in a waggon team being the thill horse. (See **Thill**)

Quotation (racing) Odds offered about a horse by a bookmaker.

—R—

RC Riding Club.

RCMP Royal Canadian Mounted Police. See under **Canadian Mounted Police**.

RDA Riding for the Disabled Association (q.v.).

Ref (racing) Refused.

RIHS Royal International Horse Show.

RO (racing) Ran on or ran out.

RSPCA Royal Society for the Prevention of Cruelty to Animals.

Race A thin white mark running down the face. (Also known as a 'stripe', 'rache', or 'rase'.)

Race card The official programme for each day's racing, issued by order of the clerk of the course, and containing the time and conditions of each race, with details of all horses still in the race, their numbers, colours, owners, trainers, ages, if appropriate, weights to be carried, and pedigrees.

Racecourse Association An association of all the racecourse owners in Britain, divided into three areas: Midland, Northern, and Southern.

Racecourse Betting Control Board Originally established under the Racecourse Betting Act of 1928 to organise and control the Totalisator. It has now become the Horserace Totalisator Board, which is responsible to the Horserace Betting Levy Board for the Totalisator.

Racecourse paddock A railed-in enclosure to which all horses running at the meeting are brought before their races. The horses' attendants are provided with badges bearing numbers corresponding with those on the race card (q.v.).

Racecourse Technical Services This is a subsidiary of the Horserace Betting Levy Board (q.v.) and is responsible for the photo-finish and race timing, the camera patrol, the public address system on courses, and the starting stalls and barrier gates.

Racehorse A horse bred for racing. (See **General Stud Book**)

Racehorse Owners' Association The only organisation which looks after the interests of flat and jumping racehorse owners in Britain.

Racehorse Trainers' Association See **National Trainers' Association**.

Racers Old-time name for footgear cut as jockey boots, made of the lightest black calf with painted tops. Minimum weight used to be about 5 oz (141 g). Used only for flat racing.

Rache See **Race**.

Racing Racing in Britain is of two kinds – flat racing and steeplechasing. Flat racing is much the older in origin, and can fairly be said to date as an organised sport from the sixteenth century; steeplechasing from 1830 onwards, when the St Albans Steeplechase was run for the first time. There are about sixty racecourses in use in Britain, some of which cater for flat racing and steeplechasing, some for flat racing only, and some for steeplechasing only. The principal courses on which there is flat racing only are Chester; Epsom (the home of the Derby); Goodwood in Sussex; Newmarket in Suffolk; and York. The principal course for steeplechasing only is Cheltenham, the home of the Cheltenham Gold Cup, the Champion Hurdle, and the National Hunt meeting. The principal course on which there are both flat racing and steeplechasing, and sometimes mixed meetings are Ascot, which belongs to HM The Queen and at which the Royal Ascot meeting is held in June; Ayr in Scotland; Chepstow in Wales; Doncaster, the home of the St Leger; Liverpool, the home of the Grand National; Newbury in Berkshire; Newcastle upon Tyne; and Sandown Park in Surrey, the home of the Eclipse Stakes.

Following the amalgamation of the National Hunt Committee with the Jockey Club in 1968, the latter is now responsible for the conduct both of flat racing and of steeplechasing. The amalgamation followed the setting up of the Horserace Betting Levy Board in 1961, as a result of which a proportion of the money betted on racing is now funnelled back into the industry. Since then, racecourse amenities and services have been improved greatly, and race courses have been encouraged to hold more meetings. With the exception (at present) of Sundays, there are now few days on which there is not a race meeting.

The charm of English racing is in its great variety. In the United States, all flat racecourses are level, left-handed and oval in shape. In Britain some are left-handed, like Chester, Epsom and York; some are right-handed, like Ascot, Goodwood and Sandown Park; Chester is almost circular; Epsom and Goodwood are downland courses with a sharp decline leading to the final half mile; Doncaster, Newbury, Newcastle and York are almost flat except for the hill on the far side of Doncaster; and there is similar variety with the steeplechase courses, with the Grand National course at Aintree almost flat in semi-urban surroundings on the edge of Liverpool, and in complete contrast to Cheltenham, set in a bowl of the Cotswolds, with Cleeve Hill as a superb backcloth.

While there is evidence of horse racing of a sort in Britain from the tenth century, it was not until the sixteenth century that there are records of annual prizes being given for racing. Two of the earliest are a Silver Bell raced for in the Forest of Galtres near York from 1530, and a Silver Bell raced for annually on Shrove Tuesday on the Roodeye at Chester, beside the north bank of the River Dee, where Chester races are still held. Later in the sixteenth century, it is on record that Queen Elizabeth I watched racing at Salisbury in the year of the defeat of the Spanish Armada.

However, credit for popularising horse racing in Britain must go to the Stuarts. James I came to Newmarket for the first time in 1605, liked it, and started it on its way as a centre for hunting, hawking and racing; but it was not until the days of the Restoration under Charles II that racing really came into its own. He loved Newmarket, founded the Newmarket Town Plate (q.v.) in 1665, rode in it himself, and won the race twice. More important, it was in the seventeenth century that English racing men began importing Arab stallions from the East to mate with home-bred mares to improve the speed, stamina and looks of the English country-bred horses. Charles II went further, and imported a number of Arabian mares to mate with the Arab stallions. These were known as the Royal mares. (See also **Thoroughbred**)

The three Arab stallions from which all Thoroughbreds now descend in tail male were, however, not brought to England until after the death of Charles II in 1685. The three, in order of arrival, were the Byerley Turk, the Darley Arabian, and the Godolphin Arabian (qq.v.), and the key names in their male lines are Herod, in the case of the Byerley Turk, Eclipse, in the Darley Arabian; and Matchem, in the Godolphin Arabian. After about 1770, it was found that the best racing results were being obtained by using home-bred stallions with home-bred mares, and Arab stallions gradually ceased to be used for racing purposes.

In the early days, races were run in heats over distances of 2-4 miles (3.2-6.4 km), and horses were not required to race until they were four years of age or more. Gradually, races of shorter distances became more popular, and horses were asked to race as three-year-olds, so that when the St Leger (q.v.), the oldest of the five Classic races for three-year-olds, was founded at Doncaster, it was of 2 miles (3.2 km), this being later reduced to just more than 1¾ miles (2.8 km).

By the beginning of the nineteenth century, there was a multiplicity of small meetings, and racing was very laxly run; but the Jockey Club, which originally had jurisdiction only over Newmarket meetings, gradually assumed control over other meetings, and under Lord George Bentinck, and later Admiral Rous, its influence spread, and it did much to clean up the Turf in Victorian days.

During the nineteenth century, steeplechasing was very much the poor relation of flat racing, in spite of the quick popularity of the Grand National, run for the first time in 1837. Steeplechasing was also bedevilled by lax control in the middle of the nineteenth century, but with the formation of the National Hunt Committee (q.v.) it became more popular again. Between the two World Wars the founding of the Champion Hurdle at Cheltenham and the Cheltenham Gold Cup brought it more to the forefront, and the advent of television made people realise what a spectacular sport it is. It has increased greatly in popularity over the last twenty-five years or so, aided by sponsorship on most National Hunt courses. (See also **Thoroughbred, racing**)

In America, racing is advised by the Jockey Club, New York, a body which exerts no jurisdiction or authority except in maintaining the integrity of the Stud Book. Official running tracks police themselves by the Thoroughbred Racing Authority Security.

Most of the major tracks are 1-mile (1.6 km) or longer, and oval, but there are some half-mile (0.8 km) tracks still operating. Formerly there were often courses for steeplechasing or hurdling just inside the 'in-field', but steeplechasing is declining at the big tracks, although it still flourishes at the hunt race meetings. Every track has its stakes races or race, but the 'big three' races (Classics) for the 'Triple Crown' remain: the Kentucky Derby; the Preakness Stakes at Pimlico, Maryland; and the Belmont Stakes at Belmont Park, New York (qq.v.). (See **Thoroughbred, racing**)

In Australia, racing is a multi-billion dollar industry. Most of the Australian Thoroughbred blood has come from England, Ireland, and New Zealand, regular importations having been made for well over a century, and are still being made. The quality now is such that America has taken considerable numbers of top Australian racing stock, and continues to purchase outstanding horses, many of which have become famous stud names in the United States.

The Stud Book is kept by the racing industry itself, and is controlled by the Thoroughbred Breeders's Association and the Australian Jockey Club, which dominates racing. All racecourses and racing stock are controlled by the AJC, and racing which does not have the official approval is not recognised. Race distances and riding weights were officially converted to the metric system in Australia in 1972.

All breeding of stud book stock is in private hands, and there is no government-owned or controlled stud in Australia, except for two small state-owned Arabian studs at Hawksbury and Gatton Agricultural colleges. Each year in the capital cities a yearling sale of stud stock is held, also of purebred unregistered stock, the largest sale being in Sydney, New South Wales. (See also **Thoroughbred, racing**)

Racing, Rules of Published annually by Weatherbys on behalf of the Jockey Club.

Racing abbreviations Bbv = broke blood vessel. F = fell. Hd = head. L = length. M = mile. Nk = neck. PU = pulled up. Ref. = refused. RO = ran out, or ran on. SH = Short head. SS = Started slowly. t = tubed. tnp = took no part. to = tailed off. ur or uns = unseated rider. wrs = whipped round start.

Racing Calendar, the Produced weekly by Weatherbys on behalf of the Jockey Club, giving details of races, entries for races, handicap weights, Jockey Club notices, etc., and other information of interest to those professionally engaged in racing. Often known as 'the Calendar'. It was first published by John Cheney in 1727, giving the race results, the pedigrees of runners, and the details of races.

Racing Calendar Office The office appointed by the Jockey Club, which is at present at Weatherbys, to which all entries for races, acceptances, declarations of forfeit and lodgement of official documents are normally made.

Racing colours These are worn by jockeys when riding in a race. Declared essential on the Turf and first registered in October 1762; the Duke of Cumberland selected 'purple', still part of the Royal colours (see **Colours, Royal**). All colours (jacket and cap) must be registered with Weatherbys, and are exclusive to the owner.

Racing girths Either narrow web, web inset with elastic, or all elastic. Except when mounted to a very light saddle, are always used in pairs.

Racing season The flat-racing season in Britain normally starts in the second half of March and ends in the middle of November. Steeplechasing starts at the end of July and ends at the beginning of the following June.

Racing seat The special position in the saddle adopted by jockeys for race riding. Leathers are very short and the seat is far forward and clear of the saddle. Steeplechase jockeys tend to adopt a safer position with longer leathers.

Rack A single-footed pace, each foot coming down singly and with great speed, a steady 1-2-3-4 with no pauses. (See also **Racking boots**)

Rack A stag-hunting term for a gap in a hedge caused by continued passing of the deer.

Rack chain Rack chains are used to restrain horses during grooming. A galvanised chain with spring hooks or, sometimes, a safer type of 'Y' piece which prevents any possibility of the horse catching his lips or nostrils in the springs.

Rack, hay This should be situated with its top on a level with the manger, to avoid dust, etc., falling on to the horse and irritating the eyes and nose.

Racking Placing hay in a feeding rack.

Racking boots Heavy rubber caps strapped over the forefeet of American Five-Gaited (q.v.) horses to protect them against injury through being struck by the hind feet when racking too fast. (See **Rack; American Saddlebred**)

Rack up, to To tether a horse to a ring in the wall.

Rag (or rake) A company or herd of young colts.

Ragged hips Prominent and unsightly hip-bones ('hat-racks'), poorly fleshed and lacking muscle.

Rails (racing) The stout, white-painted timber posts and rails surrounding all racecourses. (See **Running rails**)

Railway crossing (show jumping) A fence consisting of two gates with a red disc in the centre of each. The gates are provided with wings.

Rain scald An infection by the bacterium *Dermatophilous congolensis*, which attacks the surface of the skin over the back, leaving it raw and oozing. The oozing fluid dries and congeals on the hair of the coat, resulting in the characteristic 'paint brush' effect. It is most common in damp conditions when there is also high temperature and humidity.

Rake See **Rag**.

Rake a horse, to To slide the rider's legs

and spurs to and fro on a horse's sides; a practice inducing bucking for rodeo purposes.

Ralli cart A two-wheeled trap similar to a dog-cart but with shafts continuing along the floor to the rear of the vehicle and usually having curved sides. Built to the design of Mr Ralli of Ashtead Park, Surrey, in 1898.

Ramener Head position close to the vertical allowed by the flexion of the poll and the first two cervical vertebrae. It is obtained by the advance of the entire body toward the head, and not by the retraction of the head toward the chest.

Ram-headed A convex profile of the head, the name applied by Arab horse admirers to the head of a Barb.

Random Three horses driven in single file.

Ranelagh Club Now defunct, this was formerly a slightly more 'countrified' club than Hurlingham, noted for its clubhouse, Barn Elms, residence of the Earl of Walsingham, and which later became the headquarters of the Kit-Cat Political Club. It was noted also for its excellent cuisine and wines, and for its exotic waterfowl and beautiful gardens. It was the headquarters of the Coaching Club, and one of pre-war London's polo centres.

Range pony A comprehensive term, used on *estancias* in South America and on cattle ranches in North America for ponies used in cattle work (also known as 'cow ponies').

Rangy A term describing a horse with plenty of size and scope.

Rapping pole A pole held at either end when training a show jumper; it is raised slightly as the hindlegs are about to come over, in such a way that the horse receives a slight rap designed to encourage it to lift its legs higher on future occasions. This painful practice is banned at shows or in the vicinity of a show ground under BSJA (q.v.) rules.

Rarey, John Solomon (1827-1866) A horse-tamer and farmer from Ohio, who came to England in 1858 and 'cured' many violent-tempered racehorses. He attained his ends by a process of exhaustion, and, while the method subdued a horse for a time, the effect was not necessarily permanent. The treatment must not be compared with Galvayne's humane method.

Rase See **Race**.

Rasper A term denoting a very big fence, e.g. a double oxer.

Rasping (teeth) Known in the USA as 'floating'. The molar teeth of horses, especially after about eight years, may become long and sharp on surfaces which escape wear during mastication. Removal of the sharp edges requires the use of a gag and a long-handled rasp. It is no job for an amateur, as serious injury to the mouth may be inflicted. A veterinary surgeon should be asked to examine the teeth of all horses which show difficulty in chewing, and especially whose who 'quid' their food, i.e. those who leave the manger or feed bowl wet with chewed food dropped in it. The older the horse the more likely that his teeth will need rasping.

Rat-catcher Informal, but permissible hunting dress, usually worn during cub hunting. It consists of a hunting bowler or hunting cap, hunting tie or shirt with collar and tie, tweed riding coat, fawn breeches, black or brown boots with garter straps; spurs, hunting whip and gloves.

Rate, to To scold or rebuke a hound.

Rat tail A tail with little or no hair on the dock.

'Rat tails' Used at one time to pull on riding boots, but now fitted only on 'Jockeys' (q.v.). The modern practice is to fit tugs inside the boots.

Rattle (hunting) Said of hounds when they are pressing hard on a fox. Also the note sounded on the horn at a kill.

Rave/Raves The framework of rails or boards fitted to the sides of a cart, which enables a greater load to be carried.

Ray List or dorsal stripe (q.v.).

Razor-backed Descriptive of a horse with a sharp and prominent backbone.

'Ready' To ready a horse is to prepare it for some particular event, whether racing or a show.

Rearing The horse stands on his hind-legs, sometimes waving his front legs in the air. It is a most dangerous habit and one that should be quickly discouraged. It may be prudent to give the horse a thorough veterinary examination, and this should include his teeth. (See **Anti-rearing bit**)

Reata An American term for a rope used as a lasso.

Reata strap A strap used to hold a rope or lasso to the saddle when coiled.

Red flag Used to show the right-hand limit of an obstacle to be jumped in show-jumping or cross-country courses (or one to be negotiated in driving).

Redopp Obsolete term describing a movement where the horse canters on two concentric circles, haunches in.

Red ribbon Worn on the tail of a horse in the hunting field, this indicates a kicker. Sometimes called a 'Rogue's badge'.

Red worm See **Worms**.

Refuse, to To stop in front of any obstacle. To rein-back or to circle in front of a fence, resulting in a horse crossing its track, counts as a refusal in both show jumping and eventing.

Regularly ridden Implying in a written description that a horse is quiet to ride.

Reinagle, Philip, RA (1749-1833) Of Hungarian origin, he painted many scenes of horse and hound, also some angling and shooting pictures. The eccentric sportsman, Colonel Thomas Thornton of Yorkshire, was his patron.

Rein aids Five basic rein aids are recognised, which may be used in countless ways, and serve principally to determine direction. They are: (1) Open rein. (2) Indirect rein. (3) Direct rein of opposition. (4) Indirect (neck or counter) rein of opposition in front of the withers. (5) Indirect (or counter) rein of opposition behind the withers. Other rein aids control speed, and obtain halt and rein-back (qq.v.).

Rein-back A backward movement in which the horse raises and sets down its legs in *almost* simultaneous diagonal pairs. The movement is initiated by a foreleg. To be correct, it must be straight, with the feet lifted cleanly and without dragging, and without head raising, or a hollowing of the back. It is achieved by halting correctly, then applying the aids to move forward, but with the hands restraining the forward movement – *never* by pulling the reins backwards. As the horse responds, the contact is lightened.

Reins Leather reins can be plain, plaited, laced, or with rubber handparts, and stitched, hook-studded or buckled. Some are made of webbing or nylon. The length of a full-size rein is approximately 5 ft (1.5 m). Children's reins should be very much shorter. Widths of rein vary between ½ in. (12.7 mm) and 1 in. (25.4 mm).

Reins in both hands The normal way of conducting a horse.

Reins in one hand There are a number of recognised ways of controlling a horse thus, varying with the different schools of practice.

Rein stops These are martingale stops made of pieces of leather fixed to the rein some 10 ins (25.4 cm) from the bit to prevent the rings of a running martingale from sliding so far forward as to catch on either the rein fastening or even on a tooth.

Rejoneador A mounted matador.

Remounts A term applied generally to all horses taken in for service in an army unit.

Remouthing The process of re-making a spoiled mouth. It usually consists of re-starting and repeating the process applied when breaking a young horse.

Remuda Western American term for a herd of broken horses used daily on a ranch.

Rendlesham Benevolent Fund A fund to help steeplechase trainers and jockeys in necessitous circumstances. Administered by Weatherbys (q.v.).

Renvers Also called 'quarters-out' or 'tail to the wall', it is a movement on two tracks along the wall with the hindlegs on the original track, forelegs on an inner track, head slightly flexed in the direction of the movement, and the horse's body bent round the rider's inside leg and at an angle to the wall.

Repository A place for the sale of horses.

Resin back See **Rosinbacks**.

Resistance Any attempt by a horse to disobey the rider's aids. In dressage competitions, this may include refusal to obey the leg, opening the mouth, crossing the jaw, putting the tongue out, swinging the quarters, swishing the tail, stiffening the muscles in response to an aid or declining to go forward. Marks are deducted for resistance. In show jumping, resistance is defined precisely in BSJA rules as 'when the horse, for whatever reason, ceases to go forward, halts, rears, turns on the spot or steps back, even if this occurs as a result of deliberate action by the rider (for example, halting to adjust saddlery). The first resistance incurs a penalty of 3 faults, the second 6 faults, and the third, elimination. The same rules apply in the cross-country phase of horse trials except that the first resistance incurs 20 penalties, the second 40, and the third, elimination. In the show-jumping phase of horse trials, the first disobedience incurs 10 penalties, the second 20, and the third elimination.

Respiration rate An adult horse at rest takes 12 to 20 breaths (i.e. inspiration and expiration) per minute. The rate is higher in a younger animal. Together with the pulse, this forms the basis for assessing fitness before, during, and after exertion.

Rest-horses See **Spares**.

Restiveness This results from high spirits, temporary excitement, or vice. The offender should be treated firmly but kindly. Where the horse gives trouble by fidgeting when required to stand still, for example when being examined or groomed, a foreleg should be held or tied up, and the animal made to stand quietly.

Retainer (racing) After a jockey has completed his apprenticeship he is free to make his own riding arrangements and receive retainers (if sufficiently successful) from any owner or 'stable', at a fee to be mutually agreed. Half is normally paid in advance; the balance on termination of the agreement – usually at the end of the season. A good jockey may have a second or third retainer.

Rhenish-German Heavy Draught Now dangerously near to extinction, with less than thirty animals on the register, this breed's numbers have dropped from about 26,000 in 1949, due almost entirely to farm mechanisation. The Rhenish-German heavy horse is, however, of considerable importance. Although developed as recently as the last quarter of the nineteenth century, it is regarded as the basis of other German draught breeds, such as the Westphalian and the Hessen. Originating from a mixture of bloods – Clydesdale, Suffolk, Shire, Belgian, Boulonnais, Jutland and Ardennes – the Rhenish-German is a very powerful animal, weighing about 1 ton (1 tonne), of kindly disposition, with short, strong legs. The commonest colour is chestnut, with flaxen tail and mane, the latter double-sided.

Rhesus A factor in the blood responsible for jaundice in new born foals. Not all animals have the factor – those with being known as rhesus (or Rh) positive, and those without as rhesus (or Rh) negative. This can lead to complications if a rhesus negative mare gives birth to a *second* rhesus positive foal. These occur because she will have produced anti-rhesus bodies in response to the rhesus factor in her first rhesus positive foal (which do not affect that foal). These anti-bodies affect the second rhesus positive foal (which absorbs the anti-bodies from the now-sensitised mare) by destroying its red blood cells, leading to jaundice and death. The likelihood of this happening can be determined by blood samples taken from the mare before mating. The damage to the second foal can be prevented by not allowing it to suck the colostrum (q.v.) which contains the anti-bodies.

Rhinopneumonia An upper respiratory tract infection.

Rhinopneumonitis Infection by what is now known to be the equine herpes virus (of which there are two types). It can affect horses in two ways:

TYPE 1 VIRUS causes abortion in pregnant mares. It is *highly* infectious. The principal symptom is usually a slight nasal discharge, followed by abortion or the birth of a very weak foal. A vaccine is available against this type of infection.

TYPE 2 VIRUS is most commonly found in young animals, in which it attacks the respiratory system. Symptoms include a clear nasal discharge, increased temperature, and swollen glands around the head and neck. At present, there are no vaccines for this form of infection.

Rhum Pony A herd of Highland ponies owned by the Nature Conservancy Council, who breed them and train them for use in stalking. They came under NCC management when that body took over the island of Rhum in 1957.

Ribbed up, well A term descriptive of a deep, short, body, well rounded and with well-sprung ribs.

Ribbons Popular term for coloured rosette show awards. To win is to be 'in the ribbons'.

Ribs In all breeds, rounded and well-sprung ribs are essential. There are (in pairs) eight true and ten false ribs, except in Arabian horses, which have seventeen pairs.

Richards, Sir Gordon (1904-1986) In 1933 Richards surpassed Fred Archer's record (1885) of riding 246 winners in one season by riding 259. On 26th April, 1943, when riding Scotch Mist at Windsor racecourse, he rode his 2750th winner, this breaking another record also held by Fred Archer. He won 14 Classic races, but only won the Derby once, on Pinza in 1970, the year he retired from race riding. Sir Gordon, 26 times champion jockey, was knighted in 1953, being the first professional jockey to be so honoured.

Richmond Royal Horse Show Society Founded in 1892, the Society held an annual show at Richmond, Surrey. This no longer takes place, and the Society is amalgamated with the South of England Agricultural Society (q.v.).

Ride A lane cut through a wood. (See 'Tally over')

Rider One who, by the proper application of aids, controls and directs his horse with safety and natural comfort. (See **Riding, art of**)

Ride work, to To ride racehorses at training during the regular routine of preparation for the racecourse.

Ridge and furrow Pasture land of regular wavy formation, the result of ploughing and drainage in the days of strip farming.

Ridgeling See **Risling**.

Riding, art of A rider must so conduct himself in the saddle that, by hands, seat and balance, by lightness of touch, rhythm of movement and mental understanding, the horse and rider proceed in safety and in complete accord. (See **Riding, the basic principles of**)

Riding, the basic principles of Skill in riding involves, as in all sports, a knowledge of technique, and its execution demands balance through acquired suppleness and plenty of practice. Certain qualities, such as patience, sympathy and understanding of the mental make-up of the horse, are also necessary to give rewarding results, and a lifelong interest in this great art. It is important that a correct start is made to riding to ensure maximum comfort, safety and enjoyment for rider and horse. Lessons from a qualified instructor are recommended. Once bad habits have developed through apprehension or ignorance, they are extremely difficult to correct later on. The British Horse Society (q.v.) will supply a booklet entitled *Where to Ride*, with a list of schools approved by them. If possible the prospective beginner should take along someone with experience to make an inspection, visiting several establishments, and finally choosing one with a pleasant friendly atmosphere and capable instructors. The yard should be neat and tidy with well-fed and cared-for horses and ponies, and a well-organised programme. Certain special clothing is necessary, including a properly fitting hard hat, a pair of jodhpurs or breeches (jeans are not so comfortable), and either boots, or leather-soled shoes with adequate heels (to prevent the foot becoming caught in the stirrup in the event a fall). Gloves are not essential at this stage. Ideally the first lesson should be private. Many teachers start the beginner on a well-trained lunge (q.v.) horse, which must have a well-designed and fitted saddle, and comfortable paces. Half an hour of riding for the first three or four lessons would be sufficient, to prevent over-tiring muscles, causing stiffness and soreness. It is better to have two or three short periods a week, if possible, rather than one long one. In addition, some time may profitably be spent in the stables, under supervision, handling horses, grooming and tacking-up especially if the learner has no previous experience with horses.

Learning the basic principles of posture related to balance are begun on the lunge horse, if this is used, or, sometimes, on the lead rein, thus acquiring some feel of following the movement of the walk, slow trot and in simple transitions. Security in the saddle and control are based on balance made possible through suppleness. Correct mounting, and dismounting, adjustment of girths and stirrup leathers are practised at this stage.

During movement, balance is three-dimensional – forward and backwards, from side to side, and up and down, from the movement of the horse's back. To absorb this the rider must have flexible joints, especially the loins, hips, knees, and ankles. Correct adjustment of the stirrup leathers is essential to allow flexion of these joints. A relaxed but upright upper body must be maintained, without contraction or stiffness, enabling the rider to follow the movement of the horse. Therefore, he or she must be sitting squarely on the seat bones in the deepest part of the saddle, which should be closest to the horse's centre of gravity – i.e. just behind the withers at the halt. The rider's legs should 'hang' down close to the horse's sides, with relaxed thighs,

the ball of the foot on the stirrup iron and the heel just below the level of the toe, without being forced in any way. There should be a straight line from the ear, shoulder, hip and heel as a general guide to the outline of the rider. A neckstrap should be used to help maintain balance, and can gradually be dispensed with as confidence and balance improve. Suppling exercises which are related to individual requirements should be introduced, but used with discretion to achieve positive results. This should include progressive work without stirrups. Once rising trot is established, confidence usually develops, but this must not be practised to the exclusion of developing feel for movement and softness at sitting trot. After several lessons on the lunge, the rider may be given the reins. It is normal to want to use the arms and hands to maintain balance, as this is their normal function in everyday life. The development of a firm, independent seat without resorting to the use of the hands is the first objective in learning to ride. To start with, it will be difficult to keep them still. At this stage on the lunge, complete relaxation, comfort and confidence should be established without worrying about control.

Knowledge of the simple aids, which are the rider's means of communication with the horse, must be introduced. The natural aids are: the weight of the body, the legs, the hands, and the voice. To understand fully the effect of an independent seat, it is helpful to consider the mechanism of the horse. In order to carry the weight of the rider, a horse has to readjust his balance to the new load. If this is continually shifting about, in a direction contrary to the horse's centre of gravity, loss of control of his limbs is inevitable. Hence, if a horse increases his pace and the rider tries to stop him by pulling the reins, leaning forward, and bracing against the stirrup irons, the horse will go faster rather than slower, because of opposing aids and increasing loss of balance. Therefore the adjustment of the rider's body weight and the ability to control it at all paces, both on turns and circles, and the maintenance, quietness and softness in the saddle, are the major factors in security and control.

229

Independent use of the hands and legs will require much practice to develop co-ordination, and should be started while still on the lunge. A trained horse will respond to the rider's requests, and this is the best means of teaching a beginner to feel and learn.

The leg aids have two functions: to create impulsion and control the hind-quarters. Once the rider is capable of keeping the legs still and close to the horse's sides, he can start to apply them as aids, making sure that the weight still goes down into the heel and that the shoulders and upper body do not fall forward and stiffen. Leg aids should be applied inwards and forwards, and not in repetitive kicking from front to back. The hands, which control impulsion and the forehand, at this stage of the rider's training, should maintain a passive role, the main endeavour being to follow the movement by understanding the action of the horse's head and neck.

At the walk, the horse's head and neck move up and down from the shoulder; therefore the rider's arms, with elastic elbows, soft shoulders, fingers closed round the reins, should endeavour to follow the movement with a lightly stretched rein. While trotting, the head and neck of the horse remain still; this will cause problems for the rider to start with, as the hands should be quiet but not fixed in any way. A straight line from the horse's mouth, over the top of the thumb to the elbow, which must be bent, is a guide to the attitude which will eventually allow independent and positive use of the hand as an aid at a later stage. In the canter, the head and neck move slightly, and as at the other paces, constant contact has to be developed through practice and feel, the rider's seat remaining close to the saddle. After between twelve and eighteen lessons, the rider should be able to show some control, and maintain balance at slow paces.

Riding Classes, Children's The British Show Pony Society recommend height limits for Open Classes as follows: (1) Not exceeding 12.2 hh (127 cm) as suitable for, and to be ridden by, a child not exceeding twelve years. (2) Exceeding 12.2 hh (127 cm) but not exceeding 13.2 hh (137.2 cm), to be ridden by a child not exceeding fourteen years. (3) Exceeding 13.2 hh (137.2 cm), but not exceeding 14.2 hh (147.3 cm), to be ridden by a child not exceeding sixteen years. In Leading Rein classes the pony must not exceed 12 hh (121.9 cm) and the child must not be under the age of seven years. Novice Pony classes, Side-saddle classes, Pairs of Ponies classes and Working Hunter Pony classes all have their own special rules.

Riding Clubs, Association of Over 400 Riding Clubs in the British Isles and overseas are affiliated to the British Horse Society, which supplies information, lectures, films, etc. and co-ordinates the activities which culminate in the Riding Club Championships in show jumping, horse trials, Prix Caprilli, equitation jumping, and dressage in the summer, the Riding Clubs' Teams of Three at the Royal International Horse Show, and the Riding Clubs' Quadrille at the Horse of the Year Show.

Riding Establishments Acts, 1964 and 1970 Regulates the keeping of riding establishments, and enacts that no person shall keep a riding establishment except under licence. Requirements to justify this are detailed, and the powers of local authorities of inspection, prosecution, etc., are indicated. The Act came into operation on 1 April, 1965. In 1970 further powers were granted to local licensing authorities, providing the issue of provisional licences valid for three months, and including such regulations as not allowing responsibility for riding establishments by any one under sixteen years, or hiring out any horse aged three years or under or heavy in foal.

Riding for the Disabled Association (RDA) Established as a charity in 1969 to encourage riding for the physically and mentally disabled. Regional groups have been formed all over the country. The headquarters are at the British Equestrian Centre, Stoneleigh, Warwickshire.

Riding machine See **Rosinback riding machine**.

Riding Pony Although any pony that can be ridden may be called a riding pony, a specific type, now known as the British Riding Pony has been developed by crossing native ponies (especially Welsh and Dartmoor) with small Thoroughbreds and Arabs. This pony (which strictly speaking, is not yet an established breed) is, in effect, a child's hack, with great quality and excellent conformation, and, at its best, has not lost the bone or substance derived from native stock. Riding ponies may be entered in the National Pony Society stud book. Official classes for ridden and breeding for Riding Ponies come under the auspices of the British Show Pony Society (q.v.) (For details of ridden classes see **Riding Classes, Children's**.)

Riding off (polo) A player may be 'ridden off' the ball, provided that his opponent comes into him not at an acute angle, and applies side-to-side pressure. Charging at an angle greater than approximately 45° is prohibited as dangerous.

Riding posts See **Horse-posts**.

Riding school An enclosed space, open or covered, for the exercising and schooling of horses.

Rig A horse with a retained testicle. Such horses are mischievous, and a nuisance when running loose with mares; some are able to get mares in foal. The term can also refer to a horse inadequately operated upon.

Rig An equipage or turn-out for driving.

Right-hand course One where the horses run in a clockwise direction, as at Sandown Park and Ascot.

Rigid tree A saddle tree not of the spring type is termed rigid, denoting its lack of resilience.

Rim collar Used in hackney harness, the groove (in which the hames rest) showing on the inside (the neck side). A Kay collar, named after its designer, is neater than a rim collar, as the groove does not show, and the lining is carried smoothly from back to front.

Rim firing A cowboy practice of putting a burr under the saddle blanket to make a horse buck harder in rodeo buckjumping contests.

Ring, the (racing) Bookmakers collectively are known as 'the Ring'.

Ringbone An arthritic condition of the pastern region. 'High' ringbone affects the pastern joint. 'Low' ringbone affects the joint between the pedal bone and the pastern. The name refers to the ring of new bone which forms around the joint. There is a variety of causes, including poor conformation of the pasterns, concussion, sprains, and overlong heels due to shoes being left on too long. The symptoms include increasing lameness, more noticeable on hard going. Treatment is with anti-inflammatory drugs or, in severe cases, by de-nerving (neurectomy, q.v.).

Ringer (racing) A horse which is substituted for another.

Ringing fox One which persists in running in circles and never moving far from the home covert.

Rings See **Martingale, Irish**.

Ringworm A highly contagious skin disease caused by fungi which establish themselves around the bases of the hairs, causing them to break off, leaving a circular bald patch which is typically (but not invariably) circular. It is a highly infectious disease, transmissible to humans, appearing most frequently in younger riders where riding breeches rub around the waist. All tack, clothing and grooming kit should be thoroughly washed in an anti-fungal preparation. Treatment consists of topical anti-fungal preparation or an in-feed medication. Veterinary advice should be sought for proper control measures to be investigated.

Riot When hounds hunt any animal or bird other than their proper quarry, they are said to riot.

Rising A term used in giving the age of a horse. A horse that is, for example, nearly five years old is said to be 'rising five', and if just over five, it is said to be 'five off'.

Risling/Ridgeling A horse which has its reproductive organs only partially developed. (See **Rig**)

Ritt See **Ears, identification marks**.

Roach back A prominent malformed spinal column, also known as a hog back.

Roach back.

Roached mane American term for a hogged mane (q.v.).

'Road closed' A recognised obstacle in show jumping, usually a 'gallows' arm with the words painted boldly in contrasting colours.

Road coach (stage coach) Public passenger-carrying vehicles, which were run like those transporting the mails, but carrying many more passengers – twelve on top and four inside. In order to attract custom, road coaches were painted gaily, also having the names of destinations and stopping places on their panels and hind boots. Since payment had to be made at toll-gates, they were considerably slower than the mail coaches (q.v.), but the fares were much cheaper.

Roan Barbary The horse of King Richard II, believed to have been imported from the East. It was of great beauty and uncertain temper, but much loved by the King. It has been immortalised in the famous lines by Shakespeare in *Richard II*.

Roan (colour) A coat with an admixture of white hair which, with the body colour, lightens the general effect of the latter. Blue roan: the body colour is black or black-brown, to which the admixture of white hair gives a blue tinge; the limbs from the knee and hock downwards are black. Bay or red roan: the body colour is bay or bay-brown, to which the admixture of white hair gives a reddish tinge; the limbs as above. Strawberry or chestnut roan: the body colour is chestnut, to which the admixture of white hair gives a pinkish-red tinge.

Roarer A term describing a horse with an affliction of the larynx, who makes a deep noise when cantering or galloping. It is usually caused by malfunction of the recurrent laryngeal nerve: the vocal chords and associated cartilages are not drawn back during inspiration and the air rushing past these restricted passages results in a 'roaring' sound. Whistling is a lesser degree of the same malfunction. It can be treated by Hobdaying (q.v.), or tubing, i.e. the insertion of a tube into the windpipe.

Rockaway A town carriage of the Brougham type, although the driver's seat is placed lower, and is joined to the body of the vehicle. An extension of the roof projects over the driving seat.

Rock salt Salt is necessary from a health point of view, and a licking block is a convenient form. Blocks of iodised or plain salt should always be available for horses to lick, and are appreciated by most. Commonly known as a salt-lick. See also **Electrolytes**.

Rockwell bridle A bit having metal loops of figure-eight shape round the mouthpiece on the inside of the bit rings. To these loops is fastened a nosepiece, usually elastic, which is supported by a central strap fastening at the poll. Prevents a horse poking his nose, getting his tongue over the bit, and has a restraining effect on hard pullers. Sometimes known as 'Crocker's bit'.

Rodeo (Spanish *rodar* = to go round). Originally a round-up of cattle on American ranges, now mainly applied to special shows where cowboys give exhibitions of skill in various forms of their work, and compete in riding buckjumpers and steers, and in steer wrestling and roping. In both Northern America and Australia, professional rodeo circuits are extremely popular. The participants are frequently professional rodeo riders, as distinct from cowboys or (in Australia) stockmen.

Rodzianko gag See **Roller mouth**.

Rogue A vicious horse, and not just one who is bad mannered.

Rogue's badge Denotes blinkers worn by racehorses, but all horses running in them are not necessarily rogues. They are sometimes worn to stop horses from gazing about them. Winkers on harness are not rogues' badges. See also **Red ribbon**.

Roll cantle A roll of leather on the back of an American saddle which the rider uses to help raise himself into the saddle.

Roller (Surcingle in USA) A form of girth made of leather, jute, hemp or webbing, and used to keep a day or night rug in place. It goes right round the body, and usually has two pads either side of the spine, and fastens with one or two buckles. See also **Anti-cast roller**.

Roller bolts Four upward projections on the splinter bar, to which the traces of a pair, or of the coach wheelers, are attached.

Roller mouth A bit with rollers set round the mouthpiece. It is useful on strong horses, the movement of the bit assisting mouthing of the bit, and discouraging a horse from 'taking hold' of it. When used with gag rings it is sometimes called 'Rodzianko's gag', after the late Paul Rodzianko. The rollers can also be referred to as 'cherries'.

Roman nose See **Nose, Roman**.

Rooster pull Formerly an American cowboy game. With his horse travelling at high speed, the rider had to lean down and seize the neck of a 'rooster' buried in the ground, pull it loose and then race round a large circle.

Roots A hunting term implying any field of turnips, swede, beet, mangolds, potatoes, etc.

Rope horse A horse trained to hold a rope tight enough to prevent a steer from rising after it has been thrown.

Roseberry, Archibald Philip Primrose, 5th Earl of The only Premier to have owned a Derby winner while Prime Minister. He won with Ladas (1894), and Sir Visto (1895). He won the race a third time with Cicero in 1905, when no longer Premier.

Rosette A competition award consisting of one or more colours, presented for

various placings as well as championships and reserve championships. Cups, prize money and other awards may be added. In Britain, red usually signifies first place, and blue second, with some important exceptions, such as the Royal International Horse Show (q.v.), and the Bath and West Show (q.v.). In the USA blue ranks first and red second, but Canada reverses these colours.

Rosinante The horse of Don Quixote de la Mancha, the 'Knight of the Melancholy Countenance', hero of Cervantes' romance satirising the excesses of the last ages of chivalry. Used as a term to denote that a horse is in the last stages of usefulness.

Rosinback riding machine (or mechanic) A crane-like device used in the circus in training bareback riders. The rider is suspended from the head of a moving crane by a rope attached to a leather belt that encircles the waist, this preventing a fall when loss of balance occurs.

Rosinbacks The circus name given to bareback riding horses on which artistes stand and perform various acrobatic and other acts. The term originated from the fact that resin is rubbed into the horse's back, mainly around the quarters, to prevent the performers from slipping. It is essential for the horse to have a wide, level and un-dipped back. It must have plenty of bone, and the gait, speed and level pace at which it canters are of great importance. (See **Circus horses**)

Ross, Martin See **Ross, Violet**.

Ross, Violet (1862-1915) Under the nom-de-plume 'Martin Ross', with her cousin Edith O. Somerville (q.v.) she was the author of many books on Irish sporting life, including the well-known *Some Experiences of an Irish R.M.*

Rotten Row A straight and broad riding track in Hyde Park, London, extending from Hyde Park Corner to Alexandra Gate, and popularly known as 'The Row'. Made, probably about 1690, by William III to take him from Westminster to his palace at Kensington. It then had a surface of sorts, was lit by oil lamps, and was known as King's or Lamp Road. About 1734, it was converted to a soft surface. Apart from the obvious possible reference to the latter ('rotten' = 'soft'), there are various theories as to the origin of the name. One is that it is a corruption of *Route du Roi*, referring to the way taken by the Plantagenet kings from Westminster Palace to the Royal hunting forests; this route covered what are now Birdcage Walk, Constitution Hill and Rotten Row. Another suggestion is that after George II had constructed South Carriage Road – a shorter distance – the older way, now called Old King's Road, became the haunt of idlers, whence derived its nickname – which had certainly come into use by 1770 at the latest. A third theory is that the name derived from the Teutonic *rotteran*, to muster, since William III and the Hanoverians occasionally mustered troops in The Row. It was referred to in the *Sporting Magazine* in 1837 as Rontine (alias Rotten) Row.

Rough country Any country which is not easy to ride across i.e. woodland, moorland, or many hills.

Roughing off/Roughing up A course adopted immediately preceding the act of turning a horse out to grass, including the alteration of diet by reducing concentrates, cessation of grooming and exercise, and gradual removal of rugs, etc.

Rough-shoeing The insertion of frost-nails into shoes to secure a better hold on ice-bound surfaces.

Rouncey Mediaeval term for a riding horse of the small cob type.

Round-up The collection of cattle off the ranges in American and other ranchlands for branding, selecting for sale, etc. They are held periodically among some of the mountain and moorland breeds in the British Isles. (See **Drifts**)

Rount An early English term (and a modern American one) for a horse which is roan or flesh-coloured, inter-mixed with white or peach. Originally known also as 'grissel'.

Rous, Admiral, the Hon. Henry John (1795-1877) One of the three great names in the early history of the Jockey Club (the other two being Sir Charles Bunbury and Lord George Bentinck). A son of the 1st Earl of Stradbroke, he entered the Navy, and after a distinguished career, retired, and devoted his energies to racing. He had been elected to the Jockey Club in 1821, while still in the Navy. In 1838, he was elected Steward, and from then until his death at the age of eighty-two, exerted enormous influence on the racing scene. Because of this he was known as 'The Dictator of the Turf'. He became the unofficial Treasurer (vastly improving the finances) and Senior Steward, and in 1855 he was appointed Public Handicapper. In the same year he published *Law and Practice of Horse Racing*. As a result of his experiences as a handicapper, he introduced the 'Weight for Age' scale, which, with modifications, is still in use. He was not, however, infallible, and is quoted as saying that 'Eclipse was about good enough to win a £50 Selling Plate'! He greatly enhanced the reputation of the Jockey Club. The Rous Memorial Stakes were named after him.

Rouse (stag hunting) A term denoting that a stag has been set a-foot in cover.

Rowel A 'wheel' inserted at the head of a spur. There were many different designs of varying severity in action. Little used in modern practice and then only in mild action, except with Western horses in the USA when rowels may be severe and over-used.

Rowlandson, Thomas (1756-1827) Esteemed for his countless drawings and watercolours of English life, in many of which horses are depicted. Rowlandson is most widely known for his work of caricature or cartoon nature, notably the famous illustrations for the *Tours of Dr Syntax*. Sporting prints designed and etched by Rowlandson include hunting and racing sets, e.g. 'High Mettled Racer', a set of four published in 1879.

Rowley Mile The last mile of the Newmarket course, over which are run the 1000 and 2000 Guineas. Named after Charles II's well-known stallion Old Rowley. (See **Newmarket**; and **'Old Rowley'**).

Royal Agricultural Society of England

Founded in 1839, the Society held an annual Royal Agricultural Show in different parts of the country, popularly known as 'The Royal'. It is now permanently sited at Stoneleigh, Warwickshire.

Royal College of Veterinary Surgeons The governing body of the veterinary profession in Great Britain and Ireland, under Royal Charter granted in 1844. The Membership Diploma (MRCVS) granted by the College entitles the holder to be placed on the Register of Veterinary Surgeons maintained by the College and to practise the art of veterinary surgery and medicine. The Fellowship Diploma (FRCVS) is granted to members of not less than five years' standing on presentation of a thesis based on original research or observation. (The five years refer to the time of presentation or examination, not to the time of application as a candidate.) Candidates for Fellowship will be required to: (1) submit a thesis; or (2) pass examinations; (3) under the provisions of a by-law, veterinary surgeons of not less than twenty years' standing may apply for permission to submit published work as evidence of meritorious contributions to learning. Candidates for award by thesis must first be accepted as a provisional candidate, and then submit, with the application, the proposed course of study.

Royal colours See **Colours, Royal**.

Royal Dublin Society See **Dublin Horse Show**.

Royal George gag An alternative but incorrect term for a Nelson gag (q.v.).

Royal International Horse Show One of the premier horse shows of the world, first held at Olympia, London, in 1907, and continuing there as an annual event up to and including 1939 – with the exception of the First World War years, 1915-1919, and also 1933. There were no shows during the Second World War years 1940-1944. In 1945 the show was held at the White City, London, as the 'National' show, no international competitors being able to enter owing to post-war problems. From 1946 to 1967 it was held at the White City as the International Horse Show, and in 1968 and 1969 it

was held at Wembley Stadium, London. In 1970, it went indoors to the Empire Pool, Wembley. Then, after a brief return to the White City in 1983, it moved to the National Exhibition Centre in Birmingham. Classes are held both indoors and outdoors, and are open to Arabs, Hunters, Hacks, Cobs, Children's Riding Ponies, Hackneys, Trade Turn-outs, Riding Clubs and Show Jumpers. The right to the prefix 'Royal' was granted in 1957.

Royal mares Arab and Barb mares imported into England in the seventeenth century for the Royal Stud. These, with certain others, became the foundation mares of the English Thoroughbred.

Royal Mews Situated in Buckingham Palace Road, London. When the Royal Stables were destroyed by fire in 1537, Henry VIII ordered his Stud to be housed in the Mews of the King's Falcons at Charing Cross. The mews were moved to the present site in 1825.

Royal Society for the Prevention of Cruelty to Animals (RSPCA) (Founded 1824.) Formed to prevent cruelty to animals and to promote kindness to them.

Royal Windsor Horse Show Club, the (founded 1943) Founded to benefit charities and to promote the well-being of horses. The Society holds an annual horse show at Windsor in May.

Royal Winter Fair Held in Toronto, Canada, founded in 1925, and now an important event in the international show-jumping scene in North America.

Rubber, stable See **Stable rubber**.

Rubber-mouthed snaffle Usually a mullen mouthpiece with a chain through the centre of the rubber as a precaution against its being bitten through. Jointed metal snaffles and straight bar or mullen mouthpieces can sometimes be obtained with the mouthpieces covered in rubber. When there is no solid metal centre to the mouth it is known as a 'flexible mouth'.

Rub-down Should be given to a horse which is brought in sweating, or wet from rain. Dry straw should be used, followed by one or two dry stable rubbers. Most important parts are the ears, throat, chest, back and loins.

'Rugby' on horseback See **Buzkashi**.

Rugby pelham bit A term embracing various types of pelham (usually mullen mouth) which have a loose top ring attached closely to the cheeks. Similar to the Berkeley (q.v.).

Rugby saddle panel A short leather panel with an interior of felt.

Rugged up A term applied to a horse wearing either day or night rugs. It is important to see that the rugs fit well and are not buckled up too tightly.

Rugs (Blankets in USA) Horses may be equipped with a variety of rugs for different purposes. The most usual include day rugs, night rugs, summer sheets, anti-sweat sheets, and New Zealand rugs. See under separate headings for details.

Rug tearing Like many disagreeable habits this is a vice (q.v.). The use of a bar muzzle or the impregnation of the rug with one of the proprietary chewing inhibitors is suggested.

Rules of the road (in Britain) Ride on the left and lead on the left, keeping the ridden horse between the led animal and the traffic. BHS safety suggestions include: if riding after dark is essential, a safety lamp on the offside stirrup showing white to the front and red to the rear should be used (see *Highway Code*), the rider should wear reflective clothing, and the horse should have reflective bands on the legs above the fetlock joint. A booklet *Riding and Roadcraft*, giving fuller details and suggestions, is available from the BHS, Stoneleigh, Warwickshire.

Rumble See **Dickey**.

Run An action found in a badly broken horse, a compromise between a canter behind and a trot in front. In USA a term applied in Thoroughbreds and Quarter Horses to the fastest gait a horse can execute.

Run A hunting term referring to every occasion during which a quarry is hunted by hounds. The distance is measured by a straight line from the point of find to the point of kill; 'as hounds ran' gives the actual distance covered.

Runciman Derived from the obsolete word 'runcy' or 'rouncey' (q.v.). Thus 'runciman' would mean a runcy-keeper or runcy-dealer.

Runcy See **Rouncey**.

Runnable stag See **Warrantable**.

Runners (racing) All the horses in the list of those entered in a race, actually taking part in that race.

Runners (saddlery) Leather loops on saddlery (especially the bridle) that slide up and down and through which the strap ends pass. Also known as 'keepers'.

Running When hounds are actually in pursuit of a fox.

Running iron A ½-in. (12.7 mm) iron rod, slightly curved at one end and formerly used by cowboys for branding cattle before the introduction of modern branding irons.

Running loose A term descriptive of a racehorse which, owing to a general lack of confidence in its ability to win a race, shared by the personnel at the stable where it is trained, runs unbacked by the latter.

Running-out A term implying that a horse is out at grass.

Running-out (jumping) The action of a horse skirting round an object instead of jumping it, either when racing over fences, or when jumping in the show ring or across country.

Running rails Rails, often of plastic, placed inside the main rails on a racecourse, as a guide to jockeys and for safety.

Running rein A gag rein, running from the rider's hands, through any snaffle bit, thence to the girth.

'Running up light' Descriptive of a horse which has badly muscled quarters and sunken flanks; the result of poor condition.

Running walk An accelerated flat-footed walk, 6-8 mph (9.6-12.8 km/h). Tennessee Walking Horses (q.v.) are the best performers of this gait.

Russell, Rev. 'Jack' He inherited a love

of field sports from his father, the vicar of Iddesleigh, who kept his own pack of hounds and was a fearless rider. For some years he kept a pack of otterhounds and eventually founded the North West Devon Hunt. At the age of seventy-six, in 1871, he gave up his hounds, having hunted otter and then fox for fifty years. However, he still followed hounds, and when he became vicar of Torrington he started a harrier pack, although then over eighty years of age. He was the originator of the Jack Russell terrier, the prototype of the hunt terrier (q.v.).

Russian Heavy Draught The oldest of the Russian breeds of draught horses, and also the smallest, standing only about 14.3 hh (149.9 cm). The breed was first registered in 1952. It is based on the Belgian Ardennes imported into Russia about a hundred years ago.

Russian Trotter Obtained by crossing the Orlov Trotter (q.v.) with the American Standardbred in the late nineteenth century. Used with success in both national and international trotting races.

Rust A parasitic fungus growing on plants and grasses in the form of a yellowish powder, often having serious consequences when fed to horses.

Rustic gate parallels (show jumping) Gates of rustic material and colour, requiring a horse to negotiate both height and spread.

Rustle, to To herd, round up or steal horses or cattle.

Rutter's twitch See **Twitch, humane**.

Rutting season The stags' mating season – October.

Ryegrass A very good food in the form of hay. See **Grass; Hay**.

SANEF South African National Equestrian Federation (q.v.).

SBA Stud Book Argentino.

SH (racing) Short head.

SM Solid mouthpiece. See **SM pelham**.

SS (racing) Started slowly.

Sable Island Pony A breed of tough, hardy ponies, standing 14-15 hh (142.2-152.4 cm) found only on Sable Island, off Nova Scotia, Canada.

Saddle A pad is occasionally called a saddle by harness makers. In cart-harness a pad is always called a saddle.

Saddle This came into use in the fourth century and was either invented by the Byzantines or 'adopted' by them from the hordes of Barbarian horsemen who threatened the Roman Empire.

Saddle, astride or across Used by anyone riding astride, as distinct from side-saddle. Also called 'cross' saddle.

Saddle, basket A saddle which is fitted with a basket, attached to a pad, in which a very small child can be carried in safety.

Saddle, Danloux A saddle designed by the great French horseman Robert Danloux. Its peculiarity is a squab set under the flap in the bend of the rider's knee, and a high forward roll giving support well above the knee. It is generally used with a thick felt numnah (q.v.).

Saddle, dressage A saddle specifically designed for this equestrian discipline. The seat is dipped to allow the rider to sit deeply in the centre, and is usually shorter than a jumping saddle (q.v.). The head, unless cut back, is straight, as opposed to being sloped to the rear, to enable the stirrup bars to be positioned quite far back and also to allow the rider to sit centrally. The flaps are cut fairly straight, and the panel offers a little knee and thigh support. Dressage saddles may have either spring or rigid trees.

Saddle, felt A saddle made of thick felt with a girth attached. It is very useful for a tender-backed horse, but as it comes right down on the withers and is hot and inclined to draw, it is not recommended for long rides or for hunting. It is, however, very useful for young riders, as it provides a secure seat.

Saddle, Fulmer A dressage saddle designed by Robert Hall, formerly of the Fulmer Riding School.

Saddle, general-purpose A modern spring-tree saddle not quite as exaggerated in cut as the jumping saddle. It is used for hunting and cross-country riding, and can also be used for elementary dressage.

Saddle (harness) Made as a miniature riding saddle, this can be of many designs, and carries the back band, shaft tugs and belly band.

Saddle, hunting A term generally applied to the conventional 'English' saddle made on a rigid tree and with very little dip to the seat. The term can, of course, be applied to any saddle used for hunting. Though the hunting saddle is still used, more and more people are favouring the 'general-purpose' pattern (see above),

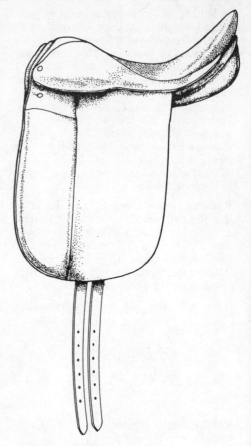

Dressage saddle.

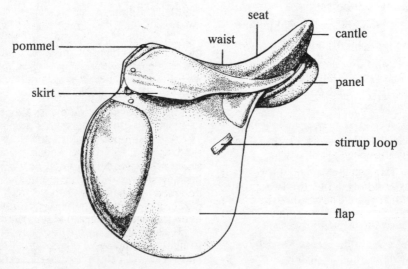

Parts of a general-purpose saddle.

which gives greater support and positions the rider more correctly in relation to the movement of the horse.

Saddle, Italian A saddle made by Italy's foremost saddlemaker, Pariani (q.v.). Also a loose (and now incorrect) term applied to a spring-tree, forward cut, jumping-type saddle.

Saddle, jumping A spring-tree, characteristically deep-seated saddle, cut well forward and having knee rolls incorporated into the panel. Its design positions the rider over the centre of gravity and

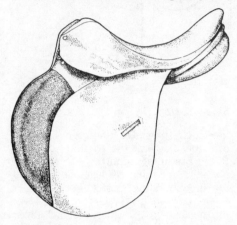

Jumping saddle.

assists him to remain with the movements of the horse. It is cut further forward than a 'general purpose' saddle and is usually lighter.

Saddle, Lane Fox A show saddle much cut back at the withers.

Saddle, McClellan An American military saddle, named after the Civil War general, formerly the standard USA trooper's saddle. It was built on a solid tree, open along the side, had a deep seat, modified fan (q.v.) and hooded stirrups. See **Stirrups, hooded**.

Saddle, McTaggart A type of forward seat saddle designed by the late Lt. Col. M. F. McTaggart. The head of the saddle is very high, to give a pronounced dip to the seat. Now obsolete.

Saddle, Morocco A military saddle used in the first half of the seventeenth century and later known as the 'Burford' saddle.

Saddle, pad A thick felt saddle without a tree. Pad-saddles of better quality are made with a fore-arch in place of a full tree; some models include an abbreviated tree made in leather and are used for exercise in training stables. Not in general use.

Saddle, Pariani See **Saddle, Italian** and **Pariani**.

Saddle, polo Slightly deeper – with a high cantle – and shorter and wider than the English hunting saddle.

Saddle, Pony Club A general-purpose saddle officially approved by the Pony Club.

Saddle, race exercise A name given to exercise saddles used in racing stables. They resemble a steeplechase saddle in appearance but are not cut so far forward. Usually serge-lined and made on a very strong tree.

Saddle, racing A small saddle with flaps cut well forward, weighing from 8 oz to 2½ lb (226 g to 1.12 kg). Steeplechase saddles are, in general, larger and can be made on a weighted tree if the rider has to carry much extra weight. Racing saddles are rarely made with stirrup bars, the leathers being passed round the tree itself. Plastics and fibreglass are commonly used in the manufacture of lightweight trees.

Saddle, Santini One of the first British-made jumping saddles following the Italian pattern. Designed by Piero Santini (q.v.). Now superseded by more modern designs.

Saddle, short A 'half' saddle built on a fore-arch rather like a driving pad and about 12 ins (30.4 cm) long. Used in training stables for horses with sore backs caused by the cantle of badly fitting saddles.

Saddle, showing Of closer fit than a hunting saddle, with straighter flaps and designed to show the horse's front to the best advantage. A show saddle is often fitted with an additional girth strap emerging from the point of the tree, to enable the saddle to be fitted further back. The best show saddles have the bars extended further to the rear, which permits the rider's knee to rest on the flap. With normally positioned bars, the leathers, and the rider's legs, would be too far forward. In the USA it is used for gaited saddle horses, Tennessee Walking horses (q.v.), Arabs and Morgans (qq.v.) and more artificial breeds. Hunters and show jumpers use English saddles.

Saddle, side- A lady's saddle upon which she sits with both legs to one side, usually the left or near-side. On this side the saddle has two projections or pommels; over one of them the rider rests the right leg, and under the lower pommel she places the left leg. The seat of the saddle is often made of doeskin.

HISTORY The history of the side-saddle is somewhat obscure. In the fifth century BC women are depicted as riding astride, and also sitting sideways on the offside. There is a spirited pottery figure of a woman playing polo, sitting astride, made in AD 620 during the T'ang Dynasty. Nicetas (1118-1205), the Greek historian, deplored the fact that women no longer rode, as formerly, on a side-saddle, but had started to ride indecently astride. In early times, in Britain, women rode astride, but there is evidence that a form of side-saddle was known and used about the mid-twelfth century. An historian during the time of Richard II (1367-1400), however, wrote: 'Likewise both noble ladies used high heads and coronets, and robes with long trains, and seats or side-saddles on their horses, by the example of the respectable Queen Anne, daughter of the King of Bohemia, who first introduced this custom into this kingdom; for before women of every rank rode as men do, with their legs astride the backs of their horses.' But this side-saddle was not the side-saddle we know today. The rider sat sideways on the horse with her feet supported by a little footrest known as a *planchette*, and in contemporary pictures both near- and offside are used. This style of saddle was used only for formal and state occasions; women still rode astride for hunting and long journeys. About 1500, Catherine de Medici, a keen hunting woman, is supposed to have introduced pommels on the top of the saddle, one on the offside, one on the near, to form a crutch

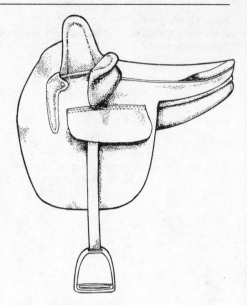

Side-saddle.

in which to wedge the right leg, and probably also – as the gossip of the day, Pierre Brantôme, reported – to show off her own very shapely legs. About 1830 the French riding master, Jules Charles Pellier or François Baucher (q.v.), added, on the near-side, a third pommel about the level of the stirrup bar, to act as a leaping head. Originally about 6 ins (15 cm) long, it was later lengthened and curved to fit the shape of a woman's left thigh, providing real security in a side-saddle. By 1860 this design was in general use. This invention made the offside pommel unnecessary, and so it gradually, over several years, became smaller, and finally disappeared. In the early part of the twentieth century, side-saddles were again considerably modified in design to meet the modern forward style of riding.

In recent years, there has been a marked revival in side-saddle riding in Britain. Restricted, for some considerable time, almost entirely to ladies' hack and hunter classes, many shows now feature classes designed specifically for side-saddle riding on both horses and ponies. The Ladies' Side-Saddle Association, formed in 1974, holds annual championships.

Saddle, slick An American saddle without any safety devices.

Saddle, stock or Western Used by mounted herdsmen and cowboys of the American West, and Mexico. It has a deep seat, high cantle (q.v.), pommel horn for attaching a rope or lariat, and full-cut flaps, fastened by double leather cinches (q.v.) pulled tight by slide knots.

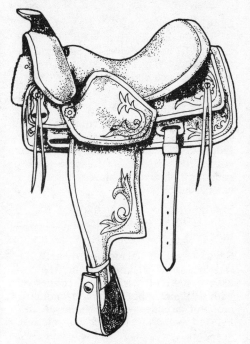

Stock or Western saddle.

Saddle, Toptani A modern spring-tree show-jumping saddle designed by Count Ilias Toptani.

Saddle, universal The name given to the British Army Trooper Saddle (used by all mounted units). A skeleton saddle panel is protected by a folded blanket. It has proved an excellent saddle for all types of backs in every condition.

Saddle, Western See **Stock saddle**.

Saddle bars Metal fittings beneath the skirts of the saddle, to which the stirrup leathers are attached. Most bars are fitted with a safety catch, or thumb piece, at the rear. Very few horsemen would recommend that this device should ever be used in the 'up' or 'locked' position, as it could prove to be dangerous. It is, therefore, largely superfluous, but remains as a relic

of the various patterns of so-called 'safety bars' which were once popular. The bars on a good saddle should be of forged steel. On cheaper saddles the bars are cast, and are therefore likely to fracture. Bars on modern spring-tree saddles are recessed to avoid bulk under the thigh.

Saddle-bracket A wall-bracket in the saddle-room on which saddles are placed.

Saddlebred, American See **American Saddlebred**.

Saddle channel The aperture between the two panels, which runs between all well-fitting saddles and horses' backs.

Saddle-cloth A shaped rectangular cloth, often made of cotton or linen check, placed under the saddle.

Saddle-flaps The cowhide side-panels of a saddle with which the rider's knees come into contact. (See **Sweat flaps**)

Saddle horn A fitting on the front of American stock or Western saddles, around which the line is twisted when a steer is roped. The 'horn' is made of metal covered with leather. It slopes forward, and the top, which is enlarged at the front, also projects forward, to help the quick release of the rope.

Saddle horse A wooden trestle-like stand upon which one or more saddles can rest securely for cleaning or storage.

Saddle-linen Unbleached linen used for lining saddle panels and bearing surfaces. It should always be put over serge and should not be used on its own. It protects the serge from wear and is more easily kept clean.

Saddle marks Marks which, when clipping, should be left in the natural position of the saddle to protect the horse's back. Nothing looks worse than a saddle mark which shows when the saddle is fitted in front of it. The term is also applied to patches of white hair under the saddle – probably caused by galls – which can be used as identification marks.

Saddle panel The cushion between the tree and the horse's back. It can either be made of felt covered in leather; or it can be stuffed with wool or plastic foam and covered in serge, serge-covered linen; or it can be leather lined. The latter is used for most modern hunting, jumping and some other saddles. Felt panels are sometimes used in show saddles. Foam or similar materials are now commonly used.

A panel can be made, according to the tree, in any of four shapes: *full panel*; *Rugby* or *short*; *Saumur* or *Witney*; and *Continental*. The FULL, which reaches almost to the bottom of the saddle-flap, is used on rigid tree saddles, is the traditional panel of the hunting saddle, and is still in use today. The short panel reaches half-way down the saddle and has a large sweat flap which carries almost to the bottom of the saddle. The SAUMUR PANEL is narrower in the waist and cut further forward and with a roll on the outside. The CONTINENTAL is similar to the Saumur but has a narrower waist and a thigh roll at the rear. The last two are those most used in modern saddles, their knee rolls and general construction affording more security to the rider and allowing him to be in close contact with the horse.

Saddlers, black The trade term applied generally to makers of cart and carriage harness, as distinct from saddles, bridles, etc. (See **Saddlers, brown**, below)

Saddlers, brown The trade term generally applied to makers of saddles, bridles, etc., as distinct from harness makers. (See **Saddlers, black**, above).

Saddlers' Company, the 'The Wardens or Keepers and commonalty of the mystery or Art of Saddlers'. The exact date is unknown, but the Company probably existed in Anglo-Saxon times. Certainly a document in the possession of the Dean and Chapter of Westminster Abbey records its existence many years before 1154. The first Saddlers' Hall was destroyed by the Great Fire of 1666, the second in 1821, and the third was destroyed by enemy action in 1940. All have been rebuilt on the same site. The Company ranks 25th in order of precedence among the City of London livery companies.

Saddle serge A special white-wool cloth used for lining saddle panels. Most modern saddles are lined with leather.

Saddle sheepskin A sheepskin numnah used under the saddle to give greater comfort to the horse; or a cover fitting over the saddle to give more security to the rider. Although comfortable, sheepskin is, however, very hot. Simulated sheepskin is now available, and is less expensive.

Saddle soap A special type of 'soap' which is applied with a damp sponge to clean, feed and preserve saddles, bridles, and harness. Glycerine soap can also be used. See **Tack cleaning**.

Saddle sores Caused by bad riding or a badly fitting saddle and harness. As prevention is better than cure, particular care should be taken to ensure that the saddle fits correctly. A horse just up from grass should not have a saddle on his back for more than an hour until the back has hardened.

Saddle stuffing Wool flock or plastic foam used for stuffing the panels of a saddle.

Saddle tree The frame upon which the saddle is built. At one time the tree was always made of beech wood, reinforced with steel plates, but nowadays laminated strips of moulded wood reinforced with light alloy are largely used. This method gives greater strength and a lighter tree. Plastic and fibreglass are other materials now in use.

Safes A term used in the saddlery trade for any piece of shaped leather which keeps undue pressure from the animal, usually behind a buckle, which would otherwise cause a gall. Girth buckle safes 'save' the saddle flap.

Safety bars Stirrup bars with a device – often activated by a spring or swivel – designed to release the stirrup leather in the event of a fall. The best-known patterns, apart from Passmore and Cole, were Allfreys, Beaufort and Cotswold. They are seldom used today. Christie's bar, a plain one tapering upwards at the rear, is used on Australian trees and is probably the most practical.

Safety-catch A movable 'latch' on the metal bar which holds the stirrup leather to the saddle. For the rider's safety, in an

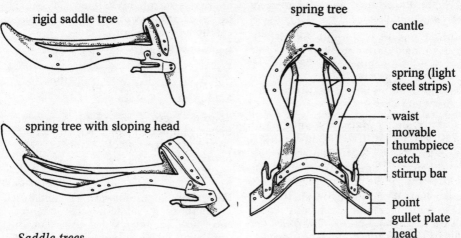

rigid saddle tree

spring tree with sloping head

spring tree

cantle

spring (light steel strips)

waist

movable thumbpiece

catch

stirrup bar

point

gullet plate

head

Saddle trees.

emergency the leather is released from the saddle.

Safety chain On a coach or carriage this can be fastened round the felloe (q.v.) of the near hind wheel to hold it if the skidpan (q.v.) breaks or jolts off.

Safety stirrups Devices in a variety of patterns designed to allow the foot to be released in the event of a fall.

Sainfoin A herb of the pea family from which good hay is made. It has a high protein content and can be fed alone or as hay with a predominant sainfoin content in a seed mixture. The plant will grow only on chalk or limestone soils. Being drought resistant it is at its best in dry summers.

St Christopher Traditionally patron saint of all who travel and thus the patron saint of all horsemen.

St Hubert Patron saint of huntsmen. Hubert was the son of Bertrand, Duc d'Aquitaine. He became so fond of the chase that he neglected his religious duties, but one day a stag with a crucifix between its horns threatened him with eternal perdition, which speedily resulted in his becoming a reformed character. The feast day of St Hubert, 3 November, is still celebrated in certain districts of France; every year, hounds and hunt attend Mass and are blessed.

St Leger The oldest (and the longest)

of the five British Classic races. It was founded in 1776 and is run annually in September on the Town Moor, Doncaster, in Yorkshire. It is for three-year-old colts and fillies over a distance of about 1 mile 6½ furlongs (1.81 km). The race was named in honour of Colonel St Leger, a leading local sportsman of the time. For the first year of its existence it was run over a 2-mile (3.22 km) course, and was won by Lord Rockingham's filly, Allabaculia. The first winner over the shortened course was a grey filly, Hollandaise.

St Simon One of the greatest racehorses and sires of the English turf. He was foaled in 1881, by the 1875 Derby winner, Galopin, out of St Angela. Although he never ran in a Classic, he was never beaten in a race, and his wins included the Ascot Gold Cup (by 20 lengths). He was leading sire nine times. Among his sons and daughters, who won seventeen Classics, were Persimmon (winner of the Derby, St Leger, and Ascot Gold Cup), and St Frusquin (winner of the 2000 Guineas), both of whom emulated him by being leading sires, as did Desmond, another son. His influence has been enormous, and famous stallions such Hyperion, Nearco, and Ribot are all in-bred to him.

Sais See **Syce**.

Salerno An Italian riding horse of quality, based on Neapolitan and Andalusian stock. It was first produced in the early eighteenth century, and was formerly used by the Italian cavalry.

Sales, bloodstock Various bloodstock sales are held during the year. The principal ones are conducted by Tattersall's at Newmarket and by Goffs in Ireland. In England there are also bloodstock sales at Ascot and Doncaster.

Salisbury, Emily Mary, Marchioness of (1749-1835) Said to be the first woman MFH, the Marchioness was Master of the Hertfordshire Hunt from 1793 until she reached her seventieth year in 1819.

Saliva tests When the performance of a horse in racing or other competitive sport is suspect, the authorities may order the saliva, blood and/or urine to be tested for evidence of doping.

Sallenders A complaint similar to mallenders (q.v.), the only difference being in location. Sallenders is found at the front of the hock.

Salmon marks A rarely-used expression denoting a certain amount of white hair on the quarters and back.

Salts See **Electrolytes**.

'Salted' In South Africa, a horse which has recovered from an attack of African Horse Sickness or has been immunised against it. A colloquial term implying acclimatised, tough, hardened etc.

Salt-lick Shaped blocks of salt which can be fitted into holders and hung in stables or on fences for horses to lick. Other minerals are sometimes added. See **Rock salt**.

Sandalwood A very hardy pony used for bareback racing. Bred in the Indonesian islands of Sumba and Sumbawa, it is named after the sandalwood which was the biggest export from the islands. Height 12.1-13.1 hh (124.4-134.6 cm).

Sandbath A natural or artificial hollow in which horses love to roll.

Sandcrack A split in the wall of the hoof which starts near the coronet or below, and penetrates the sensitive parts within, which bleed. It may occur in any part of the hoof, but it usually appears in the front of the hind hoof and on the inside

quarter of the fore hoof. It may be caused by treads or blows to the coronet, severe exertion, or faulty horn secretion.

Sandwich-case A container enclosed in a leather canteen and attached to the saddle by 'Ds'. It is used when hunting.

Sanfoin See **Sainfoin**.

Santini, Piero (1881-1960) A notable Italian horseman and writer, whose books, *Riding Reflections* (1932); *The Forward Impulse* (1937); and *The Riding Instructor* (1952) introduced the doctrine of Federico Caprilli (q.v.) on the Italian system of forward riding, thus revolutionising modern cross-country and show jumping styles. A Major in the Italian Cavalry Reserve, he won the *Croce di Guerra ad V.M.* (military cross for valour) in World War I.

Sardinia Pony Originally bred in a semi-wild state in the island of Sardinia, these hardy ponies stood between 13 and 14 hh (132.1 and 142.2 cm). Bay in colour, they were good work and ride ponies.

Sartorius, Francis (1734-1804) The son of John Sartorius Snr (q.v.) he achieved more widespread recognition with his race-match pictures and portraits of hunters and racehorses (including several of Eclipse). Having been taught by his father, he inherited many of the same limitations of technique.

Sartorius, John (Snr) (1700-1780) Son of a Nuremberg engraver, he became established in England *c.* 1720, the first of four generations of this family who used British field sports as their subject. He painted several racehorses in a stiff, primitive style for influential owners. English sporting records have been considerably enriched by the work of the Sartorius family, who ignored Continental influence and brought an English approach to sporting art.

Sartorius, John Nost (1759-1828) Son of Francis Sartorius (q.v.), and the most gifted of the family. His backgrounds, the composition of his racing and hunting pictures, and his portraits of horses being pictorially more pleasing and technically superior. Many prints were made after his works. One of his sons, John Francis

(1775-1830), also painted sporting subjects.

Satchel A leather pouch worn by a coachguard and containing a timepiece.

Saturation A theory once strongly believed by some breeders – but without any foundation in fact – that a mare repeatedly served by the same stallion will produce offspring more and more resembling the sire, through the constant interchange of blood between the unborn foal and its dam.

Saugor (cavalry school) Home for many years of the Indian Army Equitation School, it was the Indian Army counterpart of Weedon (q.v.). Situated in the Central Provinces, it was closed in 1939.

Saumur A town in Western France, home of the French cavalry school which was founded in 1763 at the instigation of Louis XV, by the Royal Corps of Caribineers. The Royal Cavalry School moved to Saumur in 1825. Initially it was the home of the famous corps of instructors, the Cadre Noir (q.v.), but in 1969 the officers of the Cadre separated from the Army to supervise tuition at the National School of Equitation at Terrefort, just outside Saumur.

Saumur panel See **Saddle panel**.

Sausage boot A stuffed leather ring strapped round the coronet as prevention against a capped elbow, which is caused by pressure of the shoe on the elbow when a horse is lying down.

Sausage boot.

Savage, to To bite or in any other way to attack another horse or a human. Horses proved to be savage to humans are very dangerous and should be destroyed.

Sawdust Sometimes used as a bedding material. To be restful it must be spread thickly. It is one of the least attractive of all forms of bedding, but one of the most comfortable. Care must be taken that it does not block drains. (See **Bedding**)

Scamperdale pelham bit An angle-mouth, straight-bar bit made popular by Sam Marsh, a well-known twentieth-century horseman. It is thought that greater control is obtained through the cheeks coming into contact with a part of the horse's mouth not hitherto affected. Its main advantage is in having the mouthpiece turned back at each end, bringing the cheekpiece further to the rear and away from the area where chafing is likely to occur.

Scarlet, hunting (incorrectly called 'pink') Its origin is uncertain. One possibility is that it was introduced by Henry VIII, who clothed his huntsmen and yeoman-prickers in habits of scarlet cloth. More likely, however, is that it began in the days of Queen Anne, when scarlet coats were usually worn by country gentlemen, who naturally rode to hounds in them. It probably became more widely popular when military men who had served in the Peninsula Wars rode in their smart scarlet in the hunting field. Hunting coats in other colours are worn by the Masters and hunt servants of family packs such as the Beaufort green and the Berkeley tawny yellow.

Scawbrig bridle A bitless schooling bridle.

Scent, fox's Hounds rarely see the fox, but hunt it by a scent which it gives off from glands just under the brush (chief source), and from the pads (feet). This is imparted in the form of an oily substance to any object touched by the fox, but hounds may receive some of it as it is carried in the air. The scent is best when the temperature of the ground is higher than that of the air. It is believed that a vixen in cub leaves no scent and is therefore practically immune from being hunted.

Sceptre A daughter of the 1896 Derby winner, Persimmon, she was out of Ornament, a full sister to Ormonde. She was one of only two fillies to win four Classics races – the 1000 and 2000 Guineas, the Oaks, and the St Leger, all in 1902. She also won the Jockey Club Stakes, the Hardwicke Stakes, and the Champion Stakes.

Schaukel Dressage movement in which the horse is required to step alternately backwards and forwards for a prescribed number of steps without halting.

Schleswig-Holstein Developed about the same time as the Rhenish-German Heavy Horse (q.v.), the Schleswig-Holstein is the smaller of the two, standing between 15.2 and 16hh (157.5-162.6 cm). The province of Schleswig-Holstein has been in both German and Danish ownership, and much Danish Jutland blood (q.v.) was used in the development of the breed. Lighter blood, such as Thoroughbred, Yorkshire Coach, and Cleveland Bay, was introduced at the end of the nineteenth century, to the overall detriment of the breed. As with the Rhenish-German, numbers declined dangerously after World War I, but revived after World War II, until mechanisation once again reduced the breed to a few hundreds in the 1970s. Since then, a great effort has been made to increase and improve the stock – the latter by the use of Breton and Boulonnais blood. More recently, Jutland blood has been used to increase substance and height.

School The area – open, enclosed, or enclosed and covered – in which a horse, ridden or otherwise, is exercised or trained. Also the exercise carried out by a horse with or without its rider for education or training. (See **Manège**)

Schooled Term applied to a steeplechaser, hurdler or hunter who has been ridden at home over fences that he is likely to meet in his work. A horse is also said to be 'schooled' or 'well-schooled' when he has been trained for his work.

School figures Movements performed by horse and rider, including the diagonal change of hand, counter change of hand, reversed change of hands, half-volte, volte or circle, figure-of-eight, serpentine and others.

Schooling The training of a horse for the task for which he is intended.

School paces Collected paces (walk, trot, canter) loftier in step and more perfect in cadence than normal paces.

School riding Riding exercises of the classical school. Alternatively, any work done in a riding school (see **Manège**).

Scissors Horse scissors used for trimming have curved blades, occasionally bent shanks, and always blunted points. Tail scissors are long and straight, like paperhanger's scissors, and are used only to cut the tail to the required length.

Scorrier snaffle Also called 'Cornish snaffle'. A 'strong' bit with four rings, the inner pair set in slots within the serrated mouthpiece. The design encourages a strong squeezing action against the lower jaw.

Scorrier snaffle bit.

Scouring Diarrhoea, i.e. loose, very moist faeces, arising from increased gut activity. There is a variety of causes, including inflammation of the intestine (enteritis), incorrect diet, bacterial or viral infection, and poisons. It is a potentially serious condition in foals, as they are often unable to deal with the fluid loss, leading to dehydration, coma and death. Minor and short-lived scouring during the dam's foaling heat is usually normal; it is due to additional substances in the mare's milk at that time.

Infective white scouring may occur one to two days after birth, in which the foal's buttocks become covered with evil-smelling, yellow-grey faeces. It is caused by a bacterial infection of the gut, for which veterinary attention is required.

Scowling Laying back the ears and perhaps showing the whites of the eyes.

Scratching When a cowboy rides a buckjumper at a rodeo he spurs his horse's sides with a continuous raking or 'Scratching' motion, backwards and forwards.

This is compulsory in all rodeo bucking contests.

Scratching (racing) Taking a horse which is lame, unfit, etc. out of a race for which there is a declaration of forfeit.

'Screw' A derogatory term implying an inferior, unsound or worn-out horse. A superior horse can be termed a screw if suffering from some unsoundness which does not affect its usefulness: e.g. whistling.

Scrotum The purse or sac which holds the testes, located between the thighs.

'Scrub, to' (racing) To try to get the best out of a horse who is lazy or unwilling or nearing the end of his tether. A horse often has to be 'scrubbed along' to keep his place in a field. This is done by the jockey moving his lower legs backwards and forwards in time with the horse's stride, and by wielding his whip so that the horse can see it, but without actually touching the animal's flanks.

Scurry A timed show-jumping competition over medium-sized obstacles. The competitor is judged over the whole course, and a specified number of seconds for any faults is added to the time taken. Refusals are not penalised, as they automatically increase the overall time. The competitor taking the least time, including any penalties, wins.

Scurry (USA) A short, quick hunting run or race on horseback.

Scut The tail of a hare.

Season, racing See **Racing season**.

Seasons, hunting See **Hunting seasons**.

Seat The position of the rider in the saddle.

Seat (of saddle) The part between the head and the cantle on which the rider sits.

Seat, classic/basic The modern seat for riding on the flat requires the rider to sit squarely, with the seat bones on the lowest point of the saddle and the hip bones pushed slightly forward so that the pelvis supports the weight of the upper body. The legs should hang down naturally, with the thighs flat on the saddle, the knees and toes pointing to the front,

the ball of the foot resting squarely on the stirrup, the heel a little lower than the toe. The upper arms should hang straight down, and the forearm, hands, and wrist should be held so that there is a straight line from the elbow through the hands to the horse's mouth. Seen from the side, a vertical line should run through the rider's ear, shoulder, hips, and heel. From front or rear, the rider is seen to be sitting squarely, with his head up.

Seat, balanced A rider's seat on a horse is said to be balanced when he is completely independent of any need of support by the reins, and when he is able to follow the horse's movements smoothly and without disturbance.

Seat, forward A style of riding over jumps first put into practice by Captain Federico Caprilli of the Italian Army. The knee, firmly and immovably in one place on the saddle, is the central pivot. The knee should be pointed and the leathers sufficiently short to give a definite 'feel' of the stirrups. The lower leg is bent backwards to a point where the foot remains behind a perpendicular line drawn from the knee downwards. The toe is held up and pointing slightly outwards, with the heel down. The rider does not sit in the saddle but rides on the fork, and during a jump he rests on the stirrup irons. He leans forward with hollow loins and not with a rounded back.

Seat, hunting Until the early years of this century the hunting seat was achieved by the use of long leathers and sitting right down in the saddle behind the line of balance. To take a fence riders would lean forward at take-off, and lie right back on landing. The modern seat has increasingly become the balanced seat required in scientific equitation. This indicates the shorter stirrup leather with the legs 'hanging' more naturally by the horse's sides and the rider sitting forward at the jump. On landing, the overall tendency is to sit balanced lightly and predominantly 'off' the saddle.

Seat, Western Straight, upright, and long-legged seat favoured by the American cowboy. It is based on balance, with very little grip, and the rider rarely 'posts' (rises to the trot).

Seating The hollowed-out part of the bearing surface of a shoe; thus a 'seated-out' shoe (q.v.) bears only on the wall of the foot.

Seaweed In its concentrated powder/meal form this is used as a feed additive. It contains the essential trace element iodine, of which the average horse requires 0.10 mg per day. Some areas of the world are severely iodine-deficient: e.g. Derbyshire in the United Kingdom; the Dakotas, Michigan, California, Colorado, Illinois, Montana, Utah, Washington, Wisconsin, New York, Iowa, and Indiana in the United States. In these areas either meal or iodised salt is fed. However, if fed to pregnant mares, excess iodine can cause toxicity and goitre in foals.

Second thigh See **Gaskin**.

Second wind See **Comes again**.

Secretariat An outstanding American racehorse, by Bold Ruler out of Somethingroyal by Princequillo. Winner of the US Triple Crown (q.v.). He raced for only two years, and set a record for the Kentucky Derby in 1973 of 1 min. 59.4 secs. He retired to stud in 1973 having won $1,316,808.

Segundo, Don Juan A Spanish authority on bridles, bits, and spurs, on which he wrote a treatise, dedicated to King George IV. (See **Segundo Bit** below).

Segundo bit One of the series of curb and pelham bits invented by Juan Segundo. Common to all of them is the large heart-shaped port designed to accommodate the tongue. In all cases the cheeks revolve independently of the mouthpiece.

Selby, James (1844-1888) A well-known and popular professional driver of London coaches. He was proprietor of the Old Times Coach, which ran between London and Brighton. In 1888 he made history by accomplishing a double journey in under eight hours.

Selby apron Worn below the Selby coaching cape (see below), and fastened at the waist with a strap and buckle. Named after James Selby (q.v., above).

Selby cape A short, loose, double-breasted, sleeved cape of box-cloth, worn, when coaching in bad weather, outside the apron so as to shoot off the rain. See **Selby, James**, above.

Selfing Breeding true to type.

Selle Français/Cheval de Selle Français/French Saddle Horse A composite term, originating in 1958, used to describe nineteen different kinds of crossbred riding horses found in the various French provinces. The Selle Français Stud Book was founded in 1965, and incorporates all the former local stud books. The breed has been developed by the crossing of English Thoroughbreds and half-bred stallions with native mares, together with Arab and Anglo-Arab and French Trotter blood, to produce a quality performance horse. There are five classifications, according to height and weight – *small*, *medium* and *large mediumweight*, ranging from under 15.3 hh (160 cm) to over 16.1 hh (162.5 cm); and *small* and *large heavyweights*, ranging from under 16 hh (162.6 cm) to over 16 h. Chestnut predominates, but all colours are permissible.

Selling handicap See **Handicap** and **Selling race**.

Selling race A race in which the winner must be offered for sale at auction immediately after the race. It is usually for horses of small ability.

Semi-mail phaeton See **Demi-mail phaeton**.

'Send on', to To arrange the transporting of hunters to a meet in advance of their riders.

Senner An extinct breed of pony which lived in the Teutonburg Forest of Hanover.

Sensory nerves These exist all over a horse's body. When they are touched they actuate movement of various muscles and produce locomotion.

Serge See **Saddle serge**.

Serpent tail A term used when the curve of the dock is concave instead of convex.

Service The mating of a mare with a stallion. (See **Stint**).

Service collar A padded leather collar which protects a mare from being bitten by a stallion during service.

Service hobbles See **Hobbles**.

Sesamoiditis Inflammation of the sesamoid bones and/or the sesamoid sheath. It is caused by faulty conformation, such as turned-out toes, excessive strain – as in pulling up suddenly, or jumping drop fences. The symptoms are heat and swelling over the flexor tendons, and lameness. In severe cases the horse will not bring the affected heel to the ground. Veterinary advice is required, but there is no permanent cure.

Sesamoids Two small bones situated at the back of the fetlock, forming part of that joint. The two branches of the suspensory ligament are attached to the sesamoids.

Set-fair, to To put down a horse's bed.

Setfast See **Azoturia**.

Set-tail A cruel fashion, popular in the USA, of breaking and setting the tails of saddle horses to give a high and showy tail carriage. The operation is painful and deprives the horse of the use of the tail as a protection against flies.

Setter Apparatus with a movable arm which when placed under the axle of a vehicle raises the wheels so that they can be washed.

Seymour, James (1702-1752) Painter of hunting, racing and other sporting scenes, and also of sporting portraits. His work is almost as well known as that of his friend John Wootton (q.v.). Some of his paintings were engraved. A Londoner of good family and means, Seymour took up art as a profession after losing money on the turf. Though his horses have the stiffness of all the artists of the period, his best work shows him to be a talented draughtsman.

Shabrack/Shabraque A trooper's housing or saddle-cloth. (See **Housing**)

Shadbelly (Swallowtail or cutaway) Tight-fitting double-breasted hunting coat in either scarlet or black, with high-cut front and sides cut away into tails.

Named after hard-riding members of the Pytchley Hunt.

Shadowroll See **Noseband, sheepskin**.

Shafts The bars between which a horse is harnessed in any single-horse vehicle.

Shagya Arabian See **Hungarian Shagya**.

Shanderidan A four-wheeled pair-horse vehicle of the waggonette type used for private parties at race meetings and picnics. The coachman operated the brakes by means of a long lever.

Shandrydan A light two-wheeled cart originating in Ireland, where the name is still sometimes used to denote a shabby or rickety conveyance.

Shanks See **Cannon bone**.

Shannon (bone) The cannon bone of the hindleg.

Shan Pony See **Burmese**.

Sharatz Piebald charger of Prince Marko of Serbia in the fourteenth century. Their exploits against the Turkish oppressors figure in many legends and epic poems of the Balkans.

Shayer, William J. (1811-1860) Born in Southampton, son of William Shayer, Snr. Painter of animal, sporting and coaching subjects. The roads of southern England generally formed the background of his coaching scenes.

Sheath A loose fold of skin situated in front of the scrotum (q.v.), containing the front and free portion of the penis, and with the anterior end open.

Shedding coat See **Casting coat**.

Shelly A term applied to the hollow in a newly cut incisor teeth.

Shelt A Highland pony used by deer-stalkers to carry carcases.

'Sheltie' See **Shetland Pony**.

Shetland Pony (Popular name 'Sheltie'.) The smallest of all breeds of pony, this is nevertheless the strongest member of the equine world in relation to its size. Records of its strength are legion, and a well-known story tells of a pony regularly carrying a 2½ cwt (127 kg) sack of meal 26 miles (41 km) across country.

The Shetland's origin is uncertain, but records of its existence in the islands north of Scotland, after which it is named, date back many centuries. Its diminutive size is thought to be due to the severe climate and poor living, but ponies of this type bred in kinder climates rarely grow over height. In the Shetlands they are used as saddle and pack ponies. Considerable demand from the coal pits caused breeding to flourish, but little attempt at selective breeding was made until the middle-to-late nineteenth century.

The Shetland is a very hardy pony, strong-willed, but biddable if handled correctly. It makes an ideal riding pony for children, and goes very well in harness, competing in FEI combined driving events. It is of pleasing appearance, with a typical pony head, bearing neat, small ears and large kindly eyes; the compact little body is supported by short legs. The mane is abundant, as is the forelock and tail. Height limits (traditionally expressed in inches) are 40 ins (101.5 cm) at three years old and 42 ins (106.5 cm) at four years and over. All colours are accepted (including piebalds and skewbalds – 'broken colours'), but black is the most common.

Shetland Pony Stud Book Society Founded in 1890 to encourage the breeding of pedigree Shetland ponies.

Shillibeer In 1829 George Shillibeer (1797-1866), an Englishman who had been a coachbuilder in Paris, introduced the first public omnibus in England. It started from 'The Yorkshire Stingo' at Paddington, London, and ran to the Bank of England and back at a single fare of one shilling. It was roomy and comfortable, and was drawn by three horses abreast. Its success was immediate and Shillibeer put others into service – calling them 'omnibuses' – but many competitors followed his example and he was ruined. When practising as an undertaker, he also introduced a new form of hearse, which bore his name.

Shim A dialect word for a white mark. In East Anglia it is often used instead of blaze (q.v.).

Shin bone See **Cannon bone**.

Shin boot A foreleg boot worn by steeplechasers to prevent the shins being knocked when jumping; or protective boots worn on all legs when jumping.

Shins, sore (periostitis) Inflammation of the *periosteum* (membrane covering the bone) of the front of the cannon bone. Occurs mostly in young racehorses and is caused by concussion, a blow, strain, or infection. There is pain, swelling, and heat. Veterinary advice is required.

Shippon A stable or cowshed.

Shirazi A pony found in Persia. Known as the 'Gulf Arab'. (See **Persian Horse**)

Shire In height and weight the Shire is the greatest of England's agricultural and trade horses. It is believed by some to be a survivor of the type known as the Great Horse used in mediaeval times, when riders with armour could weigh as much as 30 stone (420 lb; 190.5 kg). It has great strength and stamina, allied to docility, and was developed for heavy draught work in the fields and on the roads. After World War II its numbers in Britain dropped alarmingly, and by 1968 the combined breed show of Shires and Percherons had fewer than one hundred entries. Fortunately a considerable revival has taken place and the breed is no longer in danger.

Shires were first exported to the USA in 1883, and for the next eight or so years hundreds were sent, many of poor quality. The trade ceased during the depression years of the 1890s and, although it revived to some extent, the Americans found that they did not like the excessive feather on the Shire's legs. In recent years, however, the export market has opened up again, and a significant number of Shires have crossed the Atlantic. They were exported to Australia in the first ten years of this century, but proved unsuitable for Australian working conditions. Recently, interest has revived, and there are now a small number, mostly in New South Wales. Standing over 17 hh (170 cm), weighing 1 ton to 22 cwt (1.016-1.117 tonne), they are slow workers but can pull immense weights. Bays and browns predominate; blacks and greys are also seen. The shoulders should be deep and oblique, wide across the chest; hindquarters should be full-muscled. Shires often have white on the feet and lower legs, which also carry much silky fine hair ('feathers').

Shire Horse Society Founded in 1878 to promote the Old English Breed of Cart Horse (the name by which the breed was formerly known).

Shires, the (Also known as the 'Hunting Shires') Midland counties of England, which include Leicestershire, Warwickshire, Northamptonshire and parts of Lincolnshire. Shire packs are: Pytchley, Quorn, Fernie, Belvoir and Cottesmore.

Shivering An affliction of the nervous system with involuntary muscular contractions, usually of the hindlegs. It is a progressive condition and has no cure. It should not be confused with the shivering which is due to cold or excitement, or with the normal shivering of a foal for the first couple of hours after birth.

Shod too close A farriery term for driving a nail so close to the sensitive part of the foot that it presses against it. Known also as 'nail-bind'.

Shoe, bar A shoe suitable for a horse with weak heels. It is an ordinary shoe which has a bar connecting the heels, which presses on the frog. The hind surface of the bar is bevelled to reduce concussion, while the bar itself takes the weight off the weak heels and transfers it to the frog. It has the disadvantage of heaviness, thus

requiring more nails, and of providing a poorer foothold, thus restricting its use to horses working at slow paces.

Shoe, for capped elbows A shoe with a short, narrow inner heel may be used, but the condition is more easily prevented by use of a sausage boot (q.v.).

Shoe, for carriage horse These formerly consisted of plain fullered shoes in front and plain stamped shoes with calkins behind. Modern practice is to shoe with concave fullered shoes all round, with a calkin or stud on each hind heel.

Shoe, for draught horse Shoes vary according to the work done, but for general purposes, plain stamped shoes are used – generally with thickened toes – and with calkins behind.

Shoe, feather-edged (An exaggerated knocked-up shoe – q.v.). A shoe of which the inside edges are narrowed, bevelled and rounded, to avoid brushing. The wall of the foot on the inside protrudes over the shoe. It is sometimes used on horses with turned out toes. It wears quickly.

Shoe, fullered A shoe with a groove round the ground surface where the nail holes are placed, which grips the ground. The inside edge should be concave, to eliminate suction from the ground in

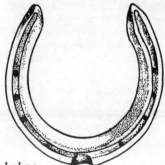

Fullered shoe.

deep going, and to prevent over-reaches. A concave-fullered shoe is the most commonly used for general purposes on riding horses.

Shoe, knocked-up A shoe in which the inner branch is narrow and the ground surface slopes downwards and inwards and is rounded off. A calkin on the hind shoe is replaced by a wedge heel. It is

Bar shoe.

used on horses which brush with the toe or with a mid-quarter shoe.

Shoe, patten A shoe with a wide, raised bar across its heel. It can be used on a horse with a sprained tendon to raise the heel and reduce pain. Also known as a 'platten' shoe.

Shoe, plain stamped A shoe with no fullering.

Shoe, polo In Great Britain these must comply with Hurlingham Polo Association rules, which allow rims and fixed or movable calkins, but not frost nails or screws. Rimmed shoes have a ground surface with a sharp rim around the inside edge to give a good grip on turf. Rimmed shoes are rarely used today. Modern polo ponies are commonly shod with concave fullered hunting shoes with the heels of the hind shoes tapped for studs.

Shoe, rocker-bar A wide-webbed shoe with a curved surface, usually thicker at the quarters and thinner at the toes and heels. It has some use in treating laminitis, as it reduces concussion.

Shoe, rolled-toe A shoe in which half the width of the web at the toe is 'set up' or 'rolled' at an angle, and which has slightly raised heels. It is used to prevent stumbling.

Shoe, rope This has a groove on the ground surface in which rests a tarred rope, the purpose being to lessen the possibility of the horse slipping on smooth pavements. Special long-headed nails are used.

Shoe, saucer A shoe which has had so much of its ground surface hollowed out that it bears only on the outer surface of the wall of the foot. Designed as a treatment for dropped sole, it is injurious and may induce coronitis. It is rarely, if ever, used nowadays.

Shoe, seated-out Where the sole of a horse's foot tends to weakness, a seated-out shoe may be used. It is slightly hollowed, thus avoiding pressure on the sole, and throwing all the shoe's bearing surface on the wall of the foot. This type of shoe has the disadvantage that stones, etc. accumulate under it, and it is inclined to be sucked off in heavy going.

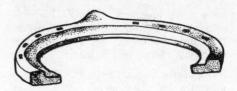

Seated-out shoe.

Shoe, for speedy cutting A shoe with the inner branch straightened from toe to quarter, and with the outer surface rounded off.

Shoe, threequarter Formerly used for shoeing feet affected with corns, or to prevent brushing, capped elbow, and cutting. Not recommended in modern farriery.

Shoe, threequarter bar A shoe with a bar across the heel, and 1-1½ ins (2.5-3.8 cm) cut off *one* heel. It can be used for treating corns, as it relieves the pressure on the corn while still supporting the heel.

Shoe-boil Capped elbow (q.v.).

Shoeing Making, fitting and fixing shoes to the feet of a horse.

OUTLINE OF STAGES IN SHOEING When the old shoe has been removed, the farrier prepares the hoof for the new one by removing the overgrowth of the wall to the correct length, and trimming ragged pieces from the frog and the sole. The rasp is then used to ensure a level bearing surface. The new shoe is fitted (preferably by 'hot shoeing'). The hot shoe is briefly applied to the hoof and the burning of the horn shows if adjustments are necessary. The shoe is cooled in water, then nailed on to the hoof. When this is completed, the clenches are smoothed with the rasp, and tapped down. The toe clips are tapped into place, and the rasp is finally used lightly on the lower wall to reduce the risk of cracking.

CORRECT FITTING OF SHOES The following five points are important when examining a newly-shod horse. Without lifting the foot, check: (1) The front and hind feet should be pairs, being the same size and shape, and with the same pastern foot axis. (NB: some horses, like some humans, have odd feet, and this should have been noted.) (2) The clenches should be even, flat and broad; the nails placed higher at the toe than the heel, and not driven into old nail holes or cracks. (3) There should be no rasping of the wall other than the small amount required when the clenches are smoothed. (4) No dumping (q.v.) should be present. (5) The clips should be low and broad, and the toe clip centred. (6) The shoe must fit the outline of the foot. (7) The heels must be of the correct length: i.e. to the end of the horn.

On lifting the foot check that: (1) The toe clip is centred and in line with the point of the frog. (2) The nails are driven home and the heads fit the countersunk holes correctly. (3) There is no excessive paring of the frog and sole. (4) The heels are not opened up, i.e. the bars are not cut out. (5) The shoe fits the foot, and the heels allow the frog to function correctly. (6) The sole has been eased at the seat of corns. (7) There is no space between the foot and the shoe. (8) The shoe is properly finished off.

Shoeing block A tripod on which a horse's foot is placed for certain shoeing processes. It is also known as a 'foot stool'.

Shoeing cage See **Trave**.

Shoeing forge (or Farrier's Shop) A forge in which only horseshoeing is practised by farriers, consisting of a fireman who makes and fits the shoes, and a doorman who prepares the feet, nails on the shoes, finishes them off (clenches up), and helps to make new shoes.

Shoes, removal of Shoes should be removed about every four weeks, otherwise the horse suffers from pinching caused by the growth of the horn of the hoof.

'Shooting your wheelers' Sending the wheelers (q.v.) or leaders in a coach team into their collars in order to draw the weight of the load.

Short 'Going short' implies restricted action, indicating some discomfort and probably lameness.

Short-coupled A term denoting a horse that is short and deep in the body with well-sprung ribs.

'Short of a rib' There is a marked space between the last rib and the point of the hip, showing a sign of slackness over the loins. This condition is found in horses of defective conformation, i.e. too long a back, hindquarters standing too far back.

'Short of blood' See **'Out of blood'**.

'Short of bone' See **Cannon bone**.

Short Tommy A short, stiff, leather thong, some 3 ft (91 cm) in length, for use on wheel-horses of a coach. Often used by box-seat passengers while the coachman was using his thong on the leaders of a team to extricate the coach from ruts and boggy patches. About 1828 Short Tommy fell into disuse, owing to the improving state of the roads.

Shoulder, point of The point immediately over the joint between the extreme lower end of the shoulder blade and the humerus, or upper arm.

Shoulder, sloping This runs obliquely from the point of the shoulder to the withers. In theory, the more sloping the shoulder, the better the ride.

Shoulder, straight A less oblique type than the above. The harness horse should have shoulders tending to straightness, being a draught horse, where the position and set of the neck collar is very important. A Hackney intended for show must have oblique shoulders for the up-and-out action which is now demanded.

Shoulder-in The horse, evenly bent round the rider's inside leg, moves at an angle of about 30° to the direction of movement. The inside front leg crosses in front of the outside front leg, and the inside hind is placed in front of the outside hind. The horse looks away from the direction in which it is moving. The movement is the basis of all lateral work. See diagram on next page.

Shoulder lameness To test for lameness, each leg is pulled forwards and backwards two or three times. If the horse rears or flinches he is probably in pain. For a further test, the horse is trotted up and down hill. Lameness in the shoulder will become more acute when ascending the hill, whereas foot lameness will be

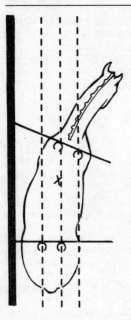

Shoulder-in (see previous page).

more apparent in the downward trot. In fore-limb lameness very careful attention must be paid to the foot before diagnosing shoulder lameness. A veterinary surgeon should be consulted.

'Shouldering the pole' An old coaching term describing the act of one of the wheelers (q.v.) pushing the pole against his partner.

Show bridle (riding) A very light, elegant bridle, either hook-studded or, more probably, sewn to the bits. Snap billets can also be used as a means of attachment.

Show bridle (stallion) A substantial brass-mounted bridle with swelled noseband and cheeks. It can be fitted with a coloured front and leather or brass rosettes.

'Showing too much daylight' See 'On the leg'.

Show jumping The first *recorded* show-jumping competition in Britain took place in 1876 at the Agricultural Hall, Islington in London, although the sport had been in existence at agricultural shows throughout the country for many years. This event had been preceded by some eleven years by competitions at the

Royal Dublin Society's show in Ireland, in Russia, and in Paris in 1866. In those days, the sport was very different from the modern version, and the result was determined solely on the rider's style. In spite of its limitations, the popularity of the sport spread, particularly in Europe, and gradually the rules were altered to place more emphasis on jumping ability than style. Courses were little more than plain fences down either side of the ring, with, perhaps, a water jump in the centre. Slats, all too easily displaced, were placed on top of the fences, and, as riders were not penalised for time penalties, jumping was extremely slow, with circling in front of fences both permitted and much practised.

Show jumping was included in the Olympic Games for the first time in 1912, and the rules became even more complicated. Each fence on the course was allotted 10 marks, with deductions being made as follows: first refusal – 2; second refusal, or fall of horse and rider – 4; third refusal or fall of rider – 6. Marks were also deducted for hitting the fences, with double deduction for hitting with the forelegs. It is no surprise to learn that each fence had its own judge. Sweden won the first Olympic team gold, France the silver, and Germany the bronze.

Following the formation of the FEI (q.v.) in 1921, the rules (qq.v.) were simplified, and, to a large extent, standardised, even though slats were still in vogue in Britain after World War II.

In Britain, the British Show Jumping Association (q.v.) was founded in 1923, with Lord Lonsdale as President and Colonel V. D. S. Williams as Secretary. This set the sport on the real road to success, and riders who were to become household names began to emerge, contributing enormously to the spread of the sport. One of the great riders of the pre-World War II era was Colonel Jack Talbot-Ponsonby, who won the first of his three King George V Gold Cups (q.v.) in 1930, and went on to become a highly successful trainer and coursebuilder after the War. Colonel Talbot-Ponsonby represented Britain before the Second World War in the increasing number of international events, and was joined by Colonel Mike Ansell, who with justification, has been described as the chief architect of modern show jumping in Britain. It was Colonel Ansell, who, following World War II (in which he was blinded) became Chairman of the BSJA in 1944. He and his committee set about putting show jumping on the map as a spectator sport in Britain. They clarified the rules, introduced the grading of horses (q.v.), chose the White City as the venue of the first big show-jumping show, and, perhaps even more significantly, were instrumental (with Tony Collings, Colonel V. D. S. Williams and others) in founding the Horse of the Year show (q.v.), first held at Harringay in London in 1949.

Although horse shows had been televised since 1947, it is generally accepted that the duel for the Puissance at the Horse of the Year Show in 1950, between Pat Smythe on the tiny Finality, who was little more than a pony, and Colonel Harry Llewellyn on the 17 hh (170 cm) Foxhunter, established show jumping as a major spectator sport in Britain. From that time onwards, riders such as Pat Smythe, Harry Llewellyn, Wilf White, and Peter Robeson, with horses such as Finality, Foxhunter, Nizefella and Craven A, became household names. The rapid rise in popularity of the sport in Britain (aided by a team gold medal at the 1952 Helsinki Olympics) was matched (and had, in fact, been preceded) by the European countries. D'Oriola of France, Goyoaga of Spain, the d'Inzeo brothers from Italy, and Thiedemann from Germany, were among the great stars of the post-war era, who became nearly as well known in Britain as in their own countries. These great riders and horses were succeeded, inevitably, by other famous names – David Broome, Harvey Smith, Marion Mould, Caroline Bradley – to name but a few.

Internationally, the most noticeable feature, however, was the remarkable domination by West Germany. In the Olympics they took the team gold medal in 1956, 1960, 1964, and 1972, the bronze in 1968 and the silver in 1976. More Olympic history was made in the 1956 Stockholm Olympics, when Pat Smythe became the first woman to compete, and to win a team medal (bronze). International show jumping expanded enormously. Individual European Men's,

Women's and Junior championships were founded in 1957 (the two former combining after 1973; the Men's World championship began in 1953, and the Women's in 1965; now, of course men and women compete in single competitions at all levels.

In the last fifteen or so years show jumping in Britain has been dominated by the professional riders. In 1975, all countries affiliated to the FEI were required to designate riders as either amateur or professional (qq.v.) – the latter being ineligible for the Olympics. The British authorities felt (correctly) that the rules left them no option but to designate most of the top riders as professionals. Most other European governing bodies applied a more liberal interpretation to the rules, which left Britain at a considerable disadvantage in subsequent Olympic games.

The more general acceptance of professionalism has had a considerable impact on the sport. Sponsorship of riders and horses is widespread, and indeed, essential. Sponsorship of individual classes and of whole shows is also a vital ingredient of the modern show-jumping scene.

Another major change has been in the length and character of the show-jumping season. Formerly restricted (in Britain) almost exclusively to the summer agricultural show season, the proliferation of indoor arenas and the popularity of major indoor shows, such as the Horse of the Year Show in October, has resulted in the sport continuing virtually non-stop throughout the year. The riders have had to make considerable adjustments; no horse can jump throughout the year, and a number of the top professionals now have what amounts, virtually, to 'indoor' and 'outdoor' horses. See also **Hickstead**; **Grading of horses**; **Show jumping in the USA**; and **Show jumping in Australia**.

Show jumping in the USA Jumping classes are a part of almost all general shows in America. The American Horse Show Association, the sport's ruling body, divides 'jumper' classes into two categories: the first awarding penalties for 'touches' and 'rubs', as well as knock-downs; the second being ridden under the more familiar (to Europeans) system. The horses ridden by American show jumpers have long been the envy of European riders, as they are nearly all fine Thoroughbred or threequarter bred animals, with great scope and suppleness. The riders, too, are much admired for their quiet, easy style, developed over years of coaching by their great national trainer, Bert de Nemethy (now retired). Riders of the calibre of Frank Chapot, William Steinkraus, George Morris, Kathy Kusner, and Neal Shapiro were all world class.

Riders in America travel much longer distances to compete around their domestic circuit than do their British counterparts. February and March sees the top competitors in Florida, whence they move to Virginia for the Upperville show, and on to Ox Ride, Connecticut, in May. During the summer the principal shows include Lake Placid, and in September there is the American Gold Cup in Philadelphia, and the American Jumping Derby in Harrisburgh, Pennsylvania. Close on the heels of these shows are the autumn competitions at Washington DC, the National Horse show in New York, and then the Toronto Winter Fair in Canada. There are, of course, many other smaller shows, at which the novice rider and horse may compete.

American teams have tended to come to Europe for the season leading up to an Olympics to gain more international experience, possibly a factor in their success. They have competed in fifteen out of the sixteen Olympic Games from 1912-1984 – more than any other country. They won the team bronze in Helsinki in 1952, the team silver in Rome, 1960, and again in Munich, 1972, and won the gold in Los Angeles in 1984. Individually, they have won the silver in 1932, the gold in Mexico, 1968, the bronze in 1972, and the gold and silver in 1984. In the World Championships they won the team bronze in 1978 and the gold in 1986.

Show jumping in Australia The sport is very popular, with classes of all standards at major shows. In past years, high jumping was a great crowd-puller, with the horses tackling a single huge fence. An unofficial world record of 8 ft 6 ins (258 cm) was jumped by Gold Meade, ridden by Jack Martin in 1946, but these competitions have largely been dropped following allegations of cruelty in training. The more traditional style show jumping has flourished, and the first Australian Olympic team competed in Tokyo in 1964. Further teams have followed and performed well, but without actually winning a medal. A number of individual Australian riders have travelled abroad to compete with considerable success in Britain, Europe and North America.

Show Jumper of the Year, Leading Annual competition at the Horse of the Year Show (q.v.), Wembley.

Show jumping, abbreviated FEI rules (1) There are no marks for style. (2) Knocking down a fence with either fore or hindlegs – 4 faults. (3) Refusals: these are cumulative and the third refusal in the whole round eliminates the competitor; first refusal – 3 faults; second refusal – 6 faults; (4) Fall of horse or rider – 8 faults. (5) A certain speed for each competition is required, and the time allowed for the course is announced. Exceeding the time allowed is penalised at the rate of ¼ fault for every second or part of a second. The time limit is double the time allowed, and exceeding the time limit is always penalised by elimination.

Show pony See **Riding Pony**.

Show presentation, Arabs
IN-HAND STALLIONS: No pulling, plaiting or trimming of manes or tails, no thinning or clipping of heels. Quarter markings are undesirable. The Arab's natural beauty must not be altered. The show bridle should be brown stitched leather with fixed noseband, brass buckles, coloured or plain browband, a stallion bit with half-moon or straight bar with fixed rings. A leather or white webbing lead is attached to the bit according to the stallion's behaviour.
IN-HAND MARES: As above as to plaiting, pulling, trimming, etc. Use the lightest possible leather bridle and bit, or a brass-mounted headcollar. Lead as above.
RIDDEN ARABS: For stallions, mares or geldings the mane and tail should be unpulled and unplaited. A light, short cheek double bridle with ½ in. (12.7 mm) or ⅜ in. (16 mm) reins is the most suitable, with

no martingale. A fairly straight-fronted leather saddle is best.

Show presentation, Hackneys

IN-HAND CLASSES: Plaiting, pulling and trimming as for hacks, hunters, etc. A show bridle of black stitched leather with fixed noseband and brass buckles; with a coloured or plain browband. A stallion bit, with either a half-moon or straight bar with fixed rings. A leather or white webbing lead attached to the bit. *Yearlings*: Manes plaited. Shown in a halter. *Two and three-year-old fillies, and brood mares*: Manes plaited, bridle with short-cheeked curb bit. *Two- and three-year old colts and stallions*: Manes plaited. Stallion tack and brown side and bearing reins.

HARNESS CLASSES: Manes thinned (never hogged) to produce even length of 4-5 ins (101-127 mm), with twelve to twenty small, neat plaits. Tails should not be cut, plaited or thinned, but washed well and brushed. Long hairs on the heels, ears and lips should be trimmed. Maximum weight of shoes: ponies not exceeding 14 hh (142.2 cm) – 1½ lb (0.67 kg); horses exceeding 14 hh – 2 lbs (0.9 kg). Lightweight black leather harness with brass mountings, and brown reins toned to a dark shade are used. A black browband with a small brass chain is preferred. No martingales are worn. Kay collars (q.v.) are correct for all two-wheeled vehicles and pairs. It is optional for the lead horse in a tandem to wear either a Kay or a breastcollar, but the former is preferable. Breast pieces are essential with Kay collars, optional with breast-collars. An overcheck is usually worn. A lightweight holly whip is preferred.

Show presentation, hacks Manes are plaited, tails pulled or plaited, and heels and lips trimmed. A double bridle is preferable, but a pelham is permitted, although unusual. No martingales are used. A light leather saddle, straight cut to set off the shoulder is worn. Coloured browbands are permissible (usually made of strips of different coloured plastic). Elegance of appearance and turn-out is of the utmost importance. Note: hacks are not normally shown in-hand.

Show presentation, hunters

IN-HAND STALLIONS: Manes are plaited (seven or nine plaits, or, if preferred, as many as possible), tails are pulled or plaited, and the heels and long hair on lips and jaw trimmed. A brown, brass-mounted stallion bridle, of stitched leather with fixed noseband, a half-moon or straight bit, and plain (uncoloured) browband is usual. A lead of leather or white webbing attached to bit is used.

IN-HAND MARES: A double bridle with plain browband, or snaffle, but the former is preferred. Using only the curb bit and chain of the double bridle is permissible.

RIDDEN HUNTERS: Manes are plaited, and tails pulled or plaited, as above. A double bridle, with no martingale, and a fairly straight-fronted, leather saddle is customary. As for Arabs, the value of quarter-markings for hunters is debatable.

Show presentation, Mountain and Moorland ponies Under NPS (q.v.) Rules brood mares may be shown in a leather headcollar, a halter, or snaffle, pelham or double bridle; youngstock may be shown in a halter, leather headcollar or snaffle bridle; stallions and colts, two years old and over, must be adequately bitted. In all Open Mountain and Moorland classes, ridden and in-hand, ponies must be shown as recommended by their breed societies – this, in most instances, means in their natural state, without plaits, etc.

Show presentation, ridden cobs Pulling, plaiting and trimming for mares and geldings as for hunters, but cobs are usually shown with hogged manes. Note: cobs are not usually shown in-hand.

Show presentation, show ponies

IN-HAND CLASSES: Manes are pulled, plaiting is optional but desirable, tails are pulled or plaited, and heels and chins trimmed. A bridle or headcollar, narrow stitched with brass fittings on the headcollar, coloured browband, and a leather or white webbing leading rein is customary. For youngstock a snaffle half-moon showing bit is used, with joiners for a leading rein; for brood mares a double bridle with curb bit only, or a snaffle. Unbroken youngstock should be shown in a headcollar without a bit to prevent possible damage to the mouth. Elegance of appearance and turn-out is important.

RIDDEN SHOW PONIES: In *Leading Rein*, *Novice* and *Child's First Pony*, a snaffle bridle may be used, with a single rein. A leather saddle is suitable, or felt one with tree if the child is really small. A leather or white webbing leading rein is used. *12.2 hh class*: A double bridle with two reins if the child is a capable rider; or a pelham with a single rein, with roundings from the snaffle to the curb bit; or a Kimblewick; and a coloured or plain browband. Martingales are not acceptable. A leather saddle with a narrow white webbing girth is customary. *13.2 hh to 14.2 hh classes*: As above, but with double rein bridle. *All classes*: Single rein – ½ in. (12.7 mm); double rein – ½ in. (12.7 mm) top, ⅜ in. (16 mm) bottom recommended. Elegance of appearance and turn-out are important. Note: The British Show Pony Society permits a plain snaffle if it is considered suitable by owners: spurs are forbidden.

Show wagon A lightweight vehicle having bicycle wheels with fine wire spokes and pneumatic tyres, and to which Hackneys are driven in shows.

Shy feeder A horse with a fickle appetite, needing to be tempted with small, varied feeds – a little added salt is helpful. Such a horse should have most of its ration at night when all is quiet and there is nothing to distract it.

Shying This may be a dangerous vice at any time. Many theories have been advanced as to its cause, including defective eyesight, fear, temper inherited from ancestors, nervousness, intended playfulness, etc.

Siamese phaeton Unlike the ordinary phaeton (q.v.), this has two identical seats, one behind the other.

Sick See **Vomiting**.

Side bone A hereditary unsoundness under the 1918 Horsebreeding Act. It affects the lateral cartilage of the foot. Calcium salts are deposited in these, which in time become bony and immobile. It is more common in heavy horses but is also found in lighter breeds. Premature formation of the condition is probably caused by concussion due to excessive road work.

Side reins These are attached to the roller for training purposes, and are used by some trainers when lungeing young horses.

Side steps A term used to indicate any movement on two tracks, where the horse proceeds sideways to a certain extent.

Side-stick A strong stick fastened at one end of the bit and at the other to the surcingle; a device used when grooming a confirmed biter.

Side-strap See **Gaiting strap**.

Side-wheeling The side-to-side roll of a pacer when in motion – the lateral fore and hindlegs strike the ground in pairs.

Siena Races Correctly known as the Palio of Siena, this race was first run in 1482 to celebrate the return of the 'reformer citizens' to the government. It was established in 1659, and held twice yearly, in July and August, after 1701 (wars etc. excepted). The course is round the main square, and the race is preceded by a procession of great pageantry, with participants in fifteenth-century costumes. The riders represent different districts of the town, and there is enormous local interest and intrigue. The Palio is the Latin word for the painted silk banner presented to the winner.

Silage Grass and other green vegetable matter preserved in clamps with the addition of diluted molasses. The grass is cut at an earlier stage than for hay, and is therefore more nutritious. It spoils rapidly on the exposure to air. Horses, once they become accustomed to it, appear to enjoy it, and it can be used as a bulk food, usually mixed in equal parts with hay. It is becoming more popular. In Europe, a certain amount of maize (corn) silage is being used.

Silks Silks or racing silks are the jockey's jacket and cap, whether for racing on the flat or steeplechasing. Real silk has been replaced by silk-nylon (lightweight), which is more hardwearing and easier to launder. It is available in over a hundred colours and shades.

Silver ring The cheap and secondary betting enclosure on a racecourse where the smaller bookmakers operate.

Simplex irons Australian pattern of safety stirrup-iron. The outside section is shaped forward in a half-moon, and allows the foot to be released in an emergency.

Sinews See **Tendons**.

Singeing The removal of long hairs, which remain in various parts of the coat after clipping (q.v.), is carried out by lamp or gas flame. Since the introduction of electric clipping machines singeing is much less practised. The long bristle-like hairs about the eyes, nostrils or lips should never be singed.

Single bank A bank with a ditch on one side.

Single-foot A very fast walk of short steps with only one foot on the ground at a time. The horse must not break into a trot, but must travel at the highest possible speed.

Single-trees See **Bars**.

Sinking fox A very tired, hunted fox.

Sire Male parent of a horse or foal.

Sire, to To beget.

Sitfast A hard, painful swelling on the back, probably caused by an ill-fitting saddle or by pressure on an incompletely healed sore. A hard lump will be apparent which will increase in size the longer it is neglected. The sitfast may be cut out by a veterinary surgeon.

Skeleton break A four-wheeled vehicle for breaking horses to double harness; it has no bodywork behind the box-seat, but a small platform on which an assistant can stand.

Skeleton bridle A harness bridle without winkers (q.v.).

Skep See **Skip**.

Skewbald Where the skin bears large irregular patches of white hair and any definite colour except black. The line of demarcation is generally well defined. See also **Piebald**.

Skid-pan An iron shoe or platform on which the tyre of a wheel rests, fastened to a four-wheeled vehicle by a strong chain, which locks the near hind wheel on steep hills. The fitting of a skid-pan was compulsory under bye-laws of the Highways and Locomotives (Amendment) Act, 1878. Also called a 'slipper', 'drag-shoe', or 'wagon-lock'.

Skin In the horse, this most important structure consists of two layers: the outer epidermis which is covered with hair, and the inner dermis containing blood vessels, nerves, hair roots, and sweat and oil glands. It protects the 'inner horse' from infection, changes of temperature, etc.

Skip A wicker or plastic basket used in stables for collecting droppings. Also known as a 'skep'.

Skirt A hound which does not follow the true line of the fox, but cuts off corners, is said to skirt, or to be a skirter.

Skirt The lower and forward part of the saddle which covers and protects the rider from the metal spring bar.

Skowronek A famous Arabian stallion bred at Volhynia in Poland in 1909. A grey horse, by Ibrahim out of Yaskoulka, he was imported to England by the late Walter Winans. He was bought from him by H. V. Musgrave Clark and subsequently acquired from him by the late Lady Wentworth. His blood has had great influence on modern Arab breeding in England. See **Arab**.

Skull caps Under Rule 146, skull caps of a pattern approved by the Stewards of the Jockey Club must be worn. They consist of a fibre-class shell, with a shock-absorbing lining, and a chin-strap/harness. Skull caps are also worn by riders in the cross-country phase of horse trials, and a number of riders are now wearing them in show-jumping classes. They are in frequent use for everyday riding.

Skyros Pony A very small, ancient breed of pony (maximum height 11 hh (111.8 cm), found on the Aegean island of Skyros. They are extremely hardy, living out on the mountains, and some are caught up annually for use in threshing the corn at harvest time. A few are now used for racing, as a tourist attraction. The predominant colour is grey, with some duns, bays and browns.

Slab-sided See **Flat-sided**.

Slack in the loins A horse of weak loins. The last rib is short and too far from the point of the hip.

Sleep Horses sleep little (about seven hours out of twenty-four) and lightly, dozing for short spells only. Some horses never lie down – the reluctance to do so is a bad and incurable habit. Some old horses are unable to do so owing to the stiffness of the spine.

Sleepy foal disease A fatal bacterial disease of newborn foals. Its symptoms are sleepiness, weakness, fever, rapid breathing and failure to suck.

Slings A special form of harness employed to suspend, and thereby to rest, a very lame horse or one with badly damaged legs or feet. It consists of a band of stout canvas which encircles the belly, with a breastcollar and breeching to keep it in place. The upper ends of the canvas have sturdy metal bars with rings attached, and pulleys with ropes or chains are attached to the roof. It is also valuable for raising a cast horse.

Slip head The head strap and cheekpieces which support the bridoon in a double bridle. Also known as a bridoon slip head.

Slipper See **Skid-pan**.

Slipping point The point at which the rider starts to time a horse to get him into his stride for a jump.

Sloan, James Todhunter ('Tod') (1874-1933) An American jockey who, in 1897, brought to Britain the 'crouching' style of flat-race riding – the extreme forward seat with very short leathers. His judgement of pace was unerring, and he practised the art of waiting in front of his field. Sloan died in obscurity, but this seat is now universal for flat-racing.

Sloping head The head of a modern general-purpose saddle has the point of the saddle tree sloped forward at an angle of about 45°. The result is to place the stirrup bar, and therefore the rider, that much further forward.

Slot The foot or footprints of a deer.

Slug A lazy horse, always requiring to be urged. (See **Jade**)

SM pelham (solid mouthpiece) A bit with a wide, flat, ported mouthpiece on which the cheeks move independently in a restricted arc.

Smith, Horace Dayer (1878-1957) Appointed Royal Riding Master to Queen Elizabeth II (then Princess Elizabeth), 'Cadogan' Smith was associated with horses for threequarters of a century. A well-known horse dealer and showring judge, winner of a great number of prizes, he bought and sold nearly twelve thousand horses. He was the author of *A Horseman Through Six Reigns*.

Smith, Thomas Assheton (1776-1858) Founder of the Tedworth Hunt. When Master of the Quorn, he jumped Billesdon Brook 'in a place like a ravine', which required 34 ft (10 m) to cover it, with a fence on the landing side. He once remarked that 'there is no fence you cannot get over *with* a fall'.

Smith, Tom (1790-1878) Master of the Hambledon, Craven, and Pytchley Hunts, Smith wrote *Extracts from the Diary of a Huntsman*, which contains a description of his famous 'all-round-my-hat' cast, consisting of a closed loop, starting on the up-wind, or the least likely, side of the check.

Snaffle bit A bit consisting of a single-jointed or unjointed mouthpiece. The latter may have a straight or curved (half-moon or mullen) bar. The rings can be either circular or D-shaped, which minimises the risk of the lips being pinched.

Snaffle bridle A common term for a bridle with any snaffle bit attached.

Snatch A once popular term for stringhalt (q.v.).

Snip An isolated white marking situated in the region of the nostrils. Its size, position and intensity should be specified when a written description is given.

Snowflake marking See **Appaloosa**.

Snubbing post A post round which a rope is wound to check the motion of a horse.

Soaping The sweat of a horse is peculiar in its white soapy richness. It is easy to see on parts such as the neck and between the hind limbs, where lathering is particularly profuse in a highly strung and excited animal.

Sobre Paso See **Paso Fino**.

Sociable A low, pair-horse, four-wheeled vehicle with doors, driven from a box-seat, for four people sitting opposite each other.

Society of Master Saddlers Saddlers formed an association in 1898, but the present Society has been incorporated only since 1968. Membership consists of Master Saddlers; Associate Members who have an interest in saddlery but are not Master Saddlers; and Trade Members whose interest lies in the wholesale trade. The Society has close ties with the Worshipful Company of Saddlers, and runs an apprenticeship scheme.

Sock A white mark extending from the coronet, a short way only up the leg. (See also **Stocking**)

Soil The nature of the soil affects the development of horses. Heavy cold clay is bad for all horses. For lighter breeds, a dry sandy sub-soil under rich loam, and sub-soils of limestone and chalk are preferable.

Soil, to To feed (possibly green food) in a stall in order to fatten a horse.

Soilings Deer enjoy wallowing in mud, generally in recognised 'soiling pits'. They frequently 'soil' when they are hunted.

Sold at halter Old-time dealer's expression indicating that the buyer bought the horse as he found it, without warranty or veterinary examination.

Sole See under **Hoof, sole of**.

Sole, bruised This is caused by a stone picked up in the foot, or treading on a large stone. Thin, brittle soles or those with weak frogs are much more sensitive to such trouble. It can be prevented by shoeing with a piece of leather or plastic between the sole and the shoe.

Sole, dropped This condition occurs in acute laminitis (q.v.), when the pedal bone rotates from its normal position, resulting in the sole becoming convex instead of concave, and protruding below the bearing surface of the hoof.

Sole, horny A plate of hard horn about ⅜ in. (9.5 mm) thick, secreted by the sensitive sole and concave on its ground surface. Its posterior position receives the horny frog. Its function is to assist in carrying the horse's weight and to protect the sensitive parts of the foot immediately in contact with it.

Sole, pricked Descriptive of a foot when a nail has been driven into the sensitive area, usually the laminae. It often results in a reaction severe enough to cause separation of the horny sole from the sensitive part of the foot. With careful attention the condition will heal up with no long-term ill-effect. It may, however, take several weeks, and patience is required.

Solid nickel The metal from which the cheapest bits and irons are made. It is rustless, but rapidly assumes a yellow colour when left exposed to the air. It is a soft metal, very easily broken and therefore unreliable.

Somer Fifteenth-century term for a packhorse, also known as a 'sumpter'.

Somerville, Dr Edith Oenone (1858-1949) Farmer, organist, philanthropist, artist and MFH, she was best known as an author, collaborating with her cousin Violet Ross (q.v.) in many books featuring Irish sporting life. The most famous is *Some Experiences of an Irish RM*.

Sorghum A cereal used for feeding in the USA.

Sorraia The native pony of western Spain and Portugal, found near the river from which it takes its name. It is of rather 'primitive' appearance, with features reminiscent of the Przewalski wild horse (q.v.). Frequently dun in colour, with a dark dorsal stripe, and often with zebra stripes on the legs. Height 12.2-13 hh (127-132.1 cm).

Sorrel In the USA a chestnut colour of lighter red or golden tones.

'Soup plates' A term describing horses' feet which are big and round, out of proportion to the size of the animal, and usually found to be low on the heel.

South African National Equestrian Federation The body which controls show jumping, horse trials, dressage and certain show classes in South Africa.

Southern Hound The last areas in which this type of hound was maintained in its purity were Devonshire, the Sussex Weald and Wales. In type it was a slightly built hound, in colour a light tan to yellow.

South of England Agricultural Society An agricultural society founded in 1967 by the amalgamation of the Sussex County Agricultural Society, the Tunbridge Wells and South-Eastern Counties Agricultural Society and the Royal Counties Agricultural Society. It also incorporates the Richmond Royal Horse Show. The permanent showground is at Ardingly, Sussex.

South Wales and Monmouthshire Agricultural and Horse Shows Association Founded in 1944 to encourage and improve Horse and Agricultural Shows, to encourage interest in, and a better understanding of, the horse amongst the general public, and to encourage the breeding and showing of all classes of horses and ponies.

Sovereign A carriage closely resembling the Clarence (q.v.), but more ornate in design.

Soviet Heavy Draught Horse Bred in all agricultural areas of the Soviet Union. The breed is based on local crossbred mares derived from Ardennes, Bityug and Percheron blood, and mated with Belgian stallions. A stallion of the breed set up a weight-pulling record by moving 22,900 lb (23 tonnes) over a distance of 21 miles (35 km).

Sowar (under horseman) A trooper in an Indian cavalry regiment.

Soya-bean meal A very high protein food (up to 45%), containing 6% oil. Used in small quantities (up to a maximum of 1lb (0.45 kg) per day for young and breeding stock, and for horses in very hard work.

Spahis Originally irregular light cavalry units in the Turkish army, but the term was applied to certain native cavalry regiments, the officers being French, in Algiers and Tunis. Disbanded in 1963.

Spanish Horse When the Saracens invaded Spain and brought with them Arabs and Barbs, this greatly improved the native stock. Subsequent crossings of this Spanish horse resulted in the Spanish jennet, famous for its beauty, great docility and obedience, possessing width of chest, powerful shoulders, a Roman nose, a long arched neck, with full flowing mane, a goose-rump, and extraordinarily high action. This action was appreciated in the Vienna High School, where they excelled at the Spanish Walk. Later the Spanish Horse deteriorated, except for the Andalusian breed (q.v.), which, until recently, provided a large proportion of remounts. The most important Andalusian stud is now at Jerez, where warmblood horses are bred.

Spanish jumping bit Another name for the Kimblewick (q.v.).

Spanish Riding School of Vienna Evidence exists of an open manège in the sixteenth century on the premises of the Imperial Palace in Vienna, which was later replaced by a covered area. Between 1729-1735 in the reign of Emperor Charles VI, the present Spanish Riding School was completed to the magnificent design of Fischer von Erlach. Here equitation based on the sixteenth- and seventeenth-century Italian and French riding masters was, and still is, actively taught and practised in its purest classical form. Movements include airs above the ground, e.g. the Levade, Capriole, and Courbette (qq.v.). The training of selected riders covers several years. The name Spanish derives from the horses of Andalusia, imported from the Spanish court of Queen Isabella in the sixteenth century, which were the foundation stock of the Lipizzaner (q.v.) stallions now used exclusively in the School. These are selected on performance. During World War II the horses were evacuated from bombed Vienna to Upper Austria, and in 1945, owing to the intervention of the US Army Commander, General Patton, they were returned to the Spanish Riding School, and to the breeding farms at Lipizza. This ensured the continuation of four hundred years of classical equitation.

Spanish School A designation for the Spanish Riding School of Vienna.

Spanish walk An artificial air in which the horse lifts its forelegs very high, and extends them straight out in front. A spectacular movement, much favoured in the circus, but not recognised as classical High School.

Spares A racing term for horses in partial training and not doing work with the main string.

Spares Spare coach horses for a road coach, which were kept at allotted 'changes' on the coach route.

Spatterdashes Long gaiters or leggings of leather or cloth, etc., which were used to keep trousers or stockings clean when riding.

Spavin The traditional description of this condition is 'visible or non-visible lumps due to degenerative joint disease, or arthritis, as it is called'. Arthritis tends to occur with increasing age or from wear and tear, excessive demands on the horse, or conformation defects. The diagnosis is by X-ray. The radiographs show how and to what extent the changes affect the horse.

Spavin, bog A puffy swelling or distension of the capsular ligament caused by increased synovial fluid (q.v.) on the inside, and slightly to the front, of the hock. The condition is caused by strain, poor conformation, or injury. It is not usually painful, and does not cause lameness.

Spavin, bone A bony growth caused by osteo-arthritis inside and just below the hock. In a young horse, it is due to stress and/or concussion, or to severe exertion. Animals with sickle or cow hocks are susceptible. A horse suffering from the condition shortens his stride and may drag his toe. The lameness diminishes with exercise. A 'spavin test' involves forcibly flexing the hock for about a minute then immediately trotting the animal; increased lameness will then be apparent.

Spavin, knee A bony growth at the back of the knee on the inner side, which occurs mostly in racehorses. It is caused by a blow or strain. There is a distinct swelling at the knee, and the horse shows signs of pain.

Spavin, occult A serious condition in which a growth occurs between the two bones of the hock just below the joint on the inner side. It is difficult to detect, hence its name. In this type of spavin, lameness does not diminish with exercise but is always present and increases. Veterinary advice is required, but the condition may not respond to treatment.

Speak Hounds do not bark, they speak.

Spectacles See **Martingale, Irish**.

Speed In the horse, this depends on type, conformation and condition. The approximate speed at which the Derby is run is 35-36 mph (56 km/h) and the time for the Grand National averages about 28 mph (44 km/h).

Speedy cut boot A boot made specially high to prevent speedy cutting (q.v.).

Speedy cutting (interfering) An injury to the inside of one leg caused by a blow from the opposite foot. The point of impact may be anywhere between the knee/hock and the coronary band. It is caused by poor action/conformation, or in tired or green animals.

Spider phaeton The lightest type of phaeton for a pair or single.

Spider phaeton.

Spiffing A coper's trick of blowing black snuff into the left nostril to start a jibbing horse.

Spire A three-year-old stag.

Spiti A characteristic breed of Indian hill pony of Mongolian origin, taking its name from the Spiti tract of very mountainous country in the Kangra district between Kulu and the central spine of the Himalayas. Breeding is mostly in the hands of the Kanyat tribe of high-caste Hindus. The pony is small, tough thickset, up to weight, and very sure-footed. It has an intelligent head, with remarkably sharp ears, a strong short back, short legs and hard round feet. The neck is short and thick, shoulders are sturdy and straightish, ribs well-sprung and quarters developed. It thrives only on the Himalayas, and is apparently tireless and very hardy. Height: 12 hh (121.9 cm); colours: grey and iron-grey. (See **Bhutan**)

Spiv/Spivvey An unattached groom who will 'do' a spare horse at race meetings (describing himself as a 'paddock assistant'); he will box one bought at a sale or lead horses to and from race meetings, sales, and shows.

Splashboard An upright protection in front of the coachman's feet in some vehicles; it may be of thick leather or wood.

Splint A small bony growth which forms between the splint bone and the cannon bone in either the fore or the hind limbs. Such formation of new bone is known as an exostosis. It seldom causes trouble in a horse over six years old, except as a result of concussion. It is generally caused by the legs having been jarred unnecessarily when the horse was still young. It may also be due to bad conformation.

Splint bones See **Metacarpals, small**.

Splinter bar A cross-timber fixed to the front of a vehicle to which the wheelers of a team are attached by their traces.

Split hoof See **Grass crack**.

Split quarter strap A strap carrying a short breeching body.

Split up behind A term applied when the quarters, viewed from behind, show

a wide dividing line from the dock to the top line of the gaskins. The cheeks *should* lie firm and close together.

Spoke brush A long, narrow brush, with thick, hard bristles, used for washing carriage wheels.

Spokes Wooden or metal bars connecting the inside rim of the wheel with the centre portion.

Sponge Separate sponges should be used for eyes and nostrils, and for the dock and sheath. An 'elephant ear' sponge is a special close-textured, small, flat sponge favoured in tack-cleaning.

Sponsorship Over the last twenty or so years, sponsorship of competition riders and/or horses by individuals/companies has become a significant, even essential, part of show jumping, eventing, dressage, etc. Races or classes at race meetings or shows are frequently supported by cash contributions from sources other than the racecourse or shows concerned. One of the earliest races to be sponsored was a 6 furlong two-year-old event at Newmarket, for which William Blenkiron Snr donated £1000 in 1866. The race was named after his Middle Park Stud.

Spoon See **'Lame hand'**.

Spoon cheek A shortened and flattened cheek to a snaffle bit. A 'full spoon cheek' extends above and below the mouthpiece; a 'half spoon' extends only beneath the mouthpiece.

'Sport of kings' An expression referring to horse racing. Originally applied to hawking.

Spots (body) Small, more-or-less circular collections of hairs differing from the general body colour, distributed over various parts of the body.

Spotted horse See **Appaloosa**.

Sprain Torn fibres in tendons, muscles, ligaments, tendon sheaths, etc., caused by abnormal stretching.

Spread fence An obstacle designed to test a horse's ability to jump width as well as height.

Spreading See **Stretching**.

'Spreading a plate' An expression indicating that a shoe has become loose in its seating.

Spring bar The name refers to the stirrup bar which has a spring-mounted safety catch or thumbpiece.

Spring double The Lincolnshire Handicap, now run at Doncaster, and the Grand National, at Aintree, constitute the Spring Double, for which bookmakers often make an ante-post book.

Springer (racing) A horse which suddenly springs into prominence in the betting on a race. A 'market springer' is a horse suddenly well backed in the betting market.

Springhalt See **Stringhalt**.

'Springing' An old coaching term for galloping.

Spring mouth A jointed snaffle bit without rings, which can be fastened on to an existing snaffle by spring clips to make the action more severe. It often has a serrated mouthpiece and is sometimes known as a 'butterfly'.

Spring tree A saddle having two highly tempered lengths of steel set into the head and extending to the cantle. It makes the seat of the saddle resilient, gives to the movement of the horse's back, and enables the rider's seat and back aids to be more easily transmitted. Used in modern jumping, general-purpose and dressage saddles. Showing and racing saddles do not have spring trees.

Sprinter A horse that gallops at great speed up to 6 furlongs (1.2 km) but can stay no further.

Spur boxes These are sometimes set in the heels of boots such as jodhpur boots, and dress boots worn with overalls (q.v.). Spurs fitted in this way are sometimes known as 'box-spurs'.

Spur rests A small triangular block of leather sometimes fitted at the top back of a riding boot counter to keep the spur point parallel with the ground.

Spurrier One who makes spurs.

Spurs An artificial and supplementary aid, believed to have been first used by the Assyrians. There are numerous different designs, and neck lengths vary with fashion. Modern spurs are of the loop and single strap pattern; others are kept in place by ankle straps. Box-spurs, worn with riding trousers, fit into a hole at the back of the heel of the boot, which keeps them in place without a strap. In polo, blunt spurs only are permitted.

Spur-shields Square-shaped safes (q.v.) which go beneath the top strap of the spur straps.

Squatter's rights, to take (USA) To be thrown.

Stable connections A racing term implying those connected with a horse running in a race, e.g. the owner, trainer, and stable staff at its training quarters.

Stable rubber A twill linen cloth about 26 ins x 33 ins (66 cm x 83 cm). Used in grooming to remove dust from the surface of the coat.

'Stables' A term used in army and racing stables for the first and last work of the day in the stables – 'Morning stables' and 'Evening stables'.

Stables A building for housing horses, usually sub-divided into loose-boxes. Modern purpose-built stables are constructed of brick, breeze-block, or, more commonly, timber. The majority of the latter are obtainable in sectional prefabricated form.

The basic requirements for stables are: (1) They should be dry, well-ventilated, well-insulated (for warmth in winter and cool in summer), and draught-free. The best materials for stable construction are those mentioned above. Windows are the prime means of ventilation; each box should have one, protected with iron bars or mesh on the inside, and opening inwards from the top. Other means of ventilation include louvre boards, cowls and tubes. Doors can also be a means of ventilation; e.g. the Dutch door type, with top and bottom portions opening separately. All stable doors should be at least 8 ft (2.44 m) high and 4 ft (1.22 m) wide. They should be hinged, opening outwards, or hung on rollers.

Door latches should be strong, horse-proof and fitted flush with the door. (2) They must have adequate drainage. (3) They should be sited in a sheltered position. (4) They should be adequately lit with well-protected electrical fittings. (5) They must have a good water supply. (6) The floors should be solid, durable and non-slip, with drainage facilities. Stable bricks of the non-slippery variety are good, laid over a solid foundation of concrete. (7) They must be at least 12 ft (3.6 m) high at the eaves. (8) They should be built on good foundations, e.g. (in order of preference) a sub-soil of gravel or deep sand, rock; stiff clay, deep loam, or marshy soils are unsuitable.) (8) The interior should be fitted with kicking boards.

Suitable sizes for loose boxes are: for horses – 12 ft x 14 ft (3.6 m x 4.2 m); for ponies – 10 ft x 12 ft (3 m x 3.6 m); foaling boxes – ideally 15 ft (4.5 m) square.

Some stables are fitted with stalls (q.v.). These are usually 5 ft 6 ins (1.6 m) wide by 11 ft (3.3 m) long, with a partition 6 ft 6 ins (1.9 m) high at the front and 5 ft (1.5 m) at the rear.

Stadium jumping An expression, used principally in America, for show jumping, more especially for the show-jumping phase of a three-day event.

Stag A male deer at four years of age and over. (See **Warrantable**)

Stag An unbroken colt or gelding over one year of age; the term is also applied to a horse castrated late in life. Rarely used in modern-day language.

Stage coach See **Road coach**.

Stage wagon A big clumsy vehicle for cumbersome loads, drawn by six, eight and even ten heavy horses. The wheels were big and very broad, to assist in improving roads by flattening the ruts.

Staggart An obsolete term for a male deer at four years.

Staggers (also known as 'Megrim') A loss of equilibrium due to a variety of causes: e.g. grass sickness, wobbler syndrome, poisoning, brain infection, or degeneration. Urgent veterinary attention is necessary.

Stag hook The hook of a hunting whip made from stag horn.

Stag-hunting See **Hunting seasons** and **Rutting season**.

Stain Another term for foil (q.v.).

Stake and bind A fence consisting of strong but thin vertical stakes interlaced horizontally with supple sapplings. (See **Cut and laid**)

Stake money The total money allotted and contributed for a race, out of which the winner and placed horses are paid.

Stale An over-trained or over-raced horse which has become lethargic and uninterested in its work.

Stale, to The act of equine urination.

Stale See **Jade/Jadey**.

Stale line The line of a fox which has passed some time earlier.

Stalking-horse A horse behind which a sportsman hides while stalking game.

Stalled A term descriptive of a horse which is surfeited with food and leaves some in his manger.

Stallion A horse, not under four years, capable of reproducing the species. An entire, ungelded horse.

Stallion hound A dog hound in a pack used as a sire.

Stallion licence Until 1983 all stallions were required to be licensed by the Ministry of Agriculture. When this ceased, the various breed societies introduced stallion registration schemes.

Stallion tack Leather roller, crupper, side reins, bridle and lead, worn when being exercised or shown.

Stalls Compartments open at the rear, in which horses must be haltered. The main disadvantage of stalls are: the risk of becoming cast (q.v.), the horse slipping the headstall and freeing himself. Chains stretching from the two pillars at the entrance to the stall will minimise the latter risk.

Stalls (racing) See **Starting stalls**.

Standard, a (show jumping) If the show

is running late or there are too many clear rounds, a competitor, after he has made a certain number of faults, may be required to retire from the event.

Standardbred The official name of the famous American trotting and pacing (q.v.) horses, bred with extreme care and scientific efficiency. The breed, although developed in the USA, is of great interest to Britain, as it traces back in direct male line to the Thoroughbred Messenger, who in turn traces back to the Godolphin Arabian, the Byerley Turk, and the Darley Arabian. Messenger stood at stud in America for twenty years, and a grandson of his, Hambletonian (by Abdallah out of a mare with Norfolk Trotter blood), became the true founding father of the Standardbreds. Ninety-nine per cent of today's Standardbreds trace back to him. Characteristics of the breed are similar to those of the Thoroughbred, but with modifications due to differences in gait and work. The Standardbred is heavier-limbed and more robust than most Thoroughbreds, with a longer body, shorter legs, and with great courage and endurance. The height is between 14 hh and 16 hh (142.2-162.6 cm). The gaits of trotting or pacing are inherited, with the pacer being slightly the faster of the two. The horses must be able to cover a mile (1.6 km) in not less than 2 mins. 20 secs, which is known as the 'standard', from which the breed takes its name. Modern Standardbreds travel considerably faster, in the region of 1 min. 52 secs over a mile.

Standing over A term descriptive of a horse that appears to 'give' at the knees. The defect is not detrimental (except in the show ring), unless it is caused by overwork.

Stand off, to A term used when a horse takes off some way in front of a jump. The opposite of 'to get under' (q.v.).

'Stands near the ground' Said of a deep-bodied, short-legged horse.

Stand up a horse, to To place an in-hand horse so that he stands level on all four legs, enabling a judge to assess his conformation.

Stanhope gig A vehicle whose seat (de-signed for two persons) rests on the boot or locker foundation. The vehicle was named after the Hon. F. Stanhope.

Stanhope gig.

Stanhope phaeton A light phaeton for a pair or for one horse. It has a full lock for turning in a limited space, and seats four people, all facing forwards.

Star Any white mark on the forehead. Size, shape, intensity, position and coloured markings (if any) of the white should be specified if a description is being given.

Star gazer A horse which holds its head too high and is liable to take its fences blindly; though a dangerous ride, a star gazer will seldom refuse a fence.

Start (racing) In flat racing in Britain there are two modes of starting a race, either by a mechanical barrier start or by starting stalls. If a barrier start is used, the starter calls over the runners and their places in the draw (previously drawn by lot at the Overnight Declarations office), and gives orders for the jockeys to move into position. Formerly, when the field was in position, a white flag was raised, denoting that the field was under starter's orders; now, however, in most cases, the signal is given by radio, but the Rules still provide for a white flag as an alternative. The starter releases the gate as soon as he considers a fair start can be made, and the white flag is lowered.

Should the tapes of the barrier be broken prematurely by a horse or jockey, or should the starting barrier fail to work properly, the starter can declare a 'no start' and order the jockeys to return to the start by means of a red re-call flag. The procedure is the same with starting stalls. The white flag is raised when all the runners are in their correct stalls, and lowered as the stalls are opened simultaneously by the starter operating the opening mechanism. These days, very few flat races are started by the mechanical barrier method.

With steeplechasing and hurdle races, the starter merely releases a single strand of rubber, which acts as the barrier, and there is no draw for the start. (See also **Starting stalls**)

Starter An official who obtains an annual licence from the Jockey Club, by whom he is employed. His duty is to give the orders necessary to secure a fair start. He has the power to remove an unruly horse from his place in the draw, to order a horse to be held behind the other runners in a barrier start, and to order a horse to be withdrawn if it refuses to enter its starting stall. He can fine jockeys who misconduct themselves at the start.

Starting gate First used in Great Britain in 1900, this is a mechanical barrier used to assist the starter in securing a fair start to a race. The gate consists of strands of rope (tapes) stretched across the course at the starting point, and secured to posts at either end. The ropes are spaced one above the other at intervals of 2 ft (0.6 m), the lowest being 4 ft (1.2 m) from the ground. These tapes fly up when the starter releases the catch from his position on the platform. (See also **Starting stalls**)

Starting price (racing) The starting price of a horse is the odds quoted about him by a bookmaker at the time of the start of the race. Starting prices normally rule all off-the-course bets unless the bets are ante-post.

Starting stalls Movable sets of stalls into which horses are placed at the starting point of a race. The front gate is opened mechanically when the starter presses an electric button, releasing the horses. These stalls are now used at almost all flat races in Great Britain and other major racing countries.

State coach Used by nobility for state occasions. Equipped with great splendour and fitted with glass side panels so that its occupants can be easily visible. See also **Lord Mayor's State Coach** and **Coronation Coach**.

Stay apparatus/mechanism A system of muscles and ligaments in the limbs which helps to support the horse while standing and which 'locks' to prevent him falling if he dozes.

Stayer A horse that can gallop at a racing pace over 1½ miles (2.4 km) or further.

Steaming (the head) Giving the horse an inhalation in cases of nasal discharge. It is achieved by putting a small quantity of hay in a bucket standing in a sack, and adding an inhalant substance such as Friar's Balsam followed by boiling water. The horse's head is then held in the opening to the sack to enable it to inhale the fumes.

Steed A popular poetic description for a horse or stallion, infrequently used by horsemen; a spirited horse.

Steeplechase A race in which the horses have to jump fences, open ditches and, under Jockey Club Rules, a water jump. There are regulations governing the height of fences, etc.

Steeplechase meetings The first organised steeplechase meeting was held in 1830, at St Albans in Hertfordshire; the first steeplechase at Aintree was run in 1836; and the first Grand National (though not so called at the time) was run in 1837.

Steeplechaser A horse who races over fences, as opposed to a flat racer or a hurdler.

Steeplechasers Boots for jockeys, of a slightly sturdier type than racers (q.v.), with fitted 'polishing tops' and a minimum weight of about 1¼ lb (0.56 kg).

Steeplechases, early Old manuscript records show that in 1752 a match was run over 4½ miles (7.2 km) of country in Ireland between O'Callaghan and Blake, the course being from Buttevant Church to the spire of St Leger Church. In 1792, a steeplechase was held in Leicestershire, the competitors being hunting men, Lord Forester, Sir Gilbert Heathcote, and Mr C. Meynell. In 1810, the first steeplechase over a made course was run at Bedford. The 3-mile (4.8 km) was run in heats over eight fences, but unfortunately there were only two runners. Mr Spence on Fugitive won from Mr Tower on Cecilia.

Stepping A horse with high action is called a 'stepper' or a 'high stepper'. This may be a natural action, but can be developed by artificial means and careful schooling.

Sterility Sterility in stallions may be due to immature behaviour, with inhibition of ejaculation; poor quality semen; infection; or hormone imbalance. In mares it may be due to faulty genital organs; infection; or hormone imbalance.

Stern A hound's tail.

Sternum The breast bone.

Steward An official supervising at a race meeting or horse show. On a racecourse there are at least three stewards. At horse shows many stewards may be needed, within the show arena, in the collecting ring, stables, and elsewhere.

Stewards' Secretary A racing official employed by the Jockey Club, whose duty it is to help and advise the Stewards of a Meeting, who in Britain are always unpaid volunteers. Stewards' Secretaries have largely the duties of stipendiary stewards, but can only advise the Stewards.

Sticky A horse which 'boggles' at its fences, half-refuses and jumps from a standstill or trot; an uncertain fencer.

'Stiff-necked' A straight running fox.

Stifle The junction of the tibia and patella, corresponding to the knee in the human. The joint is subject to arthritis, and to displacement of the patella.

Stifle lameness The horse raises his quarter on his lame side. His step is shorter and he 'saves' the lame leg by bending the stifle, hock and fetlock only slightly.

Stile An obstacle found in show jumping and cross-country courses.

Stings Stings from bees, wasps and flies may lead to reckless and perhaps dangerous galloping about. The animal should be quietened if possible, and stood in a stable. Efforts should be made to remove the sting, and the surrounding area of skin should be treated with a soothing antiseptic cream or spray.

Stint The right to pasture one or more horses on common land.

Stint The service (mating) of a mare to which she is holding (i.e. is in foal); 'has been stinted to . . . (stallion)'.

'Stipe' (racing) Slang for a steward's secretary or stipendiary steward.

Stipendiary Steward See **Stewards' Secretary**.

Stirrup, hooded Describes a stirrup with its front section covered, as sometimes used with a Western stock saddle.

Stirrup cup Liquid refreshment offered to a mounted rider, usually a hunting man or woman, and sometimes referred to as a 'jumping powder'.

Stirrup iron (derivation *stigan*, to mount, *rap*, rope) A metal fitting into which the rider's foot is placed. The period of introduction is unknown but it was a Barbarian invention. It appears to have been known in the second century and was in use by the dreaded Huns of Attila. Various patterns, sizes and metals are used. Stainless steel and named metals, such as Eglantine, Kangaroo, etc., are reliable. Solid nickel is not recommended.

Stirrup leathers See **Leathers, stirrup**.

Stirrup webs Lightweight tubular webs used instead of leathers for racing.

Stock See **Hunting tie**.

Stocked A term used to indicate that a mare has been served; it also refers to a field that is being pastured.

Stockholm tar Stockholm or fir-tar (an emollient ointment) may be applied on tow for plugging feet in cases of thrush (q.v.).

Stocking White on the leg extending from the knee or hock to the coronet. (See also **Sock**)

Stockton bit (or pelham type) A bit with a mouthpiece which slides and revolves through the cheek.

Stomach The connecting medium between the gullet and the small intestine; the stomach inclines to the left of the abdominal cavity, and is very small compared with the size of the animal. For this reason horses should always be fed little and often. They will graze for as many as twenty hours out of the twenty-four.

Stone-cold A term applied, in racing, to a horse which has run itself out, is unresponsive and quite unable to 'come again'.

Stone-horse A stallion (q.v.).

Stone wall A show-jumping or cross-country obstacle.

Stoop A fox is said to stoop when it lowers its nose to the ground on a scent.

Stophound In Stuart times, a slow form of hare-hound. The huntsman who ran with the hounds and stopped them by flinging his pole in front of the leading animals.

Stopping earth The closing of a fox earth with gorse, branches, etc., after the fox is known to have left, and to prevent its return. Blackthorn faggot, bound with wire, is the most effective barrier.

Stopping out Fox earths closed during the night preceding a hunting day, when the fox is out of them, are said to be 'stopped out'; the process is known as 'stopping out'.

Stops Metal projections on the shafts which keep the harness of a single horse at the proper point of contact with the shafts. They carry much of the weight of the vehicle when descending a hill.

Stops See **Rein stops**.

Stowed See **Ears, identification marks**.

Stradstick See **Bars**.

'Straight, the' The straight 'run-in' to the winning post from the final bend in any racecourse. The length of the straight varies on every racecourse in Great Britain.

Straight mover See **Level mover**.

Straightness The majority of horses are naturally slightly crooked or asymmetrical, with the spine bending marginally to one side. Dressage movements demand absolute straightness, which is achieved by various suppling exercises. Straightness is most easily checked by noting if the horse's hindlegs follow an identical track to those of the forelegs.

Strangles A highly contagious disease (particularly in young horses). It is caused by inhalation of the bacterium *Streptococcus equi*, which invades the lymph glands around the head and neck, especially those under the jaw. The affected areas become extremely hot and tender, and finally abscessed. The abscess eventually bursts. Symptoms include dullness, temperature raised to as much as 105°F (40.5°C) a thin, watery nasal discharge, red mucous membranes of the eye, sore throat, coughing, and difficulty in swallowing. The animal must be isolated immediately, and the veterinary surgeon called. See also **Bastard strangles**.

Strap, balance The balance strap is attached to the centre of the offside cantle of the side-saddle and runs on top of the girth and around under the belly in order to steady the saddle.

Strapper A groom or other stable assistant engaged in the grooming and general preparation of horses for riding and driving.

Strapping The full grooming of a horse, best done after exercise, when the animal is relaxed. See **Grooming**.

Strapping pad See **Grooming pad**.

Strappings A term applied to ceremonial harness, including saddles and bridles.

Strappings These are sewn on riding breeches and jodhpurs, extending above and below the inside of knee. They are sometimes referred to as 'grips' or 'patches'. The best are made of buckskin. Many modern breeches and jodhpurs have strappings of the material from which the breeches are made.

Straw The stalks of cereal plants after the grain has been thrashed out. Some barley or oat straw may be fed to horses, but it has a low nutritive value. See also **Bedding**.

Strawyard Horses being rested or recovering from an illness are sometimes turned into a yard deeply bedded with straw, and if possible leading out of a box or boxes. This assures exercising room, keeps them warm and allows handling and examination with a minimum of difficulty. The yard should be kept dry, and rotting manure removed.

Strelets This breed originated when selected native mares from the mountainous regions of the Ukraine were crossed with Anglo-Arab, Turkish, Persian or pure Arab sires. The Strelets bred true to type. The breed was described as a large Arab with all the excellent attributes of that ancient race. A supreme riding horse, it was particularly valuable for cavalry needs. It all but died out in the 1920s. In 1925, the few remaining specimens were sent to the Tersk Stud in the Northern Caucasus. There Arab stallions and cross-Arab/Don and Strelets/Kabardin mares were used to produce the Tersk (q.v.), which takes its name from the stud.

Stretching The practice of causing harness horses, especially Hackneys, to stand with their front legs stretched forwards and their hindlegs stretched backwards. In the USA many saddle horses are trained to stand in this way. The position makes the true height deceptive. Also known as 'camping' or 'spreading'.

String A term applied to two or more racehorses out at exercise together.

Stringhalt A condition in which one or both hindlegs are lifted in a jerking action, higher than the normal gait. It is an unsoundness, and usually worsens with age, but may to some extent be alleviated surgically.

Stripe A narrow white mark down the face, not wider than the flat anterior surface of the nasal bones.

Stripe See **Race**.

Stripe, dorsal A continuous black, brown or dun stripe extending from the line of the neck to the tail, and sometimes continuing down the latter. It is typical of Scandinavian and other types of north European and Asiatic breeds. Many Highland ponies are so marked. Professor Ewart, well known around the turn of the century for his work on the evolution of the horse, was of the opinion that all horses were once dun coloured with a dorsal stripe and zebra markings on the forearms.

Stripe, the Colloquial term for the dorsal stripe (see above).

Stub A wound on the sole of the foot caused by treading on a sharp and uneven surface.

Stub-bred Foxes born above ground rather than in an earth.

Stubbs, George, ARA (1724-1806) Outstanding British artist who was virtually self-taught. Son of a Liverpool currier, he received only a few weeks' professional training from Hamlet Winstanley. First made his living by painting portraits, but an obsessive interest in anatomy led to his patient dissection of horse carcasses in 1758 in a remote Lincolnshire farmhouse, and the publication in 1766 of *The Anatomy of the Horse*, with engravings by his own hand. This work ranks as a vital reference for every artist of repute who came after him. He became known as 'Mr Stubbs, the horse painter' and his portraits of famous Thoroughbreds of the day are superb. From 1760 he lived in London and received immediate and influential commissions as a painter of animal and sporting subjects. His pictures of hunting scenes are rare, though 'The Grosvenor Hunt', painted for Lord Grosvenor, is a masterpiece; but he also excelled in more tranquil studies, such as his nine compositions of 'mares and foals'. His undeniable genius reached its quintessence in several paintings of 'A Horse attacked by a Lion' and in the picture of 'A Cheetah and a Stag with Two Indians'. In addition to oils he also worked in enamels, first on copper and then on stoneware tablets made for him by Josiah Wedgwood. Stubbs published a number of mezzotint engravings. His natural son, George Townley Stubbs, was an engraver.

Stud A breeding establishment where mares and foals may be found, with or without a stallion.

Stud, at A stallion standing at a given place, or travelling, whose services are offered to mare owners for a fee.

Stud book A record book of all pedigree stock, whether of Thoroughbreds (General Stud Book) or of other breeds.

Stud-bred A foreign term referring to horses of certain breeds which have a stud book of their own.

Stud-fastening A metal stud by which the reins may be fastened to the rings of a bit. Satisfactory cleaning of the bit is facilitated by virtue of the simplicity and ease with which the rein is detached. Also known as a 'hook-fastening' and 'French clip'.

Stud groom The person in charge of a breeding stud, although the term is often applied to one who has charge of a few horses, e.g. hunters.

Studs Metal studs may be inserted in the shoe to give a more secure foothold. Standard studs for normal non-slip purposes, such as road work, hacking, harness work, etc., are low and broad, and are, in most instances, inserted into special holes punched in the heels of the hind shoes (i.e. two studs per hind shoe). If, for some reason, it is thought that the stud raises the heel excessively, special counter-sunk plug-type studs are used. These are level with the ground surface initially, but as the shoe wears, the hard tungsten of these studs wears more slowly, and thus gives grip on most surfaces. For sports such as show jumping and horse trials, where studs may need to be changed quickly to meet the demands of different surfaces, screw-in studs are available.

Stumbling A result of debility, low condition, faulty conformation, lameness, tiredness or bad horsemanship.

'Stumer' Slang for a horse who is not doing his best to win a race; a worthless horse in a particular race.

Substance See Leather.

Substance (of horse) A horse with good bone, deep through the heart, and giving the appearance of well-proportioned strength.

Sucker A foal of either sex up to weaning time, or, if unweaned, until ranking as a yearling.

Sudadero A leather flap on a Western saddle, behind which the stirrup leather runs, protecting the rider's leg from friction. Also known as a 'fender'.

Suffolk Previously known as the Suffolk Punch, the breed is always one of seven shades of chesnut (the traditional Suffolk spelling of the colour). Associated with the county of its name, the Suffolk dates back to a single horse – Thomas Crisp's Horse of Ufford, foaled in 1768. Of the British heavy breeds, the Suffolk is the only one to have been developed solely for agriculture. It is economical to keep, is active and docile, standing up to 17 hh (170 cm), with great width in front and behind. The legs are short, strong and clean, bearing no feather. Suffolks have a very strong 'pull', are round and impressive in appearance, and have an excellent temperament. They trot with an action that differs from the Shire and the Clydesdale, and has been well-described as 'a tense, slow trot, as though to ease an overflow of strength'.

Suffolk Stud Book Society Founded in 1877, and the first of the heavy horse breed societies in Britain.

Sugar-beet pulp/nuts *Must not be fed dry*. This foodstuff requires soaking for twenty-four hours, as it swells by a factor of at least three, and if this took place in the horse's stomach it could cause colic, choking, and death. If correctly prepared, a useful food, containing sugar (22%), protein (10%), and fibre (15%). See also **Poisoning, sugar-beet**.

Sulky A very light two-wheeled single-seated cart with skeleton body, used for racing trotters and pacers. In the USA it is known as a 'Bike' (q.v.).

Sullivan, Con A nineteenth-century Irish horse-whisperer, who tamed many high-spirited and dangerous blood horses, generally reckoned as 'savages'.

Sumba Ponies bred on the islands of Sumba and Sumbwa in Indonesia. They were trained to dance to the rhythm of drums, with bells attached to their knees. They are hardy and intelligent, usually dun with a dorsal stripe, and a dark mane and tail. The height varies, but averages 12.2 hh (127 cm).

Summering A term applied to the summer period during which hunters or any horses are turned out at grass for rest and green feed.

Sumpter A horse for carrying burdens. Also called 'somer' (q.v.).

Sunfishing The action of a buckjumper when it twists its body into a crescent shape in the air.

Suppletrees See **Badikins**.

Supporting rein This supports the intention of the opposite rein during any movement off a straight line, e.g. on circling to the right, the right rein indicates the direction required; the left rein assists this indication, prevents the bit being pulled through the mouth, and at the same time limits the extent of the circling.

Surcingle A surcingle is a piece of webbing or webbing and elastic, usually 2½-3 ins (63-76 mm) wide, which passes over the saddle and around the horse's belly to give greater security to the saddle, or it is fastened by a strap or buckles. Invariably used with race saddles and often seen on eventers during the cross-country phase. It can also be of hemp or jute, sewn to a rug as a method of keeping it in place. In the USA a surcingle is called a roller.

Surfeit A skin eruption akin to nettle rash (see **Urticaria**), causing irritation and loss of hair. Sometimes small blisters, which burst, appear all over the body. It is said to be due to over-feeding, impaired condition and exposure to heat.

Surrey A light, four-wheeled American carriage with two separate seats mounted on a flat bottom. Most had flat cloth tops with fringes.

Surrey.

Surrey clarence See **Clarence**.

Surtees, Robert Smith (1803-1864) A sporting author and qualified solicitor who bought a practice in London. Surtees subsequently abandoned law, founded *The New Sporting Magazine* (1831) and created the world-famous sporting character John Jorrocks (q.v.), who was the quintessence of cockney vulgarity, good-humour, absurdity and cunning. The chief works of this author are: *Hawbuck Grange, Mr Facey Romford's Hounds, Mr Sponge's Sporting Tour, Hillingdon Hall, Handley Cross, Country Life, Ask Mamma, The Horseman's Manual, Plain or Ringlets, Jorrocks's Jaunts and Jollities*, and *The Analysis of the Hunting Field*.

Suspensory apparatus Ligaments connecting the sesamoid bones which prevent the fetlock joint from touching the ground. They form part of the stay apparatus (q.v.).

Suspensory ligament Found between the two splint bones, under the back tendons, it runs from the two small flat bones of the knee nearly to the fetlock, above which it divides, but the two parts re-join about the middle of the pastern.

Swage buckle A flat, oval buckle of brass or white metal, with the tongue on a central bar. Used for headcollars etc.

Swaged-side stirrup irons The sides gradually taper towards the eye and are known as graduated sides. Claimed to be the strongest form of stirrup iron.

Swales gag A veterinary gag to keep the mouth open.

Swales three-in-one bit A riding pelham and also a driving bit featuring various mouthpieces. The mouthpiece and cheeks revolve in two rings set round the mouthpiece. There is no poll pressure, but considerable curb action is obtained.

'Swallows his head' A term used by cowboys when a bucking bronco gets its head right down between its forelegs, arches its back strongly and springs from the ground with great force.

Swallowtail coat See **Shadbelly**.

Swan-neck See **Bars**; and **Pole hook**.

Swan neck Describes the shape of a neck which tends to become ewe-necked (q.v.) at its lower end.

Sway-backed Descriptive of a horse which has wrenched the lower part of its back below the short ribs, resulting in

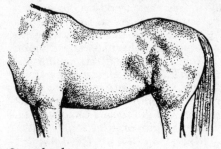

Sway back.

a marked dip behind the withers. Such a horse cannot back a load. Also termed 'bobby-backed'.

Sweat flaps An under-flap to keep sweat from the saddle flaps; it also prevents buckles from causing discomfort to the horse.

Sweating The natural result of normal exercise in warm weather or excessive exercise in any weather. It increases heat loss and thus maintains body temperature at a constant level. Nervous horses often sweat before a race or competition, and others on their return home. When back in the stable they should be dried off carefully to avoid a chill. Sweating is also a symptom associated with pain and fever.

Sweat scraper Traditionally a half-moon strip of metal to which a handle is attached; nowadays plastic/rubber versions are also available. Most useful for the quick removal of excess sweat or

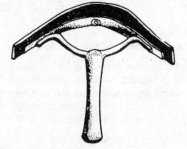

Plastic and rubber sweat scraper.

water from a horse's coat. If of metal the edge can be covered by a rubber strip which will avoid damage to prominent bones and is more comfortable for the horse.

Swedish Ardennes This strong, compact breed was first introduced in 1837, and is now used mostly for farming work. It has very little feather on the legs and stands low to the ground. The average height is 15.2-16 hh (157.5-162.6 cm).

Swedish Warmblood An outstandingly successful, quality riding horse developed some 300 years ago at the Royal Stud, Flyinge, in Sweden. Initially based on a remarkable variety of breeds from all over Europe, Russia, Turkey and Britain, the Swedish Warmblood has had further infusions in the twentieth century of Thoroughbred, Hanoverian, Trakehner, and Arab blood, to produce a breed with all-round ability, and, it seems, a particular talent for dressage. Well-known Swedish Warmblood dressage horses at international level include San Fernando, Junke, Piaff, and Wohler. Success in eventing has included a gold medal for Illuster in the 1956 Olympic Games. Rigid selection trials for conformation and performance are in operation to maintain high standards. The Swedish Warmblood stands up to 16.2 hh (165 cm).

Sweepstake (racing) A race in which the entrance fees, forfeits and other contributions of owners go to the winner and placed horses, and are added to the prize money, as opposed to a plate, in which the owners' entrance fees, etc., are kept by the racecourse.

Sweet itch An allergic examatous skin condition caused by the bites of the *Culicoides* midge. The mane and tail areas are the most severely affected, and the irritation is such that the animal will rub these areas until they are raw. When the midge is at its most active – i.e. early morning and late evening – allergic animals should be stabled. The condition is not yet fully understood. Fly repellants may help, as may anti-inflammatory drugs, but at present there is no cure.

Swell-fork A padded roll forming part of the Western saddle. It runs from the centre of the front of the saddle down either side, giving considerable added security to the seat of the rider on a bucking horse. Rodeo specifications require a 14-in. (35 cm) swell.

Swing-bars/Swingle bars/Swingle-trees/Single-trees See **Bars**.

Swing horse The middle horse in a random (q.v.), or the middle pair in a six-horse team.

Switch-tail Undocked tail with the terminal hairs pulled to a point.

Swiss Half-Bred Another European warmblood-type horse, founded on Norman and Holstein mares. In the 1960s, Swedish and Irish mares were bought by the Swiss National Stud, and a variety of stallions were used on them and their progeny – these included Swedish, Holstein, Thoroughbred, Trakehner, Selle Français and Hanoverian. Performance tests are mandatory. The Swiss Half-bred stands 16-16.2 hh (162.6-165 cm) and is an all-purpose horse with an excellent temperament.

'Swopping ends' A term used when a buckjumper bends to a half-circle or loop in the air.

Syce/Sais An Indian groom.

Syndicate (racing) A syndicate of not more than twelve persons may share an interest in a racehorse under Jockey Club rules, provided that the legal ownership of the horse is vested in not more than four members of the syndicate, who are treated as joint owners and subject to all liabilities. Under Rule 45, all syndicates have to be approved and registered by the Stewards of the Jockey Club, for which there is a registration fee.

Syndication, of stallions Generally involves a horse's capitalisation into forty shares (this being the number of mares normally covered by a stallion in a season) and the offer of some, or all, of these shares for sale.

Synovial fluid Commonly known as 'joint oil', this fluid is secreted by the membrane which lines the articular cartilage. Together with the articular cartilage, it prevents friction in joints and ensures smooth and easy working.

T

T (racing) Tubed (q.v.).

TB Universally accepted abbreviation for the Thoroughbred horse.

TNP (racing) Took no part.

TO (racing) Tailed off.

TPR Temperature, pulse, and respiration (qq.v.). Three measurements of vital importance in assessing the physical well-being of the horse. Pulse and respiration rates are much used in endurance and long-distance riding (q.v.) in which they must be within defined parameters at various stages of the competition.

TYO (racing) Two-year-old.

Tables The polished surface of the front (incisor) teeth formed by contact with the

teeth in the other jaw. The shape of the tables gives an indication of age.

Tables (show jumping) See **Bareme**.

Taboon Russian term for a large-scale breeding of steppe horses. Also known as a Kossiak.

Tack A stable word for saddlery; an abbreviation for tackle (harness).

Tack cleaning Bridles are dismantled and saddles stripped (i.e. have the girth, stirrup leathers, irons, buckle guards, etc. removed). Mud and grease are then removed with a sponge soaked in luke-warm water. The leather is then left to dry, before an application of saddle soap (q.v.). All metal parts are washed in warm water, dried, and polished with a proprietary metal polish.

Tackle spur straps A pair of straps fitting on to spur and boot by means of studs and a buckle on the former.

Tack room A room fitted with saddle racks and bridle holders for keeping saddlery and harness when not in use. Sometimes contains glass-fronted cupboards for storing bits.

Taffy Australian term for a dun colour. Correctly, taffy is liver chestnut with a yellow or silverish mane and tail.

Tag The tip of a fox's brush.

Tail carriage This should be high and gay, which is a sign of quality and breeding. It is best exemplified in the high-caste Arabian, which is unmistakeable, and has a character of its own.

Tail guard Made of rugging or leather, it covers the dock completely and is designed to prevent damage to the tail when the horse is travelling.

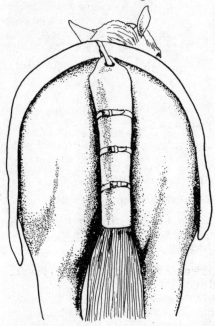

Tail guard.

Tail hounds Those which are some distance behind the main pack when running.

Tail mark A method of cutting the tail hair of ponies in the New Forest in Brit-

ain, to indicate that the marking fee (q.v.) has been paid. See **Agisters**.

Tail plaiting Usually done to enhance the appearance for show purposes.

Tail pulling Used to improve the shape and appearance of the tail. Done by first pulling the hairs from underneath the dock, followed by progressive pulling of hair evenly from both sides of the tail. The practice is not recommended for animals living out, as they need a full tail for protection from the weather.

Tail string See **Fillet string**.

Tail swishing A sign of distress, excitement, irritability or exhaustion, often noticeable during racing and show jumping and in the in-season mare.

Tail to the wall See **Renvers**.

Take hold, to A phrase indicating that a horse is taking the bit strongly, and pulling against the rider or driver.

Take-off The horse's act of lifting the forehand and striking off from the hocks when jumping; also the place from which the horse takes off when attempting a jump.

Take-off side That side of any obstacle to be jumped which is nearest to the rider.

Take with the hand To close the fingers sufficiently to increase the tension of the reins and consequently the pressure of the bit.

'Take your own line' (show jumping) A competition in which riders choose their own route around a course, with knockdowns, refusals, etc. being penalised by addition to the overall time taken.

Taking your own line A term used in foxhunting for a rider who does not remain with the field.

Tallet A hay-loft.

'Tally ho!', 'Tally o!' A hunting cry indicating that a fox has been seen. Unless the huntsman is within speaking distance, a shrill scream known as 'View Holloa' is substituted.

'Tally over', 'Tally ho over' A hunting cry

indicating that a fox has crossed a ride in a wood.

Tan An artificial riding surface, used indoors and outdoors, and consisting principally of wood bark – which gives it the tan colour from which it takes its name. The word is now falling into disuse with the upsurge of many new types of artificial and all-weather riding surfaces of varying colours.

Tandem Two horses driven one ahead of the other.

Tandem cart A dog-cart or other two-wheel trap used for driving a tandem.

T'ang horses Funeral pottery horses, lively and spirited in fashion, made during the T'ang Dynasty of AD 618-906 in China, and executed as substitutes for living animals to accompany their dead masters in their tombs.

Tanning A process in the curing of leather which prevents the hide decaying. Many hides are still tanned by the use of tannic acid, but other methods include immersion in fish oil, followed by mechanical pounding, and a drying process. The hides for saddles, bridles, harness, etc. are then coloured by the currier, in three main shades of brown – London (golden yellow), Warwick (dark brown) and Havana ('cigar coloured').

Tantivy A full gallop, riding headlong. The term originally represented the sound of a horse's feet. Sometimes erroneously applied to a flourish on the hunting horn.

Tapedero Hooded stirrup cover on a Western saddle.

Tap root The main root of a female pedigree traced to the origin.

Tar See **Stockholm tar**.

Tarbenian This is a famous breed from the neighbourhood of the small, quiet town of Tarbes at the foot of the Pyrenees, and which originated in the Iberian horse. The strain was improved at the beginning of the nineteenth century by Arab stallions imported by Napoleon Bonaparte. Later the Bourbons imported English Thoroughbred stallions which augmented the height, and this created the Bigourdan horse. The introduction of the Thoroughbred was thought by French connoisseurs to be rather a disastrous influence, and the tendency was to add more Arab blood. The Tarbenian of today is merely an Anglo-Arab (q.v.) bred for more than a century on the plains around Tarbes. The breed is light-boned, about 15 hh (152.4 cm), of good conformation and beautiful action. It is possessed of great courage, speed and intelligence, and is unexacting in food requirements. The breed produced many excellent cavalry horses, as a result of these fine qualities.

Tarpan The Forest Horse. See **Equus Przewalskii Gmelini Antonius**; and **Evolution of the horse**.

Tarporley Hunt Club The club was founded in 1762 to hunt hares, but later changed to foxhunting. Membership was limited to forty, and since 1799 the qualification for membership was property, family or residence in Cheshire. Since 1775, the Club held a yearly race meeting, except during the war years, and since 1874, steeplechases were substituted for flat races. A race is now held at the Cheshire point-to-point. Hunting songs were written year by year specifically for the Club by the well-known sporting poet Robert Eyles Egerton Warburton (q.v.) (1804-1891), and were sung after supper at Club meetings. A supper is now held during the opening week of the hunting season.

Tat A native-bred Indian pony.

Tattenham Corner The last bend on the Epsom racecourse. The winning chances of many horses running in the Derby are made or marred at this sharp left-handed turn.

Tattersall, Richard (1724-1795) Founder of the firm of that name. Tattersall went to London from his Hurstwood (Lancashire/Yorkshire borders) birthplace, and subsequently set up his business as a bloodstock auctioneer on premises he built at Hyde Park Corner. Tattersall's world famous bloodstock sales (q.v.) are now held on their premises at Park Paddocks, Newmarket. See **Sales, bloodstock**.

Tattersall bit A colt's circular bit, with

or without players or keys. Often called a foal bit or sometimes a yearling bit.

Tattersall's Committee (This has no connection with Tattersall's Sales other than the name). The committee was formed in 1795 and took its name from the fact that it met at Tattersall's auction room, which was then at their Knightsbridge premises. It had the authority to settle all questions relating to bets, commissions for bets, and any matters arising directly or indirectly out of wagers or gaming transactions on horseracing, to adjudicate on all cases of default, and, at its discretion, to report defaulters to the Jockey Club.

Tattersall's ring The chief betting ring on any racecourse to which bookmakers and the public are admitted on payment.

Tattersall's Sales See **Sales, bloodstock**.

Tattoo For identification purposes, the lips or gums are sometimes tattooed.

'Tatt's' Colloquial abbreviation of Tattersall's Sales. See **Sales, bloodstock**.

T-Cart Similar to a Stanhope phaeton (q.v.), and formerly very popular for driving polo ponies in single harness, especially in India.

Team Used alone, this term is understood to mean a four-horse team; a four-in-hand; a pair of wheelers behind a pair of leaders.

Team chasing A team sport devised by Douglas Bunn, the 'Master of Hickstead', and run for the first time at the Hickstead Easter Meeting in 1974. It consists of teams of four cross-country riders. Each team sets off together round a cross-country course, and the team which gets three of its members home in the fastest time is the winner. Now a country-wide sport, attracting many competitors and spectators.

Teaser A substitute stallion, often of little value, presented to a mare at a stud to test whether she is ready for mating to a more popular and valuable stallion.

Teeth In each jaw there are six front or biting teeth (incisors), and twelve back or grinding teeth (molars), and between these, in both jaws of horses, lie two tushes, or tusk-like teeth. They are rarely seen in mares. (See also **Ageing**; and **Age, to tell the**)

Telegraph springs Coach springs or beds (invented by John Warde (q.v.)) and first used on the coach 'Manchester Telegraph', hence the name.

Temperature The normal temperature of a horse is 100.5°F (38°C). A rectal reading should be taken by raising the dock, inserting the lubricated thermometer and rotating the instrument until three-quarters of its length is inside. It should be left in position for a suitable period of time, usually about half a minute.

Tendon boots Boots which protect the tendons against speedy cutting (q.v.). Made of leather, box-cloth or PVC, with extra padding at the rear. Perforated, cushioned tendon protectors are also available for use under exercise bandages.

Tendons Amber-coloured fibrous structures, forming bands and cords which attach the muscles to the bones of the legs. They are light, but of great strength. Tendons (also called sinews) are brought into action by the contracting and relaxing of muscles.

Tendons, bowed (Tendonitis) A strain or injury in which blood and tissue fluid is released within the superficial flexor tendons and their sheaths, causing the tendons to assume a bowed shape instead of the normal straight outline. A potentially serious injury, requiring immediate veterinary attention. First-aid measures include ice-packs and support bandages to limit the immediate inflammation. (See also **Tendons, sprained**)

Tendons, sprained/strained The rupture of some or (in extreme cases) all of the tendon fibres. It is caused by galloping or jumping in heavy going, pulling up suddenly, poor conformation (i.e. long, weak pasterns), or ringbone which restricts free joint movements. The symptoms include sudden severe lameness, swelling, and heat. A serious injury, always requiring veterinary attention, and long rest.

Tennessee Walking Horse The name indicates the purpose for which the breed was originally bred, i.e to carry plantation owners and farmers on tours of inspection of their properties. The foundation sire of the breed was Black Allan (also known as Allan F-1), foaled in 1886, the son of the trotting stallion, Allendorf and the Morgan mare, Maggie Marshall. The Walker is now used as a show and pleasure horse, where it demonstrates its two unique paces – the flat and the running walks – to advantage. Both paces are officially described as 'a basic, loose, four-cornered lick, a 1-2-3-4 beat with each of the horse's feet hitting the ground separately at regular intervals'. The running walk, the faster of the two, normally reaches speeds of 6-8 mph (9.6-12.8 km/h) and much faster in the show ring. The Tennessee Walking Horse stands 15-16 hh (152.4-162.6 cm), and is more robustly built, and rather less elegant than the American Standardbred.

Tenovitis Inflammation of the tendon sheath, not affecting the tendon as such. Symptoms include swelling, heat, and possibly a small degree of oedema.

Tent-pegging A spectacular equestrian sport, which originated in India. A soft, white wooden peg, bound with wire, is placed in the ground at an angle, leaving roughly 9 x 4 ins (23 x 10 cm) showing. It has to be taken with a sword or lance at full gallop. It was popular in the Army until recent years. In the USA it is known as 'peg-sticking'.

Terrets The two rings attached to the pad through which the driving reins pass. The centre part is not a terret, but a bearing-rein hook or pillar.

Terrier man One who accompanies the hunt (either mounted or unmounted) and has a terrier, either in a carrier on his back, or on a leash. If the fox goes to ground, the terrier must be available to go into the earth. He must also be ready to go with the pack into an extra thick covert (e.g. close-growing gorse).

Tersky A Russian horse bred and developed at the Tersk and Stavropol Studs in the North Caucasus, by crossing Strelets (q.v.) with purebred Arabs. Some cross-breds (Don/Arab and Strelet/Karbardin) were introduced later to produce a lovely horse of Arab appearance, with a good temperament, elegant paces, and great endurance. The breed stands between 14.3-15 hh (149.9-152.4 cm), and the predominant colour is grey with a silver sheen.

Test competition See **Puissance**.

Testosterone A male sex hormone secreted by the testes and responsible for the male sex characters.

Tetanus Also known as lockjaw. It is caused by the bacterium *Clostridium tetani* entering the blood stream through a wound (particularly a puncture). The symptoms are stiffness; muscular spasms including those of the jaw which clamps tightly; the horse standing stretched; and the second eyelid flicking across the eye in response to sudden noise. Immediate veterinary attention is essential. Vaccination is available and biennial boosters are necessary. The foals of vaccinated mares are immune for approximately three months following birth, after which they too, should be vaccinated. Unvaccinated animals require tetanus anti-toxin, particularly following puncture wounds; this gives temporary immunity.

Tevis Cup The foremost long-distance/endurance ride in the USA. A 100 mile (160 km) in 24 hours event, it was first held in 1955 over the very demanding course which runs from Lake Tahoe, California, through the Sierra Nevada Mountains. The Cup (which was named after Lloyd Tevis, a former President of the Wells Fargo Company) is awarded to the overall winner, and the Haggin Cup is given to the horse in the best condition among the first ten to finish. The competition was originally known as the Western States Trail Ride, but is now more commonly known as the Tevis Cup.

Thatching An old fashioned method of drying off a horse that has returned from work still hot and/or wet. Dry clean straw is spread over his back and kept in place by a sweat rug or a jute rug worn inside out. The straw is left in place until the horse is thoroughly dry.

'Thief' A racing term for a dishonest horse, i.e one which does not reproduce his good home form in public.

279

Thill A two-wheel cart harness horse as opposed to a lead chain horse. A shaft horse is termed a 'thiller', a 'thill horse', or a 'till horse'. In Eastern Counties and some other parts of England, however, the term also denotes cart-horses in tandem or team.

'This grass' An expression used when referring to the age of a horse, e.g. 'three years old this grass', meaning this coming spring.

Thongs Plaited leather, with a loop to fasten to a whip keeper and a lash at the other end. The length varies from 1-2 yds (0.9-1.8 m).

Thoroughbraces Strong leather braces connecting the rear and front C-springs and supporting the body of a C-spring-hung carriage or coach.

Thoroughbred The origin of the English Thoroughbred, the best known of all breeds, and one of the most beautiful – and certainly the fastest – horses in the world, has been the subject of a certain amount of controversy. There are two principal schools of thought, neither of which can offer absolute proof of their veracity. The first school, headed by the late Lady Wentworth, the great scholar and champion of the Arab horse, maintains that the Thoroughbred is descended from pure Arabian stock crossed with local stock. The second believes that the Thoroughbred is descended from the crossing of Arabian and *other* Oriental horses, with native British horses that had been used for racing here for many centuries. These latter were known as 'running horses', and included the Irish-bred Hobby and the Galloway from the English/Scottish borders, in addition, in all probability, to other animals of Oriental or part-Oriental blood. The difficulty of proving either theory stems from the impossibility of establishing the ancestry of these early horses with any certainty. This was due, in part, to the practice of naming horses after their owners, and the problems which then arose with changes of ownership and subsequent changes of name. There was also widespread indiscriminate use of the terms Arab, Barb and Turk when referring to Oriental horses.

Arabian horses have been in Britain for centuries, and records exist showing that they were raced here as early as 1377. It was, however, during the reign of Henry VIII that significant mention is made of the importation of horses to improve the King's racing stock; these were said to be Spanish and Italian horses, almost certainly of Oriental breeding, and they were crossed with native stock. Successive monarchs – Elizabeth I, James I and Charles I – continued the Royal interest in racing, and in the improvement of the speed and general standard of racing stock, by further imports of Oriental blood. Charles II imported a number of mares of Eastern blood, and also received gifts of mares with Oriental blood from Spain. Collectively, these were known as Royal mares, and were mated with Arabs.

But the most significant importation of Oriental horses occurred at the end of the seventeenth and the beginning of the eighteenth centuries. It was during this period that three great stallions, the Byerley Turk, the Darley Arabian and the Godolphin Arabian (qq.v.) arrived, and there is no dispute at all about their contribution to the ancestry of the modern Thoroughbred. They were crossed with English mares – some cross-breds, some Oriental – and founded the four great tail-male lines of the English racing Thoroughbred – those of Eclipse, Herod, Matchem, and Matchem's son, Highflyer. It is possible to trace the ancestry of *all* modern Thoroughbreds back in direct male line to one or more of the three great Arabian sires. On the female side, all horses in the General Stud Book (q.v.) trace to thirty or so tap-root mares, some of which were Royal mares, and some not.

The modern Thoroughbred is, of course, the supreme racing 'machine', but is also used extensively in other equestrian fields, such as horse trials, show jumping and, to a lesser extent, dressage. It is a superb hunter, and, if crossed with a heavier breed such as a Suffolk or a Welsh Cob, can produce excellent weight-carrying hunters and performance horses. The Thoroughbred has also played a significant part in the establishment and/or development of numerous other breeds, e.g. the Trakehner, and a variety of European warmbloods; American breeds such as the Quarter Horse and the Saddlebred; and Russian breeds such as the Don.

In size, Thoroughbreds range from about 14.2 hh (147.3 cm) to over 17 hh (170 cm), but average around 16.1-16.2 hh (162.5-165 cm), and may be any solid colour. They are handsome, alert horses, with great presence and quality, and with a freedom of action at all paces unsurpassed by virtually any other breed. The head is refined, the neck elegant and arched, withers pronounced, and the shoulder well sloped. The legs are clean, hard, and with good bone, and hocks well let down. The back is short, the body deep, and the quarters muscular. (See also **Thoroughbred racing**)

Thoroughbred Breeders' Association Founded by Lord d'Abernon in 1917, to encourage and ensure co-operative effort in all matters pertaining to the production and improvement of Thoroughbred horses and the interests of their breeders.

Thoroughbred racing The importance of the three great stallions, the Byerley Turk, the Darley Arabian, and the Godolphin Arabian (qq.v.), as the founding fathers of the racing Thoroughbred cannot be over-emphasised. The Byerley Turk was the great-great-grandsire of Herod, who was bred by the Duke of Cumberland in 1757, and was a marvellous sire, getting the winners of over £200,000 – a very big sum in those days. From Herod, in direct tail-male line, descend the 1836 Derby winner, Bay Middleton, the 1849 Derby winner, The Flying Dutchman, many of the best French racehorses, including Bruleur, Ksar, Tourbillon, and Djebel, and horses well known in this country like My Babu, Le Lavandou, Le Levanstell, and the 1969 Ascot Gold Cup and Prix de l'Arc de Triomphe winner, Levmoss. Other well-known horses which descend from the Byerley Turk are The Tetrarch, Hethersett, Blakeney, Julio Mariner and Sexton.

The Darley Arabian was the great-great-grandsire of Markse, the sire of the immortal Eclipse, from whom descend in tail male some 90% of the horses who race in Britain today. Tracing back to the Darley Arabian are horses of the cali-

bre of Gainsborough, Hyperion, Owen Tudor, Tudor Melody, Abernant, Aureole, St Paddy, Blandford, Donatello, Crepello, Busted, Ormonde, St Simon, Tenerani, Ribot, Relko, Phalaris, Native Dancer, Mill Reef, and the 1987 Derby winner, Reference Point.

The Godolphin Arabian's sons included Matchem, from whom descends West Australian, foaled in 1850, and the first winner of the Triple Crown (q.v.). Two of West Australian's sons were responsible for sire lines which have continued to the present day – Solon and Australian. From Solon is descended Hurry On, sire of three Derby winners, and also the Ascot Gold Cup winner, Precipitation, one of whose sons was Sheshoon.

Australian was responsible for a succession of good horses in America. From his line came Fairplay, and the brilliant Man o' War (q.v.) from whom descend such as Relic, Roan Rocket, Silver Shark, Never Say Die, Relko, and Sir Ivor.

Thoroughbred racing (Australia) Australia has the second largest Thoroughbred population in the world after America, and the racing industry is huge, with more courses in the State of Victoria than in the whole of Great Britain. The first English Thoroughbred stallion, Rockingham, arrived in 1799, and another early arrival was Northumberland in 1802. Early racing was influenced by Captain, later Admiral, Rous (q.v.), when he visited Australia as a serving naval officer. The first classic to be run in Australia was the St Leger, run at Home Bush (NSW) in 1842.

Over the years, an Australian type of racehorse has evolved by mixing old colonial stock with imported blood. This type of horse is characterised by remarkable toughness, and runs in many more races than its British counterpart.

Among the great horses bred in Australia in the last forty or so years is Shannon, foaled at the Kia-Ora Stud in NSW in 1941, who won fourteen of his twenty-five races. He was then exported to the USA where he won six more, including the Hollywood Gold Cup, before retiring to be a successful sire at the Spendthrift Farm, Kentucky. Shannon was joined at stud in Kentucky by another all-time great, Bernborough, whose illustrious racing career began in 'picnic races' in the bush in Queensland, and ended when he broke a leg as a seven-year-old when running at Melbourne's Flemington racecourse. Among his progeny were Berseen, Hook Money, and Parody Lady.

One of the most influential sires in Australian Turf history was not, however, home-bred. It was the Irish-bred Star Kingdom, foaled in 1946. This grandson of Hyperion raced in Britain as a two- and three-year-old, when he was known as Star King. His maternal grandsire was the sprinter Concerto, and from him he inherited brilliant speed, being beaten as a two-year old only by Abernant. This brilliance was, after his export to Australia in 1950, passed on to his progeny, and it is said he transformed Australian Thoroughbred breeding by 'injecting a pervasive dose of precocious speed' and, perhaps even more significantly, 'siring progeny of such sublime elegance that breeders could not ignore them, and the prejudice against home-bred stallions was broken down'. Among his progeny were the immortal Todman, in addition to Skyline, Fine and Dandy, Sky High, and Magic Knight – the first five winners of the 6 furlong (1.2 km) two-year-old Golden Slipper Stakes.

Thoroughbred racing (New Zealand) New Zealand Thoroughbreds have played an important role in Australian racing over the years. Conditions are ideal for rearing Thoroughbreds, and New Zealand-bred animals are renowned for their size, stamina and bone.

Horses were unknown in the islands until three were imported by a missionary, the Rev. Samuel Marsden, in 1814. Stock imported into New Zealand from the United Kingdom included in 1878, the famous Musket, who sired the successful Carbine and Trenton, both of whom were sold back to England. Traducer (by The Libel) arrived in New Zealand as a five-year-old, and subsequently sired nine New Zealand Derby winners, and eight Canterbury Cup winners. Of the mares, Flora McIvor (by Rous Emigrant out of Manto), foaled in 1828, went to New Zealand as a twenty-five-year-old, but none the less produced two fillies, Io and Waimea, who were to be highly influential. In later years, Phar Lap (q.v.), Tulloch (q.v.), and Balmerino (q.v.) were outstanding racehorses, while Alcimedes (by Alycidon) and his grandson, Oncidium, were also extremely successful.

Thoroughbred racing (USA) Thoroughbred racing in America did not play a significant role until after the War of Independence, when two particularly influential stallions were imported from Britain. The first was Medley (by Gimcrack), who was foaled in 1776 and arrived in Virginia as a nine-year-old. He became famous as a sire of highly influential brood mares who 'nicked' exceptionally well with the other imported horse, the remarkable Diomed (winner of the first Derby) who arrived as a twenty-one-year-old in 1798. His most distinguished son was Sir Archie (foaled in 1805), who had a good racing record and a phenomenal stud career. One of his descendants was Boston, who was leading sire from 1851-53. Possibly his most famous son, however, was Lexington, who became the greatest horse of his day, being champion sire sixteen times. His sons include Norfolk, Asteroid, and Kentucky. He was, however, pronounced ineligible for the General Stud Book in Britain, because of doubts about the pedigree of his dam, Alice Carneal. This precluded any of his stock being registered in the GSB – a ban which remained in effect until 1949. (See **Jersey Act**)

Another significant import from Britain was Eclipse (not *the* Eclipse), who founded a line which included Commando, Peterpan, Dr Fager, and more recently, Ack Ack.

The middle to late twentieth century has seen a virtual reversal, with American-bred horses coming into Britain, winning the Classics, and in some instances, remaining to stand at stud. These include the 1968 Derby winner, Sir Ivor, the 1954 winner, Never Say Die, Roberto (1972), Nijinsky (1970) and Mill Reef (1971).

Horses bred in Ireland also had a great influence on the American racing scene

– particularly those bred by the late Aga Khan during the 1930s to the 1950s. These included the Derby winners Blenheim (1930), Mahmoud (1936), Bahrain (1935), and above all, Nasrullah, who although not a Derby winner, was leading sire five times in America, and his son, Bold Ruler, eight times. Princequillo, sire of the great Mill Reef, was imported in 1954 and played an important role, and the line begun by the importation of Sickle (by Phalaris), Hyperion's half-brother, was highly significant, including as it did, Native Dancer, Raise a Native, and the 1980 Kentucky Derby winner, the filly Genuine Risk.

European horses which have influenced American bloodstock in recent years include Ribot, who was descended from St Simon (q.v.).

Thoroughpin A soft swelling near the point of the hock causing inflammation of the deep digital tendon sheath. It is due to stress or strain. Except in severe cases it rarely causes lameness but it may recur and can be treated by draining surgically. High-heeled shoes may provide relief.

Three-day event See **Horse trials**.

'Three feet of tin' A coaching term for the horn used by guards on Royal Mail coaches. Also known as 'yard of tin'. (See **Horn, coaching**)

Three-fold girth A girth made of a piece of baghide folded in three.

Three-gaited Saddlebred (USA) See **American Saddlebred**.

Threequarters brothers and sisters See **Brothers and sisters**.

Three-year-old A gelding, filly or colt is termed a 'three-year-old' between the third and fourth anniversaries of its birth, but a racehorse is so described between 1 January of the third year after birth and 31 December of the same year, e.g. a Thoroughbred foaled in April 1980 would officially become a three-year-old on 1 January 1983. (See also **Age, a horse's**)

Throat cap Form of throat covering worn by Hackneys (q.v.) to encourage wasting and fining down of the neck.

Throatlash/Throatlatch A narrow, buckled strap which is part of the bridle head, running under the throat. It should only be tight enough to prevent the bridle from slipping over the horse's ears.

Thrombosis The blocking of an artery or vein by a blood clot. It is usually due to a roughening of the vessel's lining caused by redworm larvae, bacterial infection, or injury. See also **Embolism**.

Throttle Upper part of the horse's throat or gullet.

'Throwing their tongues' When hounds vocally acknowledge the presence of the fox in covert.

'Thrown' When a horse is cast on to straw or other bed for an operation, it is said to be 'thrown'.

Thrush An inflammatory condition of the frog of the foot characterised by discharge and a foul smell; in advanced cases lameness will result. It is caused by neglect of the feet; dirty bedding and badly drained stables; the frog failing to make contact with the ground, leading to degeneration. The causative agent must be removed. Veterinary attention is required to remove the infected horn.

Thruster An aggressive rider to hounds who, though mostly selfish and without consideration of others, may be one who makes himself conspicuous by his boldness and courage in riding his own line.

Thurlow bit A pattern where, instead of the usual 'eye' or top loop in the top of the cheek, there is a slit about 1½ ins (37 mm) long in which the cheek slides.

Tibia See **Fibula**.

Ticks Insects belonging to the order *Acarina*, which live on the skin and suck blood, leading to loss of condition and anaemia. When horses are neglected or turned out to grass, ticks usually appear between the thighs, and under the mane and the root of the tail. They may transmit infectious diseases.

Tick-tack A method of signalling by hand and sign used by bookmakers and their agents on a racecourse. By this method, prices are quoted and bets laid.

Tied-in below the knee The measurement immediately below the knee is less than the measurement lower down towards the fetlock joint. A bad fault, and the horse is necessarily light of bone. A horse can also be 'tied in under the hock', giving an impression of a bad, slightly bent hindleg.

Tiercé A special form of betting in France conducted under pari-mutuel principles, the object being to select the first three to finish in a specific race which is chosen every Sunday or public holiday as the Tiercé Race.

Tie-rings (stable) Metal rings fitted to stable walls to which horses, haynets, etc. may be tied.

'Tiger' The name given to a groom of small stature who rode behind a cabriolet (q.v.), standing on the platform and holding on by the straps.

Tiger-trap A cross-country fence consisting of rails set at an angle over a deep ditch. There can be either one set of rails, or two sets forming an inverted 'V'.

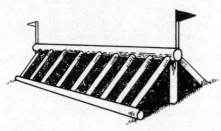

Tiger-trap.

Tilbury The horse traditionally supposed to have been ridden by Queen Elizabeth I when reviewing her troops at Tilbury. It became fashionable for other Elizabethans to prefix 'Tilbury' to the names of their horses, e.g. Tilbury Rose, Tilbury Tip, etc.

Tilbury gig A gig with the body supported at the back by three upright rails, and having seven springs. It was named after its designer.

Tilbury tugs In driving, where these are used, the shafts do not go through loops but drop into a metal reinforced tug opened at the top to receive them, and over which the belly band passes to keep them in place. They are not confined in their use to a Tilbury gig, but are used on a number of vehicles. The chief advantage in their use is that they prevent the up and down play of the shafts.

Tillemans, Peter (1684-1730) A Fleming or Dutchman who, from the age of twenty, lived in England (mainly at Richmond), painting sporting scenes and horses. Though best known for attractive compositions that include a number of people and horses, like views of racing at Newmarket, he has some good equestrian portraits attributed to him. For a while he shared the studio of his friends, Wootton and Seymour, who are thought to have owed more than a little to Tillemans' help.

Till-horse or Thill-horse A shaft horse.

Timber Any fence made of timber, e.g. a post and rail fence.

Timber splitters A term applied to horses skilled in picking their way through 'burns' with speed and safety.

Time test (racing) Official scale for calculating weight and time is: 1 length = 3 lb (1.36 kg); head (or short head) = 1 lb (0.45 kg); neck = 1 lb; 1 lb is taken to equal $1/_{15}$th of a second. For calculating weight: 1 lb = 0.06 second; 2 lb (0.9 kg) = 0.13 second; 3 lb (1.35 kg) = 0.20 second; 10 lb = (44.5 kg) = 0.66 second; 15 lb (6.8 kg) = 11 seconds.

Timor A small pony bred in the island of Timor, Indonesia. Robust, agile and of great endurance. A number were imported into Australia in the early days, and crossed with larger breeds. Usually dark coloured, and about 12hh (121.9 cm).

Tips A form of shortened shoe to protect the toes of a horse out at grass. Also known as 'grass tips'.

Tire An iron or rubber hooping confining the felloes of a wheel.

Tits A slang term for light horses. Little horses.

'Tittup' A term describing a false, fidgety, up-on-the-toes action; not a true gait. To 'tittup down the road'; 'tittuping into a jump'.

Toad eye The typical prominent eye of the true Exmoor Pony (q.v.).

Tobiano (USA) See **Pinto/Paint Horse**.

Todd bridle Similar to the Rockwell (q.v.), but having the mouthpiece joint covered in strong rubber, from which two pieces of elastic are taken to encircle the upper jaw and form a noseband. This latter is kept in place by a central strap running up the face and fastened at the poll. Prevents the tongue being placed over the bit by raising the latter in the mouth.

Toe, seedy Inflammation of the coronet which affects the horn of the hoof and causes separation of the crust. It may be detected by tapping the feet. If a hollow sound is heard, lameness is bound to occur. A farrier or veterinary surgeon should be consulted.

Toe-piece (of shoe) A toe-piece is a bar of mild steel or iron sometimes welded across the toe of a draught horse shoe. It gives a good foothold for horses pulling weight, and it also restores the balance of the foot which is altered when calkins (q.v.) are used.

Tom Thumb bit A name given to a Weymouth bit when the cheek is very short, about 2½ ins (63 mm). The action is correspondingly mild.

Tonga draught A form of pair-horse draught, used in India, similar to the curricle (q.v.). In Tonga draught the necessary elevation is given to the end of the pole by inclining it upwards from the bottom of the body of the cart.

Tongue 'Giving tongue', the cry of hounds when hunting.

Tongue grid A metal port suspended in the mouth, above the bit, by a slip head. Prevents the tongue getting over the bit.

Tongue over bit The bit should normally lie on the tongue, and if the horse will not permit this, the proper placing of the head and general control become greatly marred.

Tongue-over-bit device Two leather circles fitting round the mouthpiece, preferably of the mullen type, connected by an adjustable nose strap. To prevent this lying too low there is a central fastening attached to the ordinary cavesson. It raises the bit in the mouth and is often effective. (See also **Juba port**; and **Tongue grid**)

Tongue port See **Juba port**.

Tongue strap A racing device to keep the tongue down. It is a slotted strap through which the tongue is passed, the strap then fastening under the lower jaw. It can cause great pain if adjusted too tightly. The Jockey Club rules that no tongue strap shall be less than 1 in. (2.5 cm) wide.

Tongue-swallowing The common term for the gurgling noise sometimes made at fast paces. It happens when the neck muscles pull the larynx out of the part of its socket where it joins the pharynx. Strapping the tongue down so that it cannot move backwards is said to ease the situation. A cure can be effected by removing part of the muscles which pull the larynx.

Tony Collings Memorial Challenge Trophy Awarded to the British rider gaining the most points at horse trials organised by or affiliated to the national federation during the season.

'Tooling' (a four-in-hand) A slang expression for driving a team.

Tooth rasp A long-handled rasp or file for removing the sharp edges of teeth. See also **Rasping**.

Top boots Any form of hunting boot, whether black or brown.

Top hats Top hats came into fashion again at the end of the eighteenth century, and the hat as known today was first made by John Hetherington, a hatter, of Charing Cross, in 1797, from fine silk shag. The style became universally popular and appeared in the hunting field, where it is still regarded as correct wear. However, doubts about its protective value in the event of a fall are now increasingly voiced.

Top-latch In driving, the leather thong that binds together the top ends of the hames or seals on the horse collar.

Top line Term referring to the line of

the back, from the neck to the end of the croup (q.v.).

Top pommel or near head See **Pommel**.

Top-rein See **Overcheck** (On hackney buggy harness); also **Overcheck** (on racing harness).

Tops A term for contrasting tops of riding boots. A fashion originated by cavaliers who used to turn down the tops of their boots to expose the coloured linings.

Top weight Heaviest weight (of jockey and lead), carried by the horse which is allotted the highest weight in handicap.

Tor di Quinto Situated just outside Rome, this Italian Cavalry School was an adjunct of Pinerolo (q.v.). It was used as an international training ground for officers specialising in cross-country riding. After mechanisation in 1945, the stables became an equestrian museum.

Torisky/Toric Strong, muscular Russian horse originally bred in the Toric stud in Esthonia, and developed by crossing native mares with half-bred stallions. The Norfolk Roadster, Hatman, founded five important lines in the last quarter of the nineteenth century, and later, two Breton stallions were used. The breed is primarily a draught animal of great endurance, standing up to 15.1 hh (154.9 cm). The predominant colours are chestnut and brown.

Totalisator A mechanical device showing the number and amounts of bets staked on a race. The total pool on each race, less the Horserace Totalisator Board's percentage, is divided equally in proportion among holders of winning tickets of the pool in which the person bets. Popularly known as 'the Tote'.

Tote See **Totalisator**.

Tote double A daily double usually takes place on the third and fifth races in the programme. The backer nominates the number of the horse in the third race, for which he secures a ticket. If this horse wins, he nominates his choice for the fifth race, for which he receives a transfer ticket. The total pool subscribed for the double is then equally divided among the number of winning tickets.

Tote forecast A bet for which the punter has to nominate the first two horses – in correct order – in races where three, four, five or six horses are declared to run overnight; and in either order where seven, eight, nine or ten horses are declared overnight. A forecast pool also operates where a field of eleven or more runners declared overnight is reduced to ten or fewer by late withdrawals.

Tote place pool A pool separate from the win pool, operated by the Tote, which allows the punter to back a horse for a place only in fields of six and upwards.

Tote treble A daily treble on the second, fourth, and sixth races in the programme. The mode of operation and payout follows the Tote Double (q.v.) method.

'Touched in the wind' A horse which is unsound in wind to a slight extent only.

Touch the horn To blow the hunting horn.

Tournament A contest which reached its greatest popularity between the twelfth and fifteenth centuries. Mounted armoured combatants with blunted lances or swords engaged for a prize bestowed by the 'Queen of Beauty' or lady of the tournament. It was derived from *tourner*, to turn (French), because the riders rode in a circular arena and were, according to the rules, obliged to make many turns.

Towelling An old coaching term for the flogging of coach horses.

Towne, Charles (1763-1840) Rural scenes of great beauty painted by this Liverpool-born artist often included horses. Racing was also one of his important subjects.

Town Moor (racing) The Doncaster racecourse.

'To you' A ditch on the near-side of a fence about to be jumped is a ditch 'to you'.

Trace-bearer In driving a leather strap passing over and between the pad and the crupper with end loops to hold the traces in position; used on any pair-horse harness.

Trace clip See **Clips, types of**.

Trace horse A spare horse to assist in drawing vehicles up an incline. (See **Cockhorse**)

Traces The means of harnessing a draught horse, this consists of two thicknesses of strong leather, with adjustments usually at the shoulder end. There are various means of attachment according to the type of vehicle.

Tracheotomy (Tubing) An operation for the treatment of roaring (q.v.), or to alleviate breathing difficulty caused by abscesses in the throat. It also brings relief in strangles (q.v.). An opening is made through the skin and flesh into the trachea or windpipe, about 9-12 ins (23-30 cm) from the angle of the throat. A plated metal or plastic tube is then inserted; this must be removed and cleaned two or three times a week. The operation is simple and effective.

Track The prints of a horse's hooves on soft going are known as the 'track'. The riding-school term for making a horse follow the correct path is 'keeping a horse in the track'. (See **One-track** and **Two-track**).

Tracking-up When the imprint a horse's hind feet reach up to or beyond those of the forefeet.

Tracks, circular Tracks left by a horse moving in a circle.

Trail ride A term given to cross-country rides much favoured by American riders; also known as 'bridle-trail'.

Trail Riders of the Canadian Rockies, the Order of Established in the early 1920s and sponsored by the Canadian Pacific Railways, this Order holds annual summer meetings at remote beauty spots to encourage the riding of trails on horses through the Rockies, the finding of new trails, and to foster good fellowship and the preservation of old customs.

Trainer See **Licence, trainer's**.

Trainers' Association See **National Trainers' Association**.

Trakehner (Formerly known as the West Prussian Horse) One of the German warmblood breeds, renowned for its elegance, fine action, and good temperament. The breed was established by Friederich Wilhelm I of Prussia in the early eighteenth century at a stud in north-west Prussia. He used the native Schwerken horses of East Prussia with top quality Polish Arabs. The breed thus produced took its name from Trakehner, the name of the stud. Widely accepted as the most handsome of the German warmbloods, and somewhat lighter than most others, the Trakehner stands between 16-16.2 hh 162.6-165 cm), has a very refined 'breedy' head, with good eyes and a small muzzle. The neck is elegant and tapering, and the shoulders well-sloped. The action is very free, and the overall picture is of genuine class. Stallion selection and performance testing ensures the maintenance of high standards. Trakehners have been exported to most European countries.

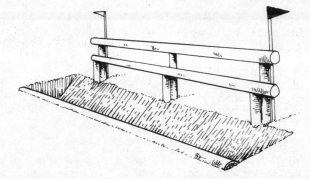

Fence with a ditch 'to you'.

There is a thriving breed society in Britain, as well as in New Zealand, Australia and the USA.

Trakener/Trakehner A type of fence used in cross-country and other events. It consists of a ditch spanned by a rail or rails in the centre.

Trandem Three horses driven abreast; known as a Manchester team.

Transitions The change from one pace to another. When ridden, these should always be smooth, straight, and balanced.

Transit tetany Stumbling gait, distress, sweating and raised respiration rate following a journey. It is caused by a lowering of the blood calcium level.

Transom plates Plates above and below the axle-tree beds on a coach.

Transverse Screened-off portion of smithy where horses were actually shod.

Trap A name loosely applied to any two-wheeled horse-drawn vehicle. Also a horse-cloth.

Trapaderos The fancy swinging pieces on cowboys' stirrups.

Trappings A term applied to ceremonial harness including saddles, bridles, and ornamental coverings.

Trave A stout wooden cage used for shoeing difficult horses. No longer in use.

Travelling boots Long boots designed to cover the leg from below the knee to below the fetlock. Made of PVC, jute or felt, with inner cushion lining.

Travelling head lad The person appointed by the trainer to be in charge when horses go to race meetings.

Travers Also called quarters in, head to the wall, or *le croupe en dedans*. Usually performed along a wall or the side of a school, but may be ridden on a circle. The horse is slightly bent around the rider's inside leg, and positioned at an angle of approximately 30° to the wall, with the hindquarters towards the centre of the school. Movement is on a three-track basis, with the outside hind foot following the track of the inside hind

foot. Travers may be ridden at walk, trot and canter.

Tread, stirrup Grooved rubber treads which fit into a stirrup iron to help keep the rider's foot in the correct position.

Treads Wounds on the coronet, caused by another horse, as is likely when one horse leads another; the condition is seldom self-inflicted. It may develop into a serious injury if neglected.

Treble A bet naming three horses in different races to make one wager.

Tree, saddle See **Saddle tree**.

Trees, boot A support inserted into leather riding boots when not being worn to preserve their shape. Trees were formerly made of wood, but now metal and plastic are used. After wear, leather boots should be treed-up immediately. Tightly rolled newspaper, used as stuffing material, makes a good emergency substitute, the boots then being hung up by the loops to dry.

Trekking See **Pony trekking**.

Trencher-fed Hounds which are trencher-fed are not kept in kennels. Each one is looked after by a farmer, subscriber, or some other person, and on hunting days the hound is collected and taken to the meet.

Tricorne A cocked hat with the brim turned up on three sides; introduced in the 1770s for riding and driving.

Triple bars (show jumping) A fence consisting of three bars of increasing height with a wide spread.

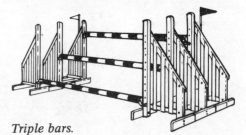

Triple bars.

Triple crown In Britain a triple crown winner is a horse who wins the 2000 Guineas, the Derby, and the St Leger. In America it is the horse who wins the

Kentucky Derby, the Preakness Stakes and the Belmont Stakes.

Trippler Gaucho term for a horse with a fast rolling gait between a trot and a canter.

Troika A Russian term for a team of three horses driven abreast, usually in an open carriage called a Caléche, which is similar to a Victoria.

Trooping the Colour This takes place on the Sovereign's official birthday on Horse Guards Parade, and is part of the ceremony correctly known as The Queen's Birthday Parade.

Tropilla (South American) From six to twelve horses, the property of an individual gaucho (q.v.). Only male horses are ridden, but a mare, usually a piebald, is made leader (madrina), and wears a specially toned bell round her neck. The riding horses become *amadrinada*, i.e. they will seldom stray from the bell-mare.

Trot A natural two-beat pace on alternate diagonals, the two beats separated by a period of suspension during which the horse is completely off the ground; the greater the speed the longer is the period of suspension. In dressage, horses are expected to show variations within the pace according to the stage of training. As in the canter, the trot may be shown as collected, medium and extended, and working (although the latter is not included in the higher standard tests). In the collected trot, the strides are short and elevated, with well-engaged quarters and hocks well-flexed, but no over-tracking (q.v.); the rider sits to the collected trot. In the extended trot, the stride is extended to its maximum, with the horse's whole frame lengthened, and with pronounced over-tracking; in medium, there is moderate extension, with the stride lengthened, but not as markedly as in the extended pace, and the outline of the horse is more rounded than in the latter. The imprints of the hind feet should fall in those of the forefeet. The working trot is between medium and collected, and performed by horses not yet ready for the more collected work. The horse must be balanced, on the bit, and moving forward with even strides showing good hock movement.

Trot, rising The rider, instead of sitting down in the saddle and feeling each hoof beat as each diagonal pair of legs meets the ground, rises in the saddle to one hoof beat, misses the next, and comes down again. Also called 'trotting light', 'posting', or 'taking the bump'.

Trotter Any horse that moves with two-beat diagonal gait at considerable speed.

Trotting Championship, the American Held at the Roosevelt Raceway, Westbury, Long Island, New York.

'Trotting light' See **Trot, rising**.

Trotting out Trotting faster than the ordinary trot, at a speed of at least 300 yards (274 m) per minute.

Trotting races (harness) Horses drawing light gigs or sulkies competing at the trot. Two types of gait are recognised: the true-trotter, which is diagonally gaited; and the pacer, which is laterally gaited. In recent years in Great Britain the sport has regained some popularity. Harness racing is much enjoyed in the USA, using the American Standardbred (q.v.). Many important meetings are held, the sport's triple crown comprising the Yonkers Futurity in New York, the Hambletonian at Du Quion and the Kentucky Futurity at Lexington. Trotting races ('the trots') are also very popular in parts of Australia.

Trotting vanner A typical tradesman's small horse of pre-motor days, much used by the railway companies. Of indiscriminate breed, it was usually a hard-wearing, short-legged type, and was formerly a light-legged cart-horse, very active and capable of a sharp trot. Dealers called them 'vanners'.

True arm Humerus bone of the foreleg of a horse.

Trumble A two-wheel 'tip' cart used on farms.

Trying board A device used at studs to discover whether a mare is ready to mate. She is presented to the stallion but separated from him by a trying board, which should be made of wood 3 ins (75 mm) thick, and 4½ ft (1.37 m) high, with a roll-top. Railway sleepers, suitably stacked, make efficient trying boards.

Tschiffely, Aimé Felix (1895-1954) Born in Switzerland, later becoming a naturalised Argentinian, he earned great fame by riding two Argentine Criollo horses, Mancha, sixteen years old, and Gato, fifteen years, some 10,000 miles (16,000 km) from Buenos Aires, South America, to Washington, USA. The journey took him two and a half years, and began on St George's Day, 1925. Great hardships were endured, including extremes of heat and cold. Gato died at the age of thirty-six; Mancha at forty. Modelled in their own skins, they are to be seen in the Colonial Museum, Buenos Aires. The expressed object of the journey was to prove the stamina of the Criollo breed (q.v.) of ponies, which Tschiffely believed to be dying out.

Tubbing Application of heat – for example to a wound on the foot – by placing the foot in a bucket or tub of warm water containing an antiseptic or other medication such as Epsom salts.

Tub-cart/Tub-car See **Governess cart**.

Tubed (horse) A roarer (q.v.) who has had a tube inserted in his windpipe by means of a tracheotomy (q.v.).

'Tucked up' A term descriptive of a wasp-waisted appearance with the loins drawn up behind the ribs. Such a tightly drawn-up condition of the abdomen points to illness, overwork, excitable temperament, or improper management.

Tufters A stag-hunting term. Several couples of experienced hounds are drafted from the pack (which is temporarily kennelled) and taken into covert to rouse and push the stag into the open. The pack is then laid on the line of exit.

Tugs In driving, circular-shaped, stoutly made loops which connect the shaft to the backband, and meet the traces in pair and team horses.

Tulloch Great New Zealand-bred racehorse. A small horse (15.2 hh/157.5 cm), he was by Khoorassan out of Florida. In spite of his small size, he was bought as a yearling by Sydney (Australia) owner, Tommy Smith. He was rated equal best two-year-old in 1956/57 with the great Todman, winning the AJC Sire Produce Stakes, and as a three-year-old winning the Victoria and Queensland Derbys, and the AJC and Victorian St Legers, as well as the very prestigious Caulfield Cup in Victoria in record time. Although suffering from an undiagnosed internal ailment, as a four-year-old he took his total prize money to £A100,000 by winning the Brisbane Cup.

Tumbril A farm cart; in some parts of England the term refers to a large trough on legs for feeding horses and cattle in the fields.

Turf, the Racing as a whole is referred to sometimes as the Turf; e.g. a credit to the Turf is the same as a credit to racing.

Turf Board, the The Turf Board is a body set up by the Jockey Club (q.v.) to coordinate and direct policy for meetings with members of the Horserace Betting Levy Board (q.v.). It now consists of the chairman, who is also senior steward of the Jockey Club, the two deputy senior stewards, six stewards, and the three Jockey Club members of the Levy Board. The senior steward of the Jockey Club and the two deputy senior stewards meet the chairman of the Levy Board and the other two Government-appointed members of the Levy Board in the Joint Racing Board (q.v.) to discuss racing priorities.

Turf pony Term used in the nineteenth century before the advent of racing grandstands. Owners and other visitors to race meetings rode 'turf ponies' alongside the rails during races.

Turk The Turkish horse was once considered the best saddle horse in the world. It was of characteristic Oriental type, having a great amount of Persian and Arab blood; the species bred in Anatolia had the highest reputation. Today the most typically indigenous Turkish horses are Kurdistan ponies, bred near Sivas, where the custom is to cross mares with Arab sires, thus producing a useful working pony, 14-14.2 hh (142.2-147.3 cm).

Turkish curb See **Mameluke bit**.

Turkoman Horse An ancient Asian breed formerly used by nomadic tribes around the Gobi desert, probably for herding livestock. Much admired by the Chinese of the Han Dynasty, and also used as mounts for the Caliph's guards in tenth century Baghadi. The Royal Horse Society of Iran, founded in 1971, encouraged the breeding of purebred Turkomans, principally for racing. The breed shows great speed and endurance. Herds of semi-wild Turkomans still roam the Russo-Iranian borders. The breed stands up to 15.3 hh (160 cm), has a long face with a straight profile, a fine silky coat, and is a light riding horse of some quality. The principal colours are bay, grey, chestnut, black, and cream gold.

'Turned' or 'Turned to the horse' A term used to indicate that a mare's last service at stud was unproductive.

Turned out A term implying that a horse is put out at grass and not stabled, usually for the summer, but may be at any time.

Turnips A root crop. When of good quality, these are useful in supplementing the food of horses standing idle or doing little work. They are best fed raw but pulped.

Turn on the quarters See **Quarters, turn on the**.

Turn-out A two- or four-wheeled vehicle.

Turpin, Dick (1706-1739) This legendary highwayman was born at Hempstead, Essex, where his father, John Turpin, kept the Bell Inn. Dick Turpin and his black mare (possibly fictitious) are featured in many romantic tales. In reality he was an unsavoury character who was wild in his early youth and before long joined a band of knaves and robbers who terrorised the countryside. His thieving included sheep-stealing and footpad robbery (highway robbery on foot). Later he took to highway robbery on horseback, sometimes using a hackney coach; he worked his trade in many parts of the country. The ultimate hue and cry for his capture was so strong that he retired from the road and became a respected horse-dealer in Yorkshire. Under the assumed name of John Palmer he rode to hounds and was liked in local society. He was arrested for stealing a racehorse named White Stockings, and executed. His 'famous ride' is apocryphal.

Tushes See Teeth.

Twici, William Huntsman to Edward II (1284-1327), who hunted in the Ashdown Forest and wrote the earliest treatise on English hunting.

Twicing The practice adopted by some trainers of long-distance horses when, on training gallops, another horse is jumped in about half-way.

Twins Twin foals are very rarely carried to term. It is a comparatively rare event for a mare to give birth to living twins, and those which do survive are sometimes weak.

Twist See **Waist (of saddle)**.

Twisted snaffle or Brisson A pattern where the mouth of the bit has serrated edges.

Twitch A method of minor restraint applied to control a restive horse for a specific purpose, such as administering medicine, performing minor operations, clipping, etc. A small loop of soft rope, fastened to the end of a long wooden handle, is passed over the upper lip, or the base of the ear, and the handle is turned until the loop becomes fast around the loose flesh. The less frequently twitches are used, the better. They tend to make a horse head shy (q.v.).

Twitch.

Twitch, humane This consists of slightly serrated wooden 'handles' held by a hinge and buckle and strap. Also known as 'Rutter's twitch'.

Two-day event See **Horse trials**.

Two Thousand Guineas Normally the first of the five Classic races of the year, it is run over a straight mile (1.6 km) at the Newmarket Spring Meeting, and is open to three-year-old colts and fillies, although fillies have rarely run in it.

Two-time A pace of two-time is marked by two hoof-beats at each stride.

Two-track A two-track movement is one in which the hindlegs follow a separate track from that made by the forelegs.

Two-tracking An American expression describing the movement in which a horse gains ground to the front and to one side simultaneously, without turning the neck or body.

Two-year-old A colt, gelding or filly having attained the second but not having reached the third anniversary of its birth. A racehorse is so described, however, from 1 January of the second year of its birth until 31 December of the same year.

Type Hunter, cob, show pony, hack, etc. as opposed to breed, e.g. Thoroughbred, Arab, Shetland, etc.

Tyres (pneumatic) These were first fitted to carriage wheels in 1845 by the Duke of Northumberland, and are said to have served him for 1000 miles (1600 km) of travel.

—U—

UR (racing) Unseated rider.

Ukrainian Riding Horse A multi-purpose horse developed after World War II, and used extensively in dressage, show jumping, driving, and in agriculture. Large mares of Gidran, Nonius, Furioso and local breeding were put to Thoroughbred, Hanoverian or Trakehner stallions to produce a powerful yet light riding-type horse with good bone, standing up to 16.1 hh (162.5 cm), and of equable temperament. The principal colours are black, chestnut and bay.

Ultra-sound treatment The therapeutic use of ultra high frequency sound waves beyond the upper limit of human hearing. Ultrasonic waves can penetrate tissue to a depth of up to 4 ins (10 cm), inducing heat, vibration and a chemical reaction. They help to reduce swelling and inflammation, break down adhesions, and remove certain breakdown products.

Unbreakable stirrup leathers (red) This generally refers to a brand of leathers made from buffalo hide and which are practically unbreakable.

Under-bitted see **Ears, identification marks**.

Undercarriage The foundation of a vehicle below the bodywork.

Under-horsed Descriptive of a rider whose horse or pony is too small for him.

Under-reach In trotting action, the front of the toe of the fore-shoe comes into contact with and scrapes away the hind toe almost up to the coronet. It may be prevented by the use of a square-shaped toe in the fore-shoe, with two clips, and the front edge of the shoe well rounded off. A flat hind shoe with a heavy toe should be used.

Undershot A deformity in which the lower jaw protrudes beyond the upper. If the incisors do not meet satisfactorily, the horse's ability to graze is impaired.

'Under starter's orders' (racing) At one time, every horse was under starter's orders when a white flag was raised, and was considered to have started in the race once this had happened. The signal is now usually given by radio.

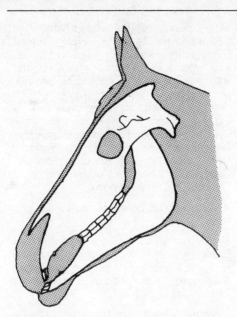

Undershot jaw.

'Under the Whip' see **Whip hand**.

Underweight By so mishandling his weight (whatever it may be) in the saddle, a rider is said to rider overweight. By light, active and alert riding he may, whatever his weight, ride underweight.

Unentered A hound which has not finished one cub-hunting season is described as being unentered.

Unicorn A team of three, with two wheelers and one leader.

United States Trotting Association Governing body of trotting harness races, found in 1938.

Unkennel see **Find**.

Un-nerved see **De-nerved; Neurectomy**.

Unsaddling enclosure Situated in the paddock adjoining the weighing room, with separate places for the first three horses finishing a race. Immediately after pulling up, the riders of the first three horses ride into the unsaddling enclosure. Other jockeys dismount in the main part of the paddock.

Unseen A term applied to horses bought on a verbal or written description without being seen by the buyer. The full expression is 'bought sight unseen'.

Unskid To remove the skid from the wheel of a coach or other heavy vehicle, necessitating backing the wheelers. (See **Skid-pan**)

'Upsides' (racing) A racing term used of horses at exercise or in a race, when running almost in a line across (side by side).

'Up to their bits' A coaching term for going freely.

Up to weight A term denoting that a horse has the substance and stamina to carry the weight of his rider with ease.

Urticaria (nettle rash) A condition in which small, inflamed, raised weals appear on the skin. Caused by stings and bites, or by an error in diet, it is sudden in onset and is distributed throughout the coat.

VEE Venezuelan equine encephalomyelitis (q.v.).

VWH Abbreviation for Vale of the White Horse (a Hunt).

Vaccination A method of preventing specific infectious diseases by injecting an antigen in solution, i.e. a solution containing the live, altered, or dead agents of the disease. This stimulates the horse's antibodies (the body's natural defences) and develops immunity to the disease-causing organism. Typical vaccines include those used against equine influenza and tetanus (q.v.). See **Influenza, equine**.

Valet, jockey's An attendant responsible for the clothes, silks, saddles, etc., of jockeys. At a big race meeting there will be several jockeys' valets present, each one looking after a number of jockeys, who rely on them for their smart turn-out.

Valeting room (hunting) A room for the use of whippers-in, for cleaning and drying hunting clothes and boots.

Van Horse Parade Society see **London Harness Horse Parade Society**.

Vanner See **Trotting Vanner**.

Vaquero Mexican cowboy.

Vardo A gipsy van.

Varmint A familiar term for a fox.

Vaulting on See **Mounting**.

Vaulting roller A roller fitted with hand-grips for the gymnastic exercises of vaulting on, off, or over a horse.

Vehicles, two-wheeled, sizes of Given below is a very general guide to the sizes of two-wheeled vehicles to fit different sized horses and ponies:

to protect the rights and privileges of Commoners. In the New Forest (Hampshire) there are seven Verderers, with statutory powers to control the wellbeing of animals (including ponies), grazing, and rights of common. The Official Verderer is appointed by the Crown, five are elected by the Commoners, and four more are nominated (one each by the Forestry Commission, the Ministry of Agriculture, Hampshire County Council and the Countryside Commission).

Vertebrae The bones of the spinal column.

Vetch A leguminous plant of the pea family, grown with rye, which supports it. If cut when in flower, certain species make good green fodder or hay. Some vetches are poisonous.

Veterinary boot A leather or plastic boot, sometimes with an adjustable, hinged shoe on the sole, allowing the frog to receive pressure but protecting the rest of the foot.

Veterinary certificate A statement of the physical condition of a horse con-

	16hh (ins/cm)	15hh (ins/cm)	14hh (ins/cm)	13hh (ins/cm)	12hh (ins/cm)
Length of shafts	76/193	72/183	67/170	62/157	58/147
Height of tug at underside of shaft	51/129	48/122	45/114	42/106	38/96
Approx. inside distance between shafts at tug stop	26/66	25/63	23/58	21/53	19/48

Velvet The hairy skin of a stag's growing antler. During the growth period, the antlers are very sensitive, but when growth is complete, the 'velvet' peels off.

Venezuelan equine encephalomyelitis An insect-born virus disease of the brain and spinal cord. Symptoms include fever, walking in circles, sitting on quarters, walking into obstacles. It was little known outside South America until 1969, when it spread to North America.

Ventilation Of great importance in stables. It is essential that sufficient pure air is admitted, but horses are particularly susceptible to draughts.

Verderers Persons appointed and elected

sequent upon an examination made by a veterinary surgeon. In 1973 the Royal College of Veterinary Surgeons and the British Veterinary Association advised their members to avoid the use of the terms 'sound' and 'soundness' because of the difficulties of their legal interpretations. Advice was given on a standard form of examination for horses on behalf of intending purchasers, and on the certificate which should be issued thereafter.

Veterinary chest A veterinary first-aid kit should include a cotton-wool roll, disinfectant solution, antiseptic cream, antibiotic aerosol, thermometer, gamgee tissue, pre-packed wound dressings, elasticated bandages, round-ended scissors, forceps, poultice, Epsom salts, and a small bowl.

Veterinary colleges and schools There are now seven of these in Great Britain: the Royal Veterinary College and Hospital (University of London); the School of Veterinary Medicine, Cambridge University; the Faculty of Veterinary Science, Liverpool University; the Royal (Dick) School of Veterinary Studies, Edinburgh University; the University of Glasgow Veterinary School; and the School of Veterinary Science, Bristol University. The course of training in each extends to at least four and a half years, and after graduation leads to the award of the diploma of Membership of the Royal College of Veterinary Surgeons (MRCVS).

Veterinary etiquette, professional Veterinary surgeons are governed by certain rules of professional conduct, the infringement of which may lead them into serious trouble with the Royal College.

It is not always understood that it is forbidden for veterinary surgeons to take over the treatment of a lame or sick horse which is already in the care of a professional colleague. Should an owner be dissatisfied with the service given by his veterinary surgeon, or feel that progress towards recovery is too slow, he has three courses of action open to him: (1) To instruct his veterinary surgeon to discontinue attendance on the case. Having done this, preferably in writing, he is at liberty to call in someone else. (2) To ask for a 'second opinion' on the case, i.e. the calling in of a second veterinary surgeon to consult with the one already in attendance. The latter cannot with reason object to such a course of action. Either the veterinary surgeon attending, or the owner, may nominate the second surgeon to be called in. (3) To inform his veterinary surgeon he wishes a 'consultant' called in. Again, the veterinary surgeon in attendance cannot reasonably object.

Veterinary profession, the The governing body of the veterinary profession in the British Isles is the Royal College of Veterinary Surgeons, whose headquarters are at 32 Belgrave Square, Lon-

don. A Royal Charter was granted in 1844 to the graduates of the two veterinary schools then in existence, forming them into an incorporate body. It declared the practice of veterinary medicine to be a profession. It provided also for the government of the profession by the formation of a Council, and for the systematic examination and enrolment of graduates. Unqualified practice became illegal on 30 July 1949, except for certain minor treatments and operations. In 1966 a new Veterinary Surgeons Act was passed, which came into operation on 15 March 1967. It dealt largely with the reconstitution of the Council, but it retained the recognition orders in respect of the veterinary schools previously included.

Since 1948, the education of veterinary students has been carried out in universities, many of which have acquired land and buildings in rural areas, for the provision of field stations were tuition can be given in natural farm surroundings.

Entry into the veterinary profession is at present very competitive, with only the most highly qualified students being accepted. Most schools require evidence that the prospective student has spent some time observing veterinary practice at close quarters, either by working in a practice during school holidays or visiting a practising veterinary surgeon for some appreciable time. The training of veterinary students involves a long and comprehensive course of study lasting a minimum of just under five years. It includes, in addition to the basic sciences, a thorough training in veterinary anatomy, animal management, veterinary hygiene and dietetics, pharmacology, bacteriology, pathology, parasitology, medicine and surgery. Additional postgraduate diplomas may also be awarded in specialist fields.

Students who graduate in veterinary medicine from one of the universities are accepted by the Royal College of Veterinary Surgeons as members, and are entitled to use the abbreviation MRCVS, in addition to those signifying the degrees granted by their respective universities.

The Fellowship of the Royal College of Veterinary Surgeons may be awarded to existing graduates by thesis, examinations or by election by the Council of the

Royal College for meritorious contribution to learning.

Veterinary students planning to specialise in equine practice require as much practical experience with the horse as possible, and the majority of veterinary surgeons who have special knowledge of equine management, medicine and surgery acquire this as a result of post-graduate training and experience. The duties of the equine practitioner fall under three main headings; clinical veterinary medicine, including preventative medicine; surgical diagnosis and treatment, including operative procedures; the diagnosis and treatment of lameness, and the use of X-rays in diagnosis.

The examination of horses for soundness both in relation to purchase and insurance has acquired an additional importance now that horses and ponies have increased so vastly in value.

Veterinary surgeon Under an Act of Parliament of 1844, this term is reserved exclusively for Members or Fellows of the Royal College of Veterinary Surgeons. Its use otherwise is illegal, the intention being to enable persons in need of veterinary aid to distinguish between practitioners trained at a veterinary college, and the unqualified.

Veterinary surgery and medicine Probably one of the most important features influencing the success of modern equine surgery is the development of the range of antibiotics. The other, nearly as important, is the revolution in the administration and safety of anaesthetics. Chloroform inhalation has practically gone out of use, and its place has been taken by other inhalants such as halothane, usually in conjunction with intravenous or intramuscular injection of a fluid containing reliable anaesthetic properties. Epidural anaesthetics (injection of local anaesthetic into the epidural space, usually between the first and second tail vertebrae, to block the spinal nerves as they emerge from the cord), aid surgery to the posterior areas of the body. Other local anaesthetics are still employed in minor surgery, usually in conjunction with a sedative injection.

The use of intravenous anaesthetics does away with much of the preliminary casting and struggling necessary when using chloroform alone; moreover the recovery period is shortened and the after-effects much reduced.

Operations upon the larynx for the relief of roaring and kindred conditions continue to be performed with a fair measure of success.

Although the anatomical structure of the horse's intestine does not lend itself to a great deal of surgery, the abdomen can be subjected to laparotomy (surgical incision of the abdominal wall). Caesarean section has been successfully carried out on mares.

Much more is known today about the equine eye and disorders of vision, and the use of modern ophthalmic instruments makes correct diagnosis of eye conditions easier.

The universal use of anti-tetanus serum and toxoid when the skin is broken make tetanus rare, with owners much more aware that vaccination is of vital importance.

The employment of X-rays in the diagnosis of lameness, fractures and the presence of foreign bodies, particularly within the foot, is now everyday practice.

Heat therapy and also the rhythmic contraction of muscles produced by application of an electric current are increasingly employed. (See **Faradism**; and **Electrotherapy**)

MEDICAL TREATMENT: in recent years, a great many new drugs and methods of treatment have superseded many of the older methods, and the stomach tube has to be used much less frequently. The knowledge regarding the causes of disease, pathology in general, and the treatment of parasitic diseases has undergone marked improvement. Antibiotics have become more numerous and varied. The laboratory is resorted to more than ever, particularly in connection with bodily secretions and excretions, and the analysis of blood. Vaccination now covers an increasing number of conditions, particularly the influenza-like conditions associated with loss of form and coughs. In the racing world as well as in connection with shows, the spread of these diseases is less likely than before, although problems still remain.

Vice Any chronic objectionable habit acquired by a horse, but particularly the following: kicking; biting; rearing; jibbing; bolting; crib-biting; wind-sucking; weaving; dung-eating, and rug-tearing. In polo, a pony showing any vice is not permitted to be ridden in a game.

'Viceroy' See **Gooch wagon**.

Victoria An open carriage only partly protected by a hood, universally popular from the 1870s onwards.

Victoria, Queen (1819-1901) Upon the death of William IV in 1837 the Royal Stud at Hampton Court was sold, but it was later re-formed for Queen Victoria by Charles Greville, and such famous horses as Sanfoin, La Flêche, Diophantus, etc. were bred there. During her girlhood and early married life, the Queen was a keen horsewoman and her diaries have many affectionate references to particular horses and ponies, and to the pleasure she derived from riding and driving. The Queen attended several race meetings, and was seen at Newmarket and Ascot, but after the death of the Prince Consort in 1861, she never went racing again.

Victoria Club A London club for bookmakers, where call-overs (q.v.) take place on races which have ante-post betting.

Vienna Riding School See **Spanish Riding School**.

View To see a fox.

View holloa (pronounced 'holler') The shout given to reach the huntsman when a fox is viewed. (See also **'Tally-ho!'**)

Vis-à-vis An open four-wheeled vehicle without hood or side doors, and with the seats facing each other. Sometimes called the Barouche Sociable. Similar to the Victoria or Calache (qq.v.).

Vitamins Organic substances necessary in small quantities for metabolism. They may, for a variety of reasons, be lacking in the normal fresh food, and are then added as supplements. Excessive amounts of vitamins may also lead to abnormalities. The principal vitamins are:

VITAMIN A (Retinol). Found in plant material as a constituent of carotene, which is converted to Vitamin A in the intestinal wall and the liver. Lack of this vitamin causes reduced resistance to infection, poor feet, weepy eyes, dull coats, retarded growth, respiratory symptoms, and reproductive problems.

VITAMIN B. This is an aggregate (complex), of which Vitamin B_1, B_2 (riboflavin), B_{12}, niacin, panthotenic acid, folic acid, biotin, and choline are of principal importance to horses. The vitamins are normally synthesised by bacteria in the large intestine; foals receive a supply in the mares's milk until, at about seven months, they have acquired sufficient gut bacteria. Good quality foodstuffs, plus the vitamins synthesised by bacteria, normally supply adequate amounts of B_1, B_2, B_6, and B_{12}. Production or absorption of B_{12}, however, may be inhibited by the presence of gut parasites. Lack of the B vitamins can cause a range of disorders, including lack of growth, anaemia, internal upsets, and neuritis.

VITAMIN C (Ascorbic Acid). Normally synthesised in the horse by the gut bacteria; also found in green foods. Deficiency said to lower disease resistance, and impair the repair of damaged tissues.

VITAMIN D (Calciferol). Necessary for the absorption of calcium and potassium. The precursor of Vitamin D is found in the horse's skin, but is valueless until converted into calciferol by the ultra-violet rays from the sun. Good quality hay contains Vitamin D, but the horse has limited storage capacity, and animals kept stabled throughout the winter may require a supplement, e.g. cod liver oil. High levels of Vitamin D may be harmful. Deficiency may result in kidney damage, bone weakness, and soft tissue calcification.

VITAMIN E (Tocopherol). Can be used, with Vitamin A and selenium, to improve the breeding performance in mares and stallions (although there is not complete agreement that it is effective), and is essential in competition horses for speed, stamina and good performance. It is said to be helpful in treating azoturia (q.v.). Under normal conditions, sufficient Vitamin E is contained in the fresh foods and grains of the diet, provided there is no shortage of selenium.

VITAMIN K. Present in green vegetation, soya-bean meal, and also produced by gut bacteria. It is essential for the normal clotting of the blood in case of injury.

Vixen A female fox. See also **Scent, fox's**.

Vladimir Heavy Draught The largest of the four principal Russian heavy draught breeds, standing up to 16.1 hh (165 cm). Evolved in the areas east of Moscow, using Clydesdales and Shires on local mares. Used in agricultural work, and for pulling Russian troikas, where its free and energetic action is seen to advantage.

Volte/Volt A circle of 6 m (20 ft) in diameter, accepted as the smallest a horse may be asked to perform on either one or two tracks. It is determined by regarding the average length of a horse from nose to tail as 3m (10 ft); thus the diameter of the smallest circle through which the animal is able to pivot is 6 m (20 ft). The word *may* be used to describe circles up to 10 m (32 ft) in diameter, but in international dressage it *always* remains 6 m (20 ft).

Voltige The exercise of vaulting, which consists of jumping off and on a galloping horse, and which may comprise a number of more or less difficult acrobatic exercises on the horse. A regular turn to be seen in the circus. Now being performed by young riders and members of the Pony Club.

Vomiting For anatomical reasons, it is almost impossible for a horse to vomit. If he does, it is a serious development, indicative of a major injury to the stomach.

Vuillier dosage system This system hinges on Galton's Law (q.v.) of ancestral contribution in bloodstock, and was propounded by Colonel Vuillier, a French Cavalry officer, in the 1920s. He traced the pedigrees of hundreds of good horses to the twelfth generation, at which stage a horse has 4096 ancestors, and he based calculations on this figure. He computed that fifteen stallions and one mare appeared in the various pedigrees with approximately the same frequency. He then worked out the average influence of each of these sixteen names in the numerous pedigrees he dissected, and thus fixed a standard dosage desirable in the make-up of the ideal racehorse. This system no longer has influence among breeders.

Vulcan mouth Descriptive of a bit whose mouthpiece is made of Vulcanite (rubber hardened by treatment with sulphur). It is not flexible but is softer in the mouth than steel.

WAHO World Arabian Horse Organisation (q.v.).

WCF Worshipful Company of Farriers.

WHP Working Hunter Pony.

WP-BR Welsh Part-bred Register.

WPCS Welsh Pony and Cob Society.

WRS (racing) Whipped round start.

WSB Welsh Stud Book.

W-mouth snaffle See **Y-mouth snaffle**.

Waggoner One who conducts a wagon.

Waggonette/Wagonette An open vehicle with the backs of the passenger seats to the wheels, with one or two seats crosswise in front. The vehicle is driven from the right-hand front seat using a single horse or pair. Popular for country use.

Waggonette brake See **Brake**.

Wagon/Waggon A four-wheeled vehicle for carrying heavy goods. A chariot.

Wagon-lock A kind of iron shoe which is placed under the rear-wheel of a wagon to slow the speed when going downhill (see **Skid-pan**).

Wain A wagon.

Wainwright A wagon-maker.

Waist (of saddle) The narrowest part of the seat just behind the head. The waist, also known as the 'twist', should be as narrow as possible to avoid spreading the rider's thighs.

'Waler' An abbreviation of New South Wales, Australia, where this mixed type of horse was originally bred. The first horses are said to have arrived in Australia in 1788 from South Africa, and were mixtures of Dutch, Barb, Arabian and Spanish blood. They were, on the whole, poor specimens in terms of conformation, with big heads, upright shoulders, and particularly poor legs and feet. However, they were tough and high-couraged. In due course, Thoroughbreds were imported from England, crossed with the earlier imports, and a better type of animal evolved. They were used for transport, and more particularly in the outback. When World War I broke out, thousands of these horses, which had come to be known as Walers, were drafted into the Army – some of them even rounded up from the herds of virtually wild animals which roamed the outback. The Waler proved an exceptional cavalry horse, and made a name for itself in many theatres of war from Palestine to France. As the need for cavalry horses declined after World War I, the Waler's numbers dropped; after World War II, the name fell into disuse, and was replaced by the Australian Stock Horse (q.v.).

Walk A pace of four-time, the sequence of hoof-beats being: near hind, near fore, off hind, off fore. A horses should be a good walker, and put his feet down fairly and squarely on the ground, all feet moving in a straight line. In dressage tests, horses are expected to show four variations in the pace:
(1) COLLECTED, in which the steps are short and elevated, with no over-tracking (qq.v.).
(2) MEDIUM, between collected and extended, with longer and lower strides with full track-up or over-track.
(3) EXTENDED, which shows the maximum length of stride and minimum elevation, with marked over-tracking.
(4) FREE WALK, which is a pace of rest, in which the horse is given complete freedom of the head and neck, with the reins at their fullest length.

Walking Horse Class (USA) An event in horse shows in the USA for Plantation or Tennessee Walking Horses (q.v.).

Walking out Taking a hound pack out on foot in the kennel, paddock or elsewhere.

Walking-out boot A leather or plastic boot enveloping the hoof and having a thick sole. It is useful for giving a horse with a damaged foot a little gentle exercise.

Walk-over If only one horse should arrive at a race meeting to run in a certain race it is allowed to 'walk over' in order to receive the prize money. Both horse and jockey must conform to the orthodox procedure, weigh-out, mount at the appointed time, ride past the Judge's Box from the correct course, and return to the unsaddling enclosure, be unsaddled and weighed-in.

Wall-eye The term used exclusively where there is such a lack of pigment, either partial or complete, in the iris, as to give a pinkish-white or bluish-white appearance. It is not indicative of blindness. Known also as 'china' or 'blue eye', and in the USA as 'glass-eye'.

Wall of hoof See under **Hoof, wall of**.

Walsall The Midlands town which is the centre of the saddlery business.

'Wap John' An old stage-coachman's term of contempt for a gentleman's coachman.

Warbles Hard lumps occurring in the saddle region during spring and early summer. They are caused by the presence of the cysts of the warble fly, which lays its eggs on a horse's legs, where they hatch. The larvae bore through the skin, and through the muscles, finally arriving on the animal's back. Here they encyst and form swellings under the skin. Eventually the larvae re-emerge, fall off the horse, and pupate. Next spring, the whole cycle starts again.

Warburton, Rowland Eyles Egerton (1804-1891) Known as 'the Poet Laureate of hunting', he rode Thoroughbred horses which he bred, and published his 'Hunting Songs' in 1846, and other verses between 1855-1879, many appearing in *Bailey's Magazine*. He was blind for seventeen years.

Ward, James, RA (1769-1859) An artist of

versatile and original talent, who was appointed engraver in mezzotint and painter to HRH the Prince of Wales (George IV) in 1794. During his long life he exhibited 298 pictures at the Royal Academy. Noted for horse portraits, hunting pictures, and landscapes.

Warde, John (of Squerries, Westerham, Kent) Born in 1752, he hunted much of the Berkshire and Oxfordshire countries between 1776-1798, and the Pytchley between 1798-1826. 'The Father of Fox-hunting', he was one of the first to prac-tise the modern fast style of hunting. He invented the Telegraph springs (q.v.).

Warendorf The centre of the German equestrian establishment. The adminis-trative offices of the National Federation, the Olympic Committee's Centre, and the Deutsche Reitschule (where young trainers are educated) are all located at Warendorf, which has a huge equestrian complex.

'Ware wire' A warning – pronounced 'wor wire' – flung over the shoulder of one hunting man to another on sighting wire in a fence.

Warmblood A collective name for a type of light horse being bred in Britain and Europe, for which the definition is 'a horse bred from Continental perfor-mance bloodlines, with acceptance as a Warmblood being dependent on the individual breed society's criteria'. Many of the European breeds are regarded as Warmbloods under this definition e.g. Hanoverians, Trakehners, etc., but purity of breeding is not essential, and part-bred horses may be registered, subject to certain conditions, based largely on performance testing and conformation inspections. The British Warmblood Society was formed in 1977, and issues two kinds of registration papers. The first (partbred papers) are for progeny with at least one parent graded (i.e. has passed inspection, in addition to being registered); the second are for progeny of parents, both of which are graded with the Society, with the proviso that the progeny must have at least 50% Warmblood lines. The latter registration is recognised by other European breed societies. Historically, in the theories of

the evolution of the horse, the term Warmblood has a rather different meaning. According to one currently held theory, following the last Ice Age, the horse family, which was then roaming over European and Asia, was divided into two groups. One group was known as the Northern or Coldblood horse (from which it is suggested that the heavy draught-horse type breeds eventually developed) and the second was the Southern or Warmblood group) from which it is claimed that the lighter, riding-type horse developed.

Warned off Newmarket Heath, to be (racing) When the Jockey Club warns a person off Newmarket Heath, that per-son is considered disqualified, and as long as the disqualification lasts, is not allowed, under Rule 205 of the Rules of Racing, to (1) act as steward or official at any recognised meeting; (2) act as author-ised agent under the Rules of Racing; (3) enter, train, run or ride a horse in any race at any recognised meeting or ride in trials; (4) enter any racecourse, stand or enclosure; (5) except with the permission of the Stewards of the Jockey Club, he employed in any Racing Stable.

Warrantable (or Runnable) A male deer should strictly not be hunted until five years old, at which age he is termed warrantable.

Warranty At sales, animals are sold with certain 'guarantees' or warranties con-cerning their suitability for the purposes for which they are being bought. A riding horse which is warranted 'quiet to ride' implies that the animal may be ridden by a reasonably experienced person, on its own, in company, and in traffic, and is sound in wind, eyes, heart and action. 'A good hunter', implies that the animal is 'quiet to ride' (as above), has been hunted and is capable of being hunted. 'Quiet to drive' implies that the animal is quiet and capable of being driven in single harness, in and out of traffic, is capable of doing a reasonable day's work, and is sound in wind, heart and action. Furthermore, it is a condition of warranty that all such war-ranted animals shall be free from any dis-ease, either infectious or contagious; that they shall be free of vices such as crib-biting, wind-sucking, weaving, etc. (unless expressly declared), and that such animal has not been tubed, fired, un-nerved or operated upon for unsoundness of any kind (unless expressly declared).

Warts Excrescences of the skin occurring most frequently on the nose, inside the hindleg, and on the sheath, which are caused by a wart virus infection. Though they mostly disappear without treatment, some may grow rapidly and ulcerate; this condition is known as equine sarcoid, or, more commonly, angleberries. Sarcoids tend to recur, even after surgical removal.

Warwick colour See **Tanning**.

Water jump.

Water Essential to the horse, who drinks between 6-12 gallons a day, depending on size and conditions – more when the weather is hot or if on dry food, less if turned out on grass with a high moisture content. Water is necessary for the maintenance of body fluids, for digestion and for maintenance of body temperature. It accounts for between 50-70% of the total bodyweight. Water should be clean, fresh, and always available except (a) after long fast work, when the horse may be dehydrated, in which case it should be allowed a little 'chilled' water (i.e. with the chill removed) every ten minutes or so, until the thirst is quenched; (b) immediately after a grain feed, as the water will either wash the grain through the stomach, or cause it to swell – both causing colic; (c) for approximately four hours before fast work. In general, stabled horses should have water available to them throughout the day; if this is not possible, then the horse must be watered a minimum of three times a day, before, but not immediately after, feeding. Water may be given in a stable bucket, or in an automatically-filling bowl – the disadvantage of the latter being that it is not possible to tell if the animal is drinking

properly (lack of drinking may be a sign of illness).

Water (hunting) A ditch or stream having no fence on either side, but containing water.

Water brush An item of grooming kit with longer bristles than a body brush. It is used damp on the mane and tail, and is good for dry brushing of the head and legs, but is applied wet for quartering.

Water jump (show jumping) An artificial obstacle, filled with water, and usually with a guard rail or small brush fence on the take-off side. A white tape, lath, or plasticine strip is fixed on the landing side, touching the water but not in it, to determine if a horse has faulted at the obstacle.

Water out, to (USA) To cool off a trotter (or pacer) after a race by walking it about, allowing it occasional drinks of water.

Wattle (hunting) A hurdle.

Weaning Foals soon start to masticate and supplement their milk diet with grass. The time for weaning is to some extent governed by circumstances, such as the condition of the mare and foal, the quantity and nutritive value of the grass, or the resentment of the mare to the foal's attention, but it usually takes place between the fourth and sixth month after the birth of the foal.

Wear A horse is said to 'wear itself well' if it carries the head and tail up and puts life in its actions. An alternative term is 'to carry both ends'.

Weatherbys 1773 is now considered the date when Weatherbys came into being, although the Mr James Weatherby who started the General Stud Book, and his relation (also) Mr James Weatherby, who was the first Keeper of the Match Book for the Jockey Club, were not at that time working together. The latter, however, held office from 1777 until his death in 1793, and a member of the Weatherby family has been Keeper of the Match Book to the Jockey Club ever since. Weatherbys act as Secretaries to the Jockey Club and publish the Racing Calendar on their behalf. They also control the registration of horses' names, issue horses' passports, produce a monthly list of horses in training, compile a register of owners' colours, trainers' licences and permits, horses' records, deal with entries, handicaps, declarations, and update the General Stud Book. In 1963, a General Stud Book office was also opened in Dublin.

Weaving A stable vice of nervous origin in which the horse rocks to and fro continually and may lift each forefoot in turn as its sways its head and forehand. It is a habit which may be copied by one from others.

Web The whole structure of the horseshoe; the word is usually applied to the width of the actual shoe, e.g. 'bend upwards half the web of the toe'.

Web martingale See **Martingale, bib**.

Webs, race See **Stirrup webs**.

Wedging See **Beaning**.

Weed A derogatory term for a horse of poor and mean conformation, and one usually lacking in stamina and carrying no flesh. Generally a Thoroughbred, or of Thoroughbred type.

Weedon (Northamptonshire) One-time headquarters of Army Cavalry training until 1940, and largely responsible (until that time) for teaching the art and science of modern equitation in England.

Weedon lane See **Jumping lane**.

Weedy A description of a long-legged animal with a mean body and generally unimpressive appearance. Such a horse does not stand up to work, is difficult to get into condition, and tends to knock its legs about in fast work.

Weighing-in Immediately after dismounting at the end of a race, every jockey must present himself to be weighed by the Clerk of the Scales. (See **Weights**)

Weighing-out Every jockey must be weighed for a specified horse by the Clerk of the Scales, at the appointed place, not less than fifteen minutes before the time fixed for the race. (See **Weights**)

Weight (show jumping) Under FEI (q.v.) rules all competitors carry a minimum of 165 lb (75 kg), including saddle.

Weight/seat aids The use of the rider's weight on one or both seat bones, combined with the loin muscles, to aid the legs in driving the horse forward.

Weight calculation Can be ascertained approximately by the following formula:

$$\frac{\text{Girth}^2 \times \text{length}}{300} = \text{Total weight in pounds}$$

(multiply by 0.45 to convert to kilograms) Girth measurement to be taken around the barrel in inches; length, from the elbow upwards to the point of buttock, also in inches.

Weight carrier A horse capable of carrying a minimum of 15 stone (210 lb; 95.2 kg). Strength, bulk of frame, and big limbs are watched for in the show ring, though these are worth nothing without quality, heart room, and action.

Weight cloth A leather and felt cloth carried on a horse's back under the saddle. The outside of a weight cloth has a series of narrow flat pockets in which lead weights can be inserted in order to increase the rider's weight to the required amount.

Weight for age race The official definition in the rules of racing is 'any race which is not a handicap or a selling race'. As in practice this lends itself to contradictions, it may be said to be 'an event open to horses of different ages in which the runners carry different weights according to their ages'. For this purpose the age is reckoned as dating from 1 January, and only years and not months are taken into consideration when allotting weight for age. As it is considered that the difference between the older and the younger horses becomes less as the year advances, a scale, varying with each month, has been published by the Jockey Club for the guidance of Clerks of the Course, but its use is not obligatory.

Weights (racing) All horses must carry a certain weight in races, either according to the conditions of the race or according to the weight allotted by the handicapper, in the case of handicaps. In flat racing the conditions of a race shall not provide for a weight of less than 7 stone (98 lb; 44 kg), and in no case shall any allowance reduce this weight below 6 stone 7lb (91 lb; 41 kg). For steeplechase and hurdle races, no horse shall carry less than 10 stone (140 lb; 63.5 kg) except in long-distance steeplechases, when the lowest weight may be 9 stone 7 lb (133 lb; 59 kg). According to rule 109, inexperienced cross-country riders may claim a special allowance in the less valuable steeple-chases and hurdle races. In weighing out, a jockey includes in his weight everything except his skull cap, whip, bridle, plates, rings or anything worn on a horse's legs.

Weights of horses A pony of about 13.2 hh (137.2 cm) weighs 480-600 lb (220-300 kg); a small hunter of about 15 hh (152.4 cm), 814-946 lb (370-430 kg); a show jumper of about 16 hh (162.6 cm), 1034-1144 lb (470-520 kg); a middleweight hunter of about 16.3 hh (170.2 cm), 1114-1232 lb (520-560 kg); a heavy hunter of about 16.3 hh (170.2 cm), 1276-1540 lb (580-700 kg). Three-fifths of the weight of a horse is distributed on the forelegs, two-fifths on the hind.

Weights on the foot The practice of shoeing harness horses heavily, causing them to give an exaggerated bend to the knees.

'Well let down' Said of hocks, when they are long and low, and drop straight to the ground.

Well ribbed-up A term signifying that the front or true ribs are flat, with the back or false ribs 'well-sprung' or hooped behind the saddle.

Well-sprung See **Well ribbed-up**.

Welsh Cob (Section D in Welsh Pony and Cob Society Stud Book) One of the nine British Mountain and Moorland breeds. An old established breed whose exact origins are obscure. It seems certain, however, that the Cob is descended, at least in part, from the early Welsh Mountain ponies (q.v.). Virtually no reli-able history of the breed exists before the twelfth century, when it is believed that Arab stallions, brought back by the Crusaders, were used on the local native ponies, and in due course, the Welsh Cob evolved. Early references in Welsh literature of mediaeval times describe a cob as 'fleet of foot, a good jumper, and able to carry a substantial weight on his back'. Infusions of Thoroughbred, Hackney, and Yorkshire Coach Horse blood came later, and the spectacular trotting action seems likely to have come from Norfolk Roadsters. Cobs were used for the heavy work on hill farms, and until as recently as thirty or forty years ago, were used in the Army for pulling heavy guns and equipment. The modern Cob is the only one of the Mountain and Moorland breeds to have no upper height limit; the minimum height is over 13.2 hh (137.2 cm). The Cob should have pony characteristics, with a quality pony head, small, neat ears, plenty of bone and substance, and free, true and forcible action, with the knee bent and the whole leg extended straight from the shoulder and as far forward as possible in the trot. The hocks are flexed under the body with straight and powerful leverage. The trot is so characteristic of the breed that, until stallion licensing was introduced in 1918, breeding stock was selected by trotting tests and matches. The Cob is a versatile breed, ideal as a family pony, able to jump well, and is excellent in harness. The Welsh Cob may be any colour except piebald or skewbald.

Welsh Mountain Pony (Section A in the Welsh Pony and Cob Society Stud Book) One of the most popular and argu-ably the most beautiful of the nine Moun-tain and Moorland breeds. The origin of the Welsh Mountain Pony is obscure, but it has, for many centuries, thrived on the hills and mountains of Wales. Its rough existence has produced the qualities of intelligence, soundness and endurance for which the breed is famed. As a child's pony it is popular and successful. The Welsh Mountain Pony has a small neat head, big eyes set well apart, a dished face-line, the muzzle fine and tapering, and soft to the touch. (The Arab-like fea-tures of the head are due, almost certainly, to Arab stallions which were turned out on the Welsh hills, especially during the eighteenth century.) The neck should be of a good length, and the shoulders deep and well laid, though the withers must not be pronounced; the back must be short and strong, with the tail well set and carried gaily. The whole should present a sprited appearance with great presence. The Welsh Mountain Pony has been used in the improvement of other breeds, such as the New Forest, and, to a lesser extent, the Dartmoor, and it has also contributed to the development of the British Riding Pony. The maximum height is 12 hh (121.9 cm) and the most common colour is grey, although any colour is permitted except piebald and skewbald. Welsh Mountain Ponies have been exported to many countries – Europe, the USA, New Zealand, and particularly Australia, where it is said (with possibly only slight exaggeration) that there are more Welsh Section As than there are in Britain.

Welsh Pony (Section B of the Welsh Pony and Cob Society Stud Book) The Welsh Pony should be an enlarged edition of the Mountain Pony, with emphasis on those points which distinguish a modern riding pony. Such ponies have always existed in Wales, some of them Mountain ponies that have grown overheight, some with a dash of blood from larger breeds in their veins. The Welsh Pony is a miniature hunter as opposed to a miniature hack, and should possess the strength, toughness, and hard, flinty bone of the true native pony. The maximum height is 13.2 hh (137.2 cm). In the past they were used mainly for shepherding and hunting on the hills. They are now ideal as a child's second pony. Welsh Ponies have played a considerable role in the development of the British Riding Pony. Welsh Ponies have been exported to Europe, the USA, New Zealand, and to Australia.

Welsh Pony and Cob Society Founded in 1901 to encourage the breeding of Welsh Ponies and Cobs.

Welsh Pony of Cob Type (Section C in the Welsh Pony and Cob Stud Book) Developed by the intermingling of Cob

blood with that of the ponies. The section C pony resembles a small Cob and the whole impression should be of strength for size and of activity. It is very sure-footed. The height may not exceed 13.2 hh (137.2 cm). They make excellent ride and drive ponies.

Wentworth, Baroness Judith Anne Dorothea Blunt-Lytton (1873-1957) Renowned as a breeder of, and publicist for, Arab horses, and for many years, up to the time of her death, the owner of the Crabbet Park Stud at Crawley, Sussex, which she inherited from her parents, Lady Anne and Wilfred Scawen Blunt. She was a distinguished poet and writer.

Westchester Cup Formerly the premium international polo trophy for competition between England and America. The first contest was played in 1886 at Meadowbrook in America. Losers of the best-of-three-matches contest challenged the winners in their own country. The competition was discontinued in 1939, but revived in 1971 as the Coronation Cup, held annually at either Windsor or Cowdray Park.

Western States Trail Ride See **Tevis Cup Ride**.

Weymouth bit This usually consists of a straight mouthpiece with a port, or it can be a straight bar or mullen mouth. The cheeks vary in length but normally correspond to the width of the mouth. The

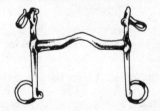

Weymouth bit.

mouthpiece slides up and down, within the cheeks, a matter of half an inch or so. The bit is worn in conjunction with a thin jointed snaffle to form the double bridle.

Weymouth, dressage bit This bit is made on the German pattern with a fixed cheek, obligatory in advanced tests, and with a very broad mouthpiece in which the port is slightly offset forward. The bridoon is usually, but not always, one with small eggbutt cheeks, and again has a broad, flat mouthpiece. Because of the mouth construction this is a mild bit.

Whalebone Before 1946, when the killing of Greenland whale was prohibited by international law, whalebone was used as the centre of good quality whips of all sorts. It has now been replaced by fibreglass and nylon. Cheaper whips are lined with steel.

Whanghee A yellow riding cane having rings or knots closely spaced and made from the stem of Chinese or Japanese plants allied to the bamboo.

Wheat Not usually fed to horses, but as it is high in Vitamin E, it may be recommended for brood mares or stallions; it is then fed in small quantities, crushed or boiled with oats, bran or chaff.

Wheel-bar See **Splinter bar**.

Wheelers Team horses nearest to the vehicle, as opposed to the leaders.

Wheel harness Harness for the wheelers (q.v.), as distinct from lead harness.

Wheelwright A man who makes wheels for wheeled vehicles.

Whelps Unweaned hound puppies.

Whicker See **Nicker**.

Whiffletree/Whippletree Other names for swingletree (q.v.). See **Bars**.

Whinny A horse's call of pleasure and expectancy.

Whip, coaching Sometimes called a team whip, though the coaching term is 'crop'. It is made of holly, and the total length is more than that of the normal driving whip. The stick is shorter than that of the latter, but the thong is long enough to reach the leaders on the hocks.

Whip, cutting Made of fibreglass, nylon or steel, covered with gut or plaited kangaroo leather and and carried mostly for racing and hacking.

Whip, dog-leg A driving whip having a near right-angle bend in the shaft. Lightly held, the head of the thong will hang down correctly for instant use.

Whip, hunting Incorrectly called a hunting crop, this is made of steel, cane or fibreglass, which may be covered in braided nylon, or gut, or with plaited kangaroo hide, with a thong and a silk or cord lash attached to the top end, and, at the lower end, a buckhorn handle for opening gates.

Whip, stock A whip with a short stock but very long thong, used by mounted stockmen when driving cattle.

Whip, trotting Whalebone whip in one piece, limited in the USA to 4 ft 8 in (142 cm).

Whipcord (cloth) A strong and durable cloth with a more pronounced rib than gaberdine. It was formerly much used for riding coats and breeches, and made with drab and white twill, the finished twill resembling plaited whipcord, hence the name.

Whip-cord See **Lash**.

Whip hand/'Under the whip' Terms signifying the offside horse of a pair or team. The offside is generally said to be under the whip, as it is in the better position to be reached easily by the whip, and can therefore be kept up to work if required. It is customary to put the sluggish horses on the offside.

Whipper-in, first The huntsman's principal assistant.

Whipper-in, second The huntsman's second assistant.

Whippletrees or Whiffletrees See **Bars**.

Whip reel A circular wooden block attached to a wall, on which to hang

Whip reel.

driving whips of the quill top variety. By use of the block, the semi-circular shape at the upper end is maintained.

Whirlicote An early conveyance for women travellers. *Stow's Commentaries* record that 'Richard the Second, being threatened by the rebels of Kent, rode from the Tower of London to the Miles End, and with him his mother, because she was sick and weak, in a *whirlicote*,' and this is described as an ugly vehicle of four boards put together in a clumsy manner. In the following year, Richard married Anne of Bohemia, who introduced riding upon side-saddles, and so 'was the riding in those whirlicotes forsaken, except at coronations and such like spectacles.'

Whisk See **Dandy brush**.

Whiskey/Whisky An early form of gig with a chair body.

Whisperer A horse-whisperer, one who tames high-spirited and dangerous horses, often reckoned as savages (see **Sullivan, Con**).

Whistling See **Roarer**.

White Very pale colour or absence of any pigment in the hairs of the coat is designated white, but in reality many white horses are simply grey horses in old age, when white hairs, increasingly with age, replace the black hairs with which the horse was born.

'White castor' A slang term for a white coaching hat.

White face When the white covers the forehead and front of the face, extending laterally towards the mouth, it is described as a white face. The extension may be unilateral or bi-lateral.

White flag (racing) See **Start, racing**

White flag (show jumping) This is used to show the left-hand limit of the obstacle to be jumped.

White horse The name applied to the figure of a horse on a hillside, formed by the removal of turf to show the underlying chalk. There are several of these to be seen in England, the most famous, perhaps, being at Uffington, Berkshire. It is traditionally supposed that this com-

memorates Alfred the Great's victory at Ashdown in AD 871.

White legs The following is an old doggerel, of which there are many versions, on white-legged horses:
> Four white legs, keep him not a day,
> Three white legs, send him far away,
> Two white legs, give him to a friend,
> One white leg, keep him to the end.

White line The band of soft horn secreted by the papillae and found on the lower border of the sensitive laminae, this is the bond of union between the wall and the sole of the foot, and its presence indicates the amount of wall the farrier has in which to place the nails.

White of the eye Where some part of the white sclerotic of the eye shows between the eyelids.

Whole coloured Where there are no hairs of any colour, other than the main colour of the horse, on the body, head or limbs.

Whorl A circle or irregular setting of coat hairs.

Whyte-Melville, George John (1821-1878) A sporting novelist, poet and soldier. The most quoted (with Adam Lindsay Gordon, q.v.) among the Victorian poets of the horse and the chase, and an authority on the science of hunting. One of his most quoted poems is 'The Old Grey Mare'. He met with a fatal accident while hunting.

Wid A dealer's term, little used now, indicating that a horse is unsound in wind.

Wide behind When both hindlegs from the feet to the quarters are separated beyond the normal.

Wielkopolski A Polish dual-purpose horse named after the area of Poznan where the breed was developed. A powerfully built animal, standing up to 16.2 hh (165 cm), the Wielkopolski is based on Poznan and Masuren blood, with infusions of Arab, Hanoverian, and Thoroughbred.

Wild Goose Chase A type of race in the seventeenth century, in which the riders, after covering 240 yards (219 m), had to follow and keep behind the leader.

He could take any course he liked and the others had to follow him, and one another, at agreed distances (i.e. two or three lengths). Triers (judges), who rode alongside, whipped those that transgressed. The chase, in its equal spacings, resembled the flight of wild geese.

Wild horse (Asiatic) See **Equus Przewalksii Przewalskii Poliakov**; and **Evolution of the horse**.

Wilson snaffle A variety of bits, all of which have four rings, come under this heading.

Wind A hound is never said to smell a fox, but to wind it.

Wind, testing for To test for soundness in wind, the horse is galloped in a circle, first on one rein, then on the other. The defect is best detected from the saddle. Alternatively, careful listening at the nostrils when the horse is halted will reveal problems. The fitter the horse, the less noise will be heard.

'Wind, thick in the' This often occurs when a horse is gross and fat. In this condition, an animal should not be given severe or fast work, which may lead to whistling (see **Roarer**). A thick wind may be the sequel to bronchitis, or may be a temporary condition – but as long as it persists, it is an unsoundness.

Wind, to Obsolete term applied to blowing the horn.

Windgalls Soft, round, fluid-filled painless swellings which may appear above and behind the fetlock joint on both sides of the limb. Caused by wear and tear, they seldom give rise to lameness. They are also known as 'wind puffs'.

Windsor Greys The popular name given to horses at the Royal Mews, Buckingham Palace, and which are so familiar in all State processions. George I, because of his interest in the famous Hanover Stud, introduced Hanoverian Cream horses into England, and these were used as Royal carriage horses. Later, before World War I, a small stud was in being at Windsor, having been started from stallions and mares supplied from the Hanover Stud. The war interfered with the supply of stock, and the stud gradually diminished, until it was finally disposed of. Some of the horses were sold, some were given to cavalry regiments, and some were destroyed. After the war, grey carriage horses were bought for the Royal carriages, and five were presented by the Queen of the Netherlands. A number of the present greys in the Mews have been given to the Queen or Prince Philip, while others have been bought. The breeds include Oldenburgs and Oldenburg-crosses. The term 'Windsor Greys' does not denote a breed. The name arose from press and public references to the 'horses from Windsor', when they appeared in London on various State occasions, later becoming 'Greys from Windsor', and then 'Windsor Greys'.

Windsor Horse Show, Royal Founded in 1944 by the Windsor Horse Show Club.

Wind-sucker A horse may, for no apparent reason, draw or suck in air and swallow it with a gulping sound. This is a disagreeable and harmful vice, and an unsoundness. It is similar to crib-biting (q.v.).

Wind-sucker's bit A straight, tubular mouthpiece with holes pierced through it.

Wings Extensions at the sides of an obstacle in show jumping.

Winkers See **Blinkers**.

Winston The chestnut gelding, owned by the Mounted Branch of the Metropolitan Police, and ridden for several years by Queen Elizabeth II (and also when she was Princess Elizabeth) at the ceremony of Trooping the Colour. Winston was by Erehwemos, and, as a seven-year-old, came from Yorkshire in 1944 to the Mounted Branch Training Establishment at Imber Court, Surrey. His fine presence and perfect temperament earned him national popularity, and he is commemorated for posterity on the coronation year crown piece, and on the Great Seal of the County Palatinate of Lancaster, where Queen Elizabeth is depicted riding him. He was killed in a street accident in 1957.

Wintering out Leaving a horse unstabled throughout the winter.

Wire Wire in a fence, whether it is plain

or barbed, constitutes a grave menace to all who follow hounds mounted.

Wire-cutters These may be of varying pattern, and are carried in a leather holster on the front of the saddle and used during a hunt for cutting wire. Cutters should be carried only by hunt officials and used with great discretion.

Wire fund In some hunts, a cap of a small amount is taken from all mounted and unmounted followers to provide money for the removal, temporarily or permanently, of wire in fences.

Wisp A grooming device made of rope, hay or straw, coiled in the form of a figure-of-eight to make a pad. Used to improve the skin and coat, to stimulate circulation and form muscle.

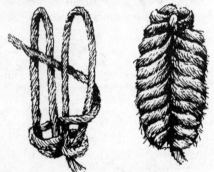

Method of making a wisp and a completed wisp.

Wither pad Usually two pads of soft material joined together and placed under the saddle, one at each side. This leaves an air passage, and is preferable to the use of one pad doubled up over the wither. Recommended in an emergency and not for permanent use. It generally denotes that the horse's saddle is a poor fit. Admirable for the prevention or relief of wither pressure. Used to advantage if there is any likelihood of the withers being wrung (q.v.).

Withers These commence at the dip at the base of the crest line of the neck, should be reasonably high and pronounced at the uppermost point of the shoulder, and should slope away gradually into the back. Good lean withers on a saddle horse are most desirable, as they ensure correct placing of the saddle.

Withers, fistulous An abscess above the vertebrae of the withers, extending down between the shoulder blades. It is caused by a blow, a bite from another horse, or an ill-fitting collar or saddle, followed by *Brucellosis* bacterial infection. Symptoms include painful swelling in the area of the withers. It is a very serious condition requiring immediate veterinary attention. See also **Poll evil**.

Withers, pinched Withers are said to be pinched when the saddle grips, rather than lies on, them.

Withers, wrung An old term for withers which are wrung or bruised by an ill-fitting saddle, although the skin is not broken.

Witney panel See **Saddle panel**.

Wobbler syndrome A progressive nervous disease appearing in animals under two years old. Initially the horse is wobbly on his hindlegs, and this may be followed by varying degrees of paralysis. It is caused by pressure on the spinal cord due to narrowing of the spinal canal through abnormal growth of the vertebrae.

Wolf teeth Rudimentary teeth which, when present, occur in front of the upper and lower molar teeth on either side of the jaw, especially the upper one. May be shed with the milk teeth, but if not, they may need removal by a veterinary surgeon.

Wolstenholme, Dean, Snr (1757-1837) and **Wolstenholme, Dean, Jnr (1798-1882)** Father and son, the Wolstenholmes were both very important and admirable painters of sport – particularly hunting – whose works are rated very highly for their representations of the old English sporting scene. Many beautiful prints after them show a great similarity in technique, and in the case of original paintings, there is sometimes doubt as to who was the painter.

Women jockeys See **Ladies' races**.

Woodland A very large covert, or series of coverts. (See **Covert**)

Wootton, John (c. 1677-1765) Talented sporting artist who also painted landscapes and battles scenes. Received training from Jan Wyck, the Dutch-born artist, and under the patronage of the Second Duke of Beaufort, studied in Italy. Painted huge hunting scenes for such stately homes as Althorp and Longleat, and was also much in demand for portraits of the racehorses of the day.

Working hunter Show class for hunters in which competitors are required to jump a course of 'natural' type fences. The class is judged on conformation and performance.

Working hunter pony A show class in which the ponies are required to jump a course of 'natural' fences, and are judged on jumping, style and manners while jumping; conformation and freedom of action; and manners. In the National Pony Society Mountain and Moorland Working Hunter Pony classes, the ponies are also judged on breed type.

'Workman' A good coachman (colloquial).

World Arabian Horse Organisation Created in 1970 with the object of acquiring and promoting information in all countries concerning the Arabian breed and its derivatives, to safeguard their interests, and to maintain throughout the world the purity of the blood of horses of the Arabian breed.

World Cup (show jumping) Held every year.

World Dressage Championships Held every four years.

World Driving Championships Held every two years.

World Show Jumping Championships Held every four years.

World Three-Day Event Championships Held every four years.

Worley, William Born in 1765, Worley had charge of the Royal Paddocks at Hampton Court during the reigns of George IV and William IV, and during the lifetime of Queen Adelaide.

Worms Horses, particularly when young, suffer frequently from worm infestation, and those grazing together on limited acreage should be dosed at regular inter-

vals under veterinary supervision. The commonest worms to cause emaciation and anaemia are STRONGYLES. Of these there are several varieties, the most common being *red worms* (see under **Worms, red**): usually about 3/8-5/8 in. (10-15 mm) in length. They may pass their larval stage in the arteries supplying the intestines and cause colic and diarrhoea. ASCARIDS are larger *round worms*, possibly 4 ins (10 cm) in length, inhabiting the large bowel and seldom causing noticeable manifestations. TAPE-WORMS are not common, but those in horses are flattened, about 3/8-7/8 in. (1-2 cm) in width and 2-2¼ ins (5-6 cm) in length. LUNGWORMS (*Dictyocaulus arnfieldi*) are found in donkeys, and the larvae may be picked up by horses from shared pasture during summer, and passed into the lungs. They may cause coughing and lung damage. Modern anthelmintics are an effective treatment for these parasites, together with correct pasture management.

Worms, red (strongyles) The most harmful of all the bowel parasites which attack the horse. They are reddish in colour, very thin, and up to three-quarters of an inch in length. They may damage blood vessels, and organs such as the liver. They are ingested as larvae which live on blades of grass, having hatched from eggs excreted in droppings. The symptoms include loss of condition, anaemia, hollow flanks, dry coat, dropped abdomen, irregular bowel actions, and, in extreme cases, colic. They may be detected in the droppings, but a 'worm count', as carried out by a veterinary surgeon, is an estimate of the number of eggs in a sample of droppings. Treatment is by anthelmintics (q.v.) prescibed by a veterinary surgeon. Control can be achieved by regular worming, regular removal of droppings from grazing, and rotation of grazing.

Worms, seat Roundworm parasites which lay eggs in the horse's anal area. They cause itchiness and sometimes lead to tail rubbing. The yellow eggs may be visible.

Worry, to Killing by biting and shaking of the quarry by hounds.

Wrangler (USA) A cowhand or cowboy.

Würtemburg A German warmblood horse bred at the state-owned Marbach stud, and which became established as a definite breed about 100 years ago. The Würtemburg's ancestry can, however, be traced back to the Marbach stud of the sixteenth century, when the Duke Christoph von Würtemburg bred horses, using Hungarian and Turkish blood. His son then introduced Andalusian and Lusitano stallions. In the next century, heavy Friesian stallions and Barb and Spanish mares were introduced, followed, in the nineteenth century, by infusions of Anglo-Norman and East Prussian blood, to instil some quality. Since World War II, Trakehner blood has been used, and the breed has developed into a good competition horse, standing up to 16 hh (162.6 cm). The Würtemburg of today is a solid horse of great depth and has an equable temperament. The principal colours of the breed are bay, brown, chestnut, and black.

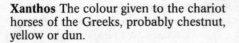

X

Xanthos The colour given to the chariot horses of the Greeks, probably chestnut, yellow or dun.

Xanthus With Balios, he drew the chariot of Achilles. Both horses were immortal, and Xanthus was given the power of speech and foretold the death of Achilles.

Xenophon (*c.* 430-350 BC) An Athenian solder, writer, historian and horseman, who wrote *Hipparchikos – The Cavalry Commander* – and *Cynegeticus* – a treatise on hunting (on foot) with and without dogs. He led the Ten Thousand Greeks from Mesopotamia to the Black Sea after the defeat of Cyrus at Cunaxa in 401 BC. Most of the principles of horsemanship and stable management which he propounded hold good to this day.

Xerxes One of Mr Jorrocks' hunters – 'a great rat-tailed brown' – sold to Captain Doleful, and the subject of a lawsuit. When driven in tandem he took the lead in front of Arterxerxes (q.v.). (See also **Jorrocks, Handley Cross, R. S. Surtees**)

Y

YSR Young Stock Register.

Y-mouth snaffle A snaffle having a double-jointed mouthpiece. Each mouthpiece has a long and a short side. The joint of the top one is on the near-side, and that of the bottom on the offside. A severe bit. Known also as a W-mouth.

Yaboo An Afghan pony.

Yankee (racing) A bet on four selections which makes six doubles, four trebles, and an accumulator (q.v.). It may be each way or win only, as desired.

Yard An open space adjoining and used in connection with stables. The word is also used comprehensively to express the business or premises of those engaged with horses, e.g. dealer's yard, livery yard, racing yard, competition yard, etc.

'Yard of tin'/'Three feet of tin' The horn used by guards of the old Royal Mail Coaches (see **Horn, coaching**). Exactly 36 ins (91.4 cm) long.

Yaud An old mare, or a decrepit horse.

Yawing The action of a horse which, when ridden, fights with its head to reach outwards and downwards. (See **Noseband, Grakle**)

Yearling A colt or filly having attained the first, but not the second, anniversary of its birth. Alternatively, a racehorse, from 1 January of the first year of birth until 31 December of the same year.

Yearling bit A name given to a Tattersall's bit, but more often to a straight or jointed breaking bit with keys.

Yearling headcollar A light headcollar, ⅞ in. or 1 in. (19 or 25 mm) in width, with adjustment at the head, nose and throat.

Yeld A Scottish term applied to brood mares which are not in foal (see **Eild**).

Yellow See **Jaundice**.

Yellow body The *corpus luteum*. (See **Oestrous cycle**)

Yellow-bounder A hired post-chaise usually painted bright yellow.

Yerk, to To lash or strike out with the heels; also to crack a whip (dialect).

'Yoi' (hunting) 'Yoi rouse 'im', 'Yoi wind 'im' are huntsmen's cheer to encourage hounds.

Yomud A Russian riding horse, descended from the ancient horses of Turkmenstan. Used for racing.

Yorksman A substitute for gloster bars (q.v.), using two corn sacks and a rolled blanket with a surcingle running its length. Sometimes used when riding a young horse for the first time.

Yorkshire boot Protective boots or coverings for the fetlocks to prevent injury to a horse liable to brush. Made from a piece of Kersey clothing, 12 in. x 9 in. (30 cm x 23 cm), it is wrapped round the fetlock and tied above the joint with tape. The margin above the fastening is folded down over the tape to form a double protective fold over the joint.

Yorkshire Coach Horse This breed originated in the East Riding of Yorkshire, and for a great number of years was indistinguishable from the Cleveland Bay (q.v.). At the end of the eighteenth century, the Yorkshire Coach horse emerged as the demand increased for a bigger and flashier type of harness horse for the more elegant vehicles appearing in the fashionable parts of London. The Thoroughbred was used on the Cleveland Bay and there was some infusion of Arab and Barb blood. The breed was itself used in the development of other breeds, including the Welsh Cob, the Holstein, and the Schleswig-Holstein. Standing about 16.1-16.3 hh (165.1-170.2 cm), bay and brown were the predominating colours. A long body on comparatively short legs gave the horse the appearance of being close to the ground. The Yorkshire Coach Horse Breed Society was formed in 1886, and produced a Stud Book. However, the arrival, of the motor car virtually saw the end of the breed, and fifty years after the Society was formed, it was wound up.

Yorkshire gallop A gallop which is between a half speed (q.v.) and a trial.

Yorkshire halter A good type of hemp halter having a throatlatch. It cannot pull over against an eye.

Young entry Before cub-hunting, young hounds are said to be 'un-entered'. During cub-hunting they are taught to hunt the fox and nothing else, and at the end of cub-hunting are 'entered', at which time they are about eighteen months old.

Y'sabella See **Isabella**.

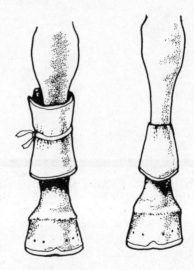

Yorkshire boot.

311

Zebra marks Striping on the limbs, neck and withers or quarters of horses. Believed to be primitive features.

Zeeland Horse See **Dutch Draught Horse**.

Zig-zag A timber jump with short units of posts and rails placed at angles to each other. The horse jumps either over the points of the 'V', or over the angled sides.

Zmudzin A Polish pony (see **Konik**).

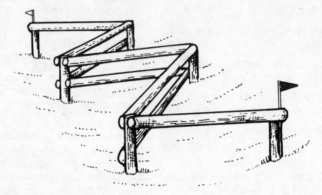

Zig-zag fence.

GLOSSARY OF FOREIGN TERMS

ENGLISH	FRENCH	GERMAN
Action, movement	l'action	die Aktion, die Bewegung
Ancestors, ancestry	l'ascendance	die Vorfahren, die Ahnen
Anglo-Arab	l'anglo-arabe	der Anglo-Araber
Arab, purebred	le pur sang arabe	der Vollblut-Araber
Arm (upper)	le bras	der Oberarm
Artificial 'airs'	les allures artificielles	die Künstilichen Gangarten
Back	le dos	der Rücken
Balance	l'équilibre	das Gleichgewicht
Bay	bai	Braun
Bedding	la litière	die Streu
Belly	le ventre	der Bauch
Black	noir	Rappe
Bloodline	la ligne	die Blutlinie
Boots	les bottines	die Streichkappen
Bowler hat	le melon	die Melone
Breed, race	la race	die Rasse
Breeder	le naisseur	der Züchter
Brick wall	le mur de brique	die Mauer, Backsteinmauer
Bridle	la bride	das Zaumzeug
Bridoon snaffle	le bridon	der Trensenzaum
Bringing in hand	la mise en main	das An-die-Hand-Stellen
Brood mare	le poulinière	die Zuchstute
Brown	brun	Schwarz
Cadence, tempo	la cadence	das Tempo
Cannon	le canon	das Rohrbein, die Röhre
Canter (gallop)	le galop	der Galopp
Canter, collected	galop rassemblé	versammelter Galopp
Canter, extended	galop allongé	starker Galopp
Chestnut	alezan	Fuchs
Circle	le cercle	der Zirkel
Coach-horse	le carossier, le postier	das schwere Kutschpferd
Collected paces	les allures rassemblées	die verkürzten, versammelten
Colt	le poulain	der Junghengst
Combined competition	le concours combiné	die kombinierte Prüfung
Conformation	le conformation extérieure	der Köperbau
Coronet	la couronne	das Kronengelenk
Course (track)	le parcours, la piste	die Sprungfolge
Cross-country	le cross	Querfeldein-Rennen
Croup	la croupe	die Kruppe
Curb bit	le mors	die Stange, Kandare
Descendants (offspring)	la descendance	die Nachkommenschaft
Disobedience	la résistance	die Widersetzlichkeit
Double obstacle	l'obstacle double	zweifaches Hindernis

ENGLISH	FRENCH	GERMAN
Dressage test	la reprise	die Prüfung
Exercise, to	sortir, promener	bewegen
Feed, to	fourrager	füttern
Fetlock	Boulet	Fesselkopf
Filly	la pouliche	die junge Stute
Flank	le flanc	die Flanke
Flexed ('in hand')	le ramener	das Beizäumen
Foal	le poulain	das Fohlen
Foot (hoof)	le sabot	der Huf
Forearm	l'avant-bras	der Vorarm
Foreleg	le membre antérieur	das Vorderbein
Forelock	le toupet	der Schopf
Forage	le fourrage	das Futter
Foxhunting	la chasse au renard	die Fuchsjagd
Foundation stock	la souche	der Stamm
Gallop, to	galoper	galoppieren
Gaskin	la jambe	der Unterschenkel
Gelding	le hongre	der Wallach
Girth	la sangle	der Sattelgurt
Grey	gris	Schmmel
Groom	le palefrenier	der Gestütswärter
Groom, to	panser	putzen
Hack	le cheval de promenade	das promenadenpferd
Half-bred	Demi-sang	Halbblut
Half-pass	appuyer	seitwärts treten
Halt; immobility	l'immobilité	das Stillstehen, Halten
Heavy horse (coldblood)	la grosse race	der schwere, kaltblütige Schlag
Height (at withers)	la taille (au garrot)	die Widerristhöle
High School	haute école	hohe Schule
Hindleg	le membre postérieur	die Hinterbeine
Hock	le jarret	das Sprunggelenk
Hoof (foot)	le sabot	der Huf
Horse	le cheval	das Pferd
Horsebox, motor	le van, la remorque	der Pferdetransport-wagon
Hound	le chien	der Hund
Hunter	le cheval de chasse	das Jagpferd
Hunting	la chasse	Jagdreiten, Reiten zu Hunden
Hunting cap	la bombe de chasse	die Jagkappe, Sturzkappe
Hunting whip	le fouet de chasse	die Hetzpeische
Huntsman	le piqueur, piqueux	der Hundsmann
Jodhpurs	les culottes Jodhpurs	die lange Reithose
Jump-off	le barrage	das Stechen
Impulsion	l'impulsion	der Schwung
Jump, to	sauter	springen
Jaw	la mâchoire	Kiefer
Jumper; show jumper	le cheval d'obstacle, le sauteur	das Springpferd
Jumps; obstacles	les obstacles	die Hindernisse
Knee	le genou	das Vorderfusswurzel
Knock down, to	déplacer	abwerfen
Light horse	le race légère	der leichte, warmblütige Schlag
Loins	la lombe, le rein	die Lende, die Niere
Long-distance ride	le raid	der Distanz-Ritt

ENGLISH	FRENCH	GERMAN
Loose-box	le box	die Box
Low school	école basse	niedere Schule
Mare	la jument	die Stute
Martingale	la martingale	das Martingal
Martingale, running	la martingale à anneaux	das Jagdmartingal
Martingale, standing	la martingale fixe	das starre Martingal
Master (of hounds)	le maître d'équipage de chasse	der Jagdherr, der Master
Muck-out, to	nettoyer le box	den Stand ausräumen
Natural paces	les allures naturelles	die natürlichen Gangarten
Neck	l'encolure	der Hals
On the bit	en main, sure la rêne	in der Hand, am Zügel
Open jumping	épreuve de chasse	Jagdspringen
Paces	allures	Gangarten
Part-bred	le demi-sang	das Halbblut
Pastern	le paturon	die Fessel, Köte
Pedigree	le certificat d'origine	der Stammbaum
Performance test	l'épreuve	die Leistungsprobe
Poll	la nuque	das Genick
Polo	le polo	das Polo
Power, strength	la puissance	die Kraft
Prize	le prix	der Preis
'Puissance' (test jumping)	épreuve de puissance	Kanonenspringen
Purebred Arab	pur-sang arabe	Arabisches Vollblut
Quarters-in	appuyer la croupe en dedans, travers	traversieren, Travers
Quarters-out	la croupe en dehors renvers	Renvers
Race	la course	das Rennen
Racehorse	le cheval de course	das Rennpferd
Race riding	équitation de courses	Rennreiten
Refuse, to	refuser	verweigern
Regular paces	les allures régulières	die regelmässigen
Reins	rênes	Zügel
Release of the reins maintaining light contact	la descente de main	Nachgeben der Hand Pferd am langen Zügel (in Selbsthaltung)
Ribs	les côtes	die Rippen
Riding boots	la botte d'équitation	der Reitstiefel, hohe Stiefel
Riding horse	le cheval de selle	das Reitpferd
Riding instructor	l'écuyer, le maitre d'équitation	der Reitmeister
Roads and tracks	parcours de routes	Prüfung auf Strassen
Rug	la couverture	die Decke
Run out, to	éviter	vorbeillaufen
Saddle	la selle	der Sattel
Scheme of marking	le barême	da Richtverfahren
School (manège)	le manège	die Reitbahn
School 'airs'	les allures d'école	die Schulgangarten
Schooling	l'entraînement	der Training
Shoulder	l'épaule	die Schalter
Shoulder-in	l'épaule en dedans	Schulterherein
Show jumping	les épreuves d'obstacles; le concours hippique	das Jagdspringen, die Springbahn.
Sire	le père, l'auteur	das Vatertier, der Vater
Soundness, health	la santé	die Gesundheit

ENGLISH	FRENCH	GERMAN
Snaffle, ordinary	le filet ordinaire	die Schultrense
Speed	la vitesse	die Schnelligkeit
Spurs	les éperons	die Sporen
Stable	l'écurie	die Stall
Stable management	soins à l'ècurie	die Stalldienst
Stallion/entire	l'étalon	Zuchhengst/Hengst
Steeplechase	le steeple	Jagdrennen
Stifle	le grasset	das Knie, Hinterknie
Stirrup irons	les étriers	Steigbügel
Stirrup leather	l'étrivière	der Steigriemen
Stop, to	s'arrêter	stehen, bleiben
Stud book	le registre général	das Gestütsbach, das Stutbuch
Stud farm	haras, le dépot d'ètalons, jumenterie	Hengstdepot
Stud groom	le palefrenier-chef	der Stutmeister
Stud manager	le directeur de haras	der Gestütsleiter
Tail	le queue	der Schweif, Schwanz
Team jumping	la coupe des equipes	Mannschaftsspringen
Thigh	la cuisse	der Oberschenkel
Thoroughbred	pur-sang anglais	Englisches Vollblut
Three-day event	composition d'un concours complet d'équitation le military	Beispiel einer Vielseitigkeitsprüfung die Military
Top hat	le haut-de-forme	der Zylinderhut
'Touch and out' (jumping)	épreuve à l'américaine	der amerikanisches Jagdspringen
Transition	la transition	der übergang
Triple bars	les triples barres	die Trippelbarre
Triple obstacle	l'obstacle triple	dreifaches Hindernis
Trot	le trot	der Trab
Trot, collected	trot rassemblé	versammelter Trab
Trot, extended	trot allongé	starker Trab
Trot, to	marcher au trot	traben
Volt	la volte	die Volte
Voltige, vaulting	la voltige	das Voltigieren
Walk	le pas	der Schritt
Walk, collected	pas rassemblé	versammelter Schritt
Walk, extended	pas allongé	starker Schritt
Walk, to	marcher au pas	schritt reiten
Water, to	abreuver	tränken
Withers	le garrot	der Widerrist

316

USEFUL CROSS-REFERENCES

The following lists of entries, grouped by subject matter, have been compiled to assist the reader in locating individual items, most of which appear in alphabetical order within the *Encyclopaedia* and are not listed under category headings elsewhere.

BITS AND BRIDLES
Angle pelham
Anti-lug big
Anti-rearing bit
Arch-mouth pelham
Arkwright bit
Australian loose-ring
  snaffle
Balding gag bridle
Balloon bit
Banbury bit
Baucher's snaffle
Bentinck bit
Berkley bit
Bitless bridle
Bocado
Bosal
Bradoon
Breathing bridoon
Bridoon
Butterfly snaffle
Buxton bit
Cambridge mouth
Chain-mouth snaffle
Cheltenham gag
Chifney – *see under*
  Anti-rearing bit
Circle cheek snaffle
Citation bridle
Cornish snaffle
Crocker's bit
Curb
D-shaped bit
Dick Christian bridoon
Dick Christian snaffle
Double bridle
Dr Bristol bit

Dravelling bit
Duncan gag
Duncombe gag
Eclipse gag
Egg link pelham
Fancy curb
Fast cheek (curb)
Fillis bridoon
Fixed cheek (curb)
Flute bit
French bridoon
French link – *see under*
  French bridoon
Fulmer snaffle
Gags
German mouthpiece
German snaffle
Globe-cheek pelham
Hack bit
Hanoverian bit
Hanoverian mouth
Harry Highover's
  pelham
Hartwell pelham
Hitchcock gag
Hunloke bit
Jaquama/Jaquima
Jointed pelham
Kimblewick
Kimblewicke
Lancer bit
Liverpool bit
'Lone Eagle'
Lowther riding bit
Lugging bit
Magenis snaffle
Mameluke bit

McGuinness snaffle
Metropolitan bit
Mouthing bit
Muscovy anti-rearing
  bit
Nagbut snaffle
Nelson gag
Newmarket bridle
Norton Perfection
Ostrich bit
Pelham
Rockwell bridle
Rodzianko gag
Roller mouth
Royal George gag
Rubber-mouthed
  snaffle
Rugby pelham bit
Scamperdale pelham
  bit
Scawbrig bridle
Scorrier snaffle
Segundo bit
Show bridle (riding)
Show bridle (stallion)
Skeleton bridle
SM pelham
Snaffle bit
Snaffle bridle
Spanish jumping bit
Spring mouth
Stockton bit
Swales gag
Swales three-in-one bit
Tattersall bit
Thurlow bit
Todd bridle

Tom Thumb bit
Turkish curb
Twisted snaffle (or Brisson)
Vulcan mouth
W-mouth snaffle
Weymouth bit
Weymouth bridle – *see under* Bridle, double
Weymouth dressage bit
Wilson snaffle
Wind-sucker's bit
Y-mouth snaffle
Yearling bit

VEHICLES

American runabout
Barouche
Barouche-sociable
Basterna
Bianconi car
Bike (USA)
Boulnois cab
Brake
Breaking cart
Britzchska
Brougham
Buckboard
Buggy
Cab
Cabriolet
Cajol
Calashe/Caleche
Cape cart
Chaise
Clarence
Coach
Cocking cart
Coffin cart
Conestoga wagon
Coronation coach
Coupé
Curricle
Dandy cart
Demi-mail phaeton
Dennett
Dog cart
d'Orsay
Dormeuse
Dos-à-dos

Drag
Dray
Droshky
Ekka
Equirotal phaeton
Float
Four-wheeled dog-cart
Gambo
Garden-seat bus
Gig
Gold State coach – *see under* Coronation coach
Gooch wagon
Governess cart
'Growler'
Hackney carriage
Hansom
Highflyer phaeton
Horse-bier
Jaunting car
Jerky
Jingle
Jogger
Knife-board bus
Lady's phaeton
Landau
Lawton gig
Litter
Liverpool gig
Lonsdale waggonette
Lord Mayor's state coach
Lurrie
Mail coach
Mail phaeton
Milord
Moff
Moray car
Murrieta gig
Norfolk car
Omnibus
Omnibus, public
Park drag
Park phaeton
Phaeton
Post-chaise
Prairie schooner
Private omnibus
Ralli cart
Road coach

Rockaway
Semi-mail phaeton
Shanderidan
Shandrydan
Shillibeer
Show wagon
Siamese phaeton
Skeleton break
Sociable
Sovereign
Spider phaeton
Stanhope gig
Stanhope phaeton
Stage coach
Stage wagon
State coach
Sulky
Surrey
Surrey clarence
Tandem cart
T-cart
Tilbury gig
Tonga draught
Trap
Trumble
Tub car/Tub cart
Tumbril
Vardo
'Viceroy'
Victoria
Vis-à-vis
Waggonette/wagonette
Waggonette brake
Wagon/waggon
Wain
Whirlicote
Whiskey/Whisky
Yellow-bounder

HORSE BOOTS

Bell boots
Brushing boots
Brushing ring
Coronet boots
Covering boots
Easy boots – *see under* Equiboots
Equiboots
Fetlock ring
French chasing boots

Heel boot
Hock boot
Jumping boots
Knee-caps
Knee-caps, jumping
Knee-caps, skeleton

Over-reach boots
Polo pony boots
Poultice boots
Racking boots
Sausage boots
Shin boot

Speedy cut boot
Tendon boots
Travelling boots
Veterinary boot
Walking-out boot
Yorkshire boot